AQA GCSE 9–1 COMBINED SCIENCE: TRILOGY HIGHER

Series Editor: Primrose Kitten

Adam Boxer
Philippa Gardom Hulme
Jo Locke
Helen Reynolds
Alom Shaha
Jessica Walmsley

Contents

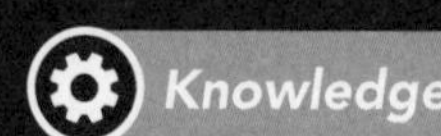

Shade in each level of the circle as you feel more confident and ready for your exam.

For answers and more practice questions visit www.oxfordrevise.com/scienceanswers

Even more practice and interactive revision quizzes are available on kerboodle

How to use this book

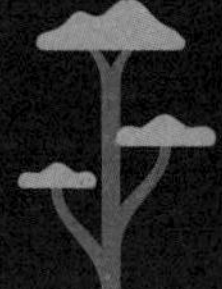

This book uses a three-step approach to revision: **Knowledge**, **Retrieval**, and **Practice**. It is important that you do all three; they work together to make your revision effective.

1 Knowledge

Knowledge comes first. Each chapter starts with a **Knowledge Organiser**. These are clear, easy-to-understand, concise summaries of the content that you need to know for your exam. The information is organised to show how one idea flows into the next so you can learn how all the science is tied together, rather than lots of disconnected facts.

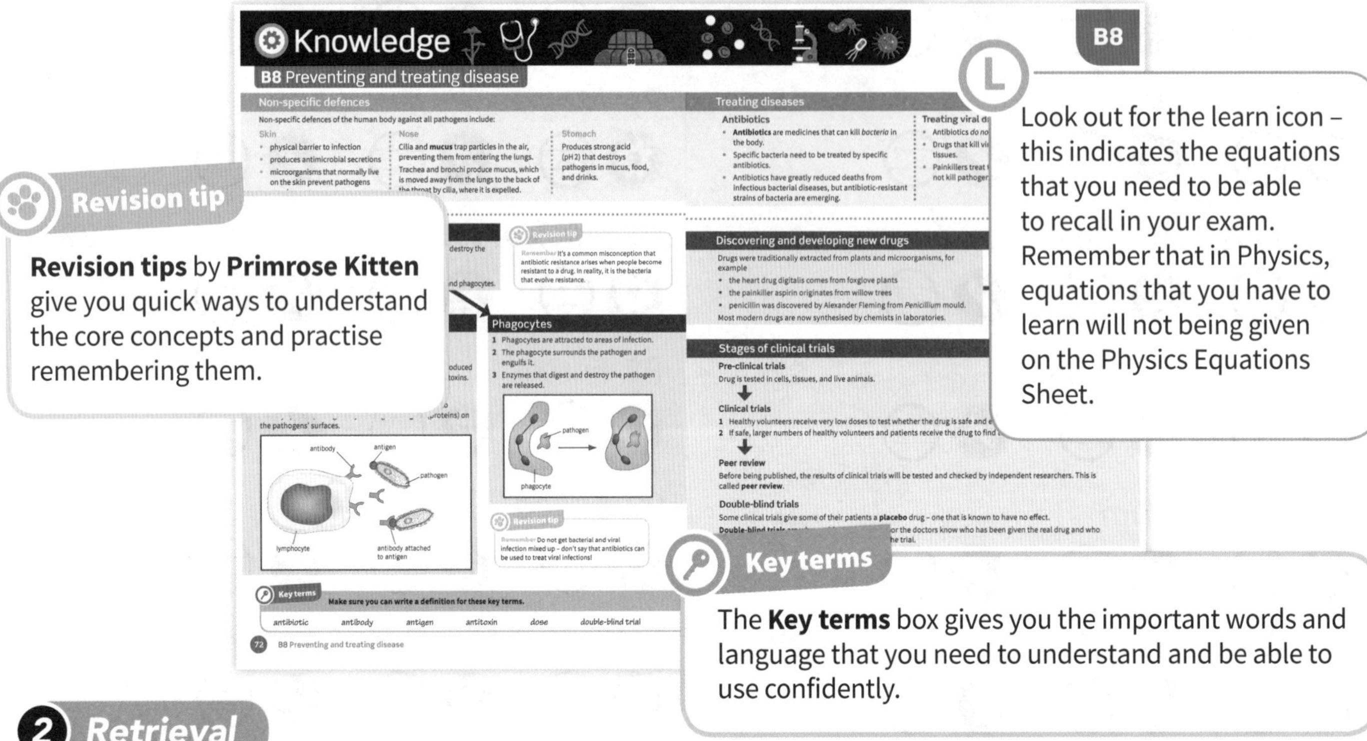

Revision tip

Revision tips by **Primrose Kitten** give you quick ways to understand the core concepts and practise remembering them.

Look out for the learn icon – this indicates the equations that you need to be able to recall in your exam. Remember that in Physics, equations that you have to learn will not being given on the Physics Equations Sheet.

Key terms

The **Key terms** box gives you the important words and language that you need to understand and be able to use confidently.

2 Retrieval

The **Retrieval questions** help you learn and quickly recall the information you've acquired. These are short questions and answers about the content in the Knowledge Organiser. Cover up the answers with some paper; write down as many answers as you can from memory. Check back to the Knowledge Organiser for any you got wrong, then cover the answers and attempt *all* the questions again until you can answer all the questions correctly.

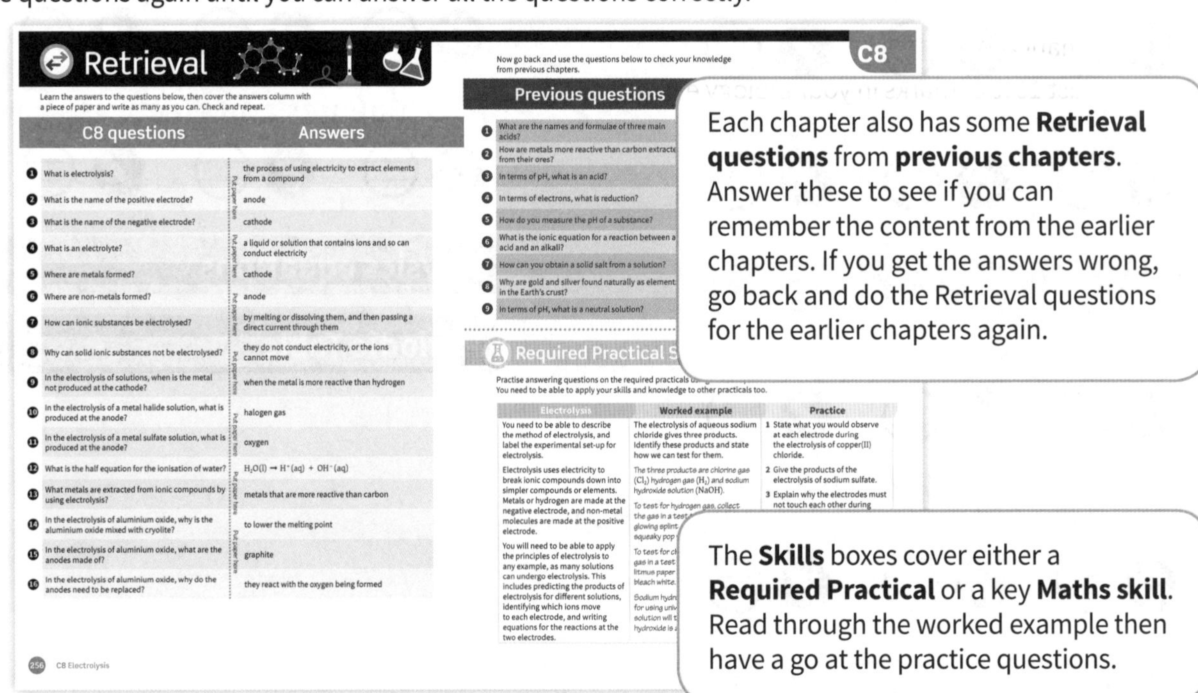

Each chapter also has some **Retrieval questions** from **previous chapters**. Answer these to see if you can remember the content from the earlier chapters. If you get the answers wrong, go back and do the Retrieval questions for the earlier chapters again.

The **Skills** boxes cover either a **Required Practical** or a key **Maths skill**. Read through the worked example then have a go at the practice questions.

Make sure you revisit the retrieval questions on different days to help them stick in your memory. You need to write down the answers each time, or say them out loud, otherwise it won't work.

3 Practice

Once you think you know the Knowledge Organiser and Retrieval answers really well you can move on to the final stage: **Practice**.

Each chapter has lots of **exam-style questions**, including some questions from previous chapters, to help you apply all the knowledge you have learnt and can retrieve.

Each question has a difficulty icon that shows the level of challenge.

 These questions build your confidence.

 These questions consolidate your knowledge.

 These questions stretch your understanding.

Make sure you attempt all of the questions no matter what grade you are aiming for.

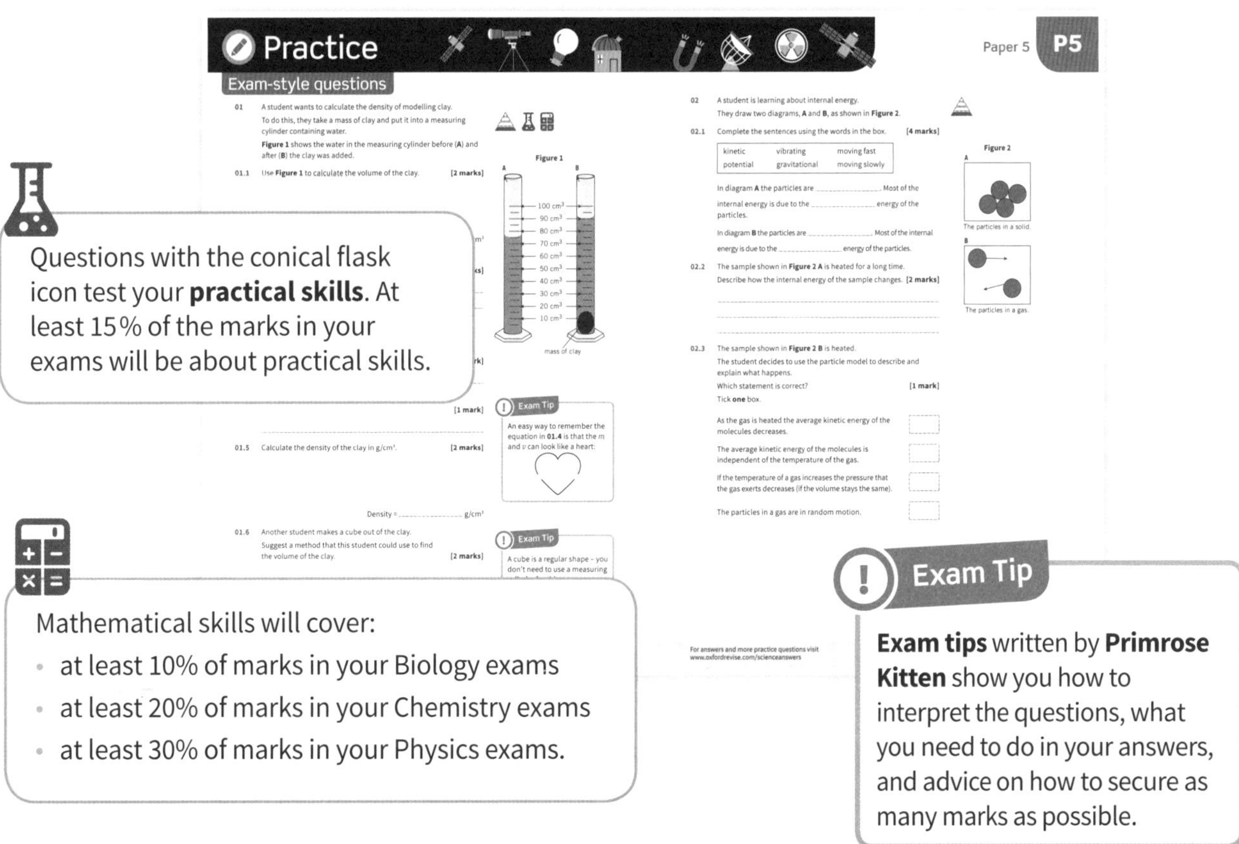
Practice
Exam-style questions
Paper 5
P5
Questions with the conical flask icon test your **practical skills**. At least 15% of the marks in your exams will be about practical skills.
Mathematical skills will cover:
• at least 10% of marks in your Biology exams
• at least 20% of marks in your Chemistry exams
• at least 30% of marks in your Physics exams.
Exam Tip
Exam tips written by **Primrose Kitten** show you how to interpret the questions, what you need to do in your answers, and advice on how to secure as many marks as possible.

All the **answers** are on Kerboodle and the website, along with even more exam-style questions. www.oxfordrevise.com/scienceanswers

Knowledge

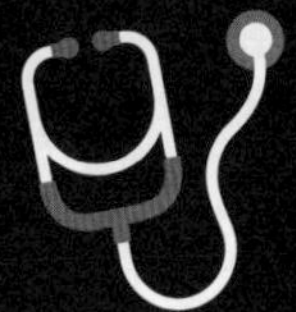

B1 Cell structure

Eukaryotic cells

Animal and plant cells are **eukaryotic** cells. They have genetic material **(DNA)** that forms **chromosomes** and is contained within a **nucleus**.

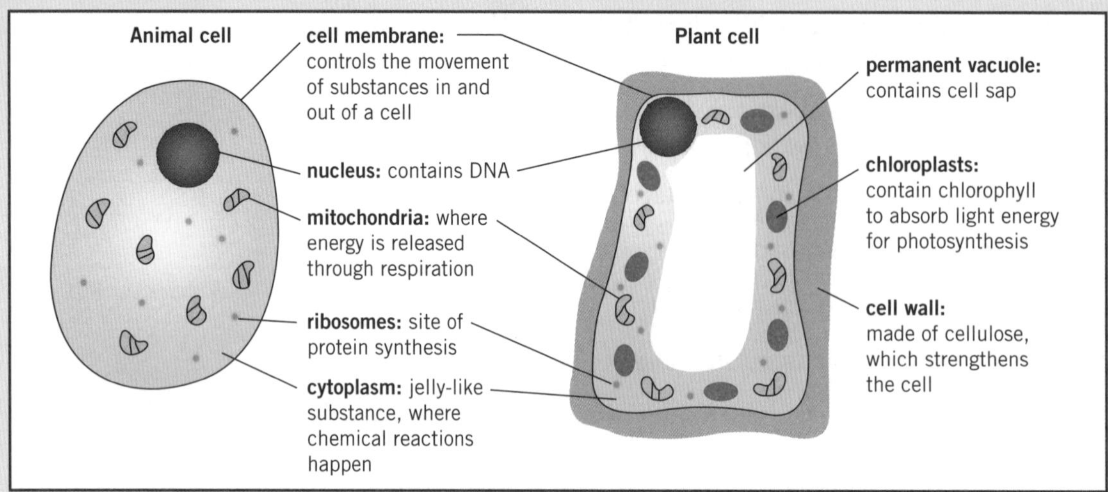

Prokaryotic cells

Bacteria have the following characteristics:
- single-celled
- no nucleus – have a single loop of DNA
- have small rings of DNA called **plasmids**
- smaller than eukaryotic cells.

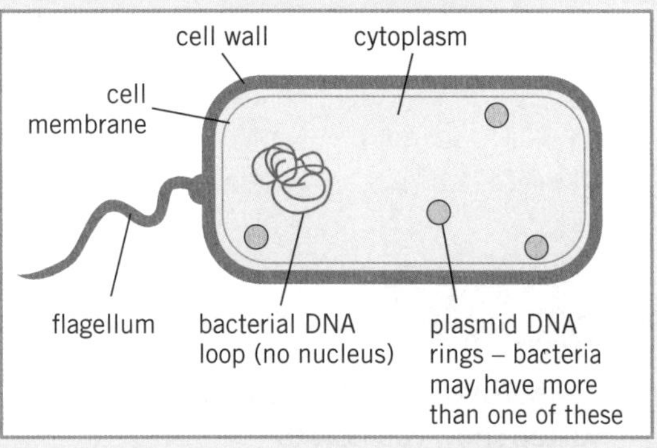

Comparing sub-cellular structures

Structure	Animal cell	Plant cell	Prokaryotic cell
cell membrane	✓	✓	✓
cytoplasm	✓	✓	✓
nucleus	✓	✓	—
cell wall	—	✓	✓
chloroplasts	—	✓	—
permanent vacuole	—	✓	—
DNA free in cytoplasm	—	—	✓
plasmids	—	—	✓

Microscopes

Light microscope	Electron microscope
uses light to form images	uses a beam of electrons to form images
living samples can be viewed	samples cannot be living
relatively cheap	expensive
low magnification	high magnification
low **resolution**	high resolution

To calculate the **magnification** of an image:

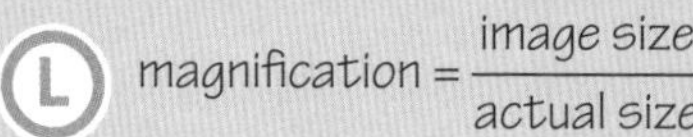

$$\text{magnification} = \frac{\text{image size}}{\text{actual size}}$$

Electron microscopes allow you to see sub-cellular structures, such as ribosomes, that are too small to be seen with a light microscope.

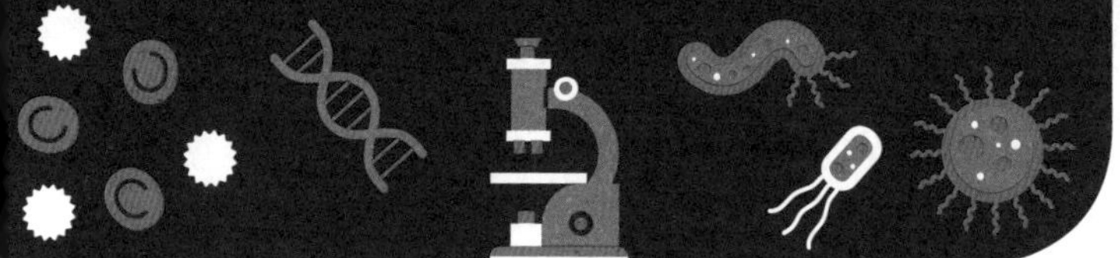

Specialised cells

Cells in animals and plants differentiate to form different types of cells. Most animal cells differentiate at an early stage of development, whereas a plant's cells differentiate throughout its lifetime.

Specialised cell	Function	Adaptations
sperm cell	fertilise an ovum (egg)	• tail to swim to the ovum and fertilise it • lots of mitochondria to release energy from respiration, enabling the sperm to swim to the ovum
red blood cell	transport oxygen around the body	• no nucleus so more room to carry oxygen • contains a red pigment called haemoglobin that binds to oxygen molecules • flat bi-concave disc shape to increase surface area-to-volume ratio
muscle cell	contract and relax to allow movement	• contains protein fibres, which can contract to make the cells shorter • contains lots of mitochondria to release energy from respiration, allowing the muscles to contract
nerve cell	carry electrical impulses around the body	• branched endings, called dendrites, to make connections with other neurones or effectors • myelin sheath insulates the axon to increase the transmission speed of the electrical impulses
root hair cell	absorb mineral ions and water from the soil	• long projection speeds up the absorption of water and mineral ions by increasing the surface area of the cell • lots of mitochondria to release energy for the active transport of mineral ions from the soil
palisade cell	enable photosynthesis in the leaf	• lots of chloroplasts containing chlorophyll to absorb light energy • located at the top surface of the leaf where it can absorb the most light energy

Key terms

Make sure you can write a definition for these key terms.

cell membrane, cell wall, chloroplast, chromosome, cytoplasm, DNA, eukaryotic, magnification, mitochondria, nucleus, permanent vacuole, plasmid, prokaryotic, resolution, ribosome

Retrieval

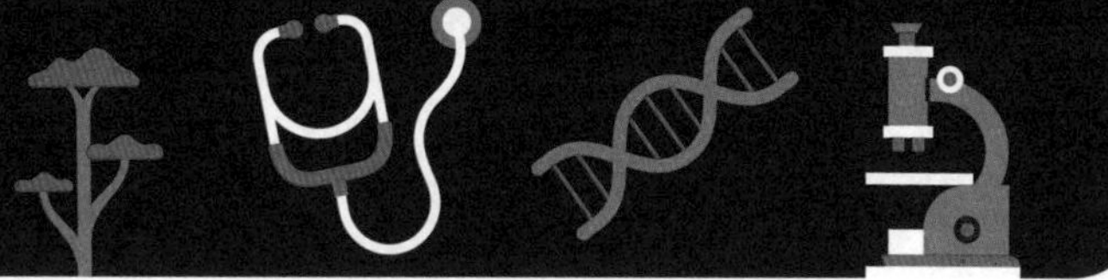

Learn the answers to the questions below, then cover the answers column with a piece of paper and write as many as you can. Check and repeat.

	B1 questions		Answers
1	What are two types of eukaryotic cell?	Put paper here	animal and plant
2	What type of cell are bacteria?		prokaryotic
3	Where is DNA found in animal and plant cells?		in the nucleus
4	What is the function of the cell membrane?	Put paper here	controls movement of substances in and out of the cell
5	What is the function of mitochondria?		site of respiration to transfer energy for the cell
6	What is the function of chloroplasts?		contain chlorophyll to absorb light energy for photosynthesis
7	What is the function of ribosomes?	Put paper here	enable production of proteins (protein synthesis)
8	What is the function of the cell wall?		strengthens and supports the cell
9	What is the structure of the main genetic material in a prokaryotic cell?		single loop of DNA
10	How are electron microscopes different to light microscopes?	Put paper here	electron microscopes use beams of electrons instead of light, cannot be used to view living samples, are much more expensive, and have a much higher magnification and resolution
11	What is the function of a red blood cell?		carries oxygen around the body
12	Give three adaptations of a red blood cell.	Put paper here	no nucleus, contains a red pigment called haemoglobin, and has a bi-concave disc shape
13	What is the function of a nerve cell?		carries electrical impulses around the body
14	Give two adaptations of a nerve cell.		branched endings, myelin sheath insulates the axon
15	What is the function of a sperm cell?	Put paper here	fertilises an ovum (egg)
16	Give two adaptations of a sperm cell.		tail, contains lots of mitochondria
17	What is the function of a palisade cell?		carries out photosynthesis in a leaf
18	Give two adaptations of a palisade cell.	Put paper here	lots of chloroplasts, located at the top surface of the leaf
19	What is the function of a root hair cell?		absorbs minerals and water from the soil
20	Give two adaptations of a root hair cell.		long projection, lots of mitochondria

Maths Skills

Practise your maths skills using the worked example and practice questions below.

Resolution

The resolution of a device is the smallest change that the device can measure.

Selecting equipment with the appropriate resolution is important in scientific investigations.

If the resolution of a digital watch is one second, one second is the smallest amount of time it can measure.

Some stop clocks have smaller resolutions, for example a resolution of 0.01 seconds. This means that they can measure times of 0.01, 1.29, or 9.62 seconds, whereas a digital watch could not.

Worked example

What is the resolution of the following equipment?

40°C
35°C
30°C

The resolution of this thermometer is 1 °C, as this is the smallest change that it can detect.

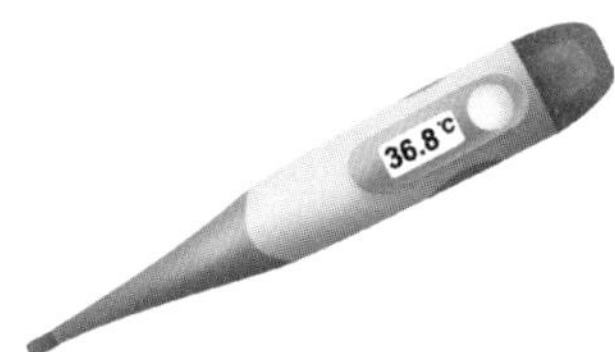

The resolution of this digital thermometer is 0.1 °C, as it can measure readings such as 1.1 °C, 8.9 °C, and 36.7 °C.

Practice

What are the resolutions of the following pieces of equipment?

1 0 1 2 3 4 5 6 7 8 9 10 11 12 13 14 15

0.1cm

2

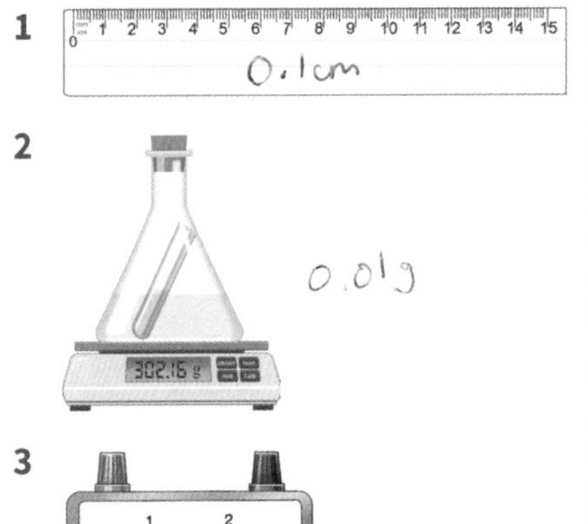

0.01g

3

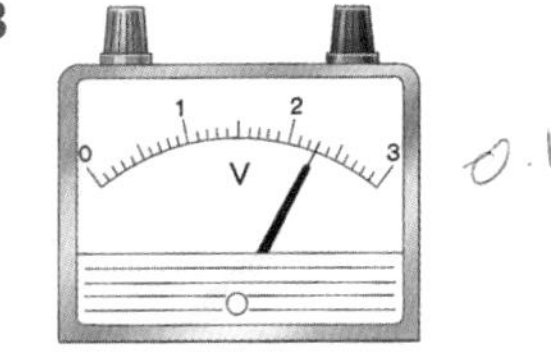

0.1V

Required Practical Skills

Practise answering questions on the required practicals using the example below. You need to be able to apply your skills and knowledge to other practicals too.

Looking at cells

In this practical you need to be able to use a light microscope to view plant and animal cells.

You should be able to

- describe how to set up a microscope
- label parts of a microscope
- describe how to focus on a slide containing a specimen
- make a labelled scientific drawing of what you observe.

You also need to be able to determine the magnification of an object under a microscope, and use this to calculate the real size of the object.

Worked example

A student wanted to determine the actual size of the cell they observed under a microscope.

They measured the size of the cell image as 15 mm, the objective lens magnification was 40×, and the eyepiece magnification was 10×.

Determine the actual size of the cell. Give your answer in standard form.

Step 1: determine the magnification

$$\text{total magnification} = \text{objective lens magnification} \times \text{eyepiece lens magnification}$$

$$\text{total magnification} = 40 \times 10 = 400$$

Step 2: put the numbers in the equation

$$\text{magnification} = \frac{\text{size of image}}{\text{actual size of object}}$$

$$400 = \frac{15}{\text{actual size of object}}$$

Step 3: rearrange the equation and find the answer

$$\text{actual size of object} = \frac{15}{400} = 0.0375\text{ mm}$$

Step 4: convert your answer to standard form

$$0.0375 = 3.75 \times 10^{-2}\text{ mm}$$

Practice

1 Describe how you could identify a cell as animal or plant by looking at it using a light microscope. Include the names and visual descriptions of any important organelles.

2 A student wrote a method for focusing a microscope image of a cell. Suggest improvements to the student's method.

'Set the microscope at the highest objective lens, then look down the eyepiece whilst you use the fine focus to find the cell.'

3 Draw a labelled image of an animal cell.

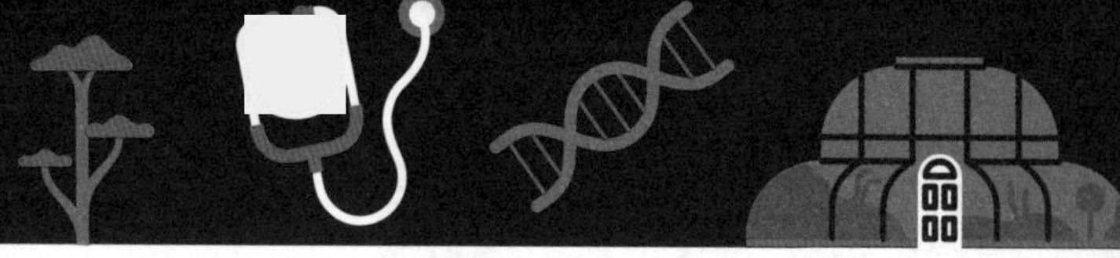

Exam-style questions

01 **Figure 1** shows a plant cell.

Figure 1

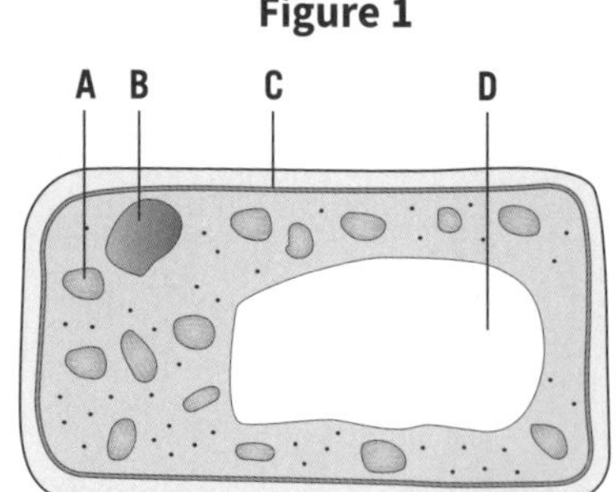

01.1 Identify parts **A**–**C**. **[3 marks]** 2

A Chloroplasts ✓

B Nucleus ✓

C Cell Wall ✗ membrane

01.2 Explain the function of part **D**. **[3 marks]**

The vacuole contains cell sap and acts ~~as a~~ to keep the cell rigid ✓✓ 2

01.3 Which feature in **Figure 1** allows you to conclude that this is a eukaryotic cell? **[1 mark]** 1

Tick **one** box. ✓

cell wall	☐
cytoplasm	☐
nucleus	☑
cell membrane	☐

> **Exam Tip**
> Labelling cells is a common exam question. Take the time to become familiar with plant cells, animal cells, and prokaryotic cells.

01.4 The cell shown in **Figure 1** was taken from a plant.

Suggest and explain where in the plant this cell would be found. **[2 marks]** 2

This would be found in a leaf, due to ✓ its chloroplasts ~~to~~ for photosynthesis ✓

> **Exam Tip**
> Plants have a range of different specialised cells, but they will all share some common features.

02 **Figure 2** shows a cheek cell viewed under a light microscope magnified at ×1350.

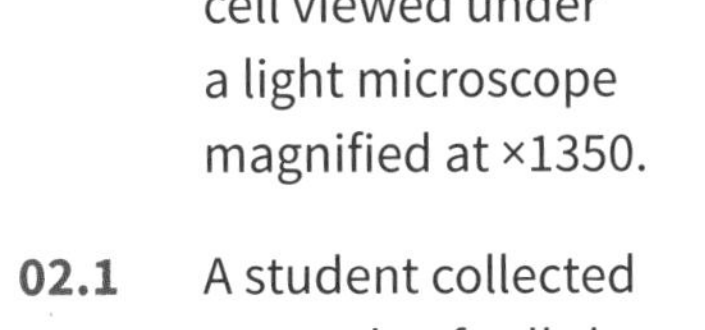

Figure 2

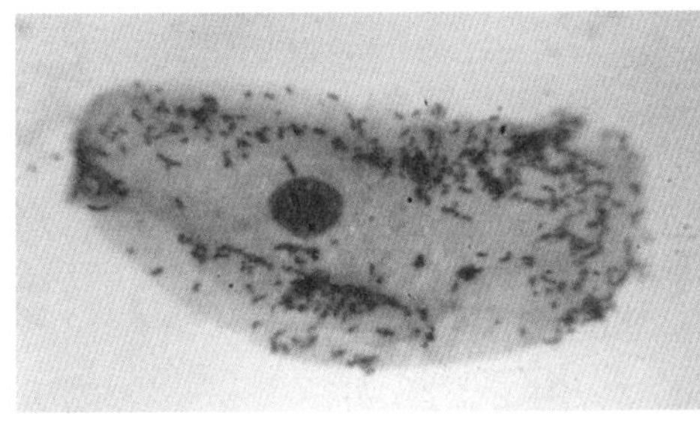

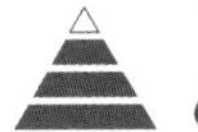  

02.1 A student collected a sample of cells by taking a saliva swab from the inside of their cheek.

Explain **one** safety measure that the student should take during this procedure. **[2 marks]**

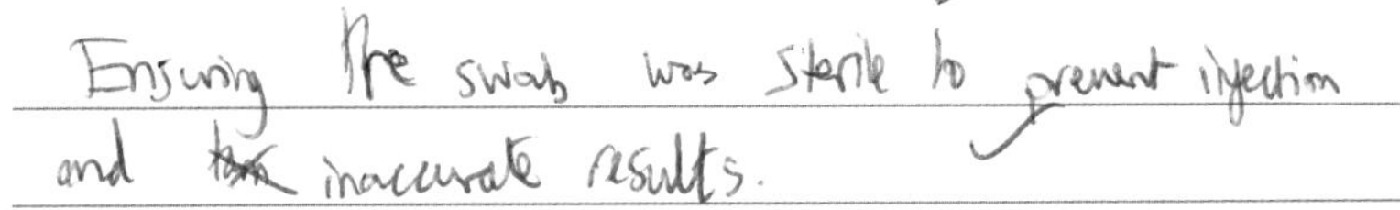

Ensuring the swab was sterile to prevent infection and inaccurate results.

> **Exam Tip**
>
> For this question 'explain' is the command word so you need to say *why* you have done something, not just what you have done.

02.2 Suggest why methylene blue dye was added to the cell sample on the slide. **[1 mark]**

To make it visible

02.3 Suggest **one** way in which the student could observe structures within the cell in greater detail. **[1 mark]**

Greater resolution microscope

02.4 Using **Figure 2**, calculate the actual length of the cheek cell.

Give your answer in micrometres. **[3 marks]**

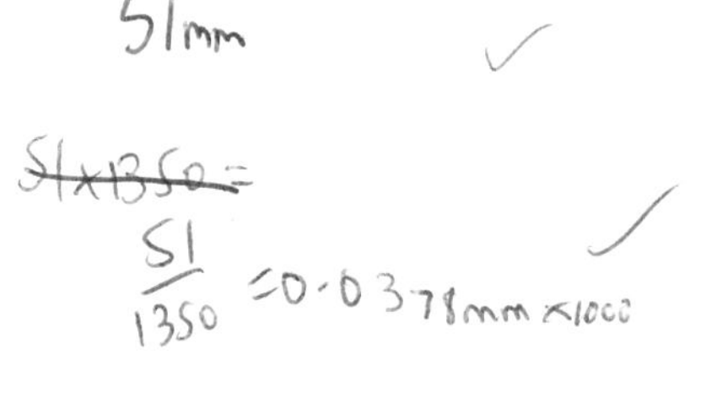

51 mm

$\frac{51}{1350} = 0.0378$ mm ×1000

378 μm

> **Exam Tip**
>
> Converting between units can be tricky. If you're not sure whether you need to divide or multiply, try to think logically and ask yourself:
>
> if 10 mm = 1 cm, does the answer look correct if I multiply or divide?

03 Plant cells have two main types of transport tissue.

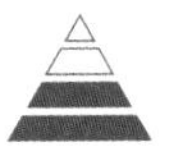

03.1 Describe what is meant by a tissue. **[1 mark]**

03.2 Xylem tissue transports water and mineral ions around the plant. Explain how the xylem tubes form. **[3 marks]**

03.3 Explain **two** ways xylem tissue is adapted to its function. **[4 marks]**

03.4 Name the other type of plant transport tissue. **[1 mark]**

> **Exam Tip**
>
> A quick way to remember what xylem carries is that x and w (for water) are close to each other in the alphabet.

04 **Figure 3** shows a single-celled organism called *Euglena*. *Euglena* are found in ponds and lakes. They survive by making their own food through photosynthesis. In low light conditions they can engulf other microorganisms, such as bacteria and algae.

Exam Tip

You may not have come across *Euglena* before. Don't let this worry you! The exam has to include a lot of content you haven't seen before, so questions like this are designed to prepare you for that.

Use the knowledge you have gained in class and practise applying it to this new situation. The more you try doing this, the better prepared you'll be for the unfamiliar contexts you will come across in the exams!

Figure 3

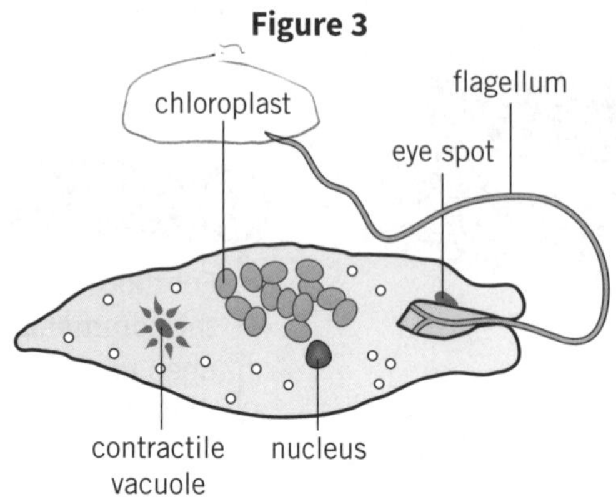

Identify which part of the *Euglena* traps light for photosynthesis. **[1 mark]**

05 Amoebas are single-celled organisms. *Naegleria fowleri,* often referred to as the 'brain-eating amoeba', is a species of amoeba that can cause sudden and severe brain infection, which normally results in fatality.

05.1 Evaluate the advantages and disadvantages of using light microscopes and electron microscopes to study amoebas. **[6 marks]**

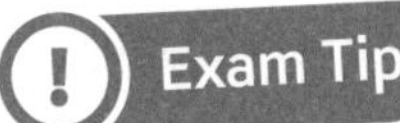

Exam Tip

This is an evaulate question. To get full marks you need to have a balanced argument and give a reasoned opinion. Try this plan:

1. advantages of light microscopes
2. disadvantages of light microscopes
3. advantages of electron microscopes
4. disadvantages of electron microscopes
5. your opinion on which one is best for the task
6. give a reason why you think this.

05.2 *Naegleria* measure approximately 10 μm in diameter. The diameter of a human egg cell is approximately 0.1 mm.
Calculate the difference in orders of magnitude between *Naegleria* and a human egg cell. **[3 marks]**

06 **Figure 4** shows some plant cells as viewed under a light microscope.

Figure 4

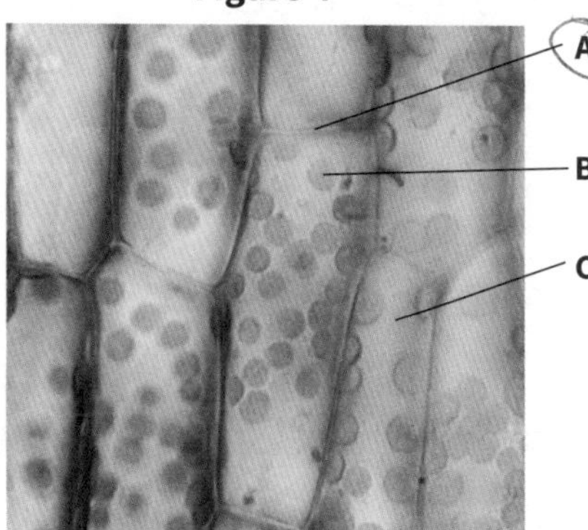

06.1 Identify the cell membrane in **Figure 4**. **[1 mark]**

06.2 Ribosomes are present in plant cells but cannot be seen using a light microscope.
Describe the function of ribosomes. **[1 mark]**

06.3 Name **one** other subcellular structure that is present in plant cells but cannot be seen in **Figure 4**. **[1 mark]**

06.4 Describe how to prepare and view a sample of plant cells using a microscope. **[6 marks]**

07 Bacteria are an example of prokaryotes.

07.1 Which of the following is the most approximate size for a prokaryote? Choose **one** answer. **[1 mark]**

100 nm 1 μm 10 μm 0.1 mm

07.2 Both plant cells and prokaryotic cells have cell walls. Describe **one** difference between the cell wall of a plant cell and the cell wall of a bacterial cell. **[1 mark]**

07.3 Describe the differences between the way genetic material is stored in a prokaryotic cell and in a eukaryotic cell. **[4 marks]**

07.4 Suggest which feature needs to be present on a bacterial cell if it needs to move in water. **[1 mark]**

Exam Tip

Very large and very small units can seem more complicated than they really are. Make sure you know the order from largest to smallest:

km > m > cm > mm > μm > nm > pm

08 Cone cells are a type of cell found at the back of the human eye. They send a signal to the brain, which it then decodes, allowing us to perceive colour. **Figure 5** shows the main adaptations of a cone cell.

Figure 5

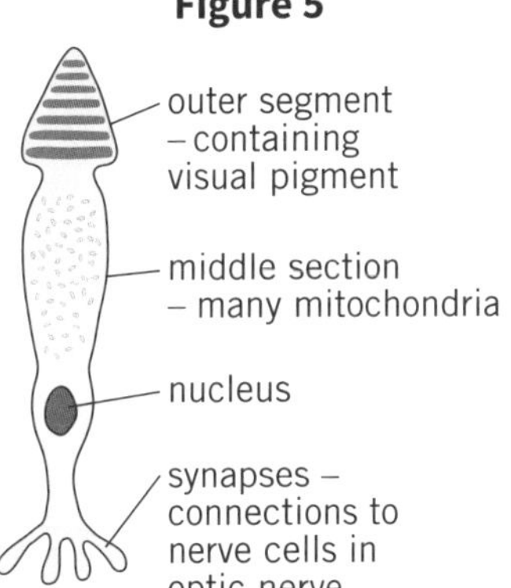

08.1 Use the information in **Figure 5** and your own knowledge to suggest and explain how the cone cell is adapted to its function. **[4 marks]**

Exam Tip

All the information you need is given to you in the question. Make sure that in your answer you go through each of the adaptations one by one.

08.2 There are approximately 6 million cone cells in the human retina. Three different types of cone cell exist:

- one to detect red light
- one to detect green light
- one to detect blue light.

Assuming there is a roughly equal number of each cone cell type in a human retina, calculate the number of 'red' cone cells present in the retinda. Give your answer in standard form. **[3 marks]**

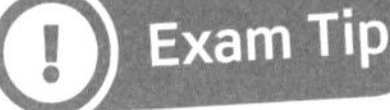

Exam Tip

Read the question carefully; if you don't give your answer in standard form you are not going to get full marks.

09 Muscle cells are an example of a specialised cell.

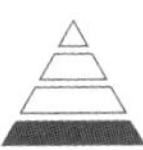

09.1 Define the term specialised cell. **[1 mark]**

09.2 The biceps contain muscle cells. Describe the function of a muscle cell. **[1 mark]**

09.3 In addition to providing movement to the skeleton, muscle tissue has other functions in the body.
Describe **one** other example of where muscles are found in the body. **[2 marks]**

09.4 Explain why muscle cells have lots of mitochondria. **[2 marks]**

09.5 Explain **one** other feature of a muscle cell. **[2 marks]**

10 A student observed some onion cells under a microscope.

10.1 Give **two** features that help the student to know that they are looking at a sample of plant cells in **Figure 6**. **[2 marks]**

Figure 6

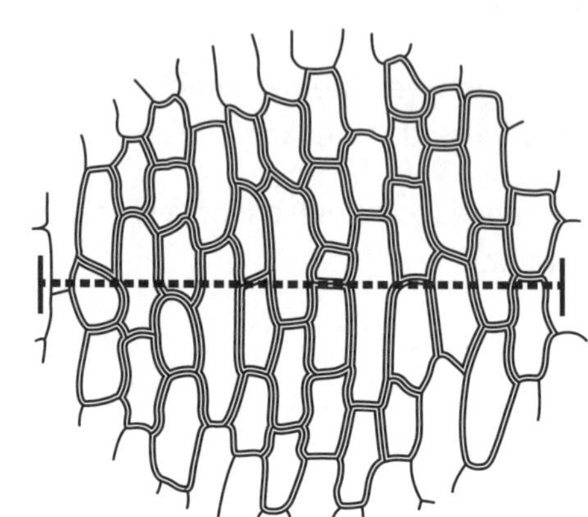

10.2 The scale ruler in the diagram represents 1000 µm.
Calculate the average width of an onion cell. **[2 marks]**

> **Exam Tip**
>
> When measuring very small things, it is better to measure a group of them and then divide the measurement – for example, measure the width of ten onion cells, then divide that measurement by ten.

10.3 These cells were observed under 100× magnification.
Identify which of the following structures may have been visible under a higher magnification using a light microscope. Choose **one** answer. **[1 mark]**

vacuole   ribosomes   chloroplasts   plasmids

11 **Figure 7** shows an animal cell.

Figure 7

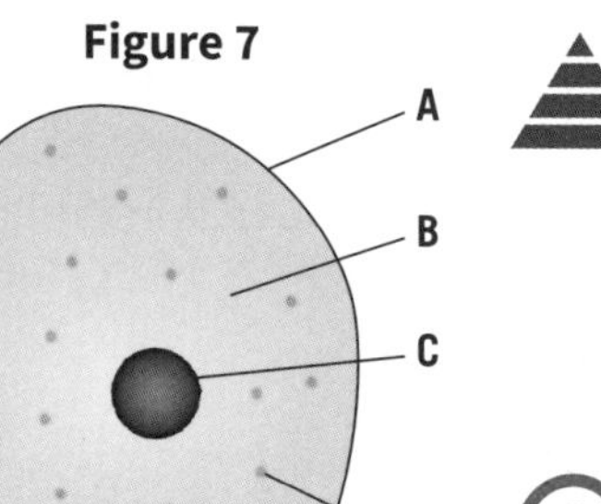

11.1 Which letter (**A–D**) represents the cell membrane? **[1 mark]**

11.2 Describe the function of the cell membrane. **[1 mark]**

11.3 **Figure 7** shows a human skin cell.
Explain how the cell would differ if it was a human nerve cell. **[4 marks]**

> **Exam Tip**
>
> Think about the function of nerve cells. Give the difference and then explain *why* this difference is important.

11.4 An animal cell has a mean diameter of 20 µm.
Estimate the length of the cell membrane in this cell. **[2 marks]**

11.5 The mean length of the molecules within the cell membrane has been estimated to be 4 nm.
If we assume that the cell membrane is one molecule thick, calculate the total number of molecules contained in the cell's membrane. **[3 marks]**

12 In general eukaryotic cells are one order of magnitude larger than prokaryotic cells.

12.1 One type of virus is 100 nm in height. One type of algal cell is two orders of magnitude larger than the virus.
Estimate the length of the cell. Give your answer in micrometres. **[1 mark]**

12.2 Compare the features found in eukaryotic and prokaryotic cells. **[6 marks]**

12.3 Cyanobacteria are a phylum of bacteria that are able to photosynthesise. Estimate the size of a cyanobacterial cell. Justify your answer. **[2 marks]**

12.4 Algae are aquatic organisms that belong to the kingdom Protista. **Figure 8** shows an algal cell.
Use **Figure 8** to suggest why some algae have been classified as plants instead. **[3 marks]**

Figure 8

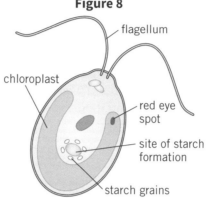

flagellum
chloroplast
red eye spot
site of starch formation
starch grains

Exam Tip

Don't panic if you've never come across protists before – look at the organelles and see if any are also found in cells that you have already learnt about.

13 Sperm cells are one type of sex cell.

13.1 Explain how a sperm cell is adapted to perform its function. **[4 marks]**

13.2 Low sperm mobility is one cause of fertility issues in males. If a male is having fertility issues, a sample of sperm can be observed through a microscope to check the mobility of the sperm.
Suggest **two** reasons why the sample is normally observed using a light microscope, rather than using an electron microscope. **[2 marks]**

13.3 A scientist studies an image of a sperm cell. The image measures 7.5 cm and has been magnified 1500×. Calculate the real size of the sperm cell. Give your answer in micrometres. **[3 marks]**

Exam Tip

When answering this question, think about what you are trying to find out when observing sperm cells.

Exam Tip

You need to remember the equations for magnification – if you need to check, you can look back at the knowledge organiser.

14 A scientist produced an image of human cheek cells. It was prepared using a light microscope.

14.1 Describe how to prepare a slide of cheek cells to view under a light microscope. **[6 marks]**

14.2 Sketch a diagram of the cell you would expect to see. Label the organelles which are visible in the cell. **[3 marks]**

14.3 Write down which additional piece of information you should include with a microscope drawing. **[1 mark]**

14.4 Some organelles will not be visible because a light microscope does not have a high enough resolution.
Define the term resolution. **[1 mark]**

14.5 Suggest how the scientist could produce an image showing the missing organelles. **[1 mark]**

Exam Tip

In this question the command word is 'sketch'. You only need to draw a rough diagram of a cell. This is not art so shading or too much detail won't get you any marks and will take up valuable time.

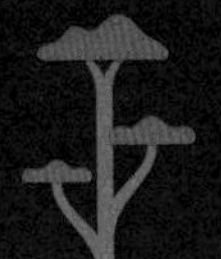
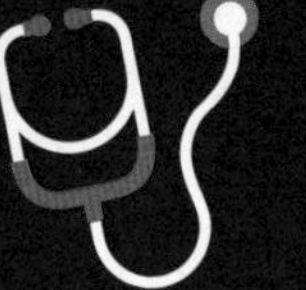

Knowledge

B2 Cell transport

Comparing diffusion, osmosis, and active transport

	Diffusion	Osmosis	Active transport
Definition	The spreading out of particles, resulting in a net movement from an area of higher **concentration** to an area of lower concentration.	The diffusion of water from a **dilute** solution to a concentrated solution through a **partially permeable membrane**.	The movement of particles from a more dilute solution to a more concentrated solution using energy from respiration.
Movement of particles	Particles move down the concentration **gradient** – from an area of *high* concentration to an area of *low* concentration.	Water moves from an area of *lower* solute concentration to an area of *higher* solute concentration.	Particles move against the concentration gradient – from an area of *low* concentration to an area of *high* concentration.
Energy required?	no – **passive process**	no – passive process	yes – using energy released during respiration
Examples	**Humans** • Nutrients in the small intestine diffuse into the blood in the **capillaries** through the **villi**. • Oxygen diffuses from the air in the **alveoli** into the blood in the capillaries. Carbon dioxide diffuses from the blood in the capillaries into the air in the alveoli. • **Urea** diffuses from cells into the blood for excretion by the kidney. **Fish** • Oxygen from water passing over the gills diffuses into the blood in the **gill filaments**. • Carbon dioxide diffuses from the blood in the gill filaments into the water. **Plants** • Carbon dioxide used for photosynthesis diffuses into leaves through the **stomata**. • Oxygen produced during photosynthesis diffuses out of the leaves through the stomata.	**Plants** Water moves by osmosis from a dilute solution in the soil to a concentrated solution in the **root hair cell**.	**Humans** Active transport allows sugar molecules to be absorbed from the small intestine when the sugar concentration is higher in the blood than in the small intestine. **Plants** Active transport is used to absorb mineral ions into the root hair cells from more dilute solutions in the soil.

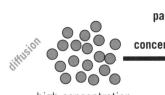

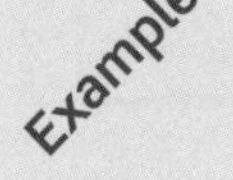
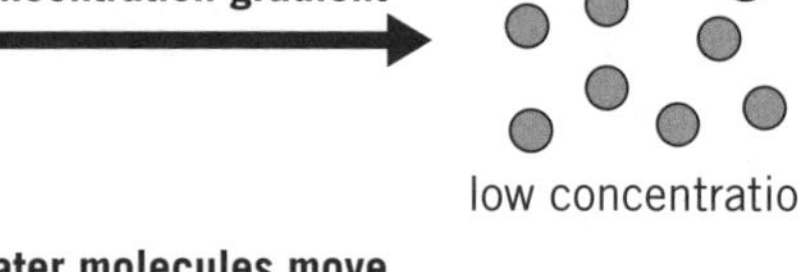

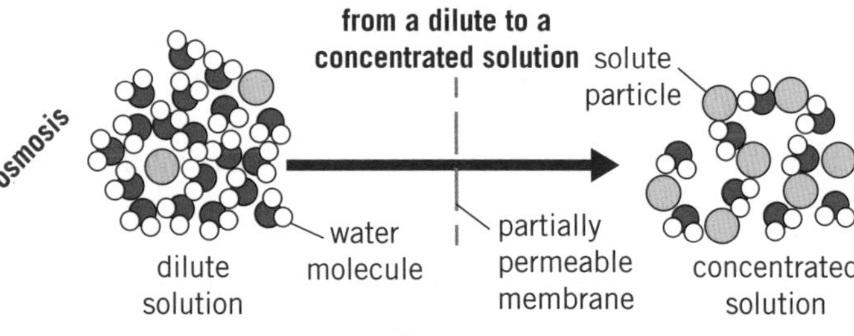

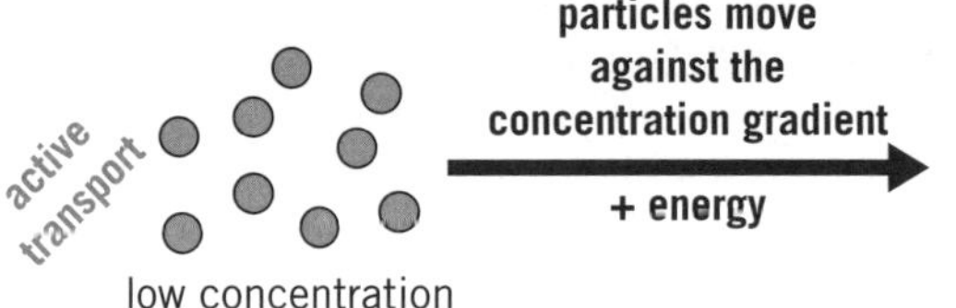

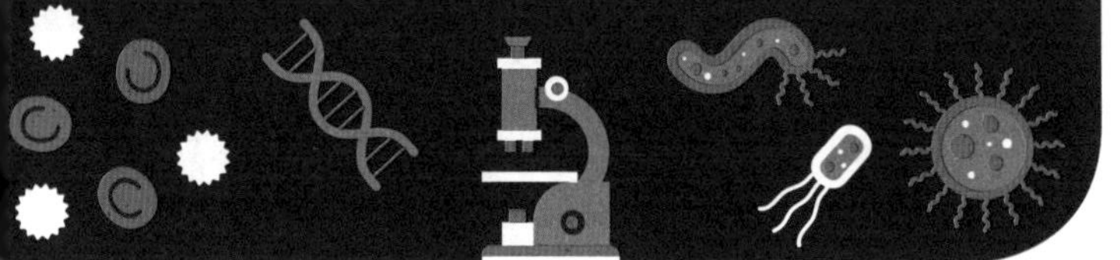

Factors that affect the rate of diffusion

① Difference in concentration

The steeper the concentration gradient, the faster the rate of diffusion.

② Temperature

The higher the temperature, the faster the rate of diffusion.

③ Surface area of the membrane

The larger the membrane surface area, the faster the rate of diffusion.

Adaptations for exchanging substances

Single-celled organisms have a large surface area-to-volume ratio. This allows enough molecules to be transported across their cell membranes to meet their needs.

Multicellular organisms have a small surface area-to-volume ratio. This means they need specialised organ systems and cells to allow enough molecules to be transported into and out of their cells.

Exchange surfaces work most efficiently when they have a large surface area, a thin membrane, and a good blood supply.

Villi in the small intestine

for absorbing nutrients

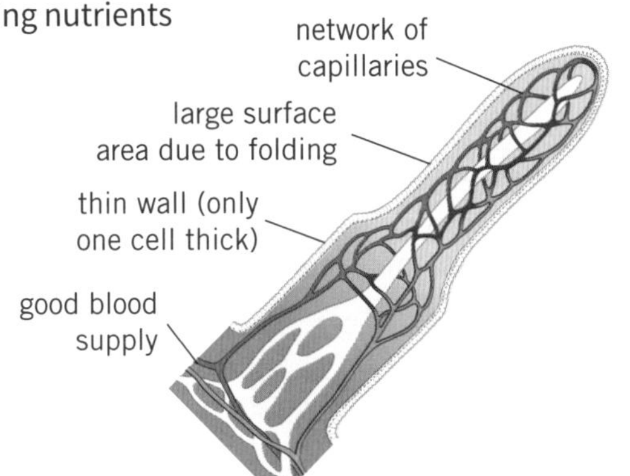

Alveoli in the lungs

for gas exchange

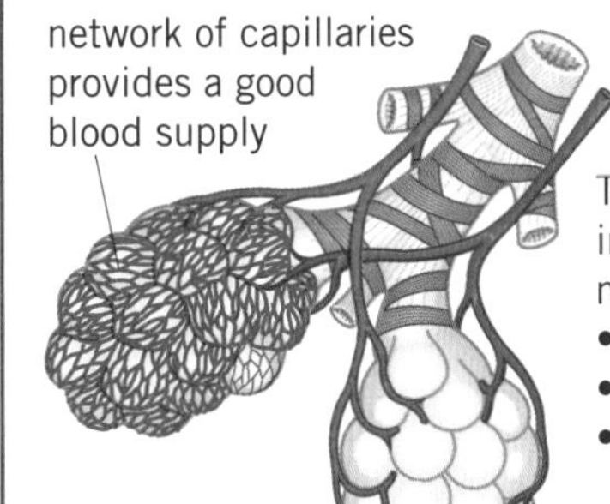

The rate of diffusion is increased because the membrane of the alveoli

- has a large surface area
- is moist
- is only one cell thick (short diffusion pathway).

Fish gills

for gas exchange

Fish gills are made up of stacks of thin filaments with

- a large surface area to increase diffusion
- a network of capillaries (good blood supply).

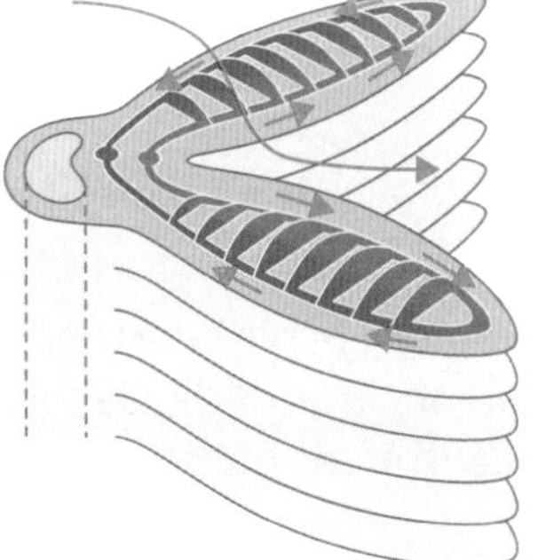

Root hair cells

for uptake of water and minerals

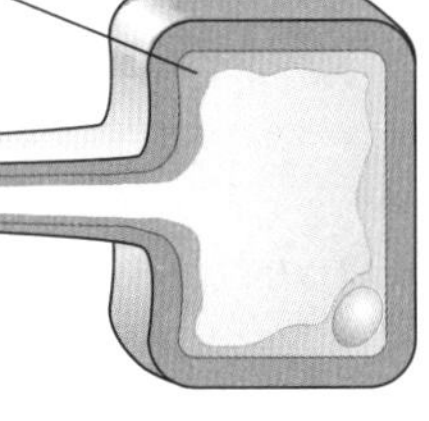

Key terms Make sure you can write a definition for these key terms.

active transport, alveoli, capillaries, concentration, diffusion, dilute, gill filament, gradient, osmosis, partially permeable membrane, passive process, root hair cell, stomata, urea, villi

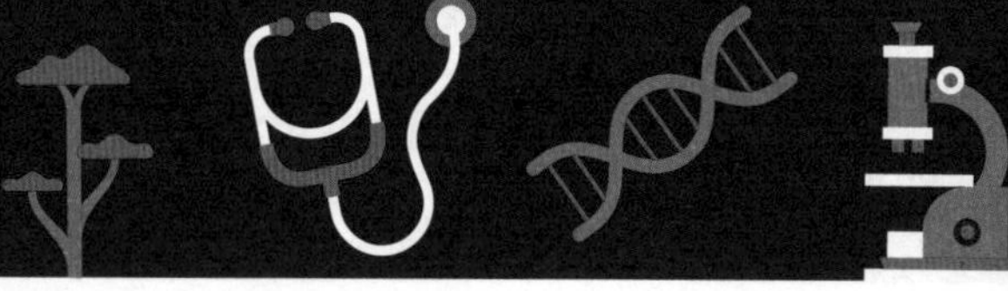

Learn the answers to the questions below, then cover the answers column with a piece of paper and write as many as you can. Check and repeat.

	B2 questions		Answers
1	What is diffusion?	Put paper here	net movement of particles from an area of high concentration to an area of low concentration along a concentration gradient – this is a passive process (does not require energy from respiration)
2	Name three factors that affect the rate of diffusion.	Put paper here	concentration gradient, temperature, membrane surface area
3	How are villi adapted for exchanging substances?	Put paper here	• long and thin – increases surface area • one-cell-thick membrane – short diffusion pathway • good blood supply – maintains a steep concentration gradient
4	How are the lungs adapted for efficient gas exchange?	Put paper here	• alveoli – large surface area • moist membranes – increases rate of diffusion • one-cell-thick membranes – short diffusion pathway • good blood supply – maintains a steep concentration gradient
5	How are fish gills adapted for efficient gas exchange?	Put paper here	• large surface area for gases to diffuse across • thin layer of cells – short diffusion pathway • good blood supply – maintains a steep concentration gradient
6	What is osmosis?	Put paper here	diffusion of water from a dilute solution to a concentrated solution through a partially permeable membrane
7	Give one example of osmosis in a plant.	Put paper here	water moves from the soil into the root hair cell
8	What is active transport?	Put paper here	movement of particles against a concentration gradient – from a dilute solution to a more concentrated solution – using energy from respiration
9	Why is active transport needed in plant roots?	Put paper here	concentration of mineral ions in the soil is lower than inside the root hair cells – the mineral ions must move against the concentration gradient to enter the root hair cells
10	What is the purpose of active transport in the small intestine?		sugars can be absorbed when the concentration of sugar in the small intestine is lower than the concentration of sugar in the blood

Now go back and use the questions below to check your knowledge from previous chapters.

Previous questions

	Previous questions	Answers
1	Give two adaptations of a root hair cell.	long projection, lots of mitochondria
2	What is the function of a red blood cell?	carries oxygen around the body
3	What type of cell are bacteria?	prokaryotic
4	What is the function of ribosomes?	enable production of proteins (protein synthesis)
5	Give two adaptations of a nerve cell.	branched endings, myelin sheath insulates the axon
6	What is the function of a sperm cell?	fertilises an ovum (egg)
7	Give two adaptations of a sperm cell.	tail, contains lots of mitochondria
8	How are electron microscopes different to light microscopes?	electron microscopes use beams of electrons instead of light, cannot be used to view living samples, are much more expensive, and have a much higher magnification and resolution

Put paper here

Put paper here

Put paper here

Required Practical Skills

Practise answering questions on the required practicals using the example below. You need to be able to apply your skills and knowledge to other practicals too.

Osmosis in cells

Different concentrations of sugar and salt solutions both affect the movement of water by osmosis, causing cells to lose or gain water and changing the mass of a tissue sample.

For this practical you need to be able to accurately measure length, mass, and volume to measure osmosis in cells.

You will need to be comfortable applying this knowledge to a range of samples, not just to the typical example of potato tissue, as osmosis happens in all cells.

Worked example

A sample of carrot was placed into a 0.75 mol/dm^3 sugar solution for 30 minutes. The mass of the carrot was recorded before and after this.

Initial mass = 6.02 g

Final mass = 3.91 g

1 Determine the percentage change in mass of the sample.

Change in mass = 3.91 − 6.02 = −2.11 g

Percentage change in mass $= \left(\frac{-2.11}{6.02}\right) \times 100 = -35\%$

(a minus sign is used because the sample has lost mass)

2 Explain why this experiment should be repeated, and give one other variable that should be controlled.

The experiment should be repeated to give a more reliable result, and to allow calculation of a mean loss in mass for the sample. The dimensions of the carrot sample need to be controlled between repeats.

Practice

1 Give one reason why it is important to dry the samples of carrot cores before they are weighed.

2 When repeating this experiment using different concentrations of sugar solution, a student found that one sample did not change mass. Suggest what this tells you about the concentration of the solution. Assume no error in the experiment.

3 Two students set up this experiment. Student A said that each sample of carrot must have the same starting mass. Student B argued that each sample must have the same length and width. Explain which student is correct.

Practice

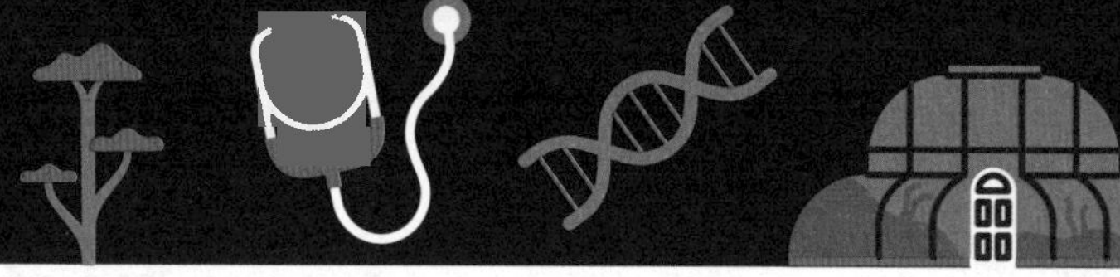

Exam-style questions

01 A group of students investigated how the mass of a potato sample changed over time, when placed into sugar solutions of varying concentrations.

They set up their equipment as shown in **Figure 1**.

Figure 1

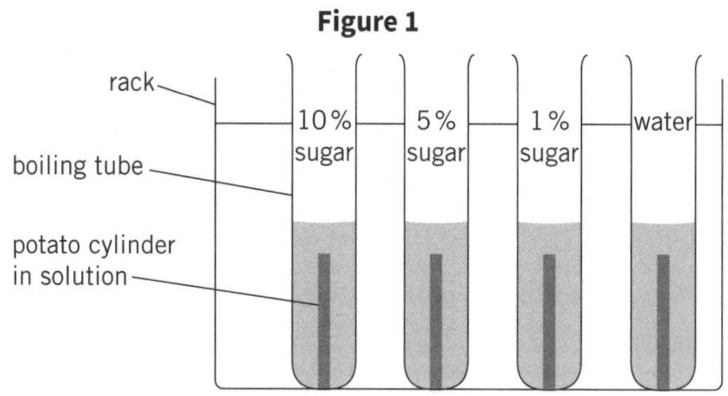

01.1 Name the independent variable in their investigation. **[1 mark]**

____

01.2 Identify **two** variables that the students controlled. **[2 marks]**

1 ______________________________

2 ______________________________

> **Exam Tip**
> Control variables are the ones we keep the same.

01.3 The students' results are shown in **Table 1**.

Table 1

Percentage solution solution	0 (water)	1	5	10
Starting mass in g	3.2	3.3	3.1	3.4
Final mass in g	3.7	3.5	2.9	2.6
Change in mass in g	+0.5	______	−0.2	−0.8
Percentage change in mass	+15.6	______	−6.5	−23.5

Complete **Table 1** by calculating the change in mass and the percentage change in mass for the 1 % sugar solution. **[2 marks]**

> **Exam Tip**
> If you're not sure what to do, try using the values given for the 5 % and 10 % solutions as trials, and see if you can get the answer.

01.4 Plot the students' results of sugar concentration against percentage change in mass on the axes in **Figure 2**.

Draw a suitable line of best fit. **[3 marks]**

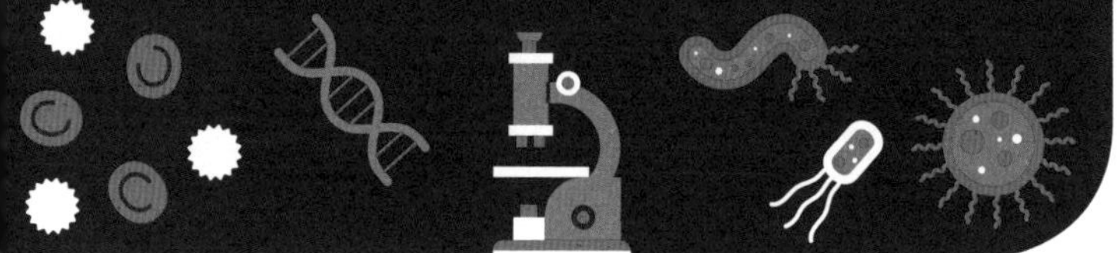

Figure 2

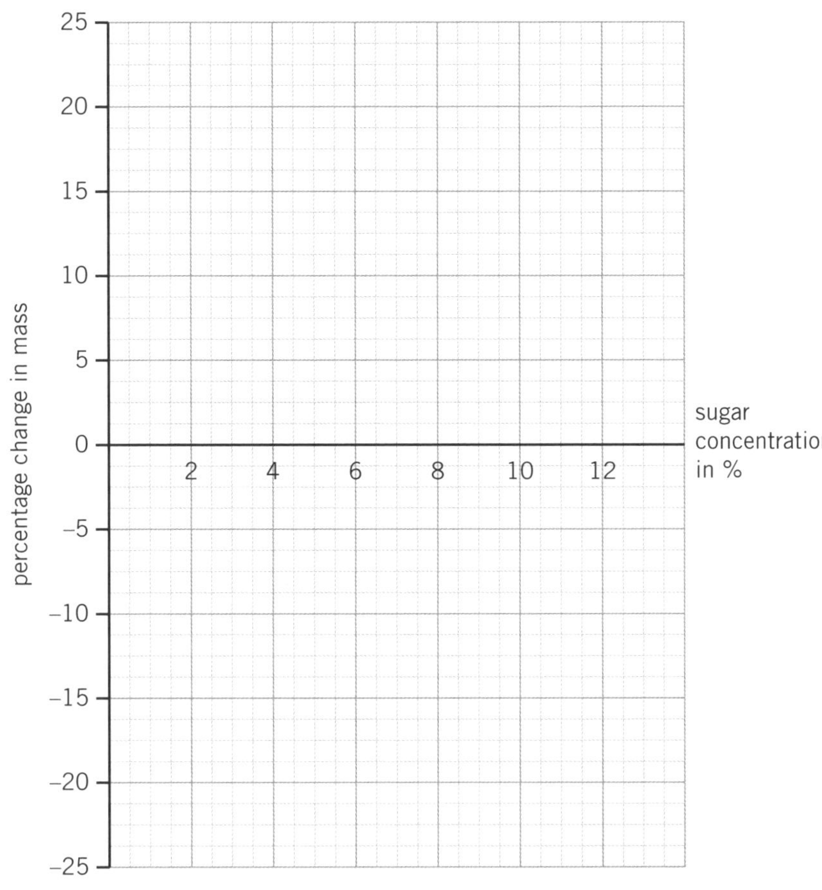

Exam Tip

Lines of best fit need to be a smooth, solid line. If it is a straight line, use a ruler.

01.5 Determine the concentration of sugar present in the potato. **[1 mark]**

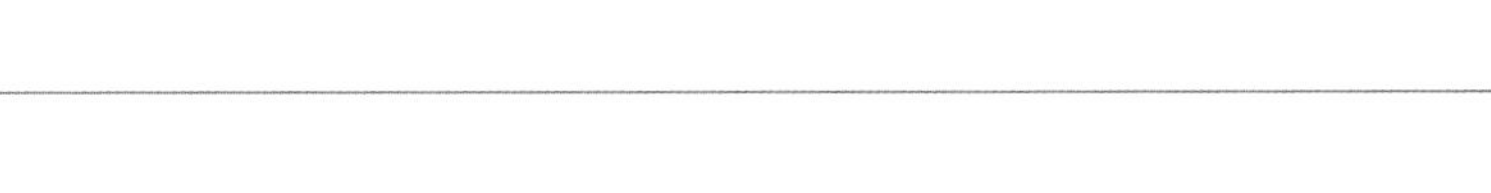

01.6 Describe what the students should do to check that their results are reproducible. **[2 marks]**

02 **Figure 3** shows a plant cell before (**A**) and after (**B**) it was placed in a solution of salt and water.

Figure 3

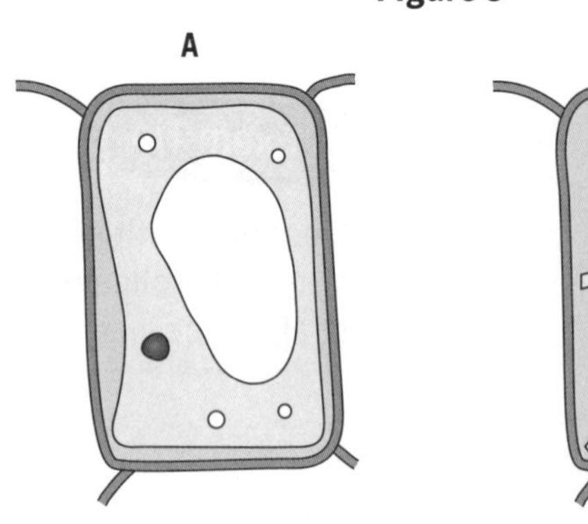

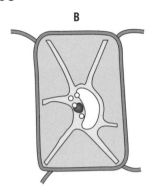

02.1 Name the type of solution that caused the differences observed in diagram **B**. **[1 mark]**

02.2 Explain the differences in the appearance of the plant cell after it was placed in the saltwater solution. **[6 marks]**

The command word here is 'explain', so you need to say *why* the changes have happened.

02.3 Suggest why the cells in **Figure 3** can only be seen in this state in a laboratory. **[1 mark]**

03 Gas exchange in fish takes place in the gills (**Figure 4**). Fish breathe by taking in oxygen from their environment through opening their mouths underwater. This allows water, containing oxygen, to pass over their gills, causing the oxygen to pass from the water into the fish's bloodstream.

Figure 4

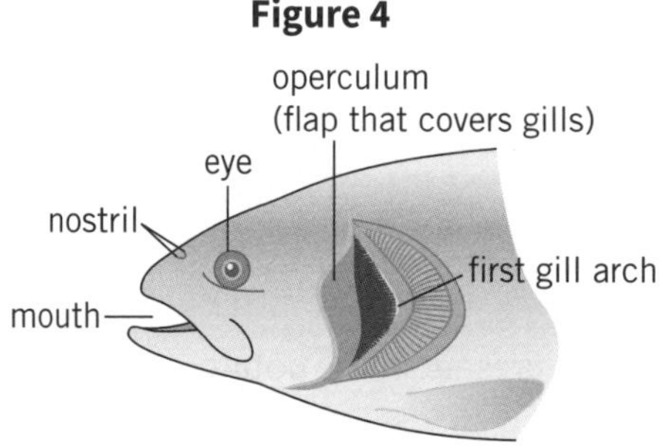

03.1 Describe what is meant by gas exchange. **[1 mark]**

03.2 Use **Figure 4** to suggest **two** ways in which fish gills are adapted for efficient gas exchange. **[2 marks]**

03.3 Students investigated the effect of temperature on the breathing rate of fish. They put same-sized fish in tanks of water at five different temperatures. They then measured the breathing rate of the fish by counting the number of times the fish opened their mouths in one minute. The fish were placed in the water tanks for five minutes before the investigation began.
Suggest why the students included this step in their investigation. **[1 mark]**

Exam Tip

Think about jumping into a swimming pool for the first time – does the temperature feel the same then as after five minutes?

03.4 The students repeated the test five times at each temperature, then calculated the mean. Their results are shown in **Table 2**.

Table 2

Temperature of water in °C	Mean number of breaths taken per minute
5	20
10	38
15	45
20	57
25	70

Exam Tip

This is a one-mark 'describe' question, so it's looking for a short answer stating *what* the pattern is.

Describe the trend shown in the results. **[1 mark]**

03.5 Identify which conclusion the students could draw from their results. Choose **one** answer. **[1 mark]**

The oxygen content of water remains the same regardless of temperature.

The oxygen content of water increases as temperature increases.

The oxygen content of water decreases as temperature increases.

04 *Crocodylus porosus* is a species of freshwater crocodile that normally lives in lakes and rivers.
This species of crocodile is also able to survive in salt water because they have special salt glands in their tongues that remove excess salt from their bodies.

04.1 Explain why *Crocodylus porosus* have to use active transport to remove excess salt from their bodies when living in a saltwater environment. **[2 marks]**

04.2 Explain why the cells in the salt glands have large numbers of mitochondria. **[3 marks]**

04.3 Suggest **one** advantage to *Crocodylus porosus* of being able to inhabit both saltwater and freshwater habitats. **[1 mark]**

05 A scientist planned to carry out an investigation to determine which variety of apple was the sweetest. The scientist had access to the following equipment:

- range of different apples
- potato borer
- scalpel
- balance
- distilled water
- test tubes
- test-tube rack
- measuring cylinder
- sucrose solutions at six different concentrations.

Plan an investigation the scientist could carry out to determine the sugar concentration of each variety of apple. **[6 marks]**

Exam Tip

Planning an experiment is an important skill to practise.

Make sure you clearly plan out what you're going to do, and think about safety.

06 Cell **A** is a spherical animal cell with a radius of 5 μm.

Cell **B** is also spherical. It has a radius of 20 μm.

06.1 Identify which statement about these two cells is true.
Choose **one** answer. **[1 mark]**

Cell **A** has a smaller surface area than cell **B**.

Cell **B** has a smaller volume than cell **A**.

Cell **A** has a smaller surface area-to-volume ratio than cell **B**.

Cell **B** has a smaller surface area-to-volume ratio than cell **A**.

06.2 Cell **A** has a surface area-to-volume ratio of 0.6 : 1. It takes 5 ms for an amino acid to diffuse out of cell **A** into the bloodstream. Assuming that the rate of diffusion is proportional to the surface area-to-volume ratio of a cell, calculate the time taken for an identical amino acid to diffuse out of cell **B**. **[5 marks]**

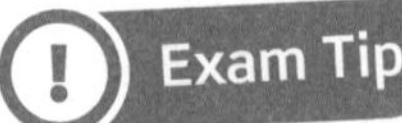

There are lots of areas of biology which use your maths skills. Make sure you practise these before your exam.

07 Plant roots absorb water from the soil by osmosis.

07.1 Define the term osmosis. **[1 mark]**

07.2 Once inside the root, water continues to move from cell to cell as it moves towards the xylem vessel. **Figure 5** shows three cells within the root. Each cell contains a different concentration of salt.

Figure 5

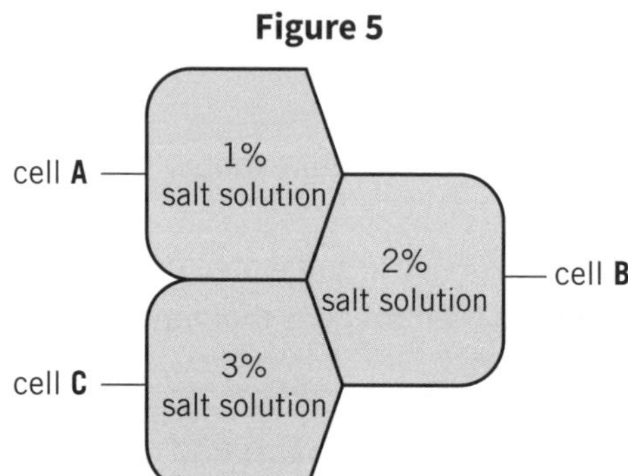

Water can move from cell to cell in any direction.
Identify which cell will gain water the fastest. Give a reason for your answer. **[2 marks]**

07.3 Xylem vessels transport water throughout the plant.
Describe the structure of the xylem vessels. **[2 marks]**

08 The alveoli in the lungs are adapted for gas exchange.
One adaptation is a large surface area-to-volume ratio.

08.1 Explain how a large surface area-to-volume ratio maximises gas exchange. **[2 marks]**

08.2 Explain **one** other way the lungs are adapted for gas exchange. **[2 marks]**

08.3 Alveoli can be modelled as spheres. The diameter of an alveolus is 300 μm. The surface area of a sphere is calculated using the formula:

$$\text{surface area} = 4\pi r^2$$

The volume of a sphere is calculated using the formula:

$$\text{volume} = \frac{4}{3}\pi r^3$$

Calculate the surface area-to-volume ratio of an alveolus. **[4 marks]**

09 In many restaurants, vegetables are prepared in advance for the evening's meals. To prevent them turning brown, chefs often leave the prepared vegetables in slightly salted water. A chef wanted to know the ideal concentration of salt water to store potatoes. The chef used the following method:

1. Cut the potato into pieces of equal volume.
2. Measure the mass of each potato piece.
3. Place each potato piece into a different concentration of salt solution.
4. Leave for two hours.
5. Remove each potato piece and blot dry.
6. Measure the new mass of each potato piece.

The chef's results are shown in **Table 3**.

Exam Tip

This can be any vegetable.

In the first exam of this new specification, the examiners used a different model for osmosis and it confused many students. Don't let changes like this cost you marks!

Table 3

Concentration of saltwater solution in M	0.0	0.5	1.0	1.5	2.0
Starting mass in g	2.8	3.0	3.1	2.9	2.9
Mass after 2 hours in g	3.1	3.0	3.0	2.7	2.4

Exam Tip

This is the difference between the starting mass and mass after two hours, not just the highest mass after two hours.

09.1 Identify the solution in which the potato gained the most mass. **[1 mark]**

09.2 Explain why this potato gained mass. **[2 marks]**

09.3 Suggest which concentration of salt solution the chef should store the potato in. Give a reason for your answer. **[2 marks]**

10 Substances such as water and ions need to move in and out of cells.

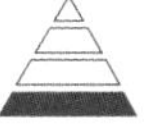

10.1 Draw **one** line between each process and the correct method of transport. **[2 marks]**

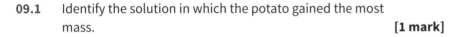

Process	Transport method
The movement of oxygen from the lungs into the bloodstream.	active transport
The movement of mineral ions from the soil into a plant root system.	osmosis
The movement of water into a plant cell.	diffusion

10.2 Complete the sentence using the correct bolded words. **[2 marks]**

Cells that carry out active transport contain **many / few** mitochondria so that there will be sufficient **chemicals / energy**.

10.3 Explain why active transport is required to move glucose from the small intestine into the bloodstream. **[3 marks]**

Knowledge

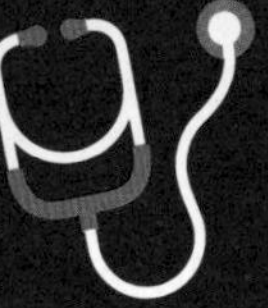

B3 Cell division

Chromosomes

The nucleus of a cell contains chromosomes.
in normal body cells the chromosomes are normally found in pairs

Each chromosome carries a large number of genes made of DNA molecules.

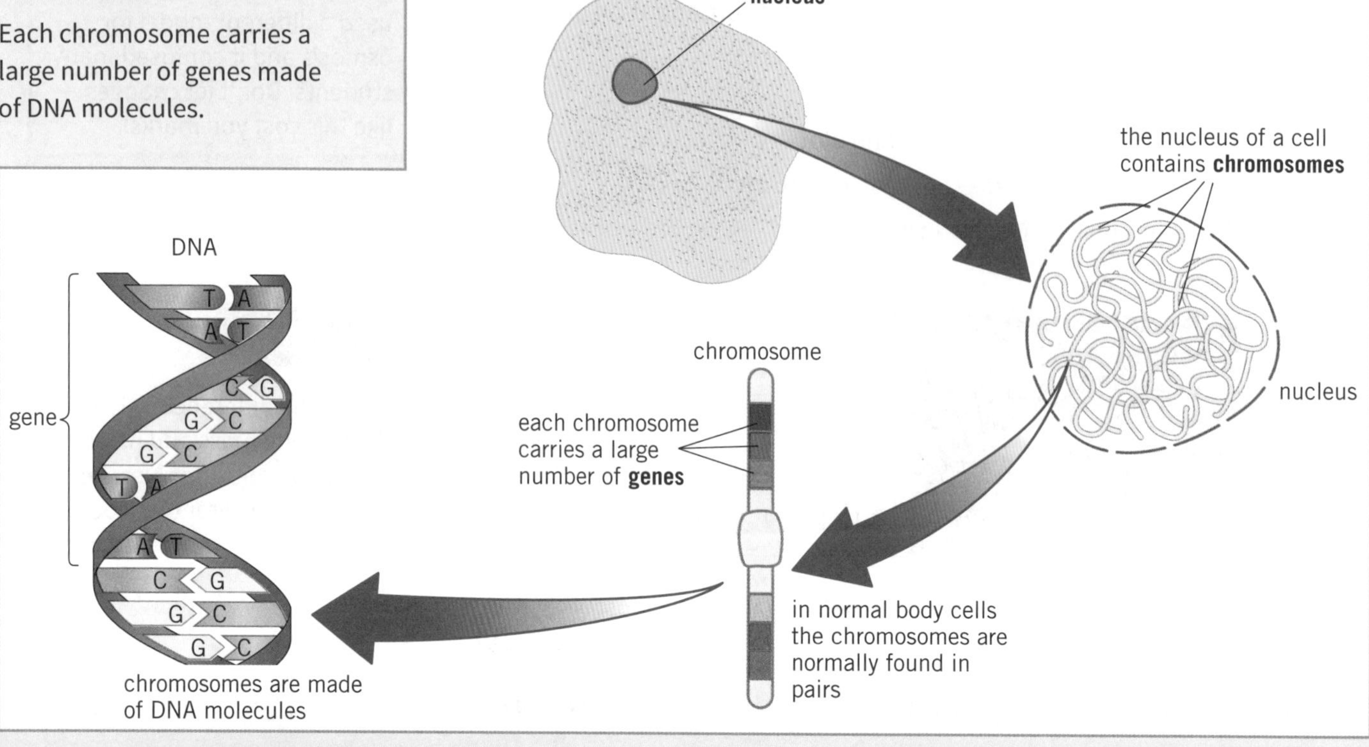

The cell cycle

Body cells divide to form two identical **daughter cells** by going through a series of stages known as the **cell cycle**.

Cell division by **mitosis** is important for the growth and repair of cells, for example, the replacement of skin cells. Mitosis is also used for asexual reproduction.

There are *three* main stages in the cell cycle:

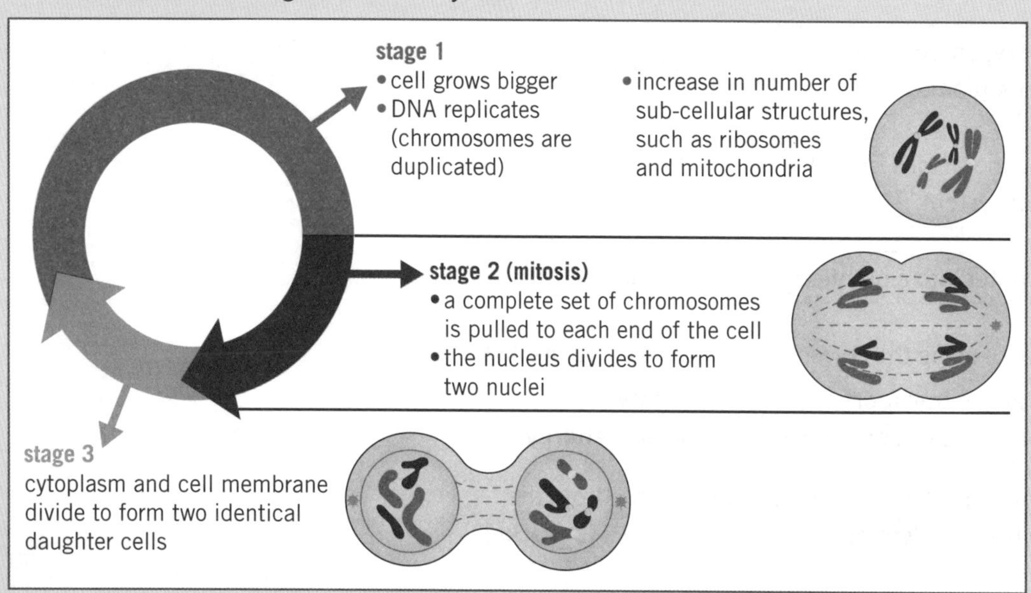

stage 1
• cell grows bigger
• DNA replicates (chromosomes are duplicated)
• increase in number of sub-cellular structures, such as ribosomes and mitochondria
stage 2 (mitosis)
• a complete set of chromosomes is pulled to each end of the cell
• the nucleus divides to form two nuclei
stage 3
cytoplasm and cell membrane divide to form two identical daughter cells

Revision tip

Remember Mitosis has a *t* in it, so that should help you remember that it makes *two* daughter cells.

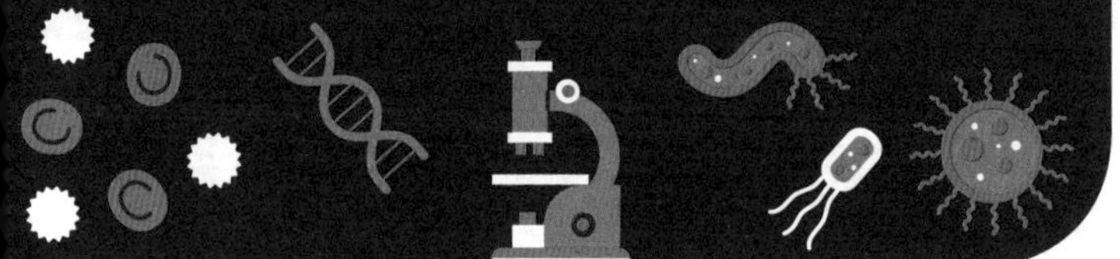

Stem cells in medicine

A stem cell is an undifferentiated cell that can develop into one or more types of specialised cell.

There are two types of stem cell in mammals: **adult stem cells** and **embryonic stem cells**.

Stem cells can be **cloned** to produce large numbers of identical cells.

Type of stem cell	Where are they found?	What can they differentiate into?	Advantages	Disadvantages
adult stem cells	specific parts of the body in adults and children – for example, bone marrow	can only differentiate to form certain types of cells – for example, stem cells in bone marrow can only differentiate into types of blood cell	• fewer ethical issues – adults can consent to have their stem cells removed and used • an already established technique for treating diseases such as leukaemia • relatively safe to use as a treatment and donors recover quickly	• requires a donor, potentially meaning a long wait time to find someone suitable • can only differentiate into certain types of specialised cells, so can be used to treat fewer diseases
embryonic stem cells	early human embryos (often taken from spare embryos from fertility clinics)	can differentiate into any type of specialised cell in the body – for example, a nerve cell or a muscle cell	• can treat a wide range of diseases as can form any specialised cell • may be possible to grow whole replacement organs • usually no donor needed as they are obtained from spare embryos from fertility clinics	• ethical issues as the embryo is destroyed and each embryo is a potential human life • risk of transferring viral infections to the patient • newer treatment so relatively under-researched – not yet clear if they can cure as many diseases as thought
plant meristem	meristem regions in the roots and shoots of plants	can differentiate into all cell types – they can be used to create clones of whole plants	• rare species of plants can be cloned to prevent extinction • plants with desirable traits, such as disease resistance, can be cloned to produce large numbers of identical plants • fast and low-cost production of large numbers of plants	• cloned plants are genetically identical, so a whole crop is at risk of being destroyed by a single disease or genetic defect

Therapeutic cloning

In **therapeutic cloning**

- cells from a patient's own body are used to create a cloned early embryo of themselves
- stem cells from this embryo can be used for medical treatments and growing new organs
- these stem cells have the same genes as the patient, so are less likely to be rejected when transplanted.

Key terms

Make sure you can write a definition for these key terms.

adult stem cell, cell cycle, chromosome, clone, daughter cells, embryonic stem cell, gene, meristem, mitosis, nucleus, therapeutic cloning

Retrieval

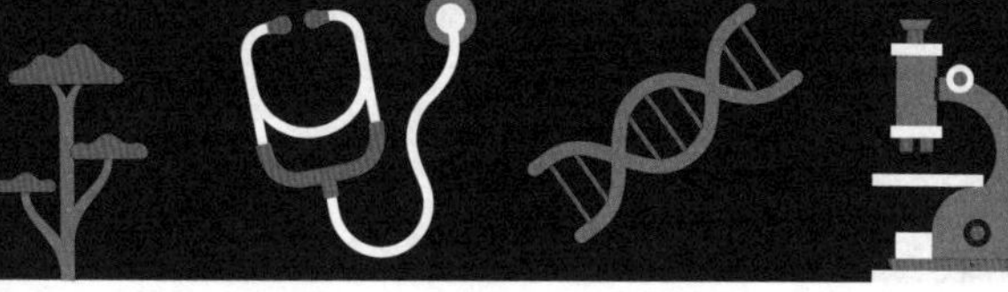

Learn the answers to the questions below, then cover the answers column with a piece of paper and write as many as you can. Check and repeat.

	B3 questions	Answers
1	What is a stem cell?	undifferentiated cell that can differentiate into one or more specialised cell types
2	What are adult stem cells?	stem cells from adults that can only differentiate into certain specialised cells
3	Where can adult stem cells be found?	bone marrow
4	What are embryonic stem cells?	stem cells from embryos that can differentiate into any specialised cell
5	Where are embryonic stem cells found?	early human embryos (usually from spare embryos from fertility clinics)
6	What is therapeutic cloning?	patient's cells are used to create an early embryo clone of themselves – stem cells from the embryo can then be used to treat the patient's medical conditions
7	Give one advantage of using therapeutic cloning.	stem cells from the embryo are not rejected when transplanted because they have the same genes as the patient
8	Give one advantage of using adult stem cells.	fewer ethical issues as obtained from adults who can consent to their use
9	Give two disadvantages of using adult stem cells.	• can take a long time for a suitable donor to be found • can only differentiate into some specialised cell types, so treat fewer diseases
10	Give two advantages of using embryonic stem cells.	• can differentiate into any specialised cell, so can be used to treat many diseases • easier to obtain as they are found in spare embryos from fertility clinics
11	Give two disadvantages of using embryonic stem cells.	• ethical issues surrounding their use, as every embryo is a potential life • potential risks involved with treatments, such as transfer of viral infections
12	What are plant meristems?	area where rapid cell division occurs in the tips of roots and shoots
13	Give two advantages of using plant meristems to clone plants.	• rare species can be cloned to protect them from extinction • plants with special features (e.g., disease resistance) can be cloned to produce many copies
14	Give one disadvantage of using plant meristems to clone plants.	no genetic variation, so, for example, an entire cloned crop could be destroyed by a disease
15	What is cell division by mitosis?	body cells divide to form two identical daughter cells
16	What is the purpose of mitosis?	growth and repair of cells, asexual reproduction
17	What happens during the first stage of the cell cycle?	cell grows bigger, chromosomes duplicate, number of sub-cellular structures (e.g., ribosomes and mitochondria) increases
18	What happens during mitosis?	one set of chromosomes is pulled to each end of the cell and the nucleus divides
19	What happens during the third stage of the cell cycle?	the cytoplasm and cell membrane divide, forming two identical daughter cells

Put paper here Put paper here Put paper here Put paper here Put paper here Put paper here Put paper here Put paper here

Now go back and use the questions below to check your knowledge from previous chapters.

Previous questions

	Previous questions	Answers
1	Where is DNA found in animal and plant cells?	in the nucleus
2	What are two types of eukaryotic cell?	animal and plant
3	What is the function of the cell membrane?	controls movement of substances into and out of the cell
4	What is the function of mitochondria?	site of respiration to release energy for the cell
5	What is the function of chloroplasts?	contain chlorophyll to absorb light energy for photosynthesis
6	Name three factors that affect the rate of diffusion.	concentration gradient, temperature, membrane surface area
7	What is the function of the cell wall?	strengthens and supports the cell
8	What is diffusion?	net movement of particles from an area of high concentration to an area of low concentration along a concentration gradient – this is a passive process (does not require energy from respiration)
9	What is osmosis?	diffusion of water from a dilute solution to a concentrated solution through a partially permeable membrane

Put paper here

Maths Skills

Practise your maths skills using the worked example and practice questions below.

Converting units

The size of a cell or organelle is most often shown in millimetres (mm), micrometres (μm), or nanometres (nm). You may be asked to convert between mm, μm, and nm. If you are converting from a smaller unit to a larger unit, your number should get smaller. If you are converting a larger unit to a smaller unit, the number should get bigger.

Worked example

- to convert mm to μm: multiply the mm reading by 1000
- to convert μm to nm: multiply the μm reading by 1000
- to convert nm into μm: divide the reading by 1000
- to convert μm into mm: divide the reading by 1000

Cell	Size in mm	Size in μm	Size in nm
red blood cell	0.007	7	7000
leaf cell	0.06	60	60 000
egg cell	0.1	100	100 000

Practice

Convert the following cell and organelle sizes to complete the table.

Structure	Size in mm	Size in μm	Size in nm
ant	3		
human hair		100	
palisade leaf cell		70	
plant cell ribosome			20
HIV virus			100
egg cell mitochondrion	0.002		

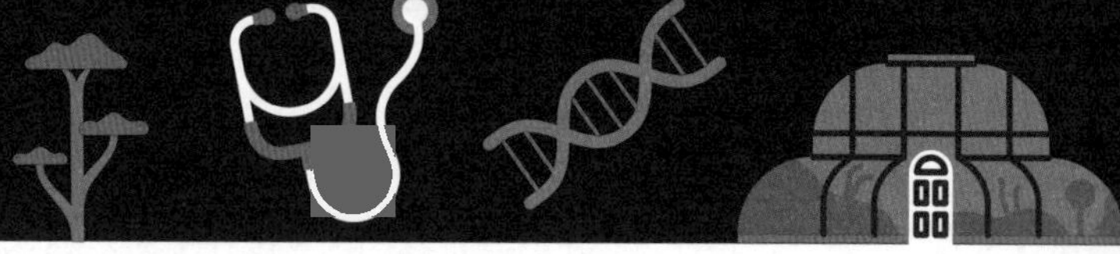

Exam-style questions

01 **Figure 1** shows some plant cells undergoing mitosis.

Figure 1

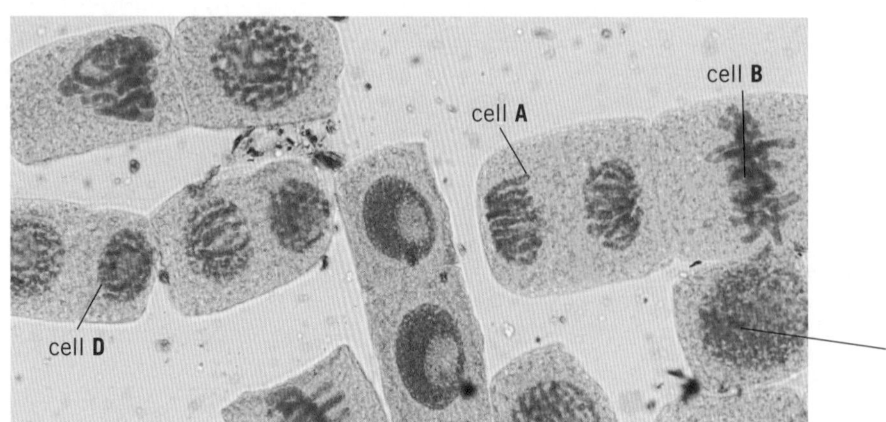

01.1 Describe what is happening in cell **C**. **[3 marks]**

____

____

____

____

> **Exam Tip**
> Think about what needs to happen to the DNA before it can divide.

01.2 Identify which sequence of cells from **Figure 1** best represents the process of mitosis. **[1 mark]**

Tick **one** box.

cell **D** → cell **A** → cell **B** → cell **C** ☐

cell **C** → cell **B** → cell **A** → cell **D** ☐

cell **A** → cell **B** → cell **C** → cell **D** ☐

cell **C** → cell **D** → cell **B** → cell **A** ☐

01.3 Cells **A**–**D** do not show the final stage of mitosis.

Describe what would happen at the next stage in this process. **[2 marks]**

____

____

____

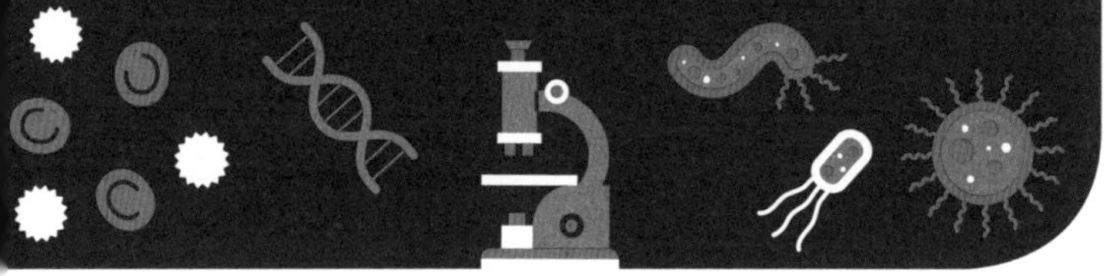

01.4 When looking at cells under a microscope, the length of different stages of the cell cycle can be estimated using the formula:

$$\text{length of stage} = \frac{\text{number of cells at that stage} \times \text{total length of time in the cell cycle}}{\text{total number of cells}}$$

The average time taken for the plant cells in **Figure 1** to complete the cell cycle is 24 hours.

One stage in the mitosis cycle is called metaphase – this is where chromosomes line up at the centre of the cell.

Using the information in **Figure 1**, calculate the time taken for the metaphase stage. **[3 marks]**

_______________ hours

Exam Tip

You may not have seen this equation before, but don't worry! You need to get used to using new and unfamiliar equations so you're ready for the exam. Just plug the numbers in and away you go!

02 People with Type 1 diabetes do not produce enough insulin. This is because the insulin-producing cells in the pancreas are destroyed by the body's immune system.

Patients with this form of diabetes have to inject themselves regularly with insulin.

Scientists hope that stem cells could be used to treat this condition one day.

02.1 Describe what is meant by a stem cell. **[1 mark]**

____

____

02.2 Suggest the role that stem cells could play in a diabetic person's body. **[1 mark]**

____

____

Exam Tip

Think about the cells that don't work properly in a diabetic person.

02.3 A group of scientists carried out a study into the use of adult stem cells to treat Type 1 diabetes.

Describe the main difference between these stem cells and an embryonic stem cell. **[2 marks]**

____

____

____

02.4 Suggest **one** reason why it is preferential to use stem cells from the actual patient instead of using cells from a donor. **[1 mark]**

____

____

02.5 The study used 23 patients. The patients taking part in the trial were tracked over a 30-month period. At the end of the investigation, 12 patients did not have to inject themselves with insulin anymore.

Calculate the percentage of patients for which the treatment was successful. **[1 mark]**

Exam Tip

A common mistake when working out percentages is forgetting to multiply the answer by 100 at the end.

______________ %

02.6 Suggest whether this technique is a successful treatment for Type 1 diabetes. **[1 mark]**

____

____

____

03 All cells in the human body contain genetic information.

03.1 Describe how the genetic material is organised in the nucleus of a human cell. **[3 marks]**

03.2 As a baby grows, its cells change in a number of ways.
Explain why mitosis and cell differentiation are important in the growth and development of a baby from a fertilised egg. **[4 marks]**

Exam Tip

Question **03.2** has four marks – you need to write two points for each section.

03.3 Describe the main steps in mitosis. **[4 marks]**

04 Scientists hope that in the future it will be possible to use stem cells to help treat patients with a number of conditions, such as diabetes.

04.1 Explain why stem cells may be able to offer treatments for conditions such as diabetes that currently have no cure. **[3 marks]**

04.2 Name where in the human body stem cells can be found that can differentiate into different types of blood cell. **[1 mark]**

04.3 There are mixed opinions about the potential use of embryonic stem cells for the treatment of human diseases. Many people feel that there are good reasons for carrying out this research, but others are opposed to these studies.
Evaluate the ethical arguments surrounding the use of embryonic stem cells in medical research. **[6 marks]**

Exam Tip

For an 'evaluate' question you need four key points:

1 advantages
2 disadvantages
3 your opinion
4 why you have that opinion.

If you don't include all of these, you won't get top marks.

05 Stem cells are found in both plants and animals.

05.1 Name the area in a plant where stem cells are located. **[1 mark]**

05.2 **Figure 2** shows a diagram of a root tip of a plant.
Identify the letter (**A–D**) in **Figure 2** indicating where stem cells are located in the root tip. **[1 mark]**

Figure 2

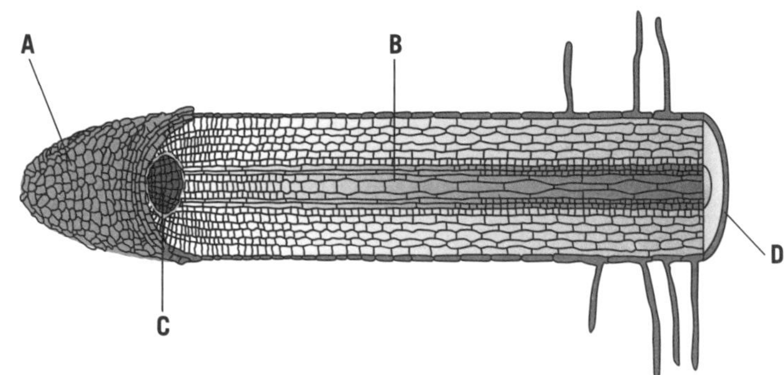

05.3 Identify the sequence that correctly describes the steps plant stem cells go through to produce a root hair cell.
Choose **one** answer. **[1 mark]**

differentiation → DNA replication → elongation → mitosis

elongation → differentiation → DNA replication → mitosis

DNA replication → elongation → mitosis → differentiation

DNA replication → mitosis → elongation → differentiation

Work through these slowly, crossing off any you know are incorrect, and hopefully that will only leave one answer!

05.4 Tick **one** box in each row to identify the differences between plant and animal stem cell differentiation. **[2 marks]**

Statement	Animal stem cells	Plant stem cells
differentiation occurs at a very early stage		
differentiation occurs throughout life		
differentiations produced are permanent		
differentiation can be reversed or changed		

Make sure that you read the question: 'Tick one box in each row' means it's not the same answer for both types of stem cell.

06 A scientist takes a cutting from a plant.

06.1 Select the statement that best describes why the meristem in the cutting allows a new plant to grow. Choose **one** answer. **[1 mark]**

Meristems contain differentiated cells.

Meristems contain undifferentiated cells.

Meristems are where new roots form.

Meristems respond to light.

06.2 Explain why this technique is a form of cloning. **[1 mark]**

06.3 Suggest **two** advantages of using this technique to produce new plants of this species, as opposed to letting the plant reproduce naturally. **[2 marks]**

07 When neurones in the brain stop producing dopamine, a person can develop Parkinson's disease. This is a disease of the nervous system. One of the symptoms experienced by sufferers is tremors (shaking).

07.1 Explain **two** ways in which nerve cells are specialised. **[4 marks]**

07.2 Dopamine is a chemical that allows neurones to communicate with each other. Suggest and explain why a person suffering from Parkinson's disease experiences tremors. **[2 marks]**

07.3 Therapeutic cloning is a type of stem cell research where scientists are trying to produce an early embryo clone from cells taken from an adult human.

The stem cells from the patient's cloned embryo can then potentially be used to produce stem cells to treat a medical condition that the person has.

This process is summarised in **Figure 3**.

Using your own knowledge and information in the question, suggest and explain how stem cell treatment could be used in the future to treat Parkinson's disease. **[3 marks]**

Figure 3

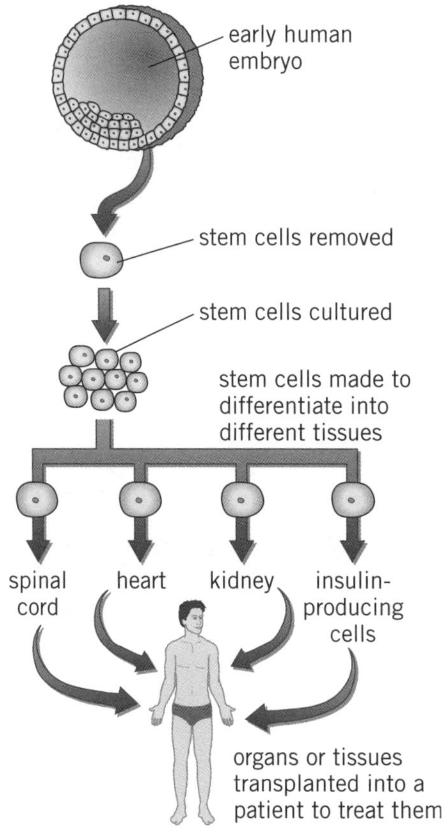

07.4 Discuss the advantages and disadvantages of using therapeutic cloning to treat Parkinson's disease. **[6 marks]**

Exam Tip

In the exam you'll come across topics you've never seen before and be expected to apply what you have learnt in your lessons. Lots of students are worried by this, but by using the questions in this book you're giving yourself a great head-start in this skill.

Don't worry if you didn't cover dopamine or Parkinson's disease in class, this is a question to show what you know about stem cell therapy.

Exam Tip

To answer **07.4**, there is lots of information already in the question.

Highlight the advantages in one colour and the disadvantages in another – this will help you easily pick out which bits you need to answer the question fully.

08 Body cells divide in a regulated series of events called the cell cycle. The length of the cell cycle varies considerably between different types of cell and the stages of an organism's development.

08.1 Identify the cell with the shortest cell cycle.
Choose **one** answer. **[1 mark]**

an adult nerve cell | a teenager's liver cell

a child's brain cell | an unborn fetal intestinal cell

08.2 Some organs in the body contain cells that have a short cell cycle throughout a person's life. Identify **one** region in the body where this happens and give a reason for your answer. **[2 marks]**

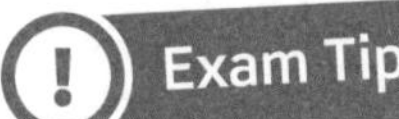

Exam Tip

In **08.2**, think of areas that frequently need new cells.

08.3 Describe the changes that occur at each stage of the cell cycle. **[4 marks]**

08.4 Suggest **one** reason why it is important that the chromosome number stays the same after mitosis. **[1 mark]**

09 Scientists can now grow a number of different types of stem cells from embryonic stem cells. Many of the stem cells are taken from spare embryos created during fertility treatments, such as in vitro fertilisation (IVF).

09.1 Identify which type of microscope a scientist would use to check that an egg cell had been fertilised and developed into a healthy embryo. Give reasons for your answer. **[2 marks]**

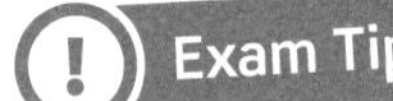

Which type of microscope can view living cells?

09.2 Suggest **one** ethical concern some people may have with using embryonic stem cells. **[1 mark]**

09.3 A human egg cell is approximately 0.1 mm in diameter. A human sperm cell is approximately 2.5 μm.
Calculate the difference in orders of magnitude between a sperm cell and an egg cell. **[2 marks]**

10 **Figure 4** shows some cells taken from the root tips of an onion viewed under a microscope.

Figure 4

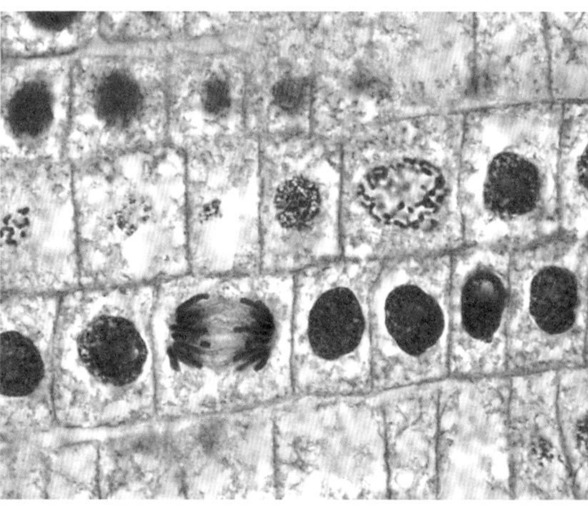

Exam Tip

Link your answers to what you can see in the image.

10.1 Describe how you can tell that these cells are undergoing mitosis. **[1 mark]**

10.2 Explain how a microscope slide of root cells should be prepared for viewing. **[4 marks]**

10.3 The root cells were viewed using a 15× eyepiece lens and a 40× objective lens.
Calculate the total magnification used to view the root cells. **[1 mark]**

Don't be tempted to use the equation for magnification in question **10.3** – it is much simpler than that, even if you haven't come across this in class.

10.4 Root hair cells are an example of a specialised cell.
Write down **one** way in which they are adapted for taking water into a plant. **[1 mark]**

Knowledge

B4 Organisation in animals

There are five levels of organisation in living organisms:

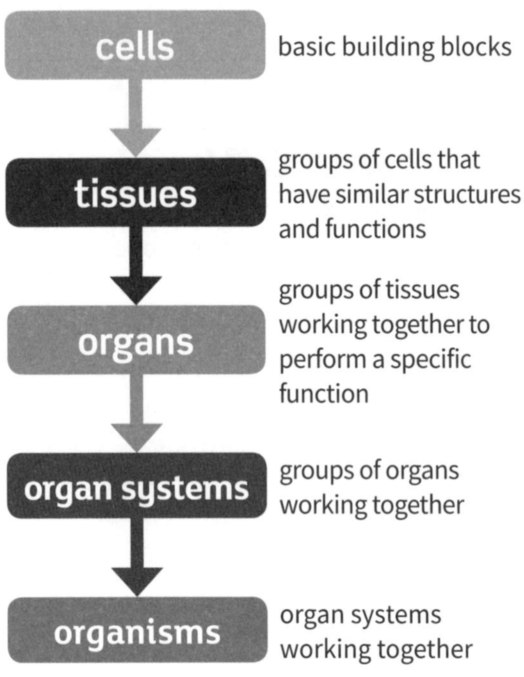

Digestive system

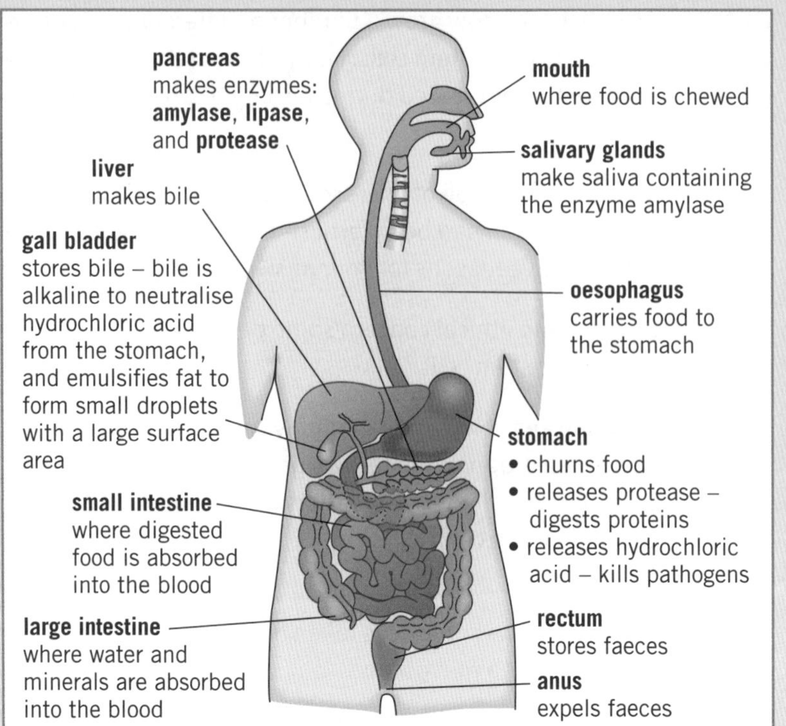

Lungs

When breathing in, air moves

1. into the body through the mouth and nose
2. down the trachea
3. into the **bronchi**
4. through the **bronchioles**
5. into the **alveoli** (air sacs).

Oxygen then diffuses into the blood in the network of **capillaries** over the surface of the alveoli.

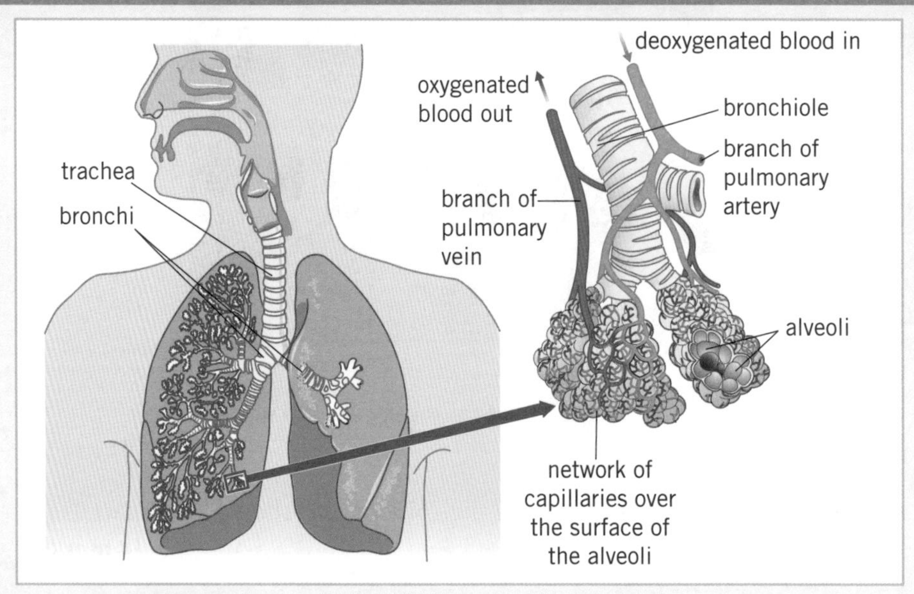

The circulatory system

Blood is a tissue made up of four main components	• red blood cells – bind to oxygen and transport it around the body • **plasma** – transports substances and blood cells around the body • **platelets** – form blood clots to create barriers to infections • white blood cells – part of the immune system to defend the body against pathogens

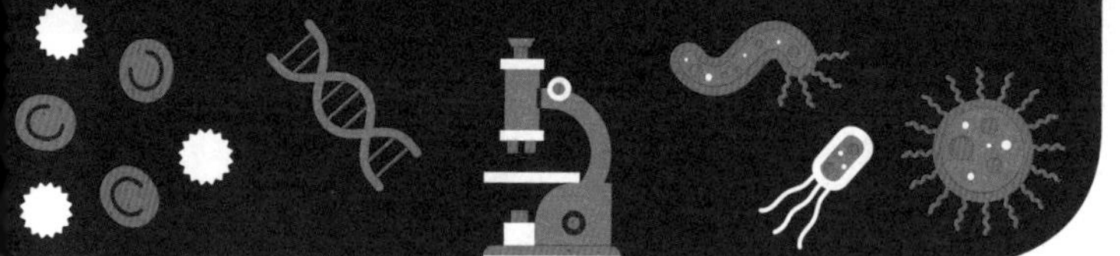

Blood vessels

The structure of each blood vessel relates to its functions.

Vessel	Function	Structure	Diagram
artery	• carries blood *away from* the heart • high pressure	• thick, muscular, and elastic walls • the walls can stretch and withstand high pressure • small lumen	thick wall; small lumen; thick layer of muscle and elastic fibres
vein	• carries blood *to* the heart • low pressure	• have valves to stop blood flowing the wrong way • thin walls • large lumen	relatively thin wall; large lumen; often has valves
capillary	• carries blood to tissues and cells • connects arteries and veins	• one cell thick – short diffusion distance for substances to move between the blood and tissues (e.g., oxygen into cells and carbon dioxide out) • very narrow lumen	wall one cell thick; tiny vessel with narrow lumen

The heart

The heart is the organ that pumps blood around your body. It is made from **cardiac** muscle tissue, which is supplied with oxygen by the **coronary artery**.

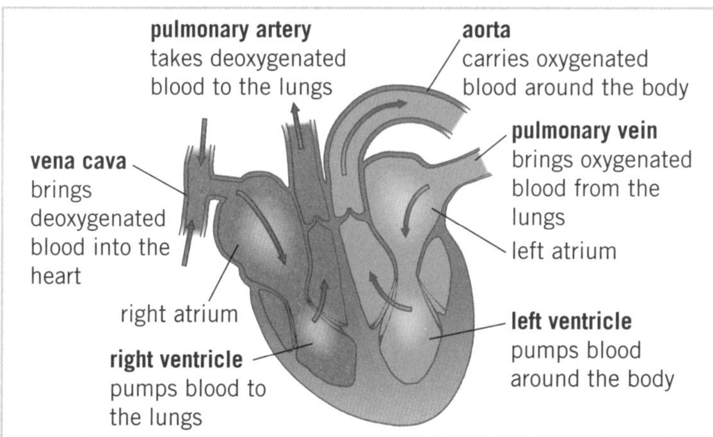

Heart rate is controlled by a group of cells in the right **atrium** that generate electrical impulses, acting as a pacemaker.

Artificial pacemakers can be used to control irregular heartbeats.

Double circulatory system

The human circulatory system is described as a **double circulatory system** because blood passes through the heart twice for every circuit around the body:

- the right ventricle pumps blood to the lungs where gas exchange takes place
- the left ventricle pumps blood around the rest of the body.

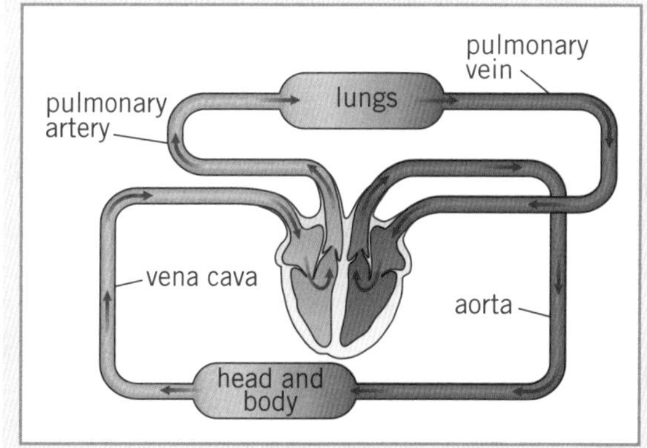

Key terms

Make sure you can write a definition for these key terms.

alveoli amylase aorta artery atrium bronchi bronchiole capillary cardiac coronary double circulatory system lipase organ organ system plasma platelet protease pulmonary tissue vein vena cava ventricle

Retrieval

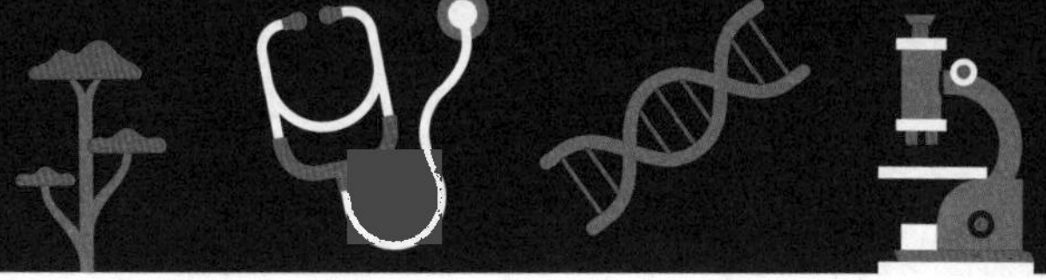

Learn the answers to the questions below, then cover the answers column with a piece of paper and write as many as you can. Check and repeat.

	B4 questions	Answers
1	Name the five levels of organisation in living organisms.	cells → tissues → organs → organ systems → organisms
2	What is a tissue?	a group of cells with similar structures and functions
3	What is an organ?	a group of tissues working together to perform a specific function
4	What is the function of bile in digestion?	neutralises hydrochloric acid from the stomach and emulsifies fat to form small droplets with a large surface area
5	What is the function of saliva in digestion?	lubrication to help swallowing – contains amylase to break down starch
6	Name three enzymes produced in the pancreas.	amylase, protease, lipase
7	Name the four main components of blood.	red blood cells, white blood cells, plasma, platelets
8	What is the function of platelets?	form blood clots – prevent the loss of blood and stop wounds becoming infected
9	Describe three adaptations of a red blood cell.	• bi-concave disc shape – large surface area-to-volume ratio for diffusion of oxygen • contains haemoglobin – binds to oxygen • no nucleus – more space for oxygen
10	How do white blood cells protect the body?	• engulf pathogens • produce antitoxins to neutralise toxins, or antibodies
11	Name the substances transported in the blood plasma.	hormones, proteins, urea, carbon dioxide, glucose
12	Why is the human circulatory system a double circulatory system?	blood passes through the heart twice for every circuit around the body – deoxygenated blood is pumped from the right side of the heart to the lungs, and the oxygenated blood that returns from the lungs is pumped from the left side of the heart to the body
13	How does the structure of an artery relate to its function?	carries blood away from the heart under high pressure – has a small lumen and thick, elasticated walls that can stretch
14	How does the structure of a vein relate to its function?	carries blood back to the heart at low pressure – doesn't need thick, elasticated walls, but has valves to prevent blood flowing the wrong way
15	How does the structure of a capillary relate to its function?	carries blood to cells and tissues – has a one-cell-thick wall to provide a short diffusion distance
16	List the structures air passes through when breathing in.	mouth/nose → trachea → bronchi → bronchioles → alveoli

Put paper here

Now go back and use the questions below to check your knowledge from previous chapters.

Previous questions / Answers

	Previous questions	Answers
1	What is the purpose of active transport in the small intestine?	sugars can be absorbed when the concentration of sugar in the small intestine is lower than the concentration of sugar in the blood
2	What is therapeutic cloning?	patient's cells are used to create an early embryo clone of themselves – stem cells from the embryo can then be used to treat the patient's medical conditions
3	What is a stem cell?	undifferentiated cell that can differentiate into one or more specialised cell types
4	Give one disadvantage of using plant meristems to clone plants.	no genetic variation, so, for example, an entire cloned crop could be destroyed by a disease
5	What is active transport?	movement of particles against a concentration gradient – from a dilute solution to a more concentrated solution – using energy from respiration

Put paper here

Put paper here

Required Practical Skills

Practise answering questions on the required practicals using the example below. You need to be able to apply your skills and knowledge to other practicals too.

Food tests

There are different ways to test for four different compounds found in food:

- ethanol test for lipids (fats) – colour change from colourless to cloudy white if present
- Benedict's test for sugars – colour change from blue to red if present
- iodine test for starch (carbohydrates) – colour change from brown to blue-black if present
- Biuret reagent test for protein – colour change from blue to purple if present.

You need to be able to identify and describe the correct method, and results, for each test.

Worked example

A student wanted to test a sample for the presence of protein using Biuret reagent. Write a risk assessment for this activity.

1 Write down general safety practices in labs:

- *wear goggles to protect your eyes*
- *wash hands at the end of the practical*
- *clear up any spills quickly*
- *do not eat any of the food.*

2 Write down what things could hurt you in the practical, and how they could hurt you:

- *Biuret reagent – irritant*
- *glass – can break*
- *pipette – can poke you in the eyes.*

3 Write down how you can prevent these hurting you:

- *wash hands after touching Biuret reagent, do not eat in the lab, and if ingested or it gets into the eyes inform a teacher immediately*
- *if glass is broken inform a teacher immediately*
- *point pipettes downwards.*

Practice

1 A student picked up solution A and added it to a sample of food. Solution A was blue and turned purple after adding to the food. Name solution A and identify the food present in the sample.

2 Benedict's test for sugar requires the solution to be heated. One way to do this is heating the test tube in a beaker of water using a Bunsen burner. Give an alternative method of heating the solution.

3 When testing a sample for protein in a test tube, a student found that the top of the sample tested positive whereas the bottom did not. Give the reason for this result.

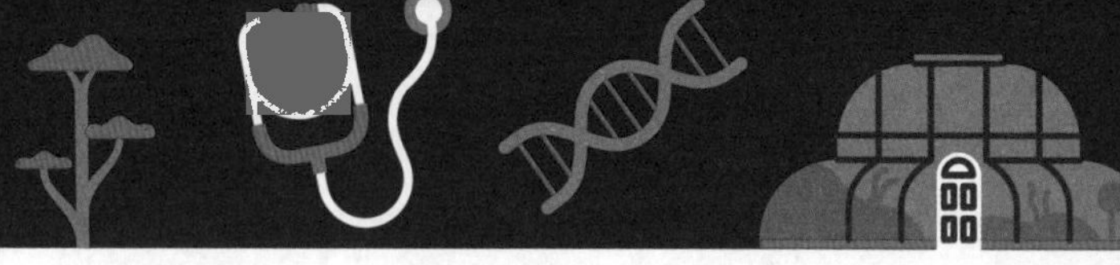

Exam-style questions

01 The events that occur during one breath – one inhalation and one exhalation – are known as one respiratory cycle.

Figure 1 shows the change in the volume of the lungs in one respiratory cycle. The data were taken when the person was resting.

Figure 1

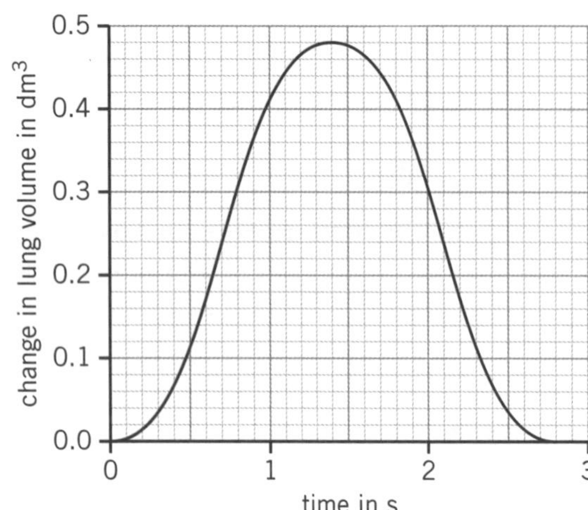

01.1 Use **Figure 1** to determine the volume of air taken in when the person inhales. **[1 mark]**

Draw lines on the graph to help you work it out.

____________ dm^3

01.2 The person's total lung volume after inhalation was 6.00 dm^3.
Calculate their total lung volume after exhalation. **[2 marks]**

____________ dm^3

01.3 Calculate how many respiratory cycles will take place in one minute.
Give your answer to two significant figures. **[3 marks]**

____________ per minute

01.4 Explain how the structures in the chest cavity cause the changes in lung volume shown between 0 s and 1 s. **[4 marks]**

____

____

____

____

____

An explain question wants to know *why* things are happening.

01.5 A doctor measured another person's resting respiratory cycle. This person had 25 respiratory cycles per minute.

Suggest and explain **one** possible cause of this difference. **[2 marks]**

'Suggest and explain' means you need to say *what* you think will happen and *why*.

02 A student carried out a number of food tests on an unknown sample.

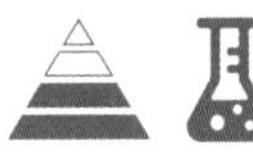

Their results are shown in **Table 1**.

Table 1

Reagent used	Result
iodine	yellow–orange
Benedict's solution	blue
Biuret reagent	purple
ethanol	cloudy white layer formed

02.1 Suggest and explain **one** safety precaution that the student should have taken when using the Biuret reagent. **[2 marks]**

The question has asked for a specific safety precaution when using Biuret reagent, so a general safety measure isn't going to get the marks.

02.2 Which of the following statements is a correct description of the student's findings? **[1 mark]**

Tick **one** box.

The food sample contains starch, protein, and fat. ☐

The food sample contains starch and sugar. ☐

The food sample contains fat and protein. ☐

The food sample contains fat and sugar. ☐

02.3 Which foodstuff is most likely to be the food sample the student tested? **[1 mark]**

Tick **one** box.

a chocolate bar	☐	spaghetti	☐
a meat burger	☐	a carrot	☐

02.4 Many people with diabetes have to follow a strict diet to control their blood glucose levels.

Explain why using Benedict's solution to test foods for glucose may not be helpful to a diabetic. **[2 marks]**

Think about which food diabetic people need to control their intake of.

____

____

____

03 Gluten is a form of protein found in some grains, for example, wheat.

03.1 Describe the structure of a protein. **[1 mark]**

03.2 Coeliac disease is a disease of the digestive system. It damages the lining of the small intestine when foods that contain gluten are eaten, resulting in a patient having a reduced number of villi. This causes a number of symptoms such as abdominal bloating and pain. A healthy person has on average 25 to 30 villi per μm^2.

Calculate the density of the villi in the small intestine of a coeliac patient who has 50 000 villi in 7200 μm^2 of small intestine. **[2 marks]**

Exam Tip

For **03.1**, coeliac disease is used as an example. You may not have covered this in class, but this is getting you used to applying what you know to new situations for the exam.

03.3 **Figure 2** compares a section of the small intestine of a person with coeliac disease and a person who does not have coeliac disease.

Figure 2

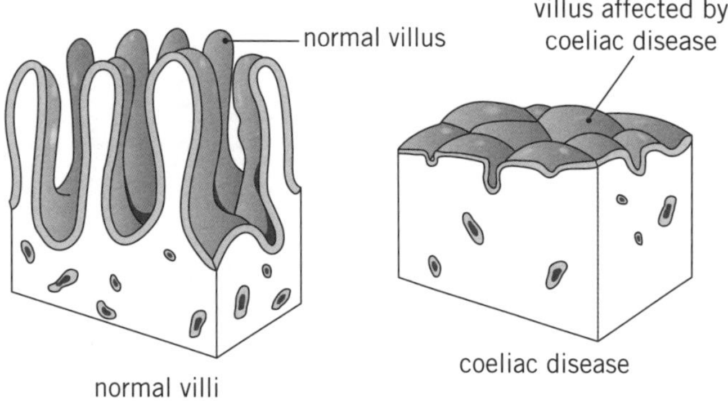

Use the information in the question, and your own knowledge, to suggest why a child with coeliac disease may not grow as tall as their peers. **[4 marks]**

Exam Tip

There is a clear difference in **Figure 2**. Think about how this difference may relate to the function of the digestive system.

04 **Figure 3** shows some organs from the digestive system.

Figure 3

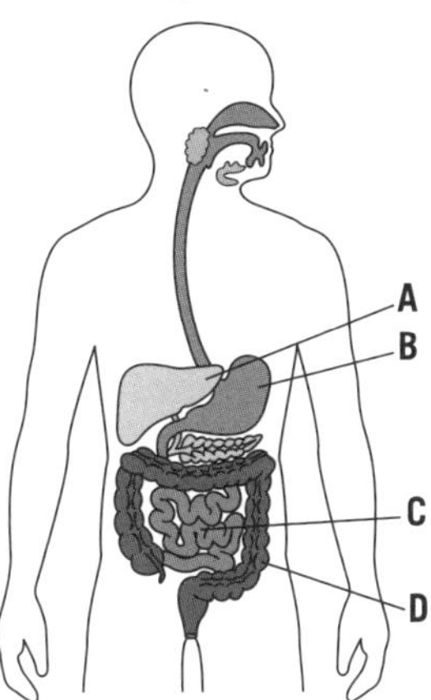

04.1 Identify organs **A** and **C** from **Figure 3**. **[2 marks]**

04.2 Identify the organ from **Figure 3** that is responsible for absorbing water from undigested food. **[1 mark]**

04.3 The stomach is made up of a number of tissues. Draw **one** line from each type of stomach tissue to its function. **[3 marks]**

Stomach tissue	Function
	churns the food and digestive juices of the stomach together
muscular tissue	
	covers the inside and outside of the stomach
glandular tissue	
	sends impulses to other areas of the body
epithelial tissue	
	produces the digestive juices

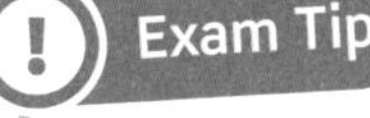

Be careful – there is one more function than you need!

04.4 Explain how the pancreas and the gall bladder work together to increase the efficiency of fat digestion. **[6 marks]**

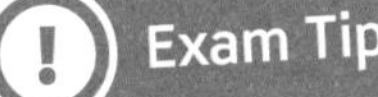

Your answer to **04.4** should relate to fat digestion, not to any other functions.

05 **Figure 4** represents cross-sectional areas through the three main types of blood vessel.

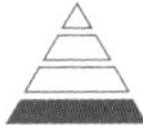

Figure 4

P

Q

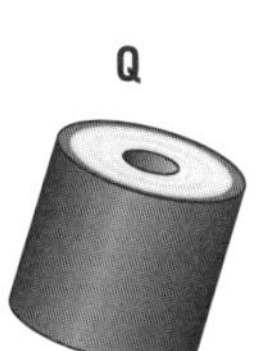

R

05.1 Identify which blood vessel in **Figure 4** represents an artery. **[1 mark]**

05.2 Explain **one** way arteries are adapted for their function. **[2 marks]**

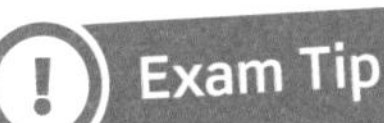

Use **Figure 4** to help with question **05.2**.

05.3 Blood in the arteries is usually bright red because it is full of oxygen. Identify the artery where this is not true.
Choose **one** answer. **[1 mark]**

aorta   vena cava   pulmonary artery   coronary artery

05.4 Give a reason for your answer to **05.3**. **[1 mark]**

05.5 Describe **two** reasons why it is important that blood is transported to every cell in the body. **[2 marks]**

06 A student was provided with an unknown food sample and the following apparatus:

- test tubes (in a test-tube rack)
- water bath
- iodine
- Benedict's solution
- Biuret reagent
- ethanol.

The food sample had been ground into a powder using a pestle and mortar. Explain how the student could test the food sample for the presence of starch, sugar, fats, and protein. **[6 marks]**

Exam Tip

Remember, don't use all of your sample in one go, clearly lay out what observations would mean positive or negative results, and don't forget safety precautions.

07 **Figure 5** shows a cross-section through the human heart.

Figure 5

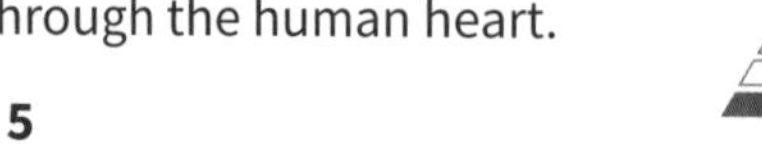

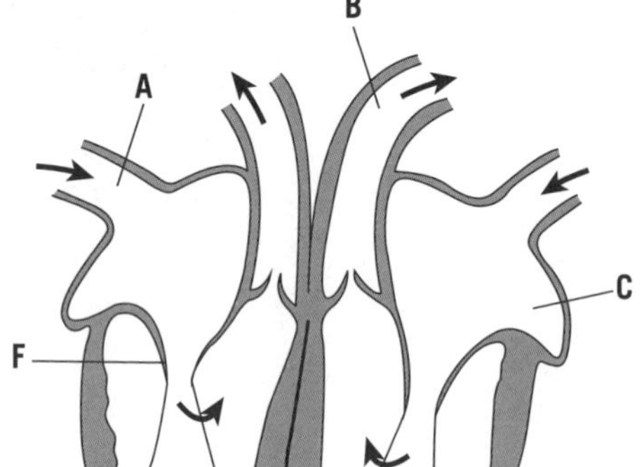

magnification: ×0.75

Exam Tip

The first thing you should do when you see a diagram of a heart is mark down your right (on the left-hand side) and left (on the right-hand side).

07.1 Identify which label is pointing to the left atrium. **[1 mark]**

07.2 Name the blood vessels labelled **A** and **B**. **[2 marks]**

07.3 Identify and describe the function of part **F**. **[2 marks]**

07.4 Humans have a double circulatory system.
Describe what this means. **[2 marks]**

08 **Table 2** shows the number of red blood cells present in people living at different altitudes above sea level.

Table 2

Height above sea level in m	Mean number of red blood cells in millions per mm^3 of blood
0	4.9
1000	5.5
2000	6.2
3000	6.8
4000	7.2
5000	7.6

08.1 Explain how a red blood cell is adapted to perform its function. **[6 marks]**

08.2 Using **Table 2**, calculate the percentage difference between the number of red blood cells present in a person living at 2000 m above sea level, and 4000 m above sea level. **[2 marks]**

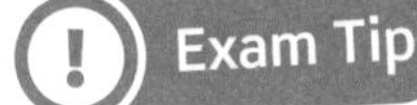

Exam Tip

When calculating percentage difference, don't forget to state whether it is an increase or a decrease.

08.3 As altitude increases, the amount of oxygen in the air decreases. Using information in **Table 2**, explain how differences in people's blood composition enable them to live at different altitudes. **[3 marks]**

09 **Figure 6** shows a section of blood vessels in the upper arm.

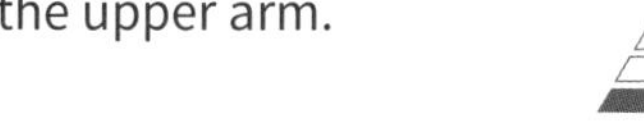

Figure 6

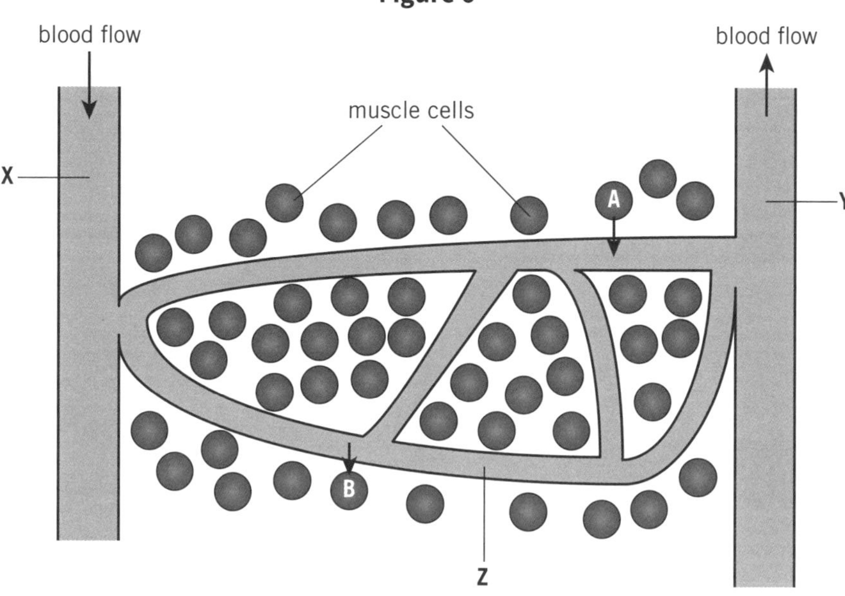

09.1 Name the blood vessel represented by label **Z**. **[1 mark]**

09.2 Describe **two** ways structure **Z** is adapted to maximise the rate of diffusion of carbon dioxide. **[2 marks]**

09.3 Identify which arrow (**A** or **B**) shows the direction of transport of carbon dioxide. **[1 mark]**

10 A student wanted to observe some of his own cells in the classroom. He was told to use skin cells from the back of his hand. He used a piece of clear sticky tape to remove some dead cells which he placed on a microscope slide.

10.1 Describe how the student should use the microscope to observe the slide. **[3 marks]**

10.2 Draw a labelled diagram of the cell the student would expect to view through the microscope. **[3 marks]**

Exam Tip

Remember this is an animal cell, not a plant cell!

10.3 Name **one** additional structure the student would be able to see if he observed the skin cells using an electron microscope. Give the function of this structure. **[2 marks]**

10.4 Suggest **one** reason why the student would not be told to observe his own blood cells in the classroom. **[1 mark]**

Knowledge

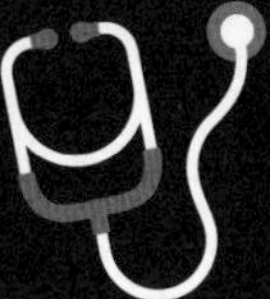

B5 Enzymes

Enzymes

Enzymes are large proteins that **catalyse** (speed up) reactions.
Enzymes are not changed in the reactions they catalyse.

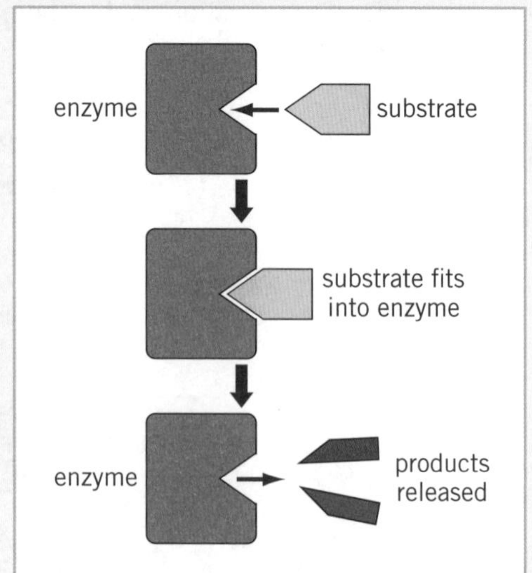

enzyme
substrate
substrate fits into enzyme
enzyme
products released

Lock and key theory

This is a simple model of how enzymes work:

1 The enzyme's **active site** (where the reaction occurs) is a specific shape.
2 The enzyme (the lock) will only catalyse a specific reaction because the **substrate** (the key) fits into its active site.
3 At the active site, enzymes can break molecules down into smaller ones or bind small molecules together to form larger ones.
4 When the products have been released, the enzyme's active site can accept another substrate molecule.

The effect of temperature on enzymes

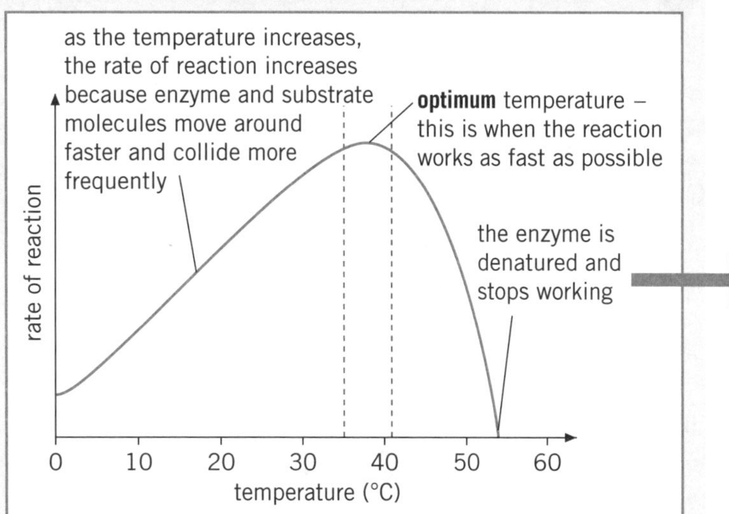

as the temperature increases, the rate of reaction increases because enzyme and substrate molecules move around faster and collide more frequently
optimum temperature – this is when the reaction works as fast as possible
the enzyme is denatured and stops working
rate of reaction
0
10
20
30
40
50
60
temperature (°C)

Denaturation

At extremes of pH or at very high temperatures the shape of an enzyme's active site can change.

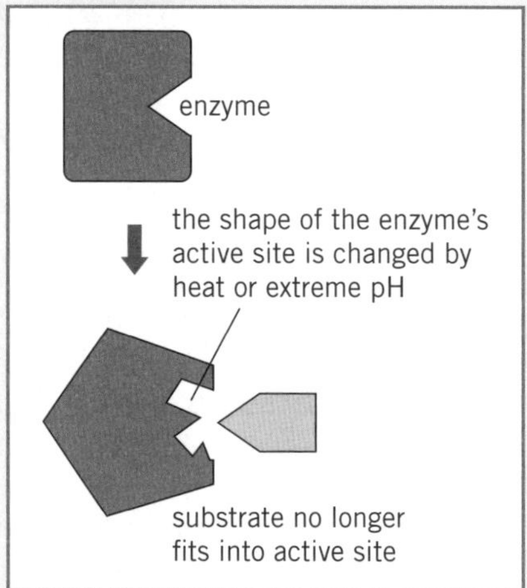

enzyme
the shape of the enzyme's active site is changed by heat or extreme pH
substrate no longer fits into active site

The substrate can no longer bind to the active site, so the enzyme cannot catalyse the reaction – the enzyme has been **denatured**.

Revision tip

Remember This is one area where biology and chemistry overlap. The first part of the graph can be explained by the collision theory you have learnt in your chemistry lessons.

Key terms Make sure you can write a definition for these key terms.

active site | amylase | catalyse | denatured | enzyme

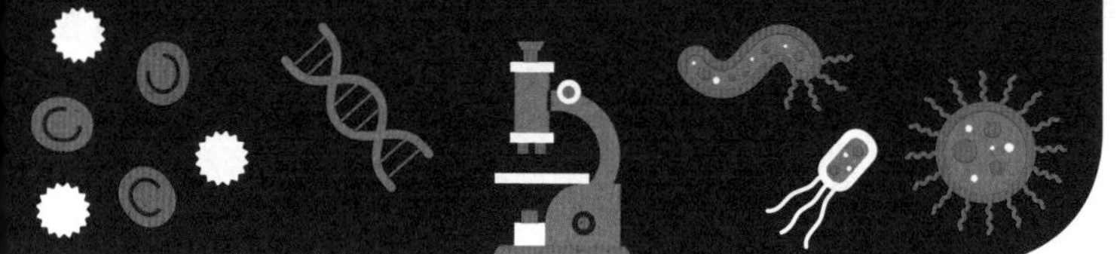

Digestive enzymes

Digestive enzymes convert food into small, soluble molecules that can then be absorbed into the bloodstream. For example, carbohydrases break down carbohydrates into simple sugars.

These products of digestion can be used to build new carbohydrates, lipids, and proteins.

Some of the glucose produced is used in respiration.

Enzyme	Sites of production	Reaction catalysed
amylase	salivary glands pancreas small intestine	starch → maltose (a simple sugar)
proteases	stomach pancreas small intestine	proteins → amino acids
lipases	pancreas small intestine	lipids → fatty acids and glycerol

The effect of pH on enzymes

Different enzymes have different optimum pH values.

This allows enzymes to be adapted to work well in environments with different pH values. For example, parts of the digestive system greatly differ in pH.

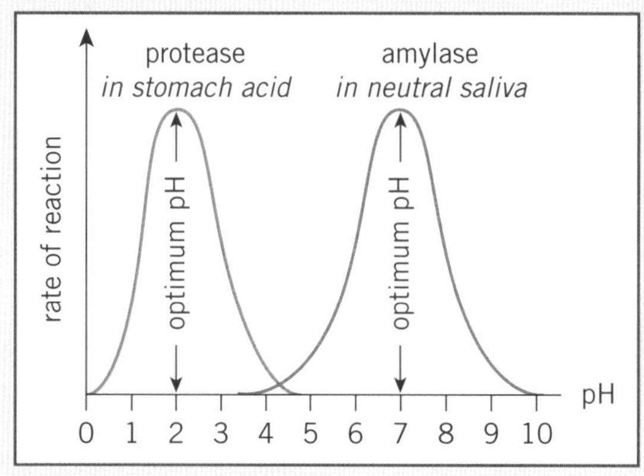

Revision tips

Remember When you're talking about enzymes, it's really important that you use the correct terms. When the active site breaks down an enzyme becomes denatured – lots of students write that the enzyme has died, or has been killed. This is incorrect and will lose you marks in the exam.

Practice The lock and key mechanism also applies when joining two substrates together. The mechanism is very similar to what you have already covered and this could be a good question to show your knowledge in a new context.

Practice These graphs are very common exam questions. Make sure you can draw them, recognise their shapes, and explain fully what is going on in each part of the graph.

lipase | optimum | protease | substrate

Retrieval

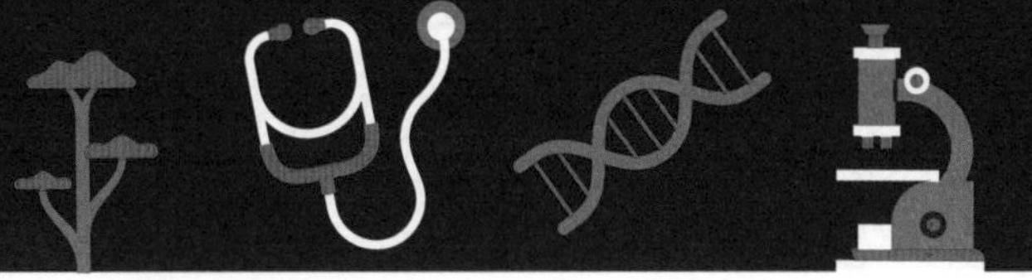

Learn the answers to the questions below, then cover the answers column with a piece of paper and write as many as you can. Check and repeat.

	B5 questions		Answers
1	What are enzymes?	Put paper here	protein molecules that catalyse specific reactions in organisms
2	What does catalyse mean?		speed up a reaction
3	Why are enzymes described as specific?	Put paper here	each enzyme only catalyses a specific reaction, because the active site only fits together with certain substrates (like a lock and key)
4	Describe the function of amylase.		to break down starch into simple sugars
5	Where is amylase produced?	Put paper here	salivary glands, pancreas, and small intestine
6	Describe the function of proteases.		to break down proteins into amino acids
7	Where are proteases produced?	Put paper here	stomach, pancreas, and small intestine
8	Describe the function of lipases.		to break down lipids into fatty acids and glycerol
9	Where are lipases produced?	Put paper here	pancreas and small intestine
10	What are two factors that affect the rate of activity of an enzyme?		temperature and pH
11	What does denatured mean?	Put paper here	the shape of an enzyme's active site is changed by high temperatures or an extreme pH, so it can no longer bind with the substrate
12	Describe the effect of temperature on enzyme activity.	Put paper here	as temperature increases, rate of reaction increases until it reaches the optimum for enzyme activity – above this temperature, enzyme activity decreases and eventually stops
13	Describe the effect of pH on enzyme activity.	Put paper here	different enzymes have a different optimum pH at which their activity is greatest – at a pH much lower or higher than this, enzyme activity decreases and stops
14	Why do different digestive enzymes have different optimum pHs?		different parts of the digestive system have very different pHs – the stomach is strongly acidic and the pH in the small intestine is close to neutral

Now go back and use the questions below to check your knowledge from previous chapters.

Previous questions

	Previous questions	Answers
1	What is the function of saliva in digestion?	lubrication to help swallowing; contains amylase to break down starch
2	Why is active transport needed in plant roots?	concentration of mineral ions in the soil is lower than inside the root hair cells – the mineral ions must move against the concentration gradient to enter the root hair cells
3	What happens during mitosis?	one set of chromosomes is pulled to each end of the cell and the nucleus divides
4	Where are embryonic stem cells found?	early human embryos (usually from spare embryos from fertility clinics)
5	How does the structure of an artery relate to its function?	carries blood away from the heart under high pressure – has a small lumen and thick, elasticated walls that can stretch
6	What is the function of a nerve cell?	carries electrical impulses around the body
7	What are plant meristems?	area where rapid cell division occurs in the tips of roots and shoots
8	Name the five levels of organisation in living organisms.	cells → tissues → organs → organ systems → organisms

Put paper here

Required Practical Skills

Practise answering questions on the required practicals using the example below. You need to be able to apply your skills and knowledge to other practicals too.

Rate of enzyme reaction	Worked example	Practice
This practical tests your ability to accurately measure and record time, temperature, volume, and pH. You will need to know how to find the rate of a reaction by using a continuous sampling technique to measure the time taken for an indicator to change colour. You will be familiar with measuring the effect of pH on the rate of reaction of amylase digesting starch, using iodine as an indicator. However, you need to be able to apply the methods of this practical to different enzymes and substrates!	A class carried out an investigation into the effect that pH has on the ability of amylase to break down carbohydrates. They timed how long it took for the amylase to break down starch at different pH values between 5 and 11. Suggest the results the class would observe. *The optimal pH of amylase is around 7, so the time taken to break down starch will be shortest at pH 7. At pH values lower than 7 it will take longer to break down the starch – it will take the longest time at pH 5, decreasing in time taken until pH 7. Above pH 7 it will take a longer time to break down the starch, and the amylase may stop breaking down the starch entirely at pH 11.*	1 A student wanted to repeat the experiment on the following day to compare their results. Suggest why using the same enzyme solution on two different days would not give comparable results. 2 Suggest how the class might have timed how long it took for the amylase to break down the starch. 3 Give one variable the class must control for this experiment to be valid.

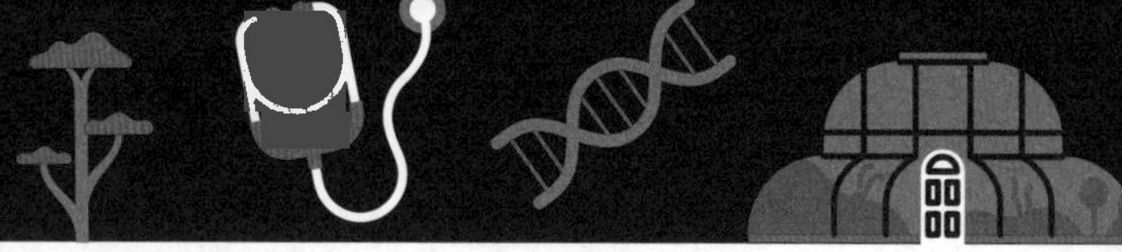

Exam-style questions

01 Lipase is an enzyme that breaks down lipids.

01.1 Name the products when a lipid is broken down. **[1 mark]**

> **Exam Tip**
> Can you think of another name for a lipid that will point you towards the answer to question **01.1**?

01.2 Name **one** organ in the body where lipase is made. **[1 mark]**

01.3 A group of students investigated the effect of temperature on the action of the enzyme lipase.

They used the following method in their investigation:

1. Add 10 cm³ of lipid solution to a test tube.
2. Add 2 cm³ of lipase solution to a second test tube.
3. Place both test tubes into a water bath set at 20 °C.
4. Leave in the water bath for five minutes.
5. Add the lipid solution to the lipase solution and mix.
6. Remove a sample of the mixture every five minutes and test for the presence of lipids. Continue until no lipid is detected.
7. Repeat the experiment every 5 °C between temperatures of 20 °C and 50 °C.

Name the independent variable in the investigation. **[1 mark]**

> **Exam Tip**
> This is the variable that you change.

01.4 Suggest why the lipase solution and lipid solution were left in the water bath for five minutes before mixing. **[1 mark]**

01.5 The students' results are shown in **Table 1**.

Table 1

Temperature in °C	Mean time taken until no lipid remained in min
20	20
25	15
30	10
35	5
40	10
45	20
50	lipid still present after 30 minutes of testing

Describe the effect on the breakdown of the lipid when the temperature was increased between 20 °C and 35 °C. **[1 mark]**

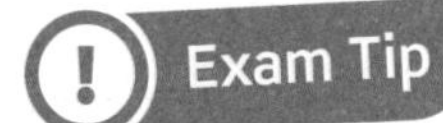

> You can make a quick sketch of the graph if you think it will help answer the question.

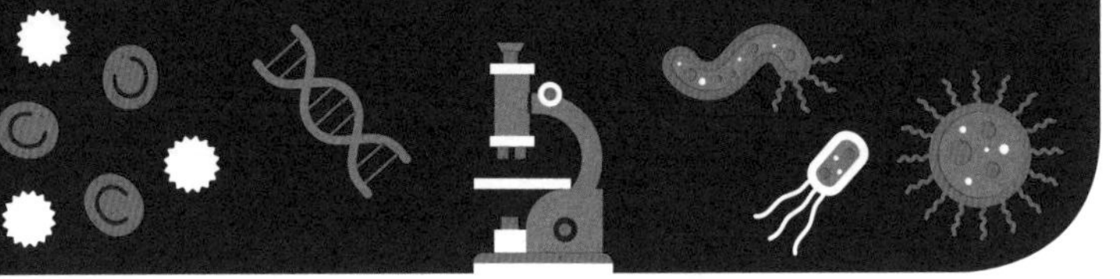

01.6 Explain the result that was observed at 50 °C. **[2 marks]**

02 **Figure 1** demonstrates the lock and key theory of enzyme action.

Figure 1

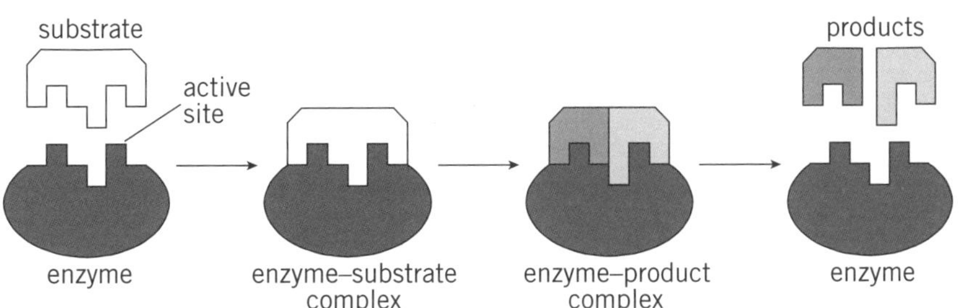

02.1 Using **Figure 1** and your own knowledge, explain what is meant by enzyme specificity. **[3 marks]**

There are lots of key words in the diagram – make sure you use them all in your answer!

02.2 Explain why you only need a small volume of an enzyme to catalyse a reaction. **[2 marks]**

An enzyme is a catalyst – think about the definition of a catalyst that you learnt in chemistry.

02.3 Describe **one** example of an enzyme-controlled reaction where small molecules are joined together to form larger ones. **[1 mark]**

02.4 Measles is an infectious disease caused by a virus. It causes sufferers to have a raised body temperature.

Using your knowledge of enzymes, suggest and explain **one** way in which this may be damaging to the body, and **one** way in which this may be beneficial to the body. **[4 marks]**

03 **Figure 2** shows how pH affects the activity of two different types of protease enzyme – enzyme **A** and enzyme **B**.

03.1 Name the substance that proteases break down into amino acids. **[1 mark]**

03.2 Describe the role of amino acids in the body. **[2 marks]**

03.3 Use **Figure 2** to identify the optimum pH of enzyme **A**. **[1 mark]**

03.4 Suggest and explain where enzymes **A** and **B** are found in the body. **[4 marks]**

Figure 2

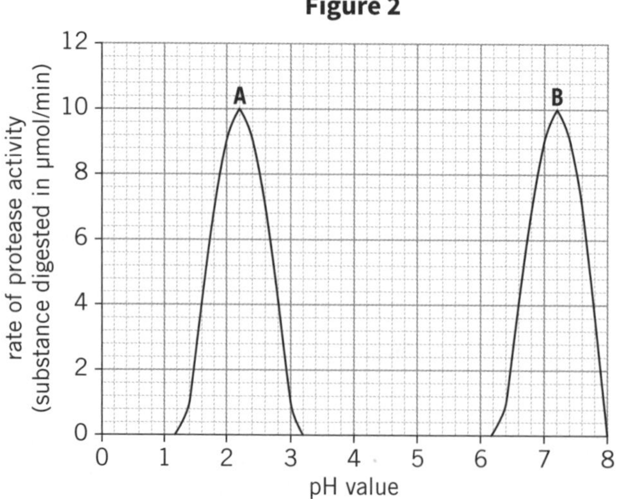

Exam Tip

Draw construction lines on your graph to show your working out.

03.5 Explain the advantage of adding enzymes to biological washing powders. **[4 marks]**

03.6 Explain why many biological washing powders recommend not washing clothes on a 60 °C cycle. **[2 marks]**

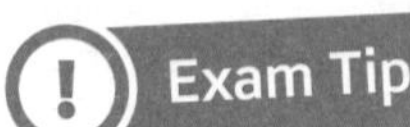

Think about enzyme action at high temperatures.

04 A student was studying the effect of pH on the enzyme activity of an unknown carbohydrase. They were provided with the following apparatus:

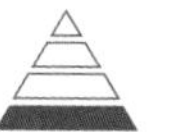

- test tubes and rack
- spotting tiles
- 10 cm³ measuring cylinder
- 3 cm³ pipettes
- glass stirring rod
- stopwatch
- safety goggles
- starch solution
- carbohydrase solution
- iodine solution
- thermometer
- pH buffer solutions.

Explain how the student could investigate the effect of pH on the rate of reaction of the enzyme. **[6 marks]**

Plan a clear step-by-step method that could be followed by another person, stating volumes and equipment, and any safety precautions.

05 Biological washing powders contain enzymes. A scientist carried out an investigation to determine if a new type of protease enzyme should be included in washing powder.

05.1 Describe the function of proteases. **[1 mark]**

05.2 Protease function can be studied by looking at the time it takes to digest cooked egg white.

1 The scientist placed a 2 cm³ piece of egg white into a test tube.

2 They then added a fixed volume of the protease enzyme to the test tube and timed how long it took for the egg white to halve in length.

3 The experiment was repeated at temperatures between 10 °C and 60 °C.

A control was also set up using water instead of protease at each temperature. The egg white in the control samples remained undigested after two hours.

Name the equipment the scientist should have used to change the temperature. **[1 mark]**

05.3 **Figure 3** shows the scientist's results.

Figure 3

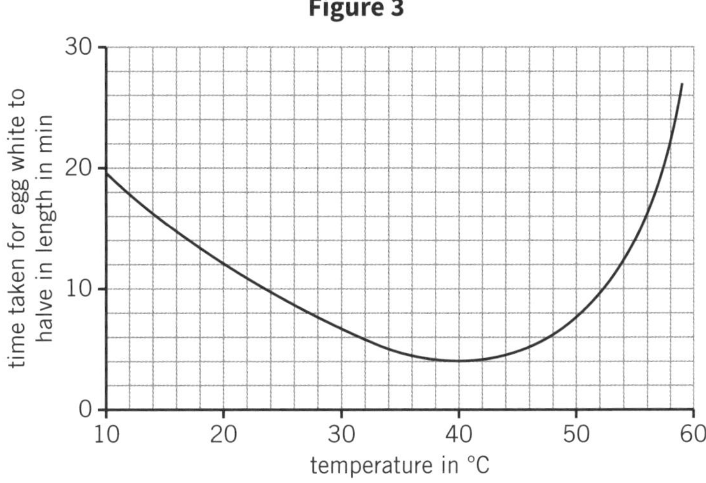

Identify the optimum temperature for protease activity. **[1 mark]**

05.4 Calculate the rate of reaction for the breakdown of the egg white by this enzyme at 20 °C. Give the unit of rate. **[3 marks]**

05.5 Using information in **Figure 3** and your own knowledge, suggest and explain **one** advantage and **one** disadvantage of using this enzyme in a biological washing powder. **[4 marks]**

Exam Tip

You may be surprised to see a question on reaction rates in biology, but it is the same method you learn in chemistry.

06 Hydrogen peroxide, H_2O_2, is a by-product of cellular respiration and is made by all living cells. Hydrogen peroxide can be harmful and is normally removed as soon as it is produced in the cell.
Cells make the enzyme catalase to remove hydrogen peroxide.
Catalase catalyses the reaction:

hydrogen peroxide → water + oxygen

06.1 Explain why catalase is referred to as a catalyst. **[2 marks]**

06.2 A group of students investigated the action of catalase on hydrogen peroxide at different temperatures. Both catalase and hydrogen peroxide are at a fixed concentration and pH. They used the following method, as shown in **Figure 4**:

1. Add 1 cm^3 hydrogen peroxide solution to a test tube.
2. Add 1 cm^3 of catalase solution.
3. Foam containing oxygen bubbles will then be produced above the surface of the liquid.
4. Measure the maximum height of the foam produced.

Describe what would happen if a lit splint was inserted into the foam. **[1 mark]**

Figure 4

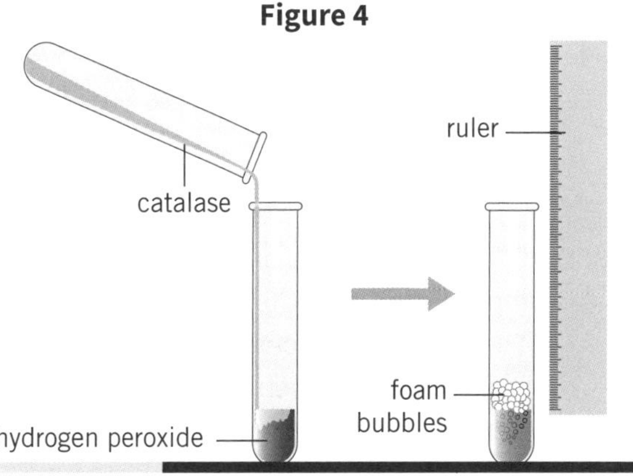

06.3 The students controlled the volumes of hydrogen peroxide and catalase used. Name **one** other control variable. **[1 mark]**

06.4 The students repeated the experiment at a range of temperatures. Their results are shown in **Table 2**.

Table 2

Temperature in °C	Maximum foam height in cm			
	Repeat 1	Repeat 2	Repeat 3	Mean
10	1.7	1.4	1.4	1.5
20	3.2	3.1	2.7	3.0
30	1.8	5.2	4.8	
40	3.9	4.3	3.8	4.0
50	1.5	1.6	1.4	1.5
60	0.0	0.0	0.0	0.0

Explain why the students carried out the experiment three times at each temperature. **[1 mark]**

Exam Tip

Whenever you're asked to calculate a mean, always look out for anomalous results.

06.5 Complete **Table 2** by calculating the mean result for 30 °C. **[1 mark]**

06.6 Explain the results at 60 °C. **[2 marks]**

06.7 The students concluded that the optimum temperature for catalase activity was between 30 °C and 40 °C.
Explain how the students could improve their investigation to find a more accurate value for the optimum temperature for catalase activity. **[2 marks]**

07 Trypsin is an example of a protease enzyme.

07.1 Name the type of molecule broken down by trypsin. **[1 mark]**

07.2 Trypsin is produced in the pancreas and released into the small intestine.
Identify the optimum pH for trypsin activity.
Choose **one** answer. **[1 mark]**

pH 2 pH 4 pH 8 pH 9

07.3 Trypsin is specific for catalysing one type of reaction.
Using the lock and key theory, explain what is meant by enzyme specificity. **[3 marks]**

Exam Tip

Key words are important for this question.

08 Cryophilic bacteria are a group of bacteria capable of growing and reproducing at low temperatures, ranging from −20 °C to +10 °C. They are found in permanently cold environments such as polar regions and the deep sea. They are able to survive because their enzymes are able to work at low temperatures.

Exam Tip

Don't worry if you've never heard of cryophilic bacteria before. This question is there for you to show that you can apply your knowledge to a new context.

08.1 On **Figure 5**, draw and label a line to represent the rate of reaction at different temperatures of an enzyme found in humans. **[2 marks]**

Figure 5

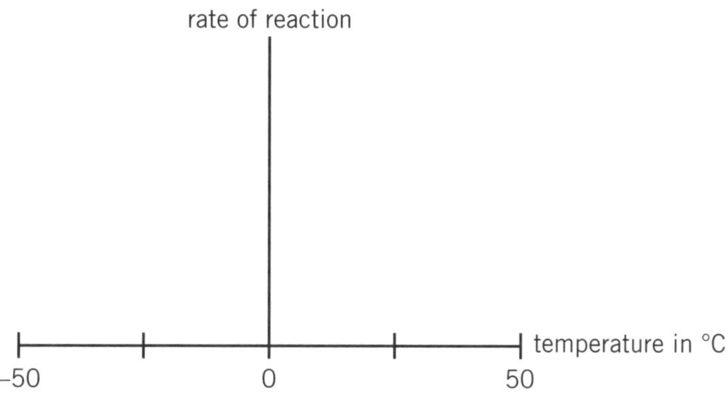

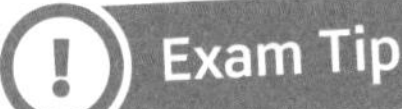

This graph may look a bit confusing, but that's just because the *y*-axis is in the middle. Treat it like any other graph.

08.2 Draw and label a second line on **Figure 5** to represent the rate of reaction at different temperatures of an enzyme found in cryophilic bacteria. **[2 marks]**

Exam Tip

This line is a similar shape to the first line, just in a different place.

09 Living cells could not function without enzyme-controlled reactions.

09.1 Explain how changing pH affects the rate of an enzyme-controlled reaction. **[3 marks]**

Exam Tip

In **09.1**, use examples such as 'at low pH…' and 'at high pH…'

09.2 The enzyme trypsin breaks down casein (a form of protein) in milk. Give the name of the group of digestive enzymes that trypsin belongs to. **[1 mark]**

09.3 Trypsin breaks down casein, changing its colour from white to clear. Some scientists took a range of milk samples and mixed them with trypsin at different temperatures. They measured the rate at which trypsin breaks down casein using a spectrophotometer. A spectrophotometer measures the amount of light transmitted through a liquid.
Suggest a method, using the spectrophotometer, to determine the optimum temperature for trypsin action. **[4 marks]**

Exam Tip

A spectrophotometer is a piece of equipment that tells you how much light you can see through things. Don't let its long name put you off!

09.4 The scientists noticed that the glass of the test tube containing the milk solution was cloudy. Suggest and explain the effect of the clouded glass on the scientists' results. **[3 marks]**

10 Large multicellular organisms require systems to exchange gases efficiently.

10.1 Select the statement that best explains why single-celled organisms do not require gas exchange organs. Choose **one** answer. **[1 mark]**

Single-celled organisms have a small surface area-to-volume ratio.

Single-celled organisms have a large surface area-to-volume ratio.

Single-celled organisms have a small surface area.

Single-celled organisms have a large surface area.

Exam Tip

Cross out any obviously wrong answers to leave you with fewer to pick from. Remember to pick the *best* answer.

10.2 Explain the changes that occur in the body causing air to be drawn into the lungs. **[4 marks]**

10.3 Explain how the alveoli are adapted for gas exchange. **[3 marks]**

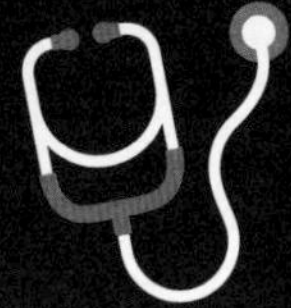

Knowledge

B6 Organisation in plants

Tissues in leaves

Leaves are organs because they contain many tissues that work together to perform photosynthesis.

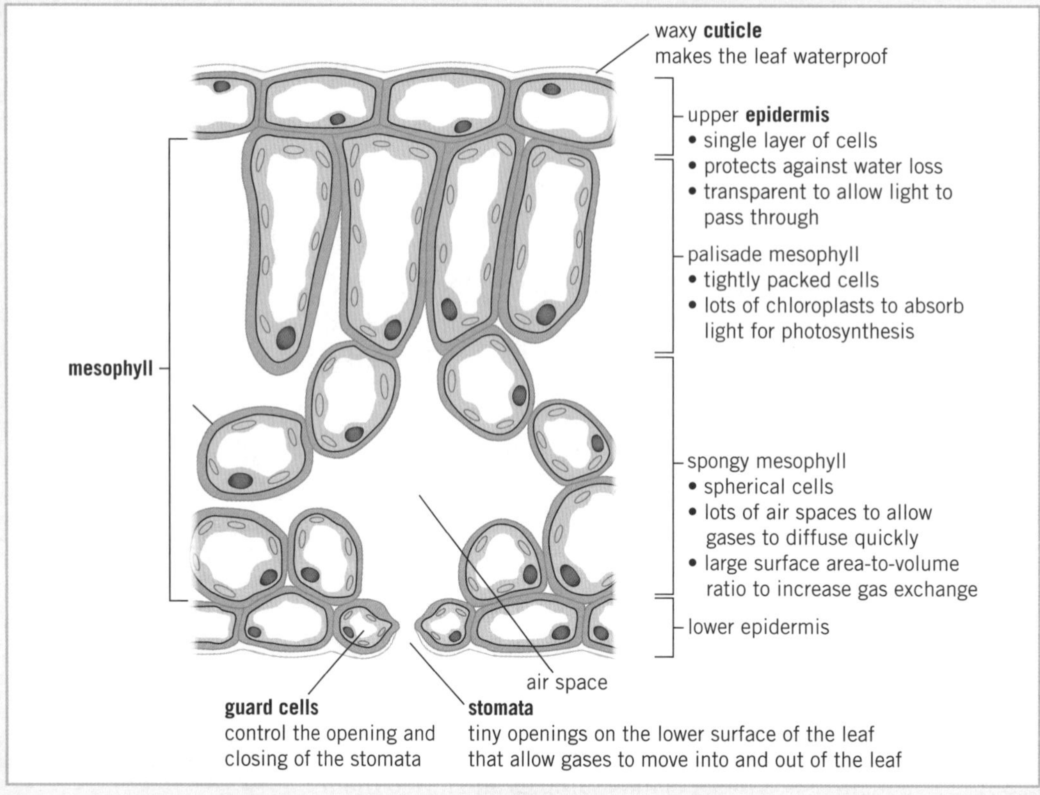

Stomata

Stomata are tiny openings in the undersides of leaves – this placement reduces water loss through evaporation.

They control gas exchange and water loss from leaves by

- allowing diffusion of carbon dioxide into the plant for photosynthesis
- allowing diffusion of oxygen out of the plant.

Guard cells are used to open and close the stomata.

When a plant has plenty of water, the guard cells become turgid. The cell wall on the inner surface is very thick, so it cannot stretch as much as the outer surface. So as the guard cells swell up, they curve away from each other, opening the stoma.

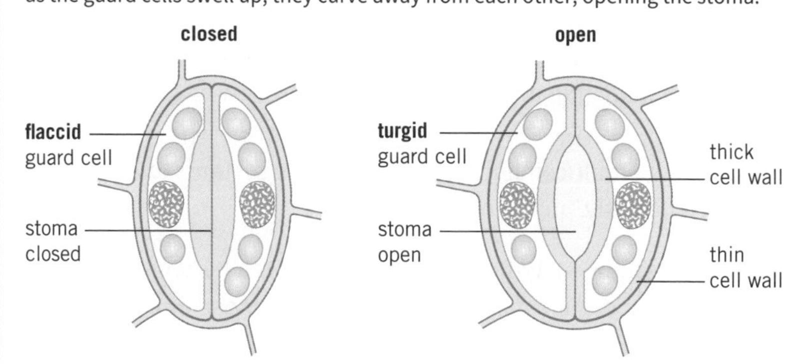

Key terms

Make sure you can write a definition for these key terms.

cuticle epidermis flaccid guard cell mesophyll phloem stomata translocation transpiration transpiration stream turgid xylem

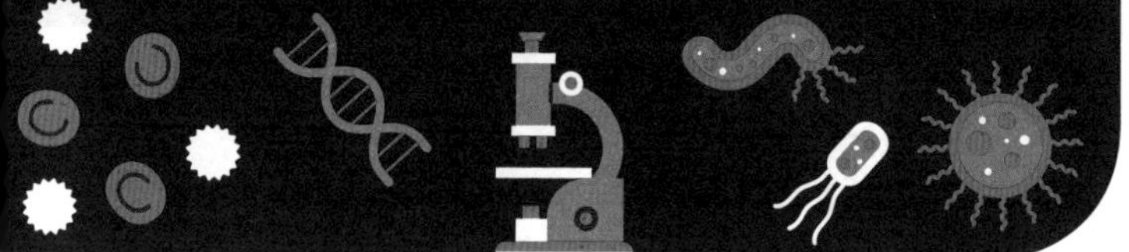

Transpiration

Description

Water is lost through the stomata by evaporation. This pulls water up from the roots through the **xylem** and is called **transpiration**. The constant movement of water up the plant is called the **transpiration stream**.

Importance

- provides water to cells to keep them **turgid**
- provides water to cells for photosynthesis
- transports mineral ions to leaves

Specialised tissues

one-way transport only

water and minerals

made of dead cells, joined together with no end walls between them

thick walls stiffened with lignin

xylem vessel

Translocation

The movement of dissolved sugars from the leaves to the rest of the plant through the **phloem**.

- moves dissolved sugars made in the leaves during photosynthesis to other parts of the plant
- this allows for respiration, growth, and glucose storage

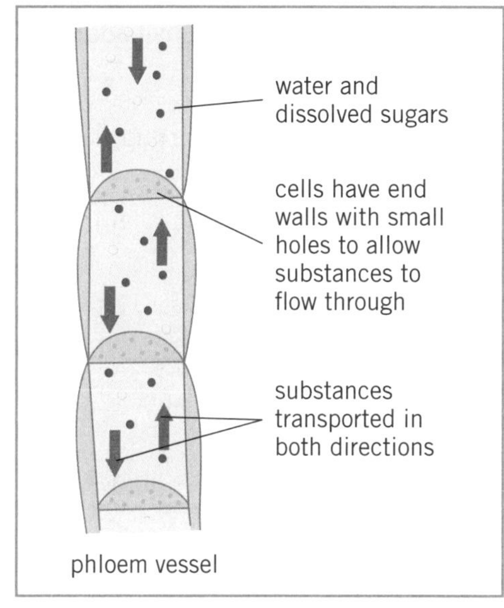

phloem vessel

Factors affecting the rate of transpiration

Factor	Effect on transpiration	Because...
temperature	higher temperatures *increase* the rate of transpiration	water evaporates faster in higher temperatures
humidity	lower humidity *increases* the rate of transpiration	the drier the air, the steeper the concentration gradient of water molecules between the air and leaf
wind speed	more wind *increases* the rate of transpiration	wind removes the water vapour quickly, maintaining a steeper concentration gradient
light intensity	higher light intensity *increases* the rate of transpiration	stomata open wider to let more carbon dioxide into the leaf for photosynthesis

Root hair cells

- increase absorption of water and mineral ions into the root by increasing the root surface area
- contain lots of mitochondria to transfer energy, which is used to take in mineral ions by active transport

Retrieval

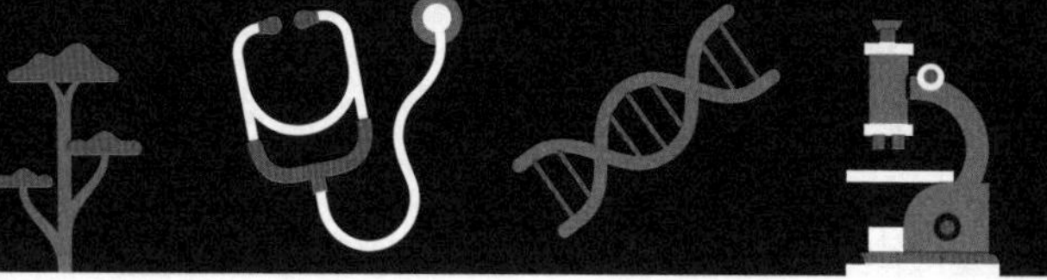

Learn the answers to the questions below, then cover the answers column with a piece of paper and write as many as you can. Check and repeat.

	B6 questions	Answers
1	Why is a leaf an organ?	there are many tissues inside the leaf that work together to perform photosynthesis
2	How is the upper epidermis adapted for its function?	• single layer of transparent cells allow light to pass through • cells secrete a waxy substance that makes leaves waterproof
3	How is the palisade mesophyll adapted for its function?	tightly packed cells with lots of chloroplasts to absorb as much light as possible for photosynthesis
4	How is the spongy mesophyll adapted for its function?	air spaces increase the surface area and allow gases to diffuse quickly
5	What is the function of the guard cells?	control the opening and closing of the stomata
6	What is the function of the xylem?	transport water and mineral ions from the roots to the rest of the plant
7	Give three adaptations of the xylem.	• made of dead cells • no end wall between cells • walls strengthened by a chemical called lignin to withstand the pressure of the water
8	What is the function of the phloem?	transport dissolved sugars from the leaves to the rest of the plant
9	What is the purpose of translocation?	transport dissolved sugars from the leaves to other parts of the plant for respiration, growth, and storage
10	Define the term transpiration.	movement of water from the roots to the leaves through the xylem
11	What is the purpose of transpiration?	• provide water to keep cells turgid • provide water to cells for photosynthesis • transport mineral ions to leaves
12	Name four factors that affect the rate of transpiration.	temperature, light intensity, humidity, wind speed
13	What effect does temperature have on the rate of transpiration?	higher temperatures increase the rate of transpiration
14	What effect does humidity have on the rate of transpiration?	higher levels of humidity decrease the rate of transpiration
15	Why does increased light intensity increase the rate of transpiration?	stomata open wider to let more carbon dioxide into the leaf for photosynthesis
16	What is the function of the stomata?	allow diffusion of gases into and out of the plant
17	Where are most stomata found?	underside of leaves
18	What is the advantage to the plant of having a high number of stomata at this location?	reduces the amount of water loss through evaporation

Put paper here

Now go back and use the questions below to check your knowledge from previous chapters.

Previous questions | Answers

	Previous questions	Answers
1	List the structures air passes through when breathing in.	mouth/nose → trachea → bronchi → bronchioles → alveoli
2	Give one advantage of using therapeutic cloning.	stem cells from the embryo are not rejected when transplanted because they have the same genes as the patient
3	How does the structure of a vein relate to its function?	carries blood back to the heart at low pressure – doesn't need thick, elasticated walls, but has valves to prevent blood flowing the wrong way
4	What does denatured mean?	shape of an enzyme's active site is changed by high temperatures or an extreme pH, so it can no longer bind with the substrate
5	How are villi adapted for exchanging substances?	• long and thin – increases surface area • one-cell-thick membrane – short diffusion pathway • good blood supply – maintains a steep concentration gradient

Put paper here

Put paper here

Put paper here

Maths Skills

Practise your maths skills using the worked example and practice questions below.

Calculating rate of transpiration

Transpiration cannot be measured directly. Instead it is determined by measuring the decrease in mass of a plant due to water loss, or by measuring the volume of water absorbed by the plant.

A potometer can be used to determine the rate of transpiration by measuring the volume of water absorbed by a plant.

The volume of water absorbed can be calculated by measuring the distance travelled by an air bubble in a given time in the potometer. The faster the bubble moves, the greater the rate of water uptake, and the greater the assumed rate of transpiration.

Worked example

A group of students used a potometer to measure the volume of water absorbed by a plant under three different conditions over 25 minutes.

Their results were

- normal conditions: 2.4 ml water absorbed
- high temperature: 3.1 ml water absorbed
- low humidity: 3.5 ml water absorbed.

Work out the transpiration rate of the plant under each condition.

transpiration rate (ml/min)

$$= \frac{\text{volume of water absorbed (ml)}}{\text{time (min)}}$$

normal conditions: $\frac{2.4}{25}$

$= 0.096$ ml/min

high temperature:

$\frac{3.1}{25} = 0.124$ ml/min

low humidity: $\frac{3.5}{25} = 0.140$ ml/min

Practice

1 The table below shows the volume of water absorbed by a plant under three different conditions in ten minutes. Calculate the transpiration rate for the plant under each condition.

Conditions	Volume of water in ml	Time in mins	Transpiration rate in ml/min
normal	1.1	10	
high temperature	1.3	10	
low humidity	1.5	10	

2 Which condition produced the highest transpiration rate? Explain this result.

3 How would you expect the volume of water absorbed to differ to that under normal conditions if a fan was set up to blow air over the plant?

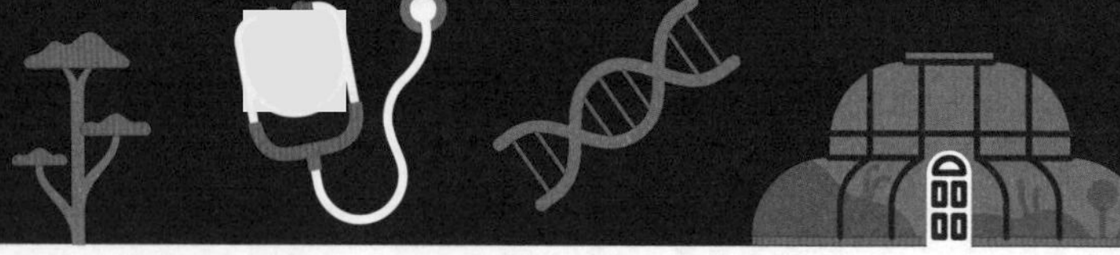

Practice

Exam-style questions

01 Four leaves of approximately the same size were removed from an oak tree.

Petroleum jelly was spread over the surface of leaves **A–C**. This acts as a waterproof agent to prevent water loss from the leaves.

All four leaves were then hung from a piece of string as in **Figure 1**.

Figure 1

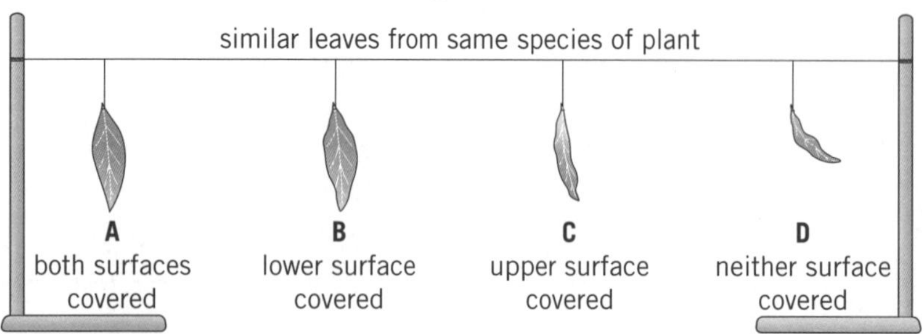

01.1 Suggest why no petroleum jelly was spread over the surface of leaf **D**. **[1 mark]**

____

01.2 The mass of each leaf was weighed at regular intervals.

Name the apparatus used to measure the mass of each leaf. **[1 mark]**

____

01.3 The results of the investigation are shown in **Figure 2**.

Figure 2

mass in g: 0, 0.5, 1.0, 1.5, 2.0, 2.5, 3.0, 3.5

time in h: 0, 5, 10, 15, 20, 25, 30

leaf **A**

leaf **B**

leaf **C**

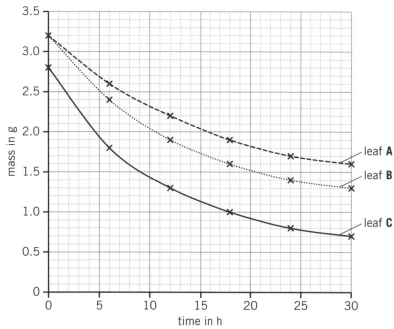

> **Exam Tip**
>
> You can use the points already plotted as a guide to find 6 and 12 hours.

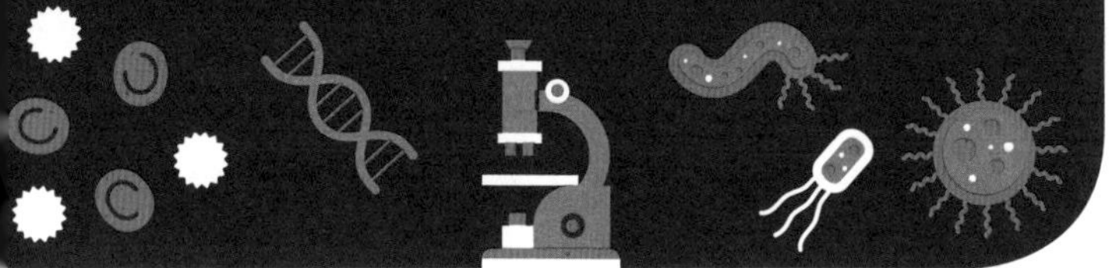

The values for leaf **D** are shown in **Table 1**.

Table 1

Leaf	Mass in g					
	start	after 6 h	after 12 h	after 18 h	after 24 h	after 30 h
D	2.7	1.6	1.0	0.6	0.4	0.3

Plot the data on **Figure 2**. Draw a line of best fit. **[3 marks]**

01.4 Identify which leaf lost water the fastest.

Give a reason for your answer. **[2 marks]**

____

____

02 **Figure 3** shows a cross-section through a leaf.

Figure 3

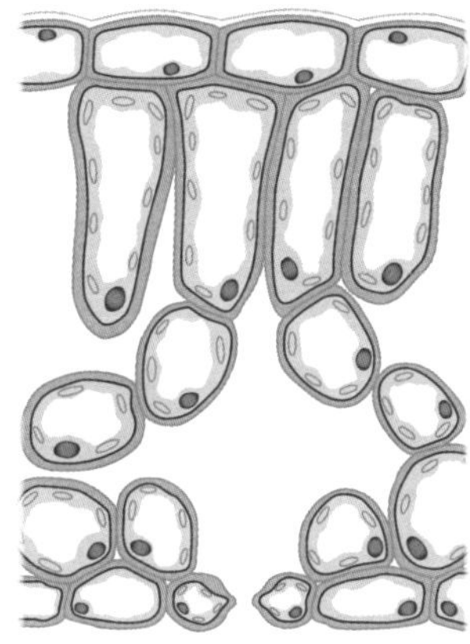

02.1 Identify and label a stoma on the diagram. **[1 mark]**

Exam Tip

Stoma is the singular of stomata.

02.2 Describe the role of guard cells in controlling water loss from a leaf. **[2 marks]**

____

____

____

02.3 A scientist calculated that the width of the cross-section they were viewing through the microscope was 250 μm.

Estimate the width of the guard cell. **[1 mark]**

Exam Tip

Start by measuring the width of the cross-section, then measure the width of the guard cell.

______________ μm

03 A group of students were studying the factors that affect the rate of transpiration in a plant. They used a potometer (**Figure 4**) to measure the rate of water uptake by a plant. The rate of water uptake can be used as an approximation of the rate of transpiration in a plant.

Figure 4

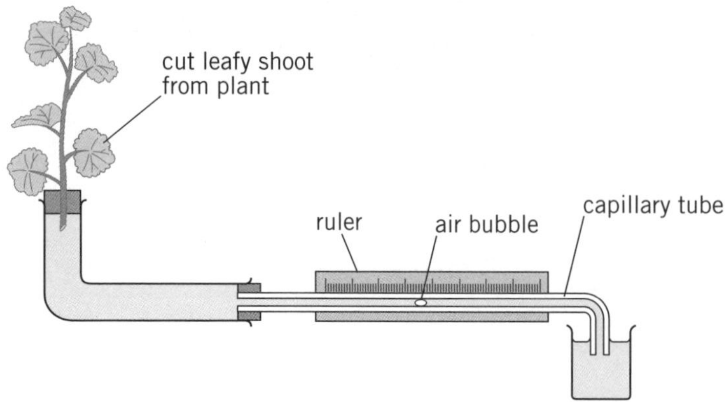

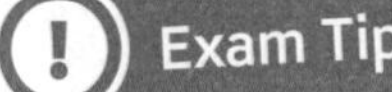

Exam Tip

You may not have seen a practical set up like this before, but don't panic!

This question is testing if you can apply your practical skills.

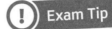

03.1 Define the term transpiration. **[2 marks]**

03.2 The students studied the rate of water uptake by the plant by measuring the distance travelled by an air bubble at 5-minute intervals over 30 minutes.
Explain why the rate of water uptake and the rate of transpiration are different. **[2 marks]**

03.3 The students' results are shown in **Table 2**.

Plot a graph of the water uptake of the plant on the axes below. Draw a suitable line of best fit. **[2 marks]**

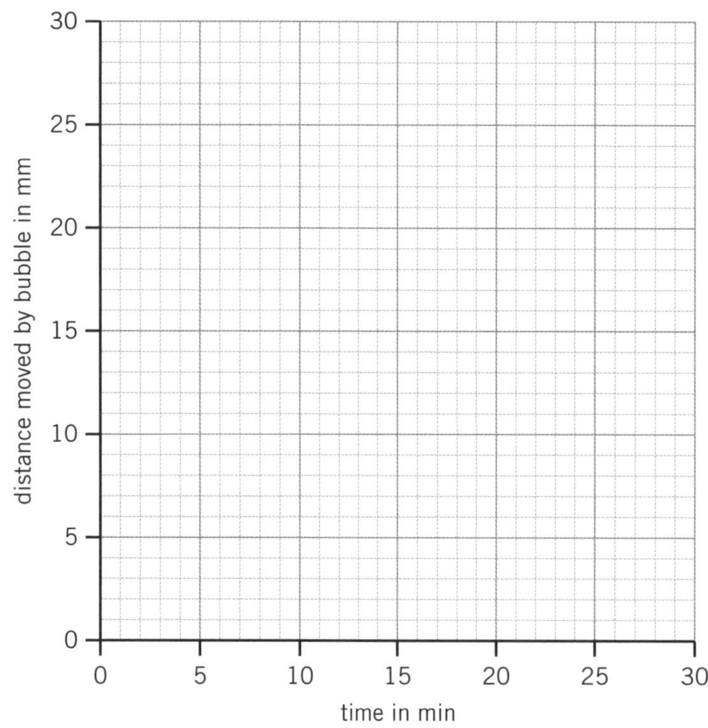

Table 2

Time in min	Distance moved by bubble from start point in mm
0	0
5	4
10	8
15	11
20	16
25	19
30	25

03.4 Describe the relationship between the distance moved by the bubble and time. **[1 mark]**

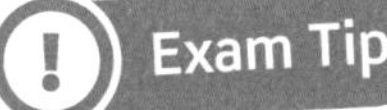

Show your working on the graph.

03.5 Use your graph to determine how long it took the bubble to move 10 mm. **[1 mark]**

03.6 Calculate the rate of water uptake by the plant between 10 and 20 min. **[4 marks]**

03.7 The experiment was carried out at room temperature.
Explain how you would expect the graph to differ if the experiment was repeated at 35 °C. **[2 marks]**

04 Plants use transport systems to move materials around inside them.

04.1 Name the structure found in stems that contains the xylem and phloem tissue. **[1 mark]**

You might not have covered greenfly in class, but apply what you know from your lessons to this new context.

04.2 Define the term translocation. **[1 mark]**

04.3 Describe the main structural differences between xylem and phloem tissue. **[4 marks]**

04.4 Suggest why plant pests such as greenfly bite into the phloem tissue in a plant. **[1 mark]**

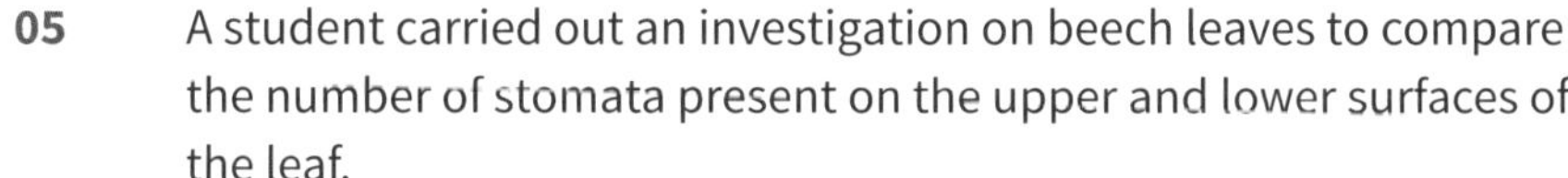

05 A student carried out an investigation on beech leaves to compare the number of stomata present on the upper and lower surfaces of the leaf.

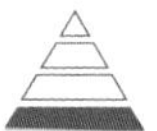

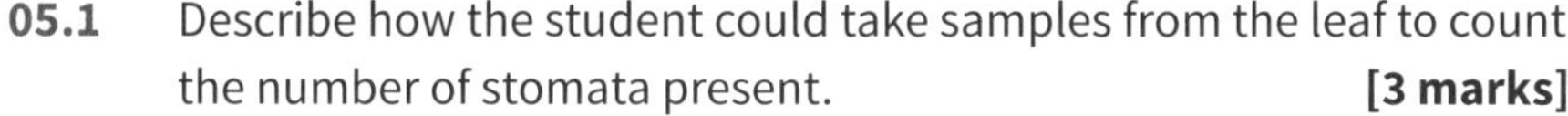

05.1 Describe how the student could take samples from the leaf to count the number of stomata present. **[3 marks]**

05.2 The student's results are shown in **Table 3**.

Table 3

	Number of stomata present					
Surface	**Sample 1**	**Sample 2**	**Sample 3**	**Sample 4**	**Sample 5**	**Mean**
Upper	1	2	2	3	2	2
Lower	36	42	35	41	37	

Calculate the mean result for the lower surface of the leaf.
Give your answer to two significant figures. **[2 marks]**

Remember significant figures and decimal places are different things. Don't get them confused!

05.3 The student concluded that most stomata are found on the lower surface of a beech leaf.
Explain why this is an advantage for a beech tree. **[2 marks]**

06 **Figure 5** shows a plant cell.

Figure 5

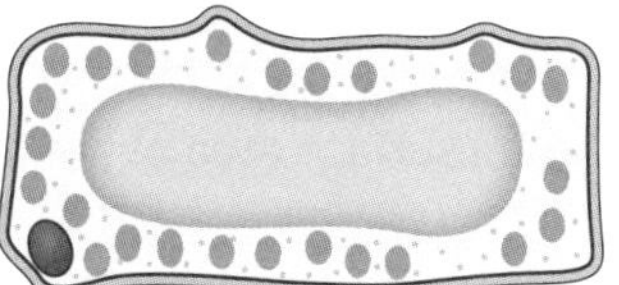

06.1 Identify which part of a plant the cell has been taken from.
Choose **one** answer. **[1 mark]**

root xylem tissue
phloem tissue palisade mesophyll

06.2 Give a reason for your answer to **06.1**. **[1 mark]**

06.3 Describe how water moves between cells in a leaf. **[2 marks]**

06.4 The main function of a leaf is to perform photosynthesis to provide food for the plant. Describe how the tissues inside a leaf are organised to maximise photosynthesis. **[6 marks]**

> **Exam Tip**
> This is a six-mark question, so make sure you give enough detail.
> Think about how the cells in a plant differ depending on their location and function.

07 As well as anchoring a plant into the ground, roots are also responsible for the uptake of water and mineral ions from the soil.

> **Exam Tip**
> 'Explain' questions are asking *why*. An answer describing what a root hair cell looks like won't get marks.

07.1 Explain how a root hair cell is adapted for the uptake of water and mineral ions. **[3 marks]**

07.2 **Figure 6** represents the movement of water and mineral ions into the root hair cell.

Figure 6

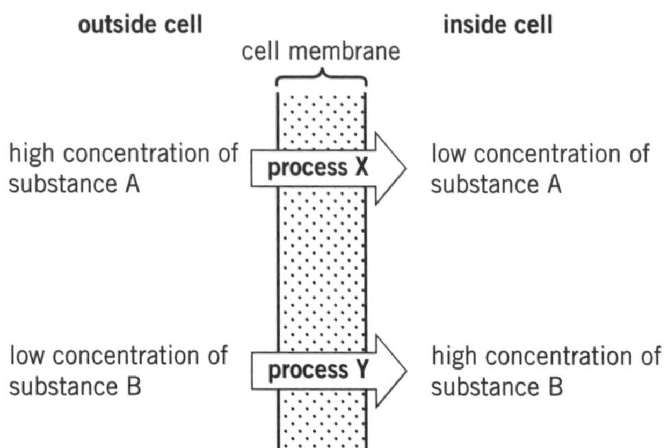

Identify and name the process (**X** or **Y**) in **Figure 6** that represents the uptake of mineral ions. Give a reason for your answer. **[2 marks]**

> **Exam Tip**
> Question **07.2** is a two-mark question – the first mark will be for identifying the process and the second mark will be for the reason.

07.3 Name the vessel that transports mineral ions around the plant. **[1 mark]**

07.4 Describe **one** use of mineral ions in a plant. **[1 mark]**

08 Scientists can use sampling and counting techniques to investigate the distribution of stomata on leaves.
Figure 7 is an observational diagram produced by a scientist when looking at a lower leaf epidermis. For each sample observed, the scientist calculated the density of stomata present in the form: *number of stomata per mm²*. Partially visible stomata were counted as present.

Figure 7

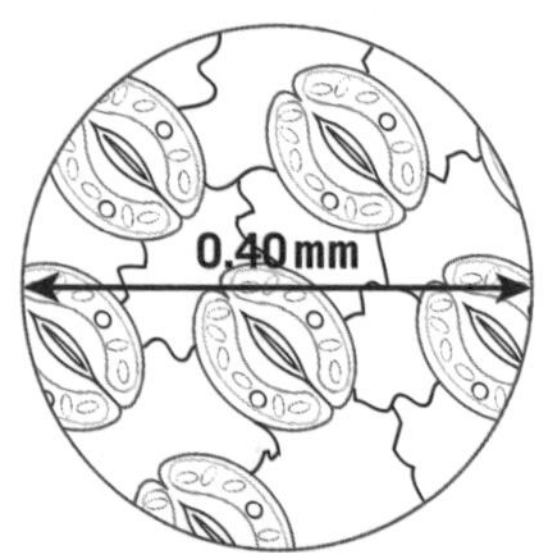

08.1 Calculate the density of stomata for the sample shown in **Figure 7**. **[5 marks]**

08.2 The scientist then estimated the total surface area of the leaf from which the sample was taken.
Suggest how the scientist estimated the leaf surface area. **[2 marks]**

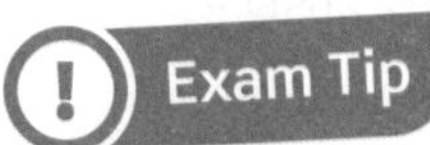

> **Exam Tip**
> For **08.1** you'll need to work out the area of the circle first.

08.3 The scientist measured the leaf's surface area to be approximately 8 cm^2.
Estimate the number of stomata that would be found on the surface of this leaf. **[3 marks]**

08.4 Suggest and explain how the scientist's results may have been different if the sample had been taken from the upper surface of the leaf. **[3 marks]**

09 Marram grass grows on sand dunes. Sand dunes are generally very dry and windy habitats. The leaves of marram grass are specially adapted to reduce water loss by transpiration.
Some of these features are shown in **Figure 8**.

Figure 8

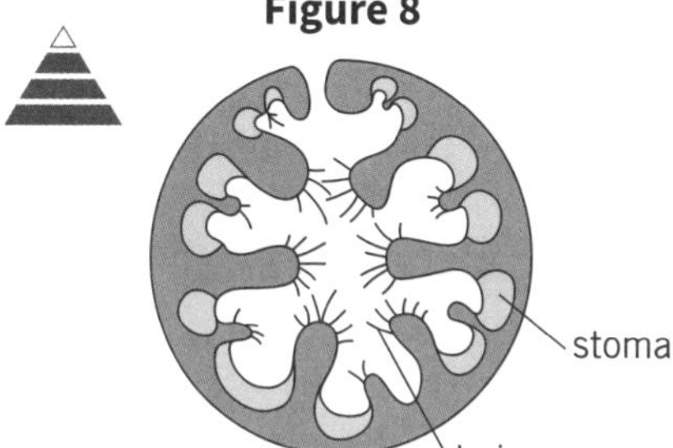

09.1 Define the term transpiration. **[2 marks]**

09.2 Identify which property of the waxy cuticle reduces the rate of transpiration. Choose **one** answer. **[1 mark]**

impermeable   large surface area   reflective   thermal insulator

09.3 Using **Figure 8**, suggest and explain how the rolled leaves, stomata, and leaf hairs work together to reduce the rate of transpiration. **[3 marks]**

Exam Tip
Make sure you refer to rolled leaves, stomata, and leaf hairs to get full marks.

10 The photograph in **Figure 9** was taken through a microscope. It shows a vascular bundle in a leaf. Vascular bundles contain both xylem and phloem tissue.

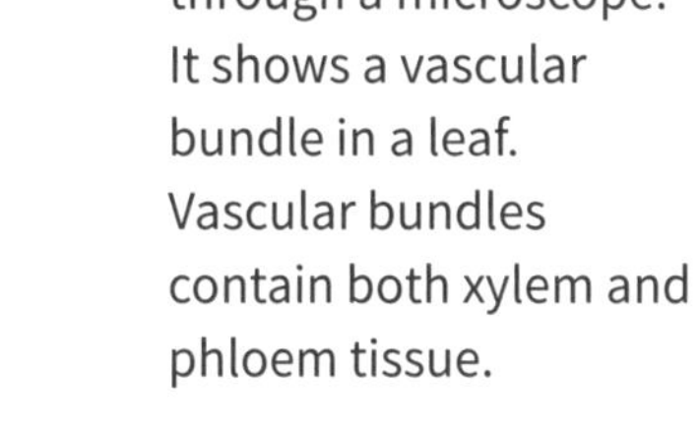

Figure 9

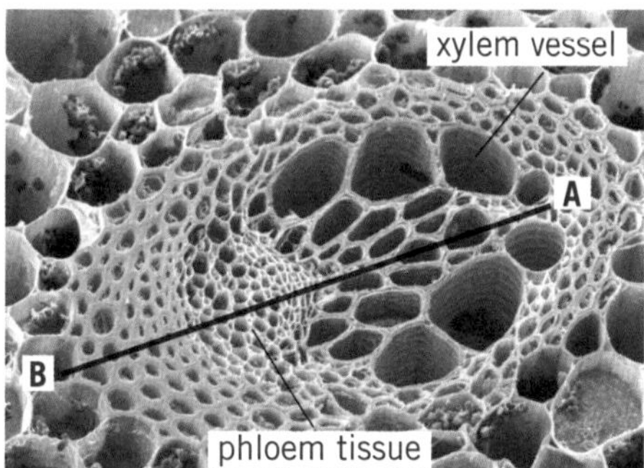

10.1 Line **A**–**B** shows the width of the vascular bundle. Vascular bundles in this species of plant have a mean width of 250 µm. Calculate the magnification of the image. **[3 marks]**

Exam Tip
Step one is to write down the equation for magnification.

10.2 Describe **one** difference between the structures of the xylem vessel and the phloem tube in **Figure 9**. **[1 mark]**

10.3 Name the chemical present in xylem vessel walls that provides the strength to withstand the pressure of the movement of water in the plant. **[1 mark]**

Exam Tip
You can still answer question **10.4** if you haven't identified the chemical.

10.4 The chemical named in **10.3** can be seen using a stain.
Use this information to plan how you could find the position of the vascular bundles in a stem. **[3 marks]**

10.5 Deer are a concern in managed woodlands. They eat tree bark and new tree shoots, and rub their antlers on tree trunks to leave a scent marker to warn other deer away from the area.
Explain the reasons why protective collars are placed around tree saplings in areas of managed woodland. **[6 marks]**

Exam Tip
The question has given you a description of the problem. Take each part of the problem and explain what protective collars can do to solve it.

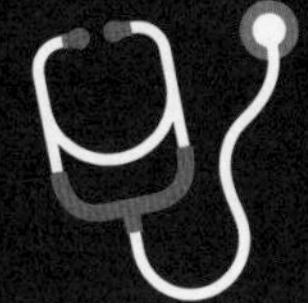

B7 The spread of diseases

Pathogens

Microorganisms that cause disease are called **pathogens**.

There are four types of pathogen:
- bacteria
- fungi
- protists
- viruses.

Pathogens can be spread
- in the air
- in water
- through direct contact.

Viruses live and reproduce rapidly inside an organism's cells. This can damage or destroy the cells.

Viruses	Spread by	Symptoms	Prevention and treatment
measles	inhalation of droplets that are produced by infected people sneezing and coughing	• fever • red skin rash • complications can be fatal	• painkillers to treat the symptoms • young children are vaccinated to immunise them against measles
HIV (human immunodeficiency virus)	exchange of body fluids such as • sexual contact • blood when drug users share needles	• flu-like symptoms at first • virus attacks the body's immune cells, which can lead to AIDS – when the immune system is so damaged that it cannot fight off infections or cancers	• antiretroviral drugs – are very damaging to the body • barrier methods of contraception, such as condoms • using clean needles
TMV (tobacco mosaic virus – plants)	• direct contact of plants with infected plant material • animal and plant vectors • soil: the pathogen can remain in soil for decades	• mosaic pattern of discolouration on the leaves – where chlorophyll is destroyed • reduces plant's ability to photosynthesise, affecting growth	• removing infected plants

Bacteria reproduce rapidly inside organisms and may produce **toxins** that damage tissues and cause illness.

Bacteria	Spread by	Symptoms	Prevention and treatment
Salmonella	bacteria in or on food being ingested	*Salmonella* bacteria and the toxins they produce cause • fever • abdominal cramps • vomiting • diarrhoea	• poultry are vaccinated against *Salmonella* bacteria to control spread
gonorrhoea	direct sexual contact – gonorrhoea is a **sexually transmitted disease** (STD)	• thick yellow or green discharge from the vagina or penis • pain when urinating	• treatment with antibiotics (many antibiotic-resistant strains have appeared) • barrier methods of contraception

Make sure you can write a definition for these key terms.

bacterium | communicable disease | fungicide | fungus | herd immunity

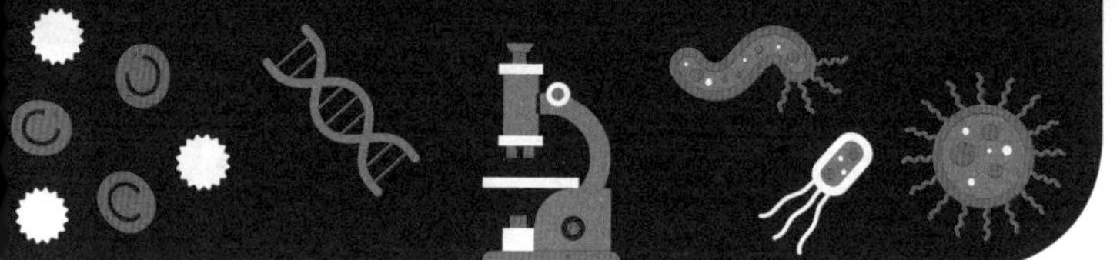

Fungi	Spread by	Symptoms	Prevention and treatment
rose black spot	water and wind	• purple or black spots on leaves, which turn yellow and drop early • reduces plant's ability to photosynthesise, affecting growth	• **fungicides** • affected leaves removed and destroyed

Protists	Spread by	Symptoms	Prevention and treatment
malaria	mosquitos feed on the blood of infected people and spread the protist pathogen when they feed on another person – organisms that spread disease by carrying pathogens between people are called **vectors**	• recurrent episodes of fever • can be fatal	• prevent mosquito vectors breeding • mosquito nets to prevent bites • anti-malarial medicine

Controlling the spread of communicable disease

There are a number of ways to help prevent the spread of **communicable diseases** from one organism to another.

Hygiene

Hand washing, disinfecting surfaces and machinery, keeping raw meat separate, covering mouth when coughing/sneezing, etc.

Isolation

Isolation of infected individuals – people, animals, and plants can be isolated to stop the spread of disease.

Controlling vectors

If a vector spreads a disease, destroying or controlling the population of the vector can limit the spread of disease.

Vaccination

Vaccination can protect large numbers of individuals against diseases.

Revision tip

Remember Communicable diseases is another way of saying infectious diseases.

Vaccination

Vaccination involves injecting small quantities of dead or inactive forms of a pathogen into the body.

This stimulates lymphocytes to produce the correct antibodies for that pathogen.

If the same pathogen re-enters the body, the correct antibodies can be produced quickly to prevent infection.

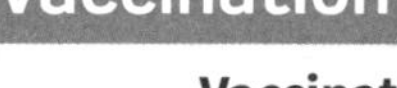

Herd immunity

If a large proportion of a population is vaccinated against a disease, the disease is less likely to spread, even if there are some unvaccinated individuals.

pathogen protist sexually transmitted disease (STD) toxin vaccination vector virus

Retrieval

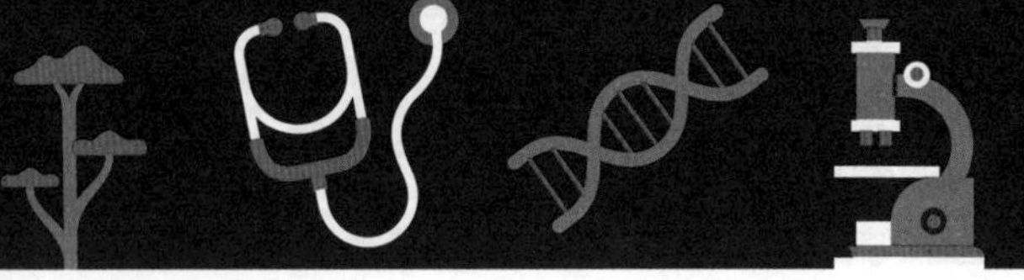

Learn the answers to the questions below, then cover the answers column with a piece of paper and write as many as you can. Check and repeat.

	B7 questions	Answers
1	What is a communicable disease?	a disease that can be transmitted from one organism to another
2	What is a pathogen?	a microorganism that causes disease
3	Name four types of pathogen.	bacteria, fungi, protists, viruses
4	How can pathogens spread?	air, water, direct contact
5	How do bacteria make you ill?	produce toxins that damage tissues
6	How do viruses make you ill?	reproduce rapidly inside cells, damaging or destroying them
7	Name three viral diseases.	measles, HIV, tobacco mosaic virus
8	Name two bacterial diseases.	*Salmonella*, gonorrhoea
9	Name one fungal disease.	rose black spot
10	Describe an example of a protist disease.	malaria – caused by a protist pathogen that is spread from person to person by mosquito bites, and causes recurrent fevers
11	Name four methods of controlling the spread of communicable disease.	good hygiene, isolating infected individuals, controlling vectors, vaccination
12	What does a vaccine contain?	small quantities of a dead or inactive form of a pathogen
13	How does vaccination protect against a specific pathogen?	vaccination stimulates the body to produce antibodies against a specific pathogen – if the same pathogen re-enters the body, white blood cells rapidly produce the correct antibodies
14	What is herd immunity?	when most of a population is vaccinated against a disease, meaning it is less likely to spread

Put paper here

Now go back and use the questions below to check your knowledge from previous chapters.

Previous questions | Answers

	Previous questions	Answers
1	Why are enzymes described as specific?	each enzyme only catalyses a specific reaction, because the active site only fits together with certain substrates (like a lock and key)
2	How is the palisade mesophyll adapted for its function?	tightly packed cells with lots of chloroplasts to absorb as much light as possible for photosynthesis
3	What is the function of a root hair cell?	absorbs minerals and water from the soil
4	What is cell division by mitosis?	body cells divide to form two identical daughter cells
5	What is the function of the phloem?	transport dissolved sugars from the leaves to the rest of the plant
6	Where are adult stem cells found?	bone marrow
7	What is the purpose of plant transpiration?	• provide water to keep cells turgid • provide water to cells for photosynthesis • transport mineral ions to leaves
8	Describe the effect of pH on enzyme activity.	different enzymes have a different optimum pH at which their activity is greatest – at a pH much lower or higher than this, enzyme activity decreases and stops

Put paper here

Maths Skills

Practise your maths skills using the worked example and practice questions below.

Calculating percentage change

To calculate percentage change you need to work out the difference between the two numbers you are comparing.

Then, you divide the difference by the original number and multiply the answer by 100.

If your answer is a negative number, this equals a percentage decrease.

percentage change = $\frac{\text{difference}}{\text{original number}} \times 100$

Worked example

In 2009, the number of deaths in England caused by MRSA was 800. In 2010, the number of deaths had fallen to 500.

Calculate the percentage change in the number of deaths caused by MRSA between 2009 and 2010.

Work out the difference in the two numbers you are comparing:

$500 - 800 = -300$

Divide the difference (–300) by the original number:

$\frac{-300}{800} = -0.375$

Multiply by 100: $-0.375 \times 100 = -37.5$

Percentage change in deaths caused by MRSA = –37.5%

Practice

The table below gives information about the number of deaths per year in England from MRSA and *Clostridium difficile* over four years.

Year	MRSA	*C. difficile*
2007	1800	8100
2008	1730	5300
2009	800	3890
2010	500	4570

1. Calculate the percentage change in deaths caused by MRSA from 2007 to 2008.
2. Calculate the percentage change in deaths caused by *C. difficile* from 2007 to 2008.
3. Calculate the percentage change in deaths caused by *C. difficile* from 2009 to 2010.

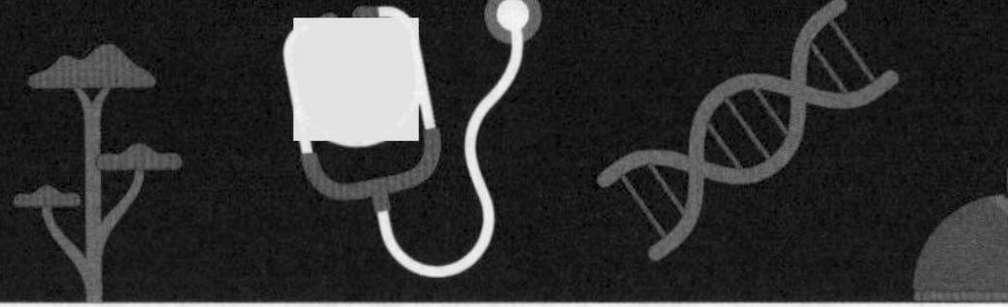

Practice

Exam-style questions

01 **Figure 1** shows a simplified image of human immunodeficiency virus (HIV).

Figure 1

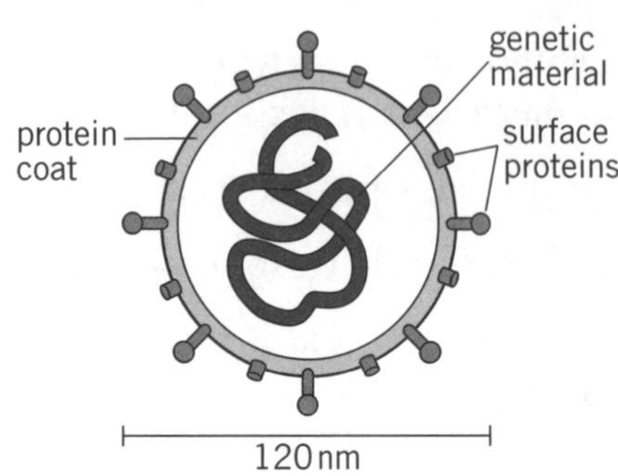

01.1 Give **two** ways this virus can be spread between people. **[2 marks]**

1 ______________________________

2 ______________________________

> **Exam Tip**
> The question is asking about the spread of HIV in particular, so make sure your answer is specific to this example.

01.2 Using the information from **Figure 1**, explain how you can tell this is a viral cell and not a bacterial cell. **[4 marks]**

____

____

____

____

01.3 Describe how a virus spreads within the body. **[4 marks]**

____

____

____

____

01.4 HIV infects white blood cells, which measure approximately 15 μm in diameter.

Calculate how many times larger a white blood cell is than a HIV particle.

Give your answer in terms of order of magnitude. **[4 marks]**

> **Exam Tip**
> You have to look back at some of the information given in the first part of the question. Not everything you need will be given to you in the same place.

Difference = ______________

01.5 In 2005, there were 8000 new cases of HIV in the UK. By 2016 this figure had fallen to 4300.
Suggest and explain **two** reasons why the number of new cases of HIV has fallen by such a significant amount. **[4 marks]**

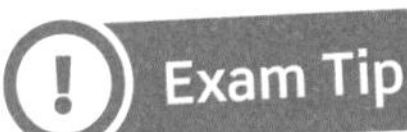

This is a four-mark question, so look at the marks available:
1 first suggested reason
2 explanation for first suggested reason
3 second suggested reason
4 explanation for second suggested reason.

02 Diseases are caused by different types of pathogen.

02.1 Draw **one** line from each disease to the correct pathogen type that causes the disease. **[3 marks]**

Disease	Pathogen type
Salmonella	virus
rose black spot	bacteria
malaria	fungus
measles	protist

Exam Tip

Only draw one line to and from each box. Any more will mean you don't get the marks, even if one of the lines is correct.

02.2 Give **one** symptom caused by measles. **[1 mark]**

02.3 Describe how measles is spread. **[1 mark]**

02.4 In 2018, there were 14.4 reported cases of measles per million people in the United Kingdom. The UK population in 2018 was 66 million.

Calculate the number of cases of measles in the UK in 2018. **[1 mark]**

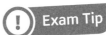

Exam Tip

This is only a one-mark question – if the way to answer it isn't obvious then you're over-thinking it!

______________ cases

02.5 In Ukraine in 2018, the number of cases of measles was 1204 per million people.

Calculate how many more cases of measles there were per million people in the Ukraine compared to the UK in 2018. **[1 mark]**

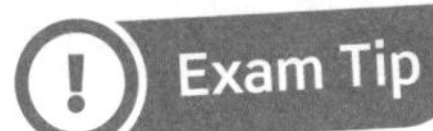

Use data and examples in your answer.

______________ cases

03 Malaria is a disease that kills over 400 000 people worldwide each year.

03.1 Give the type of pathogen that causes malaria. **[1 mark]**

03.2 Name the vector that is responsible for transmitting malaria. **[1 mark]**

03.3 Sub-Saharan Africa is known as a malarial hotspot.
Discuss the steps a traveller should take when visiting this region to minimise the risk of contracting a fatal malarial infection. **[6 marks]**

04 Diseases can often be recognised by the symptoms they cause.

04.1 Draw **one** line from each disease to the correct symptoms. **[3 marks]**

Disease	Symptoms
tobacco mosaic virus	purple or black spots on leaves
gonorrhoea	discolouration of leaves
rose black spot	fever, vomiting, diarrhoea
Salmonella	yellow or green discharge from sexual organs

Exam Tip

Start with the ones you know, then use elimination to try to work out the rest.

04.2 Complete the following sentences about sexually transmitted diseases. **[4 marks]**

______________ and ______________ are two examples of sexually transmitted diseases. They are spread through sexual intercourse. Some forms of contraception, such as ______________, are effective at preventing the spread of these types of diseases. This is because they provide a ______________, preventing the pathogens being passed from one person to another.

04.3 A school suffers from an outbreak of whooping cough, an infectious disease spread by droplet infections or direct contact with an infected person or contaminated surface.
Tick **three** steps that would help the school to control the spread of the infection. **[3 marks]**

Send infected children home.	
Prevent visitors from coming into the school.	
Employ a new school nurse.	
Wash surfaces down with disinfectant.	
Teach students about the benefits of vaccination.	

05 The spread of many diseases, such as the common cold and some forms of food poisoning, can be avoided through good hygiene practices.

05.1 Describe how each of the following approaches prevents the spread of pathogens: **[4 marks]**

- washing hands before preparing food
- covering face when coughing or sneezing
- wiping down surfaces with disinfectants
- isolation of infected people.

Exam Tip

Make it clear in your answer which point you are referring to.

05.2 Some raw meat products contain pathogens.
Suggest and explain **two** ways in which a restaurant could minimise the risk of infection for its customers. **[4 marks]**

05.3 *Salmonella* bacteria are sometimes found in uncooked chicken.
Explain how the *Salmonella* bacteria cause you to feel unwell if you eat an infected meat product. **[3 marks]**

05.4 Suggest and explain **one** way to stop the supply of infected meat to the UK market. **[2 marks]**

06 Rose black spot is a serious disease that affects rose plants.

06.1 Name the type of pathogen that causes rose black spot disease. **[1 mark]**

Exam Tip

The name of rose black spot gives you a clue to the symptoms.

06.2 Give **two** symptoms of rose black spot disease. **[2 marks]**

06.3 Explain why a plant infected with rose black spot disease does not grow properly. **[2 marks]**

06.4 A commercial flower grower notices that several of her plants are infected with rose black spot disease.
Give **two** possible treatment options available to the grower to prevent further spread of the infection. **[2 marks]**

07 Around half of the human population live in regions that are exposed to malaria. In 2015, there were over 200 million cases of malaria worldwide.

07.1 Give **one** symptom of malaria. **[1 mark]**

07.2 Many people believe that malaria is caused by mosquitoes.
Explain why this statement is **not** correct. **[2 marks]**

07.3 **Figure 2** shows the number of deaths worldwide due to malaria between the years 2000 and 2015.

Figure 2

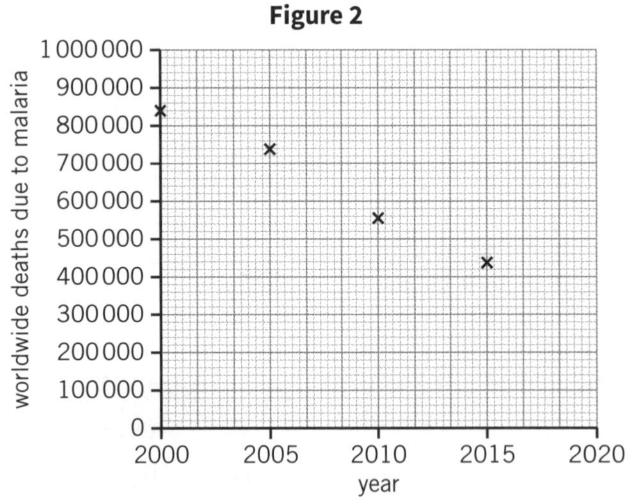

Describe the trend shown by the data.
Suggest **two** reasons for this trend. **[3 marks]**

Exam Tip

Drawing a line of best fit can help you describe the trend.

07.4 Predict the number of worldwide deaths due to malaria in 2020. **[2 marks]**

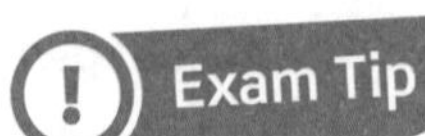

Exam Tip

You'll need to draw on the graph to answer this.

07.5 Gross domestic product (GDP) is a measure of the wealth of a country. In general, the larger the GDP, the higher the standard of living in a country. **Figure 3** shows GDP data against the number of cases of malaria per 100 000 population for different countries.

Figure 3

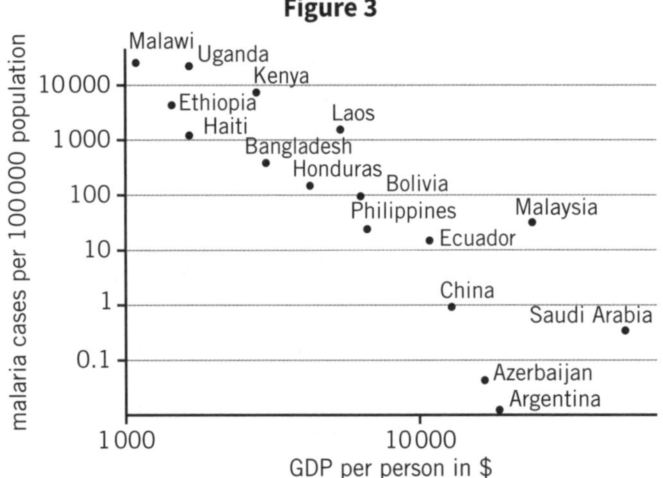

Describe the relationship shown by this scatter diagram. **[2 marks]**

Exam Tip

For questions **07.5** and **07.6**, you'll need to use examples from the figure.

07.6 Suggest and explain **two** reasons for this relationship. **[4 marks]**

08 The tobacco mosaic virus (TMV) infects tomato plants and causes a distinct mosaic pattern on the leaves.

08.1 Explain why this is an example of a communicable disease. **[2 marks]**

08.2 Explain the effects of the virus on the growth of a tomato plant. **[4 marks]**

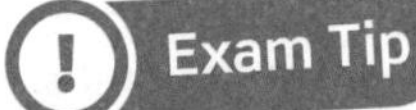

Exam Tip

Think about the effects of the virus, and how these might have knock-on effects.

08.3 Using your knowledge of TMV, identify which of the cell components TMV infects. Choose **one** answer. **[1 mark]**

nucleus mitochondrion chloroplast cell wall

Mitochondrion is the singular of mitochondria.

08.4 TMV does not usually kill the plant it has infected, but it significantly reduces the plant's yield. TMV is most commonly spread between plants by mechanical transmission – through workers' hands and tools. Some species of insects also act as vectors for TMV. TMV is also able to survive in soil for around 50 years.
Using the information given, suggest and explain **two** ways farmers could try to prevent the spread of TMV. **[4 marks]**

09 **Figure 4** shows a graph of the number of deaths worldwide due to HIV between 1990 and 2015.

Figure 4

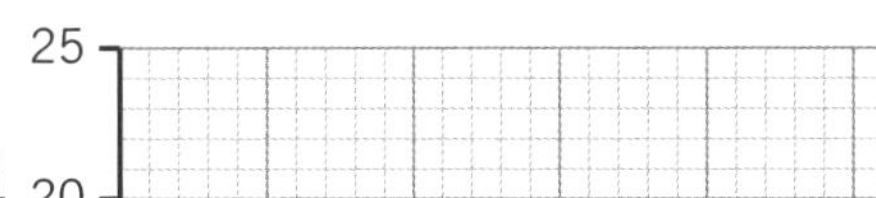

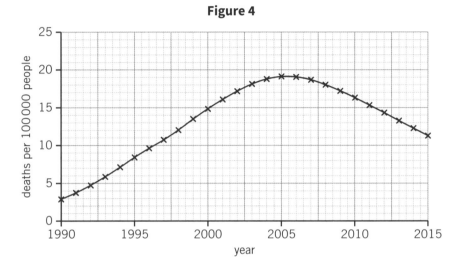

09.1 Explain how an infection with HIV can lead to death. **[3 marks]**

09.2 Name the type of drug used to treat HIV infections. **[1 mark]**

09.3 Describe the worldwide trend in deaths linked to HIV between 1990 and 2015. **[2 marks]**

Exam Tip

This graph changes direction halfway. Make sure you refer to this in your answer to **09.3**, and use data to back up what you say.

09.4 Suggest and explain **one** reason for the trend between 2005 and 2015. **[2 marks]**

09.5 Using information in **Figure 4**, calculate the number of worldwide deaths per 100 000 people due to HIV infection in 2008. **[1 mark]**

09.6 Calculate the percentage increase in deaths linked to HIV between 1998 and 2005. **[3 marks]**

10 Rose black spot is a disease that affects roses. It leads to yellow and black patterns on the leaves.

10.1 Identify the type of pathogen that causes rose black spot. **[1 mark]**

fungus virus bacteria protist

10.2 Identify the correct chemical that can be used to treat rose black spot. **[1 mark]**

insecticide herbicide fungicide pesticide

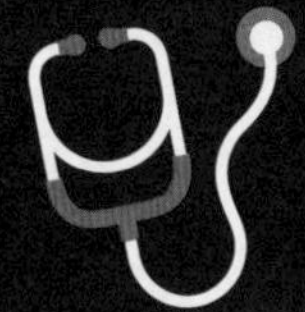
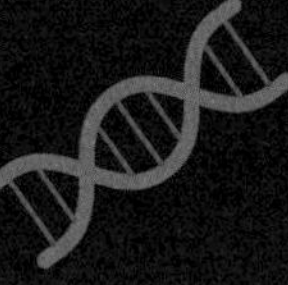

Knowledge

B8 Preventing and treating disease

Non-specific defences

Non-specific defences of the human body against all pathogens include:

Skin

- physical barrier to infection
- produces antimicrobial secretions
- microorganisms that normally live on the skin prevent pathogens growing

Nose

Cilia and **mucus** trap particles in the air, preventing them from entering the lungs.

Trachea and bronchi produce mucus, which is moved away from the lungs to the back of the throat by cilia, where it is expelled.

Stomach

Produces strong acid (pH 2) that destroys pathogens in mucus, food, and drinks.

White blood cells

If a pathogen enters the body, the immune system tries to destroy the pathogen.

The function of **white blood cells** is to fight pathogens.

There are two main types of white blood cell – lymphocytes and phagocytes.

Revision tip

Remember It's a common misconception that antibiotic resistance arises when people become resistant to a drug. In reality, it is the bacteria that evolve resistance.

Lymphocytes

Lymphocytes fight pathogens in two ways:

Antitoxins

Lymphocytes produce **antitoxins** that bind to the toxins produced by some pathogens (usually bacteria). This *neutralises* the toxins.

Antibodies

Lymphocytes produce **antibodies** that target and help to destroy specific pathogens by binding to **antigens** (proteins) on the pathogens' surfaces.

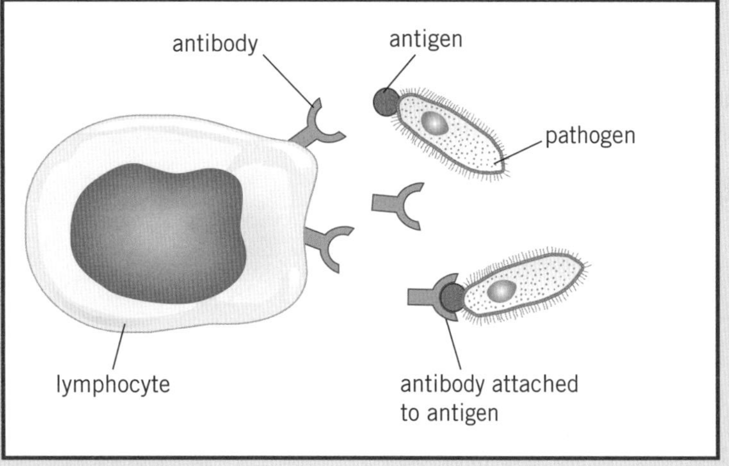

Phagocytes

1. Phagocytes are attracted to areas of infection.
2. The phagocyte surrounds the pathogen and engulfs it.
3. Enzymes that digest and destroy the pathogen are released.

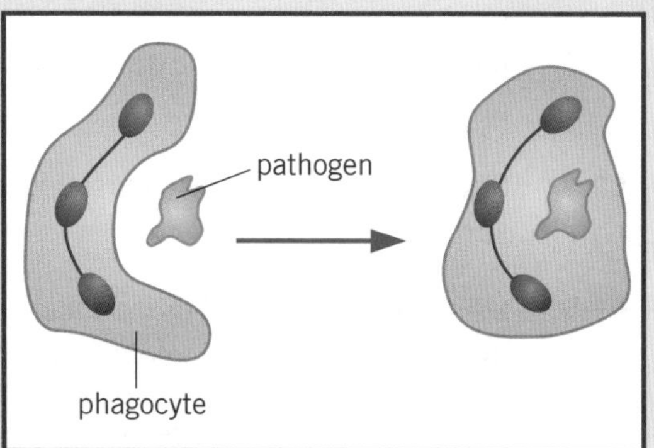

Revision tip

Remember Do not get bacterial and viral infection mixed up – don't say that antibiotics can be used to treat viral infections!

Key terms

Make sure you can write a definition for these key terms.

antibiotic antibody antigen antitoxin dose double-blind trial

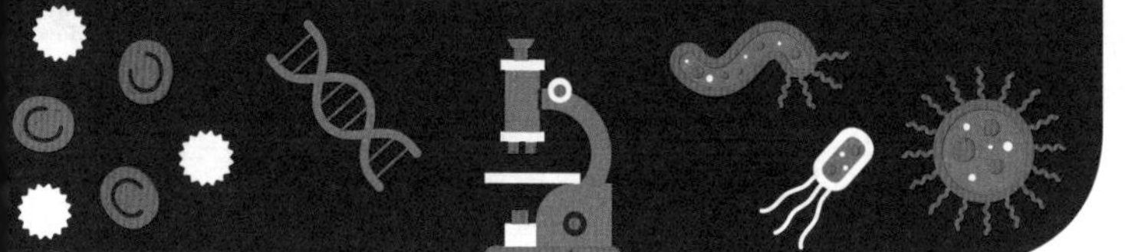

Treating diseases

Antibiotics

- **Antibiotics** are medicines that can kill *bacteria* in the body.
- Specific bacteria need to be treated by specific antibiotics.
- Antibiotics have greatly reduced deaths from infectious bacterial diseases, but antibiotic-resistant strains of bacteria are emerging.

Treating viral diseases

- Antibiotics *do not* affect viruses.
- Drugs that kill viruses often damage the body's tissues.
- Painkillers treat the symptoms of viral diseases but do not kill pathogens.

Discovering and developing new drugs

Drugs were traditionally extracted from plants and microorganisms, for example

- the heart drug digitalis comes from foxglove plants
- the painkiller aspirin originates from willow trees
- penicillin was discovered by Alexander Fleming from *Penicillium* mould.

Most modern drugs are now synthesised by chemists in laboratories.

New drugs are extensively tested and trialled for

- **toxicity** – is it harmful?
- **efficacy** – does it work?
- **dose** – what amount is safe and effective to give?

Stages of clinical trials

Pre-clinical trials

Drug is tested in cells, tissues, and live animals.

Clinical trials

1 Healthy volunteers receive very low doses to test whether the drug is safe and effective.

2 If safe, larger numbers of healthy volunteers and patients receive the drug to find the optimum dose.

Peer review

Before being published, the results of clinical trials will be tested and checked by independent researchers. This is called **peer review**.

Double-blind trials

Some clinical trials give some of their patients a **placebo** drug – one that is known to have no effect.

Double-blind trials are when neither the patients nor the doctors know who has been given the real drug and who has been given the placebo. This reduces biases in the trial.

Retrieval

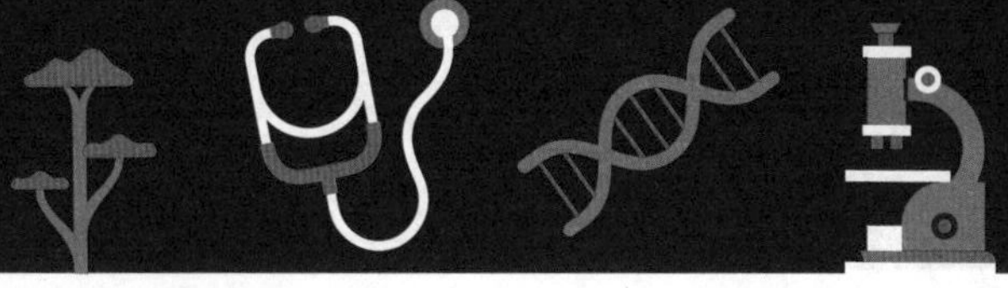

Learn the answers to the questions below, then cover the answers column with a piece of paper and write as many as you can. Check and repeat.

	B8 questions	Answers
1	What non-specific systems does the body use to prevent pathogens getting into it?	• skin • cilia and mucus in the nose, trachea, and bronchi • stomach acid
2	What three functions do white blood cells have?	phagocytosis, producing antibodies, producing antitoxins
3	What happens during phagocytosis?	phagocyte is attracted to the area of infection, engulfs a pathogen, and releases enzymes to digest the pathogen
4	What are antigens?	proteins on the surface of a pathogen
5	Why are antibodies a specific defence?	antibodies have to be the right shape for a pathogen's unique antigens, so they target a specific pathogen
6	What is the function of an antitoxin?	neutralise toxins produced by pathogens by binding to them
7	What does a vaccine contain?	small quantities of a dead or inactive form of a pathogen
8	How does vaccination protect against a specific pathogen?	vaccination stimulates the body to produce antibodies against a specific pathogen – if the same pathogen re-enters the body, white blood cells rapidly produce the correct antibodies
9	What is herd immunity?	when most of a population is vaccinated against a disease, meaning it is less likely to spread
10	What is an antibiotic?	a drug that kills bacteria but not viruses
11	What do painkillers do?	treat some symptoms of diseases and relieve pain
12	What properties of new drugs are clinical trials designed to test?	toxicity, efficacy, and optimum dose
13	What happens in the pre-clinical stage of a drug trial?	drug is tested on cells, tissues, and live animals
14	What is a placebo?	medicine with no effect that is given to patients instead of the real drug in a trial
15	What is a double-blind trial?	a trial where neither patients nor doctors know who receives the real drug and who receives the placebo

Put paper here

Now go back and use the questions below to check your knowledge from previous chapters.

Previous questions | Answers

	Previous questions	Answers
1	What is an organ?	group of tissues working together to perform a specific function
2	Why is a leaf an organ?	there are many tissues inside the leaf that work together to perform photosynthesis
3	How do white blood cells protect the body?	• engulf pathogens • produce antitoxins to neutralise toxins, or antibodies
4	Describe an example of a protist disease.	malaria – caused by a protist pathogen that is spread from person to person by mosquito bites, and causes recurrent fevers
5	Name four factors that affect the rate of transpiration.	temperature, light intensity, humidity, wind speed
6	Where is amylase produced?	salivary glands, pancreas, and small intestine
7	What happens during the third stage of the cell cycle?	the cytoplasm and cell membrane divide, forming two identical daughter cells

Put paper here

Maths Skills

Practise your maths skills using the worked example and practice questions below.

Standard form

Standard form is a way of writing very large or very small numbers. For example, in biology, we can use standard form when working with the size of cells and organelles as they are so small.

When writing a number in standard form, you first write a digit between 1 and 10, then you write × 10^n, where the power of ten expresses how big or small the number is.

For large numbers, positive powers of ten shift the digit to the left:

$23\,000\,000 = 2.3 \times 10^7$

For small numbers, negative powers of ten shift the digit to the right:

$0.000\,000\,23 = 2.3 \times 10^{-7}$

Worked example

Examples of powers of 10:

10^1	10
10^3	1000
10^7	10 000 000
10^{-3}	0.001
10^{-7}	0.000 000 1

1 What is 700 000 written in standard form?

700 000 can be written as $7 \times 100\,000$

$100\,000 = 10 \times 10 \times 10 \times 10 \times 10 = 10^5$

so $700\,000 = 7 \times 10^5$

2 What is 0.0004 written in standard form?

0.0004 can be written as 4×0.0001

$0.0001 = 10^{-4}$

So $0.0004 = 4 \times 10^{-4}$

Practice

1 The World Health Organisation estimates that 3×10^8 people are infected with malaria every year. Convert this number to an expanded figure.

2 Scientists estimate that malaria kills 2×10^6 people every year. Convert this number to an expanded figure.

3 The table below gives data relating to diabetes in the UK. Write the figures in the table in standard form.

	Figure	Standard Form
population of UK in 2015	65 000 000	
number of people diagnosed with diabetes	3 450 000	
estimated number of people with undiagnosed diabetes	549 000	

Practice

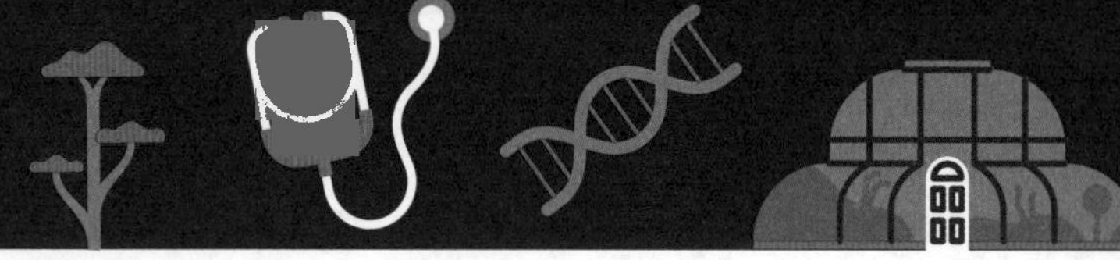

Exam-style questions

01 Most children in the UK are vaccinated against tetanus.

Tetanus is a serious disease caused by a bacterial toxin that affects the nervous system.

01.1 Name the component in the vaccine that will make a child immune to tetanus. **[1 mark]**

____

01.2 A few weeks after vaccination, a child becomes infected with the bacteria that cause tetanus.

Figure 1 shows the number of tetanus antibodies present in the child's blood.

Use your knowledge of vaccination to complete the graph to show what you think will happen to the number of tetanus antibodies present in the child's blood. **[2 marks]**

Figure 1

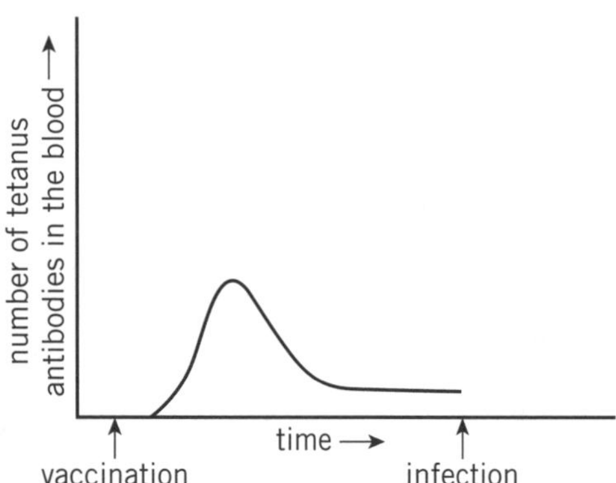

01.3 Alongside tetanus, mumps is another disease for which vaccination is available.

Explain the advantages of vaccinating a large proportion of the population against mumps. **[2 marks]**

____

____

____

> **Exam Tip**
>
> This question only asks about *advantages*, don't waste time writing down any disadvantages.

01.4 Another vaccination offers protection against the bacteria that cause some strains of meningitis.

Explain why a person who has only received vaccinations against tetanus and mumps would not have protection against meningitis. **[3 marks]**

____

____

____

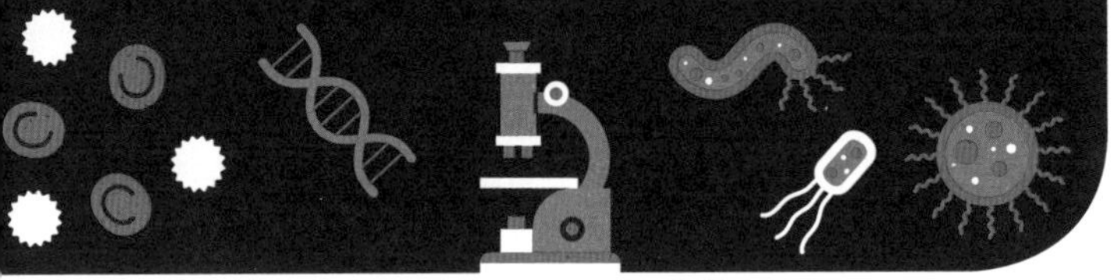

02 **Figure 2** shows a section of nasal epithelium (tissue from the nose).

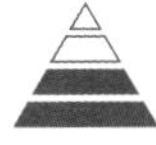

Figure 2

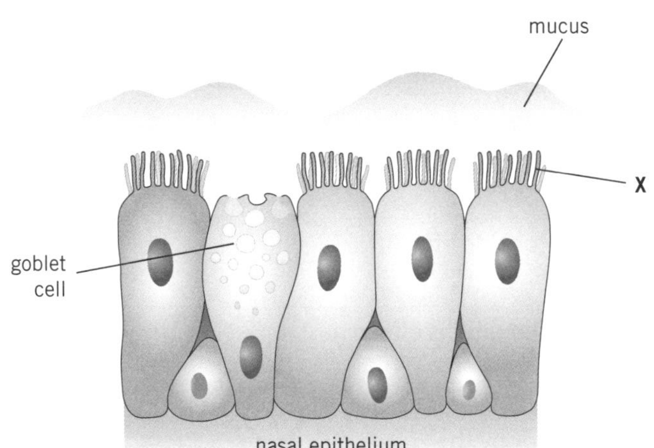

02.1 Describe why this is an example of a tissue. **[1 mark]**

____

____

02.2 Suggest the function of the goblet cells. **[1 mark]**

____

Think about the location and the name of the cell.

02.3 Identify structure **X** in **Figure 2** and explain its role in defence against disease. **[3 marks]**

____

____

02.4 The skin is another example of a non-specific defence against disease.

It acts as a barrier to microorganism entry.

Explain how the skin protects itself after its surface is punctured. **[3 marks]**

____

____

____

02.5 Describe **one** other way the skin protects the body from disease. **[2 marks]**

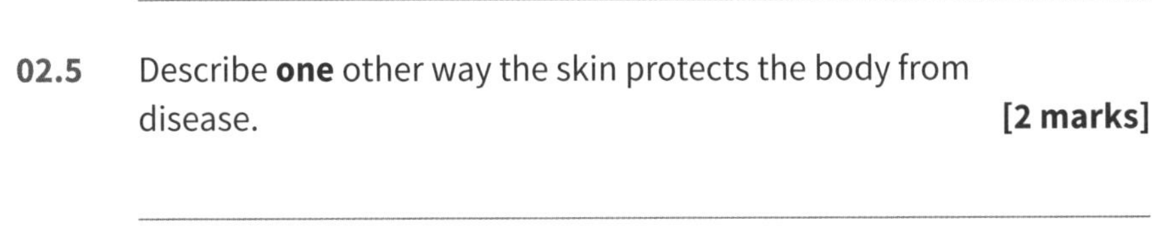

____

____

This question is asking for you to say *what* happens, not *why*.

03 Before a medical drug can be licensed to be prescribed by a doctor, it has to undergo a number of stages of testing.

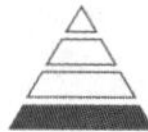

03.1 Draw **one** line from each stage of drug testing to its purpose. **[3 marks]**

Stage of drug testing	Purpose of test
small dose on healthy volunteers	to find out if the drug is toxic
cells	to determine the optimum dose
large numbers of patients	to check for side effects
small number of patients	to prove the drug is effective

03.2 Drug trials are very expensive. They are often paid for by the company that wishes to manufacture the drug.
Suggest **one** reason why people who are employed by the manufacturing company should not take part in the trial. **[1 mark]**

Exam Tip

This may sound like a question in a business exam, but it's relevant for science as well.

03.3 Describe what is meant by a double-blind trial. **[3 marks]**

03.4 Describe **one** reason why the placebo drug in a double-blind trial should contain an existing treatment for the condition being targeted. **[1 mark]**

04 Since the discovery of penicillin as an antibiotic drug, many other antibiotics have been created.

04.1 Describe how penicillin was discovered. **[3 marks]**

04.2 Explain why an antibiotic drug should not be prescribed to treat a measles infection. **[2 marks]**

04.3 Penicillin and erythromycin are two types of antibiotic drugs.
Explain why doctors have a range of antibiotic drugs available to prescribe. **[2 marks]**

04.4 Erythromycin is taken orally in tablet form. It is possible to cover the tablet in a coating that affects the rate at which the drug is absorbed into the bloodstream.

Figure 3 shows the level of erythromycin in the bloodstream over time for both forms of the tablet – coated and uncoated. Erythromycin is taken every 12 hours.

Figure 3

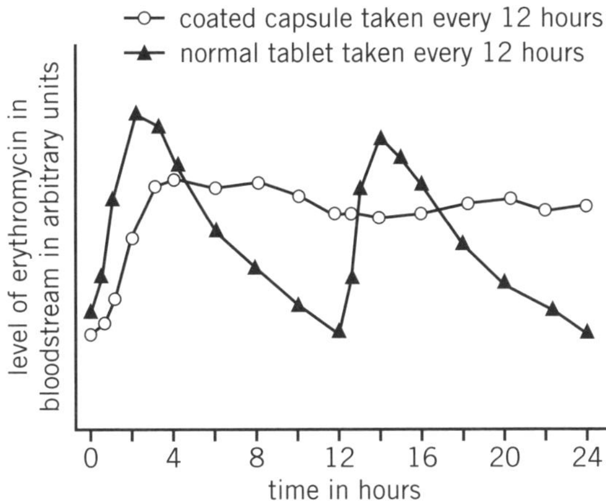

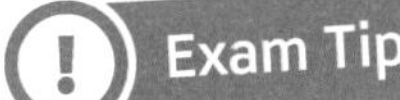

Exam Tip

For this question, it's important you describe both lines carefully, use data from the graph, and talk about any changes that you can see over time.

Using **Figure 3**, compare the effects of the two types of tablet on a patient suffering from a bacterial infection. **[6 marks]**

05 Before medical drugs can be used on patients, they undergo a number of stages of testing.

05.1 One important test is for drug efficacy. Describe what is meant by this term. **[1 mark]**

05.2 Before clinical trials, drugs are tested in the laboratory. During laboratory trials the drugs are not tested on people. Name **two** ways a drug could be tested during this stage of the trials. **[2 marks]**

05.3 Clinical trials consist of several stages of testing. During the first phase (Phase 1) of clinical trials the potential new drug is tested on healthy volunteers. Describe what happens during the next phase (Phase 2) of testing. **[2 marks]**

05.4 Phase 2 clinical trials are where most drugs fail. Only 31% of drugs that enter Phase 2 studies go on to Phase 3. A pharmaceuticals company develops 13 compounds that are successful after Phase 1 of clinical trials. Estimate how many compounds the company will advance to Phase 3. **[2 marks]**

Exam Tip

In **05.4** and **05.5**, make sure you show your working – you can get some marks even if you get the answer wrong.

05.5 Cancer drugs have the lowest overall rate of success during clinical trials. Only 5.1% of the drugs that enter Phase 1 are ultimately approved. In 2018, 59 new cancer drugs were approved for use in patients. Estimate the number of drug compounds that were successfully tested in the laboratory to produce this number of new treatments. **[3 marks]**

06 Measles used to be a very common disease in children. It spreads quickly through groups of people through droplet infection.

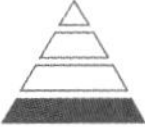

06.1 Describe why measles cannot be treated using antibiotics. **[1 mark]**

06.2 People who have been infected with measles may be advised to take aspirin. Identify the plant that aspirin originates from. **[1 mark]**

foxglove   willow tree   mould   tomatoes

06.3 Explain why aspirin may be beneficial for a person with measles, even though it does not cure the disease. **[2 marks]**

06.4 The best way to prevent the spread of measles is through a national vaccination programme.
Describe how the measles vaccine works. **[4 marks]**

06.5 In 2017–2018, 91.2% of children in the UK were vaccinated against measles. This was the lowest recorded vaccination level since 2010–2011.
Suggest how this will affect the number of people who are infected with measles. **[2 marks]**

07 Diphtheria is a highly contagious condition that affects the nose, throat, and skin. It is transmitted through droplet infection, or by sharing items such as cups or cutlery with an infected person.

Figure 4 shows the number of diphtheria cases in England and Wales, and the number of deaths due to the illness, between 1914 and 2014.

Figure 4

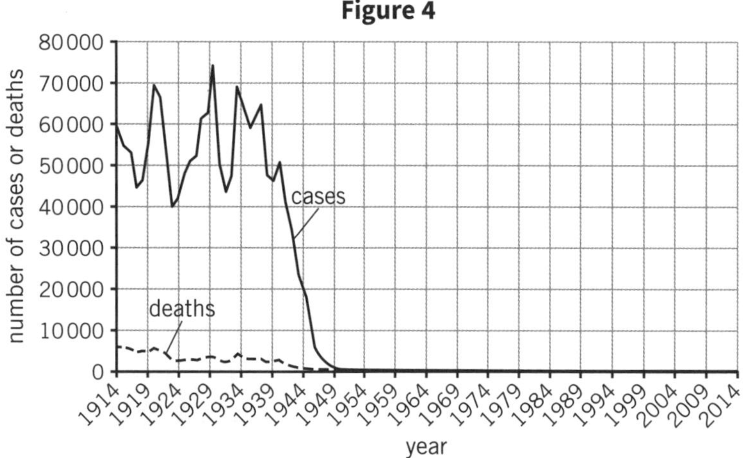

07.1 Identify the highest annual number of deaths due to diphtheria. **[1 mark]**

Exam Tip

Draw lines on the graph to help you work this out.

07.2 Suggest **two** reasons why the year with the highest number of deaths due to diphtheria does not correspond to the year with the highest number of cases of diphtheria. **[2 marks]**

Exam Tip

In **07.2** don't just think about the number of cases, but also what happens when people get ill.

07.3 Calculate the percentage change in the number of cases of diphtheria between 1914 and 1944. **[2 marks]**

07.4 Using **Figure 4**, suggest and explain which year the diphtheria vaccine was introduced in England and Wales. **[3 marks]**

07.5 Due to the effective childhood vaccination programme, diphtheria is an extremely rare disease in England and Wales. However, there were 14 confirmed cases of diphtheria in 2014.
Suggest why diphtheria has not been eliminated entirely as a disease from England and Wales. **[3 marks]**

08 The human body uses a number of defence mechanisms to protect itself against disease.

08.1 Identify which of the following is a non-specific defence mechanism. Choose **one** answer. **[1 mark]**

antibody production

antitoxin production

presence of hydrochloric acid in the stomach

production of bile

08.2 A student reads that *'a link exists between a person's white blood cell count and their risk of developing a communicable disease'.*
Explain why this statement is true. **[6 marks]**

Exam Tip

You must refer to the question in your answer.

09 An increasing number of strains of bacteria are resistant to all known antibiotics. Scientists are working to develop new forms of antibacterial drugs to meet this challenge.
Describe the main steps scientists follow to develop a new medicine, so that it is available to be prescribed by a doctor. **[6 marks]**

10 Fatty material can build up inside our arteries. This prevents blood flow and can lead to cardiovascular disease (CVD).

10.1 Explain whether this is an example of a communicable disease. **[2 marks]**

10.2 A double-blind clinical trial was carried out to investigate the effect of a drug on the mass of the fatty deposits in patients with CVD.
Explain what is meant by a double-blind trial. **[2 marks]**

10.3 The doctors measured the mass of the fatty deposits before and after treatment with the drug. The mean change in mass of the fatty build-up in patients was calculated.
The results are shown in **Table 1**.

Table 1

Group	Mean change in mass of fatty deposit in mg	Uncertainty in change in mass in mg
placebo	+10	±20
treatment	−50	±50

Exam Tip

±20 means that it can be 20 above *or* below the value.

Describe the results of this trial. **[4 marks]**

10.4 Evaluate the success of the drug as a treatment for CVD. **[4 marks]**

Knowledge

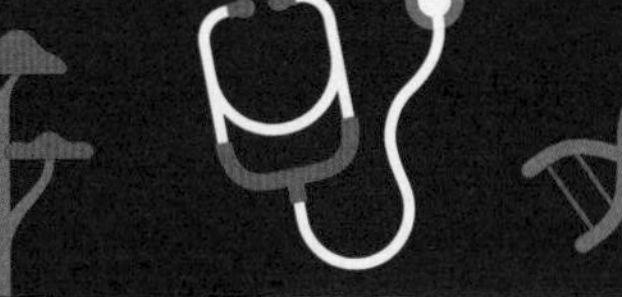

B9 Non-communicable diseases

Health issues

Health is the state of physical and mental well-being.

The following factors can affect health:

- communicable and non-communicable diseases
- diet
- stress
- exercise
- life situations.

Different types of disease may interact, for example

- defects in the immune system make an individual more likely to suffer from infectious diseases
- viral infection can trigger cancers
- immune reactions initially caused by a pathogen can trigger allergies, for example skin rashes and asthma
- severe physical ill health can lead to depression and other mental illnesses.

Coronary heart disease

Coronary heart disease (CHD) occurs when the coronary arteries become narrowed by the build-up of layers of fatty material within them.

This reduces the flow of blood, resulting in less oxygen for the heart muscle, which can lead to heart attacks.

Treating cardiovascular diseases

Treatment	Description	Advantages	Disadvantages
stent	inserted into blocked coronary arteries to keep them open	• widens the artery – allows more blood to flow, so more oxygen is supplied to the heart • less serious surgery	• can involve major surgery – risk of infection, blood loss, blood clots, and damage to blood vessels • risks from anaesthetic used during surgery
statins	drugs that reduce blood **cholesterol** levels, slowing down the deposit of fatty material in the arteries	• effective • no need for surgery • can prevent CHD from developing	• possible side effects such as muscle pain, headaches, and sickness • cannot cure CHD, so patient will have to take tablets for many years
replace faulty heart valves	heart valves that leak or do not open fully, preventing control of blood flow through the heart, can be replaced with biological or mechanical valves	• allows control of blood flow through the heart • long-term cure for faulty heart valves	• can involve major surgery – risk of infection, blood loss, blood clots, and damage to blood vessels • risks from anaesthetic used during surgery
transplants	if the heart fails a donor heart, or heart and lungs, can be transplanted **artificial hearts** can be used to keep patients alive whilst waiting for a heart transplant, or to allow the heart to rest during recovery	• long-term cure for the most serious heart conditions • treats problems that cannot be treated in other ways	• transplant may be rejected if there is not a match between donor and patient • lengthy process • major surgery – risk of infection, blood loss, blood clots, and damage to blood vessels • risks from anaesthetic used during surgery

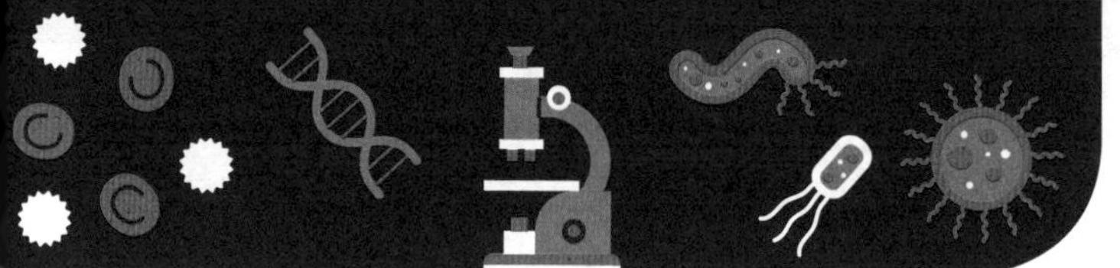

Risk factors and non-communicable diseases

A **risk factor** is any aspect of your lifestyle or substance in your body that can increase the risk of a disease developing.

Some risk factors cause specific diseases. Other diseases are caused by factors interacting.

Risk factor	Disease	Effects of risk factor
diet (obesity) and amount of exercise	Type 2 diabetes	body does not respond properly to the production of insulin, so blood glucose levels cannot be controlled
	cardiovascular diseases	increased blood cholesterol can lead to CHD
alcohol	impaired liver function	long-term alcohol use causes liver cirrhosis (scarring), meaning the liver cannot remove toxins from the body or produce sufficient bile
	impaired brain function	damages the brain and can cause anxiety and depression
	affected development of unborn babies	alcohol can pass through the placenta, risking miscarriages, premature births, and birth defects
smoking	lung disease and cancers	cigarettes contain carcinogens, which can cause cancers
	affected development of unborn babies	chemicals can pass through the placenta, risking premature births and birth defects
carcinogens, such as ionising radiation, and genetic risk factors	cancers	for example, tar in cigarettes and ultraviolet rays from the Sun can cause cancers
		some genetic factors make an individual more likely to develop certain cancers

Cancer

Cancer is the result of changes in cells that lead to uncontrolled growth and division by mitosis.

Rapid division of abnormal cells can form a **tumour**.

Malignant tumours are cancerous tumours that invade neighbouring tissues and spread to other parts of the body in the blood, forming secondary tumours.

Benign tumours are non-cancerous tumours that do not spread in the body.

Treatment of non-communicable diseases linked to lifestyle risk factors – such as poor diet, drinking alcohol, and smoking – can be very costly, both to individuals and to the Government.

A high incidence of these lifestyle risk factors can cause high rates of non-communicable diseases in a population.

Key terms Make sure you can write a definition for these key terms.

artificial heart   benign   carcinogen   cholesterol   coronary heart disease   health   malignant   risk factor   statin   stent   transplant   tumour

Retrieval

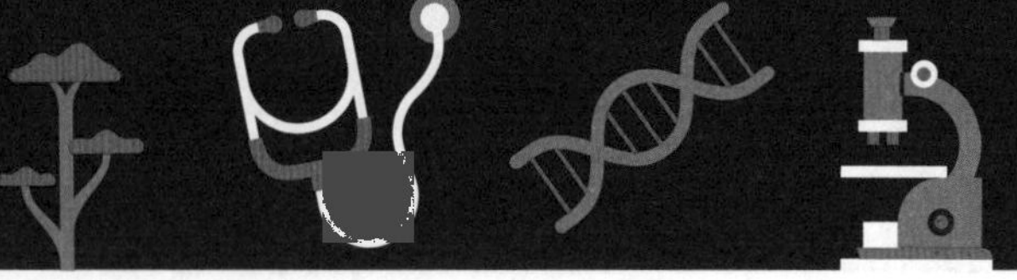

Learn the answers to the questions below, then cover the answers column with a piece of paper and write as many as you can. Check and repeat.

	B9 questions	Answers
1	What is coronary heart disease?	layers of fatty material that build up inside the coronary arteries, narrowing them – resulting in a lack of oxygen for the heart
2	What is a stent?	a device inserted into a blocked artery to keep it open, allowing more blood and oxygen to the heart
3	What are statins?	drugs that reduce blood cholesterol levels, slowing the rate of fatty material deposit
4	What is a faulty heart valve?	heart valve that doesn't open properly or leaks
5	How can a faulty heart valve be treated?	replace with a biological or mechanical valve
6	When do heart transplants take place?	in cases of heart failure
7	What are artificial hearts used for?	keep patients alive whilst waiting for a transplant, or allow the heart to rest for recovery
8	Define health.	state of physical and mental well-being
9	What factors can affect health?	disease, diet, stress, exercise, life situations
10	What is a risk factor?	aspect of lifestyle or substance in the body that can increase the risk of a disease developing
11	Give five risk factors.	poor diet, smoking, lack of exercise, alcohol, carcinogens
12	What is cancer?	a result of changes in cells that lead to uncontrolled growth and cell division by mitosis
13	What are malignant tumours?	cancerous tumours that can spread to neighbouring tissues and other parts of the body in the blood, forming secondary tumours
14	What are benign tumours?	non-cancerous tumours that do not spread in the body
15	What two types of risk factor affect the development of cancers?	lifestyle and genetic risk factors
16	What is a carcinogen?	a substance that can cause cancers to develop

Put paper here

Now go back and use the questions below to check your knowledge from previous chapters.

Previous questions / Answers

	Previous questions	Answers
1	What is a communicable disease?	disease that can be transmitted from one organism to another
2	What is a pathogen?	microorganism that causes disease
3	What is a double-blind trial?	a trial where neither patients nor doctors know who receives the real drug and who receives the placebo
4	Describe the function of lipases.	to break down lipids into fatty acids and glycerol
5	What are antibiotics?	drugs that kill bacteria but not viruses
6	What do painkillers do?	treat some symptoms of diseases and relieve pain
7	Give one example of osmosis in a plant.	water moves from the soil into the root hair cell
8	Where are most stomata found?	underside of leaves
9	Why is the human circulatory system a double circulatory system?	blood passes through the heart twice – deoxygenated blood is pumped from the right side of the heart to the lungs, and the oxygenated blood that returns is pumped from the left side of the heart to the body

Put paper here

Put paper here

Put paper here

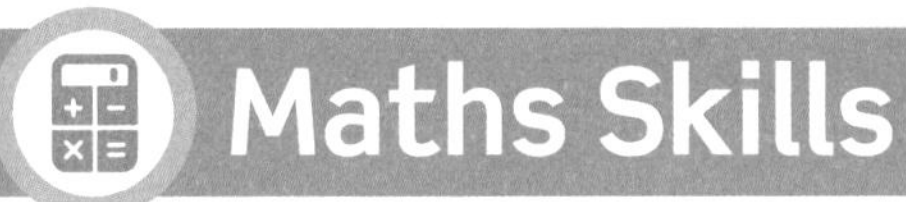

Maths Skills

Practise your maths skills using the worked example and practice questions below.

Calculating rate of blood flow

The rate of blood flow in the body changes in response to things like exercise and illnesses.

Blood flow increases during exercise to deliver oxygen to working muscles and to remove waste products.

The rate of blood flow can be reduced by non-communicable diseases such as coronary heart disease.

To calculate rate of blood flow:

$$\text{rate of blood flow (ml/min)} = \frac{\text{volume of blood (ml)}}{\text{time (min)}}$$

Remember to add units to your answer. Rate of blood flow can be measured in ml/min or l/hr – check the question to see which units you need to use.

Worked example

1660 ml of blood is pumped through a vein in 4 min.

Calculate the rate of blood flow through the vein in ml/min.

$$\frac{1660}{4} = 415 \text{ ml/min}$$

You may have to convert millilitres to litres if given a large volume.

To do this, divide the volume in ml by 1000.

Practice

1 3540 ml of blood is pumped through an artery in 3.5 min.

Calculate the rate of blood flow through the artery in ml/min.

2 11 540 ml of blood is pumped through an artery in 12.5 minutes.

Calculate the rate of blood flow through the artery in ml/min.

3 670 l of blood is pumped through the heart in 1 hr.

Calculate the rate of blood flow through the heart in ml/min.

Practice

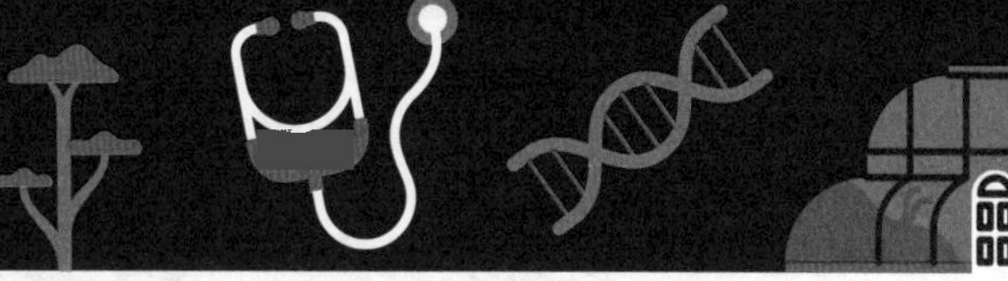

Exam-style questions

01 **Figure 1** shows the main causes of death in the UK in 2012 for people under the age of 75.

The total number of deaths recorded in this period was 150 000.

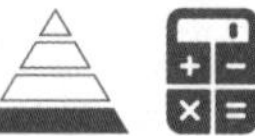

Figure 1

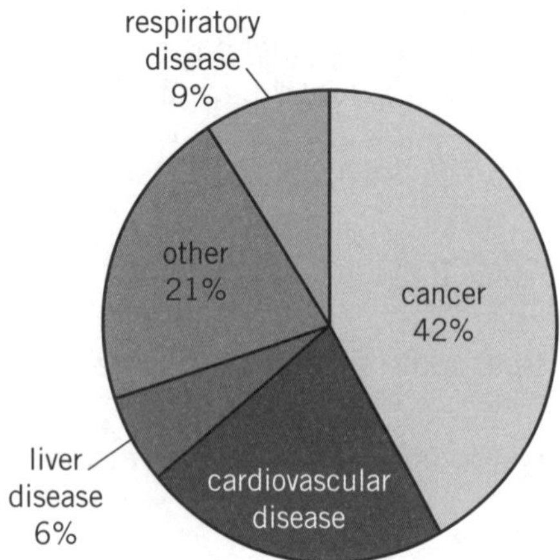

01.1 Describe what is meant by cardiovascular disease (CVD). **[1 mark]**

____

____

01.2 Determine the percentage of people under the age of 75 who died in 2012 due to CVD. **[1 mark]**

______________ %

01.3 Calculate the number of people under the age of 75 who died in 2012 due to CVD. **[2 marks]**

Exam Tip

The total number of people is given in the first part of the question.

______________ people

01.4 Explain **three** ways a person could reduce their risk of CVD. **[6 marks]**

1 ______________________________

____

2 ______________________________

____

3 ______________________________

____

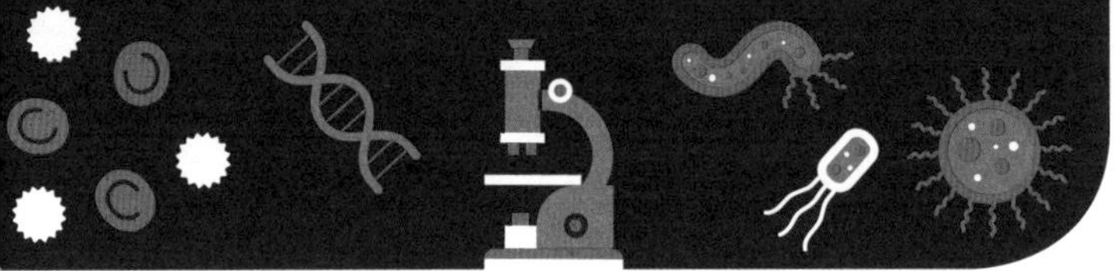

02 If a patient has a blocked blood vessel they may be treated using a stent or by undergoing bypass surgery. This is where another piece of blood vessel is used to replace the damaged vessel.

02.1 Describe how stents are used to treat blocked blood vessels. **[4 marks]**

____

____

____

____

02.2 Evaluate the use of stents to treat blocked blood vessels by explaining the risks and benefits of having a stent. **[4 marks]**

____

____

____

____

____

02.3 **Figure 2** shows the proportion of patients suffering complications following surgery to treat cardiovascular disease (CVD). This information was collected by analysing the health records of 2500 patients, half of whom received a stent and half of whom received a bypass operation.

Figure 2

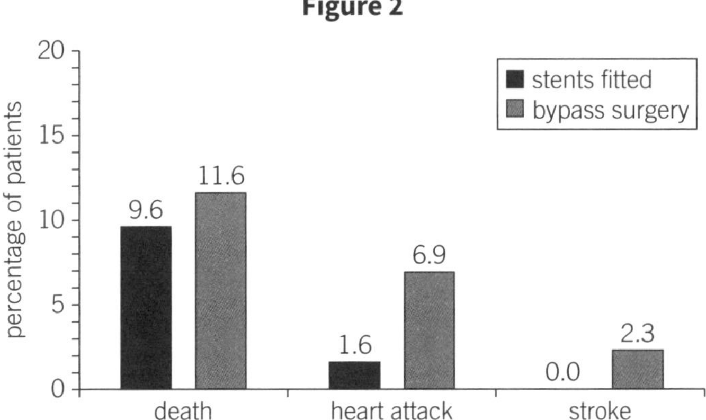

Calculate how many more patients died following a bypass operation compared to those who received a stent. **[3 marks]**

Exam Tip

The y-axis on the graph gives you the percentage to use in this question.

______________ patients

03 **Figure 3** shows the effect of three key risk factors on the mortality rate of 35 000 people with cardiovascular disease (CVD) in a region of Finland. The data are all relative to the number observed in the first year of the study.

In 1972:

- 31 500 people had cholesterol levels above the recommended maximum level
- 11 200 people were smokers
- 28 000 people had high blood pressure
- 650 people died due to CVD.

Figure 3

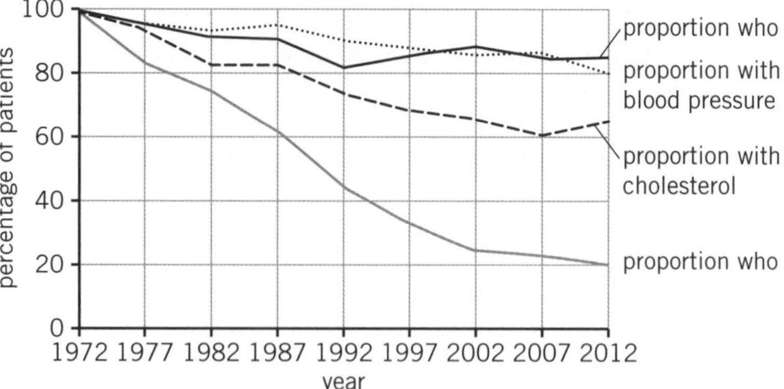

03.1 Describe the main trends shown in the three key risk factors for CVD between 1972 and 2012. **[2 marks]**

03.2 Suggest and explain **two** reasons for the trends shown in **Figure 3**. **[4 marks]**

03.3 Explain how a high level of cholesterol can cause a heart attack. **[3 marks]**

03.4 Name the drug used to reduce blood cholesterol levels. **[1 mark]**

03.5 Calculate the number of deaths due to CVD in this region of Finland in 2012. **[3 marks]**

03.6 A student writes the following conclusion based on **Figure 3**:

'*The data gathered in Finland prove that smoking, high blood pressure, and high levels of cholesterol are three key risk factors linked to cardiovascular disease.*'

Explain the extent to which you agree or disagree with this conclusion. **[3 marks]**

Writing 'I agree' or 'I disagree' isn't going to be enough to get the marks here – you need to say why you think that.

04 To reduce the number of deaths from non-communicable diseases, scientists study large volumes of data to search for possible links between risk factors and disease.

04.1 Describe the difference between a risk factor that shows a correlation with the incidence of a disease and a risk factor that shows causation of a disease. **[2 marks]**

04.2 Give **one** risk factor for a disease that you cannot control. **[1 mark]**

04.3 Unprotected exposure to sunlight is a risk factor for developing skin cancer. Explain what is meant by the term cancer. **[2 marks]**

04.4 Explain how sun exposure increases a person's risk of developing skin cancer. **[2 marks]**

04.5 Smoking is a risk factor for the development of tumours. Most tumours caused by smoking are malignant. Explain the difference between a benign and a malignant tumour. **[3 marks]**

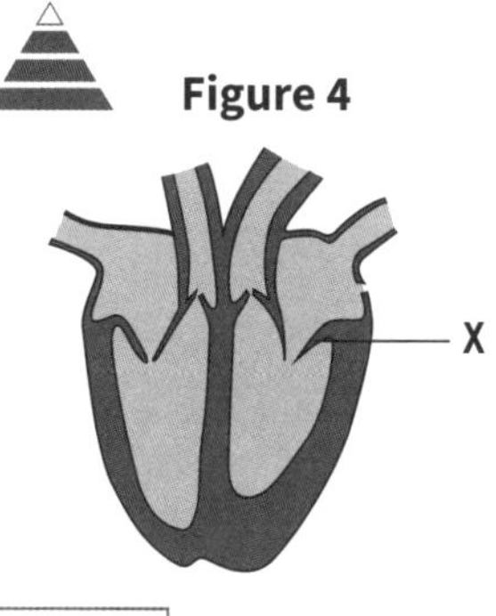

Figure 4

05 Every year many patients need to have heart valve replacements.

05.1 Describe the function of the heart valve labelled **X** in **Figure 4**. **[2 marks]**

05.2 Over time valves can become leaky.
Explain how this can cause health issues. **[3 marks]**

05.3 **Table 1** gives information about two types of heart valve.

Table 1

Type of heart valve	mechanical heart valve	biological heart valve
Material	titanium	usually cow or pig tissue, but can be from a human donor
Lifespan	20 years	10–15 years
Additional medication	anti-coagulation medication to prevent blood clotting around the valve	not required

A 20-year-old patient requires a heart valve replacement.
Using **Table 1** and your own knowledge, evaluate the advantages and disadvantages of each type of heart valve. **[6 marks]**

Exam Tip

Make sure you refer to *all* of the information given in **Table 1** – put a little tick next to it when you've used it.

06 One measure of a person's health is their body mass index (BMI), which is calculated using the following formula:

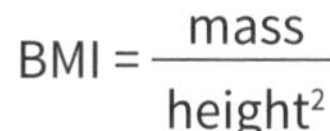

$$\text{BMI} = \frac{\text{mass}}{\text{height}^2}$$

Exam Tip

It's just the height that is squared and not everything.

06.1 A student has a mass of 48 kg and is 1.5 metres tall.
Calculate the student's BMI. **[2 marks]**

06.2 Using **Table 2**, identify which weight category the student belongs to. **[1 mark]**

Table 2

Weight category	BMI in kg/m^2
underweight	<18.5
healthy weight	18.5–24.9
overweight	25–29.9
obese	30–34.9
severely obese	35–39.9
morbidly obese	≥40

06.3 In the UK in 2016, 26 % of adults were classified as obese.
Explain the effects of obesity on the body. **[6 marks]**

06.4 One public health campaign aims to increase levels of exercise amongst the population by getting people to choose to walk or cycle to work, rather than take public transport or drive.
Explain how this campaign could help to reduce obesity levels in the population. **[2 marks]**

06.5 It typically costs £2 billion to develop a new drug and get it onto the market.
Evaluate the costs and benefits to society of the availability of an anti-obesity drug that suppresses a person's feeling of hunger. **[6 marks]**

> **Exam Tip**
> Think about ways that reducing obesity can reduce the cost of healthcare.

07 If a person has a high level of cholesterol in their blood, it increases their risk of a heart attack or a stroke.

07.1 Explain how the build-up of cholesterol can cause a heart attack. **[4 marks]**

07.2 Give **one** factor that can affect the level of cholesterol in a person's blood. **[1 mark]**

07.3 Statins reduce blood cholesterol levels. They are commonly prescribed to people who have high levels of blood cholesterol. However, statins cause negative effects in some patients.

One study showed the following information for every 10 000 people treated with statins:

- 275 fewer cases of heart disease occurred than had been predicted
- 10 fewer cases of oesophageal cancer than had been predicted
- 25 extra patients experienced acute kidney failure compared to mean levels
- 75 extra patients experienced liver dysfunction, compared to mean levels
- 300 patients developed cataracts
- 150 patients experienced muscle weakness.

Explain why doctors prescribe statins despite the risks to patients of developing another medical condition. **[2 marks]**

> **Exam Tip**
> Use data from the question in your answer.
> This isn't testing what you know, it's testing your analysis and interpretation skills.

07.4 In the year of the study, 4 200 000 people (from a population of 60 000 000) in the UK experienced liver dysfunction.
Evaluate whether taking statins causes a significant increase in the risk of liver dysfunction. **[5 marks]**

08 Atherosclerosis is one form of cardiovascular disease (CVD). Patients with this form of the disease have a build-up of fatty material on the inner walls of their arteries.

08.1 Explain how atherosclerosis increases the risk of a heart attack. **[2 marks]**

08.2 Describe **one** mechanical technique doctors can use to lower the risk of a heart attack for a patient with atherosclerosis. **[3 marks]**

08.3 Patients with CVD are often advised to take aspirin daily. An effect of aspirin is to reduce the ability of platelets to stick together.
Suggest and explain the benefits of a person with atherosclerosis taking this drug. **[4 marks]**

> **Exam Tip**
> Read the question carefully, there is information that will help you with your answer.

09 Fresh cow's milk is a mixture containing water, lipids, protein, and lactose sugar. It also contains some vitamins and minerals.

Exam Tip

This test has a colour change – don't forget to include the start and end colours.

09.1 Describe the chemical test that could be used to show that there is protein present in milk. **[2 marks]**

09.2 Lactose cannot be absorbed into the body. It must be digested by the enzyme lactase into the sugars glucose and galactose, which can then be absorbed.
Suggest why lactose cannot be absorbed into the blood. **[1 mark]**

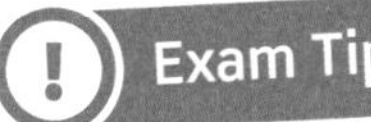

Exam Tip

Anything that ends in *–ase* is an enzyme.

09.3 Lactase can be added to fresh milk to pre-digest the lactose. This makes 'lactose-free' milk, which is suitable for people who do not produce enough lactase of their own.

A company that produces lactose-free milk investigated the effect of temperature on lactase. Their results are shown in **Table 3**.

Table 3

Temperature in °C	Time taken to digest lactose in min
25	20
30	14
35	11
40	11
45	29
50	no digestion

Explain why no digestion occurred at 50 °C. **[3 marks]**

09.4 Using the information provided, suggest the optimum temperature for the company to heat milk to, prior to adding the lactase enzyme. Give a reason for your answer. **[2 marks]**

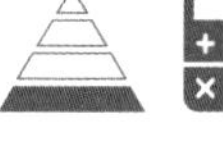

10 A student looked down a microscope to observe some actively dividing cells from a root tip. They estimated that there were 700 cells in their field of view. The student counted 36 cells that were going through mitosis.

10.1 If one complete cell cycle is 25 hours, estimate how long mitosis takes. Use the equation: **[3 marks]**

length of cell cycle stage =

$$\frac{\text{observed number of cells at the stage}}{\text{observed total number of cells}} \times \text{total length of cell cycle}$$

10.2 Describe the main steps in the cell cycle. **[4 marks]**

Knowledge

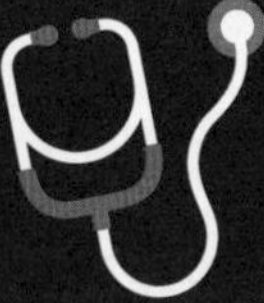

B10 Photosynthesis

Photosynthetic reaction

Photosynthesis is a chemical reaction in which energy is transferred from the environment as light from the Sun to the leaves of a plant. This is an **endothermic** reaction.

Chlorophyll, the green pigment in **chloroplasts** in the leaves, absorbs the light energy. Leaves are well-adapted to increase the rate of photosynthesis when needed.

Rate of photosynthesis

A **limiting factor** is anything that limits the rate of a reaction when it is in short supply.

The limiting factors for photosynthesis are

- temperature
- light intensity
- carbon dioxide concentration
- amount of chlorophyll.

Less chlorophyll in the leaves reduces the rate of photosynthesis. More chlorophyll may be produced by plants in well-lit areas to increase the photosynthesis rate.

carbon dioxide + water $\xrightarrow{\text{light}}$ **glucose** + oxygen

$$6CO_2 + 6H_2O \xrightarrow{\text{light}} C_6H_{12}O_6 + 6O_2$$

Limiting factors and photosynthesis rate

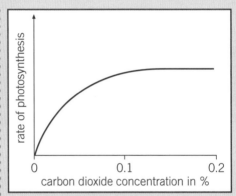

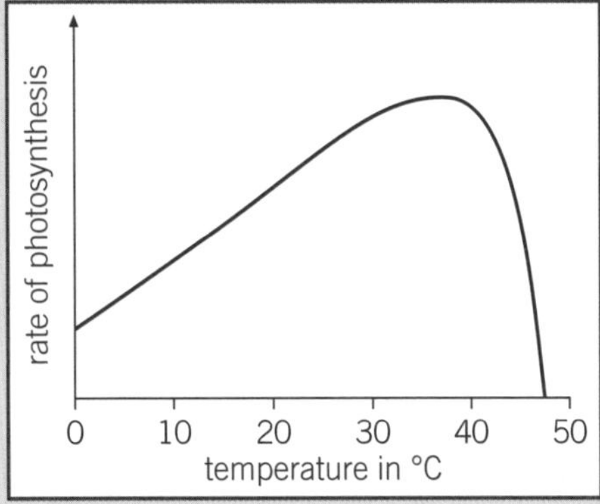

rate of photosynthesis

0 0.1 0.2

carbon dioxide concentration in %

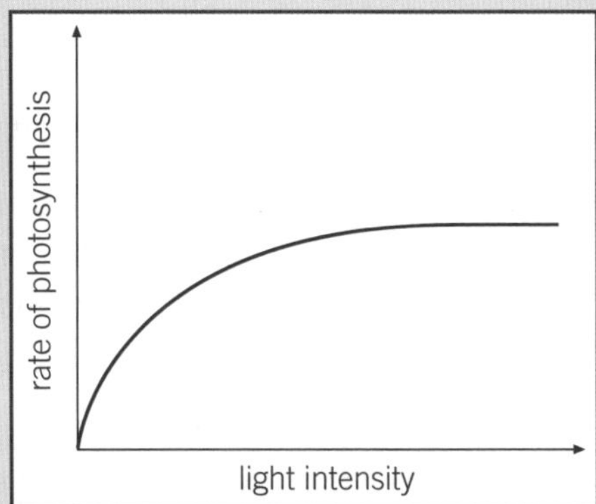

- At low temperatures the rate of photosynthesis is low because the reactant molecules have less kinetic energy.
- Photosynthesis is an enzyme-controlled reaction, so at high temperatures the enzymes are denatured and the rate quickly decreases.

- Carbon dioxide is used up in photosynthesis, so increasing carbon dioxide concentration increases the rate of photosynthesis.
- At a certain point, another factor becomes limiting.
- Carbon dioxide is often the limiting factor for photosynthesis.

- Light energy is needed for photosynthesis, so increasing light intensity increases the rate of photosynthesis.
- At a certain point, another factor becomes limiting.
- Photosynthesis will stop if there is little or no light.

Key terms

Make sure you can write a definition for these key terms.

carbon dioxide *chlorophyll* *chloroplast* *endothermic*

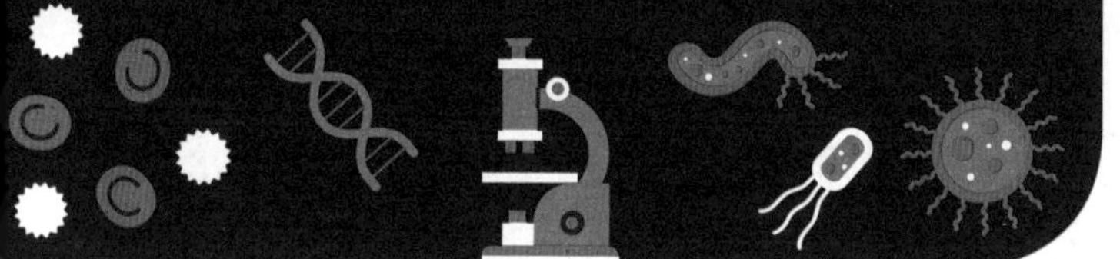

Interaction of limiting factors

Limiting factors often interact, and any one may be limiting photosynthesis.

For example, on the graph the lowest curve has both carbon dioxide and temperature limiting photosynthesis. Temperature is limiting for the middle curve, and the highest curve shows photosynthesis rate increases when both temperature and carbon dioxide are increased until another factor becomes limiting.

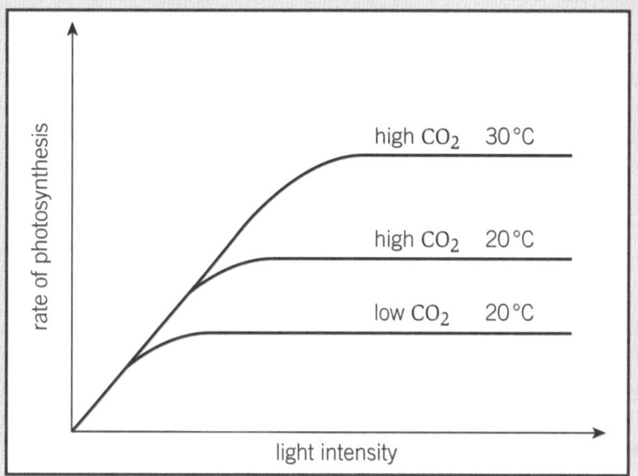

Inverse square law

As the distance of a light source from a plant increases, the light intensity decreases – this is called an inverse relationship. This relationship is not linear, as light intensity varies in inverse proportion to the square of the distance:

$$\text{light intensity} \propto \frac{1}{\text{distance}^2}$$

For example, if you double the distance between a light source and a plant, light intensity falls by three-quarters.

Revision tip

Remember The inverse square law may look complicated but you will have covered it in maths, and it works exactly the same way in science. Make sure you follow the rules of BIDMAS and use your calculator carefully.

Greenhouse economics

Commercial greenhouses control limiting factors to get the highest possible rates of photosynthesis so they can grow plants as quickly as possible or produce the highest yields, whilst still making a profit.

Revision tip

Practice Make sure you learn the shapes of the graphs of limiting factors. In an exam you may be asked to sketch them (the axes and shape of the line), describe them (use words to show the shape), or explain them (say *why* the shape is how it is).

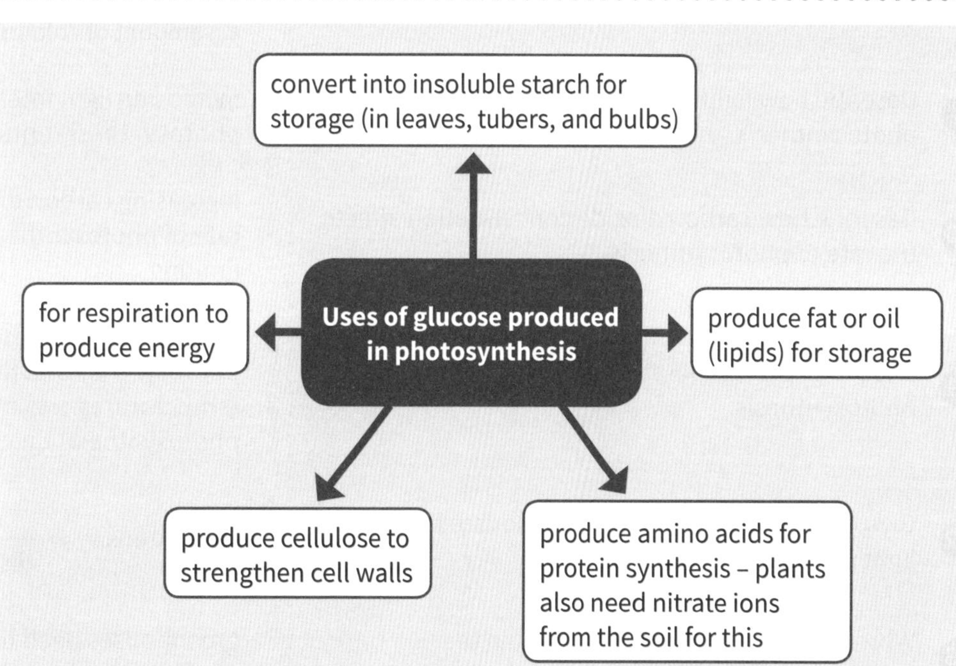

glucose | inverse square law | limiting factor | photosynthesis

Retrieval

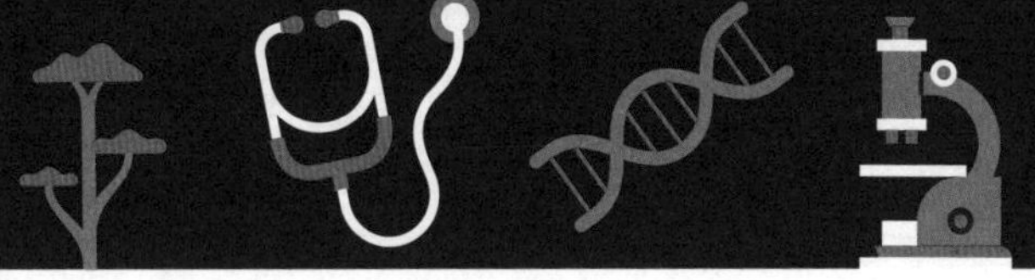

Learn the answers to the questions below, then cover the answers column with a piece of paper and write as many as you can. Check and repeat.

	B10 questions	Answers
1	Where does photosynthesis occur?	chloroplasts in the leaves of a plant
2	What is the name of the green pigment in the leaves?	chlorophyll
3	What type of reaction is photosynthesis?	endothermic
4	What type of energy is used in photosynthesis?	light energy
5	Give the word equation for photosynthesis.	carbon dioxide + water → glucose + oxygen
6	Give the balanced symbol equation for photosynthesis.	$6CO_2 + 6H_2O \rightarrow C_6H_{12}O_6 + 6O_2$
7	Define the term limiting factor.	anything that limits the rate of a reaction when it is in short supply
8	Give the limiting factors of photosynthesis.	• temperature • carbon dioxide concentration • light intensity • amount of chlorophyll
9	Describe how light intensity affects the rate of photosynthesis.	increasing light intensity increases the rate of photosynthesis until another factor becomes limiting
10	Describe how carbon dioxide concentration affects the rate of photosynthesis.	increasing carbon dioxide concentration increases the rate of photosynthesis until another factor becomes limiting
11	Describe how temperature affects the rate of photosynthesis.	increasing temperature increases the rate of photosynthesis as the reaction rate increases – at high temperatures enzymes are denatured so the rate of photosynthesis quickly decreases
12	Give the equation for the inverse square law for light intensity.	light intensity $\propto \frac{1}{\text{distance}^2}$
13	Why are limiting factors important in the economics of growing plants in greenhouses?	greenhouses need to produce the maximum rate of photosynthesis whilst making profit
14	How do plants use the glucose produced in photosynthesis?	• respiration • convert it into insoluble starch for storage • produce fat or oil for storage • produce cellulose to strengthen cell walls • produce amino acids for protein synthesis

Put paper here

Now go back and use the questions below to check your knowledge from previous chapters.

Previous questions

	Previous questions	Answers
1	What is a stent?	a device inserted into a blocked artery to keep it open, allowing more blood and oxygen to the heart
2	How is the upper epidermis adapted for its function?	• single layer of transparent cells allow light to pass through • cells secrete a waxy substance that makes leaves waterproof
3	Why do different digestive enzymes have different optimum pHs?	different parts of the digestive system have very different pHs – the stomach is strongly acidic, and the pH in the small intestine is close to neutral
4	Name the substances transported in the blood plasma.	hormones, proteins, urea, carbon dioxide, glucose
5	How do viruses make you ill?	reproduce rapidly inside cells, damaging or destroying them
6	What factors can affect health?	disease, diet, stress, exercise, life situations
7	What are benign tumours?	non-cancerous tumours that do not spread in the body
8	Why are antibodies a specific defence?	antibodies have to be the right shape for a pathogen's unique antigens, so they target a specific pathogen

Put paper here

Put paper here

Put paper here

Required Practical Skills

Practise answering questions on the required practicals using the example below. You need to be able to apply your skills and knowledge to other practicals too.

Rate of photosynthesis

You should be able to accurately measure changes in the rate of photosynthesis of a plant, and how the rate changes in response to changes in the environment.

This requires being able to describe how to measure the rate of a reaction or biological process by collecting a gas produced. For example, collecting bubbles of oxygen produced by pondweed to compare the volume of gas produced at different light intensities.

It is important to understand how different factors affect rates of photosynthesis, including light intensity, temperature, and carbon dioxide concentration.

Worked example

A student used an inverted test tube to investigate the number of bubbles released from a piece of pondweed in a beaker of water in a ten-minute period. They repeated each measurement five times.

1 Identify the dependent variable in this experiment.

Number of bubbles released.

2 Explain how the student could use this set-up to investigate how light intensity affects the rate of photosynthesis.

Carry out the experiment described above with a switched-on lamp placed exactly 10 cm from the pondweed. Record number of bubbles produced over the 10 mins, repeating experiment 5 times. Move lamp 10 cm further away from the pondweed, and repeat the same experiment. Calculate the mean number of bubbles produced for each light intensity, and compare the results.

Practice

1 Suggest how the student could change the experiment to give a more accurate measurement of the gas released.

2 Explain how temperature affects the rate of plant photosynthesis.

3 Name a piece of equipment that could be used to investigate how temperature affects the amount of gas released by the pondweed.

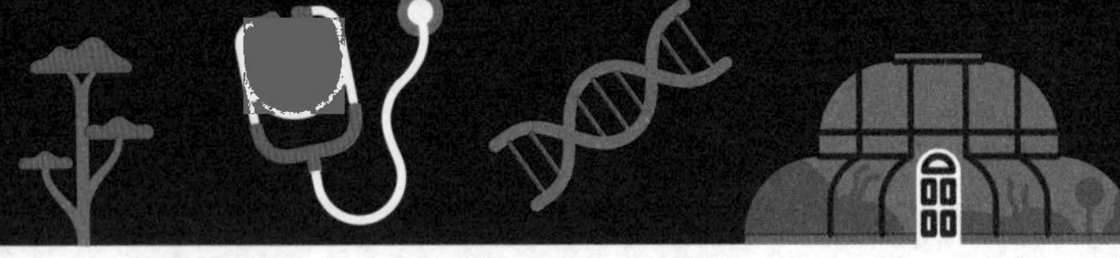

Exam-style questions

01 A student set up the apparatus in **Figure 1** to investigate the effect of light intensity on photosynthesis in pondweed.

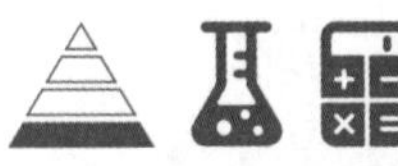

Exam Tip

Figures can give you lots of information that you may not have thought of. For example, why is it an LED light source in **Figure 1**? Why is the pondweed not just in water?

Figure 1

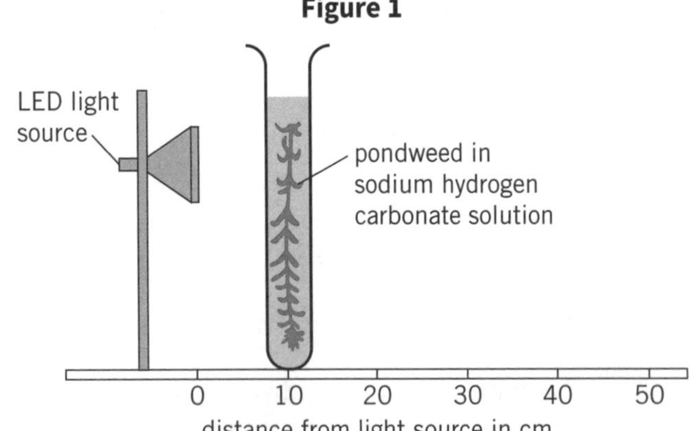

01.1 Identify the independent variable in this investigation. **[1 mark]**

____

01.2 Give the reason the pondweed was placed in a solution of sodium hydrogen carbonate. **[1 mark]**

____

01.3 The student measured the rate of photosynthesis of the pondweed by counting the number of oxygen bubbles produced in one minute.

Describe how you could test the bubbles to show they contained oxygen. **[2 marks]**

____

____

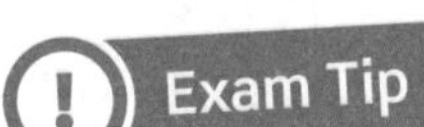

Exam Tip

You'll need a little bit of chemistry here!

01.4 The student's results are shown in **Table 1**.

Plot the data on **Figure 2**. **[2 marks]**

Table 1

Distance from light source in cm	Number of bubbles produced per minute
10	15
20	8
30	4
40	2
50	0

Figure 2

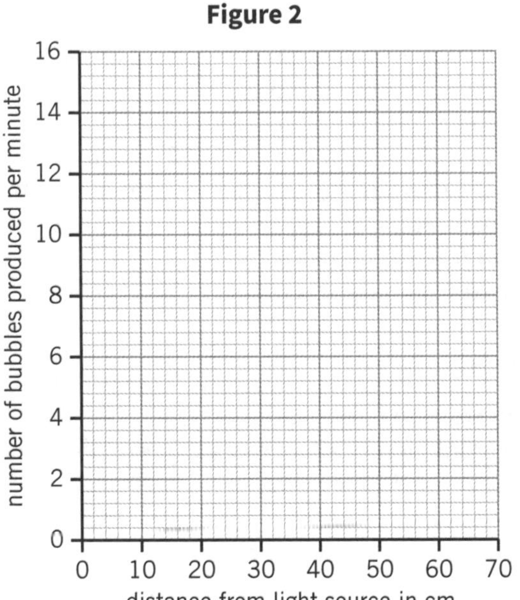

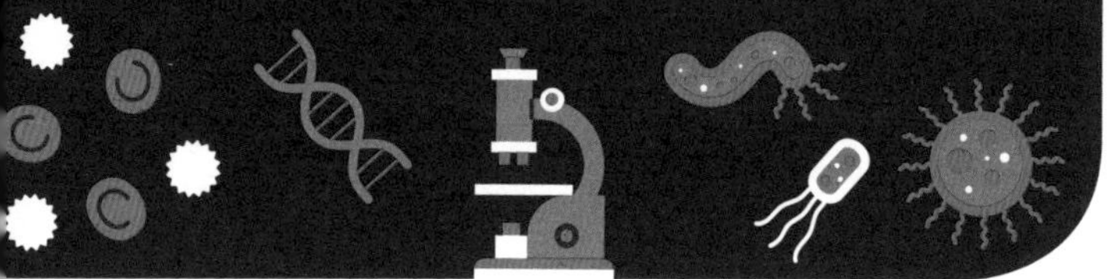

01.5 Describe the trend shown by your graph in **Figure 2**. **[1 mark]**

____

____

> **Exam Tip**
> For a one-mark question you only need to give a simple answer, such as describing an increase or decrease.

01.6 Use **Figure 2** to determine the rate of photosynthesis at 25 cm. **[1 mark]**

____

01.7 The student stated that counting bubbles was not an accurate way of measuring the volume of oxygen produced.

Write down **one** reason why the student is correct. **[1 mark]**

____

> **Exam Tip**
> Think about the size of a single bubble.

01.8 Suggest **one** improvement the student could make to improve the accuracy of this investigation. **[1 mark]**

____

02 Plants produce glucose by the process of photosynthesis.

02.1 Complete the following chemical equation that describes the process of photosynthesis. **[2 marks]**

$$6CO_2 + \_\_\_\_\_\_ \xrightarrow{\text{light}} \_\_\_\_\_\_ + 6O_2$$

> **Exam Tip**
> Balancing this equation can seem tricky – the easiest thing to do is to learn the numbers first.

02.2 Photosynthesis is an endothermic reaction.

Explain why this is. **[3 marks]**

____

____

____

____

02.3 Describe how a carbon atom from the atmosphere can become part of a starch molecule inside a leaf. **[6 marks]**

____

____

____

____

____

____

____

____

03 **Figure 3** shows a cross-section through a leaf.

03.1 Identify the structures labelled **A** and **B**. **[2 marks]**

03.2 Explain **two** ways the leaf is adapted to absorb light for photosynthesis. **[4 marks]**

03.3 Explain **two** ways the leaf is adapted to take in carbon dioxide for photosynthesis. **[4 marks]**

Figure 3

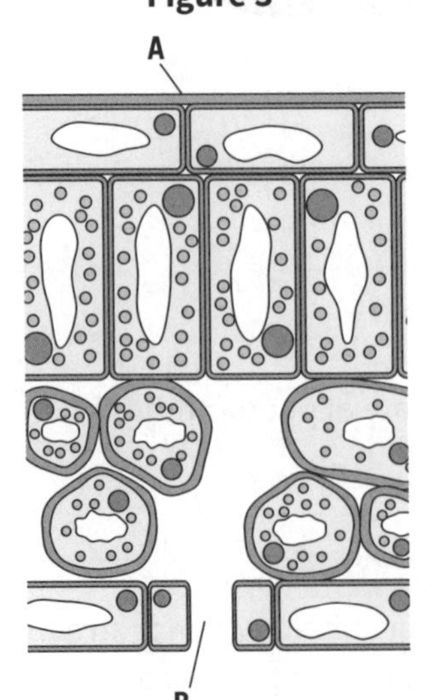

> **Exam Tip**
> You'll need to refer to specific parts of the leaf and how they act in questions **03.2** and **03.3**.

04 A tomato grower wants to know which growing conditions lead to the highest growth rate of tomato plants. They set up three experiments to measure the rate of photosynthesis in the tomatoes.

Figure 4 shows the results. All of the plants were given an adequate supply of water.

Figure 4

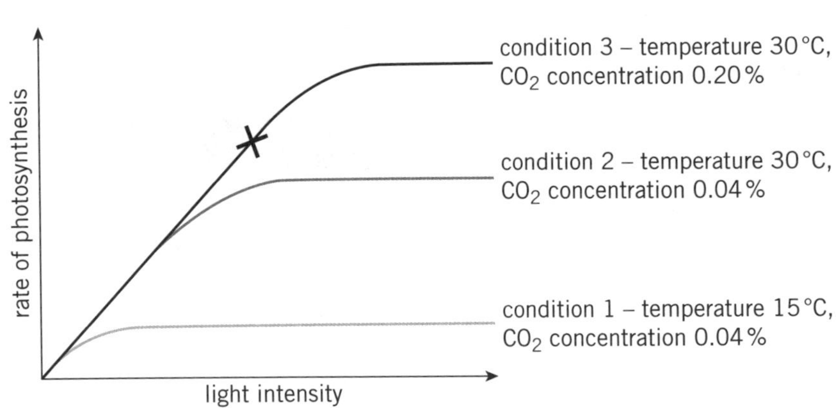

> **Exam Tip**
> Start this question by looking at the data on the graph and thinking about the differences between the conditions.

04.1 Identify the limiting factor at the point labelled **X** on the graph. Choose **one** answer. **[1 mark]**

light intensity

volume of soil added

carbon dioxide concentration

temperature

04.2 The tomato grower sets up a fourth condition at a temperature of 40 °C and a carbon dioxide concentration of 0.2 %.
Explain what will happen to the rate of photosynthesis under these conditions. **[2 marks]**

04.3 The tomato grower concludes from their investigation that increasing temperature, light intensity, and carbon dioxide concentration maximises the rate of growth of tomato plants.
Evaluate the validity of the tomato grower's conclusions. **[3 marks]**

> **Exam Tip**
> For an 'evaluate' question you need to give a justified opinion.

04.4 Explain why the tomato grower should not raise the temperature of the greenhouses above 40 °C. **[2 marks]**

05 A number of factors affect the rate of photosynthesis. Two of these factors include carbon dioxide concentration and temperature.

05.1 Name **one** other factor that limits the rate of photosynthesis. **[1 mark]**

05.2 **Figure 5** shows the effect of carbon dioxide concentration on the rate of photosynthesis. Describe and explain the shape of the graph. **[4 marks]**

05.3 Explain how temperature affects the rate of photosynthesis. **[4 marks]**

Figure 5

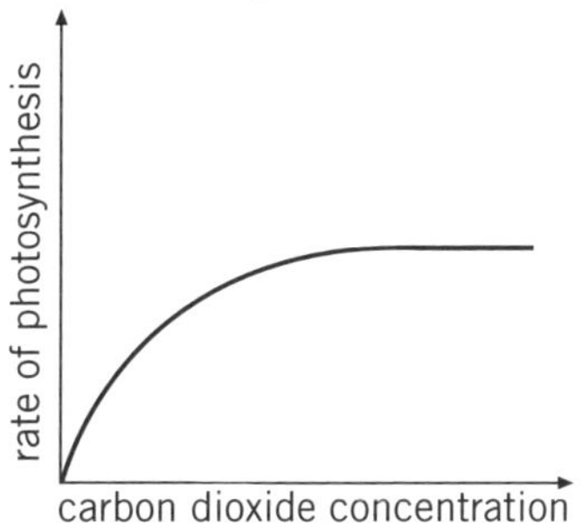

rate of photosynthesis

carbon dioxide concentration

Exam Tip

The answer to **05.2** needs to have the what *and* the why.

06 Light intensity, carbon dioxide concentration, and temperature are three of the factors that affect the rate of photosynthesis.
Design an investigation to study the effect of light intensity on the rate of photosynthesis. **[6 marks]**

Here is a list of some of the apparatus you might use:

- desk lamp
- metre rule
- funnel
- pondweed
- beaker

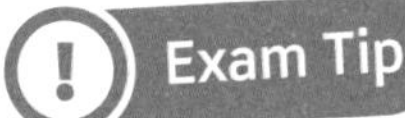

This is a required practical, so you should know this method really well!

07 Plants produce glucose through the process of photosynthesis. Some of this is used immediately in respiration. The remainder is converted into starch molecules.

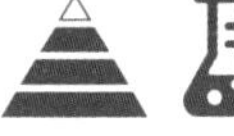

07.1 Explain why plants convert glucose into starch. **[3 marks]**

07.2 Onions store starch in bulbs.
Suggest how you could demonstrate that an onion contains starch. **[2 marks]**

07.3 Some of the glucose produced in respiration is also used to produce proteins. Explain how glucose is used to make proteins. **[4 marks]**

08 A group of students investigated the effect of temperature on the rate of photosynthesis. They carried out their investigation using pondweed. **Figure 6** shows how they set up their apparatus.
The experiment was repeated using water baths set at different temperatures.

08.1 Write down **one** factor the students must control. **[1 mark]**

08.2 Explain why the students should leave the test tube in the water bath for five minutes before taking their measurements. **[1 mark]**

Figure 6

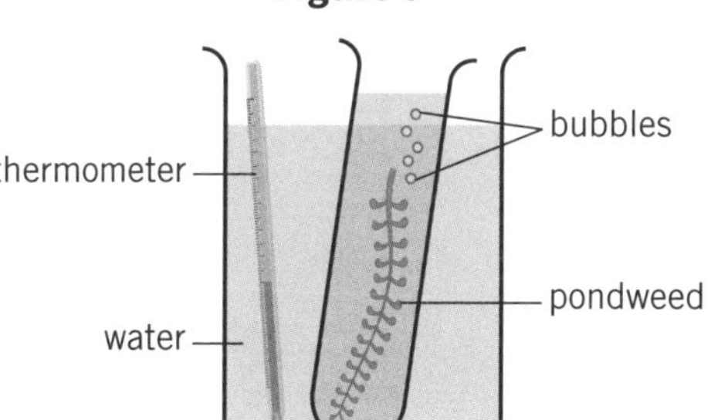

08.3 Bubbles of oxygen gas are released when the pondweed photosynthesises.

Describe **one** way the students could calculate the rate of photosynthesis. **[2 marks]**

08.4 At 60 °C no bubbles of gas were produced. Explain why. **[2 marks]**

09 A scientist investigated how light intensity affected the rate of photosynthesis of pondweed.

The scientist placed the pondweed in a beaker of water at different distances away from a table lamp. They calculated the rate of photosynthesis by counting how many bubbles were produced in one minute. The scientist's results are shown in **Table 2**.

Table 2

Distance of lamp from pondweed in m	Light intensity in arbitrary units	Bubbles produced per minute
0.20		60
0.30	11	28
0.40	6	17
0.50	4	12
0.60	3	9

Light intensity can be calculated using the inverse square law:

$$\text{light intensity} \propto \frac{1}{\text{distance}^2}$$

This is the same as the inverse square law in maths.

09.1 Calculate the light intensity when the lamp is 20 cm from the pondweed. **[1 mark]**

09.2 Plot a graph of light intensity against rate of photosynthesis on **Figure 7**. **[3 marks]**

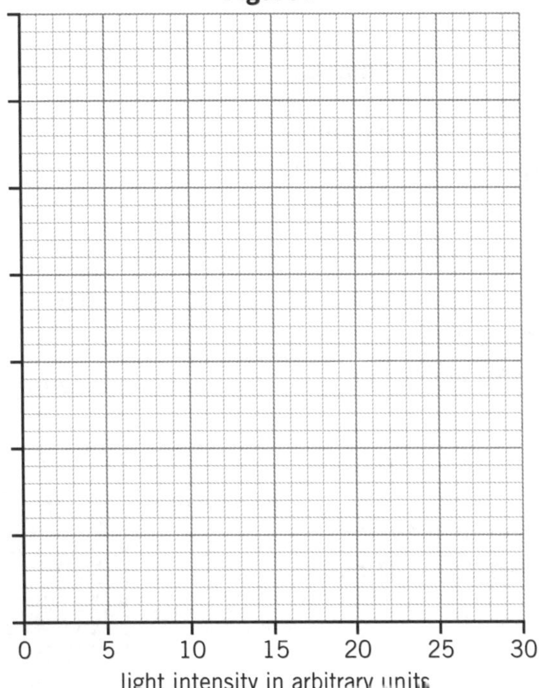

Don't worry if you've never come across arbitrary units before, it just means it doesn't really matter what the units are.

09.3 Describe the trends shown in the data collected. **[2 marks]**

09.4 The scientist concluded that during this experiment, light intensity was a limiting factor for photosynthesis.
Write down the evidence used by the scientist to form this conclusion. **[1 mark]**

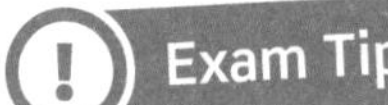

Exam Tip

Use data from the graph in your answer.

09.5 When the light is placed a distance of 0.10 m from the pondweed, carbon dioxide becomes the limiting factor.
Sketch a second graph of light intensity against rate of photosynthesis to show this effect for lamp distances of 0.10–0.60 m. **[3 marks]**

10 Plants make their own food by the process of photosynthesis.

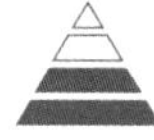

10.1 Write down the word equation for photosynthesis. **[2 marks]**

10.2 **Figure 8** shows the effect of temperature on the rate of photosynthesis.

Figure 8

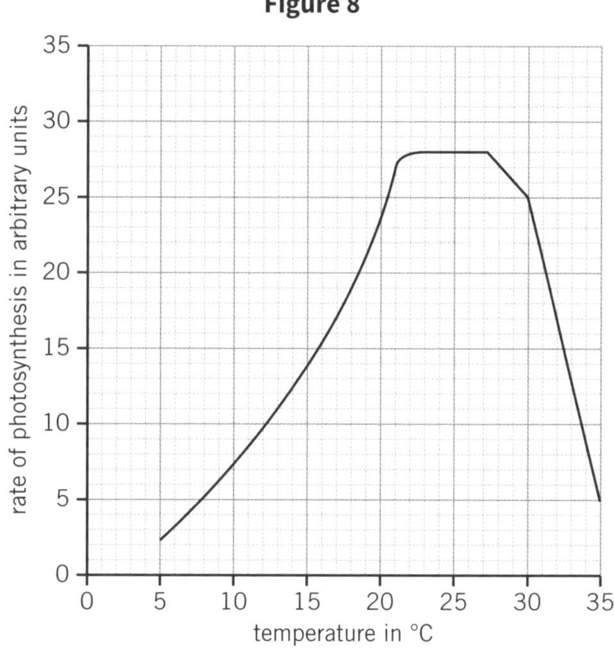

Exam Tip

Draw lines on the graph to show your working.

Using **Figure 8**, write down the range of optimum temperatures for photosynthesis. **[1 mark]**

10.3 Suggest why the rate of photosynthesis stays the same between these temperatures. **[2 marks]**

10.4 A farmer decides to use this information to set their greenhouse to the optimum conditions.
Identify the best temperature to heat the farmer's greenhouse to.
Give reasons for your answer. **[3 marks]**

Exam Tip

Question **10.4** has asked for reasons for your answer. This means the only way to get full marks on this is by describing data from the graph.

Knowledge

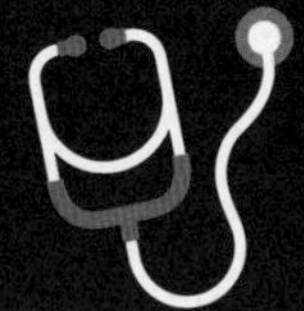

B11 Respiration

Cellular respiration

Cellular **respiration** is an **exothermic** reaction that occurs continuously in the **mitochondria** of living cells to supply the cells with energy.

The energy released during respiration is needed for all living processes, including

- chemical reactions to build larger molecules, for example, making proteins from amino acids
- muscle contraction for movement
- keeping warm.

Respiration in cells can take place aerobically (using oxygen) or anaerobically (without oxygen).

Type of respiration	Oxygen required?	Relative amount of energy transferred
aerobic	✓	complete **oxidation** of glucose – large amount of energy is released
anaerobic	✗	incomplete oxidation of glucose – much less energy is released per glucose molecule than in aerobic respiration

Aerobic respiration

glucose + oxygen → carbon dioxide + water

$$C_6H_{12}O_6 + 6O_2 \rightarrow 6CO_2 + 6H_2O$$

Anaerobic respiration in muscles

glucose → lactic acid

$$C_6H_{12}O_6 \rightarrow 2C_3H_6O_3$$

Fermentation

Anaerobic respiration in plant and yeast cells is represented by the equation

glucose → ethanol + carbon dioxide

Anaerobic respiration in yeast cells is called **fermentation**.

The products of fermentation are important in the manufacturing of bread and alcoholic drinks.

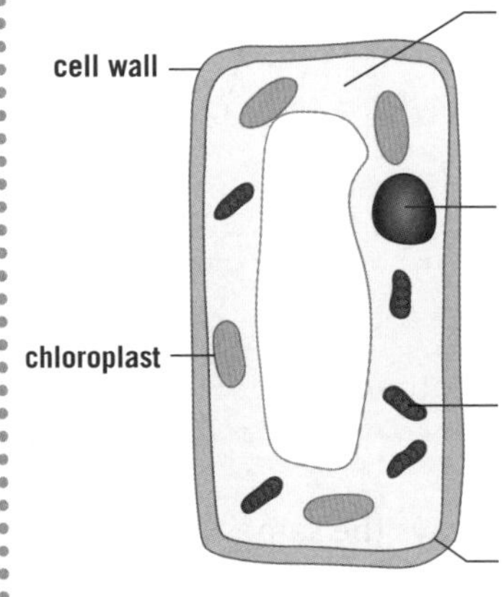

cell wall
chloroplast
cytoplasm
Where enzymes are made. Location of reactions in anaerobic respiration.
nucleus
Holds genetic code for enzymes involved in respiration.
mitochondrion
Contains the enzymes for aerobic respiration.
cell membrane
Allows gases and water to pass freely into and out of the cell. Controls the passage of other molecules.

Typical plant cell

Typical animal cell

Revision tip

Remember You need to learn the balanced symbol equations for the different types of respiration as well as the word equations.

Key terms

Make sure you can write a definition for these key terms.

aerobic anaerobic exothermic fermentation lactic acid

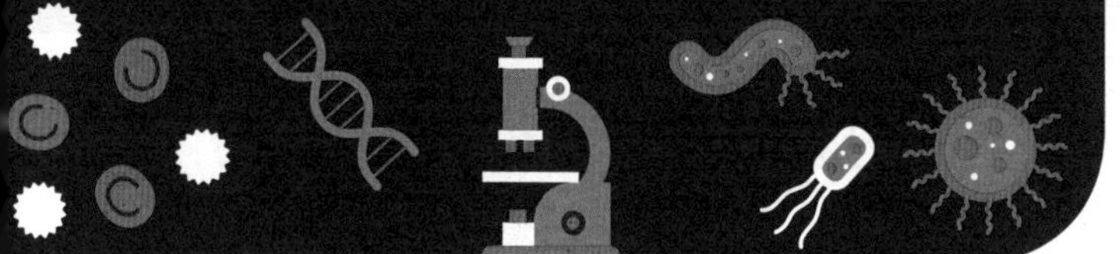

Response to exercise

During exercise the human body reacts to the increased demand for energy.

To supply the muscles with more oxygenated blood, heart rate, breathing rate, and breath volume all increase.

If insufficient oxygen is supplied, anaerobic respiration takes place instead, leading to the build-up of **lactic acid**.

During long periods of vigorous exercise, muscles become fatigued and stop contracting efficiently.

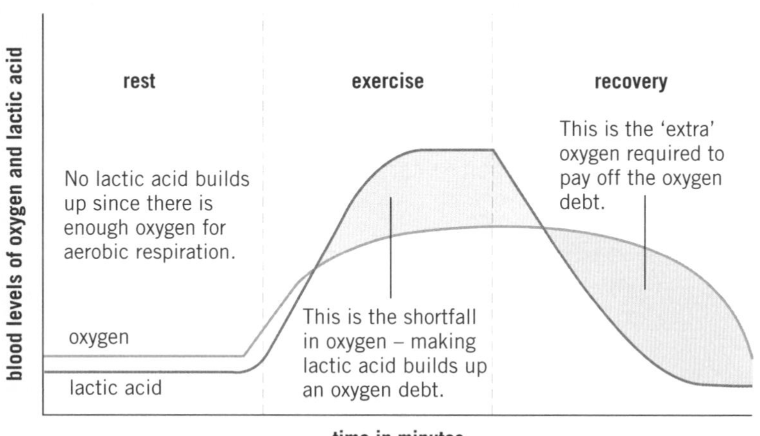

After exercise, the lactic acid accumulated during anaerobic respiration needs to be removed. **Oxygen debt** is the amount of oxygen needed to react with the lactic acid to remove it from cells.

Removal of lactic acid

lactic acid in the muscles

↓

transported to the liver in the blood

↓

lactic acid is converted back to glucose

Revision tip

Practice Don't expect questions in the exam to cover only one topic – they can link a few topics together within one question. A question on respiration could be easily linked to one on enzyme action and breakdown of carbohydrates, proteins, or lipids.

Metabolism

Metabolism is the sum of all the reactions in a cell or the body.

The energy released by respiration in cells is used for the continual enzyme-controlled processes of metabolism that produce new molecules.

Metabolic processes include the synthesis and breakdown of:

Carbohydrates

- synthesis of larger carbohydrates from sugars (starch, glycogen, and cellulose)
- breakdown of glucose in respiration to release energy

Proteins

- synthesis of amino acids from glucose and nitrate ions
- amino acids used to form proteins
- excess proteins broken down to form urea for excretion

Lipids

- synthesis of lipids from one molecule of glycerol and three molecules of fatty acid

metabolism mitochondria oxidation oxygen debt respiration

Retrieval

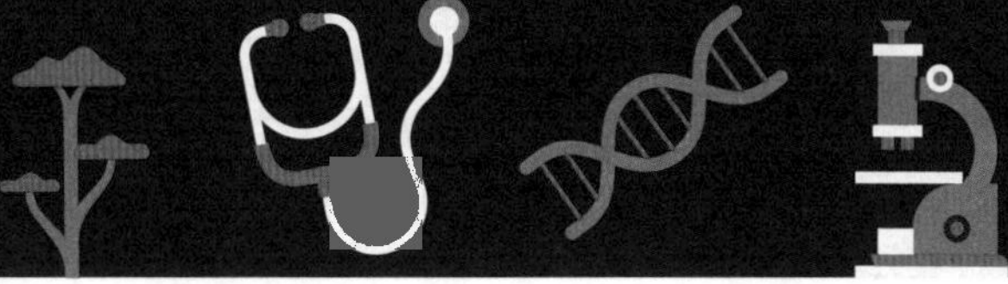

Learn the answers to the questions below, then cover the answers column with a piece of paper and write as many as you can. Check and repeat.

	B11 questions	Answers
1	Define the term cellular respiration.	an exothermic reaction that occurs continuously in the mitochondria of living cells to release energy from glucose
2	What do organisms need energy for?	• chemical reactions to build larger molecules • muscle contraction for movement • keeping warm
3	What is the difference between aerobic and anaerobic respiration?	aerobic respiration uses oxygen, anaerobic respiration does not
4	Write the word equation for aerobic respiration.	glucose + oxygen → carbon dioxide + water
5	Write the word equation for anaerobic respiration in muscles.	glucose → lactic acid
6	Write the balanced symbol equation for aerobic respiration.	$C_6H_{12}O_6 + 6O_2 \rightarrow 6CO_2 + 6H_2O$
7	Why does aerobic respiration release more energy per glucose molecule than anaerobic respiration?	oxidation of glucose is complete in aerobic respiration and incomplete in anaerobic respiration
8	What is anaerobic respiration in yeast cells called?	fermentation
9	Write the word equation for anaerobic respiration in plant and yeast cells.	glucose → ethanol + carbon dioxide
10	How does the body supply the muscles with more oxygenated blood during exercise?	heart rate, breathing rate, and breath volume increase
11	What substance builds up in the muscles during anaerobic respiration?	lactic acid
12	What happens to muscles during long periods of activity?	muscles become fatigued and stop contracting efficiently
13	What is oxygen debt?	amount of oxygen the body needs after exercise to react with the accumulated lactic acid and remove it from cells
14	How is lactic acid removed from the body?	lactic acid in muscles → blood transports to the liver → lactic acid converted back to glucose
15	What is metabolism?	sum of all the reactions in a cell or the body

Put paper here

Now go back and use the questions below to check your knowledge from previous chapters.

Previous questions

	Previous questions	Answers
1	How are the lungs adapted for efficient gas exchange?	• alveoli – large surface area • moist membranes – increases rate of diffusion • one-cell-thick membranes – short diffusion pathway • good blood supply – maintains a steep concentration gradient
2	Name four types of pathogen.	bacteria, fungi, protists, viruses
3	What non-specific systems does the body use to prevent pathogens getting into it?	• skin • cilia and mucus in the nose, trachea, and bronchi • stomach acid
4	Define health.	state of physical and mental well-being
5	Give the word equation for photosynthesis.	carbon dioxide + water → glucose + oxygen
6	How do plants use the glucose produced in photosynthesis?	• respiration • convert it into insoluble starch for storage • produce fat or oil for storage • produce cellulose to strengthen the cell wall • produce amino acids for protein synthesis
7	Give the balanced symbol equation for photosynthesis.	$6CO_2 + 6H_2O \rightarrow C_6H_{12}O_6 + 6O_2$

Put paper here

Maths Skills

Practise your maths skills using the worked example and practice questions below.

Surface area-to-volume ratio

Knowledge of surface area-to-volume ratio is important in biology, for example, it explains the body size adaptations of organisms, and is important for the rate at which transportation processes such as respiration occur.

To calculate it, you first need to calculate the surface area and volume of the object.

For the surface area of a cube, find the area of one face and multiply by six.

To find the volume of a cube, use: length × width × height

To calculate surface area-to-volume ratio:

surface area-to-volume ratio

$$= \frac{\text{surface area}}{\text{volume}}$$

Worked example

What is the surface area-to-volume ratio of the cube below?

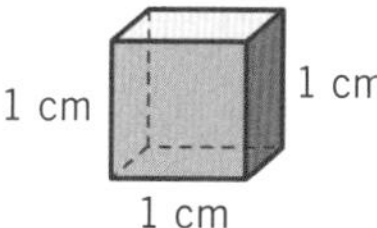

To calculate surface area (cm^2):

Area of one side of the cube = 1 × 1 = 1 cm^2

The cube has six sides, so:

surface area = 1 × 6 = 6 cm^2

To calculate volume (cm^3):

1 × 1 × 1 = 1 cm^3

Surface area-to-volume ratio:

$\frac{6}{1}$ = 6:1 ratio

Practice

Work out the surface area (cm^2), volume (cm^3), and surface area-to-volume ratio for cubes with the following dimensions.

1. 2 cm × 2 cm × 2 cm
2. 5 cm × 5 cm × 5 cm
3. 12 cm × 12 cm × 12 cm

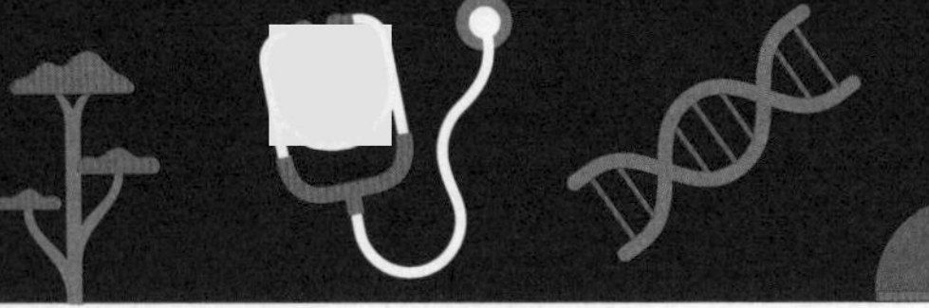

Exam-style questions

01 Animals transfer energy into a form that cells can use by the process of respiration.

01.1 Complete the following balanced chemical equation to summarise the process of aerobic respiration in animal cells. **[2 marks]**

$6O_2$ + ______________ → ______________ + $6CO_2$ + energy

01.2 Explain why respiration is described as an exothermic reaction. **[3 marks]**

____

____

____

____

01.3 Explain why fat cells do not have as many mitochondria as muscle cells. **[3 marks]**

____

____

____

____

Exam Tip

Think about the differences in function between muscle and fat cells.

01.4 Plants do not move or maintain a certain body temperature.

Describe **two** ways plants use energy from respiration. **[2 marks]**

1 ______________________________

____

2 ______________________________

____

02 A group of students investigated the effect of temperature on the rate of aerobic respiration in earthworms.

They placed the equipment shown in **Figure 1** into a water bath.

Figure 1

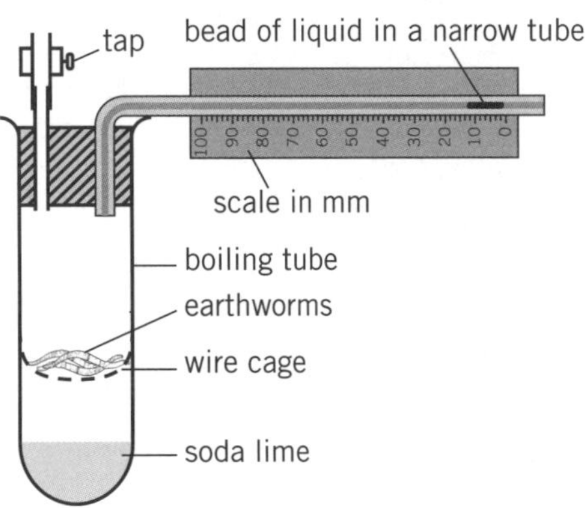

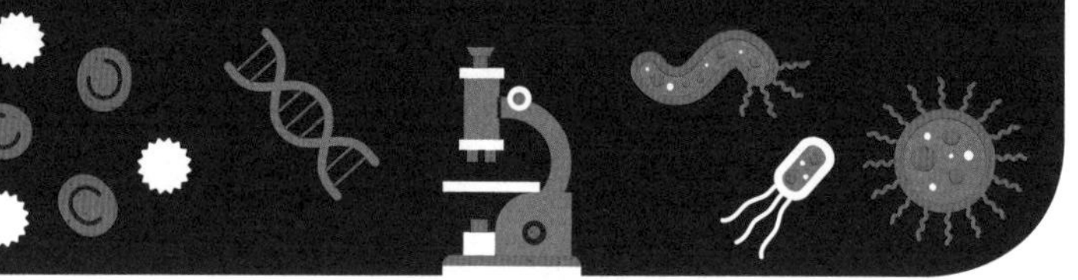

02.1 Identify the function of soda lime. **[1 mark]**

Tick **one** box.

to absorb carbon dioxide ☐

to absorb oxygen ☐

to provide the earthworms with water ☐

to provide the earthworms with nutrients ☐

02.2 Explain how this equipment can be used to measure the rate of respiration at different temperatures. **[6 marks]**

____

____

____

____

____

____

Exam Tip

You'll need a safe way to heat the boiling tube that can be controlled and measured.

02.3 Write down **one** ethical consideration needed in this experiment. **[1 mark]**

____

____

02.4 The students' results at 10 °C and 20 °C are shown in **Figure 2**.

Figure 2

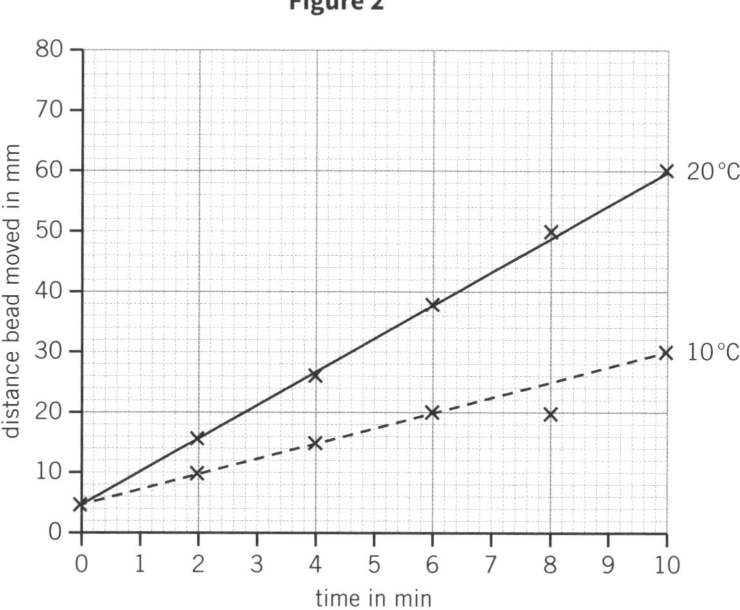

Compare the rate of respiration of earthworms at 10 °C and 20 °C. **[5 marks]**

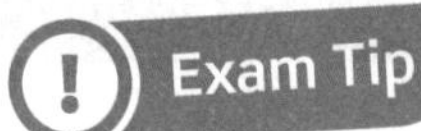

This question is worth five marks – you need to include data from both lines on the graph, and talk about the differences between the lines.

02.5 Draw a line on **Figure 2** to show what you predict the rate of respiration would be for earthworms at 25 °C.

Give reasons for your answer. **[3 marks]**

03 Yeast respires anaerobically. This reaction is called fermentation and it is used in the manufacture of some foods.

03.1 Write down the word equation for anaerobic respiration in yeast cells. **[2 marks]**

03.2 To make food products efficiently, producers need to know the optimum conditions for yeast to respire. A food scientist set up the apparatus in **Figure 3** to study how temperature affects yeast respiration.

Figure 3

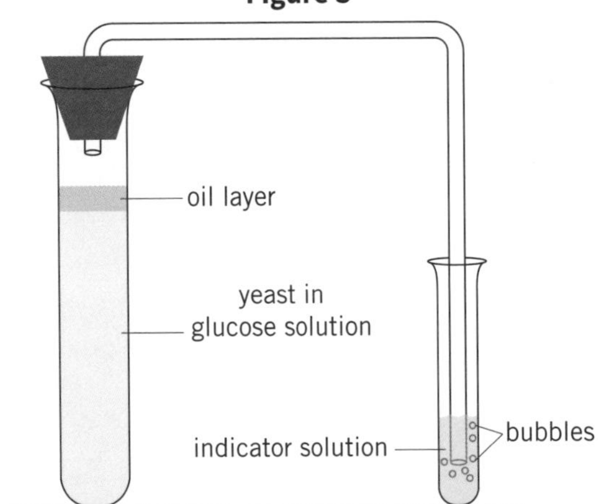

The indicator solution responds as follows:

blue — green — yellow

very low → high

carbon dioxide concentration

Suggest which colour the indicator will turn when yeast is respiring at its maximum rate. **[1 mark]**

The important thing about the oil is that it is sitting on top of the mixture.

03.3 Explain the purpose of the layer of oil. **[1 mark]**

03.4 Explain how you would use this equipment to study the effect of temperature on the rate of respiration. **[4 marks]**

03.5 Suggest how you can adapt this investigation to obtain quantitative data on the rate of yeast respiration. **[3 marks]**

04 **Figure 4** shows the concentration of lactic acid in a person's blood. The concentration of lactic acid was measured before, during, and after ten minutes of vigorous exercise.

Figure 4

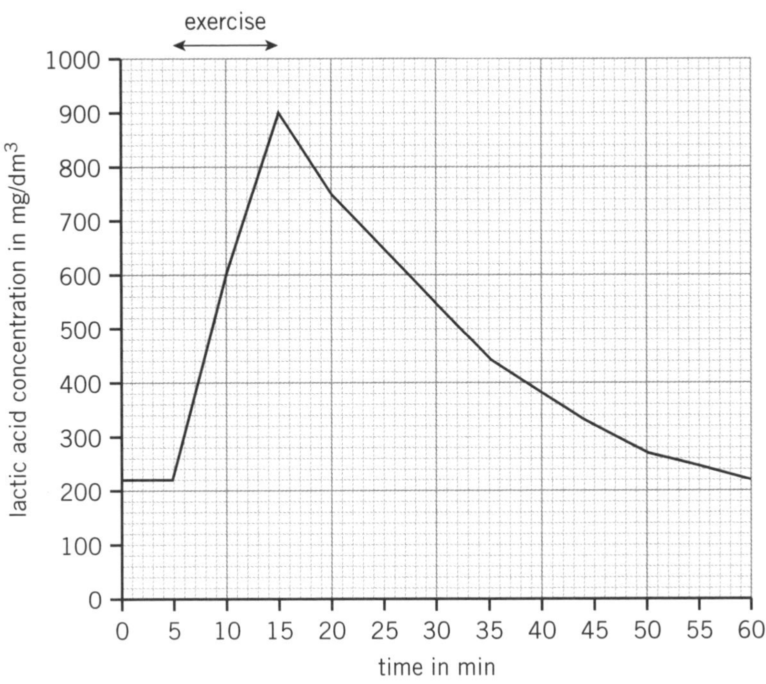

Don't forget to give the units!

04.1 Identify the level of lactic acid in the person's blood before exercise. **[1 mark]**

04.2 Explain why lactic acid was produced between 5 and 15 minutes. **[2 marks]**

04.3 Calculate the rate at which lactic acid was produced during the period of exercise. **[2 marks]**

04.4 Describe and explain the trend shown by the graph between 15 and 60 minutes. **[6 marks]**

Exam Tip

Draw a large triangle on the graph to help you calculate this. Remember to write down your working out.

05 Respiration takes place in all living plant and animal cells.

05.1 Describe the purpose of respiration. **[2 marks]**

05.2 Organisms can respire both aerobically and anaerobically. **Table 1** summarises the similarities and differences between these processes. Complete the table. **[4 marks]**

Table 1

Type of respiration	aerobic	anaerobic	
Organism it occurs in	plants and animals	plants	animals
Oxygen required?	yes	no	
Glucose required?	yes		yes
Carbon dioxide produced?	yes	yes	
Other products produced	water		lactic acid

05.3 Describe **two** ways yeast is used to produce food products using anaerobic respiration. **[4 marks]**

06 **Figure 5** shows the main components in an animal cell as seen under a light microscope.

Figure 5

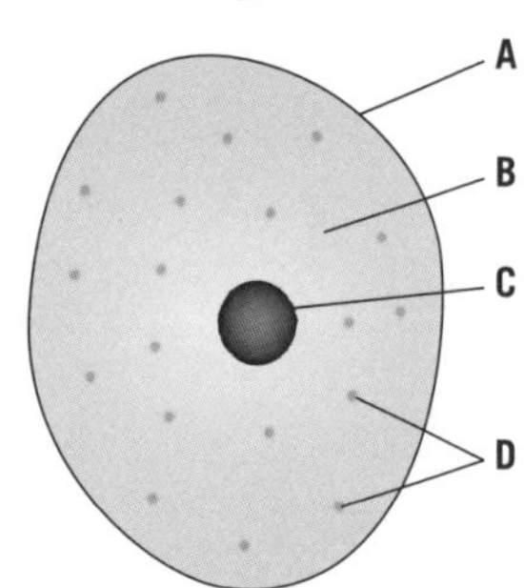

06.1 Identify (**A–D**) the part of the cell where respiration occurs. **[1 mark]**

06.2 What are the products of respiration? Choose **one** answer. **[1 mark]**

glucose + oxygen | carbon dioxide + water

glucose + carbon dioxide | water + oxygen

06.3 When a person is exercising vigorously, body cells can switch to anaerobic respiration.
Give **two** reasons why animal cells normally respire aerobically. **[2 marks]**

Exam Tip

The equation for respiration is the opposite to photosynthesis, so if you have trouble write down the one you remember and reverse it.

07 As part of a fitness test, an athlete ran as fast as possible for 15 minutes on a treadmill. The glucose and lactic acid concentrations of the athlete's blood were measured. **Figure 6** shows the results.

Figure 6

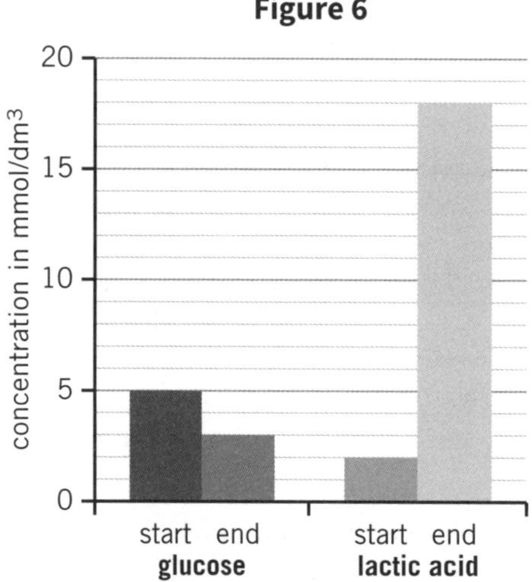

07.1 Using **Figure 6**, explain how the athlete respired over the 15 minutes of their fitness test. **[4 marks]**

Exam Tip

You'll need to use data from the graph to get full marks on this question.

07.2 Calculate the percentage change in the athlete's lactic acid concentration between the start and end of the exercise. **[2 marks]**

07.3 Explain why the athlete's heart and breathing rates increased during the fitness test. **[6 marks]**

08 All living organisms metabolise chemical compounds.

08.1 Define the term metabolism. **[1 mark]**

08.2 Explain how respiration maintains the rate of metabolism in an organism. **[3 marks]**

08.3 Two examples of metabolic reactions are the formation of lipids and the conversion of glucose into starch (in plants) or glycogen (in animals). Name the molecules required to form a lipid. **[2 marks]**

08.4 Plants convert glucose to starch, and animals convert glucose to glycogen. Explain why this is necessary. **[2 marks]**

09 Endurance athletes wish to avoid lactic acid build-up in their muscle cells.

09.1 Lactic acid build-up is a concern for marathon runners, but is not an important consideration for sprinters. Explain why. **[4 marks]**

> **Exam Tip**
> Marathons take many hours whereas sprints are generally over in under a minute.

09.2 To increase the blood's oxygen-carrying capability, many marathon runners train at high altitudes. This encourages the body to produce more red blood cells.
Explain why high-altitude training can improve the performance of an athlete. **[4 marks]**

09.3 Blood doping is an illegal practice that mimics altitude training. An athlete provides up to two litres of blood several weeks before a competition, which is then stored. The blood is then re-infused into the athlete one week before the competition.
Explain why blood doping would produce a performance enhancement for an athlete similar to the effect produced through high-altitude training. **[3 marks]**

> **Exam Tip**
> The advantage to high-altitude training is the increase in red blood cells. How could blood doping mimic this?

10 All living organisms respire.

10.1 Complete the chemical equation for aerobic respiration. **[1 mark]**

$C_6H_{12}O_6$ + ______________ → $6CO_2$ + ______________

10.2 Explain **two** reasons why animals usually respire aerobically. **[4 marks]**

> **Exam Tip**
> Think about the different types of respiration that occur when running.

10.3 Cheetahs are able to sprint very fast. After sprinting a cheetah will puff and pant for several minutes. With reference to respiration, explain why this happens. **[4 marks]**

11 Variegated leaves are leaves with areas that do not contain chlorophyll. To show that chlorophyll is needed for a plant to photosynthesise, a scientist tested a leaf for the presence of starch.

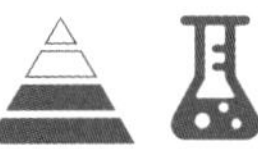

11.1 Explain why the scientist first boiled the leaf in ethanol and then washed the leaf using water. **[3 marks]**

> **Exam Tip**
> There are a few you could pick from, but only write about *one* safety procedure.
> You won't get extra marks for writing about two or three.

11.2 Describe and explain **one** safety procedure the scientist should follow when performing this experiment. **[2 marks]**

11.3 Predict and explain the results the scientist will observe when iodine is added to different areas of the leaf. **[4 marks]**

11.4 Explain how a plant produces starch. **[6 marks]**

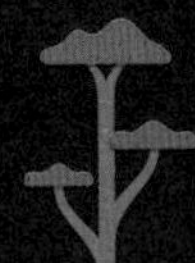
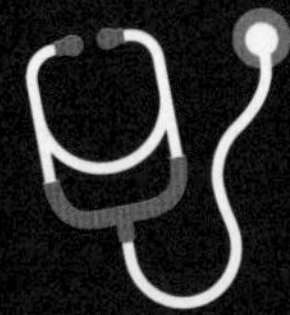

B12 The nervous system and homeostasis

The nervous system

Function

The nervous system enables humans to react to their surroundings and to coordinate their behaviour – this includes both voluntary and **involuntary** actions.

Structure

The nervous system is made up of the **central nervous system** (CNS) and a network of nerves.

The CNS comprises the **brain** and **spinal cord**.

Nervous system responses

Stimulus – a change in the environment (**stimulus**) is detected by **receptors**

→ **Receptor** – information from receptors passes along cells (**neurones**) to the CNS as electrical impulses

→ **Coordinator** – the CNS coordinates the body's response to the stimulus

→ **Effector** – **effectors** bring about a response, such as glands secreting hormones or muscles contracting

→ **Response** – the body responds to the stimulus

Homeostasis

Homeostasis is the regulation of internal conditions (of a cell or whole organism) in response to internal and external changes, to maintain optimum conditions for functioning.

This maintains optimum conditions for all cell functions and enzyme action.

In the human body, this includes control of

- blood glucose concentration
- body temperature
- water levels.

The automatic control systems of homeostasis may involve nervous responses or chemical responses.

All control systems involve

- receptor cells, which detect stimuli (changes in the environment)
- **coordination centres** (such as the brain, spinal cord, or pancreas), which receive and process information from receptors
- effectors (muscles or glands), which produce responses to restore optimum conditions.

Factors affecting reaction time

- tiredness
- distractions
- caffeine
- alcohol

Revision tips

Practice The mechanism of homeostasis makes a good six-mark question – practise writing long answers on these topics.

Practice Ensure you can sketch and label all the diagrams on these pages.

Key terms

Make sure you can write a definition for these key terms.

brain *central nervous system* *coordination centre* *effectors* *homeostasis*

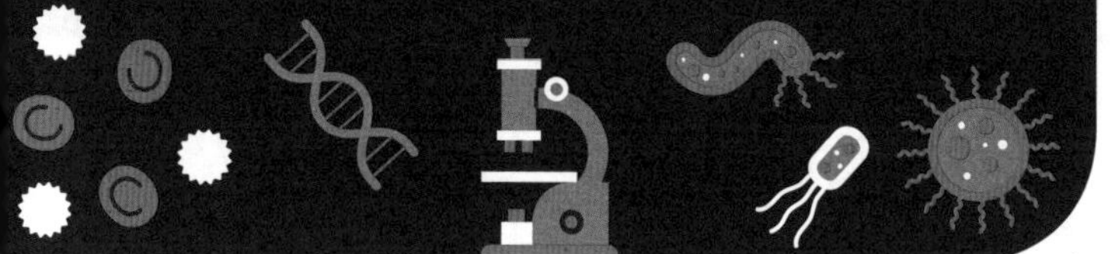

Reflex arcs

Reflex actions of the nervous system are automatic and rapid – they do not involve the conscious part of the brain.

Reflex actions are important for survival because they help prevent damage to the body.

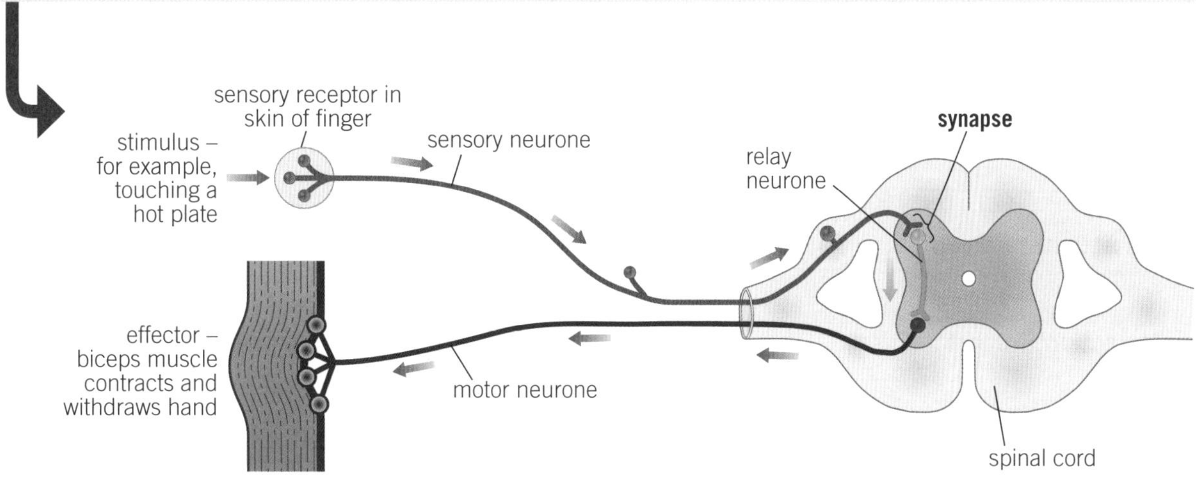

Reflex arc structures

Neurones

carry electrical impulses around the body – relay neurones connect sensory neurones to motor neurones

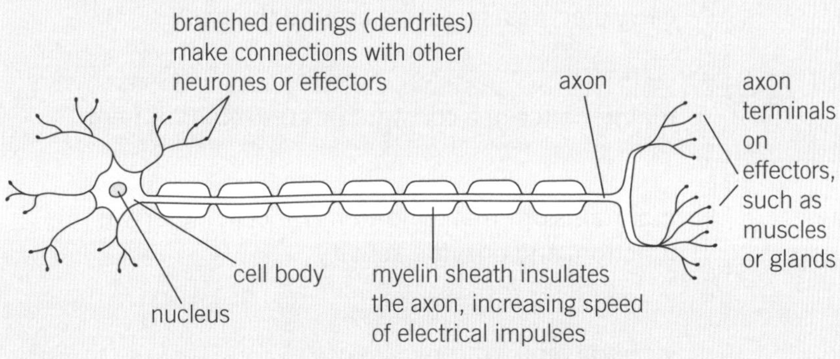

Synapses

gaps between neurones, which allow electrical impulses in the nervous system to cross between neurones

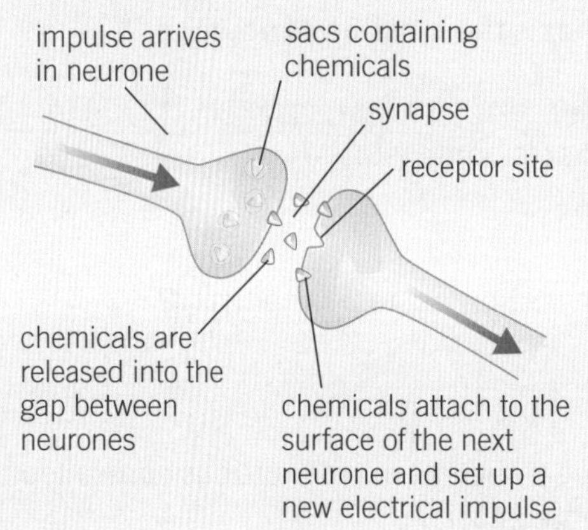

involuntary neurones receptors reflex action spinal cord stimulus synapse

Retrieval

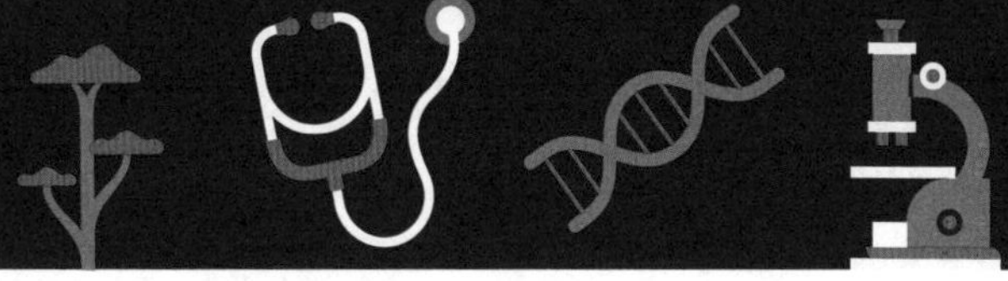

Learn the answers to the questions below, then cover the answers column with a piece of paper and write as many as you can. Check and repeat.

	B12 questions	Answers
1	What is the function of the nervous system?	enables organisms to react to their surroundings and coordinates behaviour
2	What are the two parts of the central nervous system?	brain and spinal cord
3	Why are reflex actions rapid and automatic?	they do not involve the conscious part of the brain
4	Why are reflex actions important?	for survival and to prevent damage to the body
5	Give the pathway of a nervous response.	stimulus → receptor → coordinator → effector → response
6	What is a stimulus?	a change in the internal or external environment
7	What is a synapse?	junction between two neurones where chemicals are released, allowing impulses to cross
8	What is the function of neurones?	carry electrical impulses around the body
9	What is homeostasis?	maintenance of a constant internal environment
10	Why is homeostasis important?	maintains optimal conditions for cell and organ function, and enzyme activity
11	Give three internal conditions controlled in homeostasis.	• body temperature • blood glucose concentration • water levels
12	Give three things all control systems include.	receptors, coordination centres, effectors
13	Name three coordination centres.	brain, spinal cord, pancreas
14	Name two types of effectors.	muscles and glands

Put paper here

Now go back and use the questions below to check your knowledge from previous chapters.

Previous questions / Answers

	Previous questions	Answers
1	Define the term cellular respiration.	an exothermic reaction that occurs continuously in the mitochondria of living cells to release energy from glucose
2	Give the equation for the inverse square law for light intensity.	light intensity $\propto \frac{1}{\text{distance}^2}$
3	How is lactic acid removed from the body?	lactic acid in muscles → blood transports to the liver → lactic acid converted back to glucose
4	How does the body supply the muscles with more oxygenated blood during exercise?	heart rate, breathing rate, and breath volume increase
5	Describe how light intensity affects the rate of photosynthesis.	increasing light intensity increases the rate of photosynthesis until another factor becomes limiting
6	What effect does humidity have on the rate of transpiration?	higher levels of humidity decrease the rate of transpiration
7	What is coronary heart disease?	layers of fatty material that build up inside the coronary arteries, narrowing them – resulting in a lack of oxygen for the heart

Put paper here

Required Practical Skills

Practise answering questions on the required practicals using the example below. You need to be able to apply your skills and knowledge to other practicals too.

Reaction times	Worked example	Practice
You need to be able to describe how to plan an experiment and choose suitable variables to change, to look at how different variables affect reaction times. You should be able to • write hypotheses predicting the effects of changing single variables • be able to identify independent and dependent variables • evaluate results in terms of accuracy and precision • understand how different factors affect human reaction times.	Write a method to test the effect of caffeine consumption on human reaction time. *With two people working in pairs, have the first person hold a ruler vertically with zero at the bottom. The second person should steady their arm on the edge of a bench underneath the ruler. The first person should drop the ruler, and the second person should catch the ruler between thumb and forefinger without moving their arm. Record the number on the ruler above the catcher's thumb. Repeat this at least three more times. The second person should then consume a caffeinated drink, and the entire experiment should be repeated.*	1 Give two things that must be controlled for the investigation of the effect of caffeine on reaction time to be a fair test. 2 Explain why it would not be appropriate for the same person to drop and catch the ruler in an experiment on reaction times. 3 Why should the test of reaction time be repeated multiple times before and after consumption of the caffeinated drink?

Practice

Exam-style questions

01 A student carried out an investigation to determine whether a person's reaction time was quicker with their dominant hand.

The student used the following steps:

1. The student investigator (Student **A**) held a ruler just above a second student's hand (Student **B**).
2. Student **A** let go of the ruler. Student **B** caught it as soon as possible.
3. The experiment was then repeated with Student **B**'s opposite hand.

Exam Tip

Your dominant hand is the one you write with.

01.1 Identify the dependent variable in this investigation. **[1 mark]**

____

____

01.2 Identify **one** variable that should be controlled in this investigation. **[1 mark]**

____

____

Student **A** chose ten right-handed students to test. The results are shown in **Table 1**.

Table 1

	Student	1	2	3	4	5	6	7	8	9	10	Mean
Reaction time in s	Left hand	0.25	0.23	0.39	0.26	0.27	0.22	0.25	0.27	0.25	0.25	
	Right hand	0.28	0.24	0.25	0.27	0.26	0.22	0.26	0.24	0.23	0.25	0.25

01.3 Identify the anomalous result from the experiment. **[1 mark]**

____

01.4 Complete **Table 1** by calculating the mean reaction time for the left hand results. **[1 mark]**

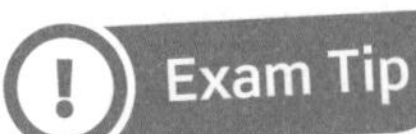

Whenever you're asked to calculate a mean, look out for any anomalous results and exclude them.

Mean = ______________ s

01.5 Student **A** reached the following conclusion:

'*Right-handed people's reaction times are more rapid when using their dominant (right) hand.*'

Explain the extent to which you agree or disagree with this conclusion. **[3 marks]**

____

____

____

____

01.6 Which type of reaction time did the experiment measure? **[1 mark]**

Tick **one** box.

reflex reaction time ☐ voluntary reaction time ☐

01.7 Give a reason for your answer to **01.6**. **[1 mark]**

____

____

01.8 The fastest measured reaction time of a human is approximately 0.1 s. Explain why a person's reaction time cannot be more rapid than this. **[3 marks]**

____

____

____

Exam Tip

To help with this question, imagine the pathway that a signal takes – is it the same the whole way?

02 To keep an organism healthy both the nervous system and the hormonal system need to work together.

02.1 Define the term homeostasis. **[1 mark]**

____

____

02.2 One purpose of homeostasis is to provide optimal conditions for enzymes to work in.

Name **two** factors that can affect the rate of enzyme action. **[2 marks]**

1 ______________________________

2 ______________________________

02.3 Homeostasis involves a number of automatic control systems.

Suggest why they are described as automatic systems. **[1 mark]**

____

____

02.4 Describe the main components of a control system. **[6 marks]**

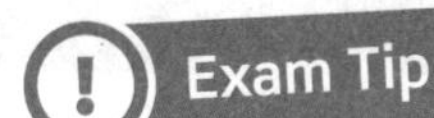

Go through each part one at a time.

03 Reflex actions are an important part of the nervous system.

03.1 Explain why the reflex arc is essential for survival. **[1 mark]**

Carefully describe what happens at each stage of the reflex action and name each part involved.

03.2 Give an example of a body function that can be controlled both consciously and unconsciously. **[1 mark]**

03.3 Describe the reflex action that would occur if you placed your hand on a hot radiator. **[6 marks]**

04 The nervous system allows humans to respond to their surroundings.

Figure 1 shows two different nerve pathways joining a big toe to the central nervous system. A touch to the big toe causes an impulse to travel through the nerve pathway.

Figure 1

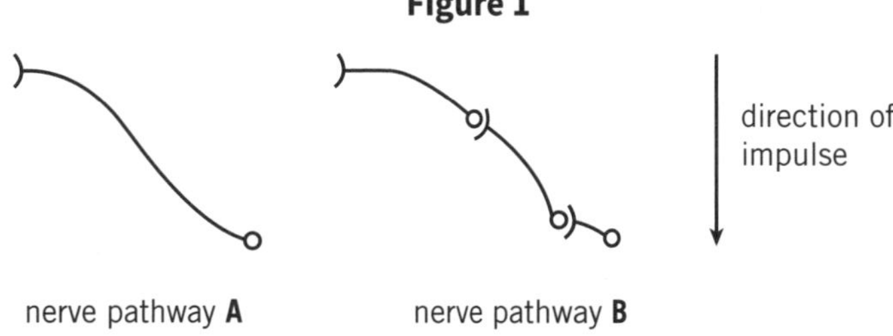

04.1 Identify the type of neurone involved in this pathway. Choose **one** answer. **[1 mark]**

sensory neurone   motor neurone   relay neurone

04.2 Nerve pathway **A** is 90 cm long. A nerve impulse travels along this pathway at 76 m/s.
Calculate how long it takes for the nerve impulse to travel the length of the pathway. Give your answer to two significant figures. **[3 marks]**

Exam Tip

The equation you need for this question is more often found in maths or physics, but there's no reason a question like this can't come up in biology.

04.3 Nerve pathways **A** and **B** are the same total length. The nerve impulse takes longer to travel along pathway **B** than pathway **A**.
Use your knowledge and information in **Figure 1** to explain why. **[4 marks]**

05 A student wanted to find out if a person's reaction time can be improved by learning a response to a stimulus. The student chose to use a computer program to measure the reaction time. This worked by displaying a symbol on the computer screen. The software measured the time it took the person to press a key after having seen the symbol.

Exam Tip

Use a highlighter to go over the text and identify the different variables.

05.1 Write down the independent and dependent variables for this investigation. **[2 marks]**

05.2 Suggest **two** variables the student should control. **[2 marks]**

05.3 The student collected the data in **Table 2**.

Table 2

Repeat number	1	2	3	4	5	6	7	8	9	10
Reaction time in s	0.34	0.32	0.34	0.30	0.29	0.29	0.45	0.26	0.27	0.25

The student collected an anomalous result. Identify the anomaly, and suggest **one** reason this may have occurred. **[2 marks]**

05.4 The student concluded that *'People are always able to react more quickly by practising their response to a situation.'*
Discuss the validity of this conclusion based on the data in **Table 2**. **[4 marks]**

06 A student carried out an investigation into the reaction times of one person. The student measured the person's reaction time by dropping a ruler and noting the drop distance.
The student dropped the ruler five times and calculated the mean drop distance to be 115 mm.

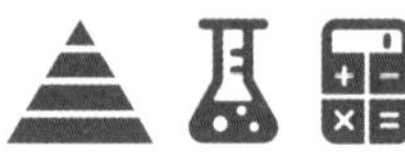

Exam Tip

Don't worry if you've never seen this equation before. There will be some things in the exam that you've never seen – it's all about your skill at applying your biology knowledge to new situations!

06.1 Use the following equation to calculate the person's reaction time.

$$\text{reaction time (s)} = \sqrt{\frac{\text{mean drop distance (cm)}}{490}}$$

Give your answer to two significant figures. **[3 marks]**

06.2 The student wanted to determine if caffeine had an impact on reaction time. Describe an approach the student could take to investigate this. **[4 marks]**

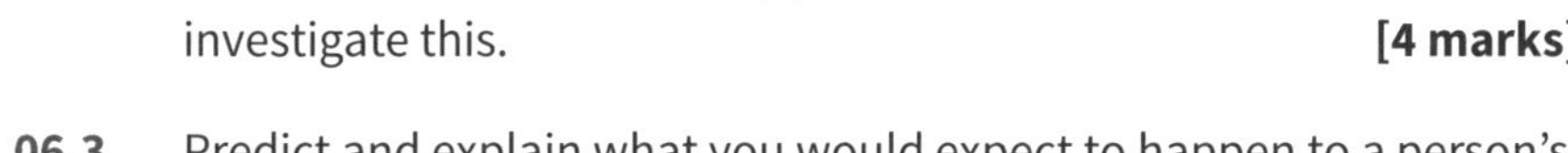

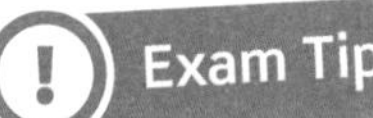

Exam Tip

The phrasing is the key to question **06.3**: *what* do you think will happen, and *why* do you think this?

06.3 Predict and explain what you would expect to happen to a person's reaction time after they consume a caffeinated drink. **[3 marks]**

06.4 The student extended the investigation to whether or not a person's dominant hand affects their reaction time. They collected the data shown in **Table 3**.

Table 3

Person tested	Repeat 1		Repeat 2	
	Left hand	Right hand	Left hand	Right hand
A (right-handed)	0.28	0.25	0.27	0.24
B (left-handed)	0.21	0.25	0.23	0.25

The student concluded that: '*Person **A**'s reaction time is shorter when using their dominant hand to respond to a situation*.'

Discuss and evaluate the validity of the student's conclusion. **[4 marks]**

07 A student shouted loudly behind their friend. The friend jumped in reaction to the noise. Explain in detail how the friend responded to the noise through the actions of their nervous system. **[6 marks]**

> **Exam Tip**
>
> In question **07**, you need to include the path the signal took and what happened at each stage.

08 As a car driver approached a set of traffic lights, the lights turned red. This caused the driver to press the brake pedal with their foot, slowing the car down.

08.1 In this response, what is the changing traffic light?
Choose **one** answer. **[1 mark]**

the coordinator   the effector   the receptor   the stimulus

08.2 In this response, what is the coordination centre?
Choose **one** answer. **[1 mark]**

the eye   the brain   a synapse   the spinal cord

08.3 Whilst the driver is waiting at the traffic lights, an insect flies close to the driver's eye. The driver's eye closes in response.
Explain how the driver's response to the insect is different to the response to the changing traffic lights. **[3 marks]**

09 If a person needs to have a dental procedure, such as a filling, a dentist will often inject the gum with an anaesthetic so the person does not feel any pain. Procaine is an example of an anaesthetic drug used by a dentist.

Figure 2 shows what happens at one of the synapses in your gum.

> **Exam Tip**
>
> You don't need to worry if you've never heard of procaine before, this is just the context for the question.

Figure 2

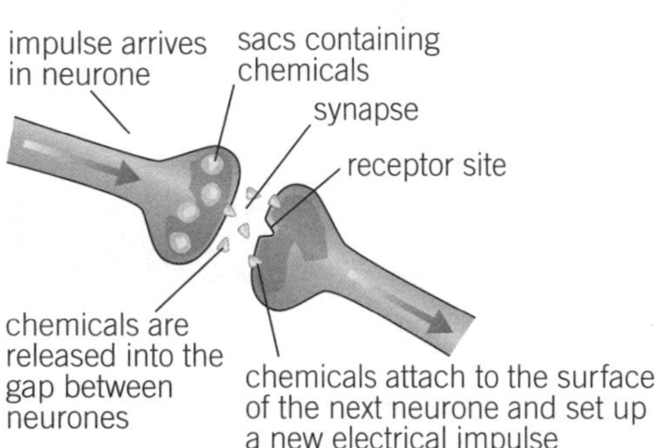
impulse arrives in neurone
sacs containing chemicals
synapse
receptor site
chemicals are released into the gap between neurones
chemicals attach to the surface of the next neurone and set up a new electrical impulse

09.1 Name the type of neurone that transmits the electrical impulse from the pain receptor. **[1 mark]**

09.2 Procaine is a competitive inhibitor. It is very similar to the chemical that is released between neurones.
Using your own knowledge and information in **Figure 2**, suggest how the drug procaine may work. **[6 marks]**

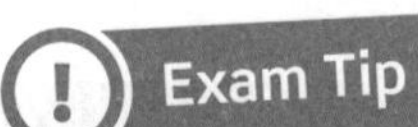

> **Exam Tip**
>
> Lots of the information you need to answer this is in **Figure 2**.

10 Multiple sclerosis (MS) is a disease that affects the nervous system. The disease causes the fatty layer surrounding the axon of a neurone to become damaged.

10.1 Name the lipid layer that surrounds the axon. **[1 mark]**

10.2 Symptoms of the disease vary between individuals, but often the disease causes difficulty in movement and feelings of numbness or tingling. Suggest, with reasons, why people with MS experience these symptoms. **[6 marks]**

Relate your answer to **10.2** with the information given in the main body of the text.

11 The nervous system controls the body's response to changes in its external environment.

11.1 Complete the following flow chart to name the main steps in a nervous response. **[1 mark]**

stimulus → ________________ → sensory neurone → CNS → motor neurone → ________________

11.2 Name the part of the nervous system that the vertebral column protects. **[1 mark]**

Exam Tip

'Describe' is what the neurones look like, not why they look this way.

11.3 Describe **two** differences between a motor neurone and a sensory neurone. **[2 marks]**

11.4 Many sports require good reactions. In relation to the nervous system, explain what reaction time depends on. **[2 marks]**

12 A group of people became ill after eating out in a restaurant. Health and safety inspectors carried out an investigation. The suspected source was food poisoning caused by bacteria on the rice. **Table 4** gives details of how four different restaurants stored their rice.

Table 4

Name of restaurant	Storage method	Time in storage in hours	Storage temperature in °C
Tom's Diner	rice in an open container	8	30
George's Hot Dinners	rice left on a hot plate	1	50
Amira's Kitchen	rice frozen in a freezer compartment	24	−5
Betty's Home Cooking	rice in a sealed container	5	20

12.1 Suggest which restaurant the diners are most likely to have eaten in. **[1 mark]**

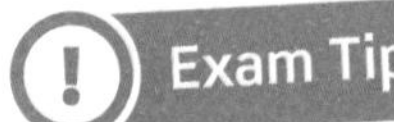

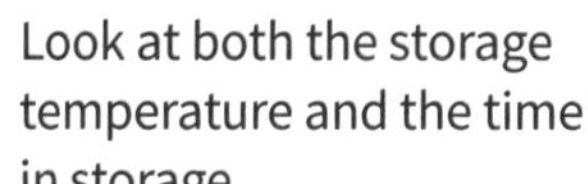

Look at both the storage temperature and the time in storage.

12.2 Explain your choice. **[2 marks]**

12.3 Name **one** way to treat food poisoning. **[1 mark]**

12.4 Explain why uncooked rice can be stored for many months in a packet or jar without spoiling. **[1 mark]**

12.5 Some diseases are contagious. Suggest and explain **two** ways you could prevent a contagious disease being spread between individuals living in the same house. **[4 marks]**

Knowledge

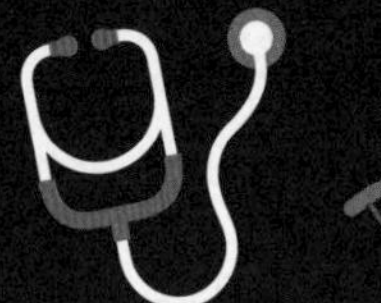

B13 Hormonal coordination A

Human endocrine system

The **endocrine system** is composed of glands that secrete chemicals called **hormones** into the bloodstream.

The blood carries hormones to a target organ, where an effect is produced.

Compared to the nervous system, the effects caused by the endocrine system are slower but act for longer.

The **pituitary gland**, located in the brain, is known as a 'master gland', because it secretes several hormones into the blood.

These hormones then act on other glands to stimulate the release of other hormones, and bring about effects.

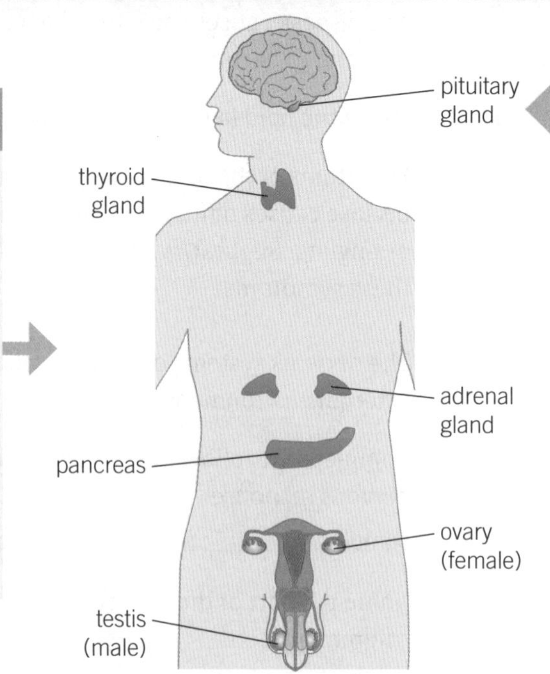

Negative feedback

Negative feedback systems work to maintain a steady state. For example, blood glucose, water, and **thyroxine** levels are all controlled in the body by negative feedback.

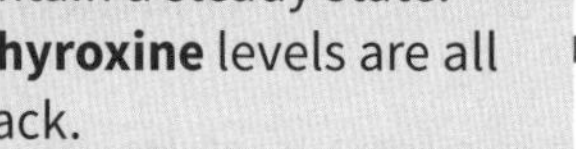

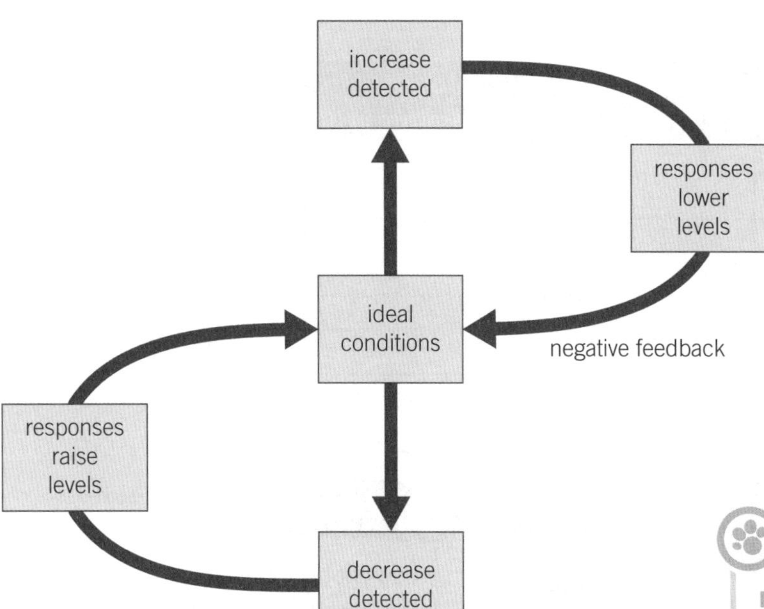

Adrenaline

- produced by **adrenal glands** in times of fear or stress
- increases heart rate
- boosts delivery of oxygen and glucose to brain and muscles
- prepares the body for 'fight or flight' response
- does not involve negative feedback, as adrenal glands stop producing **adrenaline**

Thyroxine

- produced by the **thyroid gland**
- regulates how quickly your body uses energy and makes proteins (**metabolic rate**)
- important for growth and development
- levels controlled by negative feedback

Revision tip

Remember There are lots of different hormones. For each of them you need to know where they come from, where they act, what they do once they get to where they are going, and how long they stay around for.

Key terms Make sure you can write a definition for these key terms.

adrenal gland adrenaline diabetes endocrine system glucagon hormone insulin

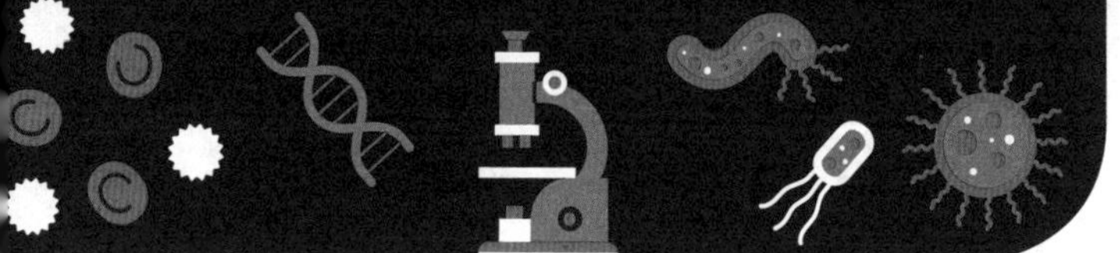

The table below describes the roles of the main hormones secreted from the different endocrine glands.

Endocrine gland	Role of the hormones
Pituitary	• controls growth in children • stimulates the thyroid gland to make thyroxine to control the rate of metabolism • in females – stimulates the ovaries to produce and release eggs, and make oestrogen • in males – stimulates the testes to make sperm and testosterone
Thyroid	• controls the rate of metabolism in the body
Pancreas	• controls blood glucose levels
Adrenal	• prepares the body for stress • involved in the 'fight or flight' response
Ovaries	• controls the development of female secondary sexual characteristics • controls the menstrual cycle
Testes	• controls the development of male secondary sexual characteristics • involved in the production of sperm

Control of blood glucose levels

Blood glucose (sugar) concentration is monitored and controlled by the **pancreas**.

This is an example of negative feedback control, as the pancreas switches production between the hormones **insulin** and **glucagon** to control blood glucose levels.

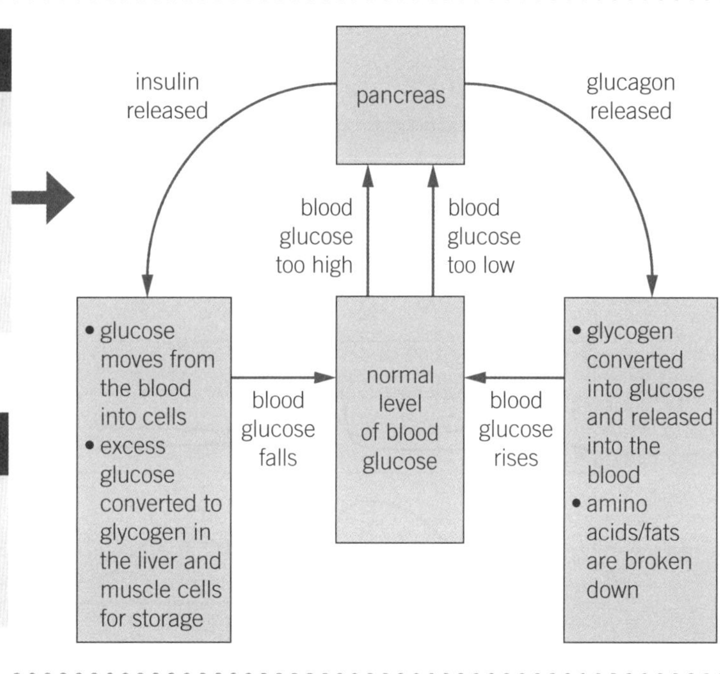

Diabetes

Diabetes is a non-communicable disease where the body either cannot produce or cannot respond to insulin, leading to uncontrolled blood glucose concentrations.

Type 1 diabetes	Type 2 diabetes
early onset	usually later onset, obesity is a risk factor
pancreas stops producing sufficient insulin	body doesn't respond to the insulin produced
commonly treated through insulin injections, also diet control and exercise	commonly treated through a carbohydrate-controlled diet and exercise

metabolic rate *negative feedback* *pancreas* *pituitary gland* *thyroid gland* *thyroxine*

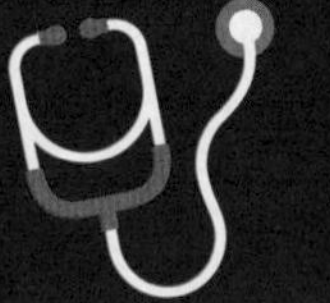

B13 Hormonal coordination B

Hormones in human reproduction

During puberty, reproductive hormones cause the secondary sex characteristics to develop:

Oestrogen

- main female reproductive hormone
- produced in the **ovary**
- at puberty, eggs begin to mature and one is released every ~28 days

Testosterone

- main male reproductive hormone
- produced by the **testes**
- stimulates sperm production

Several hormones are involved in the **menstrual cycle**. Their functions are given in the table, and their levels vary as shown in the figures.

Hormone	Released by	Function
follicle stimulating hormone (FSH)	pituitary gland	• causes eggs to mature in the ovaries • stimulates ovaries to produce oestrogen
luteinising hormone (LH)	pituitary gland	• stimulates the release of mature eggs from the ovaries (**ovulation**)
oestrogen	ovaries	• causes lining of uterus wall to thicken • inhibits release of FSH • stimulates release of LH
progesterone	ovaries	• maintains thick uterus lining • inhibits release of FSH and LH

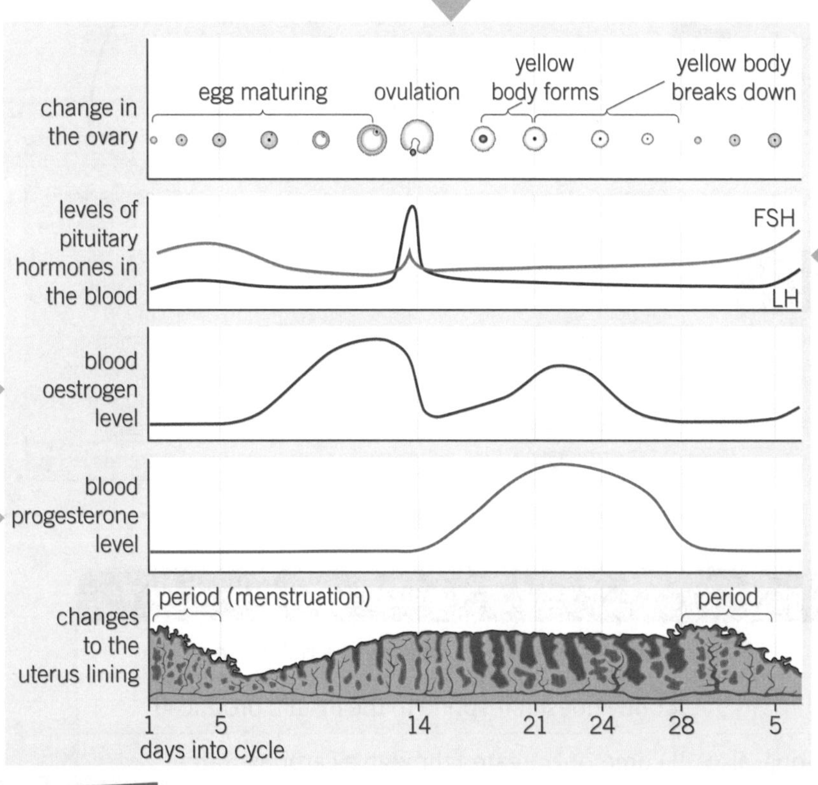

Remember The names of the different hormones can be confusing, but it's important that you use the correct names in the exam.

Practice To help you remember the key words, practise writing them out – mixing up the order of the letters can completely change the meaning, which could end up with you losing marks.

Make sure you can write a definition for these key terms.

contraception | follicle stimulating hormone | infertility
luteinising hormone | menstrual cycle | ovulation

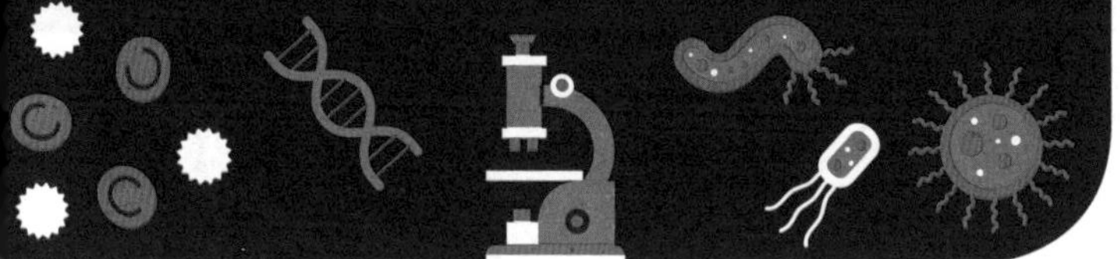

Treating infertility with hormones

Hormones are used in modern reproductive technologies to treat **infertility**.

FSH and LH can be given as a drug to treat infertility, or **in vitro fertilisation** (IVF) treatment may be used.

IVF treatment

1 mother given FSH and LH to stimulate the maturation of several eggs
2 eggs collected from the mother and fertilised by sperm from the father in a laboratory
3 fertilised eggs develop into embryos
4 one or two embryos are inserted into the mother's **uterus** (womb) when the embryos are still tiny balls of cells

Fertility treatment has some disadvantages:

- it is emotionally and physically stressful
- it has a low success rate
- it can lead to multiple births, which are a risk to both the babies and the mother.

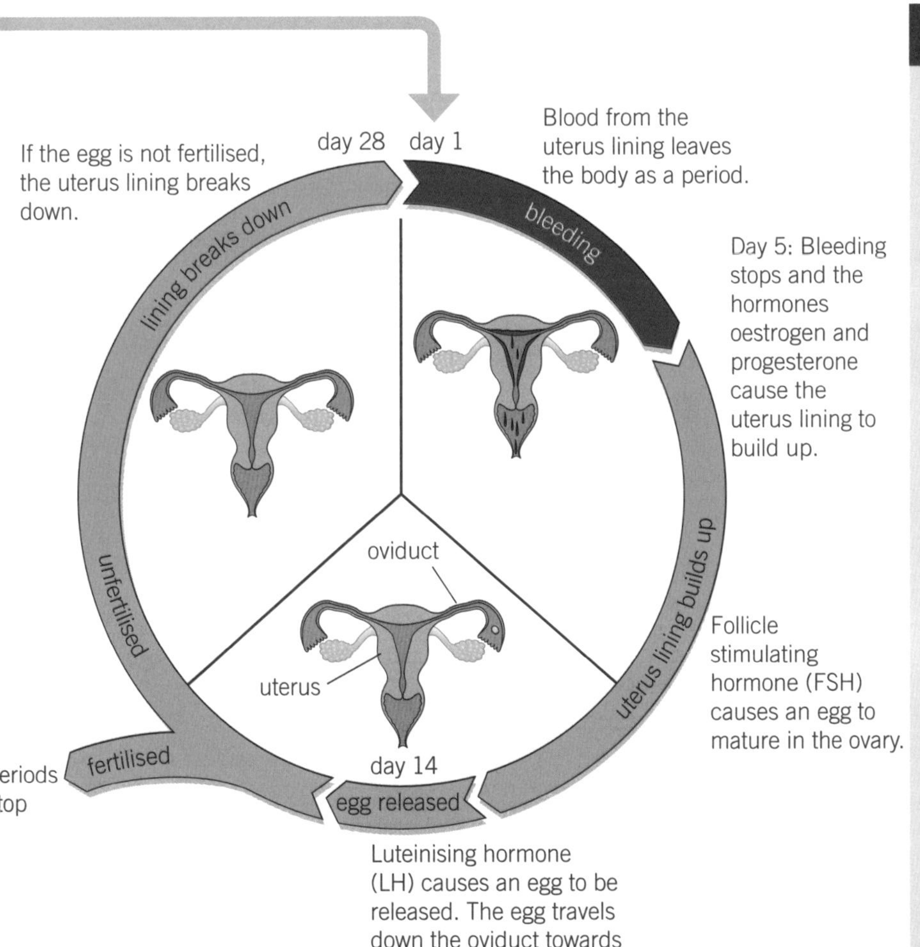

If the egg is not fertilised, the uterus lining breaks down.
day 28
day 1
Blood from the uterus lining leaves the body as a period.
lining breaks down
bleeding
Day 5: Bleeding stops and the hormones oestrogen and progesterone cause the uterus lining to build up.
uterus lining builds up
oviduct
uterus
unfertilised
Follicle stimulating hormone (FSH) causes an egg to mature in the ovary.
eriods
top
fertilised
day 14
egg released
Luteinising hormone (LH) causes an egg to be released. The egg travels down the oviduct towards the uterus.

Contraception

Fertility can be controlled by a variety of hormonal and non-hormonal methods of **contraception**.

Hormonal contraception

- oral contraceptives – contain hormones to inhibit FSH production so no eggs mature
- injection, implant, skin patch, or intrauterine devices (IUD) – slowly release progesterone to inhibit maturation and release of eggs; can last months or years

Non-hormonal contraception

- barrier methods, for example, condoms and diaphragms – prevent sperm reaching the egg
- copper IUD – prevents the implantation of an embryo
- surgical methods of male and female sterilisation
- spermicidal agents – kill or disable sperm
- abstaining from intercourse when an egg may be in the oviduct

in vitro fertilisation oestrogen ovary
progesterone testes uterus

Retrieval

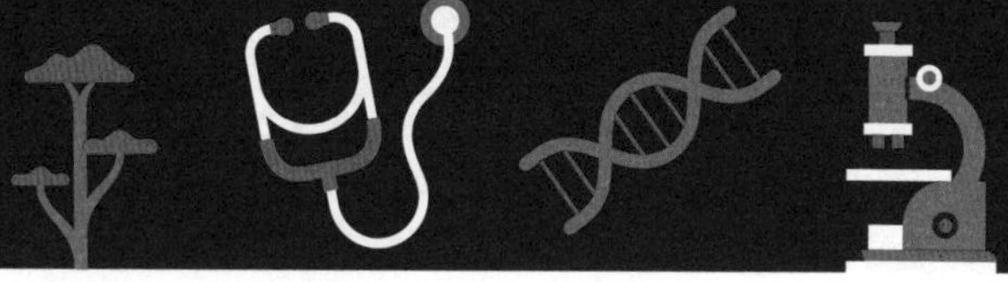

Learn the answers to the questions below, then cover the answers column with a piece of paper and write as many as you can. Check and repeat.

	B13 questions		Answers
1	What is the endocrine system?	Put paper here	system of glands that secrete hormones into the bloodstream
2	How do the effects of the endocrine system compare to those of the nervous system?		endocrine system effects are slower but act for longer
3	Where is the pituitary gland located?	Put paper here	brain
4	Which organ monitors and controls blood glucose concentration?		pancreas
5	Which hormones interact to regulate blood glucose levels?		insulin and glucagon
6	What is the cause of Type 1 diabetes?	Put paper here	pancreas produces insufficient insulin
7	What is the cause of Type 2 diabetes?		body cells no longer respond to insulin
8	What is the function of FSH?		causes eggs to mature in the ovaries, and stimulates ovaries to produce oestrogen
9	What is the function of LH?	Put paper here	stimulates the release of an egg
10	What is the function of oestrogen?		causes lining of uterus wall to thicken
11	What are the methods of hormonal contraception?		oral contraceptives, injection, implant, skin patch, IUD
12	What are the methods of non-hormonal contraception?	Put paper here	barrier methods, copper IUD, spermicidal agents, sterilisation, abstinence
13	State the disadvantages of IVF treatment.	Put paper here	• emotionally and physically stressful • low success rate • can lead to risky multiple births
14	What is the function of adrenaline in the body?		increases heart rate and boosts delivery of oxygen and glucose to brain and muscles to prepare the body for 'fight or flight'
15	What is the function of thyroxine in the body?	Put paper here	stimulates basal metabolic rate, so is important for growth and development
16	Name one hormone controlled by negative feedback.		thyroxine
17	Which endocrine glands control secondary sexual characteristics?		ovaries in females, testes in males

Now go back and use the questions below to check your knowledge from previous chapters.

Previous questions

Answers

	Previous questions	Answers
1	Why are reflex actions described as rapid and automatic?	they do not involve the conscious part of the brain
2	What are the two parts of the central nervous system?	brain and spinal cord
3	Write the balanced symbol equation for aerobic respiration.	$C_6H_{12}O_6 + 6O_2 \rightarrow 6CO_2 + 6H_2O$
4	Give the pathway of a nervous response.	stimulus → receptor → coordinator → effector → response

Put paper here

Maths Skills

Practise your maths skills using the worked example and practice questions below.

Trends in graphs

You need to be able to look at a graph and interpret what the graph tells us about the variables that have been tested.

You will often be asked to 'describe the trend' that the graph shows, or to 'describe the effect of X on Y'.

In order to do this, you will need to mention how the variable on one axis affects the variable on the other axis.

If you want to gain marks for this type of question, you have to mention the variables and also use the data from the graph, such as key dates or significant rises and falls.

Worked example

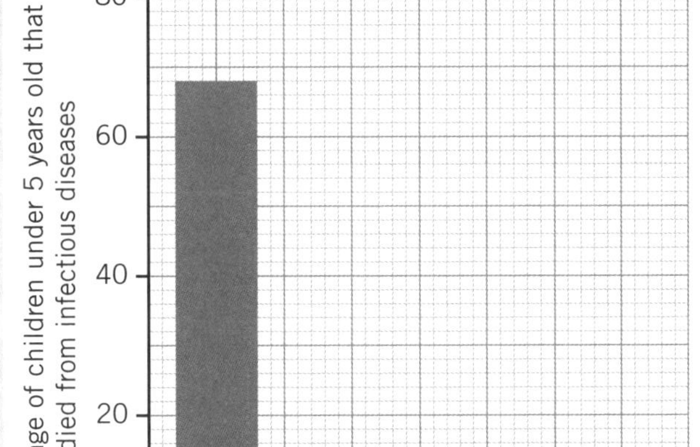

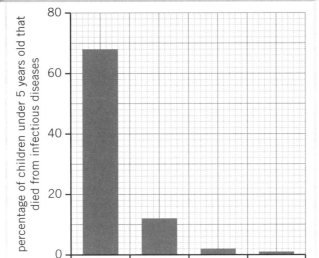

The graph shows the percentage of children under five years old who died from infectious diseases in the UK, in four different years.

Describe how the percentage of children who died from infectious diseases changed from 1750 to 1850.

To gain full marks you should include data from the graph above.

There was a significant decrease in the percentage of children under five years old who died from infectious diseases, going from 68% of children in 1750 to 12% in 1850.

An answer stating only that the percentage of children who died decreased would not get full marks.

Practice

1 The graph shows the number of deaths per million in England linked to methicillin-resistant *Staphylococcus aureus* (MRSA) between 1994 and 2010.

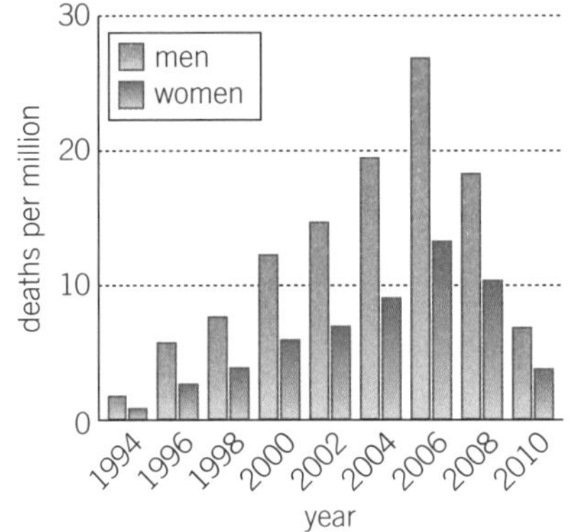

Describe the trend for deaths in women linked to MRSA.

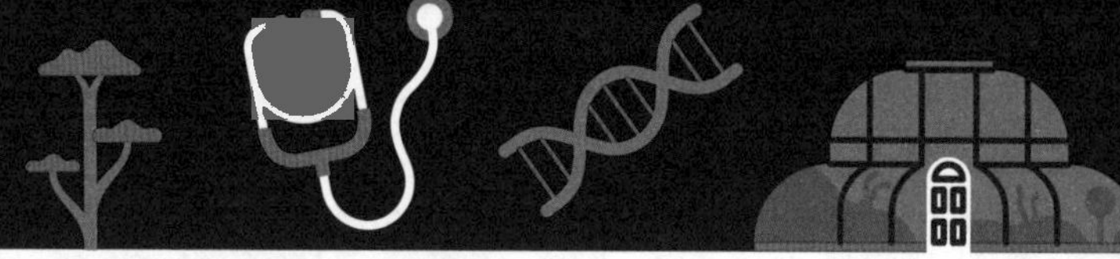

Practice

Exam-style questions

01 The graphs in **Figure 1** show changes in the levels of four hormones in a menstrual cycle.

Figure 1

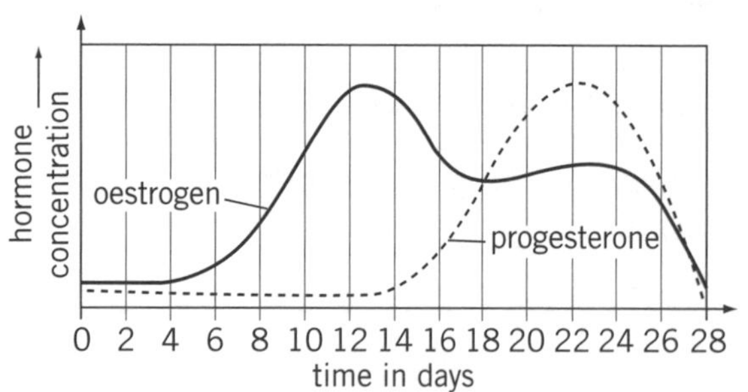

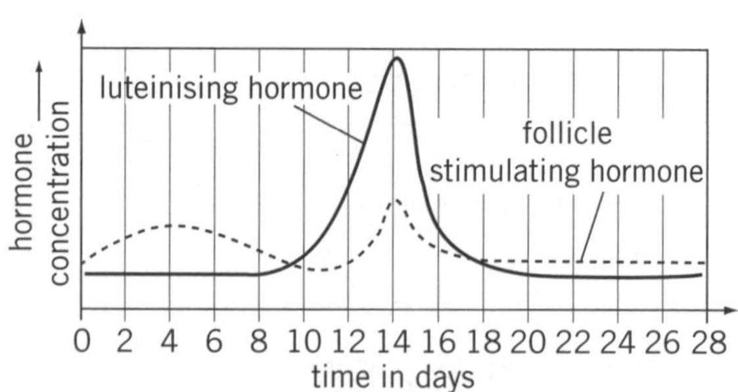

A teacher asked two students to analyse **Figure 1** and deduce on which day ovulation occurred.

One student thought that ovulation occurred on day 13, whereas the other student thought that ovulation occurred on day 14.

01.1 Use evidence from **Figure 1** and your own knowledge to explain which student was correct. **[4 marks]**

Exam Tip

With graphs that have more than one line on them it's important to be clear which set of data you're referring to.

'The line on the graph shows…' won't be enough to get the marks.

01.2 Hormones are used in a number of contraceptives.

One type of contraceptive pill keeps the level of progesterone high for most of the cycle. This tablet has to be taken each day for 21 days of the menstrual cycle.

Use evidence from **Figure 1** to suggest how this might work. **[2 marks]**

01.3 Progesterone can also be released from a contraceptive implant placed under the skin of a woman's arm. Many women who have a contraceptive implant do not have a period during the time it is implanted.

Use evidence from **Figure 1** to suggest why their periods stop. **[2 marks]**

Exam Tip

You only need to use one line in **Figure 1** to answer this question.

It can help to highlight the line you need so it stands out.

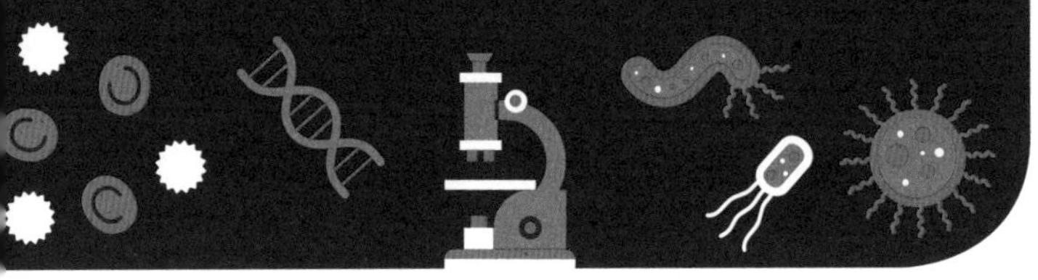

01.4 Evaluate the use of progesterone-releasing implants as a method of contraception. **[4 marks]**

Exam Tip

Remember you have to give an opinion *and* justify it.

02 The endocrine system contains many glands.

02.1 Identify the glands marked **A–E** on **Figure 2**. **[5 marks]**

Figure 2

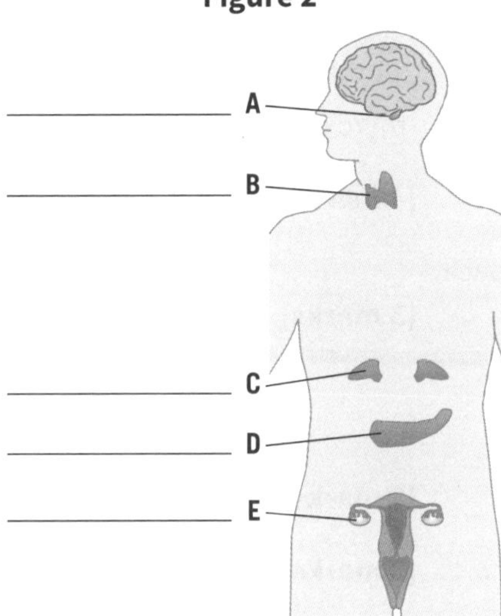

02.2 Explain why the pituitary gland is often referred to as a master gland. **[3 marks]**

02.3 Explain the role of the pituitary gland in maintaining the body's basal metabolic rate. **[6 marks]**

Exam Tip

'Explain' questions are all about the details. Discuss the names of hormones and their actions.

03 Blood glucose levels in the body are constantly controlled.

03.1 Explain why blood glucose levels need to be maintained at a constant level. **[3 marks]**

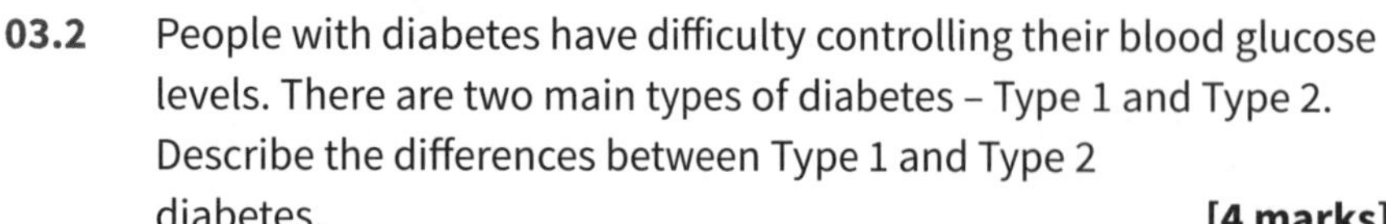

03.2 People with diabetes have difficulty controlling their blood glucose levels. There are two main types of diabetes – Type 1 and Type 2. Describe the differences between Type 1 and Type 2 diabetes. **[4 marks]**

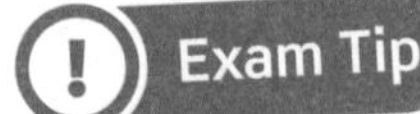

Question **03.2** is about the differences – don't waste time writing about similarities.

03.3 Compare the available treatments for Type 1 and Type 2 diabetes. **[4 marks]**

03.4 Suggest **two** actions that a government could take to reduce the number of new cases of diabetes. **[2 marks]**

04 Hormones play an important role in homeostasis.

04.1 Identify the hormone that is likely to increase after consuming a chocolate bar. Choose **one** answer. **[1 mark]**

adrenaline insulin glucagon thyroxine

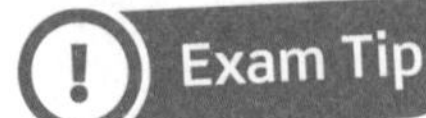

Start by crossing out any you know are wrong.

04.2 Explain your answer to **04.1**. **[4 marks]**

04.3 Many systems in homeostasis rely on negative feedback. Describe how a negative feedback system works. **[3 marks]**

05 Some couples have difficulty conceiving.

05.1 Explain **one** possible cause of infertility in females. **[2 marks]**

05.2 Explain **one** possible cause of infertility in males. **[2 marks]**

05.3 Some infertile couples receive in vitro fertilisation (IVF) treatment to increase their chances of getting pregnant. Describe the main steps involved in IVF treatment. **[4 marks]**

Exam Tip

It's important to write a balanced argument for question **05.4**. Writing about six advantages won't get you full marks.

05.4 Discuss the advantages and disadvantages of IVF treatment for those unable to conceive naturally. **[6 marks]**

05.5 **Figure 3** shows how the success rate for IVF varies with a female's age.

Figure 3

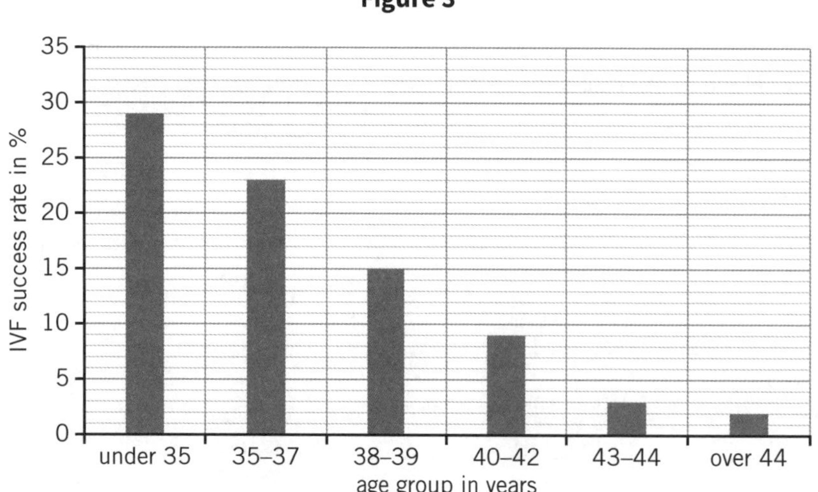

Each cycle of IVF treatment costs around £5000. In the UK, qualifying women under the age of 40 are offered up to three IVF treatments without having to pay for it, via the National Health Service (NHS). Using **Figure 3**, evaluate the arguments for and against providing IVF treatment through the NHS. **[4 marks]**

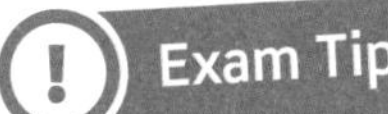

Exam Tip

Evalute means that you need to discuss the positives and negatives, and end with a reasoned opinion.

06 **Figure 4** shows how the blood glucose concentration varies in a non-diabetic person and in a person with Type 1 diabetes who is treated with insulin injections.

Figure 4

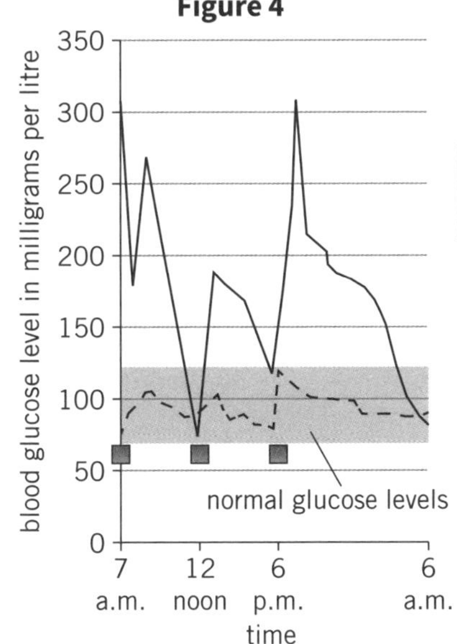

06.1 Describe why a person with Type 1 diabetes can't control their blood glucose concentration. **[1 mark]**

06.2 Compare the effect of eating a meal on a non-diabetic person with the effect on a person who has Type 1 diabetes. **[2 marks]**

Exam Tip

Look at the differences between the two lines in **Figure 4**.

06.3 Using information from **Figure 4**, suggest **one** time at which the person with Type 1 diabetes injected insulin. **[1 mark]**

06.4 Calculate the percentage change in blood glucose concentration immediately following the midday meal for a person with Type 1 diabetes. **[2 marks]**

06.5 Discuss the potential for a cure for Type 1 diabetes. **[5 marks]**

07 Blood glucose levels are maintained in a healthy person by the action of insulin and glucagon.

07.1 Name the organ that produces these hormones. **[1 mark]**

07.2 Explain how blood glucose levels are maintained in a healthy person by the action of insulin and glucagon. **[6 marks]**

07.3 In 2015, approximately 3.5 million people in the UK were living with diabetes from a total population of 65 million. 9.4% of the US population has diabetes.
Compare the rates of diabetes in the UK and the US. **[3 marks]**

Exam Tip

Use data in your answer to **07.3**. You'll have to do some calculations, but it will be needed as evidence for your comparison.

08 The body responds to changes in its internal and external environment using the endocrine and nervous systems.

08.1 Write down the name given to a change that occurs in a person's environment. **[1 mark]**

08.2 Name the hormone that is released in response to a stressful situation. **[1 mark]**

08.3 Compare the actions of hormones in the endocrine system to nerves in the nervous system. **[6 marks]**

> **Exam Tip**
> Use named hormones as examples in your answer to **08.3**.

09 Adrenaline is released in times of stress, preparing the body for 'fight or flight'.

09.1 Name the gland that releases adrenaline. **[1 mark]**

09.2 Explain **two** effects on the body caused by the release of adrenaline. **[4 marks]**

09.3 Adrenaline and thyroxine levels in the bloodstream are controlled in different ways. Explain how the level of thyroxine is controlled by the body. **[5 marks]**

10 The human menstrual cycle is controlled by the interaction of four hormones.

10.1 Select the hormone that triggers ovulation.
Choose **one** answer. **[1 mark]**

FSH LH oestrogen progesterone

10.2 Name the hormone that stimulates the release of LH. **[1 mark]**

10.3 Describe how progesterone and oestrogen control the lining of the uterus throughout the menstrual cycle. **[3 marks]**

10.4 Suggest and explain what would happen to the level of progesterone if a woman became pregnant. **[2 marks]**

11 EVD virus disease (EVD) is a highly contagious disease, caused by the Ebola virus. The disease is usually spread through direct contact with the bodily fluids of a person who has EVD. Around 50% of people who are infected with EVD die.

There have been two recent outbreaks of EVD in Africa:

- in 2014, affecting over 28 000 people
- in 2018, affecting almost 600 people.

EVD is treated by helping patients to maintain the correct balance of body fluids, supporting vital organ functions, and sustaining blood pressure and oxygen levels whilst the body's immune system fights the disease.

11.1 Suggest **two** reasons why the mortality rate is high for this disease. **[2 marks]**

11.2 Suggest **one** reason why the 2018 outbreak was much smaller than the 2014 outbreak. **[1 mark]**

11.3 A vaccine against Ebola virus is being developed, but has not yet been licensed for use. Explain how the vaccine would work. **[4 marks]**

> **Exam Tip**
> A vaccine for Ebola would work in exactly the same way as any other vaccine, this is just a new context.

12 One current treatment for people who suffer knee joint cartilage damage uses cell culture. This involves two surgical procedures:

1. Cells are harvested from an undamaged part of the cartilage and are grown in the laboratory.
2. The cells are then transplanted back into the patient.

A new technique is being researched where stem cells are removed from a patient's pelvis using a small needle. These are then transplanted into the damaged region of the knee. The stem cells differentiate and give rise to new cartilage cells, repairing the damaged region. By 2018 over 75 successful operations had taken place, with no long-term side effects yet being reported.

12.1 Explain what is meant by the differentiation of stem cells. **[1 mark]**

12.2 Write down **one** region where adult stem cells are found in the human body. **[1 mark]**

12.3 Using the information provided, and your own knowledge, give **two** advantages and **two** disadvantages of using stem cell therapy, rather than cell culture, to repair damaged cartilage. **[4 marks]**

Exam Tip

Go over the question text with two highlighter pens, pick out the advantages in one colour and the disadvantages in another – this will help you easily see what information needs to go into which part of your answer.

13 Sucrose is an example of a carbohydrate molecule. It is made when two simple sugars, glucose and fructose, bind together.

13.1 Explain why sucrose is classified as a carbohydrate molecule. **[1 mark]**

13.2 Enzymes are used to make some soft-centred chocolates. An enzyme called invertase will catalyse the breakdown of sucrose into glucose and fructose. This causes chocolate to become softer and sweeter to the taste.
Explain why invertase is an example of a catalyst. **[2 marks]**

Exam Tip

Don't worry if you've never heard of this enzyme before, just apply what you know about the action of other enzymes to this example.

13.3 Use the lock and key model to explain why invertase is only able to catalyse the breakdown of sucrose. **[3 marks]**

13.4 Suggest and explain **one** possible health benefit of adding invertase to chocolate. **[2 marks]**

14 Streptomycin is one type of antibiotic. It is used in the treatment of a number of infections, including tuberculosis (TB).

14.1 Identify the type of organism that causes TB.
Choose **one** answer. **[1 mark]**

fungi   bacteria   viruses   protozoa

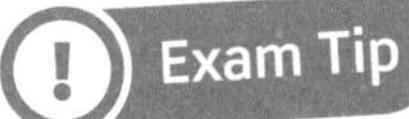

Antibiotics only work against one type of pathogen!

14.2 Streptomycin works by inhibiting protein synthesis in the target pathogen.
Name the cell component responsible for protein synthesis. **[1 mark]**

14.3 Suggest how streptomycin results in the death of the target pathogen. **[4 marks]**

Knowledge

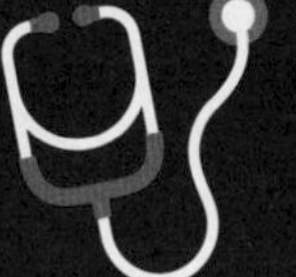

B14 Variation

Variation in populations

Differences in the characteristics of individuals in a population are called **variation**.

Variation may be due to differences in

- the genes they have inherited, for example, eye colour (genetic causes)
- the environment in which they have developed, for example, language (environmental causes)
- a combination of genes and the environment.

Mutation

There is usually a lot of genetic variation within a population of a species – this variation arises from **mutations**.

A mutation is a change in a DNA sequence:

- mutations occur continuously
- very rarely a mutation will lead to a new phenotype
- some mutations may change an existing phenotype and most have no effect
- if a new phenotype is suited to an environmental change, it can lead to a relatively rapid change in the species – this is the theory of evolution by natural selection.

Selective breeding

Selective breeding (artificial selection) is the process by which humans breed plants and animals for particular genetic characteristics.

Humans have been using selective breeding for thousands of years, since first breeding crops from wild plants and domesticating animals.

Process of selective breeding:

1 choose parents with the desired characteristic from a mixed population
2 breed them together
3 choose offspring with the desired characteristic and breed them together
4 continue over many generations until all offspring show the desired characteristic

Disadvantages of selective breeding:

- can lead to **inbreeding**, where some breeds are particularly prone to inherited defects or diseases
- reduces variation, meaning all members of a species could be susceptible to certain diseases.

The characteristic targeted in selective breeding can be chosen for usefulness or appearance, for example

- disease resistance in food crops
- animals that produce more meat or milk
- domestic dogs with a gentle nature
- larger or unusual flowers.

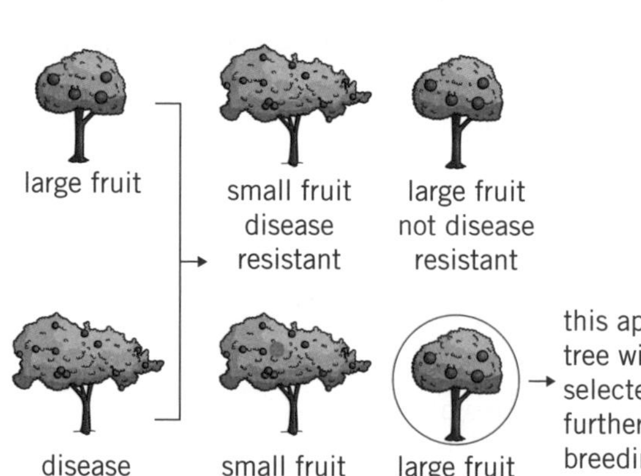

Key terms Make sure you can write a definition for these key terms.

genetically modified genetic engineering inbreeding

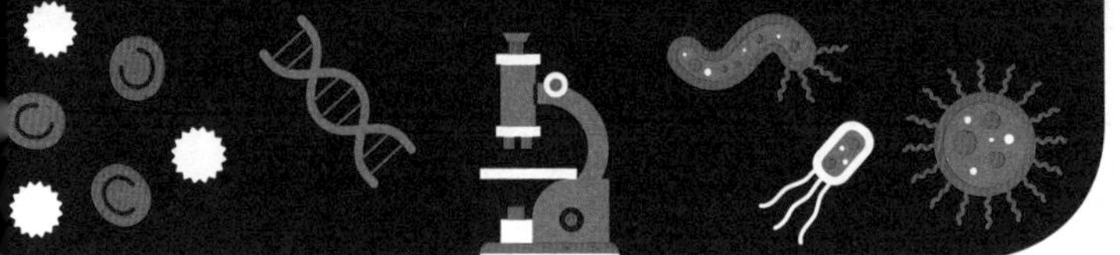

Genetic engineering

Genetic engineering is a process that involves changing the genome of an organism by introducing a gene from another organism to produce a desired characteristic.

For example:

- Bacterial cells have been genetically engineered to produce useful substances, such as human insulin to treat diabetes.
- Plant crops have been genetically engineered to be resistant to diseases, insects, or herbicides, or to produce bigger and better fruits and higher crop yields. Crops that have undergone genetic engineering are called **genetically modified** (GM).

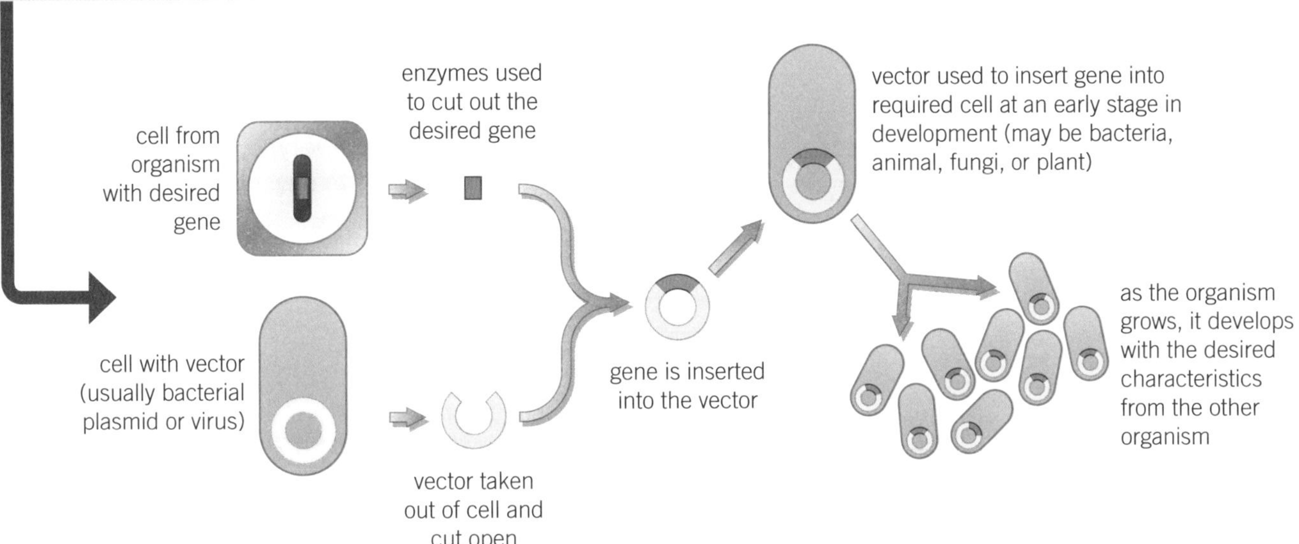

cell from organism with desired gene
enzymes used to cut out the desired gene
cell with vector (usually bacterial plasmid or virus)
vector taken out of cell and cut open
gene is inserted into the vector
vector used to insert gene into required cell at an early stage in development (may be bacteria, animal, fungi, or plant)
as the organism grows, it develops with the desired characteristics from the other organism

There are many benefits to genetic engineering in agriculture and medicine, but also some risks and moral objections.

Benefits	Risks
• potential to overcome some inherited human diseases • can lead to higher value of crops as GM crops have bigger yields than normal • crops can be engineered to be resistant to herbicides, make their own pesticides, or be better adapted to environmental conditions	• genes from GM plants and animals may spread to other wildlife, which could have devastating effects on ecosystems • potential negative impacts on populations of wild flowers and insects • ethical concerns, for example, in the future people could manipulate the genes of fetuses to ensure certain characteristics • some people believe the long-term effects on health of eating GM crops have not been fully explored

mutation   selective breeding   variation

Retrieval

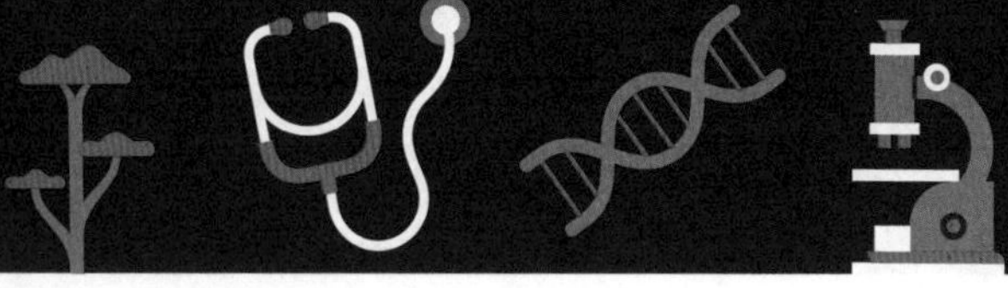

Learn the answers to the questions below, then cover the answers column with a piece of paper and write as many as you can. Check and repeat.

	B14 questions	Answers
1	What is variation?	differences in the characteristics of individuals in a population
2	What can cause variation?	genetic causes, environmental causes, and a combination of genes and the environment
3	How do new phenotype variants occur?	mutations
4	What are the effects of mutations?	most have no effect on phenotype, some influence phenotype, very few lead to new phenotypes
5	What is selective breeding?	breeding plants and animals for particular characteristics
6	Describe the process of selective breeding.	**1** choose parents with the desired characteristic **2** breed them together **3** choose offspring with the desired characteristic and breed again **4** continue over many generations until all offspring show the desired characteristic
7	What are the consequences of inbreeding?	inherited defects and diseases
8	What is genetic engineering?	modifying the genome of an organism by introducing a gene from another organism to give a desired characteristic
9	How have plant crops been genetically engineered?	• to be resistant to diseases/herbicides/pesticides • to produce bigger fruits • to give higher yields
10	What concerns are there about genetically engineered crops?	• possible detrimental effects on wild flowers and insects • the effects on human health may not be fully understood
11	How have bacteria been genetically engineered?	to produce useful substances, such as human insulin to treat diabetes
12	What are enzymes used for in genetic engineering?	cut out the required gene
13	What is used to transfer the required gene into the new cell in genetic engineering?	vector (e.g., bacterial plasmid or virus)

Put paper here

Now go back and use the questions below to check your knowledge from previous chapters.

Previous questions / Answers

	Previous questions	Answers
1	What is the cause of Type 1 diabetes?	pancreas produces insufficient insulin
2	What are the methods of hormonal contraception?	oral contraceptives, injection, implant, skin patch, IUD
3	Give three things all control systems include.	receptors, coordination centres, and effectors
4	What do organisms need energy for?	• chemical reactions to build larger molecules • muscle contraction for movement • keeping warm
5	Give three internal conditions controlled in homeostasis.	body temperature, blood glucose concentration, and water levels
6	State the disadvantages of IVF treatment.	• emotionally and physically stressful • low success rate • can lead to risky multiple births

Put paper here

Put paper here

Maths Skills

Practise your maths skills using the worked example and practice questions below.

Mean, median, mode, and range

When interpreting data, scientists often need to calculate the average or range of a set of data.

You need to be able to calculate the range, and different types of averages (mean, median, and mode).

Mean: the calculated average of the numbers.

Median: the number in the middle.

Mode: the number that occurs most often.

Range: the difference between the largest and the smallest values.

Worked example

For the following list of numbers, we can calculate the mean, median, mode, and range.

13, 18, 13, 14, 13, 16, 14, 21, 13

Mean = 15

Add all the values together, and divide by the total number of values.

13 + 18 + 13 + 14 + 13 + 16 + 14 + 21 + 13 = 135

$\frac{135}{9} = 15$

Median = 14

Write the values in order and determine which one is in the middle. If it is an even number of values, take the mean of the two values in the middle.

~~13, 13, 13, 13,~~ [14] ~~14, 16, 18, 21~~

Mode = 13

13 appears the most times in the data.

Range = 8

The largest value (21) minus the smallest value (13).

21 − 13 = 8

Practice

Stomata on a leaf can be seen using a light microscope. The number of stomata differs depending on the location on the plant.

The table below gives the number of stomata a student counted from different areas on one leaf.

Leaf area	Number of stomata	
	Upper surface	Lower surface
1	4	42
2	1	43
3	0	45
4	4	43
5	1	39

Calculate the following:

1. The mean number of stomata on the lower surface of the leaf.
2. The median number of stomata on the upper surface of the leaf.
3. The mode number of stomata on the lower surface of the leaf.
4. The range in the number of stomata on the upper surface of the leaf.

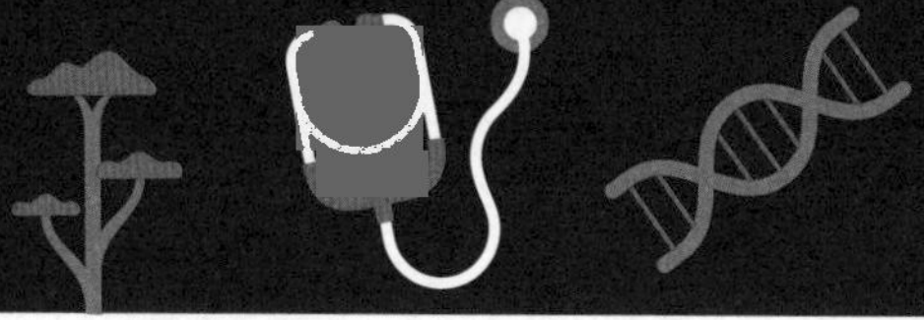

Exam-style questions

01 A market gardener grows and sells tomatoes.

The gardener wishes to selectively breed the tomato plants so that the crops have a high yield and produce sweet tomatoes.

01.1 Write down the steps that the market gardener should take to produce a sweet-tasting, high-yielding variety of tomato plant. **[4 marks]**

____

____

____

____

____

____

01.2 Suggest and explain **two** advantages to the market gardener of selectively breeding the tomato plants. **[4 marks]**

1 ____

____

2 ____

____

01.3 The gardener wishes to grow the tomato crop organically.

Suggest **one** other characteristic the gardener could selectively breed for to ensure a high yield of tomatoes is maintained.

Give a reason for your answer. **[2 marks]**

____

____

____

If a plant is grown organically then pesticides can't be used.

02 A group of students investigated the variation in height that existed amongst students in their school.

Their results are shown in **Table 1**.

Table 1

Height in cm	$100 \leq h < 120$	$120 \leq h < 140$	$140 \leq h < 160$	$160 \leq h < 180$	$180 \leq h < 200$
Number of students	12	18	36	22	6
Midpoint					

02.1 Plot an appropriate graph of these data on **Figure 1**. **[4 marks]**

Figure 1

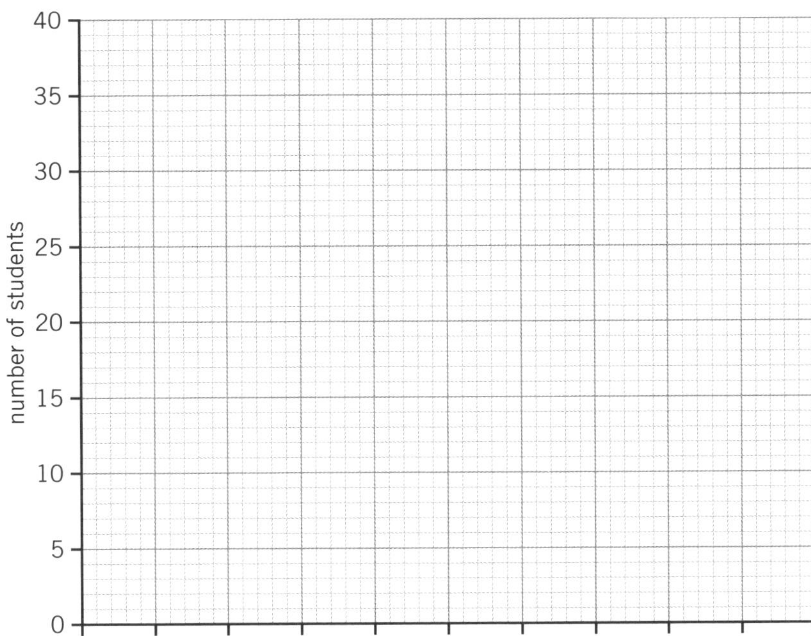

> **Exam Tip**
>
> The choice of graph is important.
>
> Bar graphs can be used to show patterns in categoric data.
>
> Line graphs can be used for continuous data.
>
> Histograms can be used to show patterns in frequency.

02.2 Explain the cause of the variation shown in the graph. **[2 marks]**

____

____

____

02.3 The mean height of a person in the UK is 168 cm.

Calculate the mean height of the students in the school. **[3 marks]**

> **Exam Tip**
>
> You may be used to using data tables to work out means in maths, but you may also be asked to use this skill in science.

______________ cm

02.4 The students concluded that the distribution of heights in their school reflects that of the whole population.

Discuss the extent to which you agree or disagree with their conclusion. **[2 marks]**

____

____

____

03 A group of scientists pooled their research data on differences caused by genetic and environmental factors. Three groups were studied:

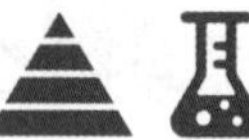

- identical twins who were brought up together
- identical twins who were brought up separately
- non-identical twins who were brought up together.

The data were summarised into the differences between the pairs studied, as shown in **Table 2**.

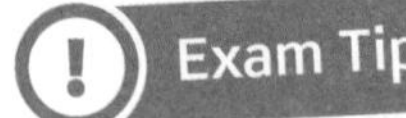

Exam Tip

This is a great question. All the information you need to get lots of marks is in the table, you just need to interpret the data.

Spend a minute thinking about what the data are showing before you answer the questions.

Table 2

Pair	Mean difference in height in cm	Mean difference in mass in kg	Mean difference in IQ
Identical twins, brought up together	1.4	1.1	4.9
Identical twins, brought up separately	1.6	3.5	8.2
Non-identical twins, brought up together	5.8	3.6	4.8

Height, mass, and IQ are all affected by both a person's genes and their environment.

Exam Tip

You need to use the data from the table to back up your answers to get top marks.

03.1 Identify the extent to which each factor is influenced by a person's genes or their environment.
Justify your answers using data from **Table 2**. **[6 marks]**

03.2 Suggest **two** possible extensions to the study that would increase the validity of any conclusions made. **[2 marks]**

04 Some plant crops have been genetically modified to improve their characteristics.

04.1 Explain what is meant by the term genetically modified. **[2 marks]**

04.2 Reorder sentences **A**–**E** to describe how crops can be modified through genetic engineering. The first and last steps have been completed for you. **[4 marks]**

Step 1: The desired gene is removed from the nucleus of a donor cell.

A The bacteria are allowed to infect plant cells.

B The foreign gene is integrated into the plant cells' DNA.

C This 'foreign' gene is inserted into a plasmid (a circular piece of DNA).

D Bacteria reproduce quickly, producing many copies of the desired gene.

E The plasmid, now containing the desired gene, is inserted into a bacterial cell.

Step 7: Plant cells grow into plants displaying the desired characteristic.

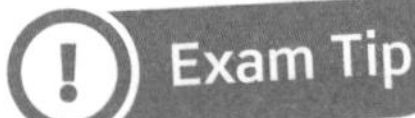

Exam Tip

Tick off each sentence as you use it, but don't cross it out completely in case you change your mind.

04.3 Give **one** advantage of the genetic modification of plant crops compared to selective breeding. **[1 mark]**

05 Most cattle and plant crops that are seen on farms today have been selectively bred.

05.1 Describe how cattle would be selected for breeding. **[4 marks]**

05.2 Some crops are genetically engineered.
Discuss the arguments for and against using genetic engineering to modify food crops. **[4 marks]**

> **Exam Tip**
> In 'discuss' questions, make sure your argument is balanced.

06 Insulin is a hormone secreted by the pancreas.

06.1 Explain the role of insulin in the body. **[2 marks]**

06.2 People with Type 1 diabetes have to inject themselves regularly with insulin. It is possible to genetically engineer bacteria so that they contain the gene for human insulin. This insulin can then be used to treat diabetes. Describe the main steps in the procedure of genetically engineering the bacteria this way. **[6 marks]**

> **Exam Tip**
> 'Describe' questions are asking for *what* happened, so go through the steps one at a time. Use key words and technical terms in the appropriate places.

06.3 Insulin used in the treatment of diabetes was originally extracted from pigs. Suggest **two** advantages of using insulin from genetically engineered bacteria rather than from pigs. **[2 marks]**

07 Two students were asked to investigate whether plant leaf surface area is affected by light intensity. They decided to study the leaves on laurel bushes found in two locations: one area was in direct sunlight and the other was partially shaded by a building. They studied eight leaves in each area.

The students recorded their results in **Table 3**.

Table 3

Location of laurel bush	Leaf surface area in cm^2								
	1	2	3	4	5	6	7	8	Average
Direct sunlight	72	72	68	72	68	68	70	70	70
Shaded	72	76	70	64	82	72	84	72	

07.1 Complete **Table 3** by calculating the average leaf surface area for the laurel bushes found in the shade. **[1 mark]**

07.2 Calculate the uncertainty in leaf surface area for the shaded leaves. **[2 marks]**

07.3 One student concluded that leaves found in the shade have a larger surface area than leaves found in well-lit areas. The second student argued that it is not possible to form a conclusion from these data. Give **two** reasons why the second student was correct. Give reasons for your answers. **[4 marks]**

07.4 Laurel leaves have a complex shape. The students estimated the surface area of a leaf by drawing around the leaf on squared paper and adding up the number of squares contained within the shape. Suggest **one** alternative approach the students could have taken to estimate the leaf surface area. **[1 mark]**

08 A scientific magazine published the following article.

> *MioneTech, a US-based biotech company, reported today that it had successfully started the first human trials of a gene replacement therapy to cure Hunter syndrome, a previously incurable disorder. This inherited disorder prevents cells breaking down some sugars, leading to developmental delays, brain damage, and possible death.*
>
> *The trial uses a form of DNA scissors called zinc finger nucleases (ZFNs), which cut both strands of the DNA double helix at a precise point. A virus is then used as the vector to transfer a 'healthy' replacement gene into the patient's DNA.*
>
> *The company claims that the revolutionary new treatment will change patients' lives for the better. People with Hunter syndrome require weekly infusions of a missing enzyme, whereas the gene replacement therapy involves a single three-hour operation.*

Exam Tip

Go through the text with a set of highlighters. Colour coding large blocks of text makes them easier to read so you can find the information you need.

08.1 People with Hunter syndrome are missing a protein from their cells. Using the information from the article, name the type of protein molecule that the replacement gene will code for. **[1 mark]**

08.2 Evaluate the ethical and social issues of using gene replacement therapy to treat Hunter syndrome. **[6 marks]**

09 Some species of tomato have been genetically engineered to be frost-resistant.

09.1 Suggest **two** advantages to a farmer of growing frost-resistant tomatoes. **[2 marks]**

09.2 To make frost-resistant tomatoes, genetic material is taken from a flounder fish. These flat fish are adapted to live in very cold water by producing an antifreeze chemical.
Describe how frost-resistant tomatoes are created using genetic modification. **[6 marks]**

10 **Figure 2** shows a litter of puppies produced from the same parents.

Figure 2

10.1 The puppies show variation.
Define the term variation. **[1 mark]**

10.2 Name **one** characteristic that is inherited. **[1 mark]**

10.3 Give **one** characteristic that is affected by genes **and** the environment. Explain your answer. **[2 marks]**

10.4 Most breeds of dog have been selectively bred for certain characteristics.
Give **one** disadvantage of selective breeding. **[1 mark]**

Exam Tip

You could easily have a six-mark question on disadvantages of selective breeding, but this question is only worth one mark. Giving too much detail for a question is a waste of time in an exam.

11.1 Identify the best description of selective breeding. Choose **one** answer. **[1 mark]**

introducing a gene from another organism to give a desired characteristic

the process by which humans breed plants and animals for particular genetic characteristics

using the differences in individuals within a population

only breeding organisms at certain times of the year

11.2 Identify the effect of selective breeding on the variation within a population. Choose **one** answer. **[1 mark]**

selective breeding increases variation in a population

selective breeding has no effect on variation in a population

selective breeding decreases variation in a population

11.3 Food crops such as wheat have been selectively bred for many years to make the plant more useful to humans (**Figure 3**).

Figure 3

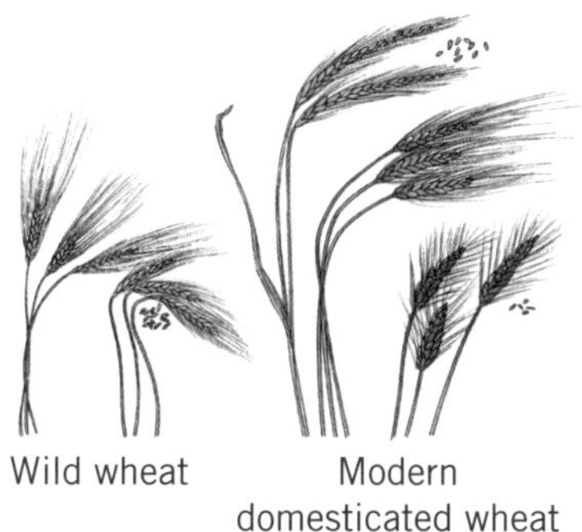

Give **one** difference between wild wheat and domesticated wheat. **[1 mark]**

11.4 Explain how wheat has been selectively bred for the characteristic named in **11.3**. **[4 marks]**

These two questions are linked. If you can't explain your answer to **11.3** in **11.4**, try to think of another answer for **11.3** that you can explain.

12 A scientist views a cell through a light microscope and an electron microscope.

12.1 Compare the advantages and disadvantages of using the two types of microscope. **[6 marks]**

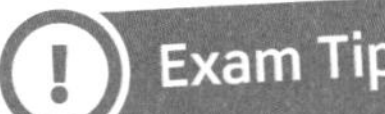

Give a balanced answer that covers both the advantages and disadvantages for the *two* types of microscope. Simply giving the advantages won't get full marks and only talking about light microscopes won't get full marks either. Ensure you cover all four parts of this question.

12.2 The scientist was unable to view a nucleus in the cell with either type of microscope.
Name the type of cell being viewed. Choose **one** answer. **[1 mark]**

plant cell   bacterial cell   animal cell

12.3 The scientist was able to view plasmid rings in the cell using the electron microscope.
Explain the function of a plasmid ring. **[2 marks]**

12.4 The light microscope used by the scientist had a resolution of 7×10^{-7} m. The resolution of the electron microscope was 5×10^{-9} m.
How many times greater was the resolution of the electron microscope than that of the light microscope? **[2 marks]**

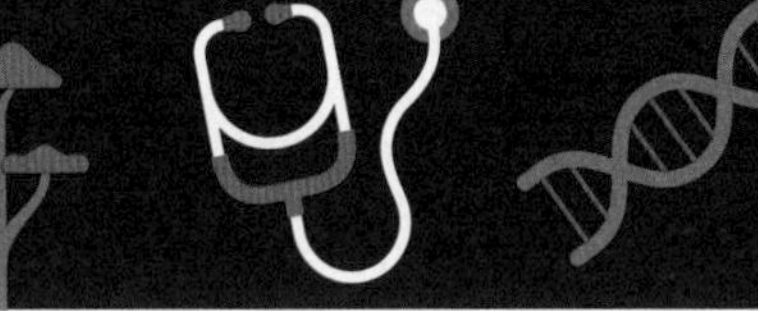

B15 Reproduction

Types of reproduction

Sexual reproduction	Asexual reproduction
two parents	one parent
cell division through **meiosis**	cell division through **mitosis**
joining (fusion) of male and female sex cells (**gametes**) – sperm and egg in animals, pollen and ovule in plants	no fusion of gametes
produces non-identical offspring that are genetically different to parents	produces offspring that are genetically identical to parent (**clones**)
results in wide variation within offspring and species	no mixing of genetic information

Meiosis

Meiosis is a type of cell division that makes gametes in the reproductive organs.

Meiosis halves the number of chromosomes in gametes, and **fertilisation** (joining of two gametes) restores the full number of chromosomes.

The fertilised cell divides by mitosis, producing more cells. As the embryo develops, the cells differentiate.

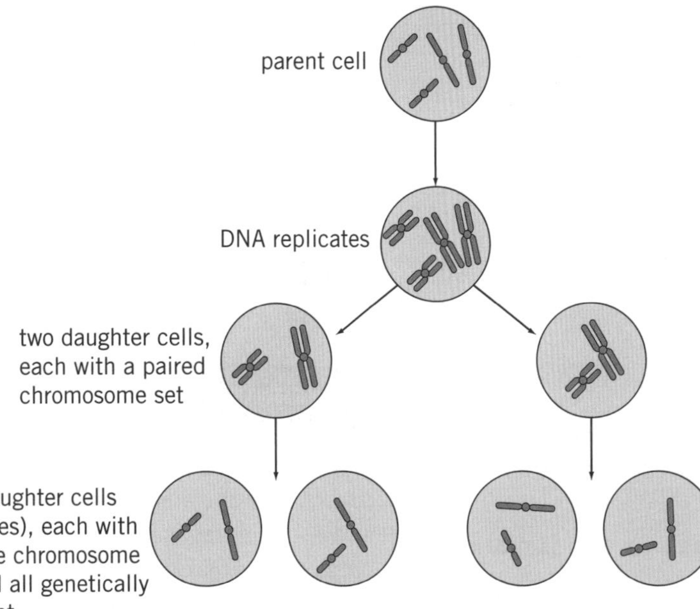

DNA and the genome

Genetic material in the nucleus of a cell is composed of **DNA**.

DNA is made up of two strands forming a **double helix**.

DNA is contained in structures called **chromosomes**.

A **gene** is a small section of DNA on a chromosome that codes for a specific sequence of amino acids, to produce a specific protein.

The **genome** of an organism is the entire genetic material of that organism.

The whole human genome has been studied, and this has allowed scientists to

- search for genes linked to different diseases
- understand and treat inherited disorders
- trace human migration patterns from the past.

Inherited disorders

Some disorders are due to the inheritance of certain alleles:

- Polydactyly (extra fingers or toes) is caused by a **dominant** allele.
- Cystic fibrosis (a disorder of cell membranes) is caused by a **recessive** allele.

Embryo screening and gene therapy may alleviate suffering from these disorders, but there are ethical issues surrounding their use.

Key terms

Make sure you can write a definition for these key terms.

allele chromosome clone DNA dominant
genome genotype heterozygous homozygous meiosis

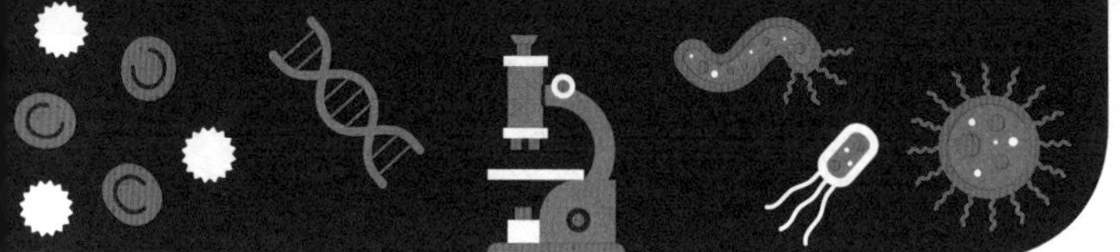

Genetic inheritance

You need to be able to explain these terms about genetic inheritance:

gamete	specialised sex cell formed by meiosis
chromosome	long molecule made from DNA found in the nucleus of cells
gene	sequence of DNA that codes for a protein – some characteristics are controlled by a single gene (e.g., fur colour in mice and red-green colour-blindness in humans), but most are controlled by multiple genes interacting
allele	different forms of the same gene
dominant	allele that only needs one copy present to be expressed (it is always expressed)
recessive	allele that needs two copies present to be expressed
homozygous	when an individual carries two copies of the same allele for a trait
heterozygous	when an individual carries two different alleles for a trait
genotype	combination of alleles an individual has
phenotype	physical expression of the genotype – the characteristic shown

Genetic crosses

A **genetic cross** is when you consider the offspring that might result from two known parents. **Punnett squares** can be used to predict the outcome of a genetic cross, for both the genotypes the offspring might have and their phenotypes.

For example, the cross bb (brown fur) × BB (black fur) in mice:

		mother	
		B	**B**
father	**b**	Bb	Bb
	b	Bb	Bb

offspring genotype: 100% Bb

offspring phenotype: all black fur (B is dominant)

Sex determination

Normal human body cells contain 23 pairs of chromosomes – one of these pairs determines the sex of the offspring.

In human females the sex chromosomes are the same (XX, homozygous), and in males they are different (XY, heterozygous).

A Punnett square can be used to determine the probability of offspring being male or female. The probability is always 50% in humans as there are two XX outcomes and two XY outcomes.

		mother	
		X	**X**
father	**X**	XX	XX
	Y	XY	XY

double helix fertilisation gamete gene genetic cross
mitosis phenotype Punnett square recessive

Retrieval

Learn the answers to the questions below, then cover the answers column with a piece of paper and write as many as you can. Check and repeat.

	B15 questions	Answers
1	What is sexual reproduction?	joining (fusion) of male and female gametes
2	What type of cell division is involved in sexual reproduction?	meiosis
3	What type of cell division is involved in asexual reproduction?	mitosis
4	What is meiosis?	cell division that produces four daughter cells (gametes), each with a single set of chromosomes
5	What are the male and female sex chromosomes in humans?	• XX – female • XY – male
6	What are the male and female gametes in flowering plants?	• pollen – male gamete • ovule – female gamete
7	What is the genetic material in cells called?	DNA
8	What is the structure of DNA?	two complementary strands forming a double helix
9	What is a gene?	small section of DNA that codes for a particular amino acid sequence, to make a specific protein
10	What are alleles?	different forms of the same gene
11	What is a recessive allele?	allele that needs to be present twice to be expressed
12	What is a dominant allele?	allele that is always expressed, even if only one copy is present
13	What is a genome?	the entire genetic material of an organism
14	Define the term homozygous.	two of the same alleles present in an organism
15	Define the term heterozygous.	two different alleles present in an organism
16	What type of allele causes polydactyly?	dominant allele
17	What type of allele causes cystic fibrosis?	recessive allele
18	How many chromosomes do normal human body cells have?	23 pairs (46)
19	Why is studying the human genome important?	• search for genes linked to certain diseases • understanding and treatment of inherited disorders • tracing past human migration

Put paper here

Now go back and use the questions below to check your knowledge from previous chapters.

Previous questions | Answers

	Previous questions	Answers
1	What happens to muscles during long periods of activity?	muscles become fatigued and stop contracting efficiently
2	Describe the process of selective breeding.	**1** choose parents with the desired characteristic **2** breed them together **3** choose offspring with the desired characteristic and breed again **4** continue over many generations until all offspring show the desired characteristic
3	What is the function of FSH?	causes eggs to mature in the ovaries, and stimulates ovaries to produce oestrogen
4	What can cause variation?	genetic causes, environmental causes, and a combination of genes and the environment
5	What is the difference between aerobic and anaerobic respiration?	aerobic respiration uses oxygen, anaerobic respiration does not
6	How have bacteria been genetically engineered?	to produce useful substances, such as human insulin to treat diabetes

Put paper here

Put paper here

Put paper here

Maths Skills

Practise your maths skills using the worked example and practice questions below.

Probability

Probability is a number that tells you how likely something is to happen.

It is important that you understand probability as this is key to genetic inheritance.

For example, you could be asked to work out the probability of a child inheriting a genetic disease from its parents using a Punnett square.

A value for probability can be expressed in the form of a fraction, decimal, or percentage.

Probability can be calculated using the formula:

$$\text{probability} = \frac{\text{number of ways the outcome can happen}}{\text{total number of outcomes}}$$

Worked example

The Punnett square shows the inheritance of sex chromosomes in a genetic cross between two parents.

	X	**Y**
X	XX	XY
X	XX	XY

male = XY

female = XX

What is the probability that the offspring from the genetic cross will be female?

- *number of ways the outcome can happen = 2*
- *total number of outcomes = 4*

$= \frac{2}{4} = 0.5$

This probability can also be expressed as a fraction $\left(\frac{1}{2}\right)$ *or a percentage (50%).*

Practice

1 The Punnett square shows the inheritance of eye colour in a genetic cross. BB and Bb represent brown eyes. bb represents blue eyes.

What is the probability that the offspring of the cross would have blue eyes?

	B	**b**
B	BB	Bb
b	Bb	bb

2 The Punnett square shows whether the offspring of a genetic cross between plants will be tall or short. TT and Tt represent tall plants, and tt represents short plants.

What is the probability that the offspring of the cross would be tall?

	T	**t**
T	TT	Tt
t	Tt	tt

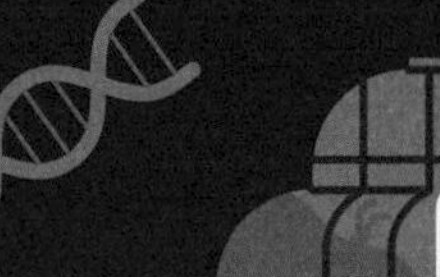

Exam-style questions

01.1 Complete the following sentences about genetic inheritance by circling the correct words. **[5 marks]**

Each human gamete contains **23 / 46 / 92** chromosomes. When a sperm and an egg fuse, a new cell called a zygote is formed. This new cell contains **23 / 46 / 92** chromosomes.

Two forms of each gene are inherited – these are called **alleles / dominant / recessive**.

One form of the gene is **allele / dominant / recessive** – this form is always expressed if present.

The other form of the gene is **allele / dominant / recessive** – a person must inherit this form of the gene from both parents if it is to be expressed.

> **! Exam Tip**
> Take each sentence one at a time. Don't let the large block of text overwhelm you.

01.2 Eye colour is controlled by a gene. Two forms of the gene exist:

- brown eyes – dominant – **B**
- blue eyes – recessive – **b**

Classify each of the possible genotypes by matching the allele combination to its correct description. **[2 marks]**

Allele combination	Description
BB	homozygous recessive
Bb	homozygous dominant
bb	heterozygous

> **! Exam Tip**
> There are lots of key words in this topic – make sure you're clear on all the different definitions.

01.3 Write down the phenotype for each of the allele combinations. **[3 marks]**

BB: ______________________________

Bb: ______________________________

bb: ______________________________

01.4 A couple is expecting a baby. The father has blue eyes and the mother has brown eyes. Select the correct statement about their new baby's eye colour. **[1 mark]**

Tick **one** box.

The baby will definitely have brown eyes. ☐

The baby may be born with brown eyes or may be born with blue eyes. ☐

The baby will definitely have blue eyes. ☐

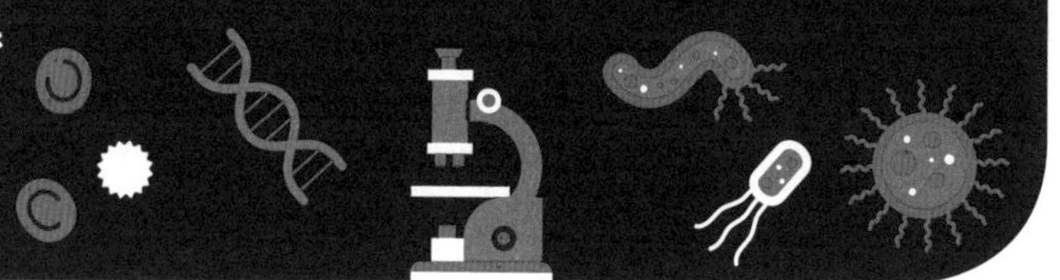

01.5 Give a reason for your answer to **01.4**. **[1 mark]**

____

____

02 **Figure 1** shows the sex chromosomes from two different people, **A** and **B**.

Figure 1

A B

02.1 Identify which image represents the chromosomes from a female. Give reasons for your answer. **[2 marks]**

____

____

> **Exam Tip**
> The sizes of the X and Y chromosomes are very different.

02.2 Use a genetic cross diagram to show how sex is inherited.

Use your diagram to show the likelihood of a couple having a female baby. **[4 marks]**

> **Exam Tip**
> Space your diagram out clearly – you get marks for showing working here.

Likelihood of having a female baby = ____________

02.3 A couple has three children.

Calculate the probability that all three children are girls. **[3 marks]**

> **Exam Tip**
> Show all of your working for this question. If you get the wrong final answer, you can still pick up some marks for the working.

Probability = ____________

02.4 A scientist studies two population groups:

- inhabitants of Manchester (population 500 000)
- inhabitants of Bath (population 90 000).

Explain which population is more likely to have a 1:1 ratio of males to females. **[3 marks]**

____

____

____

03 Polydactyly is an inherited condition. A couple is having a child. The father has polydactyly and is heterozygous for this condition. The mother does not have polydactyly.

03.1 Polydactyly can be observed in a newborn baby. Write down the characteristic that would be observed for a baby who has inherited polydactyly. **[1 mark]**

03.2 Explain how polydactyly is inherited. **[2 marks]**

> **Exam Tip**
>
> Refer back to the original question stem to help you answer question **03.3**.

03.3 Write down the allele combinations of the father and mother. **[2 marks]**

03.4 Over time, the mother and father have four more children. Draw a genetic cross diagram to show the possible alleles of the offspring. **[2 marks]**

03.5 Write down the expected ratio of children with polydactyly to children without polydactyly. **[1 mark]**

03.6 Explain why the actual ratio of children with and without polydactyly may not necessarily be the same as the ratio you gave in **03.5**. **[3 marks]**

03.7 In the USA, 1 in 3500 babies are born with cystic fibrosis. In comparison, 1 in 500 babies are born with polydactyly. Suggest and explain **two** reasons for this. **[6 marks]**

04 Many people in the population have dimples. This is because having dimples is caused by a dominant allele, **D**. The allele for no dimples is **d**.

04.1 Write down what is meant by a dominant allele. **[1 mark]**

> **Exam Tip**
>
> There is a clue in the wording of question **04.2**. 'Select as many combinations as required' tells you it's probably more than one!

04.2 Which of the following allele combinations would lead to a child having dimples? Select as many combinations as required. **[1 mark]**

DD **Dd** **dd**

04.3 A couple decide to start a family. The alleles of the mother and father are shown in **Figure 2**. Complete the Punnett square to predict the possible allele combinations that the baby could have. **[2 marks]**

> **Exam Tip**
>
> Approach Punnett squares logically – do either the rows first or the columns first.

Figure 2

	Father's alleles	
Mother's alleles	D	d
D		
D		

04.4 Calculate and explain the probability of their child having dimples. **[2 marks]**

04.5 If the parents have a second child, explain why the two children are likely to look similar but not the same. **[4 marks]**

05 Cystic fibrosis (CF) is an inherited disorder affecting over 10 400 people in the UK.

05.1 Write down **two** symptoms of CF. **[2 marks]**

05.2 Explain why a carrier (heterozygote) of CF will not suffer from the disorder. **[3 marks]**

05.3 Draw a genetic diagram to show the possible genotypes of the offspring of two carriers of CF. **[2 marks]**

05.4 Using your diagram from **05.3**, calculate the percentage probability that a child born from two carriers of CF will inherit the disorder. **[2 marks]**

05.5 Using the information below, and your answer to **05.4**, calculate the number of expected births in the UK with the genetic disorder CF in 2019:

- 1 in 25 people in the population are carriers of the CF allele
- expected number of births in 2019 is 700 000. **[5 marks]**

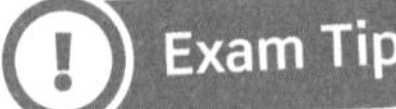

Exam Tip

Even if you didn't get the correct answer for **05.4** you can still get the full marks for question **05.5**, as an error in the previous question will be 'carried forward'. This means you wouldn't be penalised for the same mistake twice.

06 Sea anemones are animals that live in the oceans. They are closely related to corals. Sea anemones have the ability to reproduce sexually and asexually.

06.1 Name the type of cell division used in asexual reproduction. **[1 mark]**

06.2 Describe the main stages in this type of cell division. **[3 marks]**

07 Most species of tomato have 24 chromosomes present in the nuclei of their cells.

Exam Tip

Pollen cells are gametes.

07.1 Write down how many chromosomes would be present in an adult tomato cell. **[1 mark]**

07.2 Write down how many chromosomes would be present in a tomato pollen cell. **[1 mark]**

07.3 Tomato plants reproduce sexually. Identify from the list below the **two** features that are present in sexual reproduction. **[2 marks]**

there is no mixing of genetic information

two parents are required

gametes fuse together

clones are produced

07.4 Describe the main steps in the production of a tomato pollen cell. **[4 marks]**

08 The genetic material found in the nuclei of human cells is composed of the chemical DNA.

08.1 Describe the main features of the structure of DNA. **[3 marks]**

08.2 Genes are small sections of DNA. Each gene contains a code. Describe what a gene codes for. **[2 marks]**

08.3 In 2003, scientists announced that they had managed to sequence the entire human genome. Define the term genome. **[1 mark]**

08.4 Outline some of the important benefits of sequencing the human genome. **[3 marks]**

09 There are two types of cell division that occur in humans: meiosis and mitosis.

09.1 Write down where meiosis occurs in a female. **[1 mark]**

09.2 Write down where meiosis occurs in a male. **[1 mark]**

09.3 Compare the processes of mitosis and meiosis. **[4 marks]**

09.4 Explain why meiosis results in genetic variation. **[3 marks]**

09.5 Explain why the development of a fetus involves both mitosis and meiosis. **[4 marks]**

> **Exam Tip**
>
> For a 'compare' answer give a statement about mitosis and then give the comparable statement for meiosis.

10 Cystic fibrosis (CF) is a genetically inherited disorder. People who have this condition produce excess mucus in their intestines. This can block digestive juices from the pancreas from being released and can cover the villi.

10.1 Explain why people with CF are likely to be underweight if they do not follow a special diet. **[4 marks]**

10.2 Suggest why excess mucus production in the lungs leads to an increased rate of respiratory infections. **[2 marks]**

10.3 Currently there is no cure for CF. However, improved approaches to treatment have led to significant increases in life expectancy, from around 20 years old in 1980 to around 40 years old today.

A couple has a history of CF in both their families. After discovering they have conceived, the woman is offered an amniocentesis test. Amniocentesis involves taking fluid from around the developing fetus. The fluid contains fetal cells, which can be screened for the presence of the recessive allele that causes CF. The test is carried out at around 15 weeks of pregnancy.

Discuss the social, economic, and ethical considerations involved in performing an amniocentesis test for this couple. **[6 marks]**

> **Exam Tip**
>
> You are being tested to see if you can pull the important information out of a large block of text and mix it with what you have been taught:
>
> 1. read the text in full
> 2. go over the text and highlight all the social considerations in pink
> 3. highlight all the economic considerations in blue
> 4. highlight all the ethical considerations in green
> 5. make notes on any other considerations you can think of
> 6. write your answer, making sure it is balanced across the three points

11 **Figure 3** shows the family tree of five people (**1**–**5**).

Figure 3

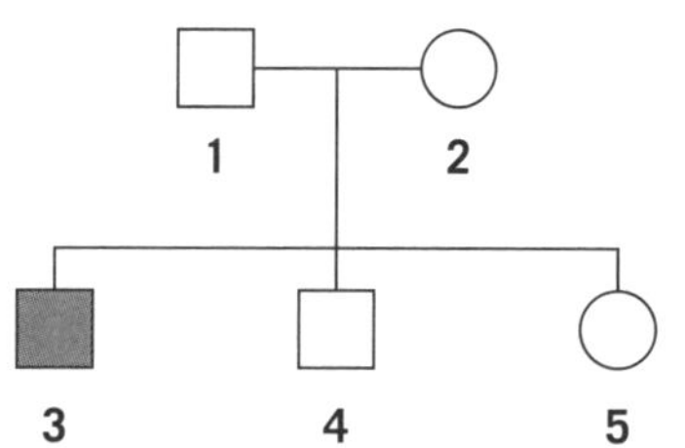

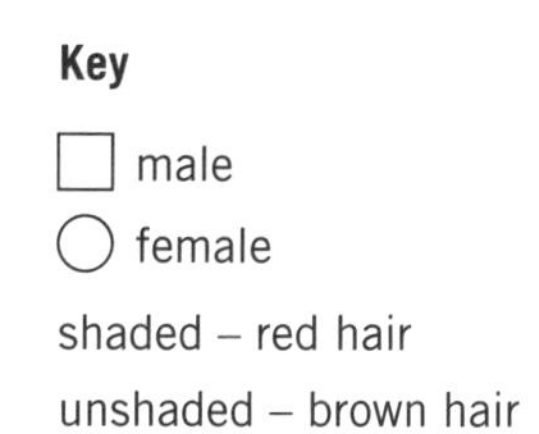

11.1 Write down the phenotype of person **4**. **[2 marks]**

11.2 Use evidence from **Figure 3** to explain whether red hair is caused by a dominant or recessive allele. **[3 marks]**

11.3 Identify the genotype of person **1**. Choose **one** answer. **[1 mark]**

homozygous dominant   homozygous recessive   heterozygous

11.4 A heterozygous female and a homozygous recessive male wish to have a child.
Draw a genetic cross diagram to calculate the likelihood of the couple having a child with red hair. Give your answer as a percentage. **[4 marks]**

> **Exam Tip**
> You need to give both the sex of the person and the colour of their hair in **11.1**.

12 Sickle cell anaemia is an inherited disorder that causes red blood cells to develop abnormally **(Figure 4)**.

Figure 4

normal
red blood cells

sickled
red blood cells

Sickle-shaped red blood cells cannot carry out their function properly.

12.1 Red blood cells are full of the protein haemoglobin. In a person with sickle cell anaemia haemoglobin does not function properly.
Describe the function of haemoglobin. **[1 mark]**

> **Exam Tip**
> Relate this to the function of red blood cells.

12.2 Suggest **one** symptom of sickle cell anaemia. **[1 mark]**

12.3 Sickle cell anaemia is caused by a recessive allele.
Draw a Punnett square diagram to explain how a couple who do not have sickle cell anaemia can have a child who has the disorder. **[4 marks]**

12.4 Due to their shape, sickle red blood cells can stick together and cause blockages.
Explain why people with sickle cell anaemia have a higher risk of developing a stroke. **[3 marks]**

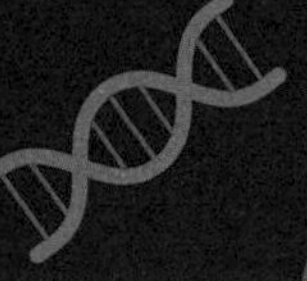

B16 Evolution

Theory of evolution

Evolution is the gradual change in the inherited characteristics of a population over time.

Evolution occurs through the process of **natural selection** and may result in the formation of new species.

Process of natural selection

The theory of evolution by natural selection states that

- organisms within species show a wide range of variation in phenotype
- individuals with characteristics most suited to the environment are more likely to survive and breed successfully
- these characteristics are then passed on to their offspring.

Key terms

Make sure you can write a definition for these key terms.

antibiotic resistance
binomial system
evolution
evolutionary tree
extinction
fossil record
natural selection
three-domain system

Evidence for evolution

The theory of evolution by natural selection is now widely accepted because there are lots of data to support it, such as

- it has been shown that characteristics are passed on to offspring in genes
- evidence from the **fossil record**
- the evolution of antibiotic resistance in bacteria.

Fossils

Fossils are the remains of organisms from millions of years ago, which are found in rocks.

Fossils can be formed from

- parts of an organism that do not decay because one or more of the conditions needed for decay are absent
- hard parts of an organism (e.g., bones) when replaced by minerals
- preservation of the traces of organisms (e.g., burrows, footprints, and rootlet traces).

Benefits of the fossil record	Problems with the fossil record
• can tell scientists how individual species have changed over time • fossils allow us to understand how life developed over the Earth's history • fossils can be used to track the movement of a species or its ancestors across the world	• many early organisms were soft-bodied, so most decayed before producing fossils • there are gaps in the fossil record as not all fossils have been found and others have been destroyed by geological or human activity – this means scientists cannot be certain about how life began on Earth

1 The reptile dies and falls to the ground

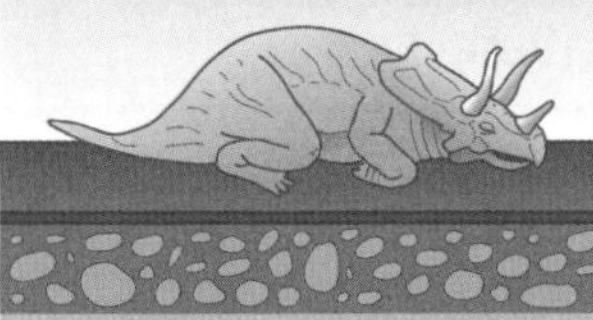

2 The flesh decays, leaving the skeleton to be covered in sand or soil and clay before it is damaged

3 Protected, over millions of years, the skeleton becomes mineralised and turns to rock. The rocks shift in the earth with the fossil trapped inside

4 Eventually, the fossil emerges as the rocks move and erosion takes place

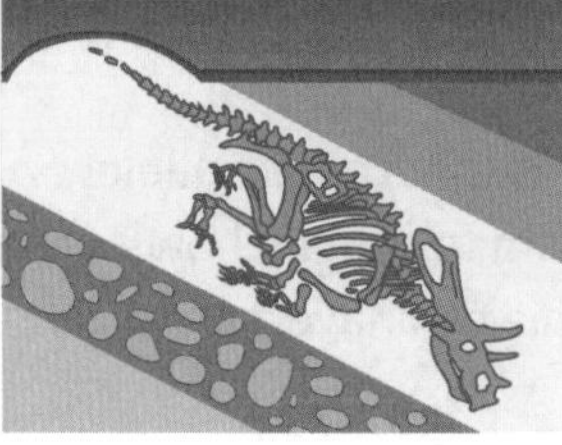

Extinction

Extinction is when there are no remaining individuals of a species still alive.

Factors that may contribute to a species' extinction include

- new predators
- new diseases or pathogens
- increased competition for resources or mates
- catastrophic events (e.g., asteroid impacts, volcanic eruptions, earthquakes)
- changes to the environment (e.g., climate change, destruction of habitats).

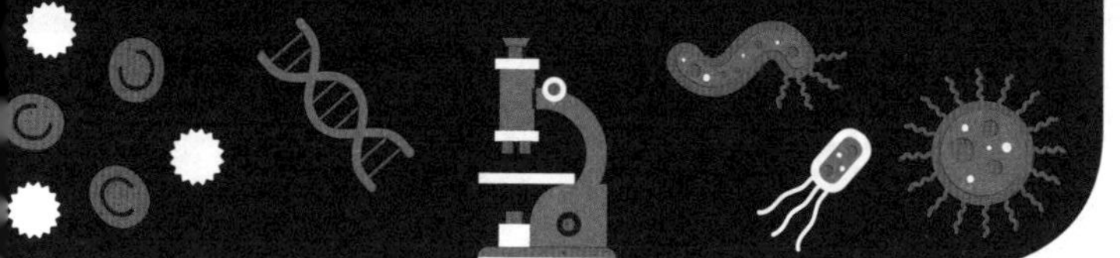

Resistant bacteria

Bacteria can evolve rapidly because they reproduce very quickly.

This has led to many strains of bacteria developing **antibiotic resistance**, such as MRSA. The development of antibiotic resistance in bacteria is evidence for the theory of evolution by natural selection.

Emergence of antibiotic resistance

The development of new antibiotics is expensive and slow, so is unlikely to keep up with the emergence of new antibiotic-resistant bacteria strains.

To reduce the rise of antibiotic-resistant strains

- doctors should only prescribe antibiotics for serious bacterial infections
- patients should complete their courses of antibiotics so all bacteria are killed and none survive to form resistant strains
- the use of antibiotics in farming and agriculture should be restricted.

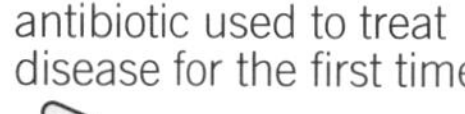

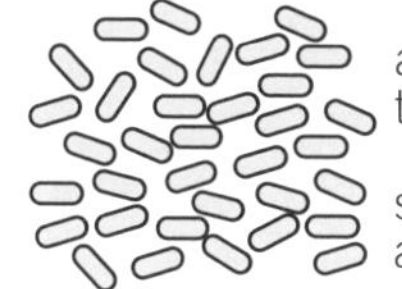

Classification of living organisms

Carl Linnaeus developed a system to classify living things into groups, based on their structure and characteristics.

New models of classification were proposed as understanding of biochemical processes developed and improvements in microscopes led to discoveries of internal structures.

There is now a **three-domain system** developed by Carl Woese, dividing organisms into

- Archaea (primitive bacteria usually living in extreme environments)
- Bacteria (true bacteria)
- Eukaryota (including protists, fungi, plants, and animals).

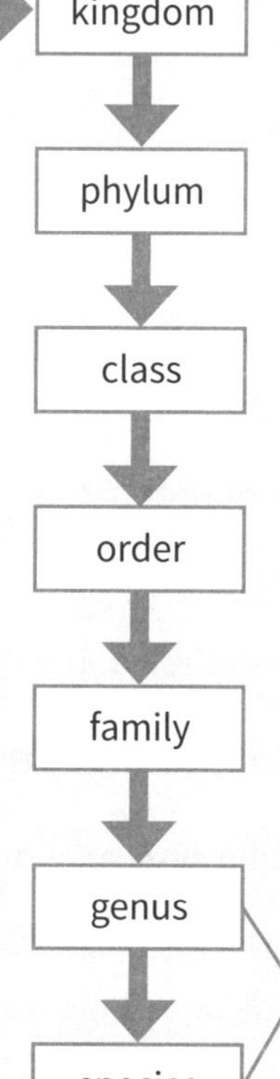

organisms are named by the **binomial system** of genus and species

Evolutionary trees

Evolutionary trees use current classification data for living organisms and fossil data for extinct organisms to show how scientists believe organisms are related.

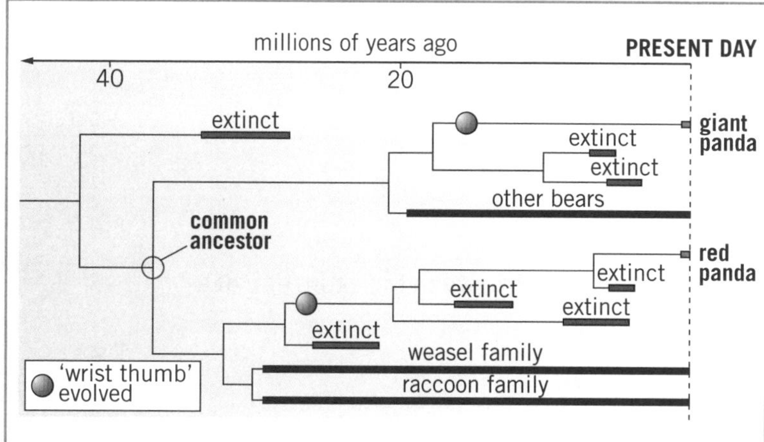

Revision tip

Remember Lots of students get the key words in this topic mixed up – evolution and natural selection are linked but are not the same, so learn the differences carefully.

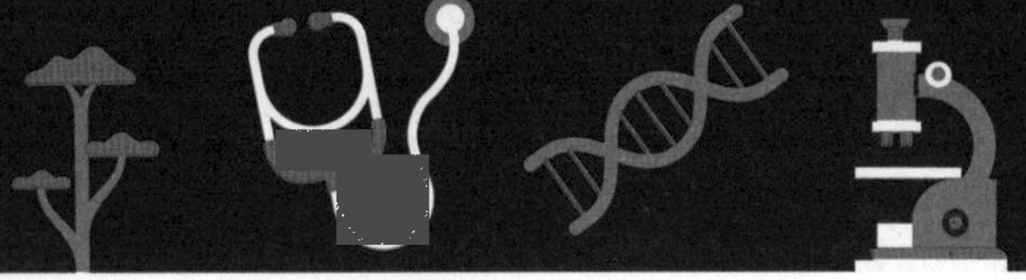

Learn the answers to the questions below, then cover the answers column with a piece of paper and write as many as you can. Check and repeat.

	B16 questions	Answers
1	What is evolution?	change in the inherited characteristics of a population over time through natural selection, which may result in a new species
2	What is the theory of evolution by natural selection?	the organisms that are best adapted to their environment are most likely to survive and pass on these characteristics to their offspring
3	What evidence supports the theory of evolution?	• parents pass on their characteristics to offspring in genes • fossil record evidence • evolution of antibiotic-resistant bacteria
4	What are fossils?	remains of organisms from millions of years ago, found in rocks
5	How might fossils be formed?	• parts of an organism do not decay because the conditions needed for decay are absent • traces of organisms are preserved • parts of an organism are replaced by minerals
6	What are the benefits of the fossil record?	can learn how species changed and how life developed on Earth, and can track the movement of species across the world
7	What are the problems with the fossil record?	• many early organisms were soft-bodied so left few fossils • gaps in the fossil record as not all fossils have been found and some have been destroyed
8	What is extinction?	no individuals of a species are still alive
9	What factors contribute to the extinction of a species?	• predators • diseases or pathogens • competition for resources or mates • catastrophic events • changes in the habitat
10	What is the binomial system?	naming of organisms by their genus and species
11	What classification system did Carl Woese introduce?	three-domain system of Archaea, Bacteria, and Eukaryota
12	Why can bacteria evolve rapidly?	they reproduce at a fast rate
13	How do antibiotic-resistant strains of bacteria develop?	mutations that allow the strain to survive and reproduce in the presence of the antibiotic

Put paper here

Now go back and use the questions below to check your knowledge from previous chapters.

Previous questions | Answers

	Previous questions	Answers
1	How do new phenotype variants occur?	mutations
2	What is cancer?	a result of changes in cells that lead to uncontrolled growth and cell division by mitosis
3	Why is studying the human genome important?	• search for genes linked to certain diseases • understanding and treatment of inherited disorders • tracing past human migration
4	Name the four main components of blood.	red blood cells, white blood cells, plasma, platelets
5	What are artificial hearts used for?	keep patients alive whilst waiting for a transplant, or allow the heart to rest for recovery
6	What is a genome?	the entire genetic material of an organism
7	What are the male and female sex chromosomes in humans?	XX – female, XY – male
8	How many chromosomes do normal human body cells have?	23 pairs (46)

Put paper here

Put paper here

Put paper here

Maths Skills

Practise your maths skills using the worked example and practice questions below.

Significant figures	Worked example	Practice
Scientists often give numbers that are expressed to two or three significant figures (s.f.). This is to avoid giving irrelevant or unnecessary figures in a very small or large number, or to avoid introducing error in a result. Significant figures can also be used to make large or complicated calculations easier. A key point to remember is that leading zeroes (before a decimal point) are *never* significant.	Zeros within a number count as significant figures. For example, 3.280 34 has 6 significant figures. Leading zeros are never significant, so 0.007 60 has 3 significant figures. **Example 1:** Round 2.837 076 to 3 s.f. First count the significant figures from left to right, giving 2.83 to 3 s.f. As the 4th digit is a 7, the answer is rounded up, giving 2.84. **Example 2:** Round 0.036 01 to 3 s.f. Number the significant figures, remembering that leading zeros are never significant. As the 4th digit is a 1, the answer is not rounded up, giving 0.0360.	**1** Round 0.009 909 to 3 s.f. **2** Round 53 879 to 2 s.f. **3** Round 0.005 089 to 1 s.f. **4** Round 98 347 to 2 s.f. **5** Round 3.5175 to 3 s.f.

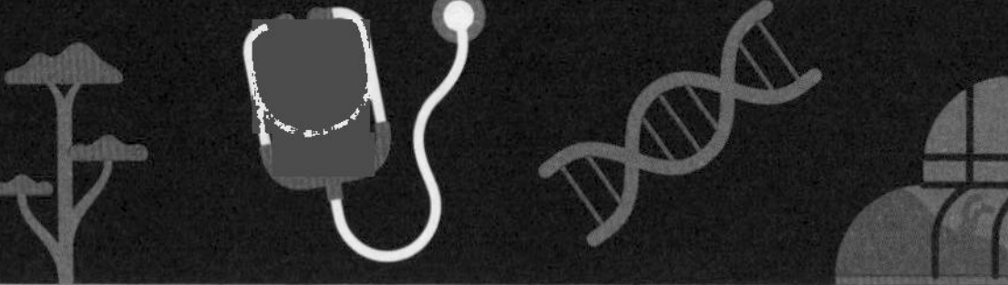

Exam-style questions

01 New species develop as a result of natural selection.

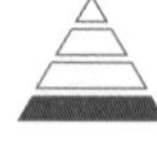

01.1 Define the term species. **[1 mark]**

____

____

01.2 **Figure 1** shows part of the evolutionary tree of primates.

Figure 1

Identify the organism in **Figure 1** that most recently shared a common ancestor with humans. **[1 mark]**

____

01.3 In 1858, Darwin proposed his theory of evolution by natural selection.

Use the words from the box to complete the passage that describes how organisms evolve by natural selection. **[4 marks]**

characteristics	die	DNA	genotype
phenotype	similarities	survive	variation

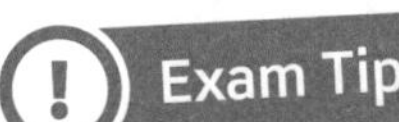

Not all the words will be used. Don't let this worry you.

Individual organisms within a species show ______________ as a result of differences in their DNA. Individuals who have characteristics that are most suited to their environment are more likely to ______________ and reproduce. The individuals pass on these favourable ______________ to their offspring. This results in more individuals displaying these favourable characteristics in their ______________.

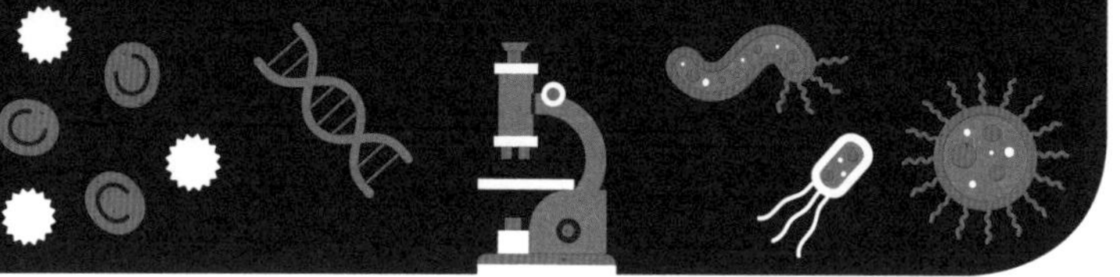

02 Some bacteria have evolved a resistance to antibiotics.

One type of antibiotic-resistant bacteria is called MRSA. MRSA infections cause dizziness, nausea, high body temperature, and skin rashes. They can be fatal.

02.1 Explain how MRSA bacteria have evolved a resistance to antibiotics. **[4 marks]**

____

____

____

____

____

____

____

Exam Tip

Do not start your answer 'MRSA bacteria have evolved a resistance to antibiotics because…'. That is just repeating the question and will gain you no marks.

02.2 **Figure 2** shows the number of fatal cases of MRSA between 1995 and 2005 in the UK.

Figure 2

number of fatal cases of MRSA (0–1800)

year (1995 1996 1997 1998 1999 2000 2001 2002 2003 2004 2005)

Calculate the percentage change in the number of fatal cases of MRSA between 1995 and 2005. **[2 marks]**

________________ %

Draw lines across from the bars at 1995 and 2005 to help to read off the values on the *y*-axis.

02.3 Suggest and explain **one** reason why the number of fatal cases of MRSA increased between 1995 and 2005. **[2 marks]**

02.4 The number of fatal cases of MRSA declined between 2006 and 2012. Suggest **two** reasons for this decline. **[2 marks]**

1

2

02.5 Antibiotics have been widely available since the mid-20th century. Explain why the evolution of antibiotic-resistant bacteria has occurred rapidly since then. **[2 marks]**

03 Dodos were flightless birds that lived on an island called Mauritius. When European sailors landed on the island, they brought dogs and rats with them. The dodo became extinct.

03.1 Describe what is meant by the term extinction. **[1 mark]**

03.2 Using the information in the question and your own knowledge, suggest why the dodo became extinct. **[4 marks]**

03.3 In 2016, the dodo genome was sequenced for the first time. Explain what is meant by the term genome. **[1 mark]**

03.4 Suggest **two** reasons for sequencing the dodo genome. **[2 marks]**

> **Exam Tip**
>
> Even if you have no knowledge of your own, the main body of the question provides you with lots of useful information, such as *flightless birds* and *dogs* and *rats*.

04 Fossils provide evidence of organisms that existed millions of years ago.

04.1 Describe **three** ways fossils can be made. **[3 marks]**

04.2 Explain why there are gaps in the fossil record. **[3 marks]**

04.3 Fossils provide evidence for Darwin's theory of evolution by natural selection. Give **one** reason why people did not believe Darwin's theory when he first proposed it. **[1 mark]**

04.4 Give **one** other piece of evidence for Darwin's theory. **[1 mark]**

> **Exam Tip**
>
> Question **04.1** is a *three*-mark question for giving *three* ways fossils can be made – so don't write lots for each method, it won't get you any extra marks.

05 A group of scientists develop a drug called 'Drug 2030' to treat bacterial infections. In trials, the drug proves highly successful at treating many bacterial infections. However, some bacteria have a natural resistance to the active agent in Drug 2030.

Exam Tip

This is a hypothetical drug to see if you can apply what you know about other drugs and developing antibiotic resistance to a new situation. Do not spend any time worrying about what this drug does, or panicking that you haven't heard of this before.

05.1 Explain how resistance to Drug 2030 could lead to changes in the population of bacteria. **[6 marks]**

05.2 Describe the features of a successful antibiotic drug. **[2 marks]**

05.3 An increasing number of strains of bacteria are becoming resistant to antibiotics.
Explain **two** steps that people should follow to help reduce the number of resistant strains of bacteria. **[4 marks]**

06 Scientists have sorted all known living organisms into groups.

06.1 Describe how organisms are classified into groups according to the Linnaean classification system. **[2 marks]**

06.2 Blue tits are common garden birds. The blue tit's scientific name is *Cyanistes caeruleus*.
Identify which **two** of the following statements are true about blue tits. **[2 marks]**

The blue tit belongs to the kingdom Animalia.

The blue tit belongs to the species Chordata.

The blue tit belongs to the phylum *caeruleus.*

The blue tit belongs to the genus *Cyanistes.*

Exam Tip

To get the four marks in question **06.3** you'll have to give the advances *and* explain the difference they made.

06.3 A number of different classification systems have been proposed. Explain **two** advances that have taken place that have led to the development of new classification systems. **[4 marks]**

07 Ammonite fossils are often found on beaches in the UK. Ammonites were marine animals belonging to the phylum Mollusca. They had a coiled external shell that provided protection. Ammonites probably fed on small plankton or vegetation growing on the sea floor.

07.1 Explain why only the shell of the animal is seen in an ammonite fossil. **[3 marks]**

07.2 The ammonites became extinct at the end of the Cretaceous period, at roughly the same time as the dinosaurs disappeared. Suggest and explain **two** reasons why ammonites became extinct. **[4 marks]**

Exam Tip

This question is more often seen asked the other way around – think about what causes organisms to evolve and then think about why they might not.

07.3 The fossil record shows that ammonites lived between approximately 200 million and 60 million years ago with little change to their basic structure.
Explain why these organisms did not evolve significantly over this period of time. **[2 marks]**

08 Carl Woese developed a three-domain system of classification.

08.1 Which of the following is a domain in Woese's classification system? Choose **one** answer. **[1 mark]**

Vertebrates | Archaea | Chordata | *Felis*

08.2 Give the name of the domain that dogs belong to. **[1 mark]**

08.3 Describe how DNA analysis helped Woese develop his classification system. **[4 marks]**

08.4 Evolutionary trees are built up through DNA analysis, similarities in characteristics, and fossil evidence.

Figure 3 shows an example of an evolutionary tree.

Figure 3

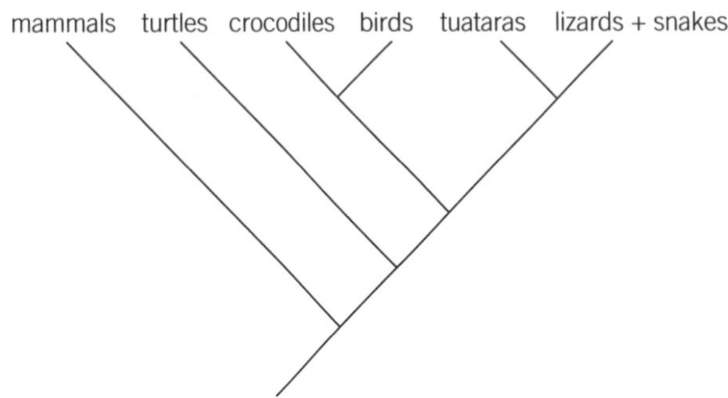

Give **three** conclusions that can be drawn from the evolutionary tree in **Figure 3**. **[3 marks]**

Exam Tip

Give evidence from the tree, just as you would from a graph.

09 **Figure 4** shows an evolutionary tree for some dinosaurs.

Figure 4

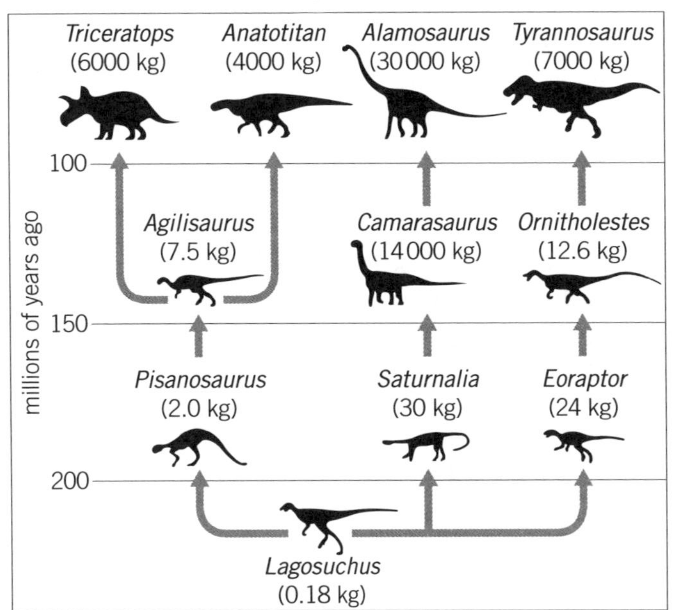

09.1 Define the term extinct. **[1 mark]**

09.2 Write down the name of the common ancestor of *Triceratops* and *Anatotitan*. **[1 mark]**

09.3 Describe the trend in the mass of the dinosaurs over time. **[1 mark]**

09.4 Estimate the time taken for *Saturnalia* to evolve into *Camarasaurus*. **[1 mark]**

Exam Tip

To help you find the common ancestor, use a highlighter or a coloured pen to trace the lines back.

10 Life on Earth began 4 billion years ago. It is estimated that 5 billion different species have lived on Earth. Of these, it is estimated that 14 million species are alive today, and that only 1.2 million species alive today have been identified and classified.

10.1 Calculate the proportion of species estimated to be alive that have not yet been identified. **[3 marks]**

10.2 Suggest **two** reasons why the proportion of species identified is only a small fraction of the total estimated number of species. **[2 marks]**

10.3 Explain why over 99% of species that ever lived can no longer be found alive on Earth. **[3 marks]**

10.4 It is estimated that 1250 species per year become extinct. Compare the current rate of extinction with the mean extinction rate since life began on Earth. **[4 marks]**

10.5 Suggest **three** reasons for the difference in extinction rates calculated in **10.4**. **[3 marks]**

> **Exam Tip**
>
> Be careful with which numbers you select for the calculation in **10.1**.

11 Overfishing in the North Sea between the 1960s and 1990s significantly depleted fish stocks.
To try to support fish populations the Government brought in a number of new rules for deep sea fishing. One of these rules requires the use of large-mesh fishing nets that contain large holes.

11.1 Suggest and explain why fishing vessels were required to use nets with large holes. **[3 marks]**

11.2 Following the period of heavy fishing in the North Sea, scientists discovered that fish species had started to breed even when they were still small. Explain how changes to the minimum fish breeding size occurred. **[6 marks]**

11.3 **Figure 5** shows the estimated North Sea cod population from 1970 to 2015.

Figure 5

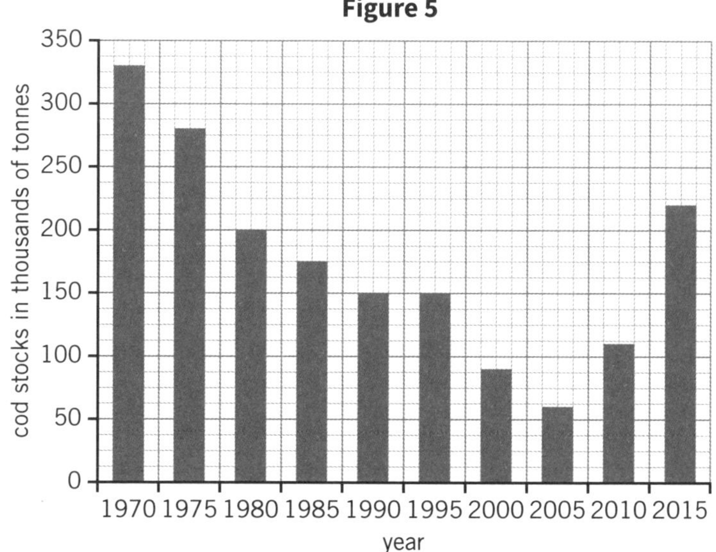

Evaluate the success of the Government's strategy to support North Sea fish stocks. **[3 marks]**

11.4 Estimate the North Sea cod stocks for the year 2020. Justify your answer. **[4 marks]**

> **Exam Tip**
>
> The y-axis is in thousands of tonnes. Be sure to use this unit in your answers – using tonnes would be incorrect.

B17 Adaptation

Ecosystem organisation

Individual organisms

Population
the total number of organisms of the same species that live in one specific geographical area

Community
group of two or more populations of different species living in one specific geographical area

Ecosystem
the interaction of a community of living organisms with the non-living parts of their environment

Competition

To survive and reproduce, organisms require a supply of resources from their surroundings and from the other living organisms there.

This can create competition, where organisms within a community compete for resources.

There are two types of competition – **interspecific competition** is between organisms of different species and **intraspecific competition** is between organisms of the same species.

Animals often compete for
- food
- mates
- territory.

Plants often compete for
- light
- space
- water and mineral ions from the soil.

Interdependence

Within a community each species **interacts** with many others and may depend on other species for things like food, shelter, pollination, and seed dispersal.

If one species is removed it can affect the whole community – this is called **interdependence**.

A stable community is one where all the species and environmental factors are in balance so that population sizes remain fairly constant.

An example of this is the interaction between predator and prey populations, which rise and fall in a constant cycle so that each remains within a stable range.

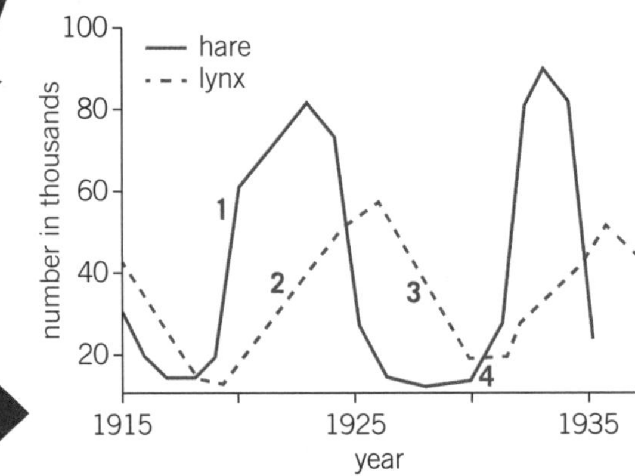

1 If the population of hares increases there is a larger food supply for the lynx.

2 This can therefore support more lynx, so more offspring survive.

3 The growing numbers of lynx eventually reduce the food supply. The number of predators starts to decrease.

4 The prey population starts to increase once more – the cycle then begins again.

Abiotic factors

Abiotic factors are non-living factors in the ecosystem that can affect a community.

Too much or too little of the following abiotic factors can negatively affect the community in an ecosystem:

- carbon dioxide levels for plants
- light intensity
- moisture levels
- oxygen levels for animals that live in water
- soil pH and mineral content
- temperature
- wind intensity and direction.

Biotic factors

Biotic factors are living factors in the ecosystem that can affect a community.

For example, the following biotic factors would all negatively affect populations in a community:

- decreased availability of food
- new predators arriving
- new pathogens
- competition between species, for example, one species outcompeting another for food or shelter, causing a decline in the other species' population.

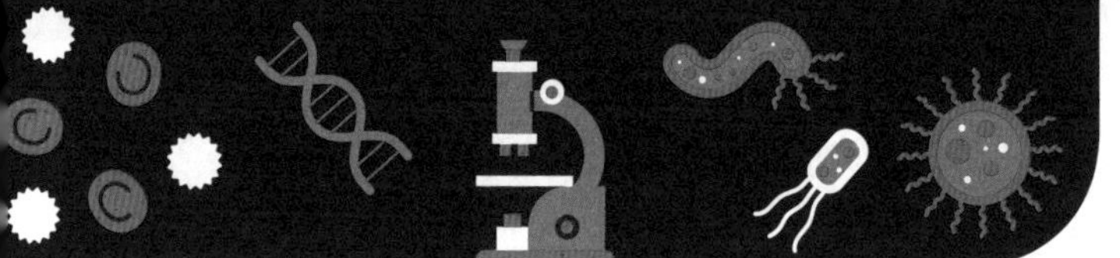

B17

Adaptations of organisms

Organisms have features – **adaptations** – that enable them to survive in the conditions in which they live. The adaptations of an organism may allow it to outcompete others, and provide it with an evolutionary advantage.

Structural adaptations

The physical features that allow an organism to successfully compete:

- sharp teeth to hunt prey
- colouring that may provide camouflage to hide from predators or to hunt prey
- a large or small body surface area-to-volume ratio.

Behavioural adaptations

The behaviour of an organism that gives it an advantage:

- making nests to shelter offspring or attract a mate
- courtship dances to attract a mate
- use of tools to obtain food
- working together in packs.

Functional adaptations

Adaptations related to processes that allow an organism to survive:

- photosynthesis in plants
- production of poisons or venom to deter predators or kill prey
- changes in reproduction timings.

You can work out how an organism is adapted to where it lives when given information on its environment and what it looks like.

For example, without the following adaptations the organisms below would be at a disadvantage in their environment.

Organism	Example adaptations
	• white fur for camouflage when hunting prey • feet with large surface area to distribute weight on snow • small ears to reduce heat loss • thick fur for insulation
	• feet with large surface area to distribute weight on sand • hump stores fat to provide energy when food is scarce • tough mouth and tongue to allow camel to eat cacti • long eyelashes to keep sand out of eyes
	• spines instead of leaves to reduce surface area and therefore water loss, and to deter consumers • long roots to reach water underground • large, fleshy stem to store water

Some organisms are **extremophiles**, which means they live in environments that are very extreme where most other organisms could not survive. For example, areas with

- very high or low temperatures
- extreme pressures
- high salt concentrations
- highly acidic or alkaline conditions
- low levels of oxygen or water.

Bacteria that live in deep sea vents are extremophiles.

Deep sea vents are formed when seawater circulates through hot volcanic rocks on the sea floor. These environments have very high pressures and temperatures, no sunlight, and are strongly acidic.

Make sure you can write a definition for these key terms.

abiotic factor · adaptation · biotic factor · community · ecosystem · extremophile · interaction · interdependence · interspecific competition · intraspecific competition · population

Retrieval

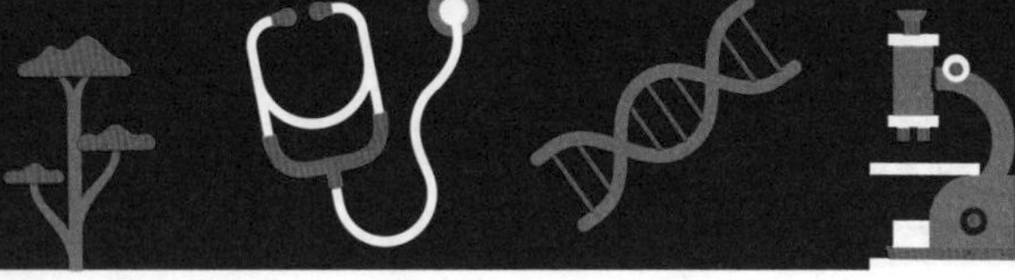

Learn the answers to the questions below, then cover the answers column with a piece of paper and write as many as you can. Check and repeat.

	B17 questions	Answers
1	What is a population?	total number of organisms of the same species that live in a specific geographical area
2	What is a community?	group of two or more populations of different species living in a specific geographical area
3	What is an ecosystem?	the interaction of a community of living organisms with the non-living parts of their environment
4	What is competition?	contest between organisms within a community for resources
5	What is interdependence?	when species in a community depend on others for resources and shelter
6	What do animals often compete for?	food, mates, and territory
7	What do plants often compete for?	light, space, water, and mineral ions
8	What is an abiotic factor?	non-living factor that can affect a community
9	List the abiotic factors that can affect a community.	• carbon dioxide levels for plants • light intensity • moisture levels • oxygen levels for animals that live in water • soil pH and mineral content • temperature • wind intensity and direction
10	What is a biotic factor?	living factor that can affect a community
11	List the biotic factors that can affect a community.	• availability of food • new predators • new pathogens • competition between species
12	What is a stable community?	when all species and environmental factors are in balance, so population sizes remain fairly constant
13	How do adaptations help an organism?	enable the organism to survive in the conditions in which it lives
14	What are the three types of adaptations?	structural, behavioural, and functional
15	What is an extremophile?	an organism that lives in a very extreme environment
16	What makes an environment extreme?	• very high or low temperatures • extreme pressures • high salt concentrations • highly acidic or alkaline conditions • lack of oxygen or water

Put paper here

Now go back and use the questions below to check your knowledge from previous chapters.

Previous questions / Answers

	Previous questions	Answers
1	What classification system did Carl Woese introduce?	three-domain system of Archaea, Bacteria, and Eukaryota
2	How might fossils be formed?	• parts of an organism do not decay because the conditions needed for decay are absent • traces of organisms are preserved • parts of an organism are replaced by minerals
3	What classification system did Carl Woese introduce?	three-domain system of Archaea, Bacteria, and Eukaryota
4	Where is the pituitary gland located?	brain
5	Describe how temperature affects the rate of photosynthesis.	increasing temperature increases the rate of photosynthesis as the reaction rate increases – at high temperatures enzymes are denatured so the rate of photosynthesis quickly decreases
6	What is the function of an antitoxin?	neutralise toxins produced by pathogens by binding to them
7	What is the function of the nervous system?	enables organisms to react to their surroundings and coordinates behaviour

Put paper here

Maths Skills

Practise your maths skills using the worked example and practice questions below.

Estimations

Estimates are often used in science before an exact calculation is done, such as when dealing with large numbers like population sizes.

For example, if you work out how many snails live in 1 m^2, you can use this value to estimate how many snails live in an area of 10 m^2.

You can also make estimates from sets of data.

To make an estimate based on a graph, try drawing a line or curve of best fit through the data points. This will enable you to draw a straight line tangent between two points, from which you can make an estimate.

Worked example

A grassy field on a farm measured 120 metres by 90 metres.

A student wanted to estimate the number of daisies growing in the field.

The student placed a 1 m × 1 m quadrat in one position in an area that daisies were found in.

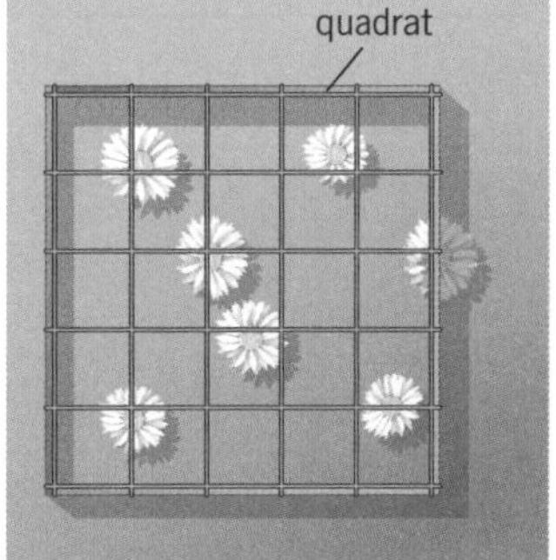

To estimate the number of daisies in the field:

Number of daisies in 1 × 1 m quadrat = 7

Area of the field (120 × 90) = 10 800 m^2

7 × 10 800 = 75 600 daisies estimated in the field

Practice

1 The average number of dandelions in a 1 metre by 1 metre square of a park is 6. The park measures 230 metres by 350 metres.

Estimate the number of dandelions in the park.

2 The average number of daisies in a 1 metre by 1 metre square of a field is 28. The field measures 180 metres by 80 metres.

Estimate the number of daisies in the field.

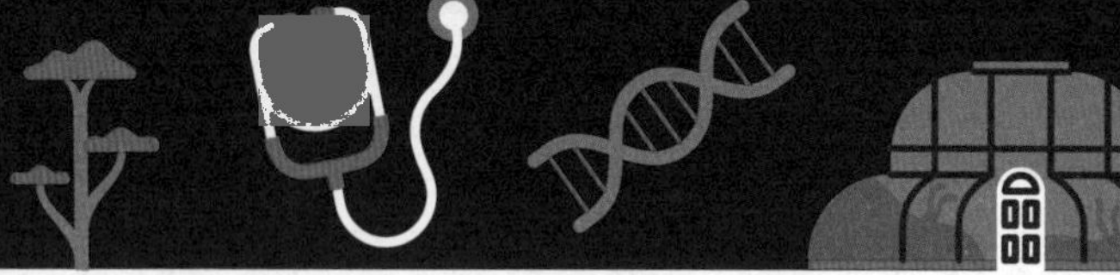

Exam-style questions

01 Over the past 50 years, scientists in Italy have been monitoring the populations of red and grey squirrels.

Red squirrels are native to the Piedmont region. Grey squirrels were introduced to the area in the mid-20th century.

To monitor the populations of these species, the scientists divided a map of the area into squares of equal size, known as cells. They then recorded the number of cells in which each species of squirrel was present.

01.1 Evaluate whether this technique provides data on population size. **[2 marks]**

____

____

____

Exam Tip

For this question, you need to give your opinion and the reason you have that opinion.

01.2 The results of the monitoring are shown in **Figure 1**.

Figure 1

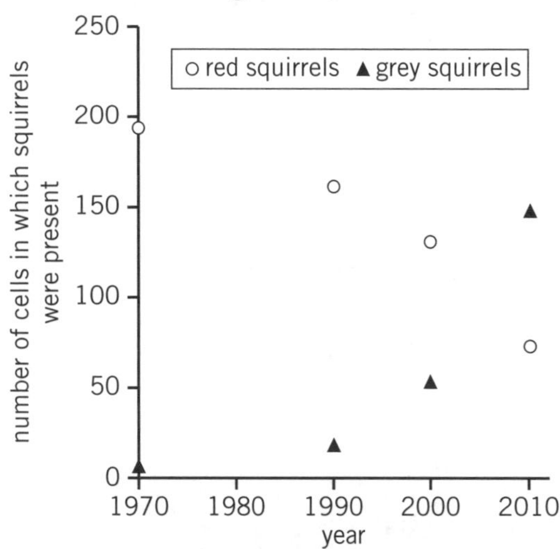

Describe the trends shown in the graph. **[3 marks]**

____

____

____

____

Exam Tip

Draw a line for the red squirrels and another for the grey squirrels to make the trend easier to see.

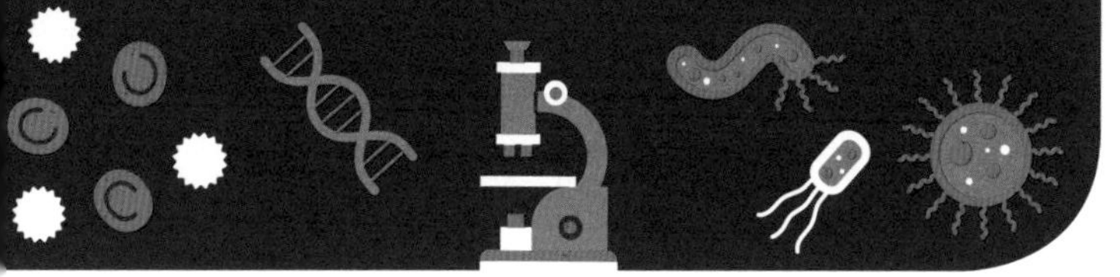

01.3 **Table 1** provides information on the two squirrel species.

Table 1

	Red squirrel	Grey squirrel
Life expectancy	7 years	2–4 years
Reproduction	up to six young, twice a year	up to nine young, twice a year
Age of sexual maturity	12 months	12 months
Survival rate of offspring	15%	40%
Health	*Parapox* virus results in high levels of fatalities	carriers of *Parapox* virus

Using **Table 1**, suggest reasons for the changes seen in squirrel populations in Italy. **[4 marks]**

Exam Tip

All the information you need to get the marks is in the table. Tick off each piece of information as you use it in your answer.

01.4 Five breeding pairs of red squirrels are introduced into a new area, where no squirrel populations currently exist.

Using data from **Table 1**, estimate the maximum number of offspring that survive from the breeding pairs after four years. **[4 marks]**

Exam Tip

Take this year by year – how many offspring are there by the end of the first year, how many by the end of the second year...

01.5 Suggest reasons why the total population of red squirrels may be higher, or lower, than the value calculated in **01.4**. **[3 marks]**

02 Common seals are found in the seas surrounding the UK.

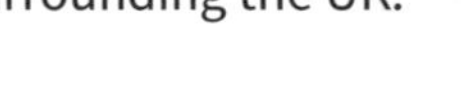

Figure 2

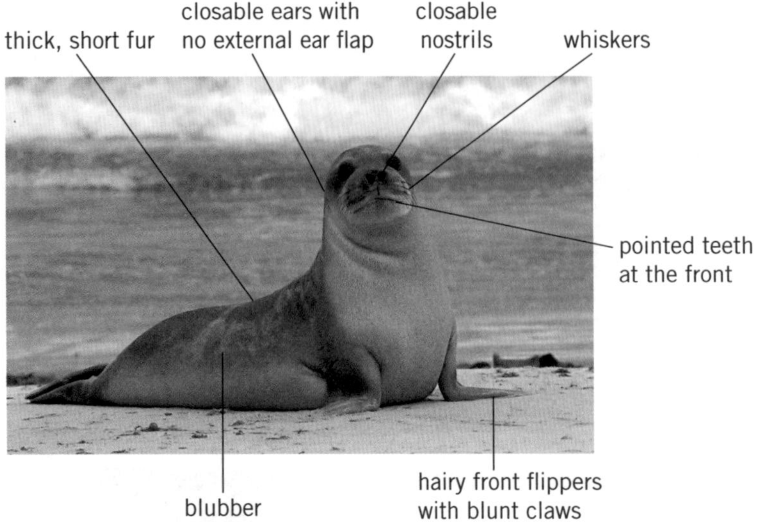

02.1 Using **Figure 2** and your own knowledge, explain **two** ways that seals are adapted for swimming. **[4 marks]**

1

2

> **Exam Tip**
>
> Even if you haven't studied seals in class, you can apply your knowledge of adaptations in other animals to answer this question.

02.2 Suggest why seals have closable ears and nostrils. **[1 mark]**

02.3 Arctic seals are another species of seal that are adapted to live in cold regions of the world.

Suggest and explain **two** ways in which Arctic seals may differ from the common seal. **[4 marks]**

1

2

03 An ecosystem is made up of a community interacting with the environment.
The size and make-up of the community are affected by the abiotic and biotic factors present in the ecosystem.
One example of an ecosystem is a woodland.

03.1 Describe what is meant by a community. **[1 mark]**

03.2 Give **one** example of an abiotic factor in a woodland. **[1 mark]**

03.3 Give **one** example of a biotic factor in a woodland. **[1 mark]**

Exam Tip

The biotic factors are the living ones.

03.4 Beech trees and ivy compete in a woodland ecosystem.
Name **two** resources these species compete for. **[2 marks]**

03.5 Describe **one** way in which beech trees support the presence of animals in a woodland. **[1 mark]**

04 Blackberry bushes are commonly found in UK hedgerows. They are often referred to as brambles as they have long, thorny, and arching stems. They can grow up to several metres tall.

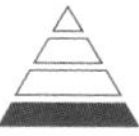

04.1 Suggest **two** ways a blackberry bush is adapted to its environment. **[2 marks]**

04.2 Blackberry seeds are found within the blackberry fruit.
Describe how blackberry seeds are dispersed. **[2 marks]**

04.3 Explain the advantages to the blackberry bush of dispersing its seeds. **[2 marks]**

05 Within a community, each species depends on other species in order to survive. This is called interdependence.

05.1 Explain the interdependence that occurs between bees and crops. **[4 marks]**

05.2 Fields of crops are fairly unstable communities.
Describe what is meant by a stable community. **[2 marks]**

05.3 Suggest and explain **two** ways a farmer could increase the stability of communities in their farmland, whilst still maximising crop yields. **[4 marks]**

06 Living organisms can be found almost everywhere on the planet.

06.1 Give the term that describes an organism that can live in an extreme environment. **[1 mark]**

06.2 Some species of fish are adapted to live at the bottom of the ocean.
One example is the angler fish.
Suggest **two** conditions that can be found at the bottom of the ocean. **[2 marks]**

06.3 The angler fish gets its name from an elongated spine that supports a light-producing organ known as a photophore. The photophore contains bacteria that can emit light through a chemical process known as bioluminescence. The photophore produces a blue-green light similar to that of a firefly.
Give the type of relationship that exists between the bacteria and the angler fish. **[1 mark]**

06.4 Angler fish are blind.
Suggest how their photophore helps them to survive. **[2 marks]**

07 Marram grass (**Figure 3**) is adapted to live in very dry conditions, such as sand dune systems. The leaves of the marram grass are adapted to survive when water is limited. In very dry conditions, the leaves of the marram grass roll up to form long tubes. This helps drain any water down towards the roots of the plant.

Figure 3

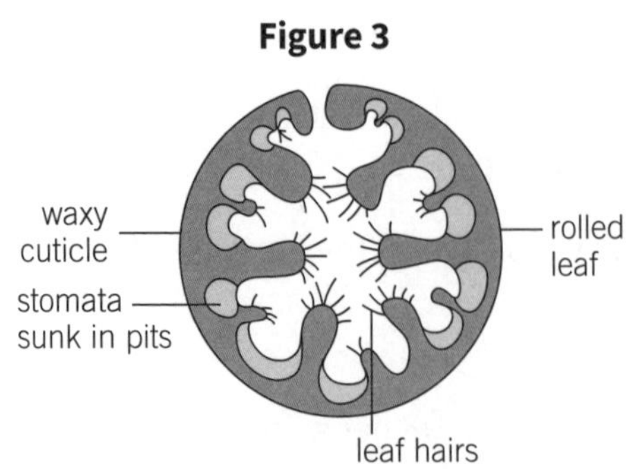

> **Exam Tip**
>
> Look at **Figure 3** – does the shape of the inside of the leaf look similar to something you have studied before?

Using **Figure 3** and your own knowledge, explain how the leaves of marram grass are adapted to survive with very limited water availability. **[6 marks]**

08 Deer can be found living in the wild in large areas of woodland in the UK.

08.1 Which of the following describes a woodland in which deer live? Choose **one** answer. **[1 mark]**

a community a population an ecosystem a habitat

08.2 Identify which of the following are examples of biotic factors that affect deer populations. Choose **two** answers. **[2 marks]**

hunting light intensity rainfall mass of grass present

08.3 Intraspecific competition is competition within a species. Identify and explain **two** resources that deer compete with each other for. **[4 marks]**

08.4 Some factors can affect a population indirectly. For example, temperature can indirectly affect a population of starfish. This is because rising temperatures kill coral, which is the food source of the starfish.

Explain how light intensity indirectly affects the size of a deer population. **[3 marks]**

> **Exam Tip**
>
> Think about what factors light intensity affects. How might this affect deer?

09 The zebra mussel is a small mussel originally native to the Caspian Sea.

A small population of these mussels was transferred to North America in the mid-1980s. One of the largest colonies exists in the Hudson River area. By the early 1990s, the biomass of the zebra mussel population exceeded the combined biomass of all other consumers in the Hudson River area.

Mussels are filter feeders: this means that they filter small organisms and organic particles out of the water. This has significantly increased the river water clarity.

Suggest and explain the positive and negative effects of the invasive species on the native populations of organisms in the Hudson River area. **[6 marks]**

> **Exam Tip**
>
> There is a large block of text here. This is very common in exams, which is why reading is great exam preparation.

> **Exam Tip**
>
> Read through the text and underline the positive effects and circle the negative effects.

10 Desert foxes and Arctic foxes show both similarities and differences in their appearance. These are summarised in **Table 2**.

Table 2

Type of fox	desert fox	Arctic fox
Habitat	desert	ice sheets
Fur colour	pale yellow	white
Ears	large	small
Feet	covered in hairs on both surfaces	covered in hairs on both surfaces
Body features	specialised kidneys that reduce water loss from the body	have a thick layer of fat underneath the skin
Average height of males	20 cm	30 cm
Average mass of males	1.0 kg	6.0 kg

10.1 Explain why the two species of fox are different colours. **[2 marks]**

Exam Tip

Think about where each species lives.

10.2 Suggest **two** reasons why the feet of the Arctic fox are covered in hairs. **[2 marks]**

10.3 The surface area : volume ratio of the foxes can be estimated by modelling their shape as a cube. Using this approach, the desert fox has a surface area : volume ratio of 3 : 10.
Estimate the surface area : volume ratio of an Arctic fox. **[3 marks]**

Exam Tip

For the desert fox we can assume each length is 20 cm.

So the volume would be $20 \times 20 \times 20 = 8000\ cm^3$, with a surface area of $6 \times (20 \times 20) = 2400$.

10.4 Explain why the two species of fox have different surface area : volume ratios. **[3 marks]**

11 Scientists classify organisms into groups.

11.1 Name **one** structure found inside a cell that scientists can use to classify organisms. **[1 mark]**

11.2 **Table 3** shows one way lions can be classified.
Name the scientist who devised this system of classification. **[1 mark]**

Table 3

Kingdom	Animalia
Phylum	Chordata
Class	Mammalia
______	Carnivora
Family	Felidae
Genus	*Panthera*
Species	*leo*

11.3 Give the name of the missing category in **Table 3**. **[1 mark]**

11.4 Use **Table 3** to give the binomial name of lions. **[1 mark]**

11.5 Explain why classification systems are useful to scientists. **[3 marks]**

Knowledge

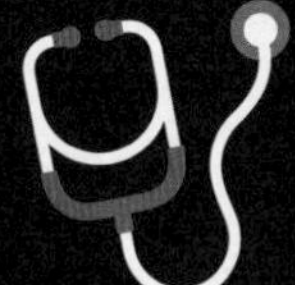

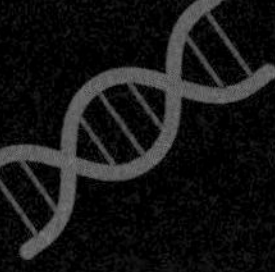

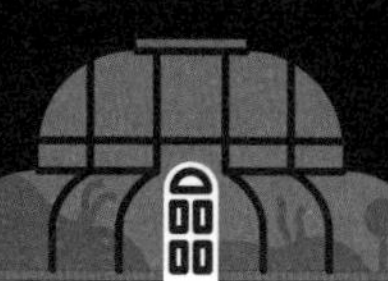

B18 Humans and the ecosystem

Levels of organisation

Feeding relationships within a community can be represented by **food chains**.

Photosynthetic organisms that synthesise molecules are the producers of all **biomass** for life on Earth, and so are the first step in all food chains.

A range of experimental methods using transects and quadrats are used by ecologists to determine the distributions and abundances of different species in an ecosystem.

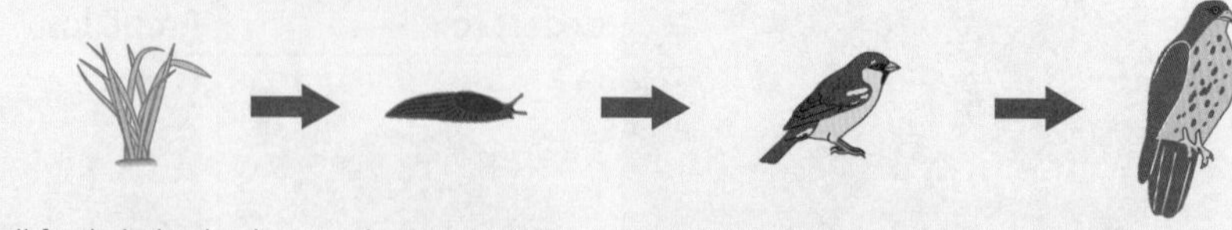

all food chains begin with a **producer**, for example, a green plant or alga producing glucose through photosynthesis

slugs are primary **consumers** – they are **herbivores** that eat producers

sparrows are secondary consumers – they are **carnivores** that eat primary consumers

hawks are tertiary consumers – they are carnivores that eat secondary consumers

Consumers that kill and eat other animals are **predators**, and those that are eaten are **prey**.

Apex predators are carnivores with no predators.

Organisms usually have more complex feeding relationships, with more than one predator or more than one food source. These can be shown in a **food web**.

How materials are cycled

All materials in the living world are recycled, which provides the building materials for future organisms.

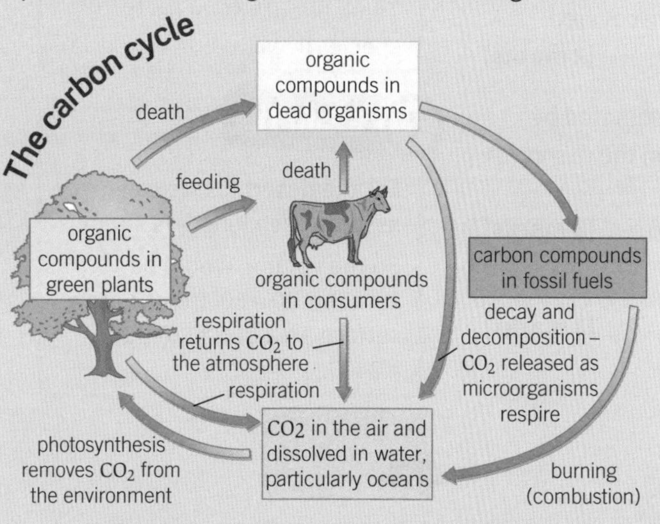

Global warming

Levels of carbon dioxide and methane in the atmosphere are increasing due to human activity, contributing to **global warming** and climate change.

Global warming is the gradual increase in the average temperature of the Earth.

This scientific consensus is based on systematic reviews of thousands of peer-reviewed publications.

Global warming has resulted in

- large-scale habitat change and reduction, causing a decrease in biodiversity
- extreme weather and sea-level changes
- migration of species to different parts of the world, affecting ecosystems
- threats to the security and availability of food.

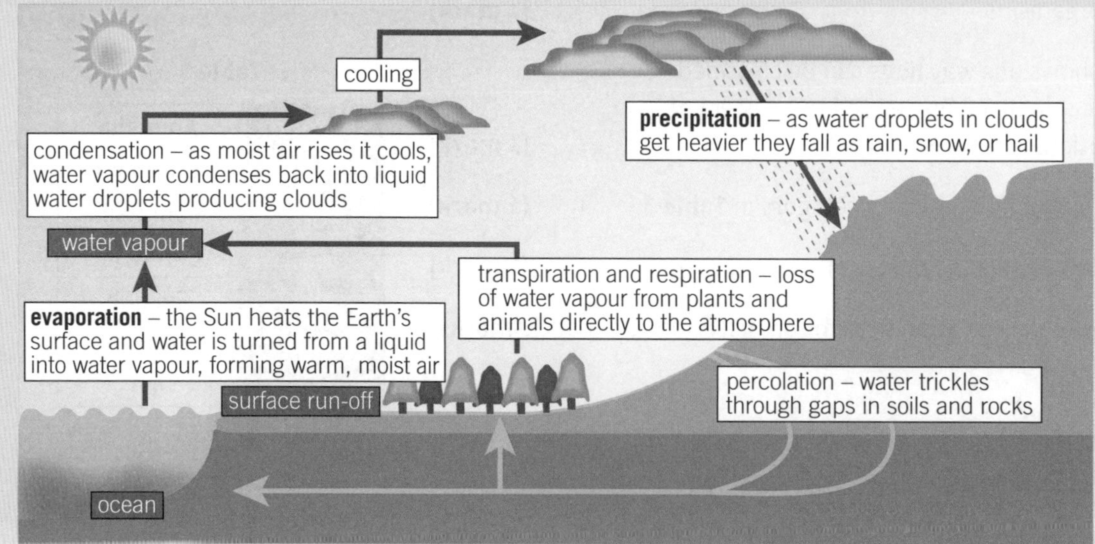

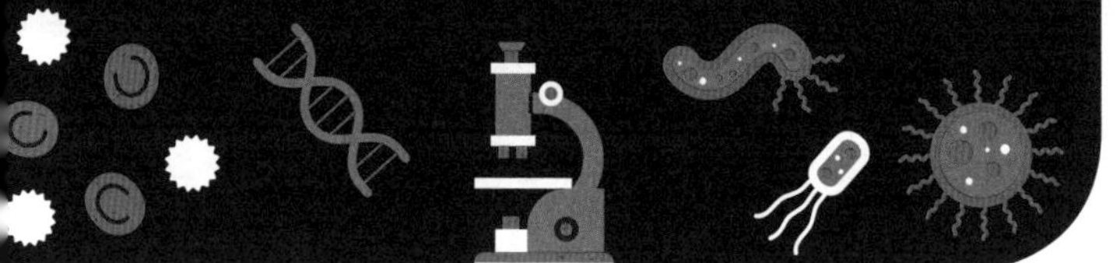

B18

Biodiversity

Biodiversity is the variety of all the different species of organisms (plant, animal, and microorganism) on Earth, or within a specific ecosystem.

High biodiversity ensures the stability of an ecosystem because it reduces the dependence of one species on another for food or habitat maintenance.

The future of the human species depends on us maintaining a good level of biodiversity. Many human activities, such as **deforestation**, are reducing biodiversity, but only recently have measures been taken to try to prevent this.

Waste management

Rapid growth of the human population and increases in the standard of living mean that humans are using more resources and producing more waste.

Waste and chemical materials need to be properly handled in order to reduce the amount of **pollution** they cause. Pollution kills plants and animals, and can accumulate in food chains, reducing biodiversity.

Pollution can occur

- in water, from sewage, fertiliser run-off, or toxic chemicals (e.g., from factories)
- in air, from smoke and acidic gases
- on land, from landfill and toxic chemicals.

Revision tip

Remember Global warming is a major *cause* of climate change – you will cover this concept in chemistry.

Maintaining biodiversity

Many habitats are currently under threat due to human activities such as deforestation, climate change, and habitat destruction.

There are a number of ways in which scientists and concerned citizens are trying to maintain biodiversity and reduce the negative impact of humans on ecosystems, including

- breeding programmes in zoos for endangered species
- protection and regeneration of rare habitats (e.g., national parks)
- reintroduction of hedgerows in agricultural areas where single crop species are grown, as hedges provide habitat for many organisms
- government policies to reduce deforestation and carbon dioxide emissions
- recycling resources rather than dumping waste in landfill.

Land use and deforestation

Rapid population growth has led to humans using much more land for building, quarrying, farming, and dumping waste. This reduces the area in which animals can live and can further destroy habitats through pollution.

For example, the destruction of **peat bogs** (areas of partially decayed vegetation) to produce garden compost has decreased the amount of this important habitat, and the biodiversity it supports. The decay or burning of peat for energy also releases carbon dioxide into the atmosphere, contributing to global warming.

Large-scale deforestation in tropical areas has been carried out to provide land for cattle and rice fields, and to grow crops for **biofuels**.

This has resulted in

- large amounts of carbon dioxide being released into the atmosphere due to burning of trees
- extinctions and reductions in biodiversity as habitats are destroyed
- climate change, as trees absorb carbon dioxide and release water vapour.

Key terms

Make sure you can write a definition for these key terms.

biodiversity biofuel biomass carbon cycle carnivore consumer deforestation evaporation food chain food web global warming herbivore peat bog pollution precipitation predator prey producer water cycle

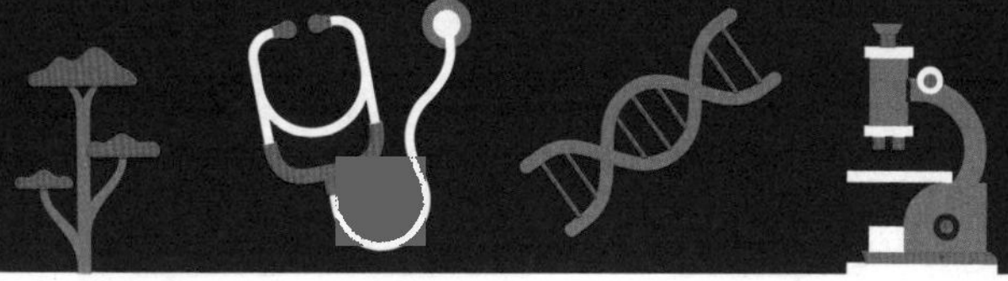

Learn the answers to the questions below, then cover the answers column with a piece of paper and write as many as you can. Check and repeat.

	B18 questions	Answers
1	What is a producer?	organism that makes its own food, usually by photosynthesis
2	What is a food chain?	representation of the feeding relationships within a community
3	What is a consumer?	organism that eats other organisms for food
4	What is a herbivore?	organism that only eats producers (plants/algae)
5	What is a predator?	organism that kills and eats other organisms
6	What is a prey organism?	organism that is killed and eaten by another organism
7	What is an apex predator?	carnivore with no predators
8	What is the carbon cycle?	process that returns carbon from organisms to the atmosphere as carbon dioxide, which can then be used by plants
9	What is the water cycle?	process that provides fresh water for plants and animals on land before draining into seas and rivers
10	What is biodiversity?	the variety of all the different species of organisms on Earth, or within an ecosystem
11	What is the advantage of high biodiversity?	ensures stability of ecosystems by reducing the dependence of one species on another
12	How are humans trying to maintain biodiversity?	• breeding programmes • protection of rare habitats • reintroduction of hedgerows • reduction of deforestation and carbon dioxide emissions • recycling resources
13	Why are more resources being used, and more waste produced, by humans?	rapid growth in human population, and increase in the standard of living
14	How are humans reducing the land available for other organisms?	building, quarrying, farming, and dumping waste
15	What are the negative impacts of the destruction of peat bogs?	• reduces amount of available habitat, causing decreases in biodiversity • burning or decay of peat releases carbon dioxide into the atmosphere
16	Why have humans carried out large-scale deforestation in tropical areas?	• to provide land for cattle and rice fields • to grow crops for biofuels
17	What gases are increasing in atmospheric levels and contributing to global warming?	carbon dioxide and methane

Put paper here

B18

Now go back and use the questions below to check your knowledge from previous chapters.

Previous questions / Answers

	Previous questions	Answers
1	What type of cell division is involved in asexual reproduction?	mitosis
2	What is the function of thyroxine in the body?	stimulates basal metabolic rate, so is important for growth and development
3	What is a biotic factor?	a living factor that can affect a community
4	What is sexual reproduction?	joining (fusion) of male and female gametes
5	What is an ecosystem?	the interaction of a community of living organisms with the non-living parts of their environment
6	What evidence supports the theory of evolution?	• parents pass on their characteristics to offspring in genes • fossil record evidence • evolution of antibiotic-resistant bacteria
7	What type of cell division is involved in sexual reproduction?	meiosis
8	How do antibiotic-resistant strains of bacteria develop?	mutations that allow the strain to survive and reproduce in the presence of the antibiotic

Put paper here

Put paper here

Put paper here

Required Practical Skills

Practise answering questions on the required practicals using the example below. You need to be able to apply your skills and knowledge to other practicals too.

Field investigations

For this investigation, you will practise applying appropriate sampling techniques in the field to look at plant population sizes. Two methods of sampling with quadrats are covered:

1 Transect lines – stretching a tape measure along the ground, placing a quadrat at even points along the measure, and recording the number of plants within each quadrat.

2 Random sampling – using tape measures to form a square area, generating random numbers corresponding to where in that area you should place the quadrat, and recording the number of plants within each quadrat.

You should be able to describe and explain the purpose of each sampling method.

Worked example

A student used a quadrat measuring 25 cm by 25 cm to sample the number of daisies in a field. The average number of daisies within a quadrat was found to be 17. The total area of the field was 320 m^2.

1 Estimate the number of daisies in the field.

25 cm = 0.25 m

area of quadrat = 0.25 × 0.25

= 0.0625 m^2

$$\frac{320}{0.0625} = 5120$$

population estimate = 5120 × 17

= 87 040 daisies

2 Give a reason why the student might use random sampling in this investigation.

Random sampling reduces any bias to the results, meaning they are more reliable.

Practice

1 A student wanted to measure how distance from a water source affected the size of a plant. Write a method to carry out this investigation.

2 A quadrat measures 15 cm by 15 cm. Give the area of the quadrat in m^2.

3 An ecologist wanted to estimate the quantity of plastic floating in the ocean. Write a method for this investigation.

Practice

Exam-style questions

01 Isle Royale is a large isolated island on Lake Superior, in the USA. It is home to populations of wolves and moose. The wolves are the only natural predators of the moose.

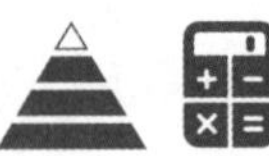

The populations of wolves and moose on the island have been monitored over a 60-year period (**Figure 1**).

Figure 1

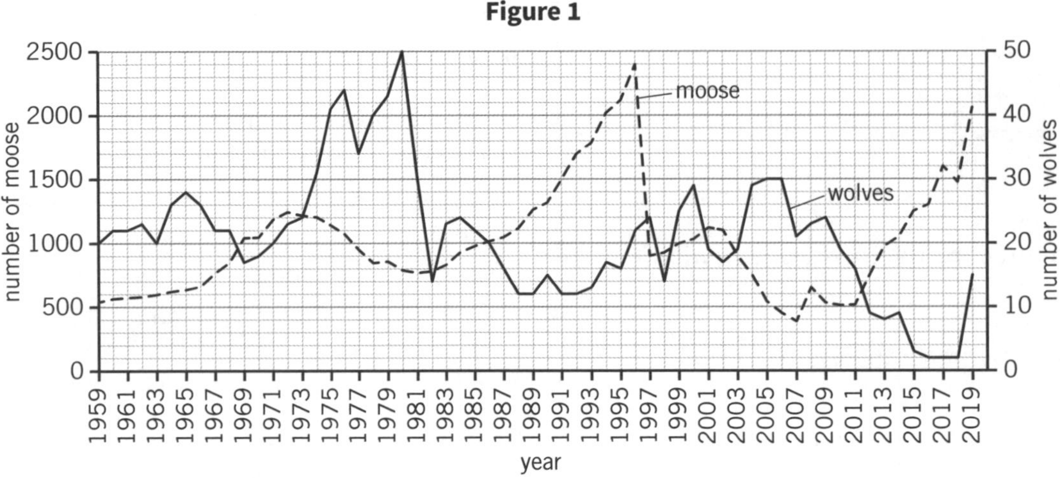

01.1 Identify the largest population of wolves on the island between 1959 and 2019. **[1 mark]**

____

01.2 The population of moose rose significantly between 1982 and 1996. Calculate the percentage increase in the moose population between 1982 and 1996. **[4 marks]**

______________ %

01.3 Explain the general population size trends in **Figure 1**. **[4 marks]**

____

____

____

____

01.4 Other than availability of moose, suggest and explain **two** factors that may affect the wolf population. **[2 marks]**

1 ______________________________

____

2 ______________________________

____

Exam Tip

There is lots of information in the question that isn't needed in the answer, for example, the fact that it is Isle Royale island on Lake Superior in the USA has nothing to do with getting you marks. Don't get put off by this extra information.

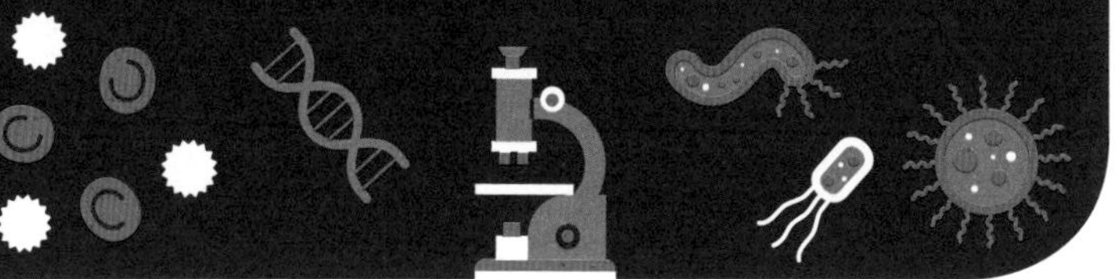

02 A group of students were asked to survey the number of daisies growing on their school field. They decided to take a series of samples using a 1 m × 1 m quadrat.

Their results are in **Table 1**.

Table 1

Sample number	1	2	3	4	5	6	7	8
Number of daisies	11	14	14	2	14	15	11	15

02.1 Write down the median number of daisies from the students' samples. **[1 mark]**

____

> **! Exam Tip**
> Rewrite the data to help you find the median.

02.2 Calculate the mean number of daisies from the students' samples. **[1 mark]**

Mean = ______________

02.3 Justify which value, the median or the mean, gives the better estimate of the average number of daisies in the school field. **[2 marks]**

____

____

____

02.4 The school field measures 350 m × 200 m.

Estimate the number of daisies in the school field. **[3 marks]**

Number = ______________

02.5 Suggest and explain **two** reasons for the difference in the number of daisies measured in Sample **4**. **[4 marks]**

1 ______________________________

____

2 ______________________________

____

> **! Exam Tip**
> There is lots of information that is not specified in the main body of the question. This leaves you lots of space to suggest reasons. As long as you've got a good explanation you can easily pick up marks in **02.5**.

03 Large areas of the Amazon rainforest have been cleared for agriculture.

03.1 Choose the word that best describes this change in land use. Choose **one** answer. **[1 mark]**

afforestation deforestation eutrophication leaching

03.2 Give **three** ways in which the removal of trees can lead to increasing carbon dioxide levels in the Earth's atmosphere. **[3 marks]**

Exam Tip

In **03.2** you will be awarded one mark per way, so don't write long sentences explaining why.

03.3 Explain why there is a difference in the level of biodiversity between rainforest regions and agricultural land. **[3 marks]**

03.4 Explain the long-term effects on the Earth's atmosphere of this change in land use. **[4 marks]**

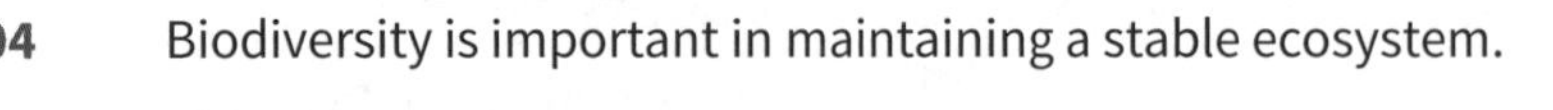

04 Biodiversity is important in maintaining a stable ecosystem.

04.1 Define what is meant by the term biodiversity. **[1 mark]**

04.2 Identify the **two** factors that can increase biodiversity. **[2 marks]**

breeding programmes deforestation

monoculture farming reintroduction of hedgerows

04.3 Explain why an area of woodland with multiple species of tree is more stable than an area containing only one tree species. **[3 marks]**

05 A student wanted to estimate the number of buttercup plants growing in a grassy field. The field measured 150 m × 60 m.

05.1 Give **two** abiotic factors that may affect the distribution of the buttercup plants. **[2 marks]**

05.2 The student found an area where buttercup plants were growing and placed a 1 m × 1 m quadrat in that area (**Figure 2**).

Figure 2

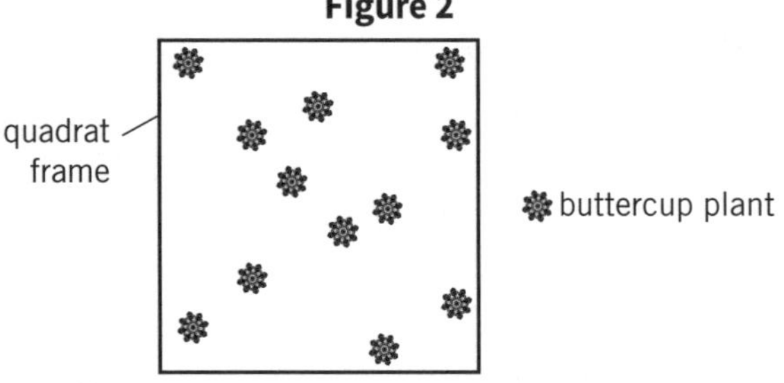

The student reported, *'My results show that there are 108 000 buttercup plants in the field.'*
Discuss the accuracy of the student's statement. **[6 marks]**

05.3 Suggest, with reasons, **two** ways the student could improve their method to give a more accurate population estimate. **[4 marks]**

Exam Tip

This is a *four*-mark question asking for *two* suggestions. This means that there are separate marks for your reasoning. If you can't explain your suggestion, try thinking of alternatives that will get you both marks.

06 Carbon is present in a wide variety of compounds in the carbon cycle.

06.1 Describe how carbon is cycled in the environment. **[6 marks]**

06.2 It is estimated that each year 166 gigatonnes of carbon are cycled through the atmosphere.
Write this value as a mass in kg, in standard form.
1 tonne = 1000 kg. **[2 marks]**

Exam Tip

First convert the value into kg, then write it in standard form.

06.3 Explain how deforestation alters the balance in the carbon cycle. **[3 marks]**

06.4 Name **one** consequence of increased atmospheric carbon dioxide. **[1 mark]**

06.5 Scientists have suggested that deforestation may lead to an increased worldwide rate of photosynthesis of plants.
Suggest how this conclusion may have been reached. **[4 marks]**

07 **Figure 3** shows a food chain of some organisms found in a park.

Figure 3

oak tree → caterpillar → sparrow → hawk

07.1 Identify the producer in this food chain. **[1 mark]**

07.2 Identify the tertiary consumer in this food chain. **[1 mark]**

07.3 Give the source of energy for this food chain. **[1 mark]**

Exam Tip

There is only one source of energy for all food chains.

07.4 Identify **one** prey organism from this food chain. **[1 mark]**

07.5 Suggest and explain **one** adaptation of the prey organism named in **07.4**. **[2 marks]**

07.6 Suggest and explain what would happen to the number of caterpillars if the hawk population was infected with a fatal virus. **[3 marks]**

08 All materials in the living world are recycled to provide the building blocks for future organisms. Water is one example of a material that is recycled.

08.1 Describe the main steps in the water cycle. **[6 marks]**

08.2 Identify and explain **two** ways in which animals return water to the environment. **[4 marks]**

08.3 Explain the importance of the water cycle to living organisms. **[4 marks]**

08.4 Other than water, name **one** material that is recycled. **[1 mark]**

Exam Tip

When describing the water cycle, be clear about where the water starts, where it ends up, and the links between each of the stages.

09 A group of students investigated the plants and animals present in a city park. They completed a line transect over 10 m to one side of a footpath. The number of organisms at each point was noted. They presented their data on a kite diagram (**Figure 4**).

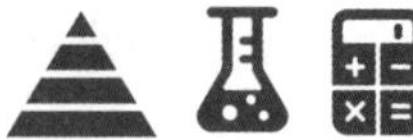

Figure 4

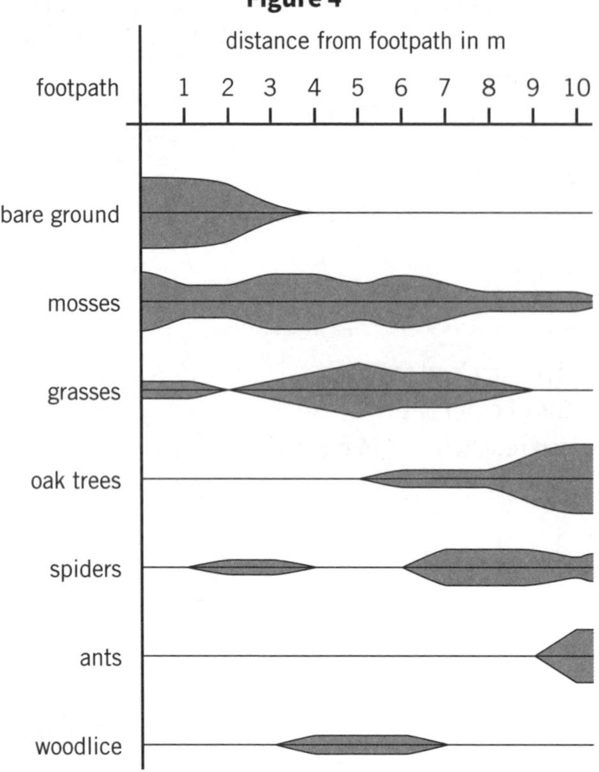

09.1 Describe a procedure the students could have followed to collect these data. **[6 marks]**

09.2 Identify which animal species had the highest population. **[1 mark]**

09.3 Write down **two** conclusions the students could draw from their data. **[2 marks]**

09.4 Suggest and explain **one** way the students could gather further evidence to support their conclusions. **[2 marks]**

10 The carbon cycle is essential for life on Earth.

10.1 Describe the main processes in the carbon cycle. **[6 marks]**

10.2 Explain how **two** human activities are causing changes to the natural balance of the carbon cycle. **[4 marks]**

11 Scientists believe that many human activities are contributing to global warming.

11.1 Suggest and explain **three** changes that could be made to decrease the current rate of global temperature increase. **[6 marks]**

11.2 Explain **two** biological consequences of global warming. **[6 marks]**

11.3 **Figure 5** shows the global mean temperature increase between 2009 and 2018, compared to the 20th-century mean value.

Figure 5

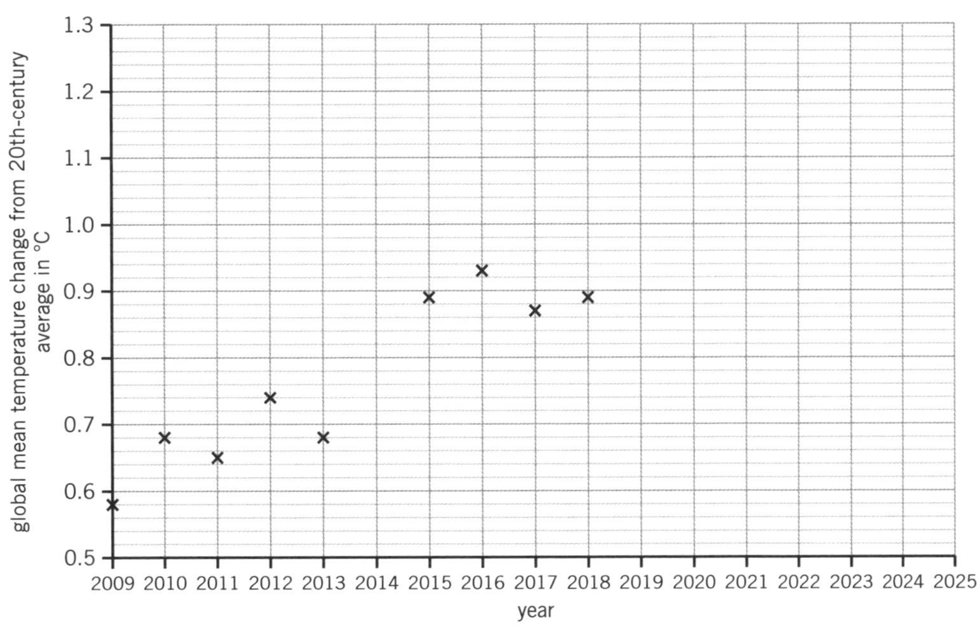

Estimate the increase in global mean temperature in 2014 and 2025, compared to the 20th-century average. **[3 marks]**

11.4 Explain which of your estimated values is likely to be the most accurate. **[2 marks]**

Exam Tip

Draw a line of best fit and use that to help with your estimate.

12 **Table 2** shows the percentage recycling rate in the UK over five years.

Table 2

Year	Recycling rate in %
2010	40.4
2011	42.9
2012	43.9
2013	44.1
2014	44.9

12.1 Name **two** materials that can be recycled. **[2 marks]**

12.2 Explain **two** environmental benefits of recycling. **[4 marks]**

12.3 The UK was set a target to recycle at least 50% of household waste by 2020.
Based on the data in **Table 2**, evaluate the likelihood that this target will be met. **[4 marks]**

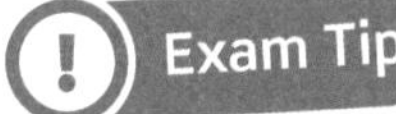

You'll have to back up what you say with a calculation based on data from **Table 2**.

Knowledge

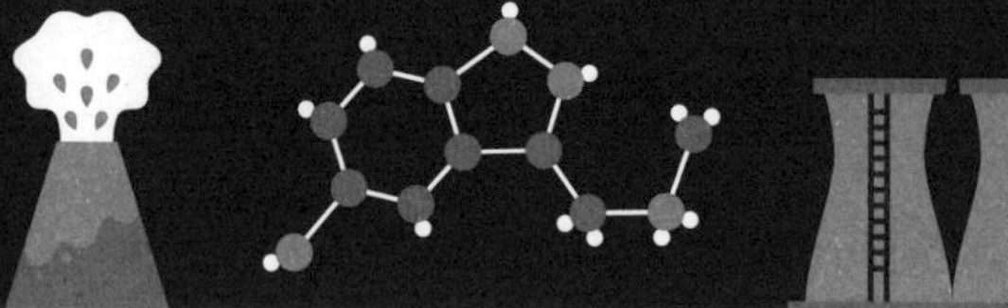

C1 The atom

Development of the model of the atom

Dalton's model

John Dalton thought of the **atom** as a solid sphere that could not be divided into smaller parts. His model did not include **protons**, **neutrons**, or **electrons**.

The plum pudding model

Scientists' experiments resulted in the discovery of sub-atomic charged particles. The first to be discovered were electrons – tiny, negatively charged particles.

The discovery of electrons led to the plum pudding model of the atom – a cloud of positive charge, with negative electrons embedded in it. Protons and neutrons had not yet been discovered.

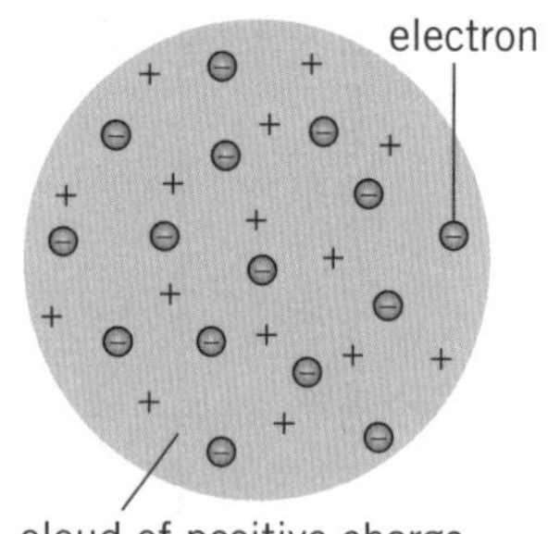

Alpha scattering experiment

1. Scientists fired small, positively charged particles (called alpha particles) at a piece of gold foil only a few atoms thick.
2. They expected the alpha particles to travel straight through the gold.
3. They were surprised that some of the alpha particles bounced back and many were deflected (alpha scattering).
4. To explain why the alpha particles were repelled the scientists suggested that the positive charge and mass of an atom must be concentrated in a small space at its centre. They called this space the **nucleus**.

scientists predicted:

gold atoms

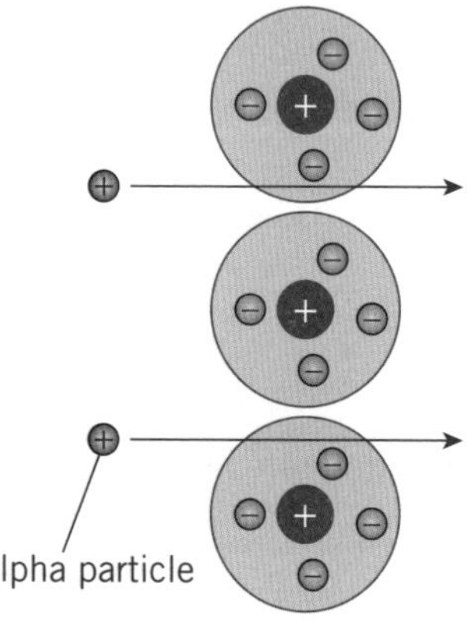

actually observed:

gold atoms

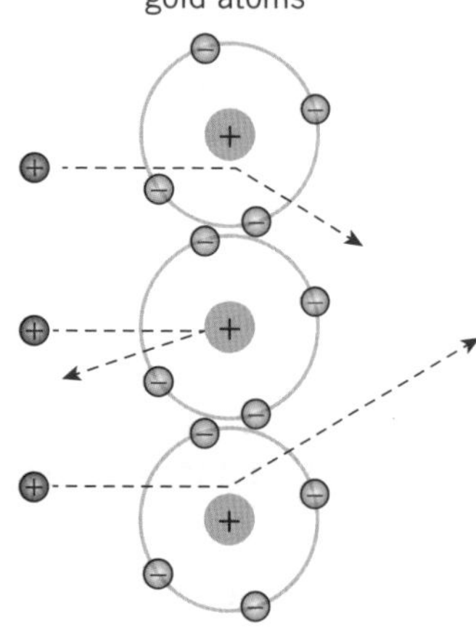

Nuclear model

Scientists replaced the plum pudding model with the nuclear model and suggested that the electrons **orbit** (go around) the nucleus, but not at set distances.

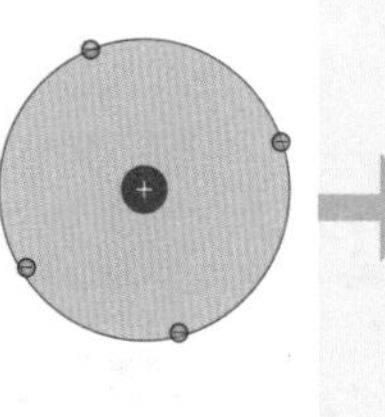

Electron shell (Bohr) model

Niels Bohr calculated that electrons must orbit the nucleus at fixed distances. These orbits are called **shells** or **energy levels**.

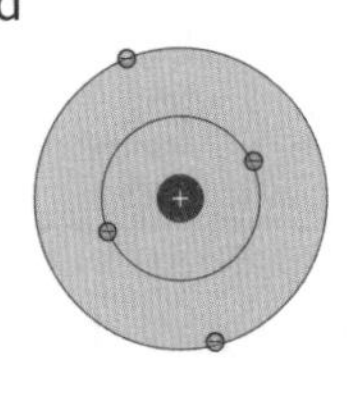

The proton

Further experiments provided evidence that the nucleus contained smaller particles called protons. A proton has an opposite charge to an electron.

The neutron

James Chadwick carried out experiments that gave evidence for a particle with no charge. Scientists called this the neutron and concluded that the protons and neutrons are in the nucleus, and the electrons orbit the nucleus in shells.

Relative mass

One property of protons, neutrons, and electrons is **relative mass** – their masses compared to each other. Protons and neutrons have the same mass, so are given a relative mass of 1. It takes almost 2000 electrons to equal the mass of a single proton – their relative mass is so small that we can consider it as 0.

Size

The atom has a radius of 1×10^{-10} m. Nuclei (plural of nucleus) are around 10 000 times smaller than atoms and have a radius of around 1×10^{-14} m.

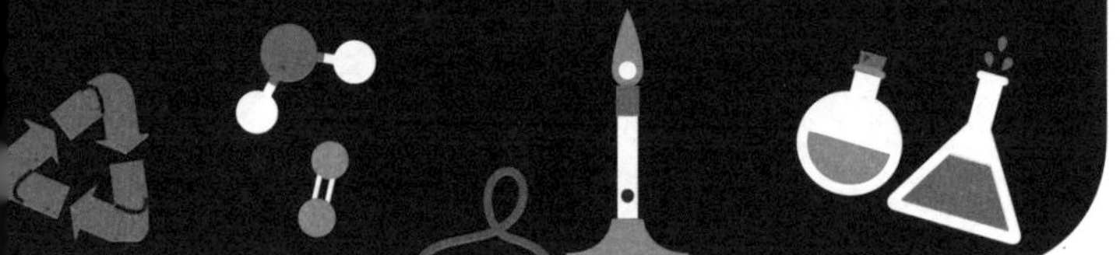

Atoms and particles

The Periodic Table lists over 100 types of atoms that differ in the number of protons, neutrons, and electrons they each have.

	Relative charge	Relative mass	
Proton	+1	1	= atomic number
Neutron	0	1	= mass number – atomic number
Electron	–1	0 (very small)	= same as the number of protons

All atoms have equal numbers of protons and electrons, meaning they have no overall charge:

total negative charge from electrons = total positive charge from protons

Drawing atoms

Electrons in an atom are placed in fixed shells. You can put

- up to two electrons in the first shell
- eight electrons each in the second and third shells.

You must fill up a shell before moving on to the next one.

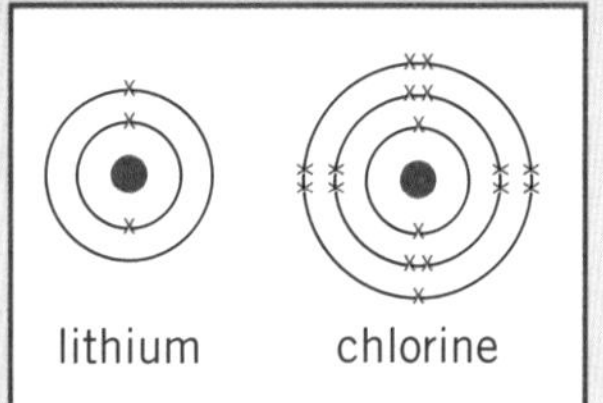

Elements and compounds

Elements are substances made of one type of atom. Each atom of an element will have the same number of protons.

Compounds are made of different types of atoms chemically bonded together. The atoms in a compound have different numbers of protons.

Isotopes

Atoms of the same element can have a different number of neutrons, giving them a different overall mass number. Atoms of the same element with different numbers of neutrons are called **isotopes**.

The **relative atomic mass** is the average mass of all the atoms of an element (note that **abundance** means the percentage of atoms with a certain mass):

$$\text{relative atomic mass} = \frac{(\text{abundance of isotope 1} \times \text{mass of isotope 1}) + (\text{abundance of isotope 2} \times \text{mass of isotope 2})...}{100}$$

Mixtures

- A mixture consists of two or more elements or compounds that are not chemically combined together.
- The substances in a mixture can be separated using physical processes.
- These processes do not use chemical reactions.

Separating mixtures

- filtration – insoluble solids and a liquid
- crystallisation – soluble solid from a solution
- simple distillation – solvent from a solution
- fractional distillation – two liquids with similar boiling points
- paper chromatography – identify substances from a mixture in solution

Key terms

Make sure you can write a definition for these key terms.

abundance *atom* *atomic number* *compound* *electron* *element* *energy level* *isotope* *neutron* *nucleus* *orbit* *proton* *relative atomic mass* *relative charge* *relative mass* *shell*

Retrieval

Learn the answers to the questions below, then cover the answers column with a piece of paper and write as many as you can. Check and repeat.

	C1 questions	Answers
1	What is an atom?	smallest part of an element that can exist
2	What is Dalton's model of the atom?	atoms as solid spheres that could not be divided into smaller parts
3	What is the plum pudding model of the atom?	sphere of positive charge with negative electrons embedded in it
4	What did scientists discover in the alpha scattering experiment?	some alpha particles were deflected by the gold foil – this showed that an atom's mass and positive charge must be concentrated in one small space (the nucleus)
5	Describe the nuclear model of the atom.	dense nucleus with electrons orbiting it
6	What did Niels Bohr discover?	electrons orbit in fixed energy levels (shells)
7	What did James Chadwick discover?	uncharged particle called the neutron
8	Where are protons and neutrons?	in the nucleus
9	What is the relative mass of each sub-atomic particle?	proton: 1, neutron: 1, electron: 0 (very small)
10	What is the relative charge of each sub-atomic particle?	proton: +1, neutron: 0, electron: −1
11	How can you find out the number of protons in an atom?	the atomic number on the Periodic Table
12	How can you calculate the number of neutrons in an atom?	mass number – atomic number = neutrons
13	Why do atoms have no overall charge?	equal numbers of positive protons and negative electrons
14	How many electrons would you place in the first, second, and third shells?	up to 2 in the first shell, and up to 8 in each of the second and third shells
15	What is an element?	substance made of one type of atom
16	What is a compound?	substance made of more than one type of atom chemically joined together
17	What is a mixture?	two or more substances not chemically combined
18	What are isotopes?	atoms of the same element (same number of protons) with different numbers of neutrons
19	What are the four physical processes that can be used to separate mixtures?	filtration, crystallisation, simple or fractional distillation, chromatography
20	What is relative mass?	the average mass of all the atoms of an element

Required Practical Skills

Practise answering questions on the required practicals using the example below.
You need to be able to apply your skills and knowledge to other practicals too.

Chromatography

This practical shows the separation of coloured substances by making paper chromatograms. You need to be able to describe the method of chromatography, including the solutes and solvents involved, and define the stationary and mobile phases.

Food colourings are often used for this practical, but remember any coloured mixture could be used in an exam question.

Worked example

A student carried out a paper chromatography experiment to determine what inks make up a sample. They observed the following results.

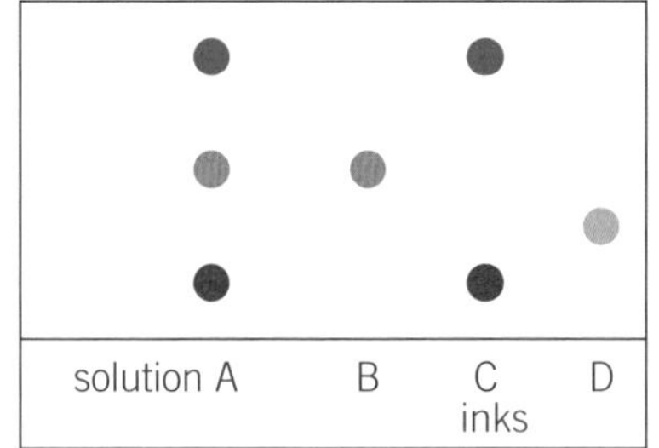

1 Determine which of the inks (B, C, and D) are present in solution A.

Compare the spots on the chromatogram to determine which inks make up solution A – the spots for inks B and C all align with spots for solution A, so these are all present in solution A.

2 Give a reason why an original line is drawn in pencil.

Pencil does not interact with the mobile phase, and therefore will not interfere with the chromatogram.

Practice

1 Two students were setting up a chromatography experiment. Student A wanted to leave the experiment until the solvent front had moved three-quarters of the way up the paper, and student B wanted to leave it for 15 minutes. Which method do you agree with? Give an explanation for your answer.

2 A student carried out a chromatography experiment on an ink. Their chromatogram showed that the ink was made up of three dyes. Sketch the student's chromatogram.

Practice

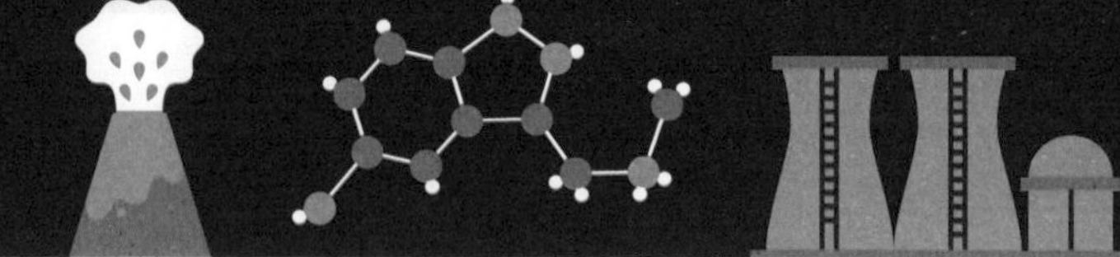

Exam-style questions

01 Different scientists made different contributions to the development of the model of the atom.

01.1 Draw **one** line from each scientist to the contribution they made. **[2 marks]**

Scientist		Contribution
		the nucleus contains neutrons
Niels Bohr		atoms contain electrons
James Chadwick		electrons orbit the nucleus at certain distances
		atoms are tiny spheres

01.2 Describe the alpha particle scattering experiment, and how it showed that the mass of an atom was concentrated in a positively charged nucleus. **[6 marks]**

Exam Tip

Ensure you cover how the results showed the presence of a nucleus.

____

____

____

____

____

____

____

____

01.3 An atom of potassium has the symbol ${}^{39}_{19}\mathrm{K}$.

What is the atomic number of potassium?

Tick **one** box. **[1 mark]**

19 ☐ 39 ☐

20 ☐ 58 ☐

02 A student has a mixture of isopropanol and water. **Table 1** gives some physical properties of isopropanol.

Table 1

Property	Value
Melting point of isopropanol	−89 °C
Boiling point of isopropanol	80.3 °C
Solubility of isopropanol in water	high

02.1 Name the method that the student should use to separate the mixture to collect pure samples of each substance. **[1 mark]**

____

02.2 Explain how to separate the substances using the method given in **02.1**. **[6 marks]**

> **Exam Tip**
> Use data from the table in your answer, and clearly link it to the method of separation.

02.3 Ethanol has a boiling point of 78.4 °C and a melting point of −114.7 °C.

Suggest why this method could not be used to separate a mixture of isopropanol and ethanol. **[1 mark]**

03 Models of the atom have changed over time.

03.1 Compare the plum pudding model of the atom to the earlier model. **[3 marks]**

> **Exam Tip**
> You'll need to mention things that are the same and things that are different.

03.2 Explain how experimental evidence led scientists to suggest the nuclear model of the atom. **[6 marks]**

04 **Table 2** gives some information about four different atoms. The atoms are represented by the letters **W**, **X**, **Y**, and **Z**. These letters are not the chemical symbols of the elements.

Table 2

Atom	Number of protons	Number of neutrons	Number of electrons
W	16	16	
X	17	20	17
Y	18	22	18
Z	17	18	17

04.1 Give the number of electrons in atom **W**. **[1 mark]**

04.2 Give the atomic number of atom **X**. **[1 mark]**

04.3 Give the letter of the atom that has the greatest mass number. **[1 mark]**

04.4 Give the letters of the **two** atoms that are isotopes of the same element. **[1 mark]**

05 **Figure 1** shows the electronic structure of an atom. The atom has no overall charge.

Figure 1

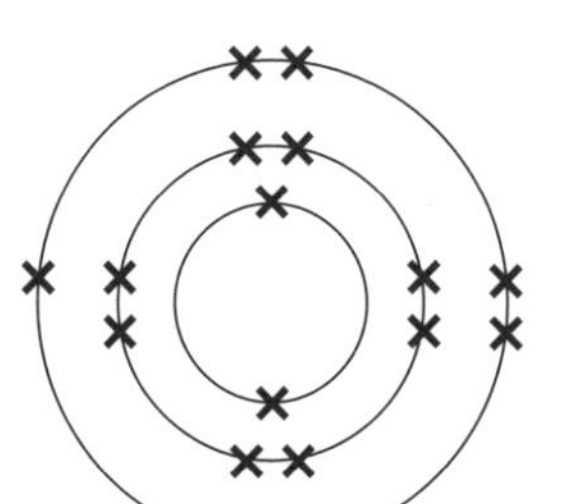

05.1 Identify the number of protons in the nucleus of the atom. **[1 mark]**

05.2 Give the atomic number of the atom. **[1 mark]**

Exam Tip

Remember protons have a positive charge and electrons have a negative charge.

05.3 **Figure 1** shows a chlorine atom. Chlorine has a relative atomic mass of 35.5. Explain why the relative atomic mass of chlorine is not a whole number. **[2 marks]**

05.4 Two isotopes of copper are copper-63 and copper-65. **Table 3** shows the abundance of each isotope.

Table 3

Copper isotope	Percentage abundance
copper-63	69.2
copper-65	30.8

Calculate the relative atomic mass of copper. Give your answer to three significant figures. **[3 marks]**

Exam Tip

If you're not sure how to answer this then think of having 69.2 atoms that have a mass of 63 and 30.8 atoms that have a mass of 65. Then work out the average mass of those 100 atoms.

05.5 Suggest why the relative atomic mass of copper on the Periodic Table is different from the value calculated in **05.4**. **[1 mark]**

06 **Figure 2** shows the electronic structure of an atom. The atom has 12 neutrons.

Figure 2

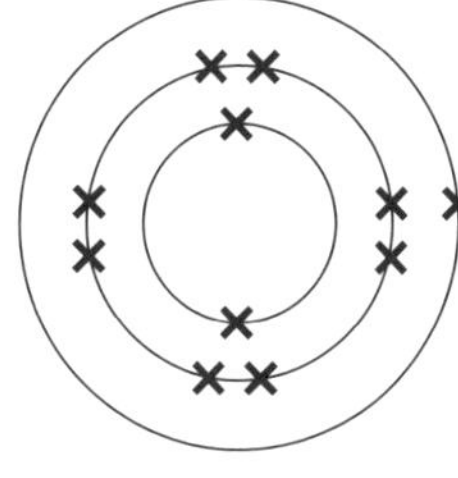

> **Exam Tip**
> You'll need to reference electrons, protons, and neutrons in your answer.

06.1 Determine the mass number of the atom. Explain how you worked out your answer. **[2 marks]**

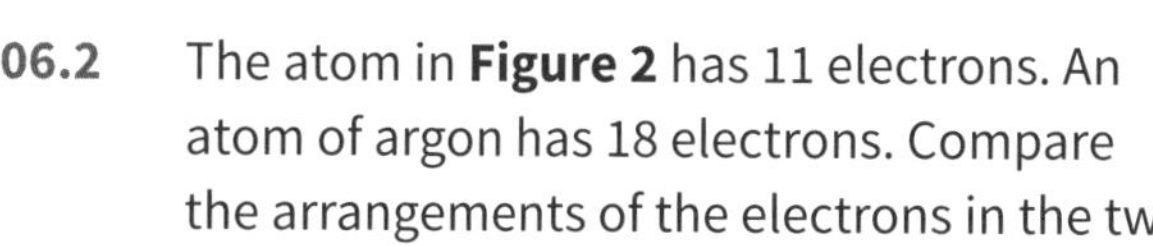

06.2 The atom in **Figure 2** has 11 electrons. An atom of argon has 18 electrons. Compare the arrangements of the electrons in the two atoms. **[6 marks]**

06.3 The radius of an argon atom is 71 pm. Determine the radius of an argon nucleus. Give your answer in pm, and in standard form. **[2 marks]**

07 **Table 4** shows data for three isotopes of an element. The total percentage abundance of all three isotopes is 100%.

Table 4

Isotope	Number of protons	Number of neutrons	Percentage abundance
L	14	14	92.20
M	14	15	4.68
N	14	16	

> **Exam Tip**
> Significant figures often come up in exams. This is something you might not have covered in your science lessons, so you need to ensure that you can use what you know from maths in a science context.

07.1 Calculate the relative atomic mass of the element. Give your answer to three significant figures. **[5 marks]**

07.2 Draw the complete electronic structure of the element represented in **Table 4**. **[2 marks]**

07.3 Compare the properties of isotope **L** and isotope **N**. **[2 marks]**

08 An atom of silicon has 14 electrons.

08.1 Give the relative charge of an electron. **[1 mark]**

08.2 **Figure 3** shows the energy levels (shells) of the electrons in a silicon atom. Complete the diagram by drawing the 14 electrons in the correct shells. **[1 mark]**

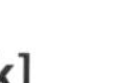

> **Exam Tip**
> Start from the centre and work your way out.

Figure 3

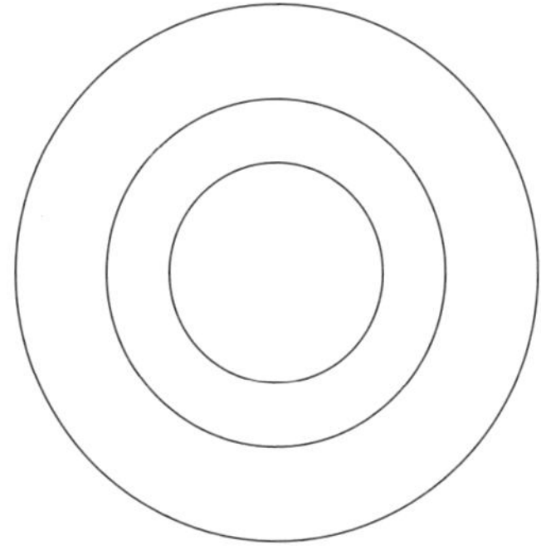

08.3 Name the scientist who suggested that electrons orbit the nucleus at specific distances. **[1 mark]**

09 Magnesium exists as three isotopes.

The symbols of the three isotopes are $^{24}_{12}Mg$, $^{25}_{12}Mg$, and $^{26}_{12}Mg$.

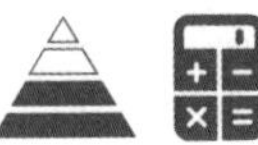

09.1 Define the term isotope. **[1 mark]**

09.2 Which statement about the three isotopes of magnesium is true?

Choose **one** answer. **[1 mark]**

The three isotopes have the same mass number.

The three isotopes have the same atomic number.

Each isotope has a different number of electrons.

Each isotope has a different number of protons.

Exam Tip

Start by crossing off the ones you know are incorrect.

09.3 The relative abundances of the three isotopes of magnesium are shown in **Table 5**.

Table 5

Isotope	Percentage abundance
$^{24}_{12}Mg$	79.0
$^{25}_{12}Mg$	10.0
$^{26}_{12}Mg$	11.0

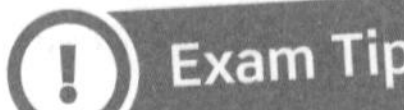

Exam Tip

The percentage abundances add up to 100.

Calculate the relative atomic mass of magnesium.

Give your answer to three significant figures. **[3 marks]**

10 **Table 6** gives some information about the most common isotopes of some elements.

Table 6

Element	Number of protons	Number of neutrons
neon	10	10
calcium	20	20
zinc	30	34
zirconium	40	50
tin	50	70
lanthanum	57	82

10.1 Write the name of the element that has an atomic number of 40. **[1 mark]**

10.2 Write the name of the element that has a mass number of 40. **[1 mark]**

10.3 Write the electronic structure of a calcium atom. **[1 mark]**

10.4 Plot the data from **Table 6** as a scatter graph on **Figure 4**. **[2 marks]**

Exam Tip

To write electronic structures, start from the inside shell, then write down the number of electrons in each shell, followed by a comma.

Figure 4

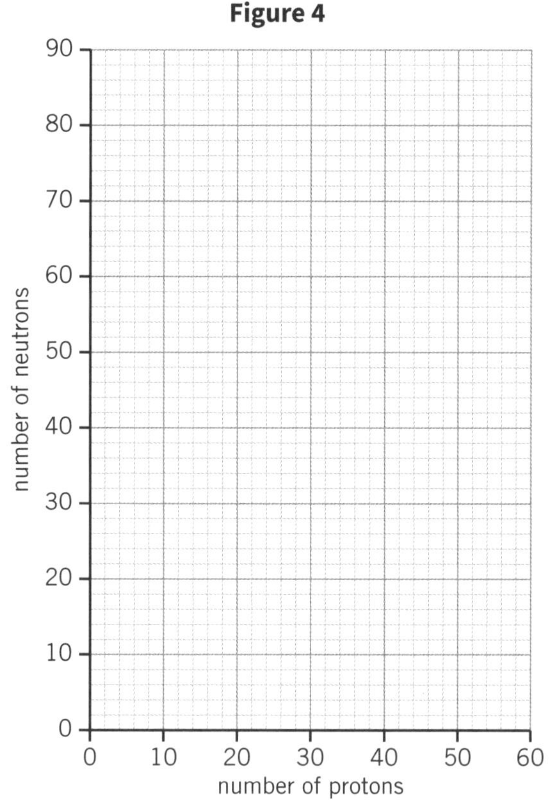

> **Exam Tip**
> Use crosses to plot your points.

10.5 Draw a curve of best fit on your graph. **[1 mark]**

10.6 Describe the relationship shown on the graph. **[2 marks]**

> **Exam Tip**
> Lines of best fit need to be smooth and continuous.

11 A scientist uses the following symbols to represent some substances.

potassium atom: ● chlorine atom: ■

sodium atom: ◆ water: ▲

11.1 Which symbol represents a compound? **[1 mark]**

11.2 The scientist uses the symbols to draw a representation of four samples they have (**Figure 5**).

Figure 5

sample **A** sample **B** sample **C** sample **D**

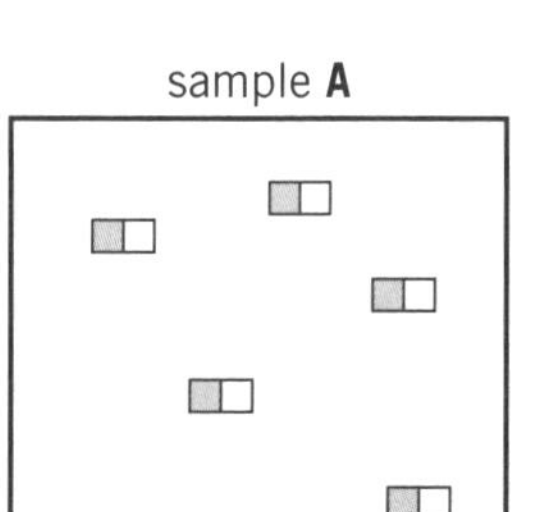

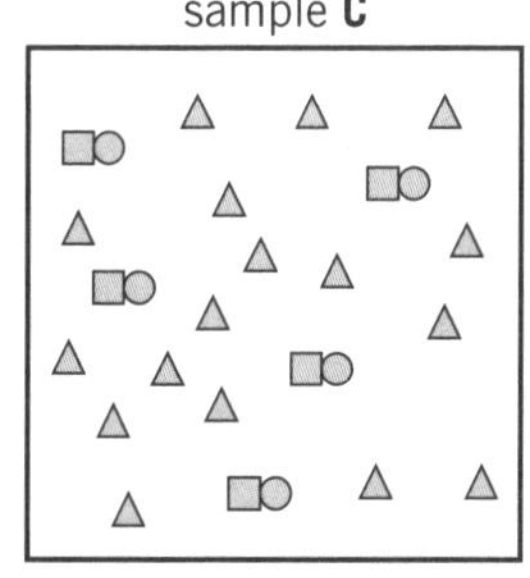

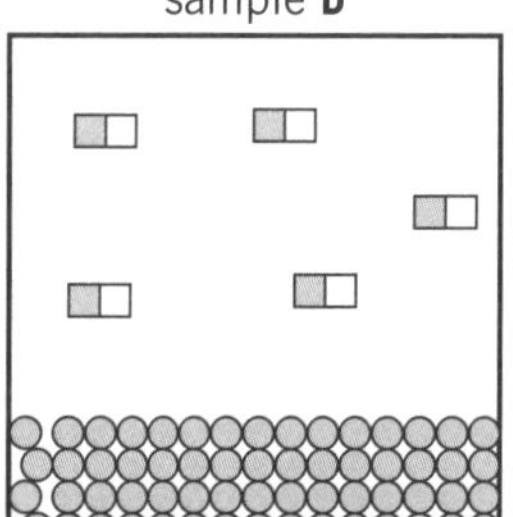

Identify the sample that contains a pure element. **[1 mark]**

> **Exam Tip**
> Look carefully at the key when answering this question.

11.3 Identify the sample that contains a mixture of two compounds. **[1 mark]**

11.4 Identify the sample that contains a mixture of two elements. **[1 mark]**

11.5 The scientists uses their symbols to draw the following representation of the compound sodium chloride.

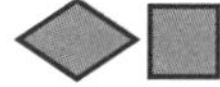

Write the chemical formula for this compound. **[1 mark]**

  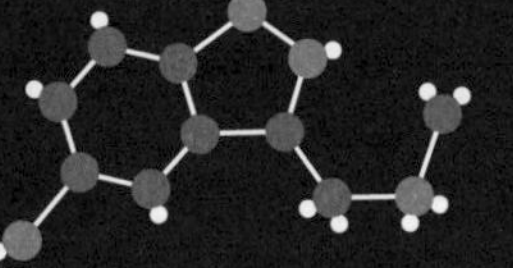 

Knowledge

C2 Covalent bonding

Particle model

The three states of matter can be represented in the particle model.

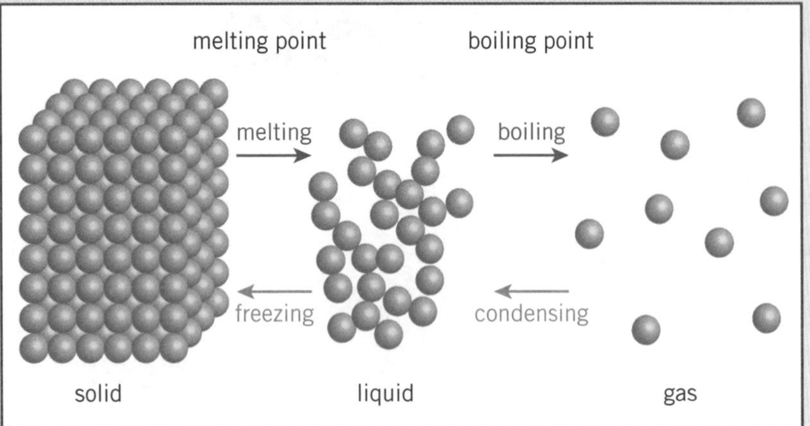

This model assumes that:

- there are no forces between the particles
- that all particles in a substrate are spherical
- that the spheres are solid.

The amount of energy needed to change the state of a substance depends on the forces between the particles. The stronger the forces between the particles, the higher the melting or boiling point of the substance.

Covalent bonding

Atoms can share or transfer electrons to form strong chemical bonds.

A **covalent bond** is when electrons are *shared* between **non-metal** atoms.

The number of electrons shared depends on how many extra electrons an atom needs to make a full outer shell.

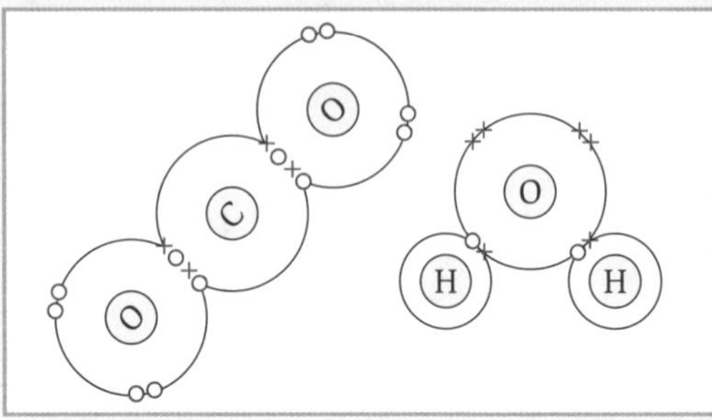

If you include electrons that are shared between atoms, each atom has a full outer shell.

Single bond = each atom shares one pair of electrons.

Double bond = each atom shares two pairs of electrons.

Covalent structures

When atoms form covalent bonds different types of structures can be formed. The structure depends on how many atoms there are and how they are bonded. There are three main types of covalent structure:

Structure and bonding

Giant covalent

Many billions of atoms, each one with a strong covalent bond to a number of others.

An example of a giant covalent structure is diamond.

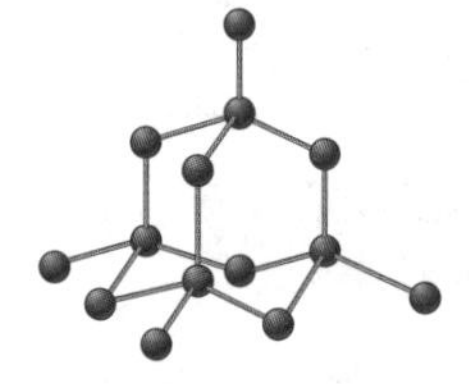

Small molecules

Each molecule contains only a few atoms with strong covalent bonds between these atoms.

Different molecules are held together by weak **intermolecular forces**.

For example, water is made of small molecules.

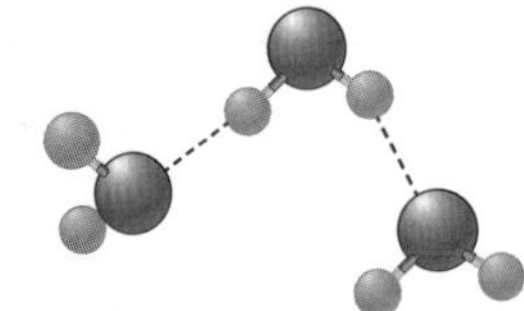

Large molecules

Many repeating units joined by covalent bonds to form a chain.

The small section is bonded to many identical sections to the left and right. The 'n' represents a large number.

Separate chains are held together by intermolecular forces that are stronger than in small molecules.

Polymers are examples of long molecules.

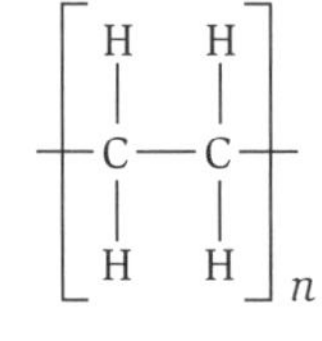

Key terms **Make sure you can write a definition for these key terms.**

boiling point · covalent bond · delocalised electrons · double bond · large molecules · melting point · nanotube · non-metal

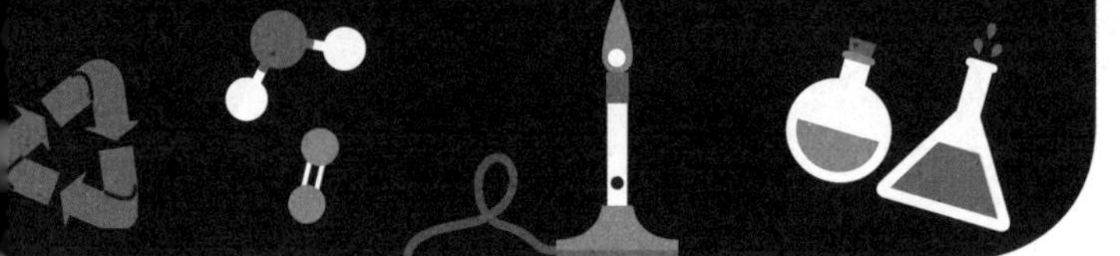

Properties	Giant covalent	Small molecules	Large molecules
	High melting and boiling points because the strong covalent bonds between the atoms must be broken to melt or boil the substances. This requires a lot of energy. Solid at room temperature.	Low melting and boiling points because only the intermolecular forces need to be overcome to melt or boil the substances, not the bonds between the atoms. This does not require a lot of energy as the intermolecular forces are weak. Normally gaseous or liquid at room temperature.	Melting and boiling points are low compared to giant covalent substances but higher than for small molecules. Large molecules have stronger intermolecular forces than small molecules, which require more energy to overcome. Normally solid at room temperature.

Most covalent structures do not conduct electricity because they do not have **delocalised electrons** or ions that are free to move to carry charge.

Graphite

Graphite is a giant covalent structure, but is different to other giant covalent substances.

Structure

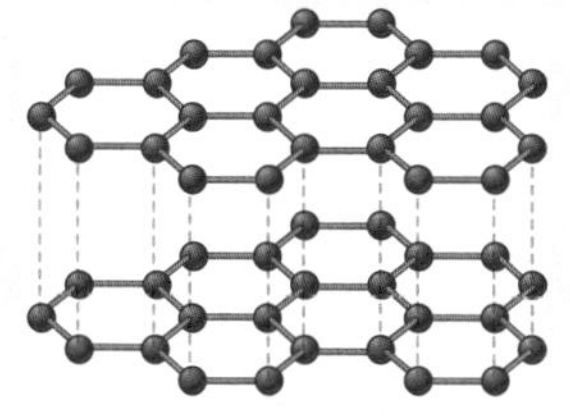

Made only of carbon – each carbon atom bonds to three others, and forms hexagonal rings in layers. Each carbon atom has one spare electron, which is delocalised and therefore free to move around the structure.

Hardness

The layers can slide over each other because they are not covalently bonded. Graphite is therefore softer than diamond, even though both are made only of carbon, as each atom in diamond has four strong covalent bonds.

Conductivity

The delocalised electrons are free to move through graphite, so can carry charges and allow an electrical current to flow. Graphite is therefore a conductor of electricity.

Graphene

Graphene consists of only a single layer of graphite. Its strong covalent bonds make it a strong material that can also conduct electricity. It is also used in composites and high-tech electronics.

Fullerenes

- hollow cages of carbon atoms bonded together in one molecule
- can be arranged as a sphere or a tube (called a **nanotube**)
- molecules held together by weak intermolecular forces, so can slide over each other
- conduct electricity

Spheres

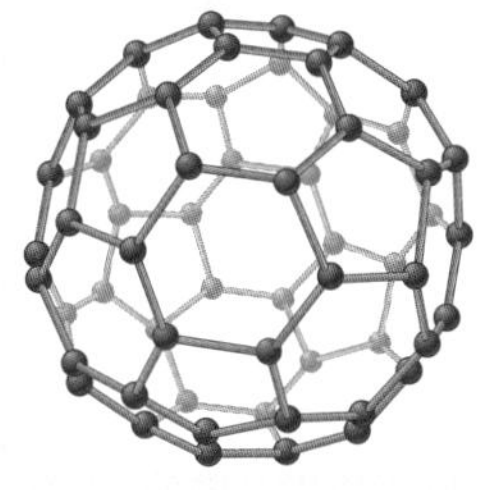

Buckminsterfullerene was the first fullerene to be discovered, and has 60 carbon atoms.

Other fullerenes exist with different numbers of carbon atoms arranged in rings that form hollow shapes.

Fullerenes like this can be used as lubricants and in drug delivery.

Nanotubes

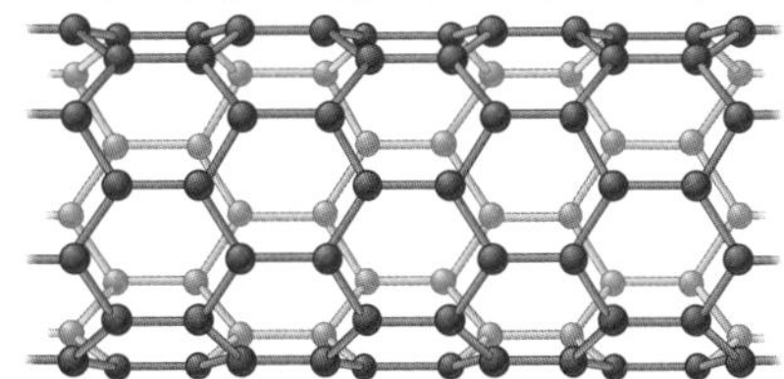

The carbon atoms in nanotubes are arranged in cylindrical tubes.

Their high **tensile strength** (they are difficult to break when pulled) makes them useful in electronics.

fullerene giant covalent graphene graphite intermolecular forces polymers single bond small molecules tensile strength

Retrieval

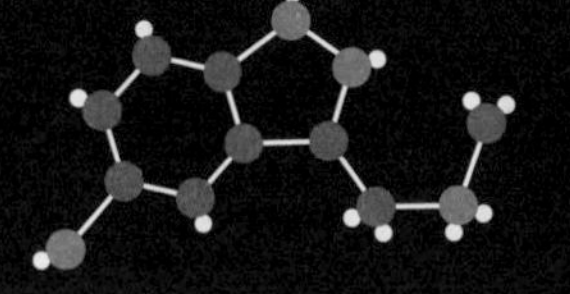

Learn the answers to the questions below, then cover the answers column with a piece of paper and write down as many as you can. Check and repeat.

	C2 questions	Answers
1	How are covalent bonds formed?	by atoms sharing electrons
2	Which type of atoms form covalent bonds between them?	non-metals
3	Describe the structure and bonding of a giant covalent substance.	billions of atoms bonded together by strong covalent bonds
4	Describe the structure and bonding of small molecules.	small numbers of atoms group together into molecules with strong covalent bonds between the atoms and weak intermolecular forces between the molecules
5	Describe the structure and bonding of polymers.	many identical molecules joined together by strong covalent bonds in a long chain, with weak intermolecular forces between the chains
6	Why do giant covalent substances have high melting points?	it takes a lot of energy to break the strong covalent bonds between the atoms
7	Why do small molecules have low melting points?	only a small amount of energy is needed to break the weak intermolecular forces
8	Why do large molecules have higher melting and boiling points than small molecules?	the intermolecular forces are stronger in large molecules
9	Why do most covalent substances not conduct electricity?	do not have delocalised electrons or ions
10	Describe the structure and bonding in graphite.	each carbon atom is bonded to three others in hexagonal rings arranged in layers – it has delocalised electrons and weak forces between the layers
11	Why can graphite conduct electricity?	the delocalised electrons can move through the graphite
12	Explain why graphite is soft.	layers are not bonded so can slide over each other
13	What is graphene?	one layer of graphite
14	Give two properties of graphene.	strong, conducts electricity
15	What is a fullerene?	hollow cage of carbon atoms arranged as a sphere or a tube
16	What is a nanotube?	hollow cylinder of carbon atoms
17	Give two properties of nanotubes.	high tensile strength, conduct electricity
18	Give three uses of fullerenes.	lubricants, drug delivery (spheres), high-tech electronics

Put paper here

Now go back and use the questions below to check your knowledge from previous chapters.

Previous questions / Answers

	Previous questions	Answers
1	What is an atom?	smallest part of an element that can exist
2	Describe the nuclear model of the atom.	dense nucleus with electrons orbiting it
3	Where are protons and neutrons?	in the nucleus
4	What is the relative mass of each sub-atomic particle?	proton: 1, neutron: 1, electron: 0 (very small)
5	What is the relative charge of each sub-atomic particle?	proton: +1, neutron: 0, electron: −1
6	How can you find out the number of protons in an atom?	the atomic number on the Periodic Table
7	How can you calculate the number of neutrons in an atom?	mass number – atomic number = neutrons
8	What are isotopes?	atoms of the same element (same number of protons) with different numbers of neutrons

Put paper here

Put paper here

Put paper here

Maths Skills

Practise your maths skills using the worked example and practice questions below.

Unit conversion

Scientists use different units depending on what is most useful to them. For example, when talking about the size of molecules it doesn't make sense to talk about them in kilometres, so we can use nanometres instead.

Whenever we do a calculation we need to make sure the units are the same, so have to do a unit conversion.

The table below shows you how some units can be compared to each other.

Unit	Standard form in m
1 metre (m)	1×10^{0} m
1 centimetre (cm)	1×10^{-2} m
1 millimetre (mm)	1×10^{-3} m
1 micrometre (μm)	1×10^{-6} m
1 nanometre (nm)	1×10^{-9} m
1 picometre (pm)	1×10^{-12} m

Worked example

Express 120 cm in metres.

When converting to a larger unit, multiply the original value by the value in metres in standard form.

$120 \times 1 \times 10^{-2} = 1.2$ m

Express 120 m in centimetres.

When converting to a smaller unit, divide the original value by the value in metres in standard form.

$= \frac{120}{1 \times 10^{-2}} = 12\,000$ cm

Practice

1 Express 400 cm in metres.

2 Express 20 m in millimetres.

3 Express 0.8 m in nanometres.

Practice

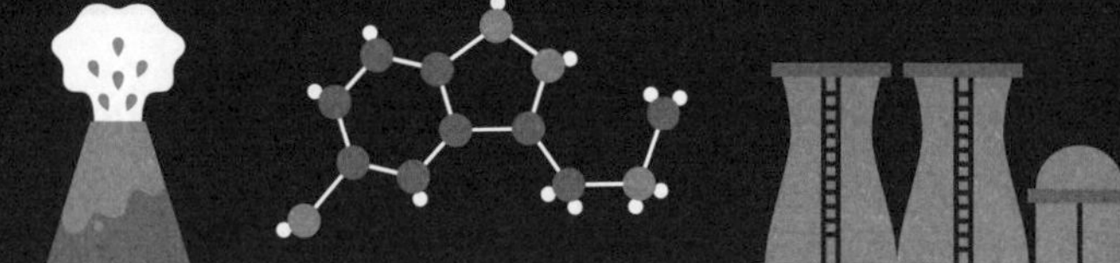

Exam-style questions

01 Silicon dioxide has a giant covalent structure. It has a high melting point and does not conduct electricity.

01.1 Draw **one** line from each property of silicon dioxide to the explanation of the property. **[2 marks]**

> **Exam Tip**
>
> Don't be tempted to draw four lines just because there are four boxes on the right.
>
> Only draw **two** lines in total, one from each of the boxes on the left.

Property	Explanation
	strong intermolecular forces of attraction
high melting point	there are no charged particles free to move
does not conduct electricity	strong covalent bonds
	electrons are free to move

01.2 **Figure 1** shows three suggested structures of silicon dioxide, SiO_2.

Figure 1

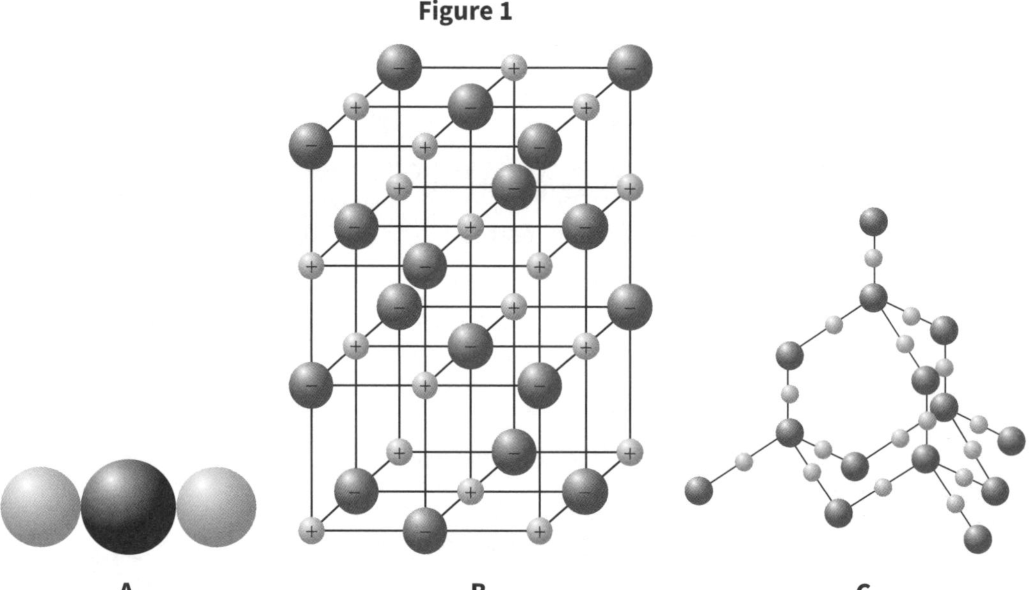

Identify which is the correct structure of silicon dioxide. **[1 mark]**

____

01.3 Silicon dioxide contains the elements silicon and oxygen.
Table 1 shows some properties of silicon and oxygen.

Table 1

Element	Melting point in °C	Boiling point in °C	Conducts electricity
oxygen	−218.8	−183	no
silicon	1414	3265	yes

Use **Table 1** and the Periodic Table to identify the types of structures of oxygen and silicon. **[2 marks]**

Oxygen gas ____________________

Silicon ____________________

Exam Tip

Look at the position of oxygen on the Periodic Table to help you identify the bonding in oxygen gas.

02 Phosphorus is a Group 5 element. It reacts with hydrogen to produce a compound called phosphine.

02.1 The electronic structure of phosphorus is 2,8,5.
Complete the dot and cross diagram in **Figure 2** to show the covalent bonding in a molecule of phosphine, PH_3.

You should show only the electrons in the outer shells. **[2 marks]**

Use crosses for hydrogen and dots for phosphorus. The groups they are in on the Periodic Table will help you work out how many electrons are in each outer shell.

Figure 2

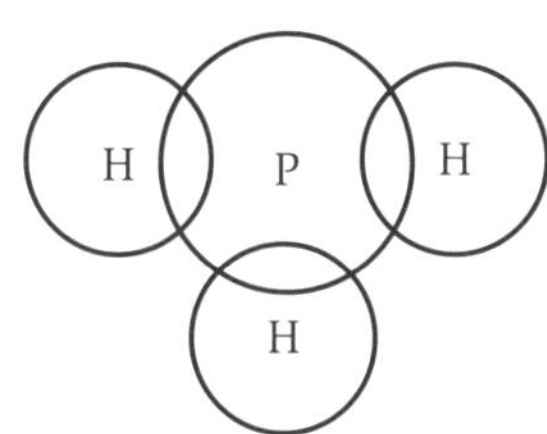

02.2 Name the type of bond or force overcome when liquid phosphine boils. **[1 mark]**

____

02.3 **Table 2** shows the boiling points of the compounds formed between hydrogen and the elements of Group 5 of the Periodic Table.

Table 2

Formula of compound	Radius of central atom in nm	Boiling point in °C
PH_3	0.110	−88
AsH_3	0.121	−55
SbH_3	0.141	−17
BiH_3	0.152	16

Identify the state that phosphine is in at room temperature. **[1 mark]**

____

02.4 Describe the trend shown in **Table 2**.
Suggest a reason for this trend. **[2 marks]**

____

____

____

Increase or decrease isn't enough – an increase or decrease in *what*?

03 Graphene is a single layer of graphite. It can be represented using a ball and stick model.

03.1 A ball and stick model is not a true representation of the structure of graphene. Give **one** reason why. **[1 mark]**

03.2 Explain why graphene conducts electricity. **[1 mark]**

03.3 Graphene is made up of carbon atoms only. One carbon atom has a mass of 1.99×10^{-23} g.
A scientist has a sheet of graphene of mass 0.240 g.
Calculate the number of carbon atoms in the sheet of graphene.
Give your answer to three significant figures. **[3 marks]**

> **Exam Tip**
> Don't be worried by very small or very big numbers – first check you can put them into your calculator correctly, then carry out the calculations.

04 Compare the physical properties of diamond and graphite.
In your answer, use ideas about bonding to explain the differences in properties. **[6 marks]**

> **Exam Tip**
> Ensure you link each property to the feature of its bonding that gives rise to that property.

05 **Table 3** shows some properties of three elements, **X**, **Y**, and **Z**.
The letters are not the chemical symbols of the elements.

Table 3

Element	Melting point in °C	Does the element conduct electricity?
X	−219	no
Y	−101	no
Z	very high	yes

05.1 Identify which element in **Table 3** could be carbon, in the form of graphite. **[1 mark]**

05.2 One of the elements in **Table 3** is chlorine.
Draw a dot and cross diagram to show the covalent bonding in a molecule of chlorine, Cl_2. You should show only the electrons in the outer shells. **[2 marks]**

05.3 One of the elements in **Table 3** is oxygen.
Draw a dot and cross diagram to show the covalent bonding in a molecule of oxygen, O_2. You should show only the electrons in the outer shells. **[2 marks]**

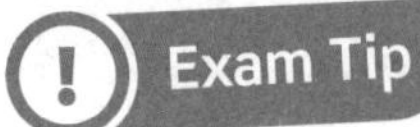

> The bonding in oxygen gas is a bit more complicated than in chlorine gas.

05.4 An oxygen atom is smaller than a chlorine atom.
Determine the letter of the element in **Table 3** that represents chlorine. Justify your choice. **[2 marks]**

06 **Figure 3** shows the ball and stick model of a compound, **X**.

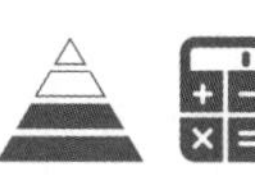

Figure 3

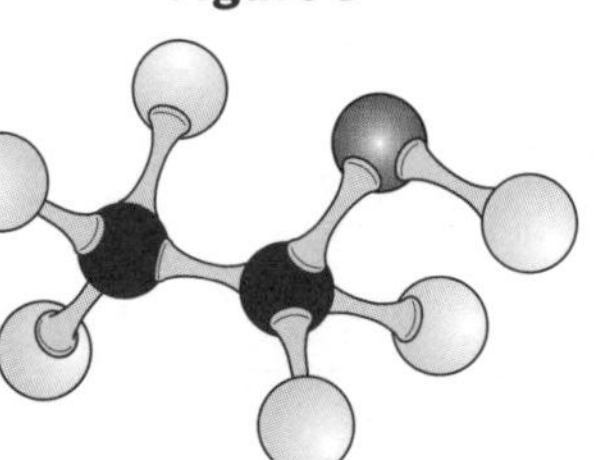

06.1 Predict **two** physical properties of compound **X**.
Explain why compound **X** has each of the properties you predicted. **[4 marks]**

06.2 In **Figure 3**, the different coloured balls represent atoms of different elements:

black = carbon   white = hydrogen   grey = oxygen.

Determine the molecular formula of compound **X**. **[1 mark]**

> **Exam Tip**
>
> Tick off the balls in the diagram once you have counted them, to make sure you don't count some twice.

06.3 A sample of compound **X** contains 6.02×10^{23} molecules.
Calculate the number of hydrogen atoms in the sample. **[1 mark]**

06.4 The boiling point of compound **X** is 78 °C and the melting point is −114 °C. Identify the state of compound **X** at 25 °C. **[1 mark]**

07 A student had samples of three substances, **P**, **Q**, and **R**. The student tested which of the substances conduct electricity.
Their results are shown in **Table 4**.

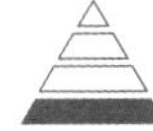

Table 4

Substance	Does it conduct electricity?
P	no
Q	no
R	yes

07.1 Give the letter of the substance in **Table 4** that could consist of nanotubes. **[1 mark]**

07.2 Give **one** other property of nanotubes. **[1 mark]**

07.3 Give **two** uses of nanotubes.
For each use, explain how the properties of nanotubes make them suitable for this use. **[2 marks]**

08 Hydrocarbons are compounds that are made up of carbon atoms and hydrogen atoms only.
Table 5 gives some data on two hydrocarbons.

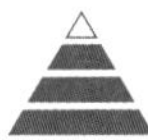

Table 5

Name of compound	Ball and stick model of molecule	Melting point in °C	Boiling point in °C
methane		−182	−162
hexane		−96	69

> **Exam Tip**
>
> You might not be used to seeing compounds drawn like this, but in reality large organic molecules are rarely sitting around in neat straight lines.

In the ball and stick models:

- black spheres represent carbon atoms
- white spheres represent hydrogen atoms

> **Exam Tip**
>
> If you're not sure, start by drawing a stick diagram, then a diagram with five overlapping circles, and then add the electrons.

08.1 Write the molecular formula of hexane. **[1 mark]**

08.2 Draw a dot and cross diagram to show the covalent bonding in a molecule of methane, CH_4. You should show only the electrons in the outer shells. **[2 marks]**

08.3 Draw the displayed formula of methane. In the formula, represent each atom with its chemical symbol and each single covalent bond with a line. **[1 mark]**

08.4 Use your own knowledge and the data in **Table 5** to compare the physical properties of methane and hexane at room temperature, 20 °C. **[6 marks]**

08.5 Explain, in terms of the forces between molecules, why hexane has a higher boiling point than methane. **[2 marks]**

09 **Table 6** gives the numbers of protons, neutrons, and electrons for some atoms and ions. The atoms and ions are represented by the letters **A** to **E**. These are not their chemical symbols. You will need to refer to the Periodic Table.

Table 6

Atom, isotope, or ion	Number of protons	Number of neutrons	Number of electrons
A	7	7	7
B	11	12	10
C	12	13	12
D	12	12	10
E	7	8	7

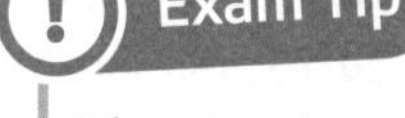

Exam Tip

The atomic number is the clue to the chemical symbol.

09.1 Write the chemical symbol of **A**, including its mass number, atomic number, and any charge. **[1 mark]**

09.2 Give the letter (**A** to **E**) of the isotope of **A** shown in **Table 6**. Write its chemical symbol, mass number, atomic number, and any charge. **[2 marks]**

09.3 Give the letter (**A** to **E**) of the ion of **C** shown in **Table 6**. Write the chemical formula of the ion of **C**, including its charge. **[2 marks]**

09.4 Give the chemical symbol of the atom in **Table 6** that has the greatest mass number.
Write its mass number and atomic number. **[2 marks]**

10 **Table 7** shows some properties of two oxides.

Table 7

Compound	Formula	Boiling or sublimation temperature in °C
carbon dioxide	CO_2	sublimes at −79
silicon dioxide	SiO_2	boils at 2230

Exam Tip

Sublimation is when a compounds turns from a solid to a gas, without becoming a liquid.

10.1 Draw a dot and cross diagram for carbon dioxide. You should show only the electrons in the outer shells. **[2 marks]**

10.2 Explain the difference in the boiling and sublimation temperatures shown in **Table 7**. **[3 marks]**

11 **Table 8** shows the strengths of the covalent bonds in six molecules.

Table 8

Element	Formula of molecule	Bond strength in kJ/mol
nitrogen	N_2	944
oxygen	O_2	496
hydrogen	H_2	436
chlorine	Cl_2	242
bromine	Br_2	193
iodine	I_2	151

11.1 Suggest a reason for the difference in bond strengths for Cl_2, Br_2, and I_2. Use the Periodic Table to help you answer this question. **[2 marks]**

11.2 Explain the difference in bond strengths for N_2, O_2, and H_2. Include dot and cross diagrams in your answer. **[4 marks]**

12.1 Use the data below to estimate the density of the nucleus of the lithium atom, $^{7}_{3}Li$.

Assume that the nucleus is spherical.

Give your answer in kg/m and to one significant figure.

mass of a proton = 1.7×10^{-27} kg

mass of a neutron = 1.7×10^{-27} kg

atomic radius of a lithium nucleus = 1×10^{-14} m^3

density = $\frac{\text{mass}}{\text{volume}}$

volume of a sphere = $\frac{4}{3}\pi r^3$ (where r = radius) **[4 marks]**

Exam Tip

You may not have used this equation in chemistry before, but all you need to do is plug the numbers in.

12.2 In **12.1** you assumed that a lithium nucleus is spherical. Give **one** other assumption you made. **[1 mark]**

12.3 Is this assumption valid? Explain your answer. **[2 marks]**

12.4 **Figure 5** shows a simple model of lithium.

Figure 5

This model also assumes that lithium atoms are spherical. Give **one** other assumption of this simple model of lithium and explain why the assumption is a limitation of the model. **[2 marks]**

Knowledge

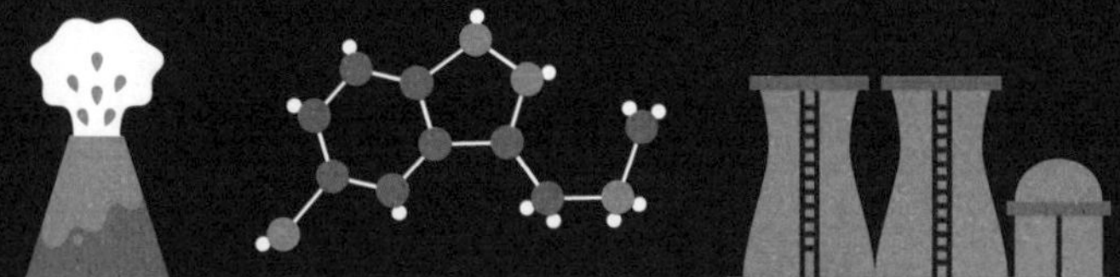

C3 Ionic bonding, metallic bonding, and structure

Ions

As well as sharing electrons, atoms can gain or lose electrons to give them a full outer shell. The number of protons is then different from the number of electrons. The resulting particle has a charge and is called an **ion**.

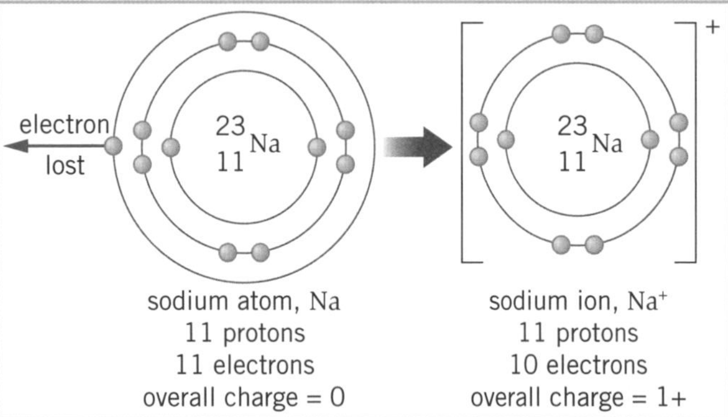

Ionic bonding

When metal atoms react with non-metal atoms they **transfer** electrons to the non-metal atom (instead of sharing them).

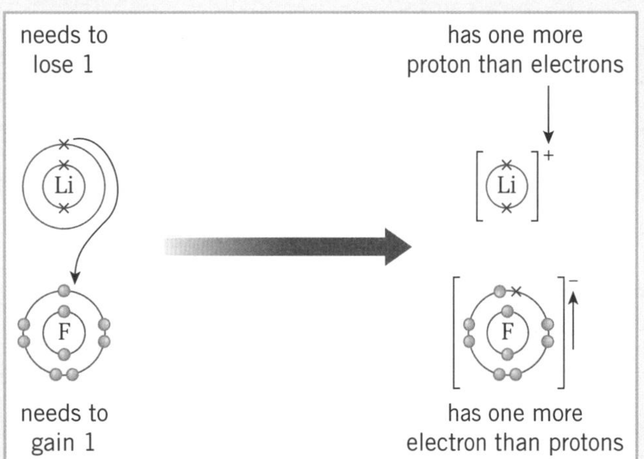

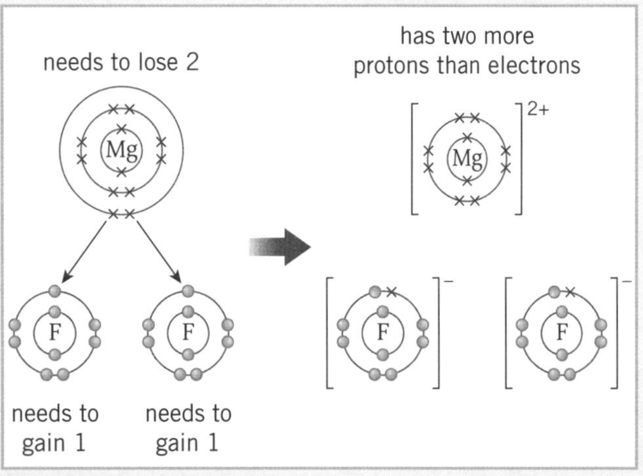

Metal atoms lose electrons to become positive ions. Non-metal atoms gain electrons to become negative ions.

Ionic structure

Giant ionic lattice

When metal atoms transfer electrons to non-metal atoms you end up with positive and negative ions. These are attracted to each other by the strong **electrostatic force of attraction**. This is called ionic bonding.

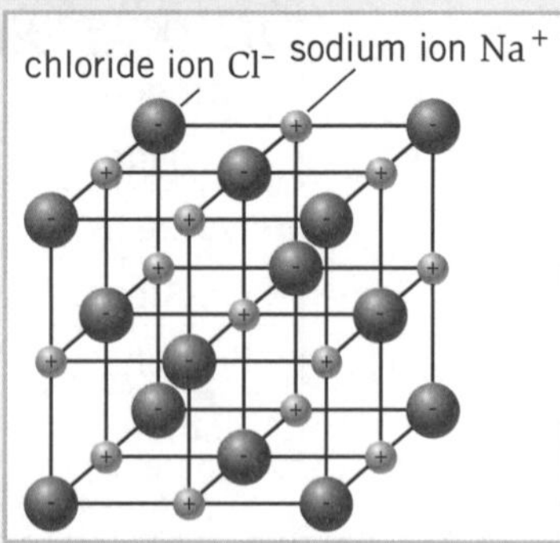

The electrostatic force of attraction works in all directions, so many billions of ions can be bonded together in a 3D structure.

Formulae

The formula of an ionic substance can be worked out

1. from its bonding diagram: for every one magnesium ion there are two fluoride ions – so the formula for magnesium fluoride is MgF_2
2. from a lattice diagram: there are nine Fe^{2+} ions and 18 S^- ions – simplifying this ratio gives a formula of FeS_2

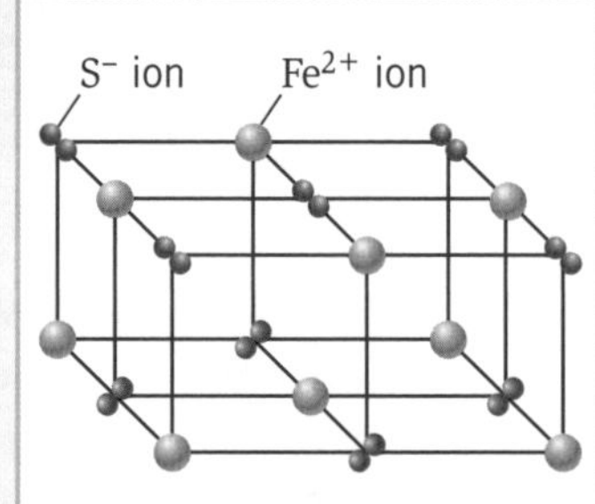

Ionic properties

Melting points

Ionic substances have high melting points because the electrostatic force of attraction between oppositely charged ions is strong and so requires lots of energy to break.

Conductivity

Solid ionic substances do not conduct electricity because the ions are fixed in position and not free to carry charge.

When melted or dissolved in water, ionic substances do conduct electricity because the ions are free to move and carry charge.

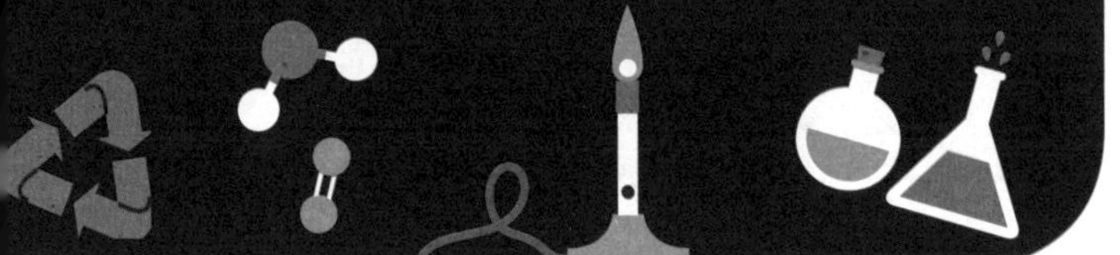

Metals

The atoms that make up metals form layers. The electrons in the outer shells of the atoms are **delocalised** – this means they are free to move through the whole structure.

The positive metal ions are then attracted to these delocalised electrons by the electrostatic force of attraction.

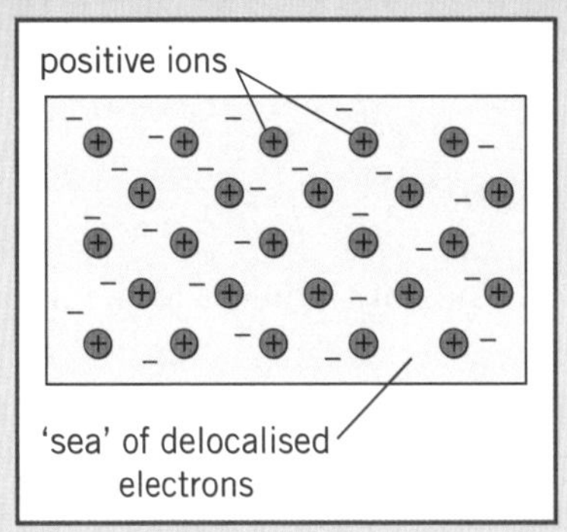

Metallic structure

Malleability

Pure metals are **malleable** (soft) because the layers can slide over each other.

Conductivity

Metals are good **conductors** of electricity and of thermal energy because delocalised electrons are free to move through the whole structure.

Melting points

Metals have high melting and boiling points because the electrostatic force of attraction between metal ions and delocalised electrons is strong so lots of energy is needed to break it.

Metallic properties

Alloys

Pure metals are often too soft to use as they are. Adding atoms of a different element can make the resulting mixture harder because the new atoms will be a different size to the pure metal's atoms. This will disturb the regular arrangement of the layers, preventing them from sliding over each other. The harder mixture is called an **alloy**.

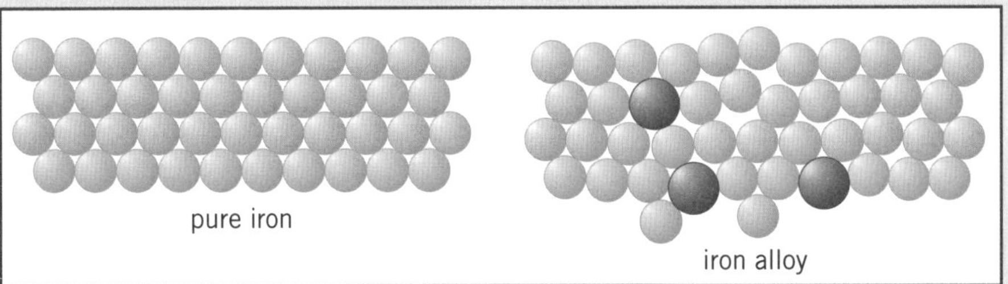

Revision tip

Practice If the difference in structure and properties between pure metals and alloys comes up in an exams, a good way to structure your answer could be:

pure → layers → sliding → soft

alloy → no layers → no sliding → hard

Revision tip

Practice Students often get the drawings for ionic and covalent bonding confused. This is a quick way to lose marks – make sure you get them the correct way around.

Key terms

Make sure you can write a definition for these key terms.

conductivity *conductor* *delocalised electron* *electrostatic force of attraction* *ion* *lattice* *layer* *malleable* *transfer*

Retrieval

Learn the answers to the questions below, then cover the answers column with a piece of paper and write down as many as you can. Check and repeat.

	C3 questions	Answers
1	What is an ion?	atom that has lost or gained electrons
2	Which kinds of elements form ionic bonds?	metals and non-metals
3	What charges do ions from Groups 1 and 2 form?	Group 1 form 1+, Group 2 form 2+
4	What charges do ions from Groups 6 and 7 form?	Group 6 form 2−, Group 7 form 1−
5	Name the force that holds oppositely charged ions together.	electrostatic force of attraction
6	Describe the structure of a giant ionic lattice.	regular structure of alternating positive and negative ions, held together by the electrostatic force of attraction
7	Why do ionic substances have high melting points?	electrostatic force of attraction between positive and negative ions is strong and requires lots of energy to break
8	Why don't ionic substances conduct electricity when solid?	ions are fixed in position so cannot move, and there are no delocalised electrons
9	When can ionic substances conduct electricity?	when melted or dissolved
10	Why do ionic substances conduct electricity when melted or dissolved?	ions are free to move and carry charge
11	Describe the structure of a pure metal.	layers of positive metal ions surrounded by delocalised electrons
12	Describe the bonding in a pure metal.	strong electrostatic forces of attraction between metal ions and delocalised electrons
13	What are four properties of pure metals?	malleable, high melting/boiling points, good conductors of electricity, good conductors of thermal energy
14	Explain why pure metals are malleable.	layers can slide over each other easily
15	Explain why metals have high melting and boiling points.	electrostatic force of attraction between positive metal ions and delocalised electrons is strong and requires a lot of energy to break
16	Why are metals good conductors of electricity and of thermal energy?	delocalised electrons are free to move through the metal
17	What is an alloy?	mixture of a metal with atoms of another element
18	Explain why alloys are harder than pure metals.	different sized atoms disturb the layers, preventing them from sliding over each other

Put paper here

Now go back and use the questions below to check your knowledge from previous chapters.

Previous questions | Answers

	Previous questions		Answers
1	Describe the structure and bonding of a giant covalent substance.	Put paper here	billions of atoms bonded together by strong covalent bonds
2	Why do atoms have no overall charge?		equal numbers of positive protons and negative electrons
3	Why can graphite conduct electricity?	Put paper here	the delocalised electrons can move through the graphite
4	Why do large molecules have higher melting and boiling points than small molecules?		the intermolecular forces are stronger in large molecules
5	What did James Chadwick discover?		uncharged particle called the neutron
6	Give three uses of fullerenes.	Put paper here	lubricants, drug delivery (spheres), high-tech electronics
7	Give two properties of nanotubes.		high tensile strength, conduct electricity
8	How many electrons would you place in the first, second, and third shells?		up to 2 in the first shell and up to 8 in the second and third shells

Maths Skills

Practise your maths skills using the worked example and practice questions below.

2D and 3D models

Scientists often use models to describe what things look like and how they act.

These models can be 2D or 3D but they are always just approximations – they are there to help you understand but have strengths and weaknesses.

Worked example

The model shows how the layers in a metal alloy are disturbed. What are the strengths and weaknesses of this model?

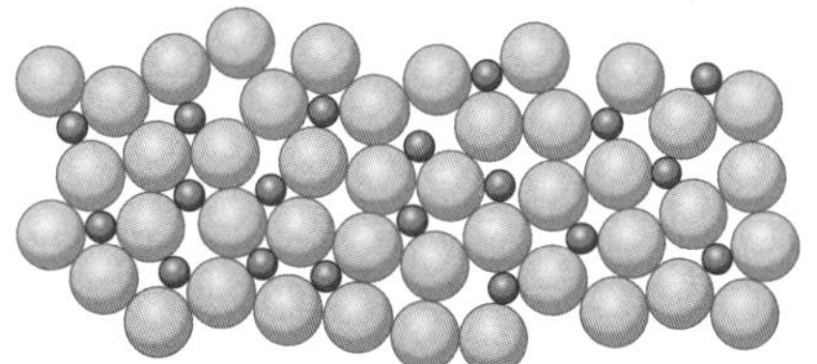

The model is in two dimensions, which helps you to see how the layers are disturbed by atoms of different sizes.

However, the metal is normally three dimensional, which this model does not show, so it is not an accurate representation of the metal's structure.

Practice

Compare and contrast the two models below showing the structure of methane.

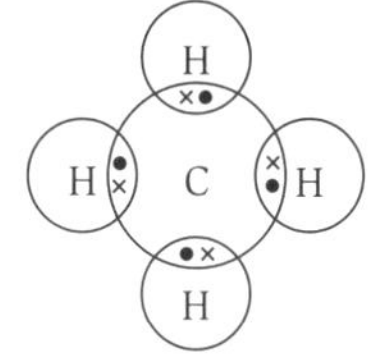

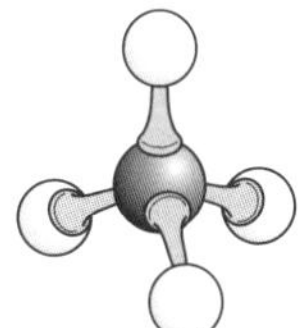

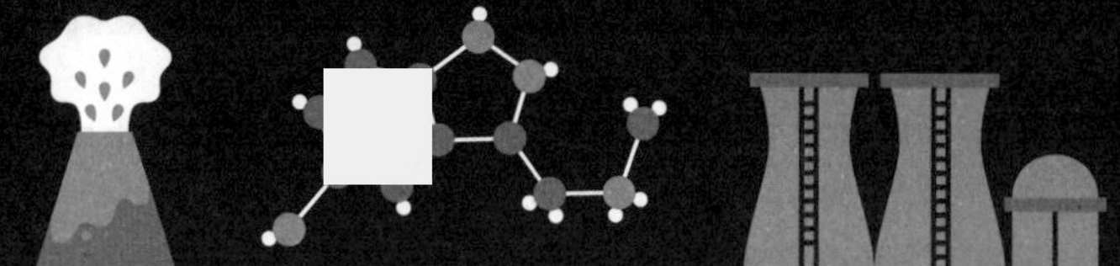

Exam-style questions

01.1 Which property is typical of metals? **[1 mark]**

Tick **one** box.

They are poor conductors of electricity. ☐

They conduct electricity in the solid state but not in the liquid state. ☐

They conduct electricity in the liquid state but not in the solid state. ☐

They conduct electricity in the solid and liquid states. ☐

> **Exam Tip**
>
> Only tick *one* box. Ticking more than one will mean no marks, even if one of the boxes you've ticked is correct.

01.2 Describe the structure of a pure metal. **[3 marks]**

____

____

____

____

01.3 Explain why the bonding in a pure metal means that metals can be shaped. **[2 marks]**

____

____

____

> **Exam Tip**
>
> This is another way of asking why pure metals are soft.

01.4 Mercury is a metal. It is a liquid at room temperature. Suggest why mercury is an unusual metal. **[1 mark]**

____

____

02 Platinum is a metal. It can be used to make jewellery.

Figure 1 shows the arrangement of particles in platinum.

Figure 1

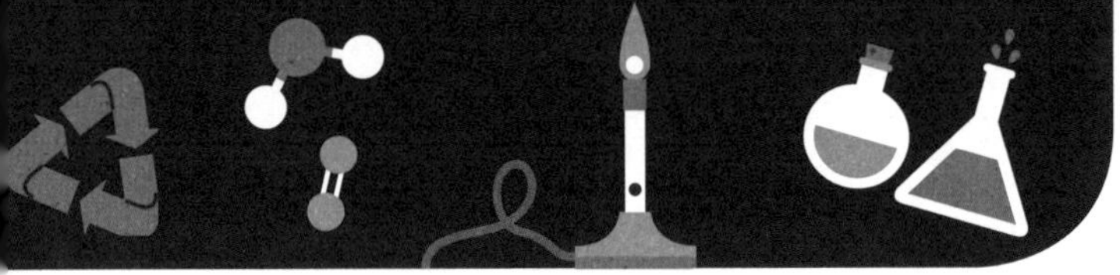

02.1 Explain why platinum can be bent and shaped.

Give your answer in terms of the arrangement of particles in the metal. **[2 marks]**

> **Exam Tip**
>
> This is a two-mark question so you need to write at least two points.

02.2 Explain why platinum has a high melting point.

Give your answer in terms of the bonding in the metal. **[3 marks]**

02.3 Pure platinum is quite soft.

An alloy of platinum that contains rhodium is harder than pure platinum.

Suggest an advantage of making jewellery from a platinum alloy instead of from pure platinum. **[1 mark]**

02.4 Explain why the platinum alloy is harder than pure platinum. **[3 marks]**

> **Exam Tip**
>
> Think carefully about the difference between the structures of pure platinum and the platinum alloy.

03 **Figure 2** shows the boiling points of three substances: ethanol (C_2H_5OH), hexanol ($C_6H_{13}OH$), and mercury. Each substance is represented by a letter (**X**, **Y**, or **Z**). The letters are not the chemical symbols of the substances.

Figure 2

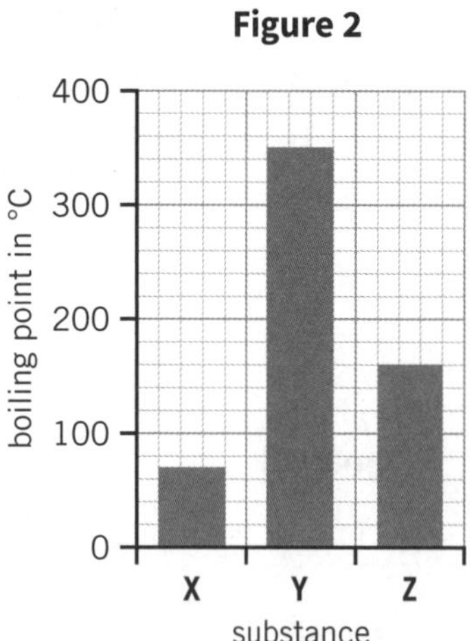

03.1 Give the boiling point of substance **Y**. **[1 mark]**

03.2 Which substance has a boiling point of 78 °C? **[1 mark]**

03.3 Suggest which letter represents each substance. Explain your answer. **[3 marks]**

! Exam Tip

Think about the structure of each of the compounds and how they will affect their boiling points.

04 Magnesium reacts with oxygen to form magnesium oxide.

04.1 **Figure 3** shows a model of magnesium atoms. Complete **Figure 3** to show the metallic bonding in magnesium. **[2 marks]**

Figure 3

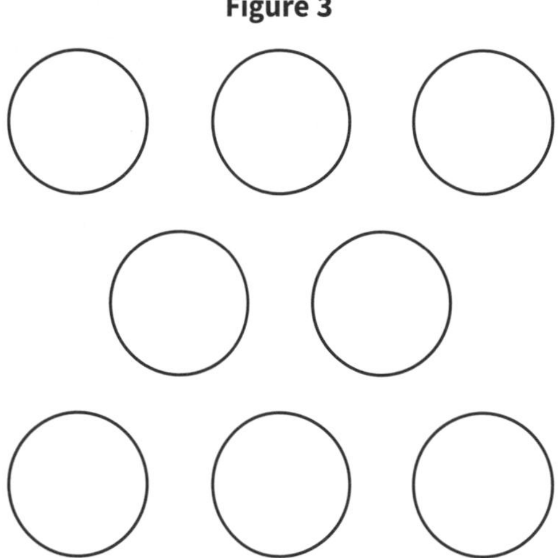

! Exam Tip

You'll need to add on positive and negative charges.

04.2 Draw a dot and cross diagram of magnesium oxide. **[2 marks]**

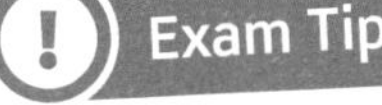

04.3 Draw **one** line from each substance to the correct property and explanation. **[2 marks]**

Substance	Property and explanation
	conducts electricity in the solid and liquid states because its electrons are free to move
magnesium oxide	conducts electricity in the liquid state only because its electrons are then free to move
magnesium	conducts electricity in the solid and liquid states because its ions are free to move
	conducts electricity in the liquid state only because its ions are then free to move

Exam Tip

Read the instruction in the question carefully. Not all of the boxes on the right hand side will have lines going into them.

04.4 Write a balanced symbol equation for the reaction between magnesium and oxygen. Include state symbols. **[3 marks]**

Exam Tip

When writing balanced equations:

1 recall the formulae
2 write down the reactants
3 work out the ions
4 determine the formulae of any products
5 check the equation is balanced
6 add state symbols

04.5 Magnesium and aluminium are two metals. They both have a low density, which makes them lightweight metals. Bicycle wheels can be made of magnesium and aluminium alloys.
Explain why an alloy of magnesium and aluminium is used instead of the pure metals. **[2 marks]**

05 **Table 1** shows the relative conductivities of some metals. The higher the relative conductivity value, the better the metal conducts electricity.

Table 1

Metal	Relative conductivity
aluminium	0.382
beryllium	0.250
lithium	0.108
magnesium	0.224
sodium	0.218
zinc	0.167

05.1 Describe the bonding in pure metals. **[2 marks]**

05.2 *'The conductivity of a metal depends on the number of delocalised electrons per atom and which period the metal is in.'*
Zinc has two electrons in its outer shell.
Evaluate the statement above using **Table 1** and the Periodic Table. **[6 marks]**

Exam Tip

You'll have to give evidence for and against this statement and then state a conclusion and justify it with data from the table.

06 **Table 2** shows the melting points of some ionic compounds.

Table 2

Compound	Melting point in °C
calcium oxide	2572
calcium sulfide	2525
calcium bromide	730
magnesium oxide	2852
magnesium sulfide	2000
magnesium bromide	711
sodium oxide	1132
sodium sulfate	884
sodium bromide	747

06.1 Describe the pattern between the charges of the ions in a compound and the melting point of the compound. **[6 marks]**

06.2 Explain the general pattern observed in **Table 2**. **[2 marks]**

> **Exam Tip**
> It might help to note the charge of each ion next to the table so that it is easy to compare the charges to the melting points.

07 **Figure 4** shows the outer electrons in an atom of magnesium and in an atom of bromine.

Figure 4

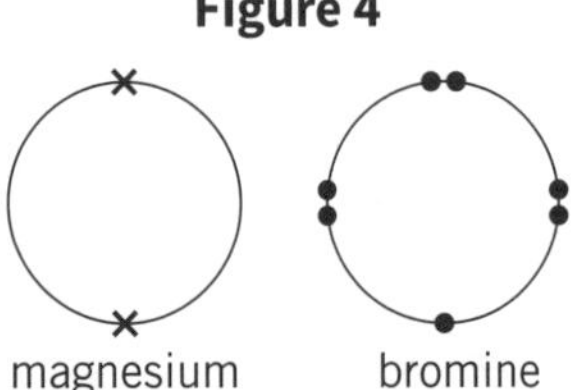

Magnesium is in Group 2 of the Periodic Table and bromine is in Group 7.

07.1 Magnesium and bromine form an ionic compound.
Describe what happens to the electrons when magnesium reacts with bromine. **[3 marks]**

07.2 Give the formulae of the ions formed in the reaction between magnesium and bromine. **[2 marks]**

07.3 Give the chemical formula of the compound formed. **[1 mark]**

07.4 Predict the physical properties of the compound formed. **[3 marks]**

> **Exam Tip**
> Bromine only needs one more electron to get a full outer shell, and magnesium has two electrons to give away. Think carefully about the ratio of bromine to magnesium.

08 **Table 3** shows the properties of five substances. Each substance is represented by a letter. The letters are not the chemical symbols of the substances.

Table 3

Substance	Melting point in °C	Does it conduct electricity in the solid state?	Does it conduct electricity in the liquid state?
A	993	no	yes
B	1085	yes	yes
C	1263	no	yes
D	1064	yes	yes
E	30	yes	yes

08.1 Use **Table 3** to deduce whether substance **C** is a metal or an ionic compound. Justify your answer. **[3 marks]**

08.2 Give the letters of **two** substances in **Table 3** that could be the element copper. Justify your answer. **[2 marks]**

08.3 Substance **E** represents the metal gallium.
Explain why the melting point of gallium is unusual compared to most other metals. **[3 marks]**

09 This question is about two compounds: caesium oxide, Cs_2O, and dichlorine monoxide, Cl_2O.

09.1 Draw a dot and cross diagram for dichlorine monoxide. **[2 marks]**

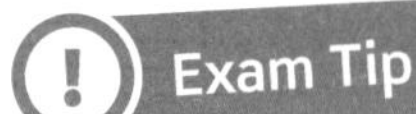

Exam Tip

Even if these compounds are unfamiliar to you, the same rules apply as to any other compound.

09.2 Describe the difference in bonding between the two compounds. **[5 marks]**

09.3 Compare **one** physical property of caesium oxide and dichlorine monoxide. Explain your predictions. **[4 marks]**

09.4 The melting point of caesium oxide is 490 °C. The melting point of barium oxide is 1923 °C. Barium is in Group 2 of the Periodic Table but the same period as caesium.
Suggest why barium oxide has a significantly higher melting point than caesium oxide. **[2 marks]**

10 **Figure 5** shows the outer electrons of a potassium atom and an oxygen atom.

Figure 5

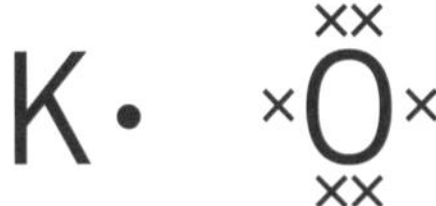

10.1 Draw a dot and cross diagram for the ionic compound formed when oxygen reacts with potassium. **[2 marks]**

10.2 Describe how the ions are bonded together in potassium oxide. **[3 marks]**

10.3 The melting point of potassium oxide is 740 °C. The melting point of oxygen is −218 °C.
Explain why the melting point of potassium oxide is much higher than that of oxygen. **[5 marks]**

10.4 The melting point of potassium is 63.5 °C.
Give **one** conclusion that can be made about metallic and ionic bonding using this data and the data from **10.3**. **[1 mark]**

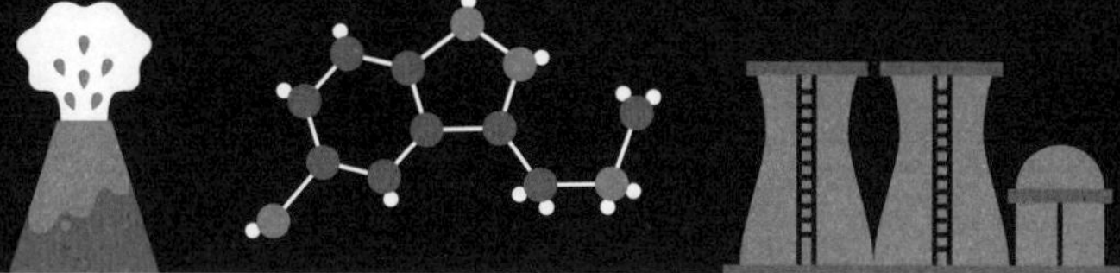

Knowledge

C4 The Periodic Table

Development of the Periodic Table

The modern Periodic Table lists approximately 100 elements. It has changed a lot over time as scientists have organised the elements differently.

The first lists of elements, Mendeleev's Periodic Table, and the modern Periodic Table have a number of differences in how they list the discovered elements.

Mendeleev was able to accurately predict the properties of undiscovered elements based on the positions of the gaps in his table.

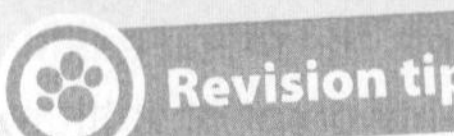

Revision tip

This topic makes a great six-mark question, or an interpret and evaluate question.

This is an area the exam board could ask you to apply your knowledge in a new context and introduce unfamiliar examples.

	First lists of elements	Mendeleev's Periodic Table	Modern Periodic Table
How are elements ordered?	by atomic mass	normally by atomic mass but some elements were swapped around	by atomic number
Are there gaps?	no gaps	gaps left for undiscovered elements	no gaps – all elements up to a certain atomic number have been discovered
How are elements grouped?	not grouped	grouped by chemical properties	grouped by the number of electrons in the outer shells
Metals and non-metals	no clear distinction	no clear distinction	metals to the left, non-metals to the right
Problems	some elements grouped inappropriately	incomplete, with no explanation for why some elements had to be swapped to fit in the appropriate groups	—

Sub-atomic discoveries

The discovery of electrons allowed scientists to work out that elements with the same number of electrons in their outer shell had similar chemical properties.

The discovery of protons allowed scientists to order the elements in the Periodic Table by their atomic number.

The discovery of neutrons led to scientists discovering **isotopes**. Isotopes explained why some elements didn't seem to fit when the Periodic Table was organised by atomic mass (like iodine and tellurium).

Group 0

Elements in **Group 0** are called the **noble gases**. Noble gases have the following properties:

- full outer shells, so do not need to lose or gain electrons
- very unreactive (**inert**) so exist as single atoms as they do not bond to form molecules
- boiling points that increase down the group.

Key terms Make sure you can write a definition for these key terms.

alkali metals chemical properties displacement groups halogens inert isotopes noble gas organised Periodic Table reactivity undiscovered unreactive

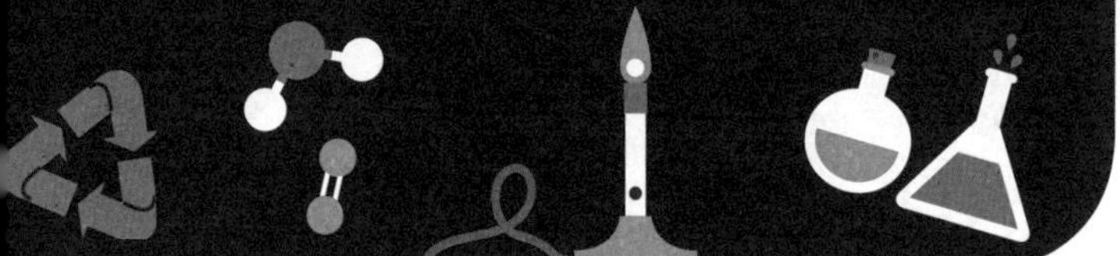

Group 1 elements

Group 1 elements react with oxygen, chlorine, and water, for example:

lithium + oxygen → lithium oxide

lithium + chlorine → lithium chloride

lithium + water → lithium hydroxide + hydrogen

Group 1 elements are called **alkali metals** because they react with water to form an alkali (a solution of their metal hydroxide).

Group 1 properties

Group 1 elements all have one electron in their outer shell. They are very reactive because they only need to lose one electron to react.

Reactivity *increases* down Group 1 because as you move down the group:

- the atoms increase in size
- the outer electron is further away from the nucleus, and there are more shells shielding the outer electron from the nucleus
- the electrostatic attraction between the nucleus and the outer electron is weaker
- so it is easier to lose the one outer electron.

The melting point and boiling point decreases down Group 1.

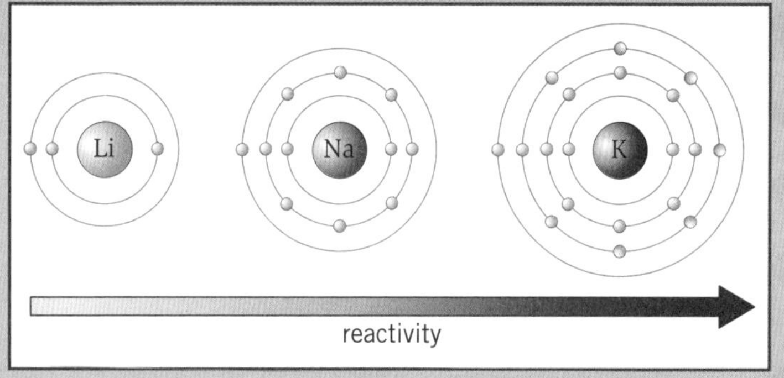

Group 7 elements

Group 7 elements are called the **halogens**. They are non-metals that exist as molecules made up of pairs of atoms.

Name	Formula	State at room temperature	Melting point and boiling point	Reactivity
fluorine	F_2	gas	increases down the group	decreases down the group
chlorine	Cl_2	gas		
bromine	Br_2	liquid		
iodine	I_2	solid		

Group 7 reactivity

Reactivity *decreases* down Group 7 because as you move down the group:

- the atoms increase in size
- the outer shell is further away from the nucleus, and there are more shells between the nucleus and the outer shell
- the electrostatic attraction from the nucleus to the outer shell is weaker
- so it is harder to gain the one electron to fill the outer shell.

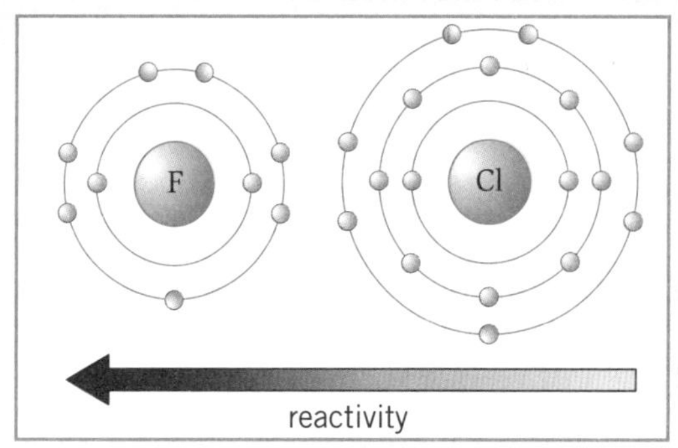

Group 7 displacement

More reactive Group 7 elements can take the place of less reactive ones in a compound. This is called **displacement**.

For example, fluorine displaces chlorine as it is more reactive:

fluorine + potassium chloride → potassium fluoride + chlorine

Retrieval

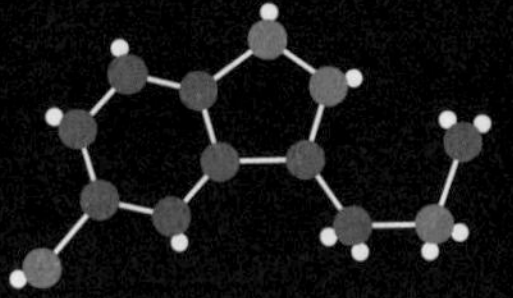

Learn the answers to the questions below, then cover the answers column with a piece of paper and write as many as you can. Check and repeat.

	C4 questions	Answers
1	How is the modern Periodic Table ordered?	by atomic number
2	How were the early lists of elements ordered?	by atomic mass
3	Why did Mendeleev swap the order of some elements?	to group them by their chemical properties
4	Why did Mendeleev leave gaps in his Periodic Table?	leave room for elements that had not yet been discovered
5	Why do elements in a group have similar chemical properties?	have the same number of electrons in their outer shell
6	Where are metals and non-metals located on the Periodic Table?	metals to the left, non-metals to the right
7	What name is given to the Group 1 elements?	alkali metals
8	Why are the alkali metals named this?	they are metals that react with water to form an alkali
9	Give the general equations for the reactions of alkali metals with oxygen, chlorine, and water.	metal + oxygen → metal oxide metal + chlorine → metal chloride metal + water → metal hydroxide + hydrogen
10	Why does the reactivity of the alkali metals increase down the group?	they are larger atoms, so the outermost electron is further from the nucleus, meaning there are weaker electrostatic forces of attraction and more shielding between the nucleus and outer electron, and it is easier to lose the electron
11	What name is given to the Group 7 elements?	halogens
12	Give the formulae of the first four halogens.	F_2, Cl_2, Br_2, I_2
13	How do the melting points of the halogens change down the group?	increase (higher melting point)
14	Why does the reactivity of the halogens decrease down the group?	they are larger atoms, so the outermost shell is further from the nucleus, meaning there are weaker electrostatic forces of attraction and more shielding between the nucleus and outer shell, and it is harder to gain an electron
15	What is a displacement reaction?	when a more reactive element takes the place of a less reactive one in a compound
16	What name is given to the Group 0 elements?	noble gases
17	Why are the noble gases inert?	they have full outer shells so do not need to lose or gain electrons
18	How do the melting points of the noble gases change down the group?	increase (higher melting point)

Put paper here

Now go back and use the questions below to check your knowledge from previous chapters.

Previous questions / Answers

	Previous questions	Answers
1	What is graphene?	one layer of graphite
2	Which type of atoms form covalent bonds between them?	non-metals
3	What charges do ions from Groups 6 and 7 form?	Group 6 form 2−, Group 7 form 1−
4	Describe the structure of a giant ionic lattice.	regular structure of alternating positive and negative ions, held together by the electrostatic force of attraction
5	What is a mixture?	two or more substances not chemically combined
6	What are four properties of pure metals?	malleable, high melting/boiling points, good conductors of electricity, good conductors of thermal energy
7	Explain why alloys are harder than pure metals.	different sized atoms disturb the layers, preventing them from sliding over each other

Put paper here

Maths Skills

Practise your maths skills using the worked example and practice questions below.

Plotting straight lines

When numerical data is plotted onto a graph you usually need to draw a line of best fit.

Sometimes this will be a straight line, but other times it will be a curve. You should draw whichever type of line fits the data.

Worked example

Early chemists carried out many experiments to work out the properties of different elements. One experiment was to heat a sample in oxygen and see how its mass changes depending on the mass of oxygen used. In one experiment, a scientist obtained the data below.

Mass of oxygen in g	Mass increase of element in g
5.0	2.1
10.0	4.0
15.0	6.2
20.0	8.1
25.0	9.8

This produces a graph with a positive correlation – as the value on the x-axis increases, so does the value on the y-axis.

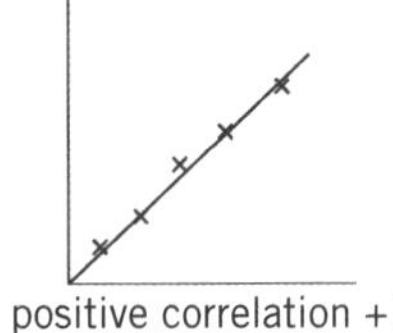

positive correlation +1

With a negative correlation the value on the x-axis increases, the value on the y-axis decreases.

Practice

In another experiment, scientists obtained the data below.

Mass of oxygen in g	Mass increase of element in g
0.0	0.0
4.0	5.2
8.0	10.1
12.0	14.7
16.0	19.8
20.0	25.1

1 Using graph paper, draw a graph for these data and include a straight line of best fit.

2 Does your graph show a positive or negative correlation?

3 In another experiment, scientists looked at how the mass of a 5.0 g element increased as it was heated.

Where does the line of best fit start on this graph, compared to on your graph?

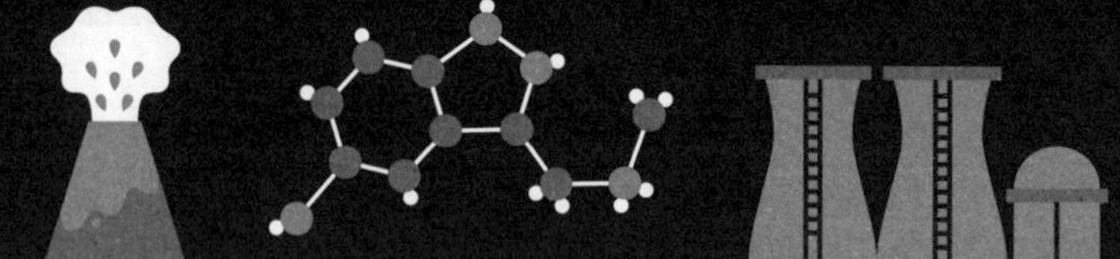

Exam-style questions

01 Rubidium is in Group 1 of the Periodic Table.

01.1 Is rubidium a compound, a metal, or a non-metal? **[1 mark]**

____

01.2 What are the products when rubidium reacts with water? **[1 mark]**

Tick **one** box.

rubidium oxide and oxygen ☐

rubidium hydroxide and oxygen ☐

rubidium chloride and hydrogen ☐

rubidium hydroxide and hydrogen ☐

> **Exam Tip**
> The formula of water might give you a clue.

01.3 Rubidium can also react with oxygen.

Write the word equation for this reaction. **[1 mark]**

____

01.4 Sodium is another element in Group 1 of the Periodic Table. Sodium reacts with bromine.

Complete the balanced symbol equation for the reaction between sodium and bromine. **[2 marks]**

$$\_\_\_\_\ \text{Na}(\_\_\_\_) + \text{Br}_2(\_\_\_\_) \rightarrow \_\_\_\_\ \text{NaBr(s)}$$

> **Exam Tip**
> All you need to add in is the numbers in front of the elements and compounds and the state symbols. Don't add in any other compounds.

01.5 Rubidium also reacts with bromine.

Explain the difference in the reactivity of sodium and rubidium with bromine. **[4 marks]**

____

____

____

02 In early versions of the Periodic Table, scientists classified the elements by arranging them in order of atomic weights.

02.1 In these early Periodic Tables, some elements were placed in groups with elements that have very different properties.

Describe **two** changes that Mendeleev made to overcome this problem. **[2 marks]**

____

____

____

02.2 Explain how the discovery of protons enabled scientists to improve the order of the elements in the Periodic Table. **[2 marks]**

> **Exam Tip**
> Think about how the Periodic Table is arranged now.

02.3 The Bohr model of the atom states that electrons orbit the nucleus in energy levels or shells.

Explain how the Bohr model helped scientists to understand why elements in the same group of the Periodic Table have similar properties. **[2 marks]**

02.4 Suggest why the discovery of neutrons helped scientists to understand why substances could have different atomic masses but identical chemical properties. **[1 mark]**

> **Exam Tip**
> For example, carbon-12 and carbon-13 have different masses but behave the same.

03 The columns of the Periodic Table are called groups. The elements in a group have similar properties.

03.1 Draw **one** line from each group to a property of the elements in this group. **[3 marks]**

Group in Periodic Table	Property
	react with water to make alkaline solutions
Group 0	react with metals to make covalent compounds
Group 1	inert
Group 7	displace more reactive elements from their compounds
	react with metals to make ionic compounds

03.2 Explain the differences in the trend in reactivity down Group 1 and Group 7. **[6 marks]**

03.3 Explain the reactivity of Group 0. **[2 marks]**

> **Exam Tip**
> The answer to **03.2** needs to have two sections. Make it clear which group you are talking about in each section.

04 Xenon is in Group 0 and Period 5 of the Periodic Table.
Under extreme conditions, xenon will react with fluorine.

04.1 Explain why xenon and fluorine are able to react. **[3 marks]**

Figure 1

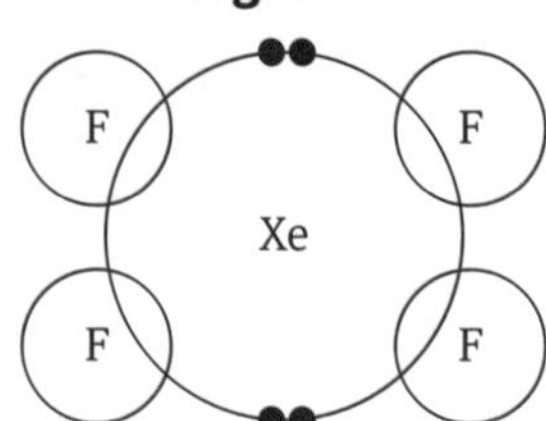

04.2 When xenon reacts with fluorine, the xenon atom is able to have 12 electrons in its outer shell. Complete the dot and cross diagram in **Figure 1** to show the product of the reaction between xenon and fluorine. **[2 marks]**

04.3 Identify the type of bonding in xenon tetrafluroide. **[1 mark]**

05 A teacher demonstrated the reaction of sodium with water.
This is the method they used:

1 Fill a big glass trough with water.

2 Use tongs to take a lump of sodium out of the oil in its storage bottle.

3 Cut off a small piece of sodium.

4 Put the bigger lump of sodium back in its storage bottle.

5 Use tongs to place the small piece of sodium on the surface of the water.

05.1 Which group of the Periodic Table is sodium in?
Choose **one** answer. **[1 mark]**

Group 1 Group 2 Group 3 Group 4

05.2 Suggest a reason for step **4**. **[1 mark]**

05.3 Suggest a reason for using tongs in step **5**. **[1 mark]**

Exam Tip

Being able to read a method and suggest improvements is an important skill in science.

05.4 In step **5**, the sodium does not start reacting with the water immediately. Suggest an improvement to step **3** to make the reaction start more quickly. **[1 mark]**

05.5 Name the gas produced in the reaction. **[1 mark]**

05.6 Describe how the teacher could show that one of the products of the reaction makes an alkaline solution in water. **[2 marks]**

05.7 Explain why the reaction of lithium with water is less vigorous than the reaction of sodium with water. In your answer, include the electronic structures of lithium and sodium. **[3 marks]**

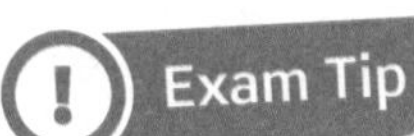

Exam Tip

First decide if caesium is more or less reactive than sodium.

05.8 Caesium is an element near the bottom of Group 1.
Predict the observations on adding caesium to water. **[1 mark]**

06 A student carried out some reactions of halogens with solutions of potassium chloride, potassium bromide, and potassium iodide.
The solutions were labelled **X**, **Y**, and **Z**.
Table 1 shows the student's results.

Table 1

Reacted with	Solution X	Solution Y	Solution Z
chlorine water	yellow solution formed	no change observed	brown solution formed
bromine water	no change observed	no change observed	brown solution formed
iodine water	no change observed	no change observed	no change observed

Deduce the identities of solutions **X**, **Y**, and **Z**. Justify your decisions. Use electronic structures to suggest an explanation for one of the reactions that occurs. **[6 marks]**

07 Four pairs of substances are reacted together:

A lithium and bromine

B lithium and fluorine

C sodium and bromine

D sodium and fluorine

Predict which pair of substances has the most vigorous reaction. Explain your prediction. **[6 marks]**

Exam Tip

For this answer you'll have to refer to the locations of the elements on the Periodic Table and their structures.

08 **Figure 2** shows the electronic structures of some Group 0 elements. Each is labelled with a letter. The letters are not the chemical symbols of the elements.

Figure 2

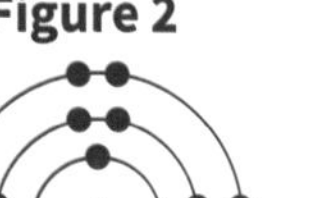

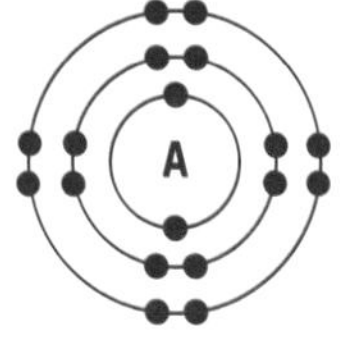
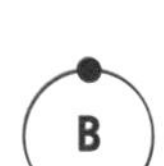

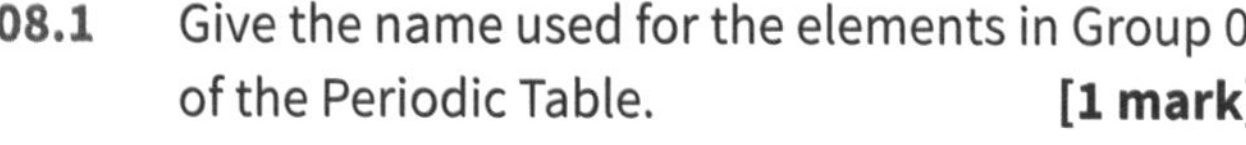

08.1 Give the name used for the elements in Group 0 of the Periodic Table. **[1 mark]**

08.2 Which letter represents a helium atom? **[1 mark]**

08.3 Give the letter of the atom of the element in **Figure 2** that has the lowest boiling point. **[1 mark]**

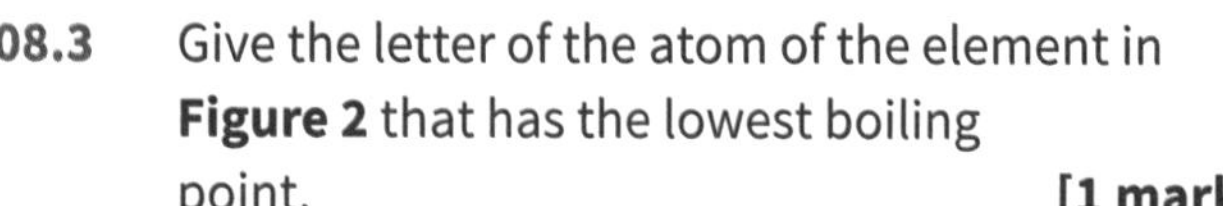

08.4 Draw the electronic structure of a neon atom. **[1 mark]**

08.5 Explain why Group 0 elements do not readily form molecules. **[2 marks]**

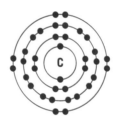

Exam Tip

You don't get marks for perfect circles, so try not to spend a long time drawing.

09 **Figure 3** shows the electronic structures of four atoms. Each atom is labelled with a letter (**P**, **Q**, **R**, or **S**). The letters are not the chemical symbols of the elements.

Figure 3

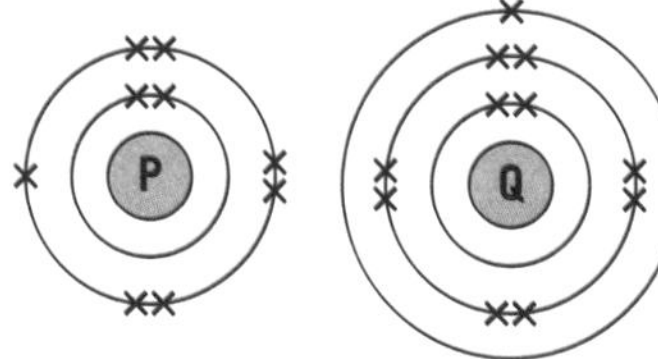

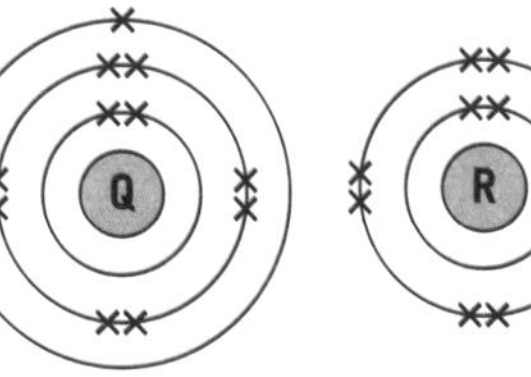

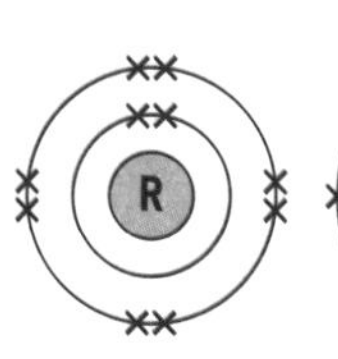

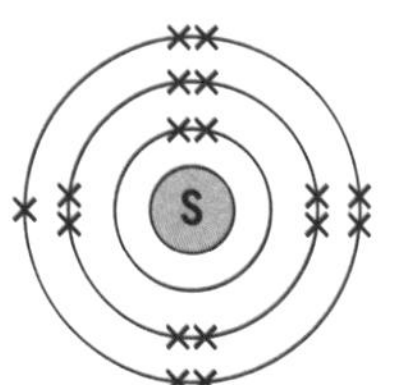

Exam Tip

Looking at the electrons in the outer shells of these elements is the key to answering the questions.

09.1 Give the letter of the atom of a Group 1 element. **[1 mark]**

09.2 Give the letter of the atom of an unreactive element. Explain why this element is unreactive. **[2 marks]**

09.3 Give the letters of **two** atoms of elements that are in the same group of the Periodic Table. **[1 mark]**

10 **Figure 4** shows the electronic structures of the atoms of three Group 2 elements.

Figure 4

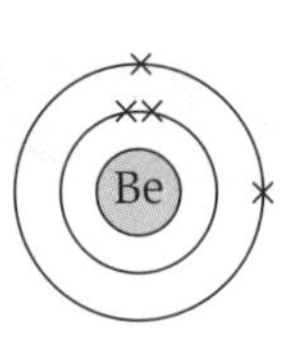

berylium

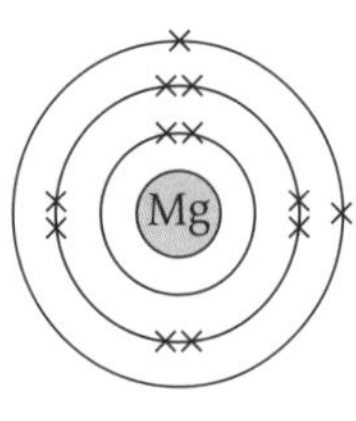

magnesium

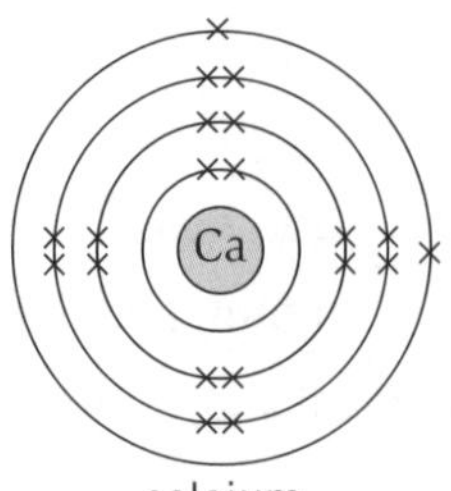

calcium

Exam Tip

In written text you can use a shorter notation to refer to the electronic structures. For example, Be would be 2,2, Mg would be 2,8,2, and Ca would be 2,8,8,2.

10.1 Predict how the reactivity of the Group 2 elements changes from the top to the bottom of the group. Justify your prediction by comparing the Group 2 electronic structures to the electronic structures of Group 1. **[4 marks]**

10.2 Describe the structure of calcium. **[3 marks]**

10.3 Magnesium reacts with steam, but does not react with cold water. Is magnesium more or less reactive than sodium? Give a reason for your answer. **[2 marks]**

Exam Tip

You'll need to know the formula for ions of magnesium and chlorine to work out the answer.

You can either learn these or work them out from the Periodic Table.

10.4 Magnesium reacts with chlorine in a similar way to sodium. Give the chemical formula of the product formed when magnesium reacts with chlorine. **[1 mark]**

11 The word equations for three reactions are given below.

Reaction 1	hydrogen + fluorine → hydrogen fluoride
Reaction 2	hydrogen + bromine → hydrogen bromide
Reaction 3	iron + bromine → iron bromide

Exam Tip

Before you answer look up each of the elements in this question on the Periodic Table.

11.1 Draw the electronic structure of the product of reaction **1**. **[2 marks]**

11.2 Explain why reaction **1** is more vigorous than reaction **2**. In your explanation, include the electronic structures of the halogens involved in the reactions. **[6 marks]**

11.3 Predict whether the product of reaction **2** or reaction **3** melts at a higher temperature. Justify your prediction. **[3 marks]**

12.1 Give the name used to describe elements in Group 1 of the Periodic Table. **[1 mark]**

12.2 Why do elements in the same group of the Periodic Table have similar chemical properties? Choose **one** answer. **[1 mark]**

They have the same number of electrons in the shell nearest the nucleus.

They have the same number of electron shells.

They have the same number of electrons in the shell furthest from the nucleus.

They have the same number of electrons.

12.3 Are Group 1 elements metals or non-metals? **[1 mark]**

12.4 Lithium is a Group 1 element. Lithium reacts with chlorine, a Group 7 element. The product is lithium chloride. Caesium is another Group 1 element, and bromine is another Group 7 element.
Name the product when caesium reacts with bromine. **[1 mark]**

> **Exam Tip**
> The location of metals and non-metals on the Periodic Table will not be given to you in the exam, you need to know this.

13 A student has a dilute potassium chloride solution.

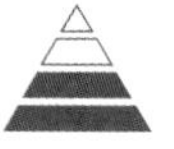

13.1 Which image shows the correct particle diagram for potassium chloride solution? Choose **one** answer. **[1 mark]**

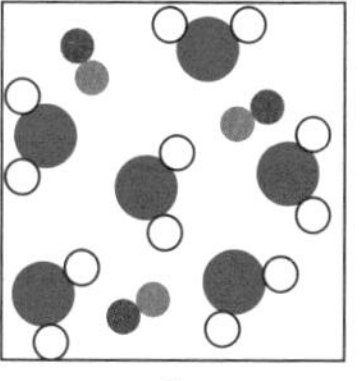
A

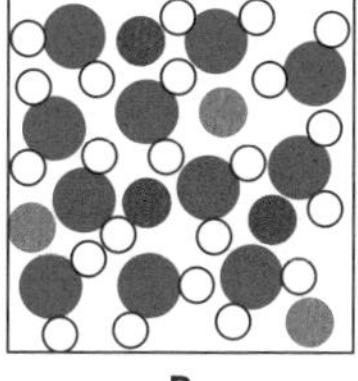
B

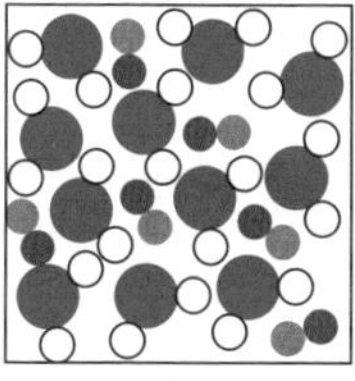
C

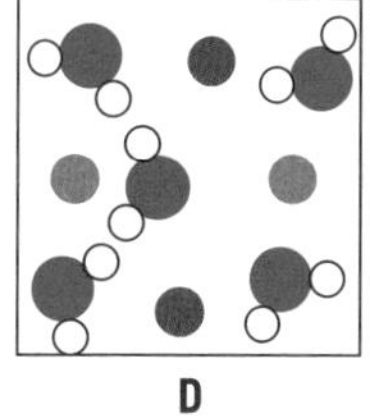
D

> **Exam Tip**
> The key phrase in this question is 'potassium chloride *solution*'. This means there will also be water in the mixture.

13.2 Write the electronic structure of the potassium ion in potassium chloride. **[1 mark]**

13.3 Describe the structure and bonding in potassium chloride. **[4 marks]**

13.4 Give the reason why potassium chloride solution can conduct electricity. **[1 mark]**

13.5 Describe a method by which potassium chloride can be separated from the solution. Your method should result in both potassium chloride and water being collected. **[6 marks]**

14 The Periodic Table lists all of the known elements.

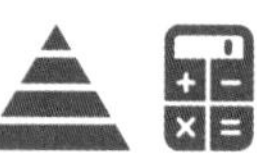

14.1 Explain how the discovery of neutrons led to a greater understanding of the Periodic Table. **[2 marks]**

14.2 On the Periodic Table, hydrogen is sometimes listed in Group 1 and sometimes listed free above the table.
Give **one** reason why hydrogen could be listed in Group 1 and **one** reason why it should not be listed in Group 1. **[2 marks]**

> **Exam Tip**
> Think about hydrogen's electronic structure and properties.

14.3 The modern Periodic Table is arranged by atomic number.
What is the atomic number of an element?

14.4 Silicon exists naturally as three isotopes: silicon-28 (92.2 %), silicon-29 (4.7 %), and silicon-30 (3.1 %).
Calculate the relative atomic mass of silicon to three significant figures. **[3 marks]**

> **Exam Tip**
> This is a key maths skill. It may look difficult, but you just need to find the average mass of 100 atoms.

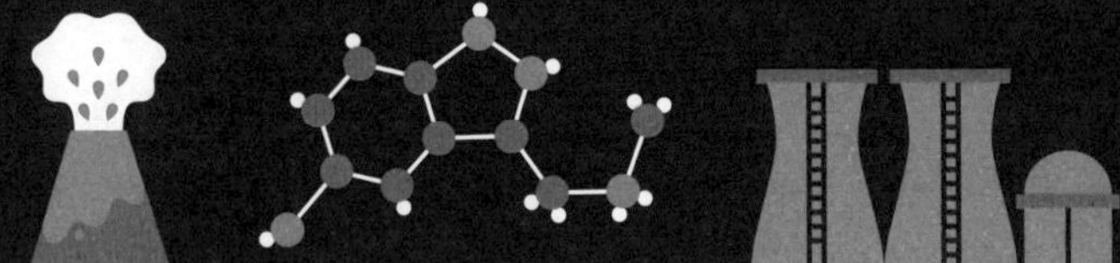

Knowledge

C5 Quantitative chemistry

Conservation of mass

The conservation of mass states that atoms cannot be created or destroyed in a chemical reaction. Atoms are rearranged into new substances. All the atoms you had in the reactants must be present in the products.

As such, when it comes to measuring the mass of a reaction, you would expect the mass at the start to be the same as the mass at the end. However, sometimes the mass can appear to change.

Decrease in mass

In some reactions the mass appears to decrease. This is normally because a gas is produced in the reaction and lost to the surroundings. For example:

sodium + water → sodium hydroxide + hydrogen

$$2Na(s) + 2H_2O(l) \rightarrow 2NaOH(aq) + H_2(g)$$

The mass of the sodium and the water at the start of the reaction will be more than the mass of the sodium hydroxide at the end of the reaction, because hydrogen atoms have been lost as a gas.

Increase in mass

In some reactions the mass appears to increase. This is normally because one of the reactants is a gas. For example:

sodium + chlorine → sodium chloride

$$2Na(s) + Cl_2(g) \rightarrow 2NaCl(s)$$

The mass of the sodium at the start of the reaction will be lower than the mass of sodium chloride at the end of the reaction. This is because atoms from the gaseous chlorine have been added to the sodium, increasing the mass.

Balancing symbol equations

When writing symbol equations you need to ensure that the number of each atom on each side is equal.

$$H_2 + O_2 \rightarrow H_2O$$

unbalanced

there are 2 hydrogen atoms on each side, but 2 oxygen atoms in the reactants and 1 in the product

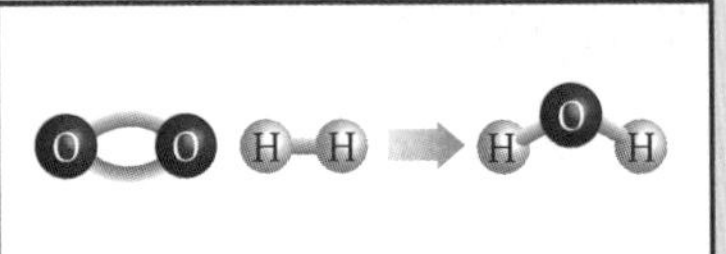

$$2H_2 + O_2 \rightarrow 2H_2O$$

balanced

there are 4 hydrogen atoms on each side, and 2 oxygen atoms on each side

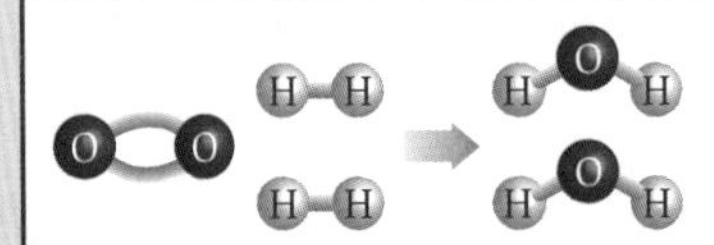

State symbols

A balanced symbol equation should also include state symbols.

State	Symbol
solid	(s)
liquid	(l)
gas	(g)
aqueous or dissolved in water	(aq)

Ratios

Look back at the reaction. In the reaction between hydrogen and oxygen, the ratio of hydrogen to oxygen molecules is 2:1. This means that for every *one* molecule of oxygen, you would need *two* molecules of hydrogen, for example:

- if you had 10 molecules of oxygen you would need 20 molecules of hydrogen
- if you had 1 mole of oxygen you would need 2 moles of hydrogen
- if you had 1.75 moles of oxygen you would need 3.5 moles of hydrogen.

A balanced symbol equation shows the ratios of the reactants and products in a chemical reaction.

Formula mass

Every substance has a **formula mass**, M_r.

formula mass M_r = sum (relative atomic mass of all the atoms in the formula)

The avogadro constant

One mole of a substance contains 6.02×10^{23} atoms, ions, or molecules. This is the **Avogadro constant**.

One mole of a substance has the same mass as the M_r of the substance. For example, the M_r (H_2O) = 18, so 18 g of water molecules contains 6.02×10^{23} molecules, and is called one mole of water.

You can write this as: moles = $\frac{\text{mass}}{M_r}$

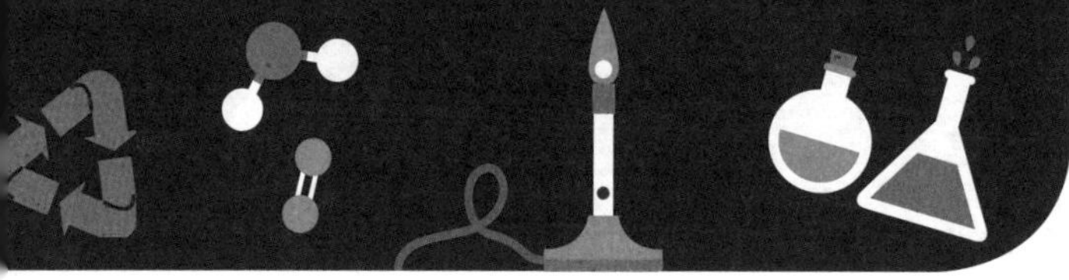

Using balanced equations

In a balanced symbol equation the sum of the M_r of the reactants equals the sum of the M_r of the products.

If you are asked what mass of a product will be formed from a given mass of a specific reactant, you can use the steps below to calculate the result.

1 balance the symbol equation
2 calculate moles of the substance with a known mass using moles = $\frac{\text{mass}}{M_r}$
3 using the balanced symbol equation, work out the number of moles of the unknown substance
4 calculate the mass of the unknown substance using mass = moles × M_r

If you are asked to balance an equation, you can use the steps below to work out the answer.

1 work out the M_r of all the substances
2 calculate the number of moles of each substance in the reaction using moles = $\frac{\text{mass}}{M_r}$
3 convert to a whole number ratio
4 balance the symbol equation

Excess and limiting reactants

In a chemical reaction between two or more reactants, often one of the reactants will run out before the others. You then have some of the other reactants left over. The reactant that is left over is in **excess**. The reactant that runs out is the **limiting reactant**.

To work out which reactants are in excess and which is the limiting reactant, you need to:

1 write the balanced symbol equation for the reaction
2 pick one of the reactants and its quantity as given in the question
3 use the ratio of the reactants in the balanced equation to see how much of the other reactant you need
4 compare this value to the quantity given in the question
5 determine which reactant is in excess and which is limiting.

Concentration

Concentration is the amount of solute in a volume of solvent.

The unit of concentration is g/dm³. Concentration can be calculated using:

$$\text{concentration (g/dm}^3) = \frac{\text{mass (g)}}{\text{volume (dm}^3)}$$

Sometimes volume is measured in cm³:

$$\text{volume (dm}^3) = \frac{\text{volume (cm}^3)}{1000}$$

- lots of solute in little solution = high concentration
- little solute in lots of solution = low concentration

Revision tip

Practice Examiners like to ask questions that bring together ideas from different places. Look at the two equations given on this page:

$$\text{concentration (g/dm}^3) = \frac{\text{mass (g)}}{\text{volume (dm}^3)}$$

$$\text{moles} = \frac{\text{mass (g)}}{M_r}$$

Can you see how these equations are linked? They both involve mass in grams. You could be asked a question that requires you to use both equations, for example, to calculate concentration of a solution when you're given the moles of the solute. You would use the equation for moles to find out the mass, then you could calculate the concentration. Being able to bring together different parts of the specification is an important skill you will need for your exam.

Make sure you can write a definition for these key terms.

Avogadro constant   balanced   calculation   concentration
conservation   dm³   equation   excess   formula mass
limiting reactant   mass   mole   ratio   state   surroundings

Retrieval

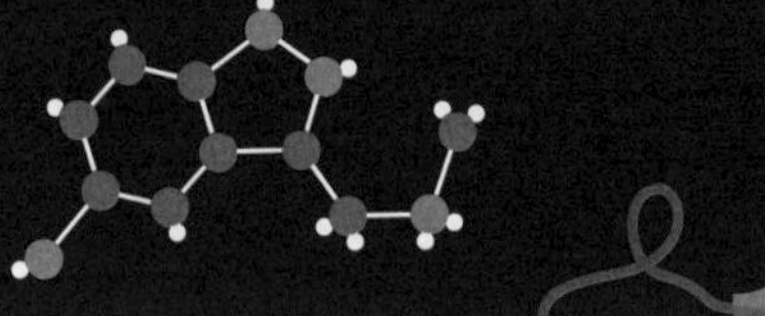

Learn the answers to the questions below, then cover the answers column with a piece of paper and write as many as you can. Check and repeat.

	C5 questions	Answers
1	What is the conservation of mass?	in a chemical reaction, atoms are not created or destroyed, just rearranged, total mass before = total mass after the reaction
2	When a metal forms a metal oxide, why does the mass increase?	atoms from gaseous oxygen have been added
3	When an acid reacts with a metal, why does the mass decrease?	a gas is produced and escapes
4	What is relative formula mass?	the sum of the relative atomic masses of each atom in a substance
5	What are the four state symbols and what do they stand for?	(s) solid, (l) liquid, (g) gas, (aq) aqueous or dissolved in water
6	How can you tell when a symbol equation is balanced?	the number of atoms of each element is the same on both sides
7	What is a mole?	mass of a substance that contains 6.02×10^{23} particles
8	Give the value for the Avogadro constant.	6.02×10^{23}
9	Which formula is used to calculate the number of moles from mass and M_r?	$\text{moles} = \frac{\text{mass}}{M_r}$
10	Which formula is used to calculate the mass of a substance from number of moles and M_r?	$\text{mass} = \text{moles} \times M_r$
11	What is a limiting reactant?	the reactant that is completely used up in a chemical reaction
12	What is a unit for concentration?	g/dm^3
13	Which formula is used to calculate concentration from mass and volume?	$\text{concentration (g/dm}^3) = \frac{\text{mass (g)}}{\text{volume (dm}^3)}$
14	Which formula is used to calculate volume from concentration and mass?	$\text{volume (dm}^3) = \frac{\text{mass (g)}}{\text{concentration (g/dm}^3)}$
15	Which formula is used to calculate mass from concentration in g/dm^3 and volume?	$\text{mass (g)} = \text{concentration (g/dm}^3) \times \text{volume (dm}^3)$
16	How can you convert a volume reading in cm^3 to dm^3?	divide by 1000
17	If the amount of solute in a solution is increased, what happens to its concentration?	increases
18	If the volume of water in a solution is increased, what happens to its concentration?	decreases

Put paper here

Now go back and use the questions below to check your knowledge from previous chapters.

Previous questions | Answers

	Previous questions	Answers
1	Why did Mendeleev leave gaps in his Periodic Table?	leave room for elements that had not yet been discovered
2	Why don't ionic substances conduct electricity when solid?	ions are fixed in position so cannot move, and there are no delocalised electrons
3	How are covalent bonds formed?	by atoms sharing electrons
4	Why does the reactivity of the halogens decrease down the group?	they are larger atoms, so the outermost shell is further from the nucleus, meaning there are weaker electrostatic forces of attraction and more shielding between the nucleus and outer shell, and it is harder to gain an electron
5	Why do most covalent substances not conduct electricity?	do not have delocalised electrons or ions
6	Give the formulae of the first four halogens.	F_2, Cl_2, Br_2, I_2
7	Why are the alkali metals named this?	they are metals that react with water to form an alkali
8	Why are metals good conductors of electricity and of thermal energy?	delocalised electrons are free to move through the metal

Put paper here

Maths Skills

Practise your maths skills using the worked example and practice questions below.

Rearranging equations	Worked example	Practice
You need to be able to rearrange and apply many equations in chemistry, for example, the equation to calculate number of moles. Chemists use moles to describe the relative numbers of particles in a given mass of substance. This can be calculated using: $\text{number of moles} = \dfrac{\text{mass (g)}}{\text{relative atomic mass } (A_r) \text{ or relative formula mass } (M_r)}$ This equation can be rearranged to find the mass of a substance, or the A_r or M_r.	What is the mass of 7.5×10^{-3} moles of aluminium sulfate? Aluminium sulfate = $Al_2(SO_4)_3$ M_r of $Al_2(SO_4)_3 = (27 \times 2) + (32 \times 3) + (16 \times 12) = 342$ *Rearrange the equation:* mass = number of moles × M_r mass = $(7.5\times10^{-3}) \times 342$ $= 2.565 = 2.6$ g	**1** Calculate the relative formula mass of H_2SO_4. **2** Calculate the number of moles of neon atoms in 0.02 g of neon. **3** Calculate the mass of copper sulfate produced through evaporating 1.5 mol copper sulfate solution.

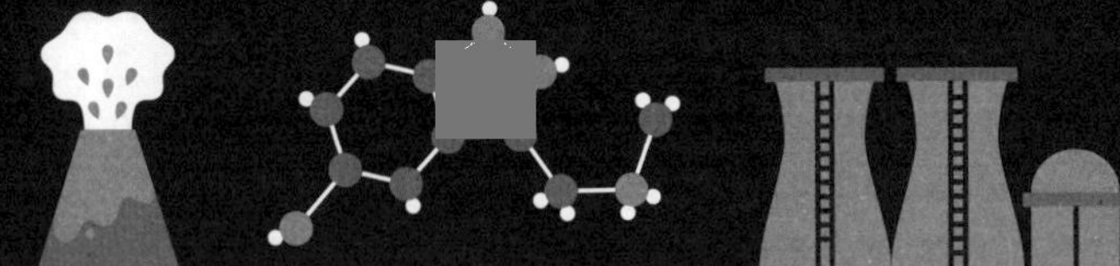

Exam-style questions

01 Methane is a compound with the formula CH_4.

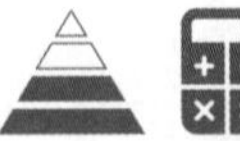

01.1 Calculate the relative formula mass M_r of methane. **[1 mark]**

Relative atomic masses A_r: $H = 1$, $C = 12$

Show your working clearly.

Relative formula mass of methane = ______________

01.2 Methane reacts with excess oxygen to make carbon dioxide and water.

Methane is the limiting reactant.

What is meant by the term limiting reactant? **[1 mark]**

Tick **one** box.

- the reactant present in the smaller mass ☐
- the reactant with the smaller relative formula mass ☐
- the reactant with the smaller molar mass ☐
- the reactant that is completely used up when the other reactant is present in excess ☐

01.3 Write a balanced symbol equation for the reaction between methane and oxygen. **[2 marks]**

____

01.4 0.13 moles of methane react with 0.25 moles of oxygen.

Which reactant is the limiting reactant? **[1 mark]**

____

01.5 How many moles of water will be produced in the reaction in **01.4**? **[1 mark]**

Exam Tip

You'll need to use the equation in **01.3** for questions **01.4** and **01.5**. If you didn't get the equation correct you can still get some marks by showing your working.

Number of moles of water = ______________

02 This question is about calcium nitrate, $Ca(NO_3)_2$.

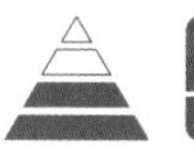

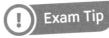

02.1 How many oxygen atoms are there in one mole of calcium nitrate?

Avogadro constant = 6.02×10^{23} **[2 marks]**

Number of oxygen atoms = ______________

Exam Tip

Take careful note of which number is inside the brackets and which is outside the brackets.

02.2 What is the relative formula mass of calcium nitrate?

Use the Periodic Table to help you. **[1 mark]**

Tick **one** box.

102 ☐

150 ☐

164 ☐

204 ☐

02.3 In a fume cupboard, a student heats some calcium nitrate in a test tube.

The calcium nitrate decomposes:

$$2Ca(NO_3)_2(s) \rightarrow 2CaO(s) + 4NO_2(g) + O_2(g)$$

Relative atomic masses A_r: Ca = 40, N = 14, O = 16.

Why is the mass of solid in the test tube lower after the chemical reaction? **[1 mark]**

____

____

Exam Tip

If you see state symbols in a question there is a good chance you need to refer to them in the answer. Look at the changes of state to find the answer to this one.

02.4 In the reaction, 22.4 g of calcium oxide is produced.

Calculate the mass of calcium nitrate that reacted. **[5 marks]**

Mass = ______________ g

03 1 cm^3 of water is equal to 1 g at room temperature and pressure.

03.1 Determine the volume in cm^3 of one mole of water. **[2 marks]**

03.2 Calculate the volume in cm^3 of one molecule of water. **[2 marks]**

03.3 Use the particle model to explain why the value calculated in **03.2** is not accurate. **[2 marks]**

Start with calculating the M_r of water.

04 Sulfur dioxide reacts with oxygen to make sulfur trioxide.

$$SO_2(g) + 2O_2(g) \rightarrow 2SO_3(g)$$

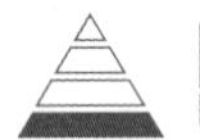

04.1 Write down what the number 3 means in the formula SO_3. **[1 mark]**

04.2 Calculate the relative formula mass M_r of sulfur dioxide, SO_2.
Relative atomic masses A_r: S = 32, O = 16 **[1 mark]**

04.3 In an experiment, 1.28 g of sulfur dioxide, SO_2, makes 1.68 g of sulfur trioxide, SO_3.
Calculate the mass of oxygen that was needed. **[1 mark]**

Even for a one-mark question it is important to show your working.

05.1 What is the Avogadro constant the measure of? **[1 mark]**

05.2 A glass contains 232 g of water.
Estimate the number of water molecules in the glass. Give your answer to three significant figures.
Relative atomic masses A_r: H = 1, O = 16 **[5 marks]**

05.3 Deduce the number of water molecules in 464 g of ice. Use your answer to **05.2**. **[2 marks]**

06 A teacher makes sodium chloride by adding burning sodium to a container of chlorine gas.

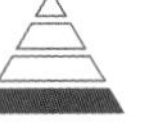

06.1 Suggest **one** safety precaution the teacher should take. **[1 mark]**

06.2 Balance the symbol equation for the reaction and add state symbols. **[2 marks]**

$$\_\_\_ \; Na \; \_\_\_ + Cl_2 \; \_\_\_ \rightarrow \_\_\_ \; NaCl \; \_\_\_$$

06.3 Describe the structure and bonding in solid sodium chloride. In your answer, outline how the ions are made and give their charges. **[6 marks]**

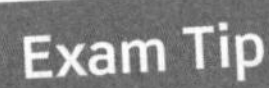

To begin it might help to think about:

- how many electrons sodium has in its outer shell and what happens to them
- the charge on the sodium ions
- how many electrons chlorine has in its outer shell and what happens to them
- the charge on the chloride ions.

07 Some students investigated the reaction of calcium carbonate with hydrochloric acid:

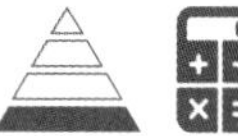

$$CaCO_3(s) + 2HCl(aq) \rightarrow CaCl_2(aq) + CO_2(g) + H_2O(l)$$

The students measured the volume of carbon dioxide gas made in 60 s. The students repeated the experiment five times. **Table 1** shows their results.

Table 1

Experiment number	Volume of carbon dioxide gas made in 60 s in cm^3
1	52
2	49
3	48
4	56
5	55

07.1 Calculate the mean volume of carbon dioxide gas. **[1 mark]**

07.2 Give the range of the values obtained in the five experiments. **[1 mark]**

07.3 What is the best estimate of the volume of gas obtained?

Choose **one** answer. **[1 mark]**

mean ± 3 mean ± 4 mean ± 6 mean ± 8

07.4 Hydrochloric acid solution contains hydrogen chloride, HCl, molecules dissolved in water. The students used 25 cm^3 of 7.3 g/dm^3 hydrochloric acid. Calculate the mass of hydrogen chloride that dissolved. Give your answer to two significant figures. **[3 marks]**

Exam Tip

Range is written slightly differently in science and in maths. In maths it is a single value whereas in science it is the two values that the numbers fall between, for example between 1 and 5.

08 A student wants to react nitric acid with potassium hydroxide to form potassium nitrate and water. The balanced symbol for the equation is:

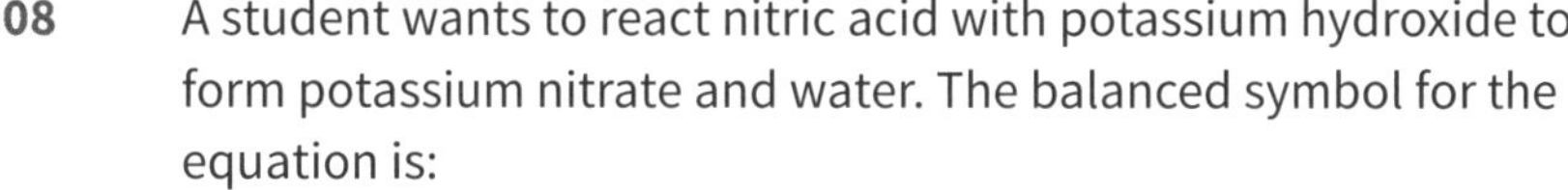

HNO_3 ____ + KOH ____ → KNO_3 ____ + H_2O ____

08.1 Complete the symbol equation by adding state symbols. **[1 mark]**

08.2 The student dissolved 14 g of potassium hydroxide in 700 cm^3 of water. Calculate the concentration of the potassium hydroxide solution in g/dm^3. **[2 marks]**

08.3 The concentration of nitric acid was 22 g/dm^3. Calculate the mass of nitric acid in 30 cm^3 of the solution. **[2 marks]**

08.4 The student reacted 30 cm^3 of nitric acid with 35 cm^3 of this solution of potassium hydroxide. Identify the limiting reactant. **[6 marks]**

Exam Tip

Always check the units given in the question. In **08.2**, the volume of water is given in cm^3, but the question asks for the answer to be given in g/dm^3.

09 Magnesium reacts with nitrogen gas, N_2, to make magnesium nitride, Mg_3N_2.

09.1 Draw a dot and cross diagram to show the bonding in a nitrogen molecule, N_2. **[2 marks]**

09.2 Two students draw diagrams of apparatus they think could be used to make magnesium nitride from magnesium and nitrogen (**Figure 1**).

Figure 1

A

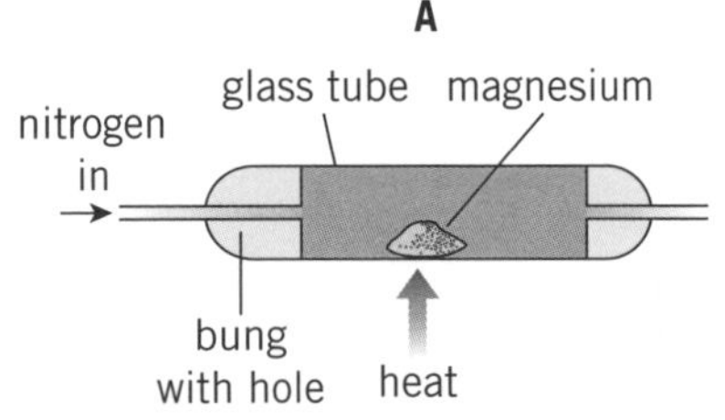

B

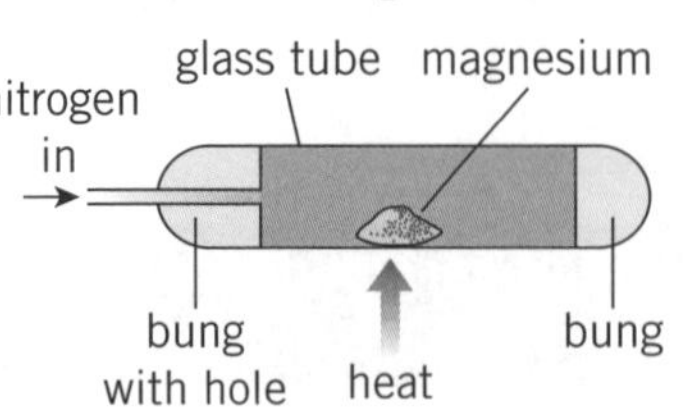

Exam Tip

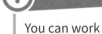

Carefully compare the two images to look for the differences.

Explain why the apparatus in **B** must **not** be used for the experiment. **[2 marks]**

09.3 A teacher made magnesium nitride from magnesium and nitrogen. **Table 2** shows the masses of the reactants that reacted and the mass of product made.

Table 2

Substance	Mass in g
magnesium	2.16
nitrogen	0.84
magnesium nitride	3.00

Use the data in **Table 2** to deduce the balanced equation for the reaction. Show all your working and use the data below.
Relative atomic masses A_r: Mg = 24, N = 14 **[5 marks]**

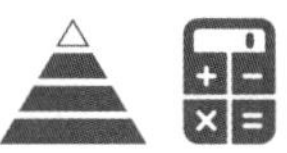

Exam Tip

You can work backwards from the mass.

10 Paracetamol and ibuprofen are painkillers.

10.1 A solution contains 500 mg of paracetamol in 5 cm³ of solution.
Calculate the mass of paracetamol in 1 dm³ of solution.
Give your answer in g. **[3 marks]**

10.2 The chemical formula of paracetamol is $C_8H_9NO_2$.
Calculate the mass of one mole of paracetamol.
Relative atomic masses A_r: C = 12, H = 1, N = 14, O = 16 **[1 mark]**

10.3 A solution of ibuprofen contains 0.10 g of ibuprofen in 5.0 cm³ of solvent. The chemical formula of ibuprofen is $C_{13}H_{18}O_2$.
Calculate the number of moles of ibuprofen in 1 dm³ of the solution.
Give your answer to three significant figures. **[4 marks]**

Exam Tip

There are lots of parts to this question. Write everything down clearly to avoid missing or repeating parts.

11 Some people take iron tablets if they do not have enough iron in their blood. **Table 3** gives some data about three types of iron tablet.

Table 3

Name of compound	Formula of iron compound in tablet	Mass of iron compound in tablet in g
iron(II) sulfate	$FeSO_4$	0.065
iron(II) fumarate	$C_4H_2FeO_4$	0.076
iron(II) gluconate	$C_{12}H_{24}FeO_{14}$	0.300

11.1 Calculate the relative formula mass of iron(II) fumarate.
Relative atomic masses A_r: Fe = 56, C = 12, H = 1, O = 16 **[1 mark]**

Check the answer to **11.2** before you try **11.3**. They are very similar methods and it's best to correct any mistakes before you move on.

11.2 Calculate the number of moles of iron(II) sulfate in one tablet.
Give your answer in standard form to two significant figures.
Relative atomic masses A_r: Fe = 56, S = 32, O = 16 **[4 marks]**

11.3 Deduce the mass of iron in one iron(II) gluconate tablet. **[4 marks]**

12 Iron is extracted from its ore in the following reaction.

Relative atomic mases A_r: Fe = 56, C = 12, O =16.

$$2Fe_2O_3 + 3C \rightarrow 4Fe + 3CO_2$$

12.1 Calculate the mass of carbon that reacts with 16.0 g of iron(III) oxide. **[5 marks]**

12.2 Calculate the mass of carbon dioxide produced in the reaction of carbon with 16.0 g of iron(III) oxide. **[4 marks]**

12.3 An industrial plant processes 3.7 tonnes of iron(III) oxide. Calculate the mass in kg of iron produced. 1 tonne = 1000 kg **[6 marks]**

12.4 Calculate the percentage by mass of iron(III) oxide that is iron. **[2 marks]**

13 A teacher demonstrates the reaction of sodium with chlorine. This is the method used:

1. Heat a small piece of sodium.
2. Fill a gas jar with chlorine.
3. Place the hot sodium in the gas jar of chlorine.

13.1 Suggest **two** safety precautions the teacher should take. **[2 marks]**

Exam Tip

Think about the substances being used in the reaction – they might give you a clue about the safety precautions required.

13.2 Explain an improvement to the order in which the steps above are carried out. **[2 marks]**

13.3 Draw a dot and cross diagram of the product of the reaction. **[2 marks]**

13.4 Describe the bonding in the product. **[3 marks]**

13.5 Explain the difference in the conductivity of electricity between sodium, chlorine, and the product of the reaction. **[6 marks]**

13.6 Predict **one** difference in the observations made if chlorine was replaced by bromine. **[1 mark]**

14 Phosphorus has 15 electrons.

14.1 Sketch the electronic structure of phosphorous. **[1 mark]**

14.2 Deduce the group number that phosphorus is in, in the Periodic Table. **[1 mark]**

14.3 Compare the properties of protons, neutrons, and electrons. Include in your answer the location of each type of sub-atomic particle within an atom. **[6 marks]**

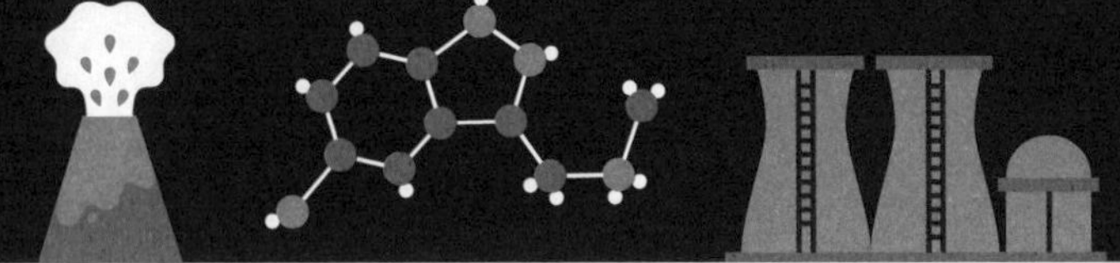

C6 Reactions of metals

Reactions of metals

The **reactivity** of a metal is how chemically reactive it is. When added to water, some metals react very vigorously – these metals have *high* reactivity. Other metals will barely react with water or acid, or won't react at all – these metals have *low* reactivity.

Reactivity series

The reactivity series places metals in order of their reactivity.

Sometimes, for example in the table below, hydrogen and carbon are included in the series, even though they are non-metals.

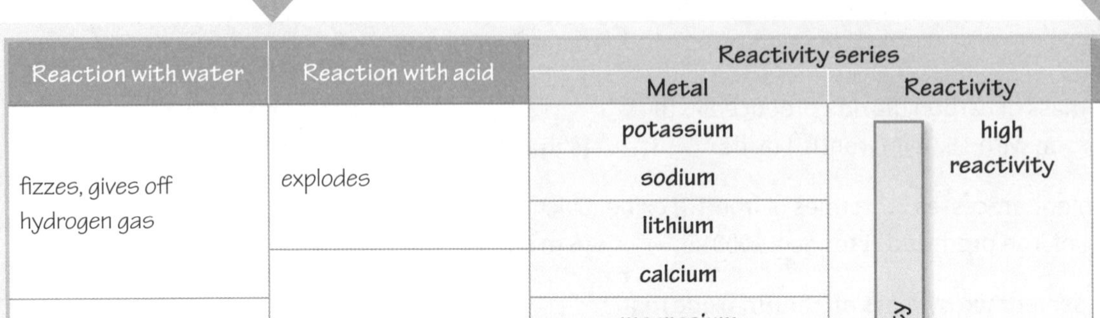

Reaction with water	Reaction with acid	Reactivity series: Metal	Reactivity series: Reactivity	Extraction method
fizzes, gives off hydrogen gas	explodes	potassium	high reactivity	electrolysis
		sodium		
		lithium		
	fizzes, gives off hydrogen gas	calcium		
reacts very slowly		magnesium	decreasing reactivity	
		aluminium		
		(carbon)		
		zinc		reduction with carbon
		iron		
no reaction	reacts slowly with warm acid	tin		
		lead		
	no reaction	*(hydrogen)*		
		copper		
		silver		mined from the Earth's crust
		gold	low reactivity	

Metal extraction

Some metals, like gold, are very unreactive meaning that they are found as pure metals in the Earth's crust and can be mined.

Most metals exist as compounds in rock and have to be extracted from the rock. If there is enough metal compound in the rock to be worth extracting it is called an **ore**.

Metals that are less reactive than carbon can be extracted by reduction with carbon. For example:

iron oxide + carbon → iron + carbon dioxide

Metals that are more reactive than carbon can be extracted using a process called **electrolysis**.

Reduction and oxidation

If a substance gains oxygen in a reaction, it has been **oxidised**.

If a substance loses oxygen in a reaction, it has been **reduced**.

For example:

iron + oxygen → iron oxide
iron has been oxidised

iron oxide + carbon → iron + carbon dioxide
iron oxide has been reduced

Key terms Make sure you can write a definition for these key terms.

displacement electrolysis extraction half equation ion ionic equation metal

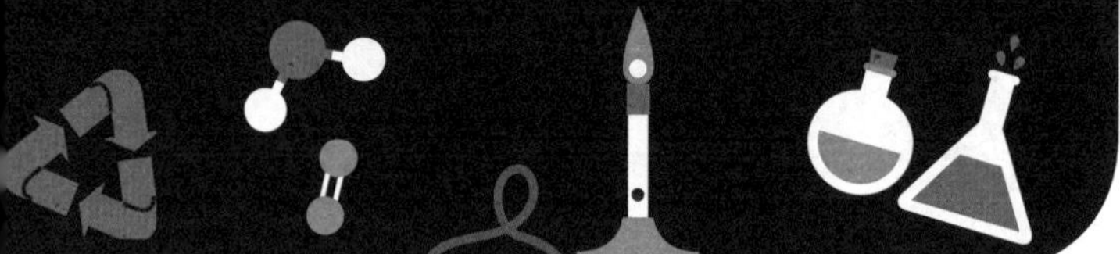

Displacement reactions

In a **displacement** reaction a *more* reactive element takes the place of a *less* reactive element in a compound.

For example:

copper sulfate + iron → iron sulfate + copper

$$CuSO_4(aq) + Fe(s) \rightarrow FeSO_4(aq) + Cu(s)$$

Iron is more reactive than copper, so iron displaces the copper in copper sulfate.

Reactivity and ions

A metal's reactivity depends on how readily it forms an **ion** by losing electrons.

In the displacement reaction of copper sulfate and iron, iron forms an ion more easily than copper.

At the end of the reaction you are left with iron ions, not copper ions.

Ionic equations

When an ionic compound is dissolved in a solution, we can write the compound as its separate ions. For example, $CuSO_4(aq)$ can be written as $Cu^{2+}(aq)$ and $SO_4^{2-}(aq)$.

The displacement reaction of copper sulfate and iron can be written as:

$$Fe(s) + Cu^{2+}(aq) + SO_4^{2-}(aq) \rightarrow Fe^{2+}(aq) + SO_4^{2-}(aq) + Cu(s)$$

The SO_4^{2-} is unchanged in the reaction – it is a **spectator ion**. Spectator ions are removed from the equation to give an **ionic equation**:

$$Fe(s) + Cu^{2+}(aq) \rightarrow Fe^{2+}(aq) + Cu(s)$$

Metals, covalent substances, and solid ionic substances do not split into ions in the ionic equation.

Steps for writing an ionic equation

1. check symbol equation is balanced
2. identify all aqueous ionic compounds
3. write those compounds out as ions
4. remove spectator ions.

Remember Half equations and ionic equations follow the same rules as full equations, they have to be balanced – this includes balancing the charges as well as the ions or compounds.

Half equations

In the displacement reaction, an iron atom loses two electrons to form a iron ion:

$$Fe(s) \rightarrow Fe^{2+}(aq) + 2e^-$$

A copper ion gains two electrons to form a copper atom:

$$Cu^{2+}(aq) + 2e^- \rightarrow Cu(s)$$

These two equations are called **half equations** – they each show half of the ionic equation.

Reduction and oxidation: electrons

Oxidation and reduction (**redox** reactions) can be defined in terms of oxygen, but can also be defined as the loss or gain of electrons.

Oxidation is the *loss* of electrons, and reduction is the *gain* of electrons.

In the example displacement reaction:

- iron atoms have been oxidised
- copper ions have been reduced.

ore oxidation reactivity reactivity series redox reduction spectator ion

Retrieval

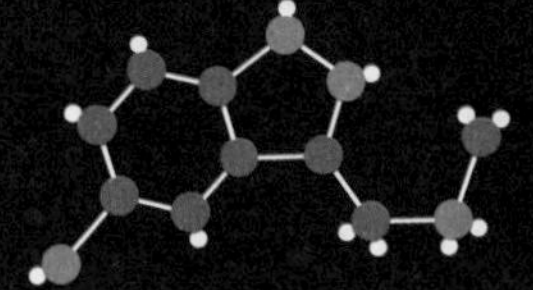
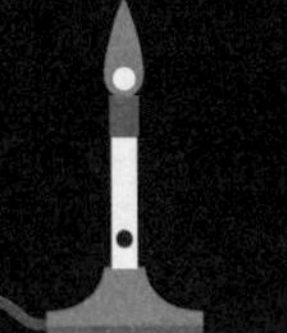

Learn the answers to the questions below, then cover the answers column with a piece of paper and write as many as you can. Check and repeat.

	C6 questions	Answers
1	What does reactivity mean?	how vigorously a substance chemically reacts
2	How can metals be ordered by their reactivity?	by comparing their reactions with water, acid, or oxygen
3	What name is given to a list of metals ordered by their reactivity?	reactivity series
4	In terms of electrons, what makes some metals more reactive than others?	they lose their outer shell electron(s) more easily
5	Why are gold and silver found naturally as elements in the Earth's crust?	they are very unreactive
6	What is an ore?	rock containing enough of a metal compound to be economically worth extracting
7	How are metals less reactive than carbon extracted from their ores?	reduction with carbon
8	In terms of oxygen, what is oxidation?	addition of oxygen
9	In terms of oxygen, what is reduction?	removal of oxygen
10	Why can metals like potassium and aluminium not be extracted by reduction with carbon?	they are more reactive than carbon
11	How are metals more reactive than carbon extracted from their ores?	electrolysis
12	What is a displacement reaction?	when a more reactive substance takes the place of a less reactive substance in a compound
13	What is an ionic equation?	equation which gives some substances as ions and has spectator ions removed
14	What type of substance is given as ions in an ionic equation?	ionic compounds in solution (or liquid)
15	What is a spectator ion?	ion that is unchanged in a reaction
16	What is a half equation?	equation that shows whether a substance is losing or gaining electrons
17	In terms of electrons, what is oxidation?	loss of electrons
18	In terms of electrons, what is reduction?	gain of electrons

Put paper here Put paper here Put paper here Put paper here Put paper here Put paper here Put paper here Put paper here

Now go back and use the questions below to check your knowledge from previous chapters.

Previous questions / Answers

	Previous questions	Answers
1	What is a unit for concentration?	g/dm^3
2	What is relative formula mass?	the sum of the relative atomic masses of each atom in a substance
3	What is a mole?	mass of a substance that contains 6.02×10^{23} particles
4	If the volume of water in a solution is increased, what happens to its concentration?	decreases
5	Why are the noble gases inert?	they have full outer shells so do not need to lose or gain electrons
6	Why do elements in a group have similar chemical properties?	have the same number of electrons in their outer shell
7	How were the early lists of elements ordered?	by atomic mass
8	What is an ion?	atom that has lost or gained electrons
9	Which kinds of elements form ionic bonds?	metals and non-metals

Put paper here

Put paper here

Put paper here

Maths Skills

Practise your maths skills using the worked example and practice questions below.

Tangents

We can obtain the gradient of a curve at a specific point on a graph by drawing a tangent. A tangent is a straight line that touches the curve at only this specified point.

To do this, you draw a tangent line on the graph, then calculate the gradient of the tangent using:

$$\text{gradient} = \frac{\text{change in } y}{\text{change in } x}$$

Tangents can also be used to calculate the rate of a reaction at a given time on a curve.

Worked example

Calculate the gradient of the line on the graph at 50 s.

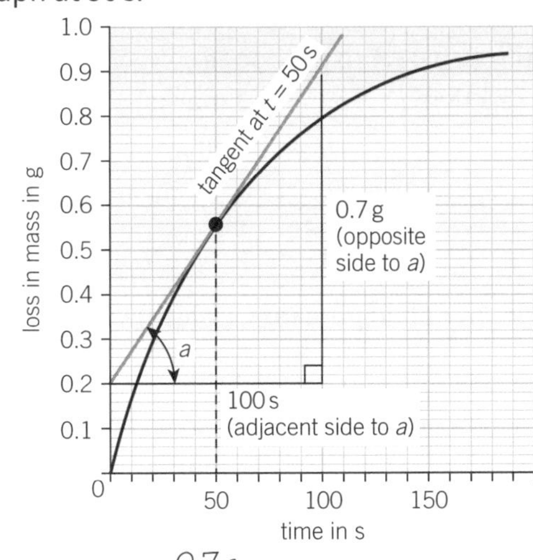

$$\text{Rate at 50 s} = \frac{0.7\,g}{100\,s} = 0.007\,g/s$$

(The gradient is the tangent of angle *a* in the right-angled triangle, i.e. opposite side divided by adjacent side.)

In this example, the gradient of the tangent is the same as the rate of the reaction at 50 s = 0.007 g/s

Practice

The graph below shows how the yield of ammonia in the Haber process changes depending on the temperature and the pressure.

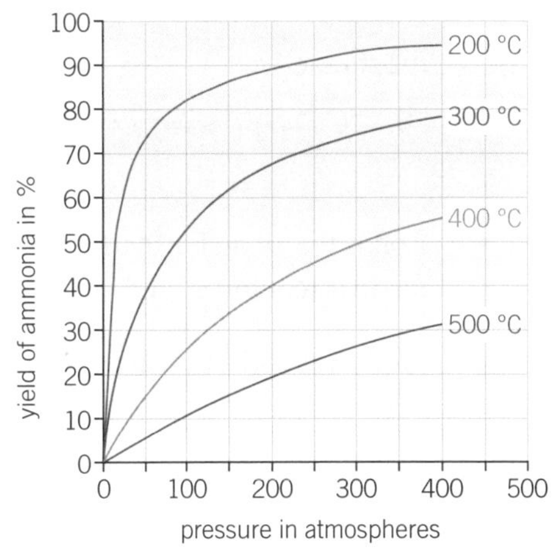

Which temperature has the steepest gradient at 50 atmospheres of pressure?

Practice

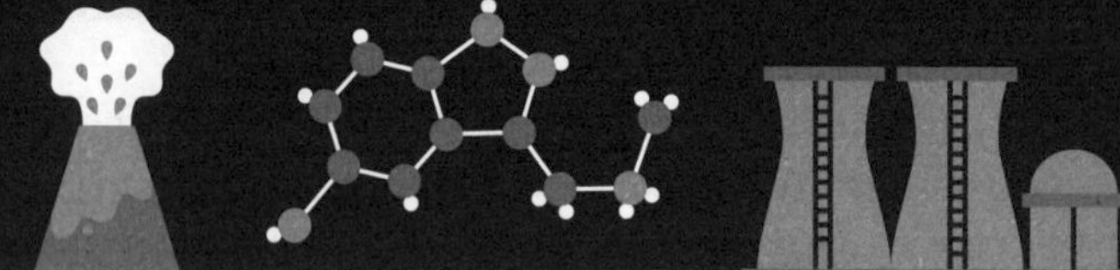

Exam-style questions

01 This question is about the reactivity series.

01.1 Which of these pairs of substances react together in a displacement reaction? **[1 mark]**

Tick **one** box.

zinc and magnesium chloride solution ☐

zinc and copper chloride solution ☐

iron and zinc sulfate solution ☐

iron and magnesium sulfate solution ☐

Exam Tip

You are expected to remember the order of elements within the reactivity series. There are lots of rhymes to help you: pick the one you like the best.

01.2 Name the gas formed when sodium reacts with water. **[1 mark]**

____

01.3 Lithium also reacts with water.

Does lithium react more vigorously or less vigorously with water than sodium? **[1 mark]**

Circle **one** answer.

more vigorously   less vigorously

Exam Tip

Identify the position of lithium and sodium on the Periodic Table to help with this question.

01.4 Lithium is added to a solution of copper chloride. Name the substance formed. **[1 mark]**

____

01.5 Use your answers to questions **01.1** through **01.4** to put copper, lithium, sodium, and zinc in order of reactivity. **[3 marks]**

most reactive   least reactive

________ > ________ > ________ > ________

02 Iron is found on Earth as iron(III) oxide. To obtain pure iron, iron(III) oxide is reacted with carbon.

02.1 Identify whether the iron is oxidised or reduced. Give a reason for your answer. **[2 marks]**

____

____

____

02.2 Balance the symbol equation for the extraction of iron from iron(III) oxide. **[1 mark]**

$\_\_\_\_ Fe_2O_3 + \_\_\_\_ C \rightarrow \_\_\_\_ Fe + \_\_\_\_ CO_2$

Exam Tip

Only write numbers in the boxes, don't try to change the formulae of the compounds already given.

02.3 Explain why you do **not** need to react gold with carbon to obtain pure gold. **[2 marks]**

03 A student pours some dilute hydrochloric acid into a beaker. The student then adds some pieces of zinc to the acid.

03.1 Describe **one** observation the student would make. **[1 mark]**

03.2 Name the **two** products of the reaction. **[1 mark]**

03.3 Write a balanced chemical equation for the reaction, including state symbols. **[3 marks]**

03.4 Explain whether zinc is oxidised or reduced in the reaction. **[2 marks]**

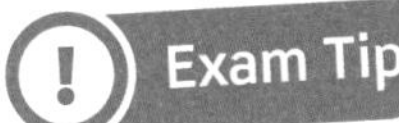

Exam Tip

If you forget the state symbols when balancing equations you won't get all of the marks.

04 **Figure 1** shows three solutions in test tubes.

Figure 1

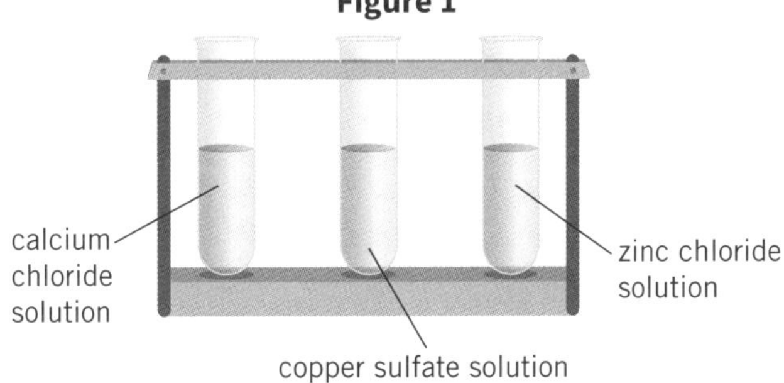

A student added small pieces of metal **X** to each test tube. **Table 1** shows the student's observations.

Table 1

Solution	Observations
calcium chloride	no change
copper sulfate	a brown solid forms on the surface of metal **X** and the blue colour of solution becomes paler
zinc chloride	a grey solid forms on the surface of metal **X**

04.1 Suggest a possible identity of metal **X**. Justify your prediction. **[3 marks]**

04.2 Write a balanced chemical equation for the reaction of metal **X** with copper sulfate solution. Use the symbol **X** to represent the metal, and assume it forms X^{2+} ions. Include state symbols in your equation. **[3 marks]**

04.3 Explain how the student could confirm the identify of metal **X**. **[4 marks]**

Exam Tip

Only giving a metal will not be enough to get all the marks, you must explain *why* you picked that one.

05 Lead is found naturally as lead sulfide, PbS. Lead sulfide is mixed with other substances in rock. This rock is called lead ore. Lead is extracted from lead ore by the steps below.

1. Lead sulfide is separated from the substances it is mixed with in lead ore.
2. Pure lead sulfide is heated with oxygen. This chemical reaction makes lead oxide and sulfur dioxide.
3. The lead oxide from step **2** is heated with carbon.

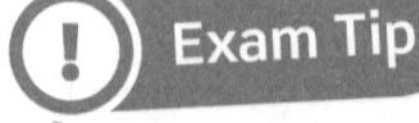

> **Exam Tip**
> First determine the mass of lead sulfide within the rock, then determine the percentage by mass of lead within lead sulfide – combine these to get the final answer.

05.1 A lead ore contains 25% lead sulfide.
Calculate the mass of lead in 240 kg of this ore.
Give your answer to two significant figures. **[4 marks]**

05.2 Write a balanced symbol equation for step **2**.
Include state symbols in your equation. **[3 marks]**

05.3 Explain whether lead oxide is oxidised or reduced in step **3**. **[2 marks]**

> **Exam Tip**
> Remember OILRIG:
> **O**xidation **I**s **L**oss (of electrons)
> **R**eduction **I**s **G**ain (of electrons)

05.4 Explain why lead is extracted from its oxide by heating with carbon but aluminium cannot be extracted from its oxide in this way. **[2 marks]**

05.5 Name **one** other metal that can be extracted from its oxide by heating with carbon. **[1 mark]**

06 Compare the displacement reactions of halogens and metals.
In your answer, include ideas about oxidation and reduction and refer to the two equations below. **[6 marks]**

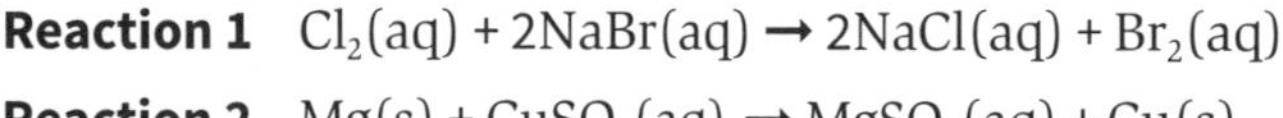

Reaction 1 $Cl_2(aq) + 2NaBr(aq) \rightarrow 2NaCl(aq) + Br_2(aq)$

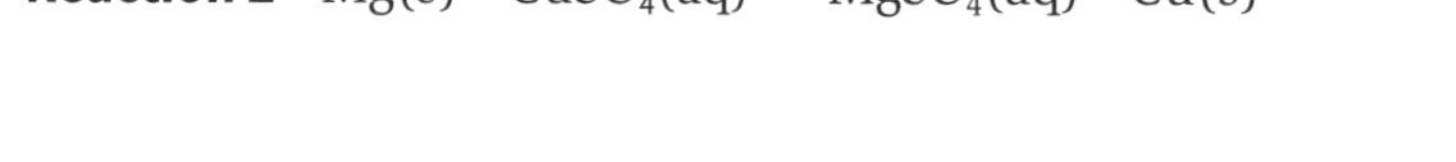

Reaction 2 $Mg(s) + CuSO_4(aq) \rightarrow MgSO_4(aq) + Cu(s)$

> **Exam Tip**
> Question **06** is asking *two* things about *two* equations – this will give structure to your answer so you don't miss anything out:
> In reaction 1 … is oxidised.
> In reaction 1 … is reduced.
> In reaction 2 … is oxidised.
> In reaction 2 … is reduced.
> Don't forget to compare the two reactions at the end.

07.1 Which of these metals has the greatest tendency to form positive ions? Choose **one** answer. **[1 mark]**

iron lithium magnesium zinc

07.2 Name the product formed in the reaction between magnesium and oxygen. **[1 mark]**

07.3 Is magnesium oxidised or reduced in the reaction in **07.2**?
Give a reason for your answer. **[2 marks]**

07.4 Magnesium cannot be extracted from the compound formed in **07.2** by reaction with carbon. Explain why. **[2 marks]**

08 A student wants to find the position of nickel in the reactivity series. The student adds small pieces of iron, lead, and nickel to dilute hydrochloric acid and to water.
The student's observations are shown in **Table 2**.

Table 2

Metal	Observations on adding the metal to dilute hydrochloric acid	Observations on adding the metal to water and leaving for a few days
iron	bubbles form slowly on the surface of the metal	red-brown flakes form on the surface of the metal
lead	no change	no change
nickel	bubbles form slowly on the surface of the metal	no change

08.1 Use the observations in **Table 2** to deduce the position of nickel in the reactivity series. Justify your decision. **[3 marks]**

08.2 The student wants to confirm the position of nickel in the reactivity series relative to iron.
Suggest how you could improve the experiment to confirm the position of nickel by using displacement reactions. In your answer, describe and explain the results you would expect. **[4 marks]**

08.3 Nickel will displace copper from a solution of copper(II) sulfate. Write an ionic equation for the displacement reaction between nickel and copper sulfate. Identify which species is reduced. **[3 marks]**

Exam Tip

As well as balancing the elements, the charges need to be balanced too.

09 A student is investigating metal displacement reactions.
The student places small pieces of metal in the depressions of a 3×3 white spotting tile. The student then adds small amounts of solutions of metal salts to the metals.
Figure 2 shows the metals and solutions of metal salts the student used.

Figure 2

magnesium + magnesium chloride solution	zinc + magnesium chloride solution	copper + magnesium chloride solution
magnesium + zinc chloride solution	zinc + zinc chloride solution	copper + zinc chloride solution
magnesium + copper chloride solution	zinc + copper chloride solution	copper + copper chloride solution

09.1 Suggest **one** improvement to the experiment that would prevent the unnecessary use of metals and solutions. **[1 mark]**

09.2 Name the metal that does **not** react with any of the solutions. Explain your choice. **[2 marks]**

09.3 Write an ionic equation with state symbols for the reaction of magnesium with copper sulfate solution. **[3 marks]**

Exam Tip

Find the metals on the reactivity series.

09.4 Write the electronic structure of magnesium before and after its reaction with copper(II) sulfate solution. **[2 marks]**

> **Exam Tip**
> This isn't drawing it out, but writing the number of electrons. It starts 2,8…

09.5 Suggest **three** advantages of doing this experiment on a spotting tile compared to using test tubes.
Give a reason for each suggestion. **[3 marks]**

10 The formula of ammonia is NH_3.
Figure 3 is a ball and stick model of an ammonia molecule.

Figure 3

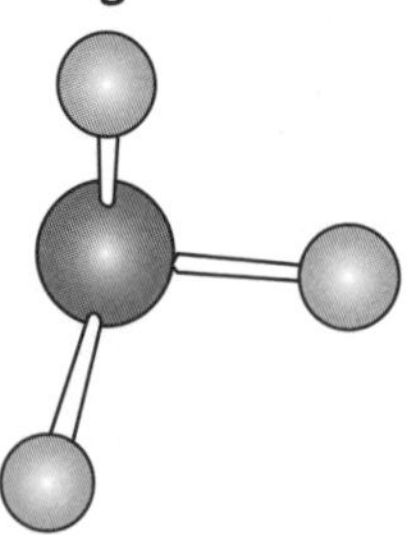

10.1 The ball and stick model is not a true representation of ammonia. Give **one** reason why. **[1 mark]**

> **Exam Tip**
> Covalent bonding has overlapping circles – ionic bonding is the one with square brackets.

10.2 Draw a dot and cross diagram to show the covalent bonds in ammonia. **[2 marks]**

10.3 Explain why ammonia does not conduct electricity. **[1 mark]**

10.4 **Table 3** shows the boiling points and formulae of two compounds.

Table 3

Name of compound	Formula	Boiling point in °C
ammonia	NH_3	−334
hydrazine	N_2H_4	114

Give the state of ammonia at 20 °C. **[1 mark]**

> You've probably never heard of hydrazine before, but this is just a new context to apply your knowledge.

10.5 Explain why hydrazine has a higher boiling point than ammonia. **[2 marks]**

11 **Table 4** shows the radii of the atoms in some metals of the reactivity series.

Table 4

Metal	Radius of atoms in metal in nm
potassium	0.231
sodium	0.186
lithium	0.152
calcium	0.197
magnesium	0.160
zinc	0.133
iron	0.126
copper	0.128

> Radii is the plural of radius.

A student studies the data in **Table 4** and makes the following conclusion:

'The bigger the atoms of a metal, the higher that metal is in the reactivity series. This is because metals high in the reactivity series lose their electrons more easily.'

11.1 Explain why bigger metal atoms are expected to be more reactive. **[4 marks]**

11.2 Evaluate the extent to which the student's conclusion is true. **[5 marks]**

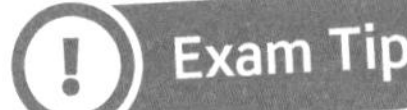

For an evaluate question you'll need to give reasons for, reasons against, your opinion, and a reason for your opinion.

12 A student carried out a displacement reaction. They used the following method.

1. Find the mass of the lead oxide powder and carbon powder.
2. Mix the two powders and place in an evaporating basin.
3. Heat strongly.
4. Find the mass of solid remaining after heating and observe the products.

12.1 Lead and its compounds are toxic.
Suggest **two** safety precautions the student should take to reduce the risk of harm from this hazard. **[2 marks]**

Exam Tip

When thinking about safety precautions there are general ones that will keep you safe in the lab and specific ones related to the chemicals used – the question has told you lead is toxic so refer to that in your answer.

12.2 Predict the **two** products of the reaction. **[1 mark]**

12.3 The total mass of solid at the end of the reaction is less than the total mass of reactants at the start. Suggest why. **[1 mark]**

13 Copper has two stable isotopes.
The chemical symbols of these isotopes are $^{63}_{29}Cu$ and $^{65}_{29}Cu$.

13.1 Give the number of protons in an atom of $^{65}_{29}Cu$. **[1 mark]**

13.2 Give the number of neutrons in an atom of $^{65}_{29}Cu$. **[1 mark]**

13.3 Give the mass number of the $^{63}_{29}Cu$ atom. **[1 mark]**

13.4 Give the number of electrons in a Cu^{2+} ion. **[1 mark]**

13.5 **Table 5** shows the relative abundances of the two isotopes.

Table 5

Isotope	Percentage abundance
$^{63}_{29}Cu$	69.2
$^{65}_{29}Cu$	30.8

Calculate the relative atomic mass of copper.
Give your answer to three significant figures. **[3 marks]**

This means working out the average mass of 69.2 atoms that have a mass of 63, and 30.8 atoms that have a mass of 65.

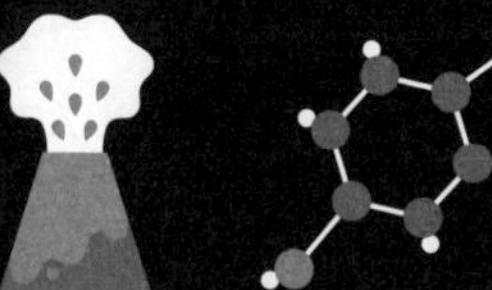
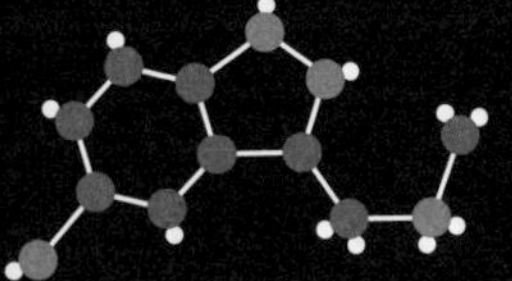

C7 Reactions of acids

Acids and alkalis

Acids are compounds that, when dissolved in water, release H^+ ions. There are three main acids: sulfuric acid, H_2SO_4, nitric acid, HNO_3, and hydrochloric acid, HCl.

Alkalis are compounds that, when dissolved in water, release OH^- ions.

The **pH** scale is a measure of acidity and alkalinity. It runs from 1 to 14.

- Aqueous solutions with pH < 7 are acidic.
- Aqueous solutions with pH > 7 are alkaline.
- Aqueous solutions with pH = 7 are neutral.

Logarithmic scales

The pH scale tells you how many H^+ ions there are in the solution. The *more* H^+ ions are present, the *lower* the pH. It is a logarithmic scale, which means that an increase of 1 on the pH scale is equal to a decrease of 10× the number of H^+ ions in solution.

For example, an acid with a pH of 3 has:

- 100× *fewer* H^+ ions in solution than an acid with pH 1
- 10× *fewer* H^+ ions than pH 2
- 10× *more* H^+ ions than pH 4
- 100× *more* H^+ ions than pH 5

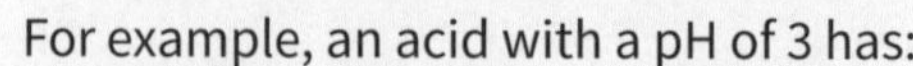

Indicators

Indicators can show if something is an acid or an alkali.

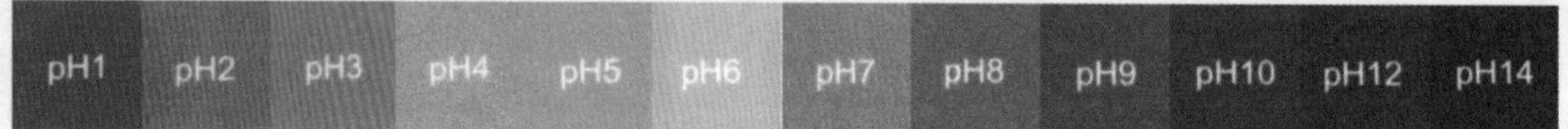

- **Universal indicator** can also tell us the approximate pH of a solution.
- Electronic pH probes, sometimes called pH meters, can give us the exact pH of a solution.

Strong and weak acids

Sulfuric acid, nitric acid, and hydrochloric acid, are all **strong acids**. This means that, when dissolved in water, every molecule splits up into ions – they are completely ionised:

- $H_2SO_4(aq) \rightarrow 2H^+(aq) + SO_4^{2-}(aq)$
- $HNO_3(aq) \rightarrow H^+(aq) + NO_3^-(aq)$
- $HCl(aq) \rightarrow H^+(aq) + Cl^-(aq)$

Ethanoic acid, citric acid, and carbonic acid are **weak acids**. This means that only a percentage of their molecules split up into ions when dissolved in water – they are partially ionised.

For a given concentration, the *stronger* the acid, the *lower* the pH.

Concentrated and dilute acids

Concentration tells us how much of a substance there is dissolved in water:

- more concentrated acids have lots of acid in a small volume of water
- less concentrated acids (dilute acids) have little acid in a large volume of water.

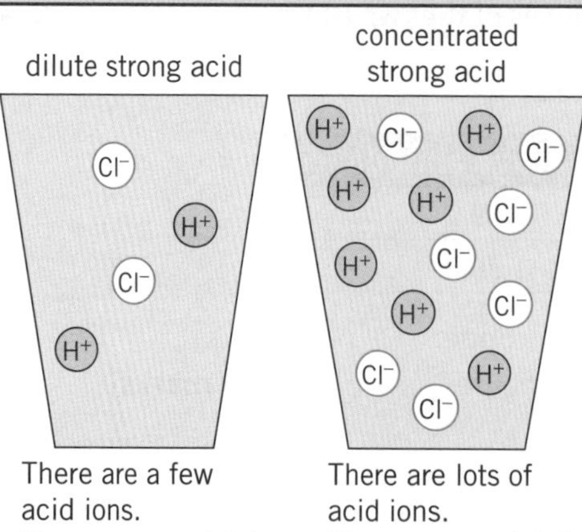

dilute strong acid: There are a few acid ions. They are completely ionised.

concentrated strong acid: There are lots of acid ions. They are completely ionised.

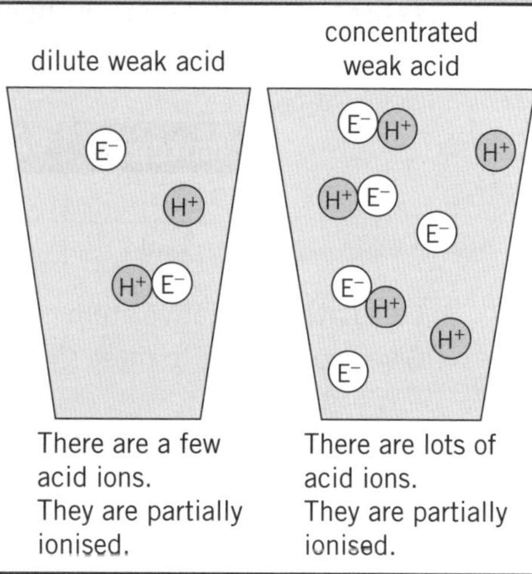

dilute weak acid: There are a few acid ions. They are partially ionised.

concentrated weak acid: There are lots of acid ions. They are partially ionised.

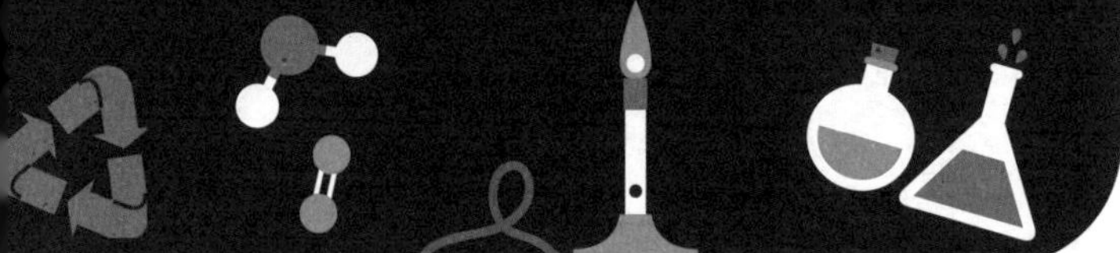

Salts

When acids react with metals or metal compounds, they form salts. A salt is a compound where the hydrogen from an acid has been replaced by a metal. For example nitric acid, HNO_3, reacts with sodium to form $NaNO_3$. The H in nitric acid is replaced by Na.

The table shows how to name salts.

Acid	hydrochloric acid	sulfuric acid	nitric acid
Formula	HCl	H_2SO_4	HNO_3
Ions formed in solution	H^+ and Cl^-	$2H^+$ and SO_4^{2-}	H^+ and NO_3^-
Type of salt formed	metal chloride	metal sulfate	metal nitrate
Sodium salt example	sodium chloride, $NaCl$	sodium sulfate, Na_2SO_4	sodium nitrate, $NaNO_3$

Reactions of acids

Neutralisation reactions

Reactions of acids with metals

Acids react with some metals to form salts and hydrogen gas.

magnesium + hydrochloric acid → sodium chloride + hydrogen

Reactions of acids with metal hydroxides

Acids react with metal hydroxides to form salts and water.

hydrochloric acid + sodium hydroxide → sodium chloride + water

The ionic equation for this reaction is always:

$$H^+(aq) + OH^-(aq) \rightarrow H_2O(l)$$

Reactions of acids with metal oxides

Acids react with metal oxides to form salts and water.

hydrochloric acid + sodium oxide → sodium chloride + water

Reactions of acids with metal carbonates

Acids react with metal carbonates to form a salt, water, and carbon dioxide.

hydrochloric acid + sodium carbonate → sodium chloride + water + carbon dioxide

Redox

The reaction of acids with metals is a redox reaction:

- the metal loses electrons – it is oxidised
- hydrogen gains an electron – it is reduced.

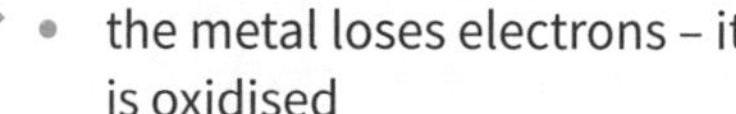

Alkalis and bases

Bases neutralise acids to form water in **neutralisation** reactions.

Some metal hydroxides dissolve in water to form alkaline solutions, called alkalis.

Some metal oxides and metal hydroxides do *not* dissolve in water. They are **bases**, but are not alkalis.

Crystallisation

You can produce a solid salt from an insoluble base by **crystallisation**.

The experimental method is:

1. Choose the correct acid and base to produce the salt.
2. Put some of the dilute acid into a flask. Heat gently with a Bunsen burner.
3. Add a small amount of the base and stir.
4. Keep adding the base until no more reacts – the base is now in excess.
5. Filter to remove the unreacted base.
6. Add the remaining solution to an evaporating dish.
7. Use a water bath or electric heater to evaporate the water. The salt crystals will be left behind.

Key terms

Make sure you can write a definition for these key terms.

acid alkali
base concentrated
crystallisation dilute
indicator ionise
logarithmic neutral
neutralisation pH
salt strong
universal indicator
weak

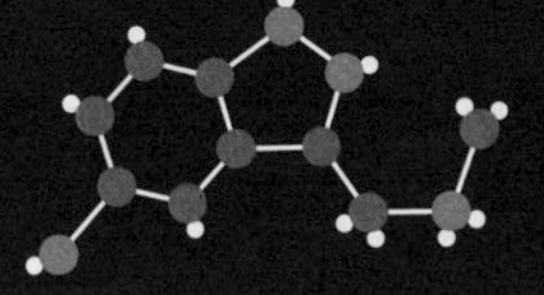

Retrieval

Learn the answers to the questions below, then cover the answers column with a piece of paper and write as many as you can. Check and repeat.

	C7 questions		Answers
1	In terms of pH, what is an acid?	Put paper here	a solution with a pH less than 7
2	In terms of pH, what is a neutral solution?		a solution with a pH of 7
3	In terms of H^+ ions, what is an acid?		a substance that releases H^+ ions when dissolved in water
4	What are the names and formulae of three main acids?	Put paper here	hydrochloric acid, HCl; sulfuric acid, H_2SO_4; nitric acid, HNO_3
5	How do you measure the pH of a substance?		universal indicator or pH probe
6	What is a strong acid?	Put paper here	an acid where the molecules completely ionise in water
7	What is a weak acid?		an acid where the molecules partially ionise in water
8	What is a salt?		a compound formed when a metal ion takes the place of a hydrogen ion in an acid
9	Which type of salts do sulfuric acid, hydrochloric acid, and nitric acid form?	Put paper here	sulfates, chlorides, and nitrates, respectively
10	What are the products of a reaction between a metal and an acid?		salt + hydrogen
11	What are the products of a reaction between a metal hydroxide and an acid?	Put paper here	salt + water
12	What are the products of a reaction between a metal oxide and an acid?		salt + water
13	What are the products of a reaction between a metal carbonate and an acid?		salt + water + carbon dioxide
14	What is a base?	Put paper here	a substance that reacts with acids in neutralisation reactions
15	What is an alkali?		a substance that dissolves in water to form a solution above pH 7
16	What is a neutralisation reaction?	Put paper here	a reaction between an acid and a base to produce water
17	What is the ionic equation for a reaction between an acid and an alkali?		$H^+(aq) + OH^-(aq) \rightarrow H_2O(l)$
18	How can you obtain a solid salt from a solution?		crystallisation
19	When an acid reacts with a metal, which species is oxidised?	Put paper here	the metal
20	When an acid reacts with a metal, which species is reduced?		hydrogen

Now go back and use the questions below to check your knowledge from previous chapters.

Previous questions | Answers

	Previous questions	Answers
1	What is a half equation?	equation that shows whether a substance is losing or gaining electrons
2	Which formula is used to calculate the number of moles from mass and M_r?	moles = $\frac{\text{mass}}{M_r}$
3	Which formula is used to calculate concentration from mass and volume?	concentration $\left(\frac{g}{dm^3}\right) = \frac{\text{mass (g)}}{\text{volume (dm}^3\text{)}}$
4	What is an ore?	rock containing enough of a metal compound to be economically worth extracting
5	What is a displacement reaction?	when a more reactive substance takes the place of a less reactive substance in a compound
6	Why does the reactivity of the alkali metals increase down the group?	they are larger atoms, so the outermost electron is further from the nucleus, meaning there are weaker electrostatic forces of attraction and more shielding between the nucleus and outer electron, and it is easier to lose the electron
7	What is an ionic equation?	equation which gives some substances as ions and has spectator ions removed
8	How do the melting points of the noble gases change down the group?	increase (higher melting point)
9	How do the melting points of the noble gases change down the group?	addition of oxygen

Put paper here

Required Practical Skills

Practise answering questions on the required practicals using the example below. You need to be able to apply your skills and knowledge to other practicals too.

Making salts	Worked example	Practice
This required practical tests whether you can safely separate and purify a chemical mixture, to produce a salt. You will need to be able to describe the uses of filtration, evaporation, and crystallisation to make pure, dry samples of soluble salts. Exam questions can ask about the production of any salt, not just the examples you are familiar with. You should also be able to describe how substances can be tested for purity.	A salt is formed when an acid reacts with a base. **1** Write a word equation for the production of magnesium nitrate. *magnesium carbonate + nitric acid → magnesium nitrate + water + carbon dioxide* **2** Identify one hazard of working with sulfuric acid, and describe two ways to prevent this hazard. *Concentrated sulfuric acid is corrosive, so can cause burns.* *To prevent any hazards, eye protection should be worn at all times and dilute sulfuric acid should be used.*	**1** Describe the colour changes that occur when copper oxide is mixed with sulfuric acid. **2** A student made a sample of copper sulfate by reacting copper oxide with sulfuric acid. After evaporating the copper sulfate solution and leaving it to crystallise, the student found two different crystals in the basin. Small white crystals formed around the edges and larger blue crystals formed in the middle. Name the two types of crystal. **3** The student used filter paper in the production of their copper sulfate sample. Describe the function of the filter paper.

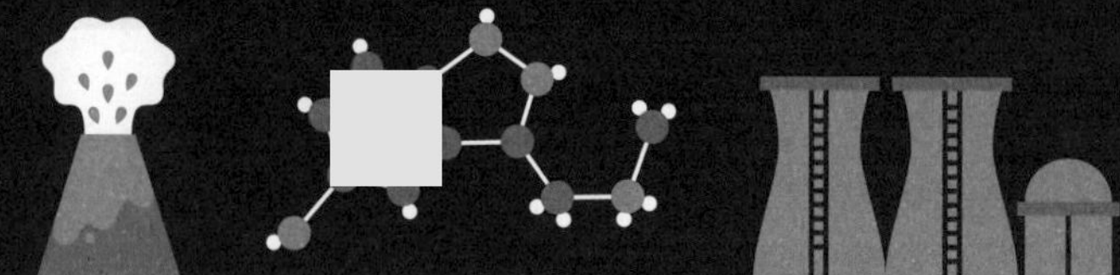

Exam-style questions

01 This question is about the pH scale and neutralisation.

01.1 Draw **one** line from each pH to a solution that might have this pH. **[3 marks]**

pH	Solution that might have this pH
	weak acid
1	strong acid
5	neutral solution
9	weak alkali
	strong alkali

01.2 Which solution has the lowest pH?

Tick **one** box. **[1 mark]**

1 g/dm^3 solution of ammonium hydroxide ☐

1 g/dm^3 solution of citric acid ☐

1 g/dm^3 solution of ethanoic acid ☐

1 g/dm^3 solution of hydrochloric acid ☐

> **Exam Tip**
>
> It is important that you can recall the list of strong and weak acids from the specification.

01.3 Give the name and formula of the ion that is produced by acids in aqueous solution. **[2 marks]**

Name: ______________________________

Formula: ______________________________

01.4 Give the name of the product that is always formed when an acid reacts with a base. **[1 mark]**

____

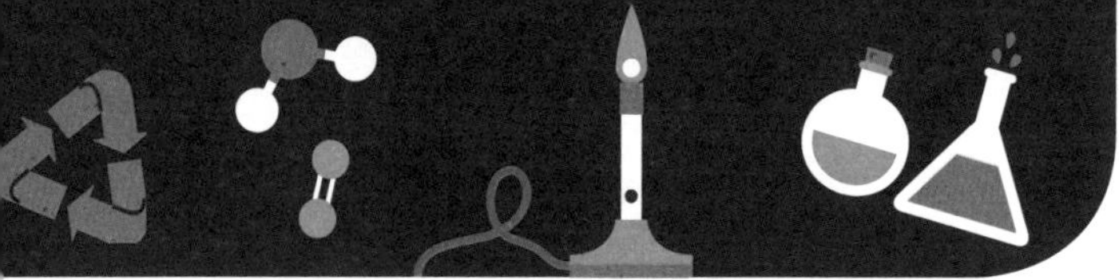

02 A student has two solutions of hydrochloric acid.

Table 1 shows the pH of each solution.

Table 1

Solution	pH
A	1
B	2

02.1 Which statement about the two solutions is correct?

Tick **one** box. **[1 mark]**

The H^+ concentration in solution **B** is ten times the H^+ concentration in solution **A**. ☐

The H^+ concentration in solution **A** is ten times the H^+ concentration in solution **B**. ☐

The H^+ concentration in solution **A** is half the H^+ concentration in solution **B**. ☐

The H^+ concentration in solution **A** is double the H^+ concentration in solution **B**. ☐

> **Exam Tip**
> Remember pH is a log scale, so it goes up by a factor of 10 each time.

02.2 What are the products of the reaction of copper carbonate with hydrochloric acid? **[1 mark]**

____

> **Exam Tip**
> There will be *three* products from this reaction – it is important that you can recall and apply all of the general salt equations.

02.3 Give the chemical formula of the salt produced in the reaction between hydrochloric acid and copper carbonate. **[1 mark]**

____

03 Some students wanted to make zinc chloride, $ZnCl_2$. This is the method they used:

1 Add excess zinc oxide to hydrochloric acid.
2 Filter the mixture.
3 Pour the filtrate into an evaporating basin.
4 Heat the evaporating basin and its contents until all the water has evaporated.

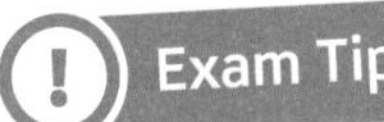

> **Exam Tip**
> This is similar to a Required Practical that you should have done in class – the different reactants might worry you at first but the method is exactly the same.

03.1 Suggest **two** improvements to step **1** to speed up the reaction. **[2 marks]**

03.2 Describe how the students would know when to stop adding zinc oxide in step **1**. **[1 mark]**

03.3 Give a reason why the mixture is filtered in step **2**. **[1 mark]**

03.4 Write down what the students should use to heat the evaporating basin and its contents in step **4**. **[1 mark]**

03.5 Suggest an improvement to step **4** to make larger zinc chloride crystals. **[2 marks]**

03.6 Write a balanced chemical equation for the reaction that occurs in step **1**. **[3 marks]**

03.7 In step **1**, the students had 25.0 cm^3 of hydrochloric acid. This volume contains 0.0125 moles.
Calculate the maximum mass of zinc chloride that could be made.
Give your answer to one significant figure. **[5 marks]**

In exams you will frequently use other parts of the question to find the information you need to answer later parts. If you get used to this now it will be easier in the exam.

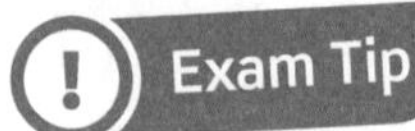

This is the reaction between zinc oxide and hydrochloric acid.

04 Magnesium reacts with dilute sulfuric acid.

$$Mg(s) + H_2SO_4(aq) \rightarrow MgSO_4(aq) + H_2(g)$$

04.1 Explain which substance is oxidised in the reaction of magnesium with sulfuric acid. Include a full balanced ionic equation, with state symbols, in your answer. **[5 marks]**

04.2 Magnesium also reacts with hydrochloric acid. Give the formulae of the **two** products of the reaction. **[2 marks]**

Hydrochloric acid is HCl, so one product will be the same and one will be different.

05 This question is about strong and weak acids.

05.1 Name **one** weak acid and **one** strong acid. **[2 marks]**

05.2 A solution of hydrochloric acid with a hydrogen ion concentration of 1×10^{-3} g/dm^3 has a pH of 3. Deduce the pH of hydrochloric acid with a hydrogen ion concentration of 1×10^{-5} g/dm^3. Explain your answer. **[3 marks]**

05.3 A technician made up solutions of two acids, represented by the formulae HX and HZ.

- Solution **A** contains a weak acid of formula HX.
  20% of the HX molecules are dissociated in solution.
  The concentration of the solution is 5 g/dm^3.
- Solution **B** contains a strong acid of formula HZ.
  100% of the HZ is dissociated in solution.
  The concentration of the solution is 2 g/dm^3.

Deduce which solution has the lower pH, solution **A** or solution **B**.
Explain your answer. **[4 marks]**

Exam Tip

This may seem like a really hard question but remember that pH is a log scale – 1 pH unit = a hydrogen ion concentration change by a factor of 10.

06 Sulfuric acid reacts with magnesium to form magnesium sulfate.

06.1 The chemical formula of sulfuric acid is H_2SO_4. What is the charge of the sulfate ion, SO_4, in sulfuric acid? **[1 mark]**

06.2 Give the chemical formula of magnesium sulfate. **[1 mark]**

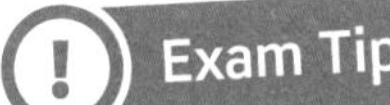

Exam Tip

Sulfuric acid is a neutral compound so the charges on the ions within sulfuric acid must be equal to zero.

06.3 Manganese is a metal that forms 2+ ions.
Manganese reacts with hydrochloric acid. Give the formula of manganese chloride. **[1 mark]**

06.4 Name the gas released when magnesium and manganese react with acids. **[1 mark]**

07 A student wanted to make large copper sulfate crystals from copper hydroxide and an acid.

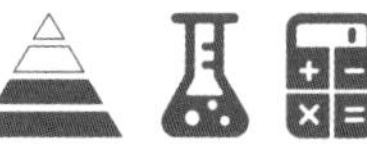

07.1 Name the acid the student should use. **[1 mark]**

Exam Tip

The second part of the salt name should point you towards the acid used.

07.2 Describe how the student could make a sample of copper sulfate crystals from copper hydroxide and the acid. In your answer:

- Name the pieces of apparatus required.
- Give a reason for each step. **[6 marks]**

07.3 Write a balanced symbol equation with state symbols for the reaction between the acid and copper hydroxide, $Cu(OH)_2$. **[3 marks]**

07.4 The student used 30 cm^3 of 32.5 g/dm^3 copper hydroxide solution. Calculate the moles of copper hydroxide that were used in the reaction. $M_r(Cu(OH)_2) = 97.5$ **[4 marks]**

07.5 Calculate the maximum mass of copper sulfate that the student could produce. Give your answer to two significant figures.
$M_r(CuSO_4) = 159.5$ **[5 marks]**

08 This question is about the pH scale. A student measured the pH of some solutions. **Table 3** shows the results the student obtained.

Table 3

Solution	pH
A	7
B	2
C	10
D	5
E	12

Exam Tip

Take this question part by part: pH before, pH as it was added, and then pH at the end.

08.1 Name **two** ways of measuring the pH of a solution. **[2 marks]**

08.2 Give the letter of the neutral solution. **[1 mark]**

08.3 Give the letter of the most alkaline solution. **[1 mark]**

Exam Tip

Getting the ratio of ions correct in sodium sulfate is an area where students often make mistakes.

08.4 Give the letter of the solution that has the highest concentration of hydrogen ions, H^+. **[1 mark]**

08.5 Some alkali is added to solution **A**. Write down whether the pH increases, decreases, or stays the same. **[1 mark]**

09 The elements calcium and oxygen react together to form an ionic compound called calcium oxide. Use the Periodic Table to help you answer this question.

09.1 Deduce the charge on a calcium ion and write its formula. **[1 mark]**

09.2 Deduce the charge on an oxide ion and write its formula. **[1 mark]**

09.3 Predict **three** properties of calcium oxide. Explain why calcium oxide has each of these properties. **[6 marks]**

Exam Tip

Look at the groups that calcium and oxygen are in and determine the number of electrons in their outer shells. This will tell you how many electrons they lose or gain and then you can work out the charge.

10 **Table 4** shows the pH of some acid solutions. Two of the solutions contain citric acid and two of the solutions contain hydrochloric acid.

Table 4

Solution	Concentration in g/dm^3	pH
W	0.1	5
X	0.1	3
Y	1.0	3
Z	1.0	1

10.1 Give the letter of the solution that has the highest hydrogen ion concentration. **[1 mark]**

10.2 Determine the letters of the **two** solutions of citric acid. Justify your decision. **[4 marks]**

10.3 Hydrochloric acid is a strong acid. Citric acid is a weak acid. Describe the difference between a weak acid and a strong acid. **[1 mark]**

10.4 Name **one** other weak acid and **one** other strong acid. **[2 marks]**

10.5 A student states that:

'*The pH of a weak acid is always higher than the pH of a strong acid.*'

Evaluate this statement. **[6 marks]**

Exam Tip

pH is a measure of hydrogen ion concentration: the more acidic the higher the concentration of hydrogen ions.

11 This question is about the elements in Group 0 of the Periodic Table.

11.1 Give the general name for the elements in Group 0. **[1 mark]**

11.2 An argon atom has 18 electrons. Write the electronic structure for argon. **[1 mark]**

11.3 Explain why the Group 0 elements are unreactive. **[1 mark]**

11.4 Describe the trend in boiling points from top to bottom of Group 0. **[1 mark]**

Exam Tip

When you're asked to 'write' the electronic structure this isn't drawing circles, it's listing the number of electrons in each shell starting from the centre.

12 An ion has the formula $^{69}_{31}Ga^{3+}$.

12.1 Give the number of protons in the ion. **[1 mark]**

12.2 Give the number of neutrons in the ion. **[1 mark]**

12.3 Give the number of electrons in the ion. **[1 mark]**

12.4 Give the name of **one** other element that is in the same group of the Periodic Table as gallium. **[1 mark]**

Exam Tip

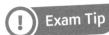

The charge on this ion will affect the number of electrons, not the number of protons.

13 Calcium chloride ($CaCl_2$) can be made by the reaction between calcium carbonate and hydrochloric acid.

13.1 Write a balanced symbol equation, with state symbols, for the reaction. **[3 marks]**

13.2 To make calcium chloride, a student added 10.0 g of calcium carbonate to a solution containing 5.0 g of HCl.
Deduce the limiting reactant. Justify your answer. **[5 marks]**

13.3 Calculate the maximum mass of calcium chloride that could be formed in the reaction. **[3 marks]**

13.4 Suggest why the student will probably make less than the maximum possible mass of calcium chloride. **[1 mark]**

14 Phosphoric(V) acid, H_3PO_4, is a weak acid.

14.1 What is meant by the term weak acid? **[1 mark]**

14.2 Phosphoric(V) acid can react with magnesium metal:

$$\_\_\_\_ Mg(s) + \_\_\_\_ H_3PO_4(aq) \rightarrow Mg_3(PO_4)_2(aq) + \_\_\_\_ H_2(g)$$

Balance the symbol equation. **[1 mark]**

14.3 Identify which species is oxidised and which species is reduced. **[2 marks]**

14.4 Phosphoric(V) acid can also react with sodium hydroxide.

$$\_\_\_\_ NaOH(aq) + H_3PO_4(aq) \rightarrow \_\_\_\_ (aq) + \_\_\_\_ H_2O(l)$$

Give the formula of the salt produced in this reaction, and then balance the equation. **[3 marks]**

14.5 A teacher reacted 25 cm^3 of 0.5 mol/dm^3 phosphoric(V) acid with a 0.15 mol/dm^3 solution of sodium hydroxide.
Calculate the volume of sodium hydroxide solution that reacted with the phosphoric(V) acid. **[5 marks]**

Exam Tip

You are expected to know a list of strong and weak acids.

Strong acids include hydrochloric acid, nitric acid, and sulfuric acid.

Weak acids include ethanoic acid, citric acid, and carbonic acid.

Knowledge

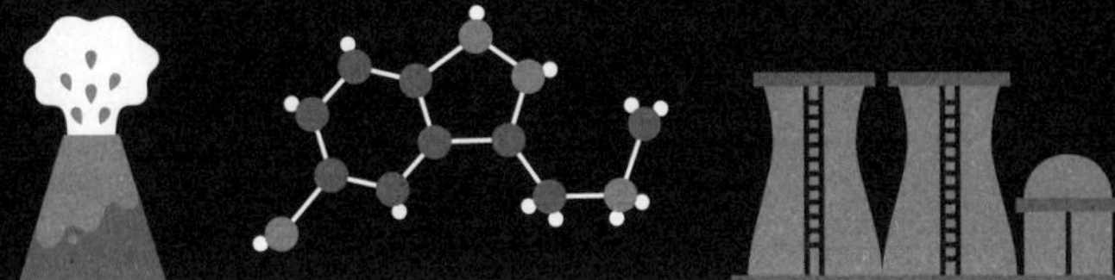

C8 Electrolysis

Electrolysis

In the process of **electrolysis**, an electric current is passed through an **electrolyte**. An electrolyte is a liquid or solution that contains ions and so can conduct electricity. This causes the ions to move to the **electrodes**, where they form pure elements.

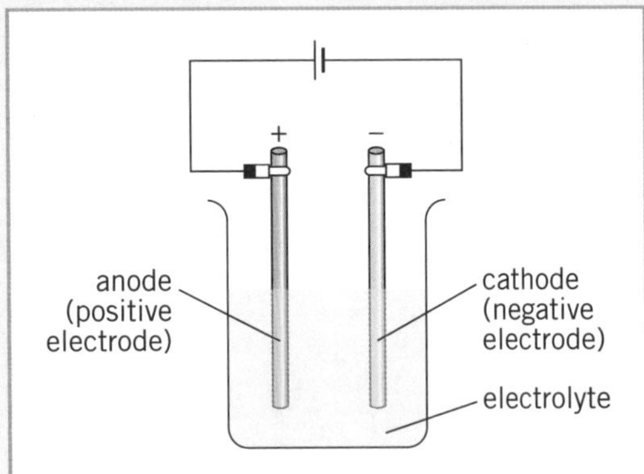

Electrolysis of molten compounds

Solid ionic compounds do not conduct electricity as the ions cannot move. To undergo electrolysis they must be molten or dissolved, so the ions are free to move.

When an ionic compound is molten:

- the positive metal ions are *attracted* to the **cathode**, where they will *gain* electrons to form the pure metal
- the negative non-metal ions are *attracted* to the **anode**, where they will *lose* electrons and become the pure non-metal.

For example, molten sodium chloride, NaCl, can undergo electrolysis to form sodium at the cathode and chlorine at the anode.

Half equations

sodium chloride → sodium + chlorine

$2NaCl(l) \rightarrow 2Na(s) + Cl_2(g)$

- at the cathode:

$2Na^+(l) + 2e^- \rightarrow 2Na(s)$

- at the anode:

$2Cl^-(l) \rightarrow Cl_2(g) + 2e^-$

Remember The anode is where electrons are lost, and the cathode is where electrons are gained – it never happens the other way around.

Electrolysis of aqueous solutions

Solid ionic compounds can also undergo electrolysis when dissolved in water.

- It requires less energy to dissolve ionic compounds in water than it does to melt them.
- However, in the electrolysis of solutions, the pure elements are not always produced. This is because the water can also undergo ionisation:

$$H_2O(l) \rightarrow H^+(aq) + OH^-(aq)$$

Products at the anode

In the electrolysis of a solution, if the non-metal contains oxygen then oxygen gas is formed at the anode:

- The $OH^-(aq)$ ions formed from the ionisation of water are attracted to the anode.
- The $OH^-(aq)$ ions lose electrons to the anode and form oxygen gas.

$4OH^-(aq) \rightarrow O_2(g) + 2H_2O(l) + 4e^-$

If the non-metal ion is a halogen, then the halogen gas is formed at the anode.

$2Cl^-(aq) \rightarrow Cl_2(g) + 2e^-$

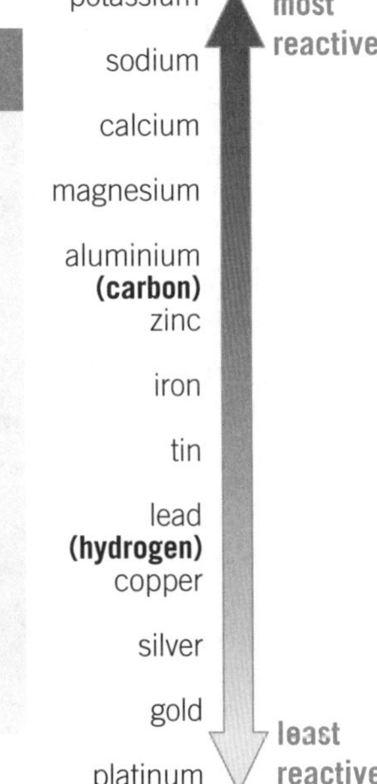

Products at the cathode

In the electrolysis of a solution, if the metal is *more* **reactive** than hydrogen then hydrogen gas is formed at the cathode:

- The $H^+(aq)$ ions from the ionisation of water are attracted to the cathode and react with it.
- The $H^+(aq)$ ions gain electrons from the cathode and form hydrogen gas.

$2H^+(aq) + 2e^- \rightarrow H_2(g)$

- The metal ions remain in solution.

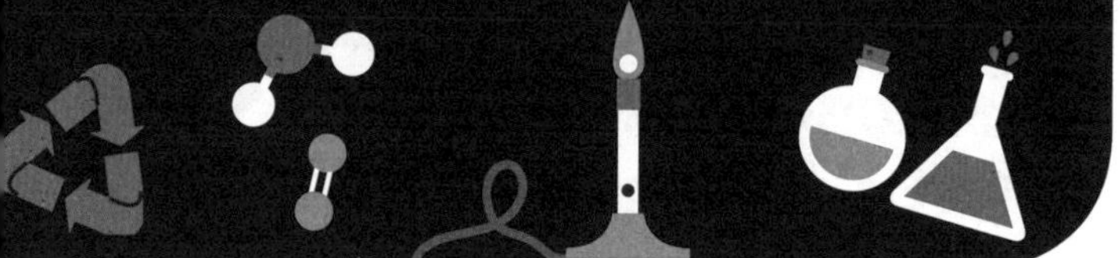

Electrolysis of aluminium oxide

Electrolysis can be used to extract metals from their ionic compounds.

Electrolysis is used if the metal is more reactive than carbon.

Aluminium is extracted from aluminium oxide by electrolysis.

1 The aluminium oxide is mixed with a substance called **cryolite**, which lowers the melting point.
2 The mixture is then heated until it is molten.
3 The resulting molten mixture undergoes electrolysis.

aluminium oxide → aluminium + oxygen

$$2Al_2O_3(l) \rightarrow 4Al(l) + 3O_2(g)$$

cathode: pure aluminium is formed

$$Al^{3+}(l) + 3e^- \rightarrow Al(l)$$

anode: oxygen is formed

$$2O^{2-}(l) \rightarrow O_2(g) + 4e^-$$

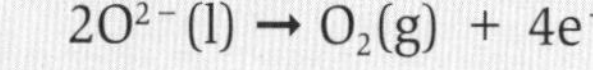

Revision tip

Practice This makes a good six-mark question. Make sure you can do the half equations, know the key words, and know what the electrodes are made of.

In the electrolysis of aluminium, the anode is made of graphite.

The graphite reacts with the oxygen to form carbon dioxide and so slowly wears away. It therefore needs to be replaced frequently.

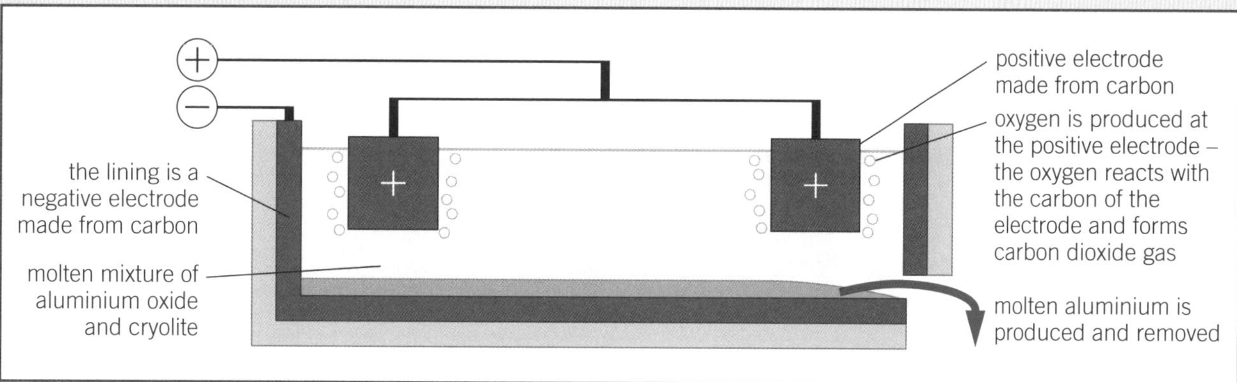

Revision tip

Remember In an exam, don't PANIC.

Here is an easy way to remember which electrode is which:

Positive
Anode
Negative
Is
Cathode

Key terms Make sure you can write a definition for these key terms.

anode cathode cryolite electrode electrolysis electrolyte reactivity

Retrieval

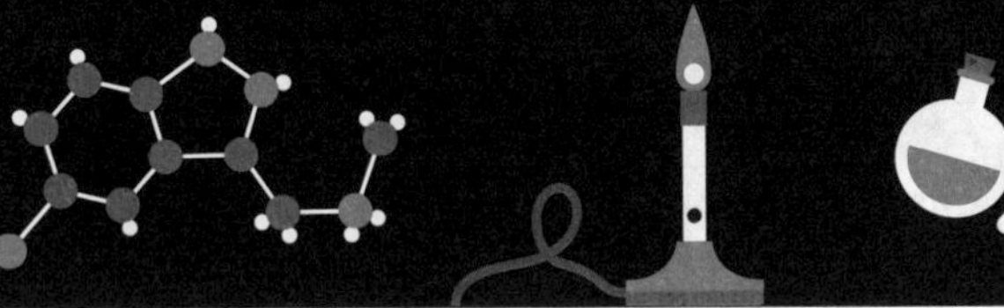

Learn the answers to the questions below, then cover the answers column with a piece of paper and write as many as you can. Check and repeat.

	C8 questions	Answers
1	What is electrolysis?	the process of using electricity to extract elements from a compound
2	What is the name of the positive electrode?	anode
3	What is the name of the negative electrode?	cathode
4	What is an electrolyte?	a liquid or solution that contains ions and so can conduct electricity
5	Where are metals formed?	cathode
6	Where are non-metals formed?	anode
7	How can ionic substances be electrolysed?	by melting or dissolving them, and then passing a direct current through them
8	Why can solid ionic substances not be electrolysed?	they do not conduct electricity, or the ions cannot move
9	In the electrolysis of solutions, when is the metal not produced at the cathode?	when the metal is more reactive than hydrogen
10	In the electrolysis of a metal halide solution, what is produced at the anode?	halogen gas
11	In the electrolysis of a metal sulfate solution, what is produced at the anode?	oxygen
12	What is the half equation for the ionisation of water?	$H_2O(l) \rightarrow H^+(aq) + OH^-(aq)$
13	What metals are extracted from ionic compounds by using electrolysis?	metals that are more reactive than carbon
14	In the electrolysis of aluminium oxide, why is the aluminium oxide mixed with cryolite?	to lower the melting point
15	In the electrolysis of aluminium oxide, what are the anodes made of?	graphite
16	In the electrolysis of aluminium oxide, why do the anodes need to be replaced?	they react with the oxygen being formed

Put paper here

Now go back and use the questions below to check your knowledge from previous chapters.

Previous questions / Answers

	Previous questions	Answers
1	What are the names and formulae of three main acids?	hydrochloric acid, HCl; sulfuric acid, H_2SO_4; nitric acid, HNO_3
2	How are metals more reactive than carbon extracted from their ores?	electrolysis
3	In terms of pH, what is an acid?	a solution with a pH of less than 7
4	In terms of electrons, what is reduction?	gain of electrons
5	How do you measure the pH of a substance?	universal indicator or pH probe
6	What is the ionic equation for a reaction between an acid and an alkali?	$H^+(aq) + OH^-(aq) \rightarrow H_2O(l)$
7	How can you obtain a solid salt from a solution?	crystallisation
8	Why are gold and silver found naturally as elements in the Earth's crust?	they are very unreactive
9	In terms of pH, what is a neutral solution?	a solution with a pH of 7

Put paper here

Put paper here

Put paper here

Required Practical Skills

Practise answering questions on the required practicals using the example below. You need to be able to apply your skills and knowledge to other practicals too.

Electrolysis	Worked example	Practice
You need to be able to describe the method of electrolysis, and label the experimental set-up for electrolysis. Electrolysis uses electricity to break ionic compounds down into simpler compounds or elements. Metals or hydrogen are made at the negative electrode, and non-metal molecules are made at the positive electrode. You will need to be able to apply the principles of electrolysis to any example, as many solutions can undergo electrolysis. This includes predicting the products of electrolysis for different solutions, identifying which ions move to each electrode, and writing equations for the reactions at the two electrodes.	The electrolysis of aqueous sodium chloride gives three products. Identify these products and state how we can test for them. *The three products are chlorine gas (Cl_2) hydrogen gas (H_2) and sodium hydroxide solution ($NaOH$).* *To test for hydrogen gas, collect the gas in a test tube and insert a glowing splint – it should burn with a squeaky pop noise.* *To test for chlorine gas, collect the gas in a test tube and insert damp litmus paper – the litmus paper will bleach white.* *Sodium hydroxide can be tested for using universal indicator – the solution will turn purple as sodium hydroxide is an alkali.*	**1** State what you would observe at each electrode during the electrolysis of copper(II) chloride. **2** Give the products of the electrolysis of sodium sulfate. **3** Explain why the electrodes must not touch each other during electrolysis.

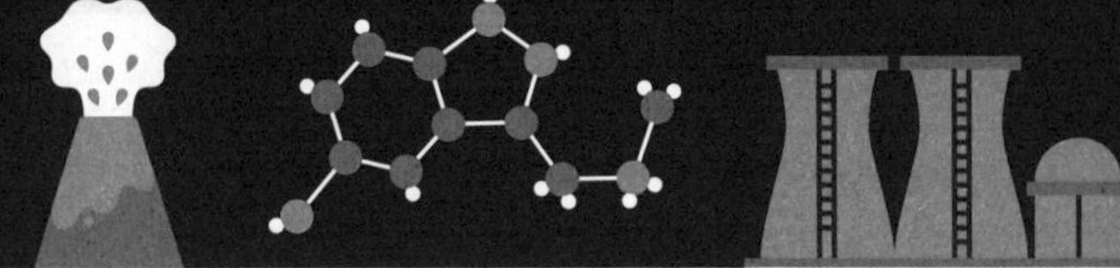

Exam-style questions

01 A student investigated the electrolysis of sodium chloride solution.

Figure 1 shows the apparatus used.

Figure 1

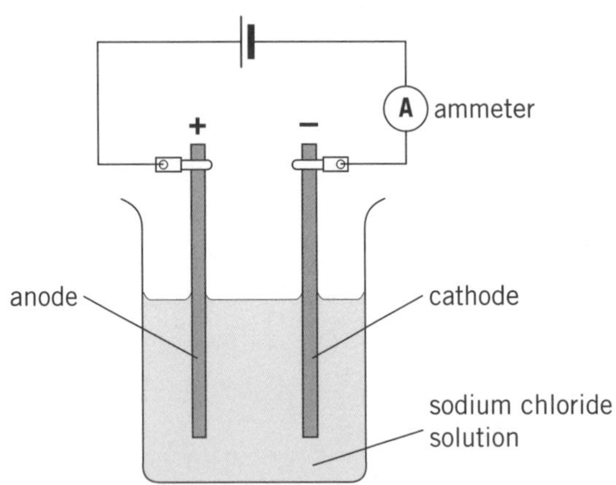

01.1 Name the substance that is produced at the cathode. **[1 mark]**

Exam Tip

The answer is not sodium. Use the reactivity series and the formula of salty water to work out the other product.

____

01.2 Write a half equation, including state symbols, for the reaction that occurs at the anode. **[3 marks]**

____

01.3 The student wanted to investigate if changing the concentration of sodium chloride solution affects the current that flows.

Table 1 shows the student's results.

Table 1

Concentration of sodium chloride solution in g/dm^3	Current in amps
0.2	0.20
0.4	0.33
0.6	0.43
0.8	0.47
1.0	0.52

Identify the independent variable and the dependent variable in the investigation. **[2 marks]**

Independent variable: ______________________________

Dependent variable: ______________________________

Exam Tip

'Independent' is the one we change and 'dependent' is the one we measure. A good way to remember this is that your results *depend* on the dependent variable.

01.4 Suggest **one** control variable in the investigation. **[1 mark]**

____

01.5 Plot the data from **Table 1** on **Figure 2**.

Draw a line of best fit. **[3 marks]**

Figure 2

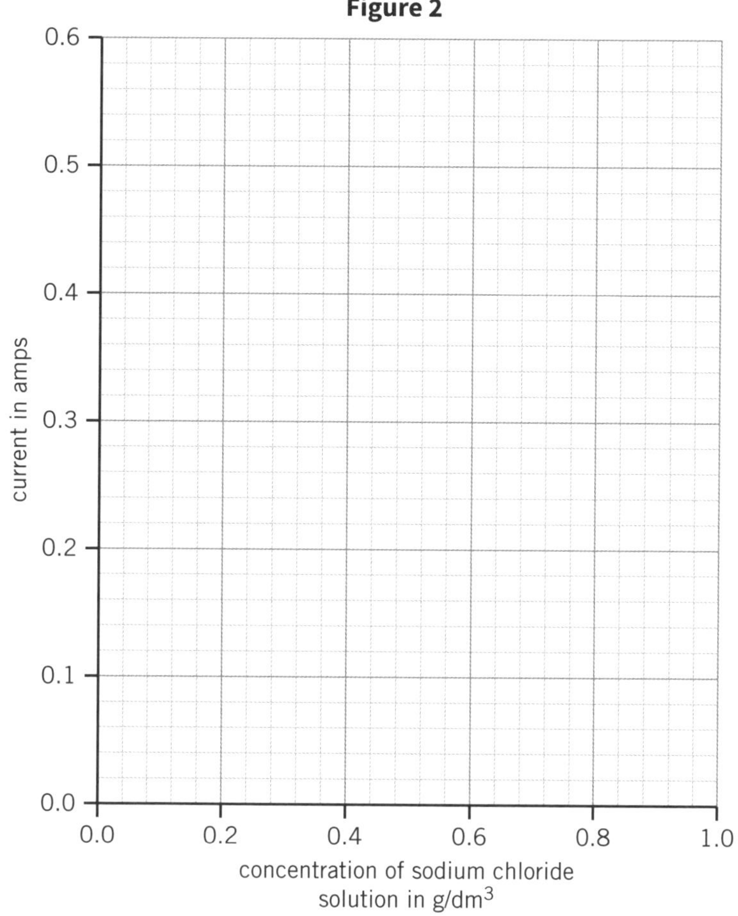

Use crosses to plot your points because this clearly shows the examiners which point you are aiming for. Circles can easily be misinterpreted as they can cover a range of points or be too small to be seen by the examiner.

01.6 Describe the pattern shown on your graph.

Suggest **one** reason for this pattern. **[2 marks]**

Pattern: ______________________________

____

Reason: ______________________________

____

Use data from the graph to support your reason.

02 Molten zinc chloride is electrolysed using inert electrodes.

02.1 Name the electrode that positively charged ions move towards during electrolysis. **[1 mark]**

____

02.2 What are the products at the anode and cathode? **[1 mark]**

Tick **one** box.

anode	**cathode**	
zinc	chlorine	☐
chlorine	zinc	☐
zinc	hydrogen	☐
chlorine	hydrogen	☐

Exam Tip

The first step is to work out the charges on the ions within zinc chloride.

02.3 Explain why solid zinc chloride cannot be used for electrolysis. **[3 marks]**

____

____

____

____

02.4 The symbol equation for the reaction is:

$ZnCl_2$ ____ → Zn ____ + Cl_2 ____

Complete the symbol equation by adding state symbols. **[1 mark]**

03 Potassium is extracted from its ores by electrolysis.

03.1 Suggest why electrolysis is used to extract potassium. **[1 mark]**

03.2 In the electrolysis of molten potassium sulfate, name the electrode that solid potassium metal will form at. **[1 mark]**

03.3 The electrolysis of molten potassium sulfate is an expensive industrial process. Give a reason why. **[1 mark]**

03.4 Aqueous potassium sulfate solution can also be electrolysed. Write the half equations for the electrolysis of aqueous potassium sulfate. **[6 marks]**

Exam Tip

Look at the reactivity series to help you answer this.

03.5 Suggest why an aqueous solution of potassium sulfate cannot be used to extract potassium. **[1 mark]**

04 **Figure 3** shows an electrolysis cell for the industrial extraction of aluminium.

Figure 3

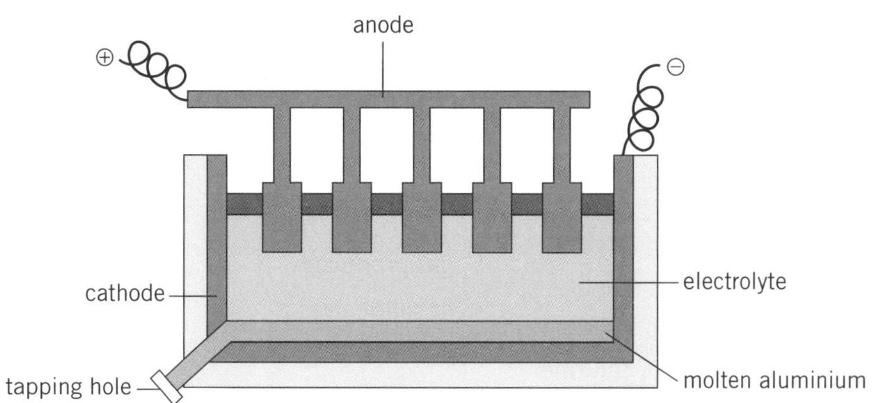

04.1 Explain why aluminium cannot be extracted by heating its ore with carbon. **[1 mark]**

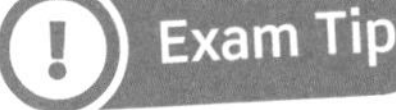

Exam Tip

Think about the element that the electrodes are made from.

04.2 Name the material that the anode and cathode are made from. **[1 mark]**

04.3 Explain why the anode must be replaced regularly. **[1 mark]**

04.4 Name the **two** substances that are mixed together in the electrolyte. **[2 marks]**

04.5 Write a half equation, including state symbols, for the reaction that occurs at the cathode. **[3 marks]**

Exam Tip

Make sure the number of electrons matches the charge on the ions, and that the equation is balanced.

04.6 Suggest why industrial aluminium electrolysis cells are often sited near power stations that generate electricity from renewable sources. **[1 mark]**

05 This question is about lead bromide electrodes.

05.1 Define the term inert electrode. **[2 marks]**

05.2 The charge on a lead ion is 2+.
Deduce the formula of lead bromide. **[1 mark]**

05.3 An electrolysis reaction happens when electricity is passed through molten lead bromide using inert electrodes.
Describe what happens in this reaction.
Include in your answer the name of the products of the electrolysis reaction and an explanation of how the products are made. **[6 marks]**

Exam Tip

Split your answer into two parts: what happens at the anode and what happens at the cathode.

06 A chemist tried to pass an electric current through a solid, a liquid, and a solution. **Table 2** shows the chemist's results.

Table 2

Substance	State	Observations at anode	Observations at cathode
sodium chloride	solid	no change (did not conduct electricity)	
sodium chloride	liquid	smell of chlorine	silver-coloured liquid produced
sodium chloride	concentrated solution	gas produced did not relight glowing splint smell of chlorine	gas produced lit splint gives a squeaky pop
sodium chloride	dilute solution	gas produced relit glowing splint smell of chlorine	gas produced lit splint gives a squeaky pop

06.1 Explain the observations in solid and liquid sodium chloride. **[3 marks]**

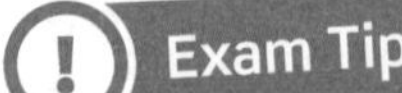

Exam Tip

There are two gases produced here, not one gas that gives two positive results.

06.2 Write a half equation, including state symbols, for the reaction that occurs at the cathode for concentrated sodium chloride. **[3 marks]**

06.3 Suggest an explanation for the observations at the anode and cathode for dilute sodium chloride solution. **[6 marks]**

07 Aluminium is manufactured by electrolysis.

07.1 Suggest why reduction with carbon is not an appropriate method to manufacture aluminium. **[1 mark]**

07.2 In the electrolysis of aluminium, what is the cathode made of? **[1 mark]**

Exam Tip

The electrodes are made of carbon.

07.3 A mixture of aluminium oxide and cryolite forms the electrolyte. Explain the purpose of the cryolite. **[3 marks]**

07.4 Explain why aluminium is produced at the cathode. **[2 marks]**

07.5 In the electrolysis of aluminium oxide, explain why the anode has to be replaced regularly. **[2 marks]**

08 A student sets up an electrolysis experiment in a Petri dish, as shown in **Figure 4.**

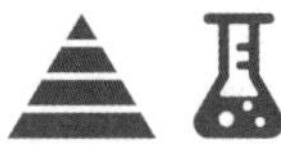

Figure 4

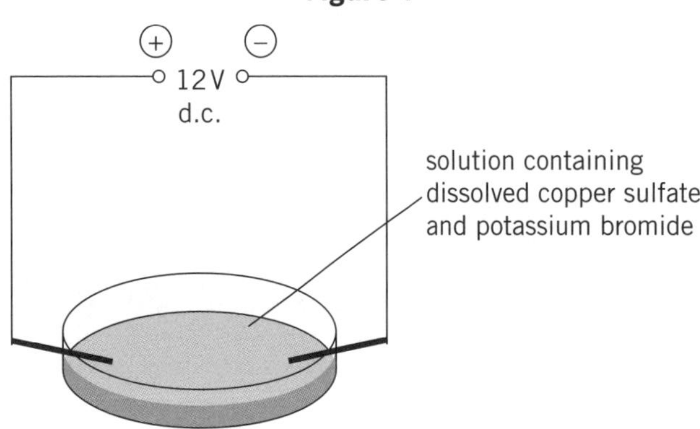

Table 3 shows the results.

Table 3

Electrode	Observations
anode	
cathode	brown flaky solid and then bubbles

08.1 Give the name of the brown flaky solid. **[1 mark]**

08.2 Predict the name of the gas that forms bubbles at the cathode. **[1 mark]**

08.3 Describe a test you could do to show that your prediction in **08.2** is correct. Include the expected results of this test. **[2 marks]**

08.4 Predict and explain the observations expected at the anode. Include half equations in your answer. **[8 marks]**

08.5 Suggest **two** reasons for carrying out the electrolysis in a Petri dish, rather than in a larger and taller electrolysis cell. **[2 marks]**

> **Exam Tip**
> Use the diagram to determine the ions in the electrolyte.

09 A student has a mixture of coloured liquids. The student wants to identify which substances are in the mixture.

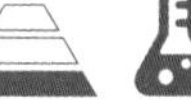

09.1 The student thinks that there are two substances dissolved in water. They carry out a chromatography experiment to identify whether this is correct. They use water as the solvent.
Sketch the chromatogram the student would see if there are two substances dissolved in water. Label the sample and the solvent front. **[2 marks]**

> **Exam Tip**
> Don't forget to label everything in your diagram.

09.2 The student finds that the mixture only contains one substance dissolved in water. They carry out another chromatography experiment to identify the substances. Their chromatogram is shown in **Figure 5**.

Figure 5

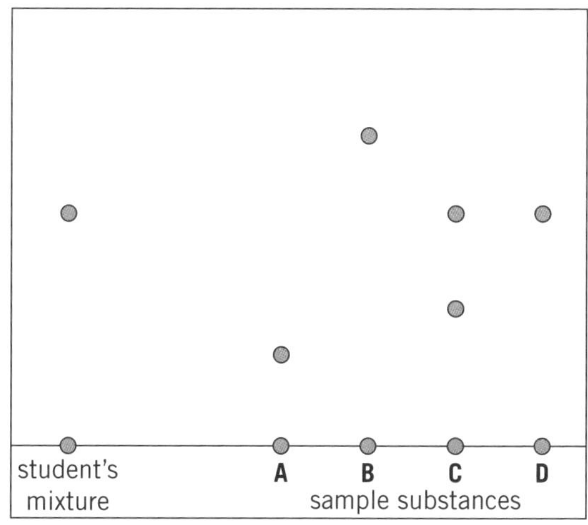

Identify the substance in the student's mixture. **[1 mark]**

> **Exam Tip**
> Use a pen to draw horizontal lines across the chromatogram for each spot – this will help you identify which spots appear in more than one sample.

09.3 The student wants to separate the substance from the water it is dissolved in. The substance has a boiling point of 78 °C. Explain why fractional distillation has to be used to extract the substance from the water. **[5 marks]**

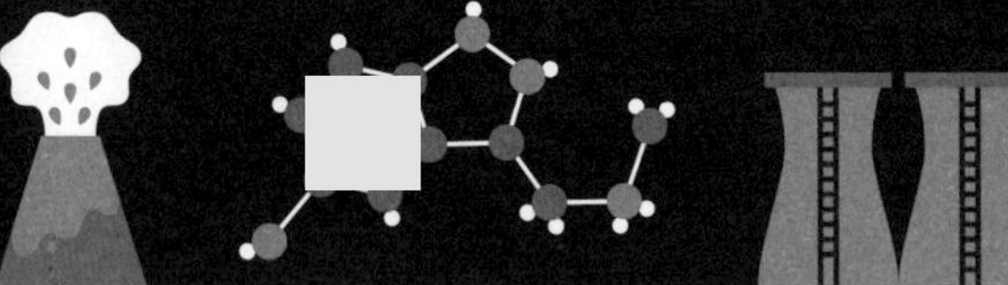

Knowledge

C9 Energy changes

Energy changes

During a chemical reaction, **energy** transfers occur.

Energy can be transferred:

- to the surroundings – **exothermic**
- from the surroundings – **endothermic**

This energy transfer can cause a temperature change.

Energy is always conserved in chemical reactions.

This means that there is the same amount of energy in the Universe at the start of a chemical reaction as at the end of the chemical reaction.

The surroundings

When chemists say energy is transferred from or to "the surroundings" they mean "everything that isn't the reaction".

For example, imagine you have a reaction mixture in a test tube. If you measure the temperature around the test tube using a thermometer, the thermometer is then part of the surroundings.

- If the thermometer records an increase in temperature, the reaction in the test tube is exothermic.
- If the thermometer records a decrease in temperature, the reaction in the test tube is endothermic.

Reaction profiles

A **reaction profile** shows whether a reaction is exothermic or endothermic.

The **activation energy** is the minimum amount of energy that particles must have to react when they collide.

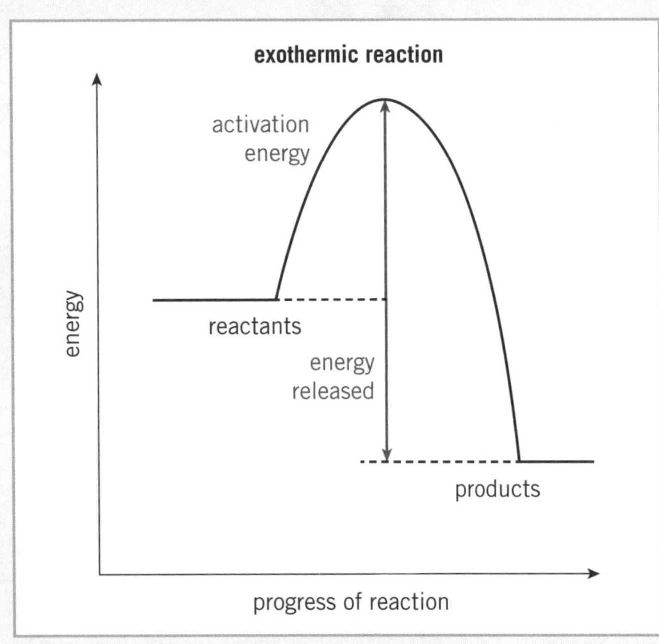

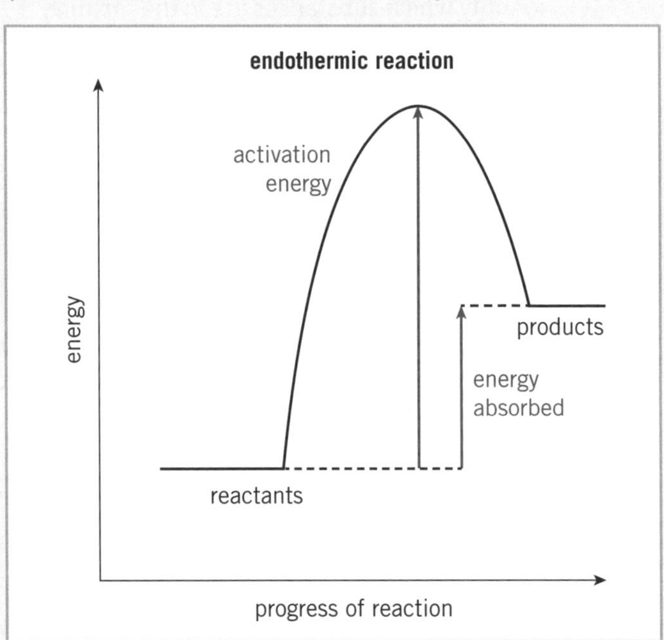

A summary of exothermic and endothermic reactions is given in the table.

Reaction	Energy transfer	Temperature change	Example	Everyday use	Bonds
exothermic	to the surroundings	temperature of the surroundings increases	• **oxidation** • **combustion** • **neutralisation**	• self-heating cans • hand warmers	more energy released when making bonds than required to break bonds
endothermic	from the surroundings	temperature of the surroundings decreases	• **thermal decomposition** • citric acid and sodium hydrogen carbonate	• sports injury packs	less energy released when making bonds than required to break bonds

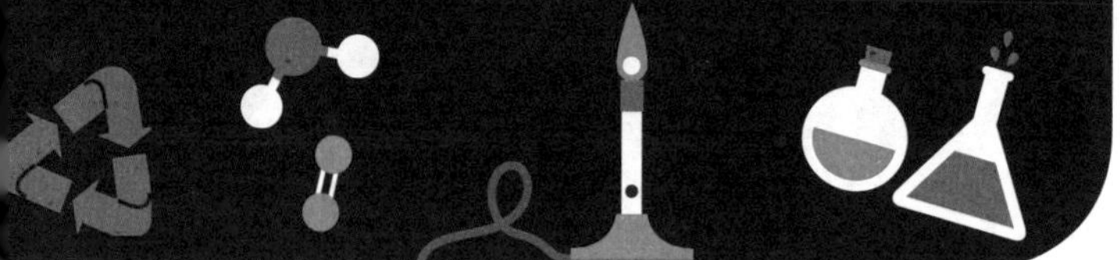

Bonds

Atoms are held together by strong chemical bonds. In a reaction, those bonds are broken and new ones are made between different atoms.

- Breaking a bond requires energy so is endothermic.
- Making a bond releases energy so is exothermic.

Breaking bonds

If a lot of energy is released when making the bonds and only a little energy is required to break them, then overall energy is released and the reaction as a whole is exothermic.

Making bonds

If a little energy is released when making the bonds and a lot is required to break them, then overall energy is taken in and the reaction as a whole is endothermic.

Bond calculations

Different bonds require different amounts of energy to be broken (their bond energies). To work out the overall energy change of a reaction, you need to:

1. work out how much energy is required to break all the bonds in the reactants
2. work out how much energy is released when making all the bonds in the products.

overall energy transferred = *energy required to break bonds* − *energy required to make bonds*

- A positive number means an endothermic reaction.
- A negative number means an exothermic number.

Revision tip

Practice Drawing everything out helps to count the correct number of bonds.

Worked example

The combustion of methane in oxygen is an exothermic reaction. Determine the energy released in kJ/mol.

$$CH_4 + 2O_2 \rightarrow CO_2 + 2H_2O$$

- the C — H bond has a bond enthalpy of +413 kJ/mol
- the O = O bond has a bond enthalpy of +498 kJ/mol
- the C = O bond has a bond enthalpy of +804 kJ/mol
- the O—H bond has a bond enthalpy of +464 kJ/mol.

For the reactants

There are four C—H bonds, so 4 × 413 = 1652 kJ/mol
There are two O = O bonds, so 2 × 498 = 996 kJ/mol
The total for the reactants is 1652 + 996 = 2648 kJ/mol

For the products

There are two C = O bonds, so 2 × 1608 kJ/mol
There are four H—O bonds, so 4 × 1856 kJ/mol
The total for the products in 3465 kJ/mol
Overall energy transferred = 2648 − 3465 = −817 kJ/mol

Key terms

Make sure you can write a definition for these key terms.

activation energy *bond energy* *combustion* *endothermic* *exothermic* *neutralisation* *oxidation* *reaction profile* *thermal decomposition*

Retrieval

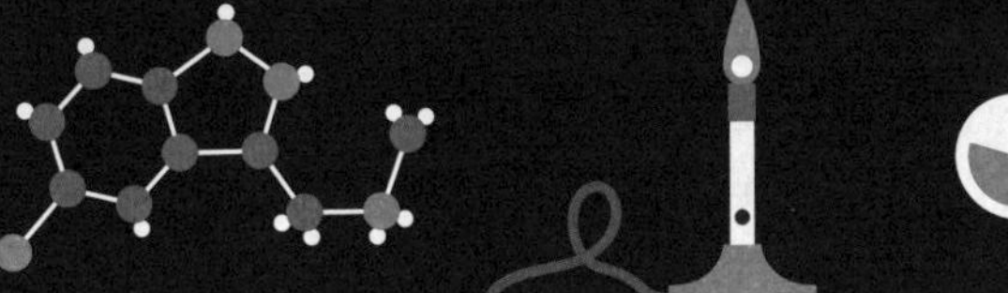

Learn the answers to the questions below, then cover the answers column with a piece of paper and write as many as you can. Check and repeat.

	C9 questions	Answers
1	What is an exothermic energy transfer?	energy transfer to the surroundings
2	What is an endothermic energy transfer?	energy transfer from the surroundings
3	What is a reaction profile?	diagram showing how the energy changes in a reaction
4	What is the activation energy?	minimum amount of energy required before a collision will result in a reaction
5	What is a bond energy?	the energy required to break a bond or the energy released when a bond is formed
6	In terms of bond breaking and making, what is an exothermic reaction?	less energy is required to break the old bonds than is released when making the new bonds
7	In terms of bond breaking and making, what is an endothermic reaction?	more energy is required to break the old bonds than is released when making the new bonds

Put paper here

Put paper here

Put paper here

Now go back and use the questions below to check your knowledge from previous chapters.

Previous questions

Answers

	Question	Answer
1	What is the half equation for the ionisation of water?	$H_2O(l) \rightarrow H^+(aq) + OH^-(aq)$
2	In the electrolysis of solutions, when is the metal not produced at the cathode?	when the metal is more reactive than hydrogen
3	How can metals be ordered by their reactivity?	by comparing their reactions with water, acid, or oxygen
4	How can ionic substances be electrolysed?	by melting or dissolving them, and then passing a direct current through them
5	What is a base?	substance that reacts with acids in neutralisation reactions
6	What is an alkali?	substance that dissolves in water to form a solution above pH 7
7	In the electrolysis of aluminium oxide, why do the anodes need to be replaced?	they react with the oxygen being formed
8	What does reactivity mean?	how vigorously a substance chemically reacts
9	What are the four state symbols and what do they stand for?	(s) solid, (l) liquid, (g) gas, (aq) aqueous or dissolved in water

Put paper here

Put paper here

Put paper here

Required Practical Skills

Practise answering questions on the required practicals using the example below. You need to be able to apply your skills and knowledge to other practicals too.

Temperature changes

This practical tests your ability to accurately measure mass, temperature, and volume to investigate changes during chemical reactions. You should be able to describe how to measure temperature change after mixing a strong acid with a strong alkali.

You also need to know:

- general equations for reactions of acids
- how to determine the formula of ionic compounds from the charges of their ions
- formulas of ions involved in neutralisation reactions.

Worked example

Write a method to investigate how the volume of sodium hydroxide added to hydrochloric acid affects the temperature change of the reaction.

Place a polystyrene cup inside a beaker. Pour 30 cm^3 of dilute hydrochloric acid into the cup, place the lid on the cup and insert a thermometer through a hole in the cup. Record the temperature of the acid. Pour 5 cm^3 sodium hydroxide solution into the cup and stir the solution. Record the highest temperature the reaction reaches on the thermometer. Repeat the experiment, increasing the amount of sodium hydroxide each time by 5 cm^3, up to 40 cm^3. Repeat the entire experiment two times to get repeat measurements.

Practice

1 Describe the function of the beaker in the experiment.

2 Is the reaction in this experiment exothermic or endothermic? Explain your answer.

3 Give a balanced equation for the reaction between sodium hydroxide and hydrochloric acid.

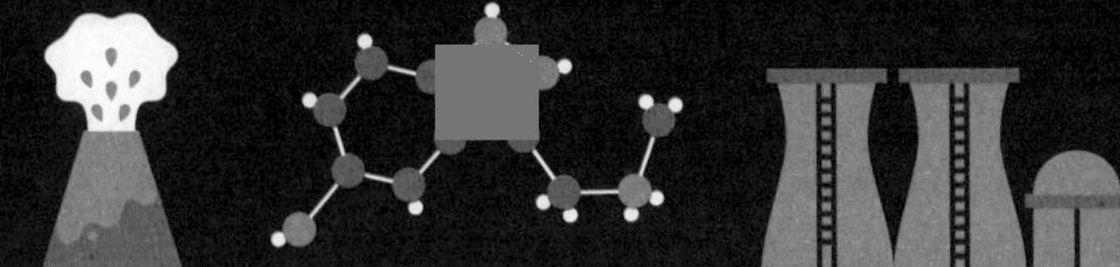

Exam-style questions

01 This question is about endothermic and exothermic reactions.

01.1 Draw **one** line from each reaction to show whether it is endothermic or exothermic. **[4 marks]**

Reaction	Endothermic or exothermic
thermal decomposition	
citric acid with sodium hydrogencarbonate	endothermic
neutralisation	exothermic
combustion	

> **Exam Tip**
>
> Read the instructions carefully; you may see the word *one* in bold and think you only need to draw one line but read the whole thing and you'll see that you need *four* lines, one from each box on the left-hand side.

01.2 Which statement is true for an exothermic reaction? **[1 mark]**

Tick **one** box.

It transfers energy to the surroundings. ☐

It transfers energy from the surroundings. ☐

The energy of the products is higher than the energy of the reactants. ☐

The temperature of the surroundings decreases. ☐

01.3 Iron oxide reacts with aluminium to produce aluminium oxide and iron. The reaction occurs at a high enough temperature that the iron produced is molten.

Identify whether the reaction is exothermic or endothermic. **[1 mark]**

____

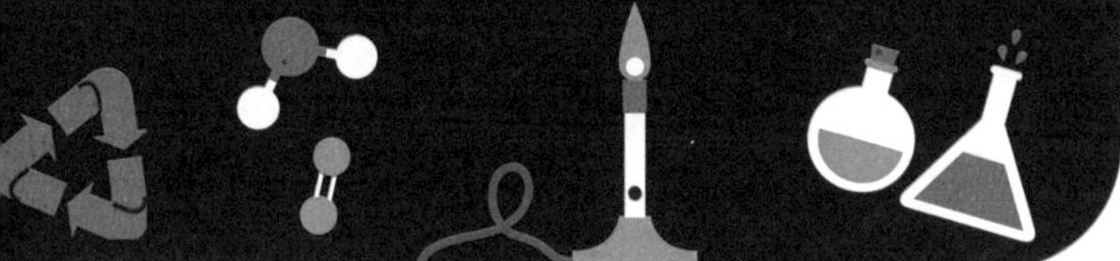

02 Hydrogen reacts with chlorine to form hydrochloric acid. The reaction is exothermic.

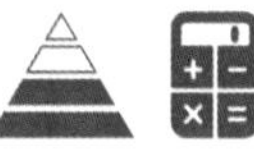

Figure 1 shows the reaction profile for the reaction.

Figure 1

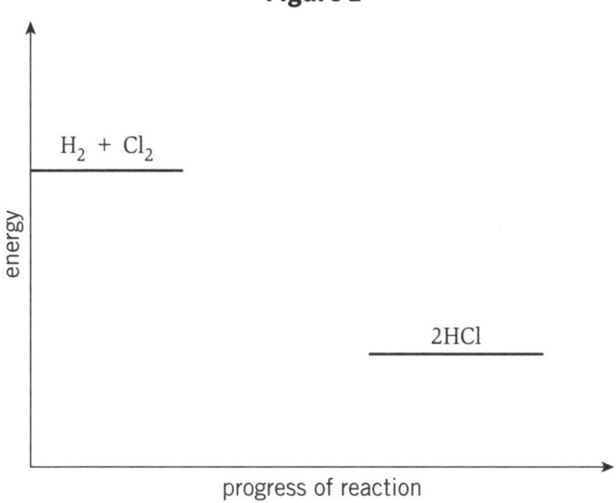

02.1 Complete the reaction profile to show how the energy changes as the reaction proceeds.

Draw an arrow to show the overall energy change of the reaction.

The arrow and line do **not** need to be to scale. **[2 marks]**

02.2 Explain how the reaction profile in **Figure 1** shows that the reaction is exothermic. **[2 marks]**

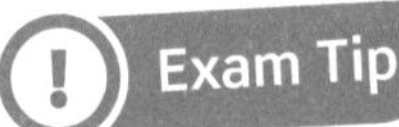

Exam Tip

You need to refer to the position of the products and reactants in your answer.

____

____

____

02.3 The displayed formulae for the reaction are:

$$\text{H—H} + \text{Cl—Cl} \rightarrow 2\ \text{H—Cl}$$

Table 1 shows some bond enthalpies.

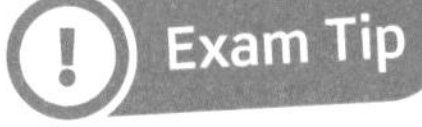

Exam Tip

Don't forget there are 2 H—Cl bonds.

Table 1

Bond	H—H	Cl—Cl	H—Cl
Energy in kJ/mol	436	242	431

Calculate the overall energy change of the reaction. **[3 marks]**

Bond energy = ______________ kJ/mol

03 Some students dissolved four substances in water. This is the method used:

1 Transfer 100 cm³ of water to a beaker.

2 Measure the temperature of the water.

3 Add 1 spatula measure of the substance, in powder form, to the water.

4 Measure the new temperature of the water.

Table 2 shows their results.

> **Exam Tip**
>
> This is a Required Practical. You may have done it by mixing acid and alkali – try to remember what you put the acid into. Even though you use a beaker, this is not where the reaction occurs.

Table 2

Substance	Temperature of water at start in °C	Temperature of solution immediately after dissolving in °C
A	20	25
B	21	17
C	21	31
D	22	6

03.1 Suggest the apparatus that could be used instead of a beaker to improve step **1**. Give a reason for your suggestion. **[2 marks]**

03.2 Suggest what the students should do between steps **3** and **4**. Give a reason for your suggestion. **[2 marks]**

> For **03.4**, it can be helpful to add an extra column on the right-hand side of the table to show change in temperature.

03.3 Give the letter of the substance that dissolves most exothermically. **[1 mark]**

03.4 Predict how the temperature changes would alter if the students repeated the experiment using 200 cm³ of water in step **1**. **[1 mark]**

04 **Figure 2** shows the displayed formulae for the combustion reaction of methane.

Figure 2

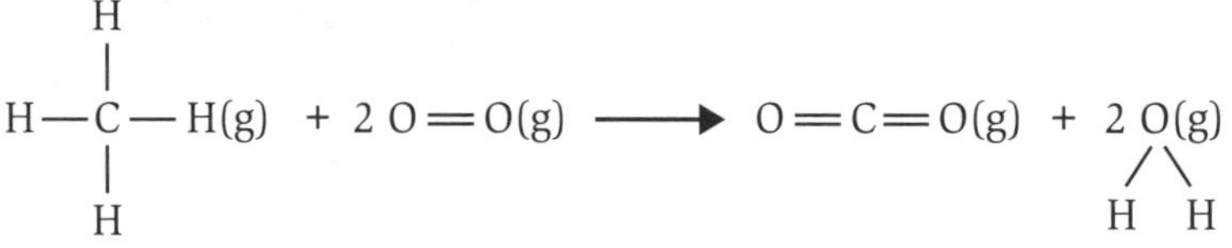

04.1 **Table 3** shows some bond enthalpy values.

Table 3

Bond	C—H	O=O	C=O	O—H
Energy in kJ/mol	412	496	743	463

> **Exam Tip**
>
> Draw out all of the compounds in full; this will help you count all the bonds. It's easy to miss that there are *four* O—H bonds in this equation.

Figure 3 is the reaction profile for the reaction shown in **Figure 2**. It is **not** drawn to scale.

Figure 3

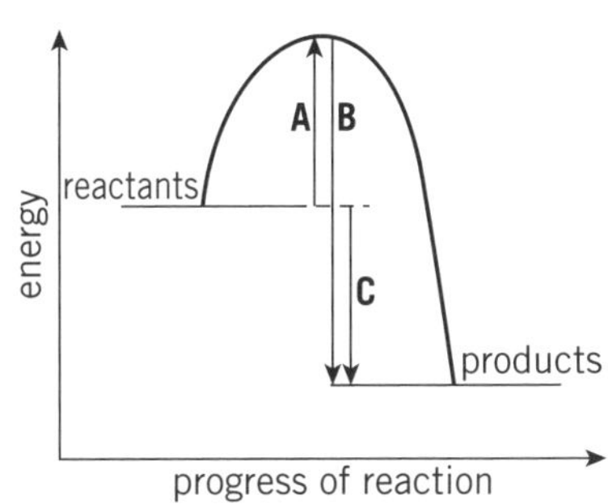

Calculate the energy change for each arrow **A**, **B**, and **C** shown in **Figure 3**. **[3 marks]**

04.2 Name the energy change represented by arrow **C**. **[1 mark]**

04.3 Define the energy change represented by arrow **A**. **[1 mark]**

05 A student wanted to compare the temperature changes when different metals reacted with hydrochloric acid. The student set up the apparatus shown in **Figure 4**.

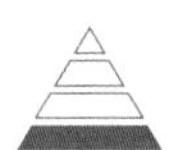  

Figure 4

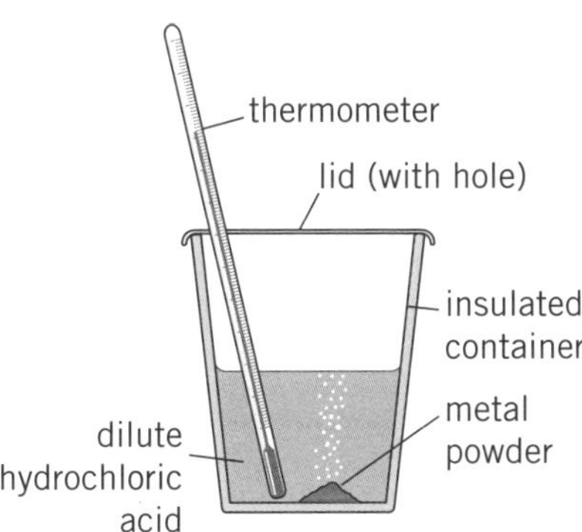

05.1 Name the dependent variable in the investigation. **[1 mark]**

05.2 Identify **two** control variables in the investigation. **[2 marks]**

Exam Tip

Control variables are all the parts of the experiment that we need to keep the same to make sure it's a fair test.

05.3 The student's results are shown in **Table 4**.

Table 4

Metal	Temperature of acid at start in °C	Temperature of mixture immediately after reaction in °C	Temperature change in °C
magnesium	19.0	36.7	
zinc	19.5	25.6	
copper	20.4	20.4	0.0

Suggest a reason for the result for copper. **[1 mark]**

05.4 Complete the missing values in **Table 4**. **[1 mark]**

05.5 State which metal reacts most exothermically with hydrochloric acid. **[1 mark]**

06 **Figure 5** shows the reaction profiles of four reactions: **A**, **B**, **C**, and **D**. The reactions profiles are drawn to scale.

Figure 5

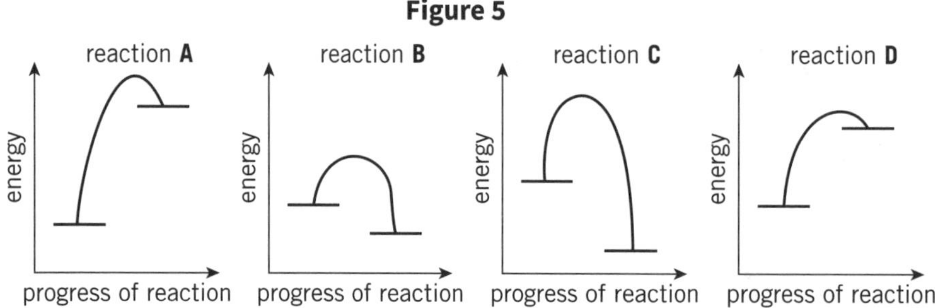

06.1 Give the letters of **two** reaction profiles that could show combustion reactions. **[1 mark]**

06.2 Give the letter of the **one** reaction with the smallest activation energy. **[1 mark]**

06.3 Give the letter of the **one** reaction that is most exothermic. **[1 mark]**

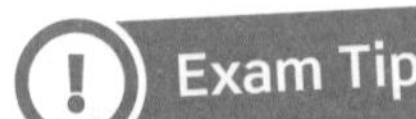

To help with this question draw arrows to show the activation energy, from where the reaction starts to its highest point.

07 Some students wanted to investigate the energy changes of the reactions of hydrochloric acid with three metal carbonates.

07.1 Write a balanced equation for the reaction of copper carbonate with hydrochloric acid. Include state symbols. **[3 marks]**

07.2 Describe a method that the students could use to carry out the investigation. In your answer name the apparatus required and identify the independent, dependent, and control variables. **[6 marks]**

07.3 State how the investigation results show which metal carbonate reacts most exothermically with acid. **[1 mark]**

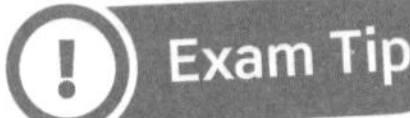

There are several steps in writing the equation in **07.1**:

1. Recall the formula for hydrochloric acid.
2. Recall the formula for a carbonate ion.
3. Determine the formula for copper carbonate.
4. Recall the general products in the equation for an acid + metal carbonate salt.
5. Determine the formula for the salt produced.
6. Balance the equation.

08 This question is about two fuels. **Table 5** gives the energy released on burning 1 mole of each of the fuels.

Table 5

Fuel name	Chemical formula of fuel	Energy transferred to the surroundings per mole of fuel burnt in kJ/mol
methane	CH_4	890
nonane	C_9H_{20}	6125

08.1 The equation for the combustion of methane is:

$$CH_4 + 2O_2 \rightarrow CO_2 + 2H_2O$$

Identify which substance is oxidised in the reaction. **[1 mark]**

08.2 The combustion products of nonane are the same as those for methane. Write a balanced chemical equation for the combustion of nonane. **[3 marks]**

08.3 Compare the environmental impacts of burning the two fuels in terms of the energy transferred per gram of fuel burnt and the energy transferred per gram of carbon dioxide produced.
Relative atomic masses A_r: C = 12, H = 1, O = 16 **[6 marks]**

Exam Tip

The numbers in the equation are getting large; always balance oxygen last as there are so many of those. If you try to start with oxygen you risk getting confused. Start with carbon, then hydrogen, and the oxygen will then be easier to sort out.

09 This question is about strong and weak acids. **Table 6** shows the pH values of four acid solutions.

Table 6

Solution	Acid	Concentration in mol/dm³	pH
W	ethanoic acid	1.0	2.4
X	hydrochloric acid		2.4
Y	ethanoic acid		4.4
Z	chloroethanoic acid	1.0	1.4

09.1 Explain what you can deduce about the concentrations of solutions **X** and **Y** from the data in **Table 6**. **[6 marks]**

Question **09.1** is asking for general comments on the concentration – you don't need to do any calculations.

09.2 Use data from **Table 6** to compare the degree of ionisation of chloroethanoic acid in aqueous solution with the degree of ionisation of ethanoic acid in aqueous solution. **[2 marks]**

09.3 Write an ionic equation for the reaction that occurs when an acid is neutralised by an alkali. **[1 mark]**

10 This question is about the reactivity series of metals.

10.1 Compare the reactions of potassium, lithium, and magnesium with cold water. **[6 marks]**

10.2 Caesium is at the bottom of Group 1 of the Periodic Table. Predict the names of the products of the reaction of caesium with water. **[1 mark]**

Base your answer on what you know about sodium or potassium.

10.3 Explain how the reactivities of the Group 1 elements are related to the tendency of the elements to form their positive ions. **[2 marks]**

11 This question is about the production of the metal lead. Methods **A** and **B** describe two processes for extracting lead.

Method A

1. Dig lead sulfide from the ground.
2. Heat the lead sulfide in air: $2PbS + 3O_2 \rightarrow 2PbO + 2SO_2$
3. Heat the lead oxide with carbon: $2PbO + C \rightarrow 2Pb + CO_2$

Method B

1. Collect battery paste from used batteries.
   The paste is a mixture of lead sulfate and lead oxides.
2. React the paste with an alkaline solution.
   One product is a soluble sulfate solution.
3. Heat the remaining mixture with carbon, for example:

$$2PbO + C \rightarrow 2Pb + CO_2$$

11.1 Name the substance that is reduced in step **3** of method **A**. **[1 mark]**

11.2 Write a balanced chemical equation for step **2** of method **B**.

- The reactants are lead sulfate and sodium hydroxide.
- The products are lead hydroxide and sodium sulfate. **[3 marks]**

This is a short two-mark question so you don't need a detailed explanation.

11.3 Suggest **two** advantages of method **B** compared to method **A**. **[2 marks]**

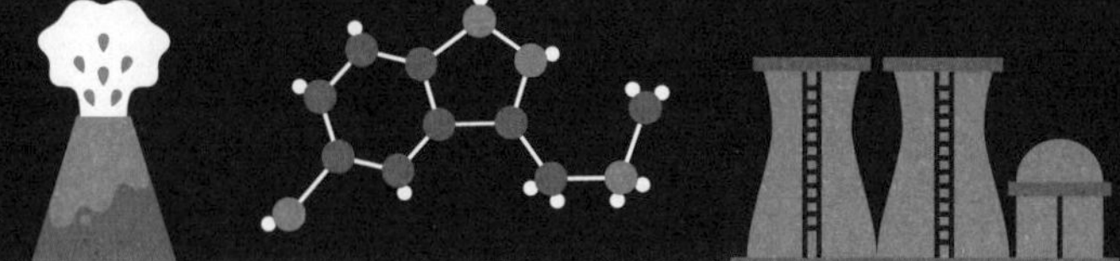

Knowledge

C10 Rate of reaction

Rates of reaction

The **rate of a reaction** is how quickly the reactants turn into the products.

To calculate the rate of a reaction, you can measure:

- how quickly a reactant is used up

$$\text{mean rate of reaction} = \frac{\text{quantity of reactant used}}{\text{time taken}}$$

- how quickly a product is produced.

$$\text{mean rate of reaction} = \frac{\text{quantity of product formed}}{\text{time taken}}$$

For reactions that involve a gas, this can be done by measuring how the mass of the reaction changes or the volume of gas given off by the reaction.

Change in mass

The reaction mixture is placed on a mass balance. As the reaction proceeds and the gaseous product is given off, the mass of the flask will decrease.

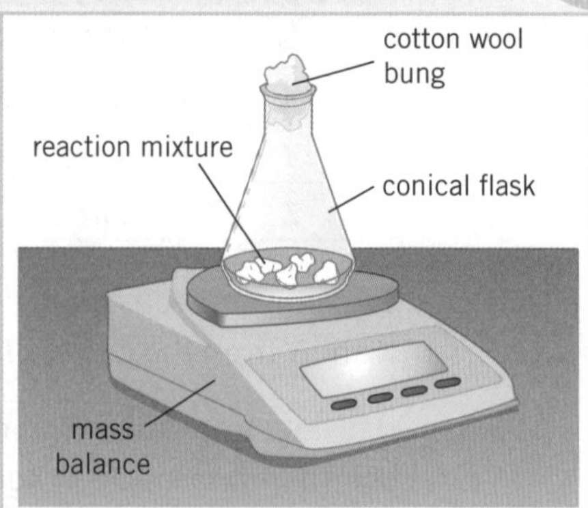

The rate for the reaction is then:

$$\text{rate} = \frac{\text{change in the mass}}{\text{time taken}}$$

The mass is measured in grams and time is measured in seconds. Therefore, the unit of rate is g/s.

Volume of gas produced

The reaction mixture is connected to a gas syringe or an upside down measuring cylinder. As the reaction proceeds the gas is collected.

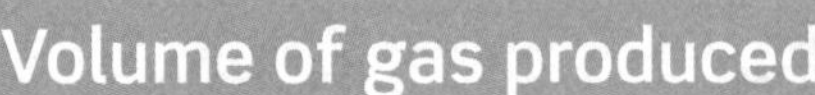
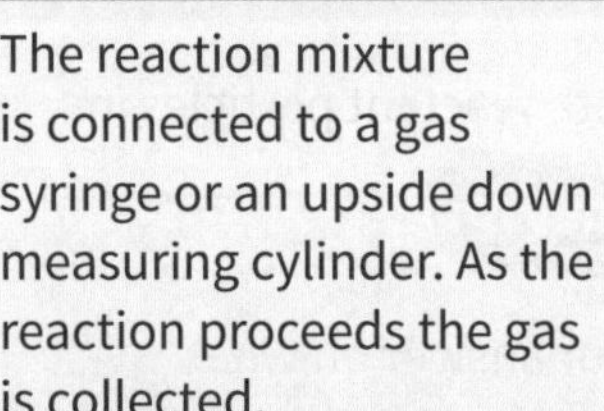

The rate for the reaction is then:

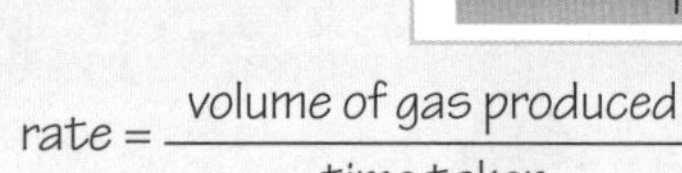

$$\text{rate} = \frac{\text{volume of gas produced}}{\text{time taken}}$$

Volume is measured in cm^3 and time in seconds, so the unit for rate is cm^3/s.

Calculating rate from graphs

The results from an experiment can be plotted on a graph.

- A steep gradient means a high rate of reaction – the reaction happens quickly.
- A shallow gradient means a low rate of reaction – the reaction happens slowly.

Mean rate between two points in time

To get the mean rate of reaction between two points in time:

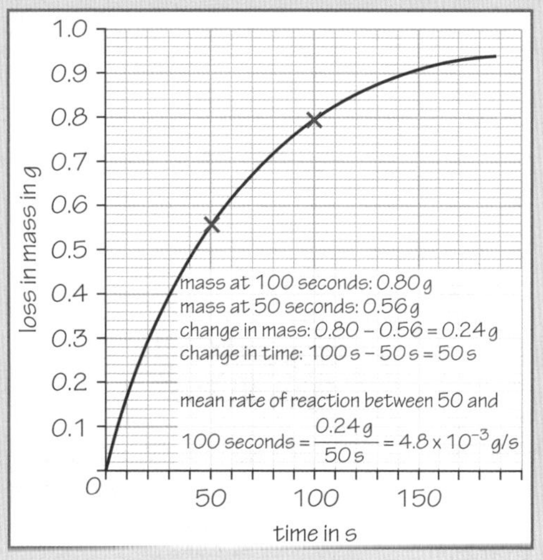

Mean rate at specific time

To obtain the rate at a specific time draw a **tangent** to the graph and calculate its **gradient**.

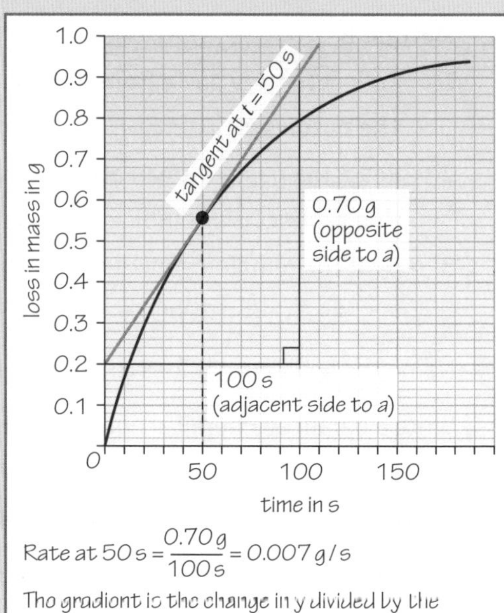

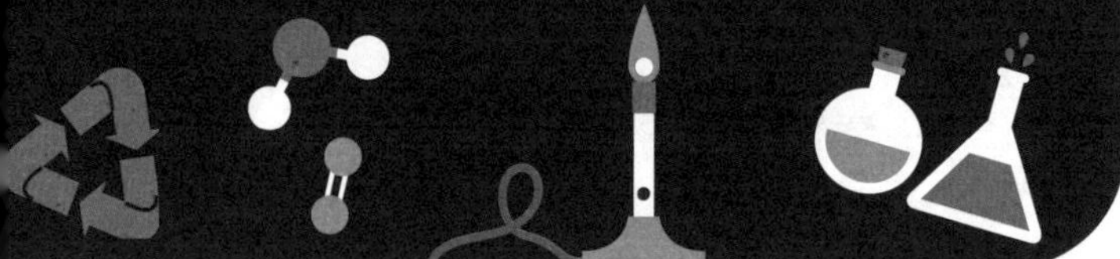

Collision theory

For a reaction to occur, the reactant particles need to collide. When the particles collide, they need to have enough energy to react or they will just bounce apart. This amount of energy is called the **activation energy**.

You can increase the rate of a reaction by:

- increasing the **frequency of collisions**
- increasing the energy of the particles when they collide.

Revision tip

Practice When drawing a tangent to determine the gradient of a curve, draw the biggest triangle that you can fit on your graph – this will give you a more accurate result.

Factors affecting rate of reaction

Condition that increases rate	How is this condition caused?	Why it has that effect
increasing the temperature	heat the container in which the reaction is taking place	1 particles move faster, leading to more frequent collisions 2 particles have more energy, so more collisions result in a reaction note that these are two separate effects
increasing the concentration of solutions	use a solution with more solute in the same volume of solvent	there are more reactant particles in the reaction mixture, so collisions become more frequent
increasing the pressure of gases	increase the number of gas particles you have in the container or make the container smaller	less space between particles means more frequent collisions
increasing the surface area of solids	cut the solid into smaller pieces, or grind it to create a powder, increasing the surface area – larger pieces decrease the surface area.	only reactant particles on the surface of a solid are able to collide and react; the greater the surface area the more reactant particles are exposed, leading to more frequent collisions

Catalysts

Some reactions have specific substances called **catalysts** that can be added to increase the rate. These substances are not used up in the reaction.

A catalyst provides a different reaction pathway that has a lower activation energy. As such, more particles will collide with enough energy to react, so more collisions result in a reaction.

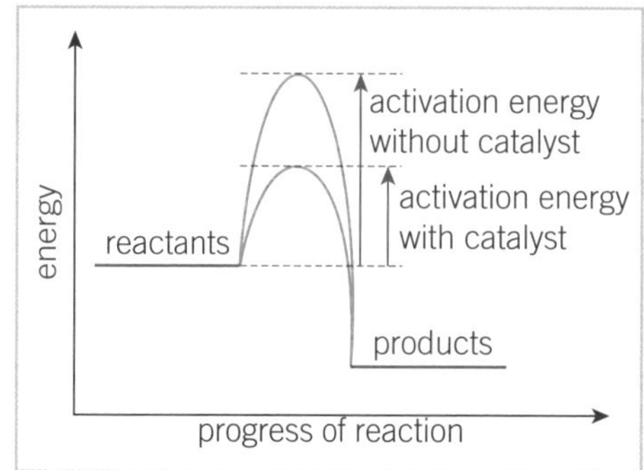

Key terms Make sure you can write a definition for these key terms.

activation energy, catalyst, collision, collision theory, frequency of collision, gradient, rate of reaction, tangent

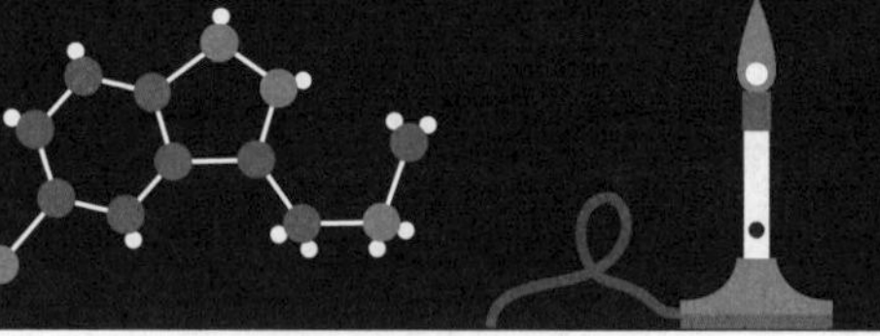

Retrieval

Learn the answers to the questions below, then cover the answers column with a piece of paper and write down as many as you can. Check and repeat.

	C10 questions	Answers
1	What is the rate of a reaction?	how quickly reactants are used up or products are produced
2	What is the equation for calculating the mean rate of reaction?	$\text{mean rate} = \frac{\text{change in quantity of product or reactant}}{\text{time taken}}$
3	What is the unit for rate of reaction in a reaction involving a change in mass?	g/s
4	What is the unit for rate of reaction in a reaction involving a change in volume?	cm^3/s
5	What is the activation energy?	the minimum amount of energy colliding particles need to have before a reaction will take place
6	What effect does increasing concentration have on the rate of reaction?	increases
7	Why does increasing concentration have this effect?	more reactant particles in the same volume lead to more frequent collisions
8	What effect does increasing pressure have on the rate of reaction?	increases
9	Why does increasing pressure have this effect?	less space between particles means more frequent collisions
10	What effect does increasing surface area have on the rate of reaction?	increases
11	Why does increasing surface area have this effect?	more reactant particles are exposed and able to collide, leading to more frequent collisions
12	What effect does increasing temperature have on the rate of reaction?	increases
13	Why does increasing temperature have this effect?	particles move faster, leading to more frequent collisions – particles have the same activation energy, so more collisions result in a reaction
14	What is a catalyst?	a substance that increases the rate of a reaction but is not used up in the reaction
15	How do catalysts increase the rate of a reaction?	lower the activation energy of the reaction, so more collisions result in a reaction

Put paper here

Now go back and use the questions below to check your knowledge from previous chapters.

Previous questions | Answers

	Previous questions	Answers
1	What is an exothermic energy transfer?	energy transfer to the surroundings
2	What is the activation energy?	minimum amount of energy required before a collision will result in a reaction
3	What is electrolysis?	the process of using electricity to extract elements from a compound
4	In terms of bond breaking and making, what is an endothermic reaction?	more energy is required to break the old bonds than is released when making the new bonds
5	In terms of H^+ ions, what is an acid?	a substance that releases H^+ ions when dissolved in water
6	What is an electrolyte?	a liquid or solution that contains ions and so can conduct electricity
7	What are the products of a reaction between a metal hydroxide and an acid?	salt + water
8	What name is given to a list of metals ordered by their reactivity?	reactivity series
9	In the electrolysis of aluminium oxide, what are the anodes made of?	graphite

Put paper here

Required Practical Skills

Practise answering questions on the required practicals using the example below. You need to be able to apply your skills and knowledge to other practicals too.

Rates of reaction

From this practical, you should be able to describe two ways in which the rate of a reaction can be measured. These are:

1. measuring the production of a gas
2. measuring changes in the colour or turbidity of a solution

You need to be able to describe the method for collecting gas with an inverted measuring cylinder, and for measuring the colour or turbidity change in a reaction. There are different methods of measuring rates of reaction, but remember that these principles are applicable to all of them.

Worked example

Silver chloride is an insoluble salt that can be made in the following reaction. Suggest a how the rate of this reaction could be measured.

$$AgNO_3(aq) + NaCl(aq) \rightarrow NaNO_3(aq) + AgCl(s)$$

The reactants are both colourless solutions. Solid silver chloride will form as a precipitate and make the solution appear cloudy.

One way of measuring the rate of the reaction is to look at the rate of production of silver chloride precipitate. This could be measured by placing the beaker with the reacting solution on a piece of white paper with a black cross printed on it, and measuring the time taken for the cross to disappear.

Practice

1. Give three factors that can affect the rate of a reaction.
2. Give two methods that can be used to determine the rate of a reaction where a gas is produced.
3. Suggest another method to measure the rate of the production of silver chloride precipitate.

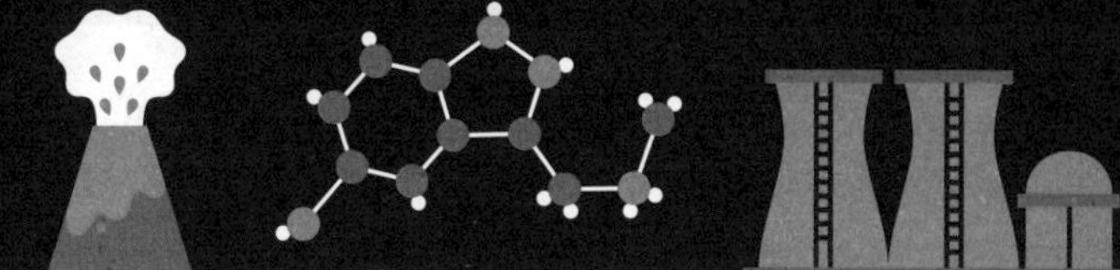

Practice

Exam-style questions

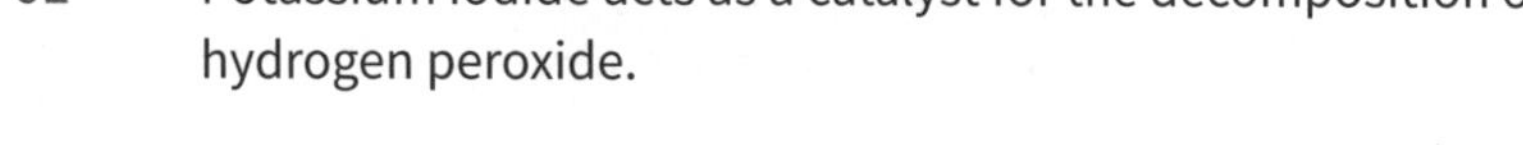

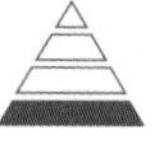

01 Potassium iodide acts as a catalyst for the decomposition of hydrogen peroxide.

01.1 What does a catalyst do? **[1 mark]**

Tick **one** box.

Decreases reaction rate by providing a pathway with a higher activation energy. ☐

Decreases reaction rate by providing a pathway with a lower activation energy. ☐

Increases reaction rate by providing a pathway with a higher activation energy. ☐

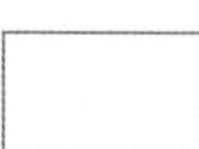

Increases reaction rate by providing a pathway with a lower activation energy. ☐

> **Exam Tip**
>
> The are two parts to **01.1**. The first part relates to reaction rate and the second part relates to activation energy. Decide how a catalyst affects reaction rate and cross off the two wrong answers. Then decide how a catalyst affects the activation energy and cross off the one remaining wrong answer.

01.2 **Figure 1** shows the reaction profile for the catalysed reaction.

Figure 1

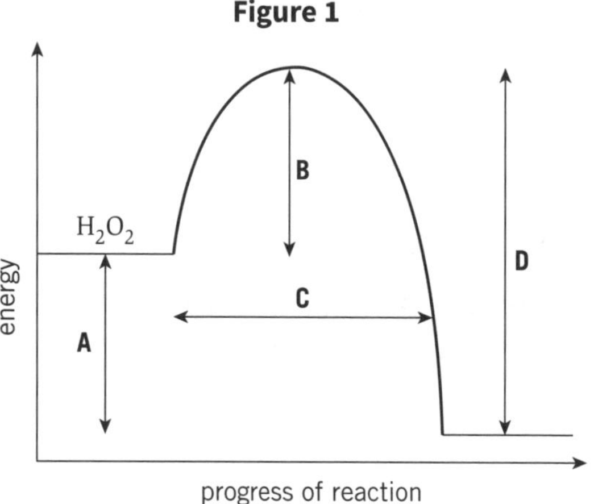

Which arrow shows the activation energy for the catalysed reaction? **[1 mark]**

____

01.3 Balance the symbol equation for the decomposition of hydrogen peroxide. Give the missing state symbol. **[2 marks]**

$$\_\_\_\_ H_2O_2(aq) \rightarrow \_\_\_\_ H_2O(\_\_\_\_) + O_2(g)$$

01.4 Why is potassium iodide not given in the balanced symbol equation? **[1 mark]**

____

02 Magnesium reacts with dilute hydrochloric acid:

$$Mg + 2HCl \rightarrow MgCl_2 + H_2$$

A student investigated how the volume of hydrogen produced changed over time.

Table 1 shows the student's results.

Table 1

Time in seconds	Total volume of hydrogen produced in cm^3
0	0
30	22
60	38
90	52
120	58
150	61
180	61

02.1 Plot the data on **Figure 2**. **[2 marks]**

02.2 Draw a line of best fit. **[1 mark]**

Figure 2

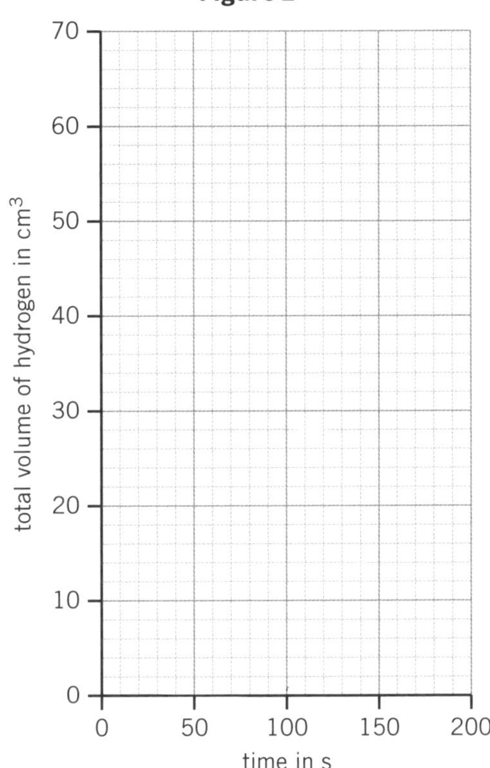

Exam Tip

It might help you if you mark 30, 60, 90 etc. on the x-axis to help you accurately plot the points.

02.3 Calculate the rate of reaction at 100 seconds.

Give your answer to two significant figures. **[4 marks]**

Exam Tip

To answer **02.3** you need to draw a tangent to the curve at 100 seconds. Then draw the largest triangle you can fit on the graph to help you determine the rate of reaction.

Rate at 100 seconds = ____________ cm^3/s

02.4 The rate of the reaction at 10 seconds is $0.83 cm^3/s$.

Suggest a reason for the difference in rate at 10 seconds and at 100 seconds. **[1 mark]**

____

____

03 Sodium thiosulfate solution reacts with hydrochloric acid. One of the products of the reaction is sulfur, which forms as a precipitate.

$$Na_2S_2O_3(aq) + 2HCl(aq) \rightarrow 2NaCl(aq) + H_2O(l) + SO_2(g) + S(s)$$

Some students investigated the rate of reaction at different temperatures. This is the method used:

1. Place 50 cm³ of sodium thiosulfate in a conical flask.
2. Start a timer then add 5 cm³ hydrochloric acid to the flask.
3. Look down through the flask at a cross drawn on a piece of paper.
4. Stop the timer when the cross disappears.
5. Repeat the experiment, each time heating the sodium thiosulfate to a different temperature.

03.1 Suggest **one** improvement that could be made to step **2** to ensure that the results at different temperatures are comparable. **[1 mark]**

03.2 One student suggests measuring the temperature of the reaction mixture after adding the hydrochloric acid instead of measuring the temperature of the sodium thiosulfate on its own.
Suggest an advantage of this idea. **[1 mark]**

03.3 Suggest why the same student in the group should carry out step **4** at every temperature. **[1 mark]**

03.4 **Table 2** shows the students' results.
Identify which result is anomalous. **[1 mark]**

Table 2

Temperature in °C	Time for cross to disappear in s
0	180
21	44
39	22
45	21
52	9
61	5

03.5 Describe how the rate of reaction changes between 0 °C and 61 °C. **[1 mark]**

03.6 Explain why the rate of reaction changes between 0 °C and 61 °C. **[2 marks]**

It may seem like **03.5** and **03.6** are asking the same question twice but describe and explain are very different: describe is *what* it looks like, explain is *why* it looks like that.

04 Calcium carbonate reacts with hydrochloric acid:

$$2HCl(aq) + CaCO_3(s) \rightarrow CaCl_2(aq) + CO_2(g) + H_2O(l)$$

Some students want to investigate how the size of the pieces of solid calcium carbonate affects the rate of the reaction.

Figure 3 shows the apparatus. This is the method used:

1. Weigh approximately 3.0 g of calcium carbonate onto a piece of paper and leave it all on the balance.
2. Place 100 cm^3 of dilute hydrochloric acid in a conical flask and place on the balance.
3. Zero the balance.
4. Add the calcium carbonate to the acid and start the stopwatch.
5. Leave the flask and its contents on the balance but remove the paper.
6. Record the time for the total mass to decrease by 0.50 g.
7. Repeat with different sized pieces of calcium carbonate.

Figure 3

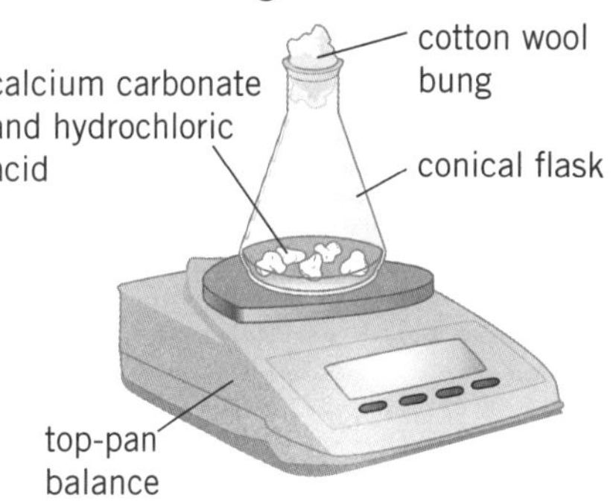

04.1 Explain why the total mass of the contents of the conical flask decreases. **[1 mark]**

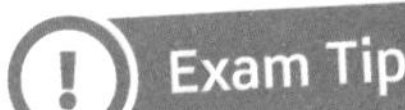

Exam Tip

Look at the state symbols of the products.

04.2 Suggest an improvement to step **5**.
Give a reason for your answer. **[2 marks]**

04.3 **Table 3** shows the students' results.

Table 3

Size of calcium carbonate pieces	Time for mass to decrease by 0.50 g in seconds
large	1280
medium	690
small	302

Explain the pattern shown in **Table 3**. **[3 marks]**

Exam Tip

The students have used the same mass of calcium carbonate. What will be the difference between one large piece of calcium carbonate and lots of small pieces of calcium carbonate?

05 Zinc is a metal. It reacts with dilute nitric acid. The products of the reaction are zinc nitrate and a gas.

05.1 Name the gas formed in the reaction. **[1 mark]**

05.2 Which one of these changes will make the reaction rate slower?
Choose **one** answer. **[1 mark]**

decreasing the acid concentration

increasing the pressure

decreasing the size of the pieces of zinc

increasing the temperature

Exam Tip

05.2 is asking about temperature and rate in the opposite way to the way it's normally asked. The chemistry is still the same so just apply your knowledge to the slightly different situation.

05.3 Predict the effect of decreasing the temperature on the rate of reaction. **[1 mark]**

06 Some students investigated the factors that affect the rate of the reaction of magnesium with excess hydrochloric acid. They followed the reaction by measuring the total volume of gas formed every 30 seconds. They changed the conditions and repeated the experiment. **Figure 4** is a graph of some of the results of the two experiments, **P** and **Q**. Curve **P** shows the results for the first experiment.

Figure 4

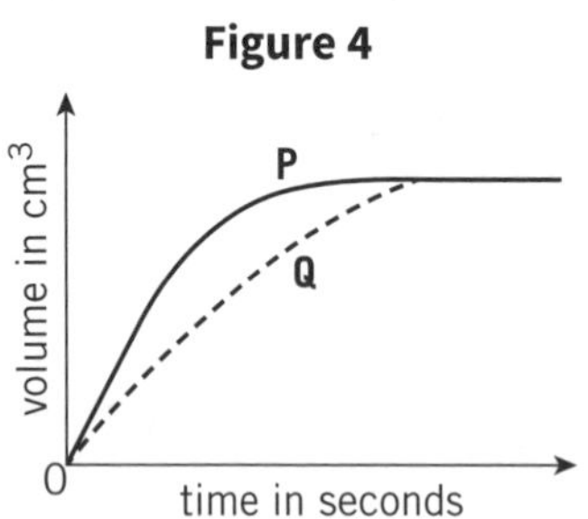

> **Exam Tip**
>
> Both reactions end at the same point, that's why the graphs level off at the same point for both lines. The rate will only affect how *quickly* a reaction finishes, not how much product is produced.

06.1 Write the balanced symbol equation with state symbols for the reaction between magnesium and hydrochloric acid. **[3 marks]**

06.2 Curve **Q** was obtained in the second experiment.
Suggest **one** variable that the students might have changed and **two** variables that they kept constant in order to obtain curve **Q**.
Justify your answer. **[6 marks]**

07 A student investigated the catalytic decomposition of hydrogen peroxide:

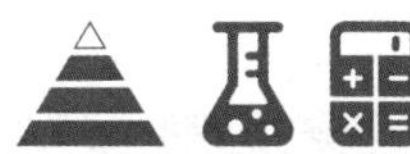

$$2H_2O_2\,(aq) \rightarrow 2H_2O(l) + O_2(g)$$

Figure 5 shows the apparatus used.

Figure 5

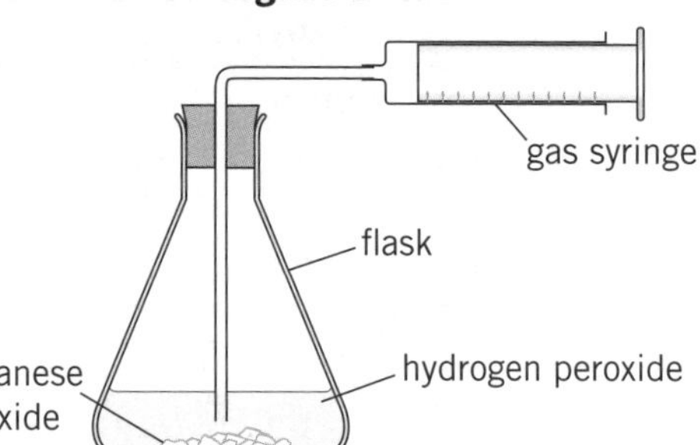

07.1 The student made a mistake in setting up the apparatus.
Describe how the student must improve the apparatus before doing the experiment.
Give a reason for making this improvement. **[2 marks]**

07.2 The student improved the apparatus set-up and collected some data. **Table 4** shows the results the student obtained.

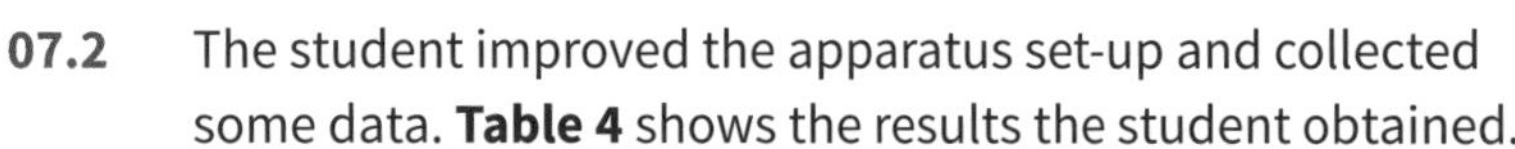

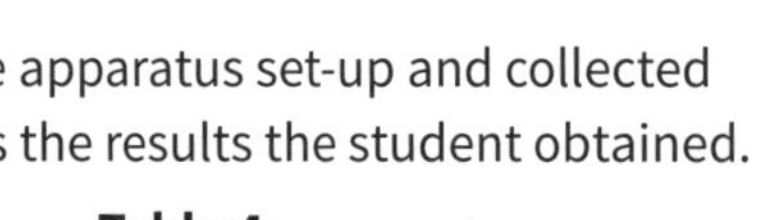

Table 4

Time in minutes	Volume of gas produced in cm^3
0	0
1	42
2	69
3	86
4	88
5	91
6	91

> **Exam Tip**
>
> The number of significant figures in your answer should match the data provided.

Calculate the average rate of reaction.
Give the unit of the rate of the reaction. **[3 marks]**

> **Exam Tip**
>
> Use the units of the variables to help you work out the units for the rate.

07.3 Predict how the mean rate of reaction would change if powdered manganese(IV) oxide was used instead of lumps.
Give a reason for your prediction. **[2 marks]**

08 A student investigates the effect of concentration on the rate of reaction between nitric acid and sodium carbonate.

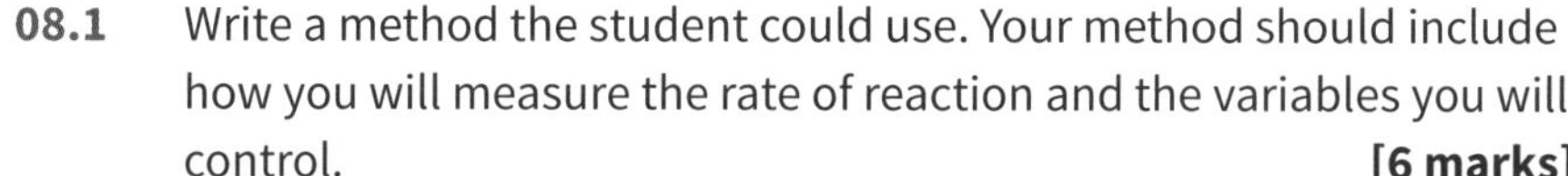

08.1 Write a method the student could use. Your method should include how you will measure the rate of reaction and the variables you will control. **[6 marks]**

Exam Tip

There are a few different methods to measure the rate of a reaction. Make sure that you clearly state which method you are using and use it consistently throughout your answer. It is easy to get confused and switch methods halfway through.

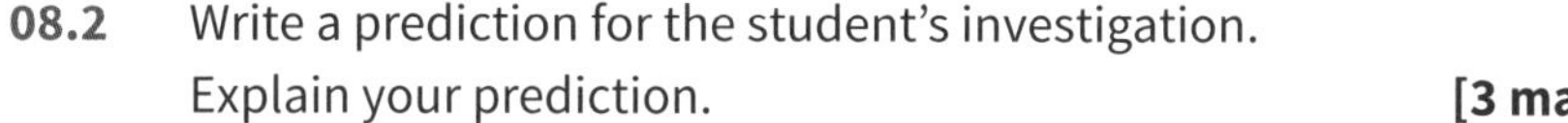

08.2 Write a prediction for the student's investigation. Explain your prediction. **[3 marks]**

08.3 Another student investigated the effect of the surface area of sodium carbonate on the rate of the reaction. Their results are shown in **Table 5**.

Table 5

Sodium carbonate	Time taken to produce 500 cm^3 of carbon dioxide in s	Mean rate of reaction in _____
solid pieces	195	2.7
powder	42	

Give the unit of the rate of reaction. **[1 mark]**

08.4 Calculate the mean rate of reaction for powdered sodium carbonate. Give your answer to three significant figures. **[2 marks]**

08.5 Give **one** other factor that will affect the rate of the reaction between nitric acid and sodium carbonate. **[1 mark]**

09 Sodium thiosulfate reacts with hydrochloric acid in the following reaction:

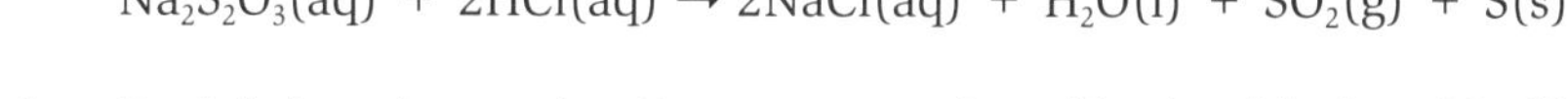

$$Na_2S_2O_3(aq) + 2HCl(aq) \rightarrow 2NaCl(aq) + H_2O(l) + SO_2(g) + S(s)$$

09.1 Explain how increasing the concentration of hydrochloric acid will affect the rate of the reaction. **[1 mark]**

09.2 Explain how increasing the temperature will affect the rate of the reaction. **[4 marks]**

09.3 The rate of the reaction between sodium thiosulfate and hydrochloric acid can be determined by measuring how long it takes for the reaction mixture to become cloudy.
A student uses a light sensor and data logger to measure the turbidity of the reaction.
Sketch a graph of time against turbidity to show the rate of the reaction at **two** different temperatures. **[4 marks]**

Exam Tip

Sketching graphs doesn't mean plotting points – the labelled axis and the line are all that you need.

Knowledge

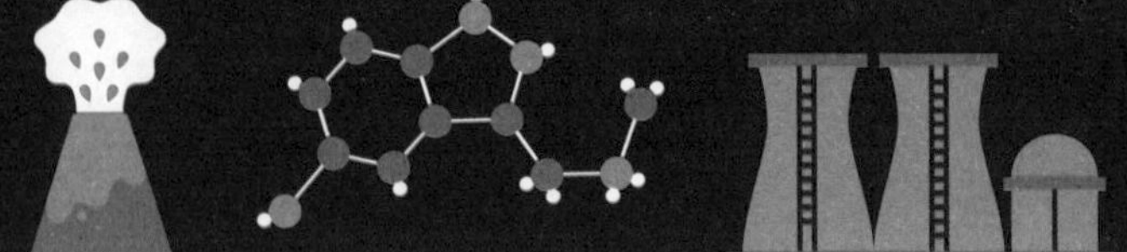

C11 Equilibrium

Reversible reactions

In some reactions, the products can react to produce the original reactants. This is called a **reversible reaction**. When writing chemical equations for reversible reactions, use the $\rightleftharpoons$ symbol.

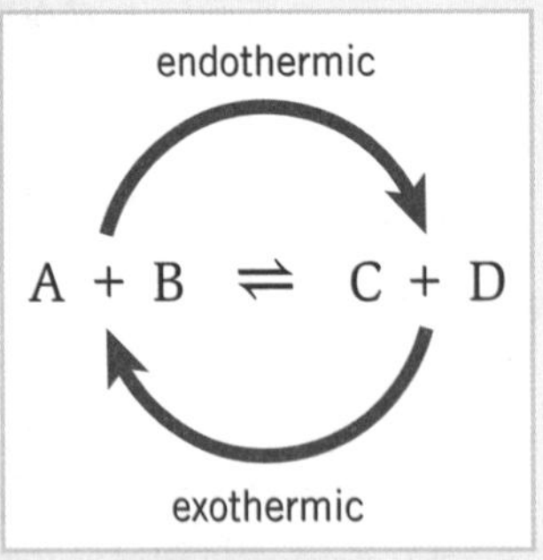

In this reaction:

- A and B can react to form C and D – the forward reaction
- C and D can react to form A and B – the reverse reaction.

The different directions of the reaction have opposite energy changes.

If the forward reaction is *endothermic*, the reverse reaction will be *exothermic*.

The same amount of energy is transferred in each direction.

Equilibrium

In a **closed system** no reactants or products can escape. If a reversible reaction is carried out in a closed system, it will eventually reach **dynamic equilibrium** – a point in time when the forward and reverse reactions have the same rate.

At dynamic equilibrium:

- the reactants are still turning into the products
- the products are still turning back into the reactants
- the rates of these two processes are *equal*, so overall the amount of reactants and products are constant.

Dynamic equilibrium

At dynamic equilibrium the amount of reactant and product are constant, but not necessarily equal.

You could have a mixture of reactants and products in a 50:50 ratio, in a 75:25 ratio, or in any ratio at all. The **conditions** of the reaction are what change that ratio.

How dynamic equilibrium is reached

Progress of reaction	Start of reaction	Middle of reaction	At dynamic equilibrium
Amount of A + B	high	decreasing	constant
Frequency of collisions A + B	high	decreasing	constant
Rate of forward reaction	high	decreasing	same as rate of reverse reaction
Amount of C + D	zero	increasing	constant
Frequency of collisions C + D	no collisions	increasing	constant
Rate of reverse reaction	zero	increasing	same as rate of forward reaction

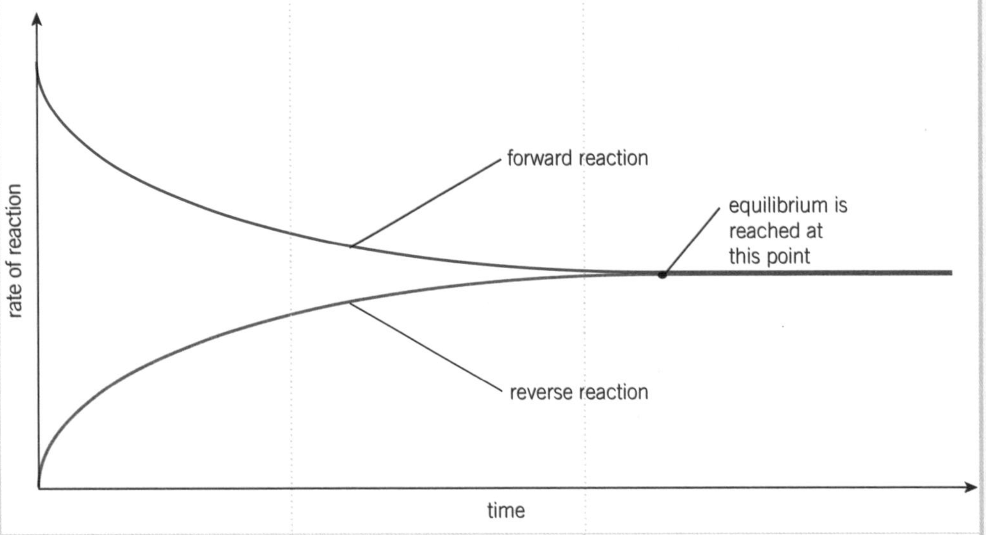

Reaction conditions

The conditions of a reaction refer to the external environment of the reaction. When the reaction occurs in a closed system, you can change the conditions by:

- changing the concentration of one of the substances
- changing the temperature of the entire reaction vessel
- changing the pressure inside the vessel.

Le Châtelier's principle

At equilibrium, the amount of reactants and products is constant. In order to change the amounts of reactant and product at equilibrium the *conditions* of the reaction must be changed. The closed system will then counteract the change by favouring either the forward reaction or the reverse reaction. This is known as **Le Châtelier's principle**.

For example, lowering the concentration of the product in the system causes the forward reaction to be **favoured** to increase the concentration of the product.

Revision tip

Remember
Equilibrium is all about opposites balancing out – whatever we do to a reaction, the reaction will try to correct it and do the opposite to go back to how it was before.

Changing concentrations

Change	Effect	Explanation
decrease concentration of product	favours the forward reaction	opposes the change by making *less* reactant and *more* product
increase concentration of product	favours the reverse reaction	opposes the change by making *more* reactant and *less* product
decrease concentration of reactant	favours the reverse reaction	opposes the change by making *more* reactant and *less* product
increase concentration of reactant	favours the forward reaction	opposes the change by making *less* reactant and *more* product

Changing temperature

The effect of changing the temperature depends on which direction is exothermic and which direction is endothermic.

This varies from reaction to reaction – some are exothermic in the forward direction, but others will be exothermic in the reverse direction.

Change	Effect	Explanation
increase temperature of surroundings	favours the endothermic reaction	opposes the change by decreasing the temperature of the surroundings
decrease temperature of surroundings	favours the exothermic reaction	opposes the change by increasing the temperature of the surroundings

Changing pressure

The effect of changing the pressure depends on which side of the reaction has more molecules of gas (e.g., the reaction $2A(g) + B(g) \rightleftharpoons A_2B(g)$ has three molecules of gas on the reactant side and one molecule on the product side). If both sides have the same number of molecules, then changing the pressure will have no effect.

Change	Effect	Explanation
increase the pressure	favours the reaction that results in fewer molecules	decreasing the number of molecules within the vessel opposes the change because it decrease pressure
decrease the pressure	favours the direction that results in more molecules	increasing the number of molecules within the vessel opposes the change because it increase pressure

Key terms

Make sure you can write a definition for these key terms.

closed system *conditions* *dynamic equilibrium* *Le Châtelier's principle* *reversible reaction*

Retrieval

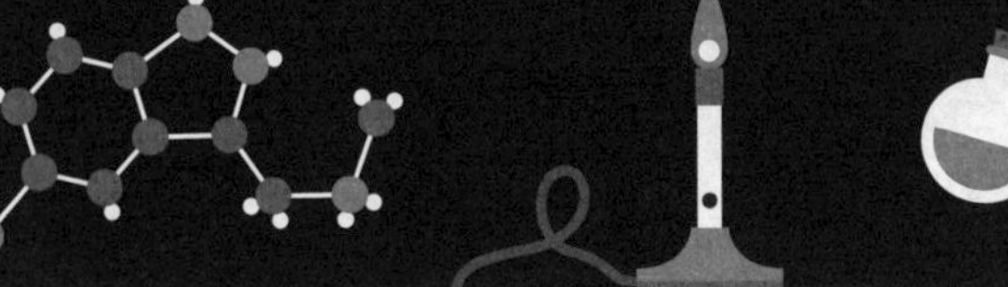

Learn the answers to the questions below, then cover the answers column with a piece of paper and write down as many as you can. Check and repeat.

	C11 questions	Answers
1	What is a reversible reaction?	when the reactants turn into products and the products turn into reactants
2	Which symbol shows a reversible reaction?	$\rightleftharpoons$
3	What is dynamic equilibrium?	the point in a reversible reaction when the rate of the forward and reverse reactions are the same
4	What are the three reaction conditions that can be changed?	concentration, temperature, pressure
5	What is Le Châtelier's principle?	the position of equilibrium will shift to oppose external changes
6	What is the effect of increasing the concentration of reactants on a reaction at dynamic equilibrium?	favours the forward reaction
7	What is the effect of decreasing the concentration of products on a reaction at dynamic equilibrium?	favours the forward reaction
8	What is the effect of increasing pressure on a reaction at dynamic equilibrium?	favours the reaction that leads to the fewest molecules
9	What is the effect of decreasing pressure on a reaction at dynamic equilibrium?	favours the reaction that leads to the most molecules
10	What is the effect of increasing temperature on a reaction at dynamic equilibrium?	favours the endothermic reaction
11	What is the effect of decreasing temperature on a reaction at dynamic equilibrium?	favours the exothermic reaction

Now go back and use the questions below to check your knowledge from previous chapters.

Previous questions

	Previous questions	Answers
1	What is the activation energy?	the minimum amount of energy colliding particles need to have before a reaction will take place
2	How do catalysts increase the rate of a reaction?	lower the activation energy of the reaction, so more collisions result in a reaction
3	What is the unit for rate of reaction in a reaction involving a change in mass?	g/s
4	What effect does increasing temperature have on the rate of reaction?	increases
5	What is an endothermic energy transfer?	energy transfer from the surroundings
6	What is a reaction profile?	diagram showing how the energy changes in a reaction

Put paper here

Put paper here

Maths Skills

Practise your maths skills using the worked example and practice questions below.

Gradients

The gradient of a straight line on a graph tells you how steep it is.

To determine the gradient:

1. pick two points on the line
2. subtract the smallest y-axis value from the largest y-axis value of your two points
3. take the two x-axis values from your two points and subtract the smallest from the largest
4. divide your answer from **2** by your answer from **3**.

If you have a positive correlation, your gradient will be positive. If you have a negative correlation your gradient will be negative.

Worked example

The graph below shows how the mass of solid copper objects varies with their volume.

Calculate the gradient of the graph.

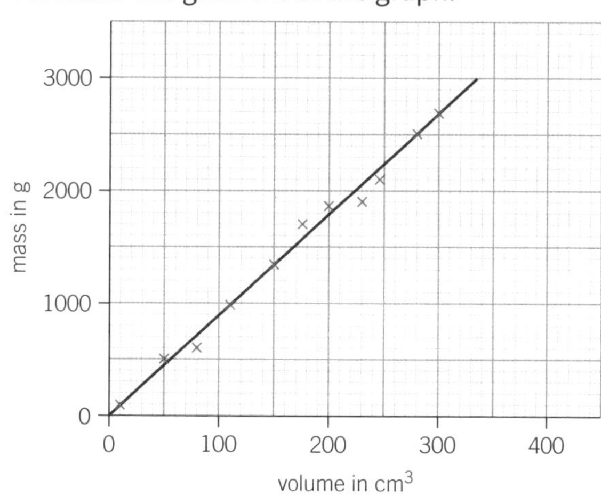

Step 1: *pick two points on the line.*

Step 2: *subtract the y-axis values:*

2500 – 1000 = 1500

Step 3: *subtract the x-axis values:*

280 – 110 = 170

Step 4: *divide the y value by the x value:*

$\frac{1500}{170} = 8.8\ g/dm^3$

Practice

The graph below shows the temperature over time of a liquid being heated.

Calculate the gradient of the graph.

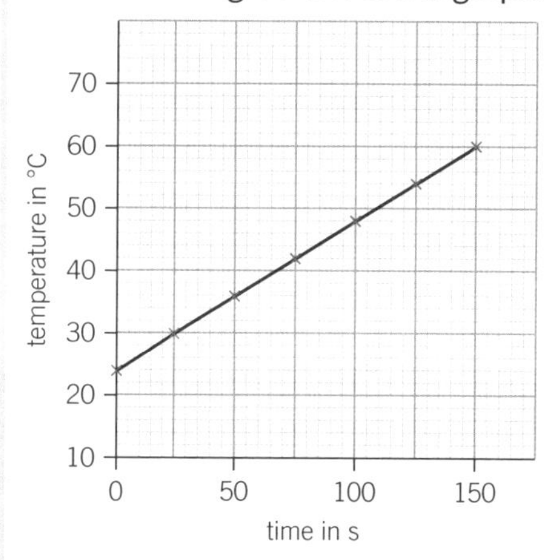

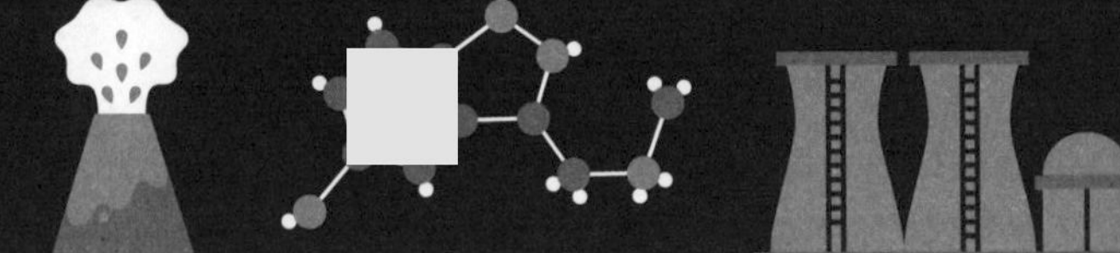

Practice

Exam-style questions

01 Ammonia is formed from the reversible reaction between nitrogen and hydrogen.

$$N_2(g) + 3H_2(g) \rightleftharpoons 2NH_3(g)$$

01.1 The forward reaction transfers 92 kJ of energy to the surroundings.

State how much energy is transferred by the reverse reaction. **[1 mark]**

____

> **Exam Tip**
> Energy is always conserved.

01.2 Define Le Châtelier's Principle. **[1 mark]**

____

____

____

01.3 The reacting mixture is placed in apparatus that prevents the escape of reactants and products.

The pressure of the reaction mixture is then increased.

What happens to the position of the equilibrium?

Tick **one** box. **[1 mark]**

It does not change. ☐

It shifts to the left. ☐

It shifts to the right. ☐

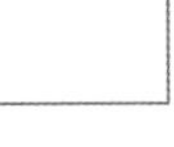

It shifts to the left and then to the right. ☐

> **Exam Tip**
> Look at the number of moles on each side of the reaction.

02 Sulfur dioxide reacts with oxygen in a reversible reaction.

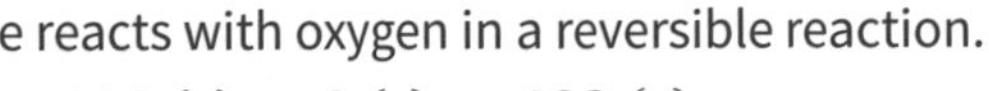

$$2SO_2(g) + O_2(g) \rightleftharpoons 2SO_3(g)$$

The forward reaction is exothermic.

02.1 Draw a dot and cross diagram to show the bonding in an oxygen molecule, O_2. **[2 marks]**

> **Exam Tip**
> Remember that oxygen gas has a double bond.

02.2 Define the term exothermic. **[1 mark]**

____

____

02.3 The reversible reaction above occurs in a closed container.

Give the effect on the position of the equilibrium for each of the following condition changes. **[4 marks]**

more SO_3 is added: ______

pressure is increased: ______

temperature is increased: ______

more O_2 is added: ______

Exam Tip

The equilibrium position shifts to counteract the change – this means the reaction will go in the opposite direction to the change made.

03 Methanol is used a fuel. It can be produced by reacting carbon monoxide with hydrogen in a reversible reaction.

$$CO(g) + 2H_2(g) \rightleftharpoons CH_3OH(g)$$

The forward reaction is exothermic.

03.1 Explain why this reaction can only reach equilibrium in a sealed container. **[3 marks]**

03.2 Identify **three** factors that will affect the position of the equilibrium reaction to produce methanol. Explain the effect that changing each of these factors has on the position of the equilibrium. **[6 marks]**

03.3 Calculate the maximum mass of methanol that can be made from 10.0 g of carbon monoxide. Give your answer to three significant figures. Use the Periodic Table to help you. **[6 marks]**

Exam Tip

Question **03.2** is a six-mark question asking for three factors – you will get one mark for each factor and one mark for explaining its effect on the equilibrium.

04 Hydrogen reacts with iodine to form hydrogen iodide.

$$H_2(g) + I_2(g) \rightleftharpoons 2HI(g)$$

04.1 State what the $\rightleftharpoons$ symbol tells you about the reaction. **[1 mark]**

04.2 The reaction reaches equilibrium in apparatus that prevents the escape of reactants and products. Describe what happens to the particles of H_2, I_2, and HI at equilibrium. **[1 mark]**

04.3 The forward reaction is endothermic. Describe the energy transfers involved in the forward reaction. **[2 marks]**

05 Some students want to investigate the reversible change:
hydrated copper sulfate $\rightleftharpoons$ anhydrous copper sulfate + water

Figure 1 shows the apparatus.

Figure 1

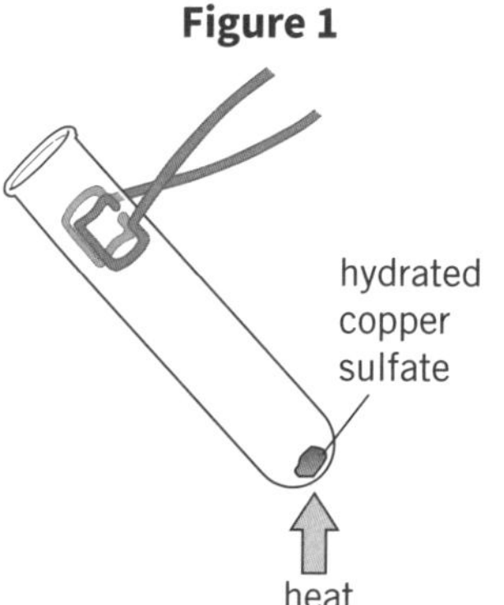

05.1 Explain why equilibrium cannot be reached using the apparatus in **Figure 1**. **[1 mark]**

05.2 Suggest a suitable piece of equipment for heating the hydrated copper sulfate. **[1 mark]**

05.3 Name the substance that leaves the test tube. **[1 mark]**

05.4 Suggest how the substance that leaves the test tube could be collected. **[3 marks]**

06 Some chemists investigated the equilibrium reaction between two solutions containing cobalt ions:

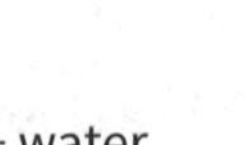

pink cobalt ion solution + chloride ions ⇌ blue cobalt ion solution + water

Figure 2 shows the apparatus.

Figure 2

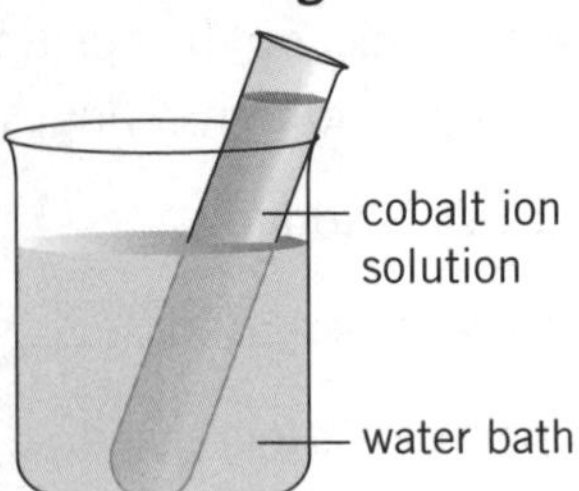

06.1 Suggest an improvement to the apparatus to make sure that all the cobalt ion solution is at the same temperature. **[1 mark]**

06.2 The chemists carried out some tests. **Table 1** shows their results.

Table 1

Test number	Action	Initial colour change
1	heat the water bath	from pink to blue
2	add ice to the water bath	from blue to pink
3	add chloride ions to the solution	
4	add water to the solution	

Write a conclusion based on the data in rows **1** and **2** in **Table 1**. **[2 marks]**

06.3 Predict the colour change that would be observed in test **3**. **[1 mark]**

06.4 Explain the prediction you made to answer **06.3**. **[3 marks]**

Exam Tip

Remember this is a reversible reaction, so the reaction will change direction to counter the change made in the environment.

07 A student sets up an equilibrium of two nitrogen oxides in a sealed gas syringe. The equilibrium is represented by the equation:

$$N_2O_4(g) \rightleftharpoons 2NO_2(g)$$

colourless　　brown

At equilibrium the substances in the syringe are light brown in colour. The student recorded their observations when they moved the plunger of the gas syringe (**Table 2**).

Table 2

Action	Colour change
push in the syringe plunger	light brown to colourless
pull out the syringe plunger	light brown to dark brown

07.1 Explain what happens to the equilibrium when the plunger is pushed in. **[4 marks]**

07.2 The forward reaction is endothermic. The student places the syringe in an ice–water mixture.
Predict and explain the colour change observed. **[3 marks]**

07.3 The student sets another equilibrium up in a separate gas syringe:

$$H_2(g) + I_2(g) \rightleftharpoons 2HI(g)$$

Predict and explain the effect on the position of equilibrium of increasing the pressure on the equilibrium mixture. **[2 marks]**

Exam Tip

Look at the number of moles on each side of the equation.

Exam Tip

Don't use abbreviations or shorthand in your answer – in class you might be used to using LHS for left-hand side but in the exam you need to write out the words in full.

08 The reaction between two substances, **X** and **Y**, is reversible:

$$X(g) \rightleftharpoons Y(g)$$

Substance **Y** is placed in a sealed container. After some time, equilibrium is established. **Figure 3** shows how the concentrations of **X** and **Y** change as equilibrium is established.

Figure 3

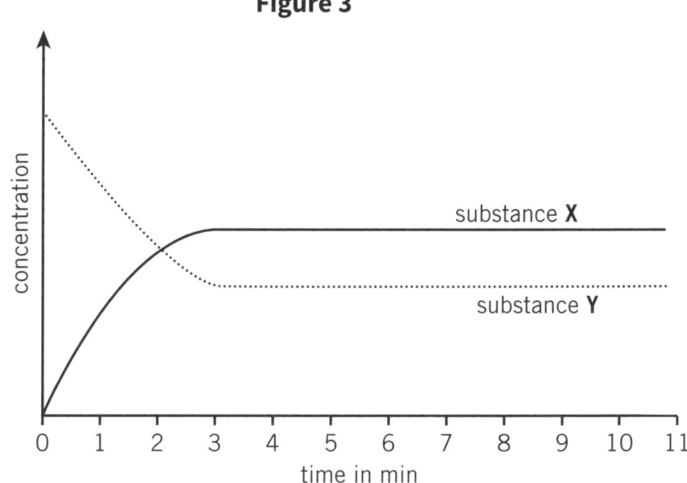

08.1 Identify the time at which the equilibrium was established. Give a reason for your answer. **[2 marks]**

Exam Tip

Use data from the graph to support your answer.

08.2 State how the rates of the forward and reverse reactions compare at equilibrium. **[1 mark]**

08.3 The system was heated for 5 minutes. At the end of the 5 minutes, it was found that there was more of substance **X** in the system than before the system was heated.
Identify which reaction is exothermic. **[1 mark]**

09 A teacher had a closed system at equilibrium that contained Cl_2 (a pale green gas), ICl_3 (yellow crystals), and ICl (a brown liquid). The teacher removed Cl_2 from the system, and left the system to reach equilibrium. At the new equilibrium, the amount of ICl had increased and the amount of ICl_3 had decreased.

09.1 Write a balanced symbol equation with state symbols for the reaction. **[3 marks]**

Exam Tip

Use two colours to highlight the text. Pick out compounds on the left-hand side of the equilibrium in one colour and compounds on the right-hand side in another.

09.2 The teacher placed the system into an ice bath. More yellow crystals formed.
Identify whether the formation of ICl_3 is exothermic or endothermic. **[1 mark]**

09.3 Explain why placing the system in an ice bath favours this reaction. **[3 marks]**

10 A student heats a sample of ammonium chloride in a test tube. The ammonium chloride breaks down into ammonia gas and hydrogen chloride gas.

solid ammonium chloride ⇌ ammonia gas + hydrogen chloride gas

As the student heats the ammonium chloride, a white solid forms at the top of the test tube (**Figure 4**).

Exam Tip

Look for the clues in the main body of the question.

Figure 4

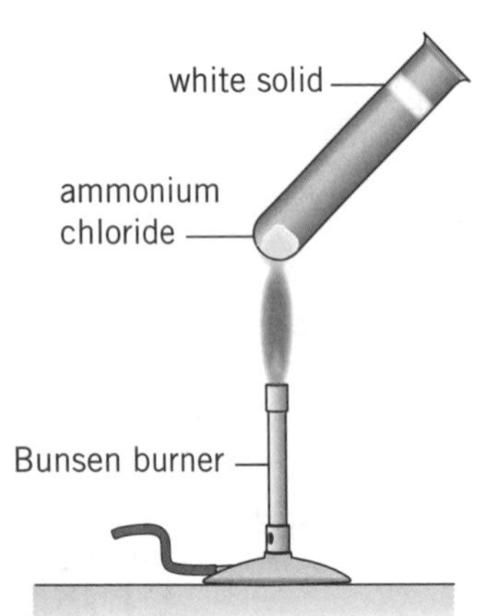

10.1 Predict what the white solid is. **[1 mark]**

10.2 Explain your prediction in **10.1**. **[3 marks]**

10.3 Another student heats hydrated blue copper(II) sulfate crystals in a test tube. Water is given off to form white anhydrous copper(II) sulfate crystals. This process is reversible.
Predict what would happen if water was added to the anhydrous copper sulfate crystals. **[1 mark]**

10.4 The student holds the test tube whilst they add the water. Predict what they would feel as water is added. **[1 mark]**

11 Ammonia, NH_3, is a gas at room temperature and pressure.

11.1 Give the number of moles of hydrogen atoms in one mole of ammonia gas. **[1 mark]**

11.2 Calculate the relative molecular mass of ammonia. **[2 marks]**

11.3 Calculate the number of moles of ammonia in a 68 g sample of the gas. **[2 marks]**

Exam Tip

You'll need to look up the mass numbers in the Periodic Table.

11.4 Calculate the number of particles of ammonia in a 68 g sample of the gas. The Avogadro constant is 6.02×10^{23} per mole.
Give your answer to three significant figures. **[3 marks]**

12 Some metals react with water.

12.1 Describe the expected observations in the reaction of potassium and water. **[2 marks]**

12.2 Name the products of the reaction of lithium with water. **[2 marks]**

12.3 Describe the expected observations when copper is placed in a test tube of water. **[1 mark]**

13 A student wanted to make sodium chloride crystals from sodium hydroxide and hydrochloric acid solutions:

$$NaOH(aq) + HCl(aq) \rightarrow NaCl(aq) + H_2O(l)$$

The student used the following method:

1. Use a measuring cylinder to transfer 25 cm^3 of sodium hydroxide into a conical flask.
2. Add 1 cm^3 of indicator.
3. Add dilute hydrochloric acid from a burette until the indicator changes colour.
4. Pour the mixture from the flask into a beaker.
5. Heat the beaker and its contents until half the water has evaporated.
6. Allow the rest of the water to evaporate by leaving the beaker in a warm, dry place.

13.1 Suggest and explain **one** improvement to step **1** and **one** improvement to step **2**. **[4 marks]**

13.2 Describe what the students should do between steps **3** and **4**. Give a reason for this extra step. **[2 marks]**

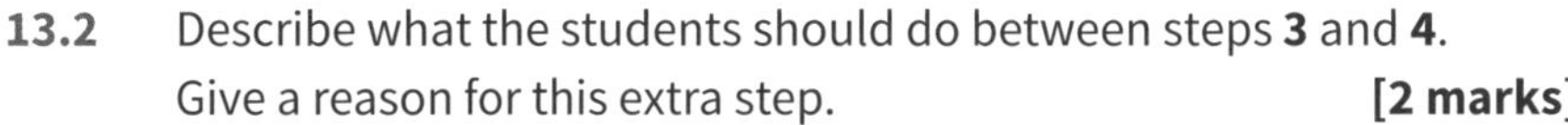

13.3 The students start with 0.025 mol of sodium hydroxide. Calculate the maximum mass of sodium chloride they can expect to make. Give your answer to two significant figures. **[4 marks]**

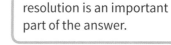

> **Exam Tip**
> If you do not give your answer to two significant figures, then you won't get full marks. The correct resolution is an important part of the answer.

14 Sulfuric acid is produced in a multi-step process called the contact process. One step within the contact process involves the reaction between sulfur dioxide and oxygen.

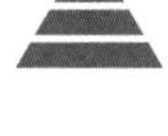

14.1 Complete and balance the symbol equation for the reaction between sulfur dioxide and oxygen. **[3 marks]**

$$\_\_\_\_(g) + O_2(\_\_\_\_) \rightleftharpoons \_\_\_\_SO_3(g)$$

> **Exam Tip**
> Only write in the gaps! Do not try to add in extra numbers or letters outside the gaps.

14.2 Increasing the temperature of the reaction vessel causes the equilibrium position to shift to the left. Identify which reaction is exothermic. **[1 mark]**

14.3 What does this suggest about the energy transfers involved in the chemical reaction? **[1 mark]**

14.4 In industry, the reaction is carried out at 450 °C rather than room temperature. Suggest what effect this will have on the yield of sulfur trioxide. **[1 mark]**

14.5 Suggest why the reaction is carried out at 450 °C. **[1 mark]**

14.6 Vanadium pentoxide is used as a catalyst for the forward reaction. Explain how the catalyst increases the rate of the forward reaction. **[3 marks]**

14.7 Suggest and explain **one** other condition that would favour the formation of sulfur trioxide. **[3 marks]**

14.8 Suggest a reason why this condition may not be used in the industrial process. **[1 mark]**

Knowledge

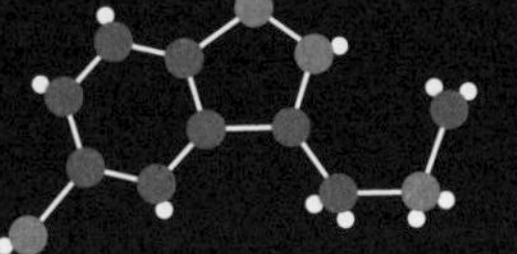

C12 Crude oil and fuels

Crude oil

Crude oil is incredibly important to our society and economy. It is formed from the remains of ancient biomass – living organisms (mostly plankton) that died many millions of years ago.

Raw crude oil is a thick black liquid made of a large number of different compounds mixed together. Most of the compounds are **hydrocarbons** of various sizes. Hydrocarbons are molecules made of carbon and hydrogen only.

Combustion

Hydrocarbons are used as **fuels**. This is because when they react with oxygen they release a lot of energy. This reaction is called **combustion**. Complete combustion is a type of combustion where the only products are carbon dioxide and water.

Properties

Whether or not a particular hydrocarbon is useful as a fuel depends on its properties:

- **flammability** – how easily it burns
- **boiling point** – the temperature at which it boils
- **viscosity** – how thick it is

Its properties in turn depend on the length of the molecule.

Chain length	Flammability	Boiling point	Viscosity
long chain	low	high	high (very thick)
short chain	high	low	low (very runny)

Alkanes

One family of hydrocarbon molecules is called **alkanes**. Alkane molecules only have single bonds in them. The first four alkanes are:

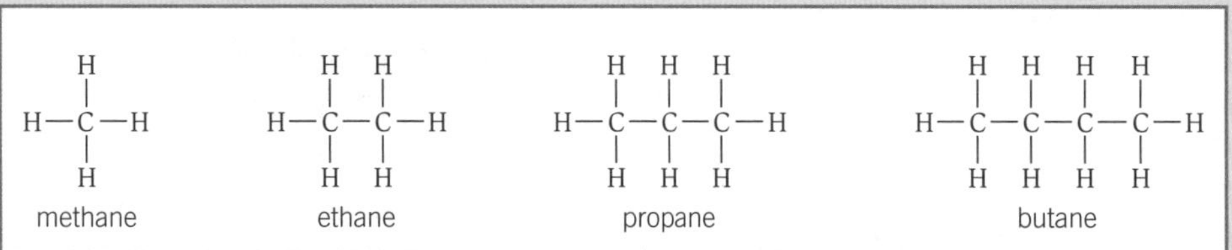

The different alkanes have different numbers of carbon atoms and hydrogen atoms. You can always work out the molecular formula of an alkane by using C_nH_{2n+2}.

Revision tip

Practice You can check if you've drawn compounds correctly since carbon always forms four bonds and hydrogen always forms one bond.

Revision tip

Practice Most of the topics on this knowledge organiser come up frequently as extended response questions – practice writing long answers based around fractional distillation and cracking.

Key terms Make sure you can write a definition for these key terms.

alkanes alkenes boiling point combustion cracking crude oil feedstock flammability fractional distillation fuel hydrocarbon viscosity

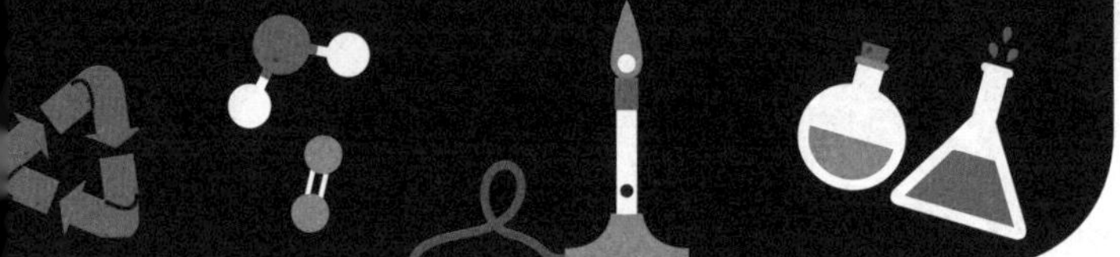

Fractional distillation

The different hydrocarbons in crude oil are separated into fractions based on their boiling points in a process called **fractional distillation**. All the molecules in a fraction have a similar number of carbon atoms, and so a similar boiling point.

The process takes place in a fractionating column, which is hot at the bottom and cooler at the top.

The process works like this:

1. Crude oil is vapourised (turned into a gas by heating).
2. The hydrocarbon gases enter the column.
3. The hydrocarbon gases rise up the column.
4. As hydrocarbon gases rise up the column they cool down.
5. When the different hydrocarbons reach their boiling points in the column they condense.
6. The hydrocarbon fraction is collected.

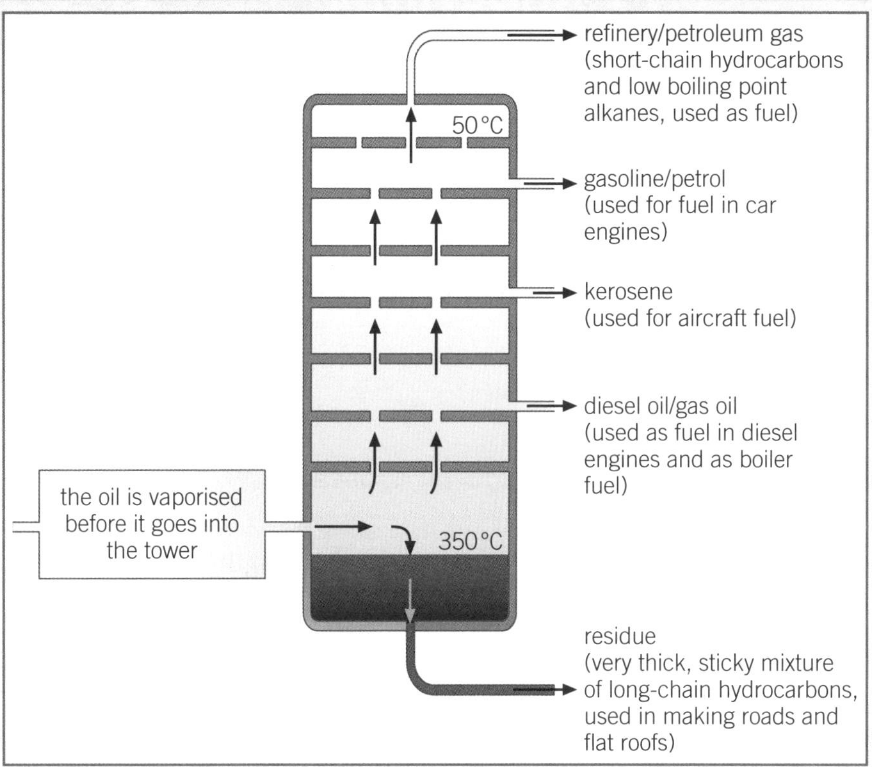

Products from fractional distillation

Many useful products come from the separation of crude oil by fractional distillation.

Fuels	Feedstock	Useful materials produced
petrol, diesel oil, kerosene, heavy fuel oil, and liquefied petroleum gases	fractions form the raw material for other processes and the production of other substances	solvents, lubricants, polymers, and detergents

Cracking

Not all hydrocarbons are as useful as each other. Longer molecules tend to be less useful than shorter ones. As such, there is a higher demand for shorter-chain hydrocarbons than longer-chain hydrocarbons.

A process called **cracking** is used to break up longer hydrocarbons and turn them into shorter ones.

Cracking produces shorter alkanes and **alkenes**.

Two methods of cracking are:

- catalytic cracking – vaporise the hydrocarbons, then pass them over a hot catalyst
- steam cracking – mix the hydrocarbons with steam at a very high temperature.

Alkenes

Alkenes are a family of hydrocarbons that contain double bonds between carbon atoms.

Alkenes are also used as fuels, and to produce polymers and many other materials.

They are much more reactive than alkanes. When mixed with bromine water, the bromine water turns from orange to colourless. This can be used to tell the difference between alkanes and alkenes.

Retrieval

Learn the answers to the questions below, then cover the answers column with a piece of paper and write down as many as you can. Check and repeat.

	C12 questions		Answers
1	What is a hydrocarbon?	Put paper here	compound containing carbon and hydrogen only
2	How is crude oil formed?		over millions of years from the remains of ancient biomass
3	What are the alkanes?	Put paper here	hydrocarbons that only have single bonds
4	What are the first four alkanes?		methane, ethane, propane, butane
5	What is the general formula for the alkanes?		C_nH_{2n+2}
6	How does boiling point depend on the chain length?	Put paper here	longer the chain, higher the boiling point
7	How does viscosity depend on chain length?		longer the chain, higher the viscosity
8	How does flammability depend on chain length?		longer the chain, lower the flammability
9	How can the different alkanes in crude oil be separated?	Put paper here	fractional distillation
10	What is a fraction?		a group of hydrocarbons with similar chain lengths
11	Name five useful fuels produced from fractional distillation.	Put paper here	petrol, diesel oil, kerosene, heavy fuel oil, liquefied petroleum gases
12	Name four useful materials produced from crude oil.		solvents, lubricants, polymers, detergents
13	What is cracking?		breaking down a hydrocarbon with a long chain into smaller molecules
14	Name two methods to carry out cracking.	Put paper here	steam cracking and catalytic cracking
15	What are the products of cracking?		short chain alkanes and alkenes
16	What are alkenes?	Put paper here	hydrocarbons with a double bond
17	What are alkenes used for?		formation of polymers
18	Describe the reactivity of alkenes compared to alkanes.		alkenes are much more reactive
19	How can you test for alkenes?		alkenes turn orange bromine water colourless

Now go back and use the questions below to check your knowledge from previous chapters.

Previous questions

Answers

	Previous questions	Answers
1	What is a reversible reaction?	when the reactants turn into products and the products turn into reactants
2	What is dynamic equilibrium?	the point in a reversible reaction when the rate of the forward and reverse reactions are the same
3	What are the three reaction conditions that can be changed?	concentration, temperature, pressure
4	What is the effect of decreasing pressure on a reaction at dynamic equilibrium?	favours the reaction that leads to the most molecules
5	What is the rate of a reaction?	how quickly reactants are used up or products are produced
6	What effect does increasing concentration have on the rate of reaction?	increases
7	What effect does increasing surface area have on the rate of reaction?	increases
8	What is a bond energy?	the energy required to break a bond or the energy released when a bond is formed
9	What is the name of the positive electrode?	anode
10	In the electrolysis of aluminium oxide, why is the aluminium oxide mixed with cryolite?	to lower the melting point

Put paper here

Maths Skills

Practise your maths skills using the worked example and practice questions below.

Finding the mean

Whenever an experiment is conducted, it is important to repeat it to establish how *precise* the values are (how close to each other they are), and how *repeatable* they are (can they be repeated).

Whenever you repeat an experiment and record repeat observations you must calculate a mean to give an average result for that observation.

However, only use values that are close together, and discard any anomalous values.

Worked example

A student burns ethanol and uses the heat released to warm up some water. As soon as the water increases by 10 °C, she stops the reaction and measures the mass of ethanol used. She repeats this three more times and records the masses: 5.1 g, 6.3 g, 6.5 g, 6.2 g.

Calculate the mean of the values.

Step 1: Establish which values to use – in this case 6.3 g, 6.5 g, and 6.2 g. The first mass (5.1 g) is ignored because it is an outlier.

Step 2: Calculate the mean.

$$\text{mean} = \frac{\text{sum of values}}{\text{total number of values}}$$

$$= \frac{(6.3 + 6.5 + 6.2)}{3} = 6.3\,\text{g}$$

Practice

1 A student measures how the mass of a magnesium strip increases when burnt in oxygen. They record the masses: 0.12 g, 0.12 g, 0.14 g, 0.11 g, 0.23 g. Calculate the mean increase in mass.

2 The volume of gas produced in three repeats of an experiment is collected, and recorded as: 54 cm^3, 58 cm^3, 55 cm^3. Calculate the mean volume of gas produced.

Practice

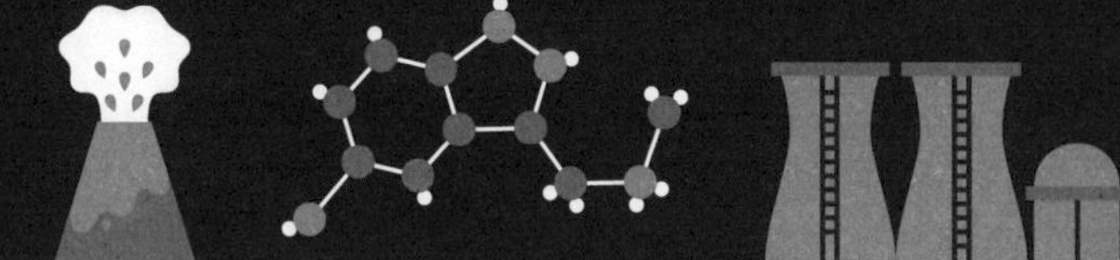

Exam-style questions

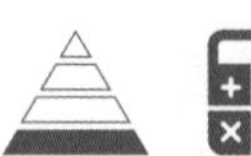

01 This question is about alkanes.

01.1 Draw **one** line from each displayed formula to the name of the alkane. **[2 marks]**

Displayed formula	Name
$\begin{array}{ccccccc} & & H & & H & & \\ & & | & & | & & \\ H & - & C & - & C & - & H \\ & & | & & | & & \\ & & H & & H & & \end{array}$	butane
	ethane
$\begin{array}{ccccccccccc} & & H & & H & & H & & H & & \\ & & | & & | & & | & & | & & \\ H & - & C & - & C & - & C & - & C & - & H \\ & & | & & | & & | & & | & & \\ & & H & & H & & H & & H & & \end{array}$	methane
	propane

01.2 What is the formula of the alkane with 22 carbon atoms?

Tick **one** box. **[1 mark]**

$C_{22}H_{42}$ ☐ $C_{22}H_{46}$ ☐

$C_{22}H_{44}$ ☐ $C_{22}H_{48}$ ☐

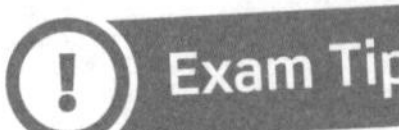

Exam Tip

Use the general formula for alkanes to figure out the number of hydrogen atoms that will be in the compound.

01.3 Decane is an alkane with 10 carbon atoms.

How do the properties of decane compare with the properties of ethane?

Tick **one** box. **[1 mark]**

Decane has a higher flammability, lower boiling point, and higher viscosity. ☐

Decane has a higher flammability, higher boiling point, and lower viscosity. ☐

Decane has a lower flammability, higher boiling point, and higher viscosity. ☐

Decane has a lower flammability, lower boiling point, and lower viscosity. ☐

Exam Tip

There are three possible differences within each answer. Go over the properties one at a time (flammability, boiling point, and then viscosity), comparing them to ethane. This should leave you with the correct answer at the end.

02 **Table 1** shows the boiling points of some alkanes.

Table 1

Name of alkane	Number of carbon atoms	Boiling point in °C
pentane	5	36
hexane	6	69
heptane	7	98
octane	8	126
nonane	9	
decane	10	174
undecane	11	196
dodecane	12	216

02.1 Plot the data from **Table 1** on **Figure 1**.

Draw a line of best fit. **[3 marks]**

Figure 1

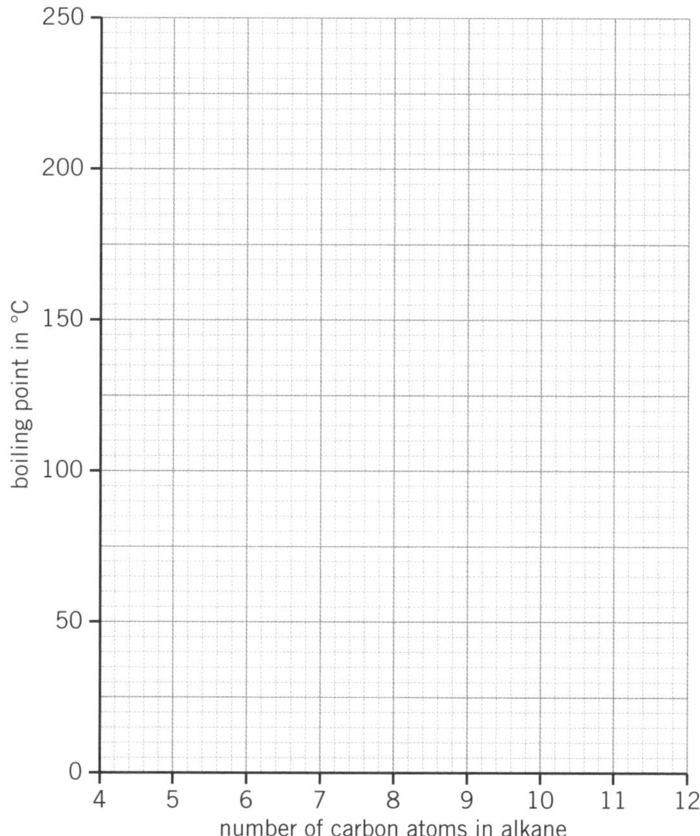

02.2 Use your graph from **Figure 1** to predict the boiling point of nonane. **[1 mark]**

____

02.3 Write a chemical equation for the complete combustion of nonane.

You do **not** need to include state symbols. **[4 marks]**

Exam Tip

The products for complete combustion are always the same. The only thing that changes with large compounds is the number of moles.

03 Many useful substances are obtained from crude oil.

03.1 Define the term fraction of crude oil. **[1 mark]**

03.2 **Figure 2** shows a fractionating column. Explain how kerosene is separated from the other fractions in crude oil by fractional distillation. **[3 marks]**

03.3 The hydrocarbons in diesel are bigger than the hydrocarbons in petrol. Compare the physical and chemical properties of diesel and petrol. **[6 marks]**

Figure 2

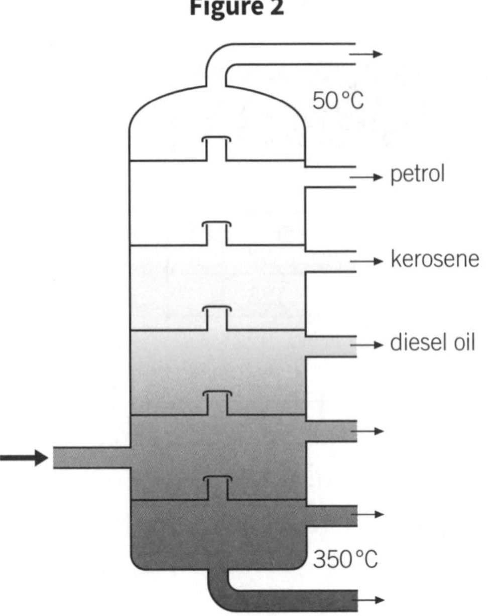

> **Exam Tip**
>
> Mark on the diagram where it is hottest and where it is coldest – this will point you towards the way they are separated in question **03.2** and the differences in properties in **03.3**.

04 Some students use the apparatus shown in **Figure 3** to crack hydrocarbons.

Figure 3

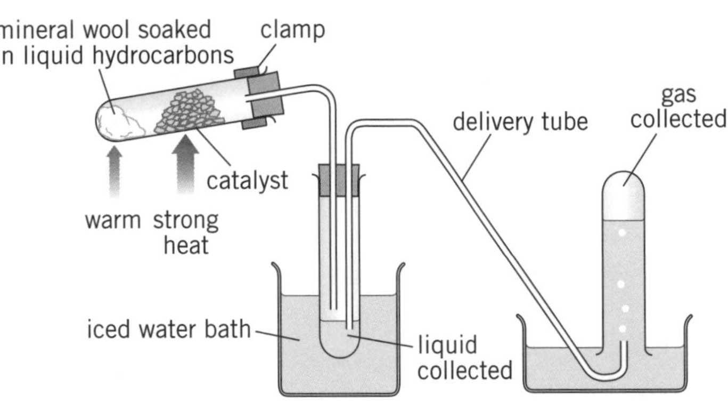

> **Exam Tip**
>
> Think about the changes that would happen if you just heated the liquid hydrocarbons.

04.1 Give a reason for heating the mineral wool soaked in liquid hydrocarbons. **[1 mark]**

04.2 Identify the error in how the students set up the delivery tube. **[1 mark]**

04.3 The equation shows one reaction that occurs in the apparatus.

$$C_{10}H_{22} \rightarrow C_5H_{12} + C_3H_6 + C_2H_4$$

One of the products of the reaction above is collected as a liquid. Write down the formula of the product that you predict is collected as a liquid. Give a reason for your prediction. **[2 marks]**

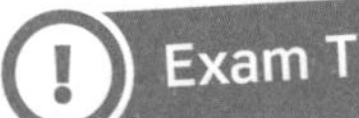

> **Exam Tip**
>
> Look at the length of the hydrocarbons to help your prediction.

04.4 The product with the formula C_3H_6 is an alkene. Describe the colour change that occurs when C_3H_6 reacts with bromine water. **[1 mark]**

05 A chemist does some tests on four hydrocarbons. The hydrocarbons have the formulae below. The chemist does not know which hydrocarbon is which.

C_2H_4 C_2H_6 C_8H_{18} $C_{17}H_{36}$

Table 2 shows the results of the tests.

Table 2

Hydrocarbon	Boiling point in °C	Observations when shaken with bromine water
A	126	no change
B	−104	orange to colourless
C	302	no change
D	−89	no change

05.1 Deduce the formula of each hydrocarbon in **Table 2**. Justify your decision. **[4 marks]**

05.2 Predict the letter of the hydrocarbon in **Table 2** that is most viscous in the liquid state. **[1 mark]**

05.3 In a cracking reaction, a molecule of $C_{20}H_{42}$ forms two compounds:

C_8H_{18} C_3H_6

Write a balanced chemical equation for the cracking reaction. Do **not** include state symbols. **[3 marks]**

06 This question is about crude oil.

06.1 Name the type of substances that crude oil is made up of. **[1 mark]**

06.2 Describe the process by which crude oil is separated into fractions. **[6 marks]**

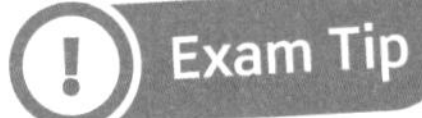

The easy examples to remember are the ones that are used in cars!

06.3 Name **one** of the fractions produced from crude oil, and give its use. **[2 marks]**

07 **Table 3** gives the formulae and boiling points of three alkanes. The alkanes have the same numbers of carbon and hydrogen atoms, but the atoms are joined together differently. Compound **X** is a straight-chain alkane. Compounds **Y** and **Z** are branched-chain alkanes

Table 3

Formula	H H H H H H H—C—C—C—C—C—C—H H H H H H H **X**	H H—C—H H H H H H—C—C—C—C—C—H H H H H H **Y**	H H—C—H H H H H—C—C—C—C—H H H H H—C—H H **Z**
Boiling point in °C	68	63	58

07.1 Name the main source of alkanes. **[1 mark]**

07.2 Calculate the relative formula mass of the alkanes in **Table 3**.
Relative atomic masses A_r: C = 12, H = 1 **[1 mark]**

07.3 Explain the relationship between boiling points and the number of branches in a molecule. **[6 marks]**

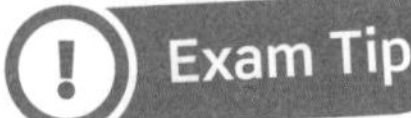

Look at the number of branches the compounds have and link the increase in branches to a change in boiling point.

08 This question is about cracking.

08.1 Compare the conditions used for steam cracking and for catalytic cracking. **[3 marks]**

08.2 The equation shows a cracking reaction:

$$C_{10}H_{22} \rightarrow C_6H_{14} + C_2H_4$$

Balance the equation by writing a number where required. **[1 mark]**

Exam Tip

Start by balancing the carbons.

08.3 Give **two** reasons for carrying out cracking reactions in industry. **[2 marks]**

09 Some alkanes are used as fuels.

09.1 Write a balanced equation for the combustion of pentane to make carbon dioxide and water only. **[3 marks]**

09.2 In certain conditions, pentane undergoes incomplete combustion:

$$2C_5H_{12} + 11O_2 \rightarrow 10CO + 12H_2O$$

Deduce the conditions in which propane undergoes incomplete combustion. Use your answer to **09.1** and the equation above. Justify your answer. **[2 marks]**

09.3 Propane is another fuel. **Figure 4** shows the displayed formula equation for its complete combustion.

Figure 4

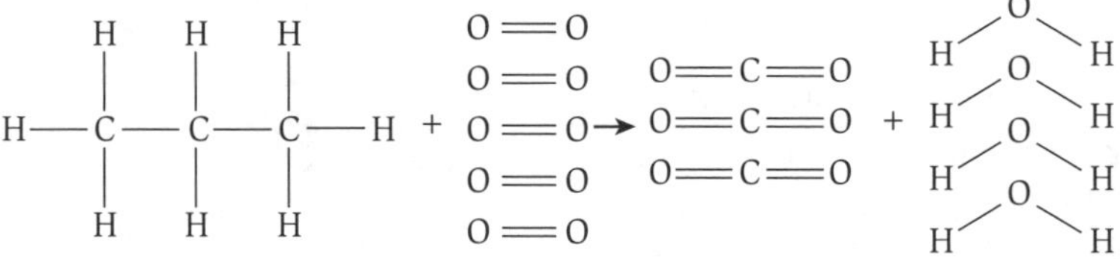

Exam Tip

Cross off each bond in the diagram as you count it — this should help you count everything only once and not miss bonds out.

Table 4 gives some bond enthalpy values.

Table 4

Bond	C–C	C–H	O=O	C=O	O–H
Energy in kJ/mol	348	412	496	743	463

Calculate the energy change for the complete combustion of one mole of propane. **[5 marks]**

10 Crude oil is a mixture of many different substances. The substances are separated using fractional distillation.

10.1 Describe what crude oil was formed from. **[1 mark]**

10.2 Name the **two** processes that occur during fractional distillation. **[2 marks]**

10.3 Outline the uses of some products obtained from crude oil. **[6 marks]**

11 The equation shows a chemical reaction:

ammonium chloride ⇌ ammonia + hydrogen chloride

11.1 Give the meaning of the symbol ⇌ . **[1 mark]**

11.2 The equilibrium moves from left to right if ammonium chloride is heated. State the condition required for the reverse reaction to occur. **[1 mark]**

11.3 State **one** feature of the apparatus required for an equilibrium to be established between ammonium chloride, ammonia, and hydrogen chloride. **[1 mark]**

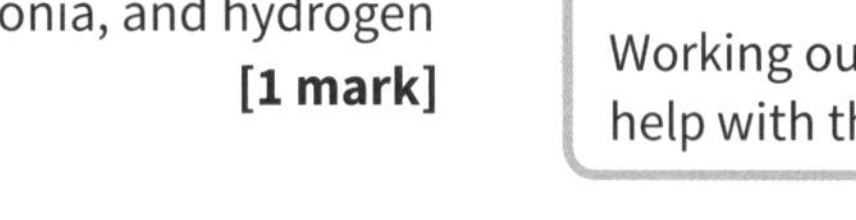

Exam Tip

Working out the states will help with this question.

12 A teacher passed an electric current through molten zinc chloride. **Figure 5** shows the apparatus.

Figure 5

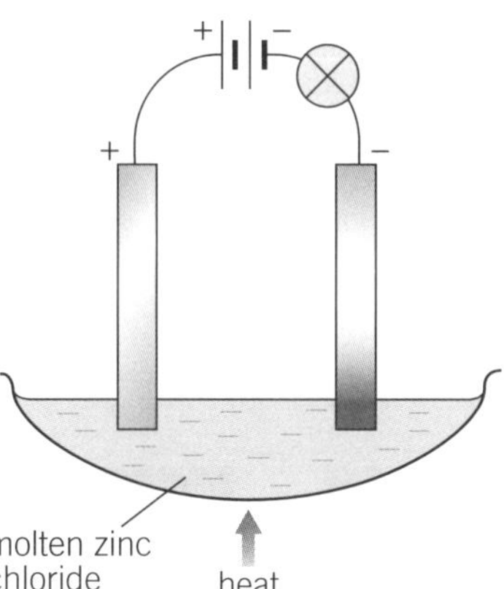

12.1 Predict the observations at the positive and negative electrodes. **[2 marks]**

12.2 Write a half equation for the reaction that occurs at the negative electrode. **[3 marks]**

Exam Tip

Start by working out the ions that will be in zinc chloride and to which electrode they will be attracted.

12.3 The teacher passes an electric current through an aqueous zinc chloride solution. Predict the products formed at the positive and negative electrodes. Zinc is more reactive than hydrogen. **[2 marks]**

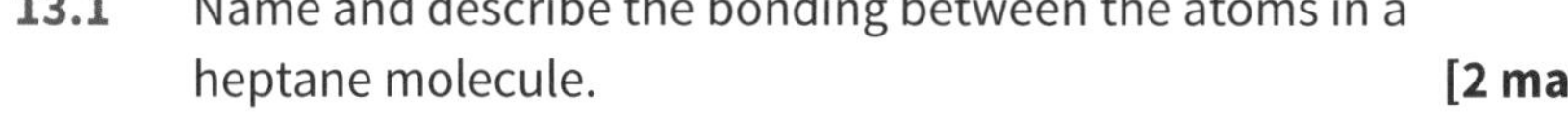

13 Heptane, C_7H_{16}, is an alkane.

13.1 Name and describe the bonding between the atoms in a heptane molecule. **[2 marks]**

13.2 Name the type of force that is overcome when heptane boils. **[1 mark]**

Exam Tip

The spelling of this force is important to get the mark here.

13.3 Calculate the mass of carbon dioxide produced when 85.0 g of heptane undergoes complete combustion. Give your answer to two significant figures. **[7 marks]**

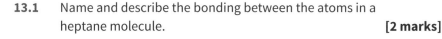

Knowledge

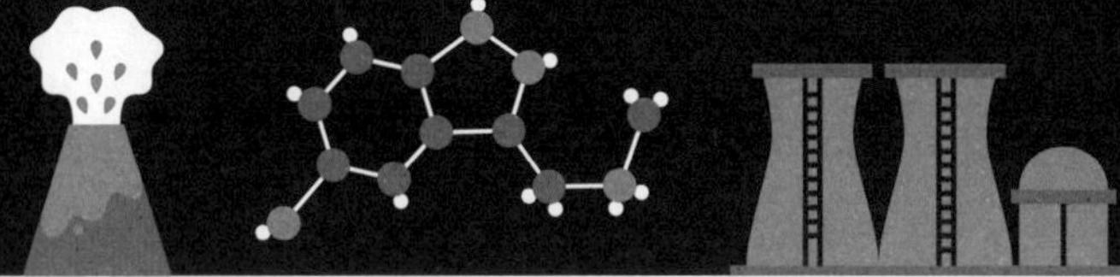

C13 Chemical analysis

Pure and impure

In chemistry, a **pure** substance contains a single element or compound that is not mixed with any other substance.

Pure substances melt and boil at specific temperatures.

An **impure** substance contains more than one type of element or compound in a **mixture**.

Impure substances melt and boil at a range of temperatures.

Jar 1

Oxygen (gas)

Jar 2

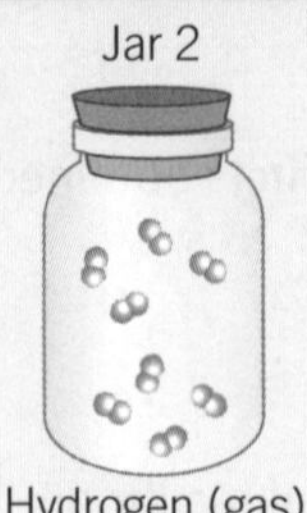

Hydrogen (gas)

Jar 3

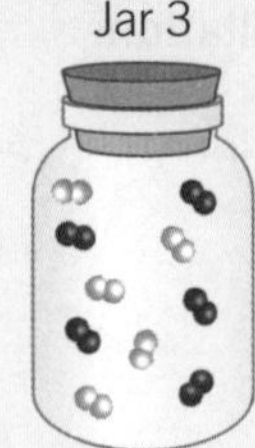

Mixture of oxygen and hydrogen (gas). The oxygen and hydrogen are not joined together. The mixture has the same properties as Jar 1 and Jar 2.

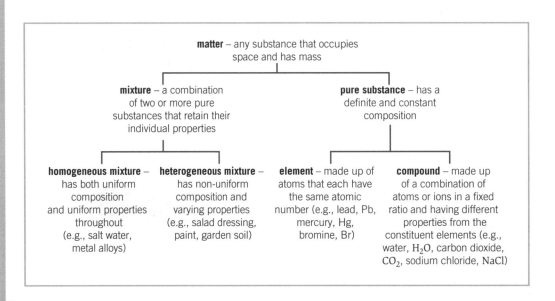

matter – any substance that occupies space and has mass

- **mixture** – a combination of two or more pure substances that retain their individual properties
  - **homogeneous mixture** – has both uniform composition and uniform properties throughout (e.g., salt water, metal alloys)
  - **heterogeneous mixture** – has non-uniform composition and varying properties (e.g., salad dressing, paint, garden soil)
- **pure substance** – has a definite and constant composition
  - **element** – made up of atoms that each have the same atomic number (e.g., lead, Pb, mercury, Hg, bromine, Br)
  - **compound** – made up of a combination of atoms or ions in a fixed ratio and having different properties from the constituent elements (e.g., water, H_2O, carbon dioxide, CO_2, sodium chloride, NaCl)

Formulations

Formulations are examples of mixtures. They have many different components (substances that make them up) in very specific proportions (amounts compared to each other).

Scientists spend a lot of time trying to get the right components in the right proportions to make the most useful product.

Formulations include fuels, cleaning agents, paints, alloys, fertilisers, and foods.

Separating mixtures

Mixtures can be separated by

- filtration – separates insoluble solids from a liquid
- crystallisation – evaporates a solvent (liquid) leaving the solute (solid)
- simple distillation – separates solvent from a solution as long as the solvent has a lower boiling point than the solute
- fractional distillation – separates two or more substances from a liquid mixture.

Key terms

Make sure you can write a definition for these key terms.

chromatography *formulation* *impure* *mobile phase* *pure*

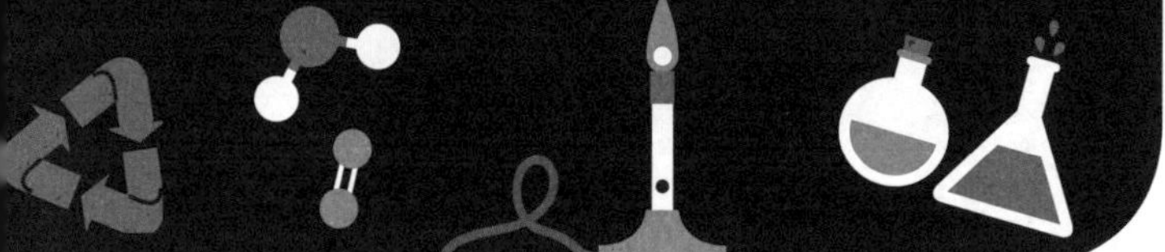

Chromatography

Chromatography is a method to separate different components in a mixture. It is set up as shown here, with a piece of paper in a beaker containing a small amount of solvent.

The **R_f value** is a ratio of how far up the paper a certain spot moves compared to how far the **solvent** has travelled.

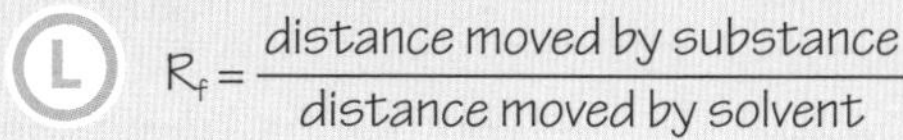

$$R_f = \frac{\text{distance moved by substance}}{\text{distance moved by solvent}}$$

It will always be a number between 0 and 1.

The R_f value depends on the solvent and the temperature, and different substances will have different R_f values. The R_f values for particular solvents can be used to identify a substance.

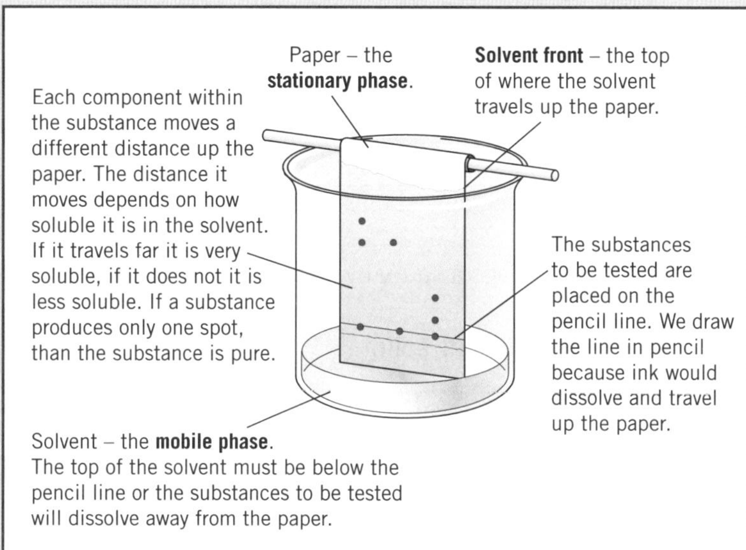
Paper – the **stationary phase**.
Solvent front – the top of where the solvent travels up the paper.
Each component within the substance moves a different distance up the paper. The distance it moves depends on how soluble it is in the solvent. If it travels far it is very soluble, if it does not it is less soluble. If a substance produces only one spot, than the substance is pure.
The substances to be tested are placed on the pencil line. We draw the line in pencil because ink would dissolve and travel up the paper.
Solvent – the **mobile phase**. The top of the solvent must be below the pencil line or the substances to be tested will dissolve away from the paper.

Revision tips

Practice Ensure you can describe the function of each piece of equipment used in chromatography, they all have an important role.

Practice Use a coloured pencil to help identify which spots appear in more than one sample by drawing horizontal and vertical lines through the spots on the chromatogram.

Testing gases

Common gases can be identified using the follow tests:

Gas	What you do	What you observe if gas is present
hydrogen	hold a lighted splint near the gas	hear a squeaky pop
oxygen	hold a glowing splint near the gas	splint re-lights
carbon dioxide	bubble the gas through limewater	the limewater turns milky (cloudy white)
chlorine	hold a piece of damp litmus near the gas	bleaches the litmus white

R_f value   solvent   solvent front   stationary phase

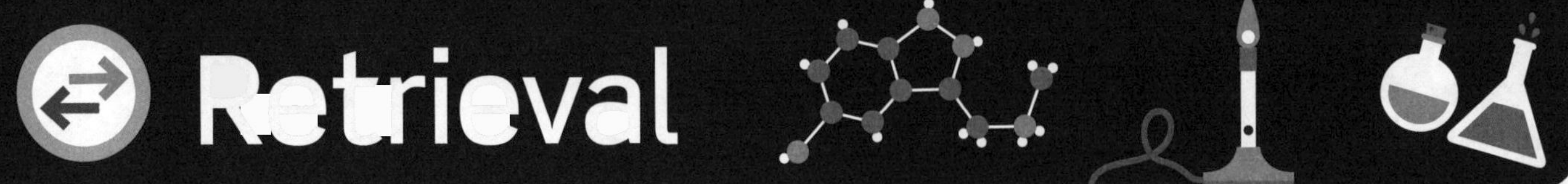

Retrieval

Learn the answers to the questions below, then cover the answers column with a piece of paper and write as many as you can. Check and repeat.

	C13 questions		Answers
1	In chemistry, what is a pure substance?	Put paper here	something made of only one type of substance
2	What is the difference between the melting and boiling points of a pure and impure substance?		pure – sharp/one specific temperature impure – broad/occur across a range of temperatures
3	What is a formulation?		a mixture designed for a specific purpose
4	What are some examples of formulations?	Put paper here	fuels, cleaning agents, paints, medicines, alloys, fertilisers, and foods
5	What is chromatography?		a process for separating coloured mixtures
6	How is R_f calculated?	Put paper here	$R_f = \frac{\text{distance moved by substance}}{\text{distance moved by solvent}}$
7	What is the test for hydrogen?		a lit splint gives a squeaky pop
8	What is the test for oxygen?		re-lights a glowing splint
9	What is the test for carbon dioxide?	Put paper here	turns limewater milky if bubbled through it
10	What is the test for chlorine?		bleaches damp litmus paper white

Now go back and use the questions below to check your knowledge from previous chapters.

Previous questions / Answers

	Previous questions	Answers
1	How is crude oil formed?	over millions of years from the remains of ancient biomass
2	Name four useful materials produced from crude oil.	solvents, lubricants, polymers, detergents
3	What are the products of cracking?	short chain alkanes and alkenes
4	What are the first four alkanes?	methane, ethane, propane, butane
5	What are alkenes used for?	formation of polymers
6	What is Le Châtelier's principle?	the position of equilibrium will shift to oppose external changes
7	What is the effect of decreasing the concentration of products on a reaction at dynamic equilibrium?	favours the forward reaction
8	What is the effect of increasing temperature on a reaction at dynamic equilibrium?	favours the endothermic reaction
9	What is the unit for rate of reaction in a reaction involving a change in volume?	cm^3/s
10	What effect does increasing pressure have on the rate of reaction?	increases

Put paper here

Required Practical Skills

Practise answering questions on the required practicals using the example below. You need to be able to apply your skills and knowledge to other practicals too.

Analysing chromatograms

Chromatography can be used to identify unknown substances. The ratio of the distance moved by a compound (centre of spot from origin) to the distance moved by the solvent can be expressed as its R_f value:

$$R_f = \frac{\text{distance moved by substance}}{\text{distance moved by solvent}}$$

Different compounds have different R_f values in different solvents. Therefore, you can compare your experimental R_f value with a value from a database and identify the substance.

Worked example

A student obtained following the chromatogram.

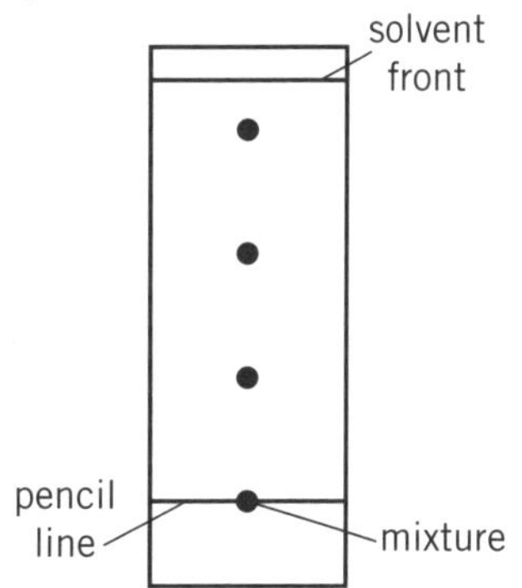

Calculate the R_f for the middle spot.

Measure the distance from the pencil line to the solvent front = 33.5 mm

Measure the value from the pencil line = 20.0 mm.

Put the values into the equation:

$$R_f = \frac{20.0}{33.5} = 0.6$$

Practice

1 Calculate the R_f value of the bottom spot from the chromatogram.

2 **Table 1** shows the R_f values of some dyes. Identify which dye produced the top spot.

Table 1

Dye	R_f
red	0.31
yellow	0.57
blue	0.82

3 A student calculated the R_f value of a spot on a chromatogram as 1.34. Is this value correct? Explain your answer.

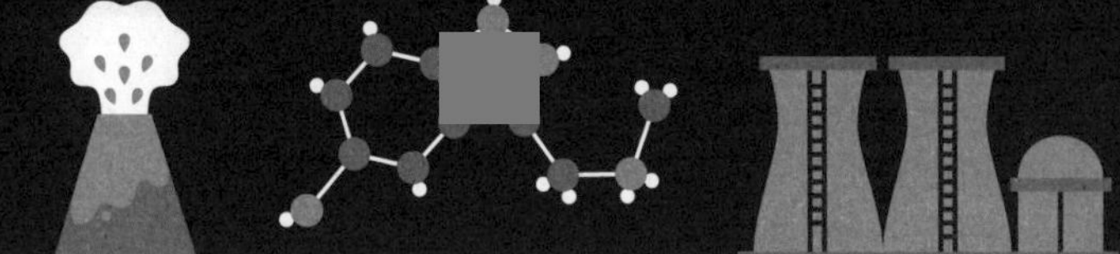

Practice

Exam-style questions

01 A student pours dilute hydrochloric acid into a test tube and adds magnesium ribbon. A gas is formed that the student collects.

01.1 Name the **two** products formed in the reaction. **[2 marks]**

1 ______________________________

2 ______________________________

> **Exam Tip**
> The question has given you a clue to one of the products: make sure you've listed a gas.

01.2 Describe the test the student can carry out to identify the gas collected. Give the expected result. **[2 marks]**

Test: ______________________________

Expected result: ______________________________

01.3 Another student reacted magnesium with sodium carbonate. A gas was formed that the student collected.

Describe the test the student can carry out to identify the gas collected. Give the expected result. **[2 marks]**

Test: ______________________________

Expected result: ______________________________

01.4 The scientist had a sample of a pale green gas. They inserted a glowing splint into the gas. The splint went out.

The scientist then put some damp litmus paper into the gas. The litmus paper turned white.

Identify the gas. **[1 mark]**

____

> **Exam Tip**
> Don't worry if you don't know which gas is pale green, it's the result of the test that is important.

02 **Table 1** shows the melting points for four substances purchased from a grocery store.

Table 1

Substance	Melting point in °C
A	90–95
B	0
C	30–32
D	47

All four substances are described as 'pure' on their containers.

02.1 Describe the difference between a chemically pure substance and a substance described as pure in everyday language. **[2 marks]**

____

____

____

____

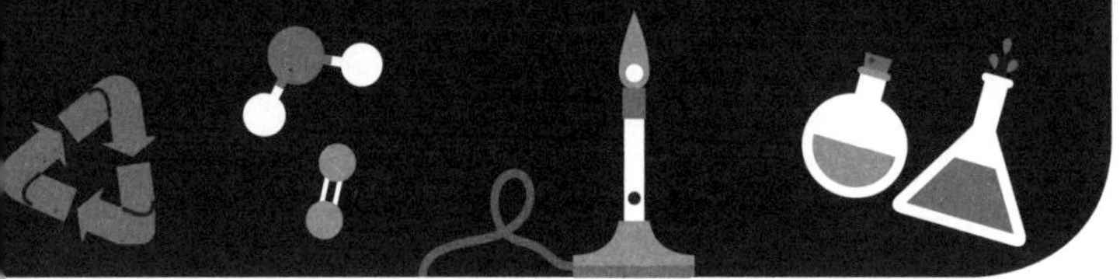

02.2 Identify the **two** substances that are chemically pure in **Table 1**. **[1 mark]**

1 ______________________________

2 ______________________________

02.3 A washing detergent was also purchased. The laundry detergent contains:

- a chemical that removes grease
- a colouring
- a fragrance.

Explain why the laundry detergent is a formulation. **[2 marks]**

____

____

____

03 All plants carry out photosynthesis. A student sets up the apparatus shown in **Figure 1** to investigate the products of photosynthesis.

Figure 1

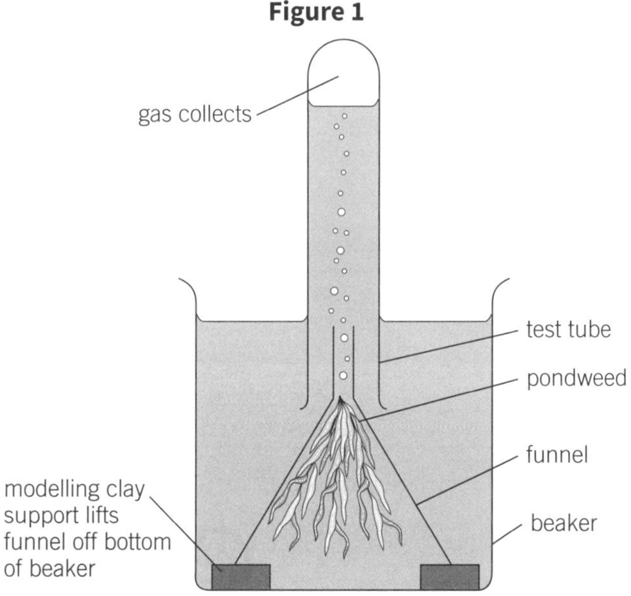

The student collects some of the gas in the test tube and inserts a glowing split. The splint relights.

03.1 Use the student's result to complete and balance the symbol equation for photosynthesis. **[2 marks]**

$$\_\_\_\_\_ \ CO_2 + \_\_\_\_\_ \ H_2O \rightarrow C_6H_{12}O_6 + \_\_\_\_\_$$

Only fill in the gaps. Do not be tempted to try to write an answer outside the gaps.

03.2 Photosynthesis occurs in the leaves of plants. Pigments in the leaves help the process to occur.
A student uses paper chromatography to investigate the pigments in a leaf.
Describe a method to carry out the paper chromatography experiment.
In your answer name any equipment required. **[6 marks]**

03.3 The student finds that there are four pigments in the leaves.
Sketch the chromatogram that the student has produced. **[1 mark]**

03.4 The student wants to calculate the R_f value of one of the pigments in the chromatogram.
Give the equation to calculate the R_f value. **[1 mark]**

03.5 The solvent travelled 12.0 cm. One of the spots travelled 8.6 cm.
Use **Table 2** to identify which pigment was responsible for the spot.

Table 2

Pigment	R_f value
carotene	0.95
xanthophyll	0.72
chlorophyll a	0.65
chlorophyll b	0.45

04 Chemists use different chemical tests to identify the substances in a compound.

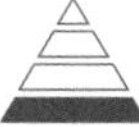

04.1 A chemist had three unknown gases. The chemist carried out three simple tests to identify the gases. Their observations are shown in **Table 3**.

Table 3

Gas	Test		
	Burning splint held at open end of tube	Glowing splint inserted into tube	Bubbled through limewater
A	no observation	no observation	cloudy
B	no observation	splint relights	no change
C	pop sound	no observation	no change

Identify the gases **A**, **B**, and **C**. **[3 marks]**

04.2 The chemist has a fourth gas. The chemist thinks the gas is chlorine.
Describe how the chemist could confirm that the gas is chlorine. **[2 marks]**

This is three marks for three short answers. Don't be tempted to explain your reasoning because you won't get any extra marks.

05 A student investigated the dyes in three felt tip pens. The dyes are soluble in water. They set up a chromatography experiment. **Figure 2** shows the apparatus the student used.

Figure 2

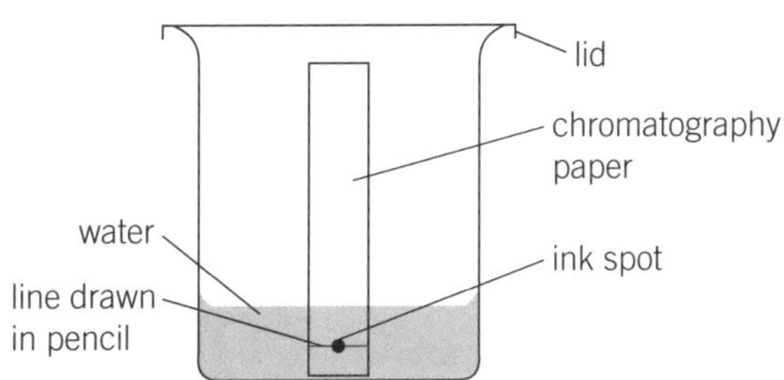

05.1 Name the mobile phase in this chromatography experiment. **[1 mark]**

05.2 The student made a mistake in setting up the apparatus. Identify the mistake and give **one** problem caused by this mistake. **[2 marks]**

> **Exam Tip**
> Look carefully at **Figure 2** to find the mistake.

05.3 Another student set up the apparatus correctly. **Figure 3** shows the chromatogram the student obtained.

Figure 3

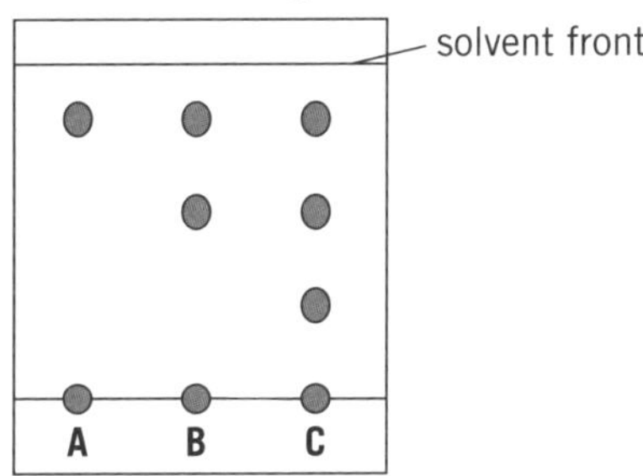

Write **two** conclusions that compare the dyes in ink samples **A**, **B**, and, **C**. **[2 marks]**

05.4 Calculate the R_f value for the spot obtained from ink sample **A**. **[2 marks]**

05.5 Circle the dye that is most attracted to the paper. Justify your answer. **[2 marks]**

06 A student carried out an experiment reacting solid magnesium with hydrochloric acid. At the end of the experiment, some of the magnesium had not reacted.

Describe how the student could separate the unreacted magnesium from the solution. Your description should include the names of any equipment used, where the substances end up, and any relevant safety precautions. **[6 marks]**

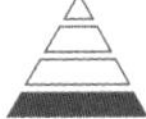

There are some easy marks to be picked up here. For example, there is an obvious safety precaution that will get you some marks.

07 Petrol is used to fuel cars. **Table 4** shows the different substances that are mixed in a sample of petrol.

Table 4

Substance	Mass of substance in 200 g of petrol in g
alkanes	110
other hydrocarbons	70
ethanol	20

07.1 Petrol is an example of a formulation.
Define the term formulation. **[1 mark]**

Exam Tip

Remember to use the general formula for alkanes.

07.2 Use data from **Table 4** to calculate the percentage by mass of ethanol in petrol. **[2 marks]**

07.3 The molecules of one alkane in petrol have seven carbon atoms.
Give the formula of this alkane. **[1 mark]**

07.4 Ethanol in petrol is made from plants. The alkanes in petrol are obtained from crude oil.
Suggest **one** advantage of including ethanol in petrol. **[1 mark]**

08 A student has a selection of mixtures:

- sodium chloride salt dissolved in water
- sand and water
- green ink.

08.1 Name the physical process that can be used to separate the sand and water mixture. **[1 mark]**

08.2 Describe a method that the student could use to obtain a sample of pure, dry sodium chloride from the mixture.
In your method include any equipment you would use. **[6 marks]**

Exam Tip

The clue is in the question.

08.3 The student thinks that the green ink is made up of a mixture of two dyes. Name the physical process the student could use to identify whether they are correct. **[1 mark]**

09 A student has an ink. The ink is made of dyes. The dyes are all mixtures. The student used chromatography to try to identify what dyes the ink is made of. A chromatogram of the ink and three dyes is shown in **Figure 4.**

Figure 4

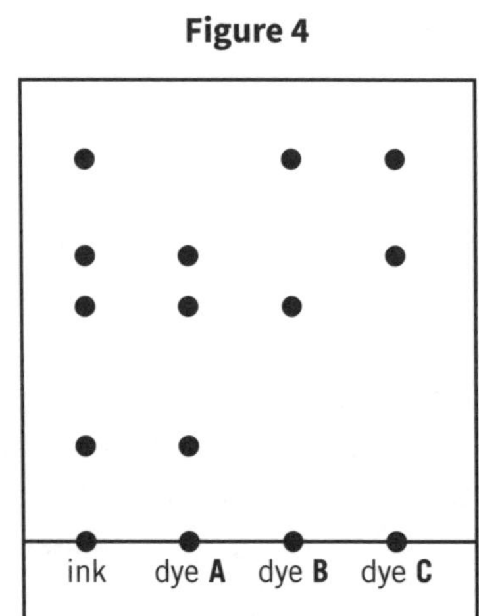

09.1 Identify **one** dye that the student's ink definitely contains. **[1 mark]**

09.2 Explain why the student cannot identify all the dyes contained within the ink from their chromatogram. **[2 marks]**

09.3 Suggest how the student could identify which dye was in the ink. **[1 mark]**

10 Companies crack long-chain hydrocarbons to produce more useful shorter-chain hydrocarbons. The equation shows an example of a cracking reaction.

$$C_{19}H\_\_\_\_ \rightarrow C_8H_{20} + C\_\_\_\_H_{10} + C_6H_{10}$$

10.1 Complete the chemical formulae in the symbol equation. **[1 mark]**

10.2 Name the homologous series that the original compound belongs to. **[1 mark]**

10.3 Identify the product from the cracking reaction that is an alkane. **[1 mark]**

10.4 Identify the product from the cracking reaction that has two double bonds. **[1 mark]**

10.5 Complete the diagram to show the possible structure for the compound with two double bonds. **[3 marks]**

C—C—C—C—C

10.6 What are the conditions required for catalytic cracking? **[1 marks]**

Each carbon will only make four bonds in total, double bonds count as two. Each hydrogen will only ever make one bond.

11 This question is about the following compounds

A C_3H_6

B C_3H_8

C CH_3CH_2COOH

D $CH_3CH_2CH_2OH$

11.1 Name compound **A**. **[1 mark]**

11.2 Name the homologous series that compound **D** belongs to. **[1 mark]**

11.3 Calculate the number of moles in 10.0 g of compound **C**. **[3 marks]**

11.4 Compare the chemical properties of compounds **C** and **D**. **[6 marks]**

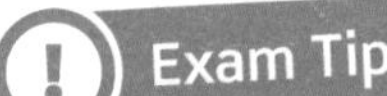

Remember that the relative atom masses of these elements are:

C = 12

H = 1

O = 16

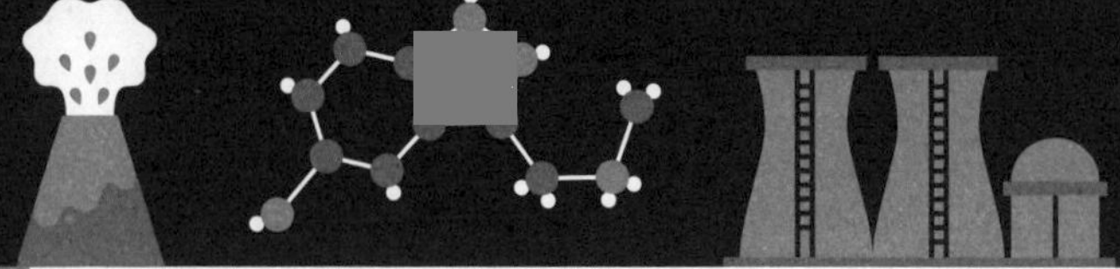

C14 The Earth's atmosphere

The Earth's changing atmosphere

The table below shows how the composition of the atmosphere has changed over the course of the Earth's entire 4.6 billion year history.

Period	Proportions of gases	Evidence
about 4.6 billion years to about 2.7 billion years ago	• **carbon dioxide, CO_2** Released by volcanoes. Biggest component of the **atmosphere**. • **oxygen, O_2** Very little oxygen present. • **nitrogen, N_2** Released by volcanoes. • **water vapour, H_2O** Released by volcanoes. Existed as vapour as Earth was too hot for it to condense. • **other gases** Ammonia, NH_3, and methane, CH_4, may also have been present.	Because it was billions of years ago there is very little evidence to draw upon.
about 2.7 billion years ago to about 200 million years ago	• **carbon dioxide, CO_2** Amount in atmosphere begins to reduce because: • water condenses to form the oceans, in which CO_2 then dissolves • algae (and later plants) start to photosynthesise carbon dioxide + water $\xrightarrow{\text{light}}$ glucose + oxygen $6CO_2 + 6H_2O \longrightarrow C_6H_{12}O_6 + 6O_2$ • CO_2 precipitates in the oceans as solid carbonates (sediments) that form rocks • CO_2 taken in by plants and animals. When they die, the carbon in them is locked up as fossil fuels. • **oxygen, O_2** Starts to increase as a product of photosynthesis. • **nitrogen, N_2** Continues to increase. Nitrogen is a very stable molecule so any process that produces it causes the overall amount to build up over time. • **water vapour, H_2O** Starts to decrease. As the Earth cools, the vapour condenses and forms the oceans.	Still limited as billions of years ago, but can look at processes that happen today (like photosynthesis) and make theories about the past.
about 200 million years ago until the present	• **carbon dioxide, CO_2** about 0.04% • **oxygen, O_2** about 20% • **nitrogen, N_2** about 80% • **water vapour, H_2O** Very little overall. Collects in large clouds as part of the water cycle. • **other gases** Small proportions of other gases such as the noble gases. 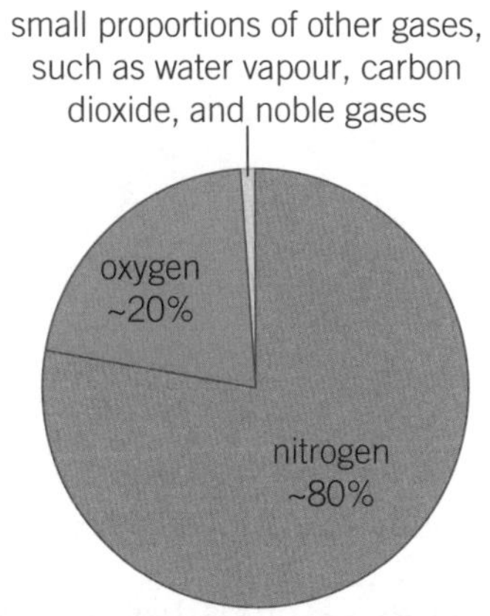 [Pie chart: small proportions of other gases, such as water vapour, carbon dioxide, and noble gases; oxygen ~20%; nitrogen ~80%]	Ice core evidence for millions of years ago and lots of global measurements taken recently.

Make sure you can write a definition for these key terms.

acid rain   atmosphere   carbon footprint   global climate change

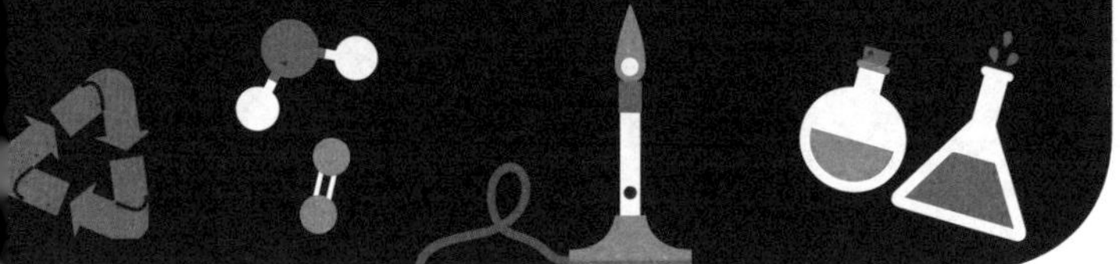

The information on this page shows how very recent human activity (in the past 150 years or so) is increasing the amount of CO_2 in the atmosphere.

Greenhouse gases

Greenhouse gases, such as carbon dioxide, methane, and water vapour, absorb radiation and maintain temperatures on the Earth to support life.

However, in the last 150 years, more greenhouse gases have been released due to human activities.

- carbon dioxide – combustion of fossil fuels, deforestation
- methane – planting rice fields, cattle farming.

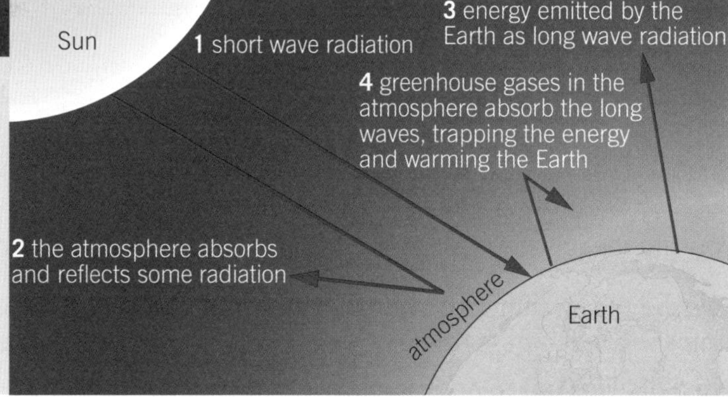
Sun
1 short wave radiation
3 energy emitted by the Earth as long wave radiation
4 greenhouse gases in the atmosphere absorb the long waves, trapping the energy and warming the Earth
2 the atmosphere absorbs and reflects some radiation
atmosphere
Earth

Global warming

Scientists have gathered peer-reviewed evidence to demonstrate that increasing the amount of greenhouse gases in the atmosphere will increase the overall average temperature of the Earth. This is called **global warming**.

However, it is difficult to make predictions about the atmosphere as it is so big and complex. This leads some people to doubt what scientists say.

Global climate change

Global warming leads to another process called **global climate change** – how the overall weather patterns over many years and across the entire planet will change.

There are many different effects of climate change, including:

- sea levels rising
- extreme weather events
- changes in the amount and time of rainfall
- changes to ecosystems and habitats
- polar ice caps melting.

Carbon footprints

Increasing the amount of greenhouse gases in the atmosphere increases the global average temperature of the Earth, which results in global climate change.

As such, it is important to reduce the release of greenhouse gases into the atmosphere. The amount of carbon dioxide and methane that is released into the atmosphere by a product, person, or process is called its **carbon footprint**.

Other pollutants released in the combustion of fuels

Pollutant	Origin	Effect
carbon monoxide	incomplete combustion of fuels	colourless and odourless toxic gas
particulates (soot and unburnt hydrocarbons)	incomplete combustion of fuels, especially in diesel engines	**global dimming**, respiratory problems, potential to cause cancer
sulfur dioxide	sulfur impurities in the fuel reacting with oxygen from the air	**acid rain** and respiratory problems
oxides of nitrogen	nitrogen from the air being heated near an engine and reacting with oxygen	acid rain and respiratory problems

global dimming *global warming* *greenhouse gas* *particulate* *pollutant*

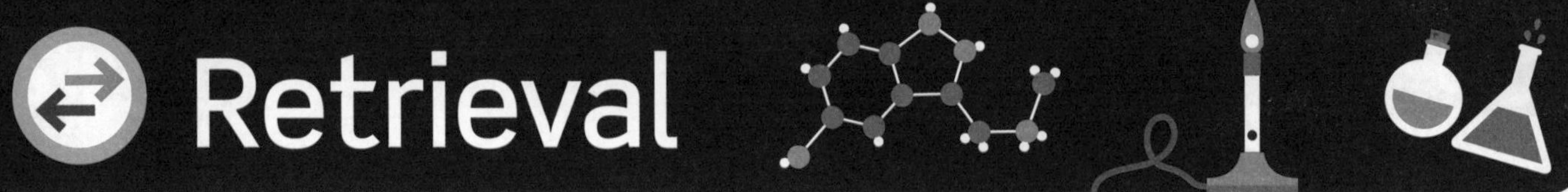

Retrieval

Learn the answers to the questions below, then cover the answers column with a piece of paper and write as many as you can. Check and repeat.

	C14 questions		Answers
1	What is the atmosphere?	Put paper here	a layer of gas surrounding the Earth
2	What was the early atmosphere composed of?		mostly carbon dioxide
3	How did the oceans form?	Put paper here	water vapour condensing as the Earth cooled
4	How did the amount of carbon dioxide in the atmosphere decrease to today's levels?		dissolved in the oceans, photosynthesis, converted to fossil fuels, precipitated as insoluble metal carbonates
5	When did life start to appear, and what was the impact of this on oxygen in the atmosphere?	Put paper here	about 2.7 billion years ago; amount of atmospheric oxygen increased as it was released in photosynthesis
6	How has the amount of nitrogen in the atmosphere changed over time?		increased slowly as it is a very stable molecule
7	Why can scientists not be sure about the composition of the Earth's early atmosphere?	Put paper here	it was billions of years ago and evidence is limited
8	What is the current composition of the atmosphere?		approximately 80 % nitrogen, 20 % oxygen, and trace amounts of other gases such as carbon dioxide, water vapour, and noble gases
9	What is a greenhouse gas?	Put paper here	a gas that traps radiation from the Sun
10	What type of radiation do greenhouse gases absorb?		longer wavelength infrared radiation
11	Name three greenhouse gases.	Put paper here	methane, carbon dioxide, water vapour
12	Give two ways recent human activities have increased the amount of atmospheric carbon dioxide.		burning fossil fuels, deforestation
13	Give two ways recent human activities have increased the amount of atmospheric methane.	Put paper here	rice farming, cattle farming
14	What is global warming?		an increase in the overall global average temperature
15	What is global climate change?	Put paper here	the change in long-term weather patterns across the planet
16	What are some possible effects of climate change?		sea levels rising, extreme weather events, changes in the amount and time of rainfall, changes to ecosystems and habitats, polar ice caps melting
17	What is a carbon footprint?	Put paper here	the amount of carbon a product, process, or person releases into the atmosphere over its lifetime
18	How is carbon monoxide formed, and what is the danger associated with it?		incomplete combustion; colourless and odourless toxic gas
19	How are particulates formed, and what are the dangers associated with them?	Put paper here	incomplete combustion; global dimming, respiratory problems, potential to cause cancer
20	How is sulfur dioxide formed, and what are the dangers associated with it?		sulfur impurities in fossil fuels react with oxygen during combustion; acid rain, respiratory problems
21	How are oxides of nitrogen formed, and what are the dangers associated with them?	Put paper here	atmospheric oxygen and nitrogen react in the heat of a combustion engine; acid rain, respiratory problems

Now go back and use the questions below to check your knowledge from previous chapters.

Previous questions / Answers

	Previous questions	Answers
1	In chemistry, what is a pure substance?	something made of only one type of substance
2	What is the difference between the melting and boiling points of a pure and impure substance?	pure – sharp/one specific temperature impure – broad/occur across a range of temperatures
3	What is the test for hydrogen?	a lit splint gives a squeaky pop
4	What is the test for chlorine?	bleaches damp litmus paper white
5	What is a hydrocarbon?	compound containing carbon and hydrogen only
6	How can the different alkanes in crude oil be separated?	fractional distillation
7	What is a fraction?	a group of hydrocarbons with similar chain lengths
8	Name five useful fuels produced from fractional distillation.	petrol, diesel oil, kerosene, heavy fuel oil, liquefied petroleum gases

Put paper here

Put paper here

Put paper here

Maths Skills

Practise your maths skills using the worked example and practice questions below.

Plotting curves

Remember that you need to draw a line of best fit when numerical data are plotted on a graph.

Some data will need a curved line of best fit, rather than a straight one.

It is important to remember that you draw the line that best fits the data.

Worked example

The alkanes have the boiling points given below.

Plot the data on a graph, and draw an appropriate line of best fit.

Number of carbon atoms	Boiling point in °C
1	−162.0
2	−89.0
3	−42.0
4	0.0
5	36.0
6	69.0

A graph displaying this data will have a curved line of best fit.

The graph shows a positive correlation – as the number of carbon atoms increases, so does the boiling point.

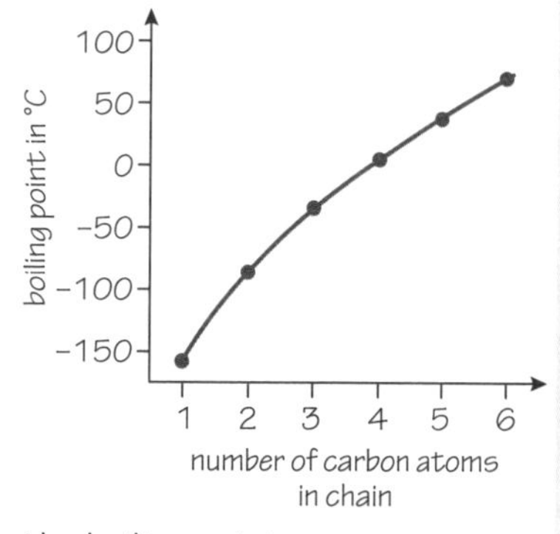

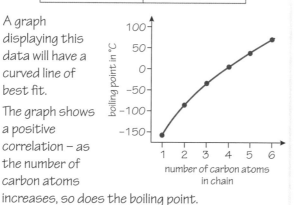

Practice

A different group of hydrocarbons have the boiling points given below.

Number of carbon atoms	Boiling point in °C
4	5.1
5	44.7
6	72.8
8	106.0
9	112.4
10	115.6

1 Plot a graph of these results. Draw an appropriate line of best fit.

2 Use your graph from **1** to predict the boiling point of a hydrocarbon in this group with seven carbon atoms.

3 Does your graph show a positive or negative correlation?

Practice

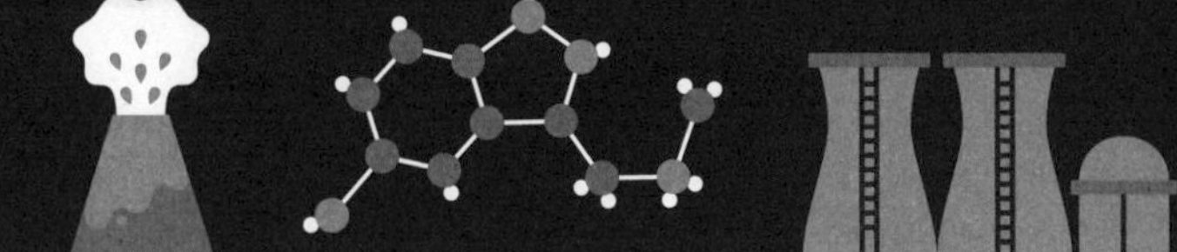

Exam-style questions

01 **Table 1** and **Figure 1** show the average concentration of carbon dioxide in the atmosphere every January from 2010 to 2019.

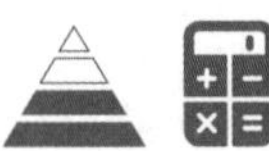

Table 1

Year	Average concentration of CO_2 in January in parts per million
2010	389
2011	391
2012	393
2013	395
2014	398
2015	400
2016	403
2017	406
2018	408
2019	411

Figure 1

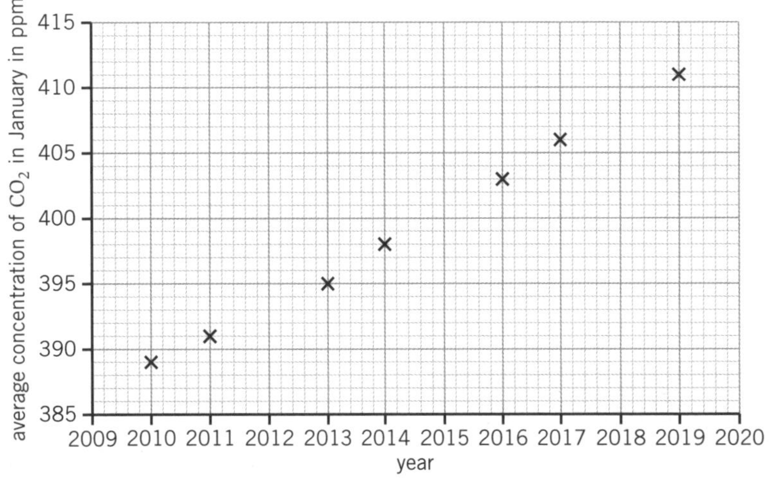

> **Exam Tip**
> Place a clear ruler over the points and see where most of them fit the line with an equal number on either side.

01.1 Complete **Figure 1** and draw a line of best fit. **[2 marks]**

01.2 Describe the trend shown by the graph. **[1 mark]**

____

____

> **Exam Tip**
> This is a one-mark question, so a simple description of the shape is all that is needed.

01.3 Describe how **two** human activities are responsible for the trend shown in **Figure 1**. **[4 marks]**

1 ______________________________

____

____

2 ______________________________

____

____

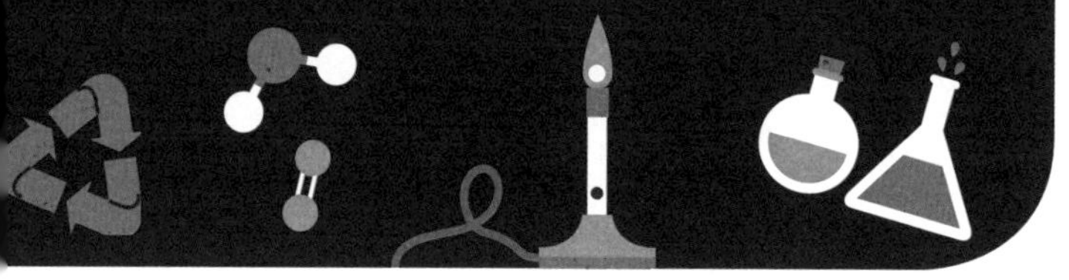

02 This question is about air pollutants.

02.1 Which pollutant is formed in car engines from the reaction between two gases that occur naturally in the atmosphere? **[1 mark]**

Tick **one** box.

carbon dioxide	☐	oxides of nitrogen	☐
carbon particles	☐	sulfur dioxide	☐

Exam Tip

Think about which gases are found at the highest levels in the atmosphere.

02.2 Carbon monoxide is also produced in car engines.

Name the process that produces carbon monoxide. **[1 mark]**

____

02.3 Balance the symbol equation for the incomplete combustion of a fuel. **[1 mark]**

$$\_\_\_\ C_4H_{10}(g) + \_\_\_\ O_2(g) \rightarrow \_\_\_\ CO(g) + \_\_\_\ H_2O(l)$$

Exam Tip

Start with the carbons, then the hydrogens and leave the oxygens until last.

02.4 Draw **one** line from each pollutant to an effect of the pollutant. **[3 marks]**

Pollutant	Effect
	poisoning of humans
oxides of nitrogen	
	global dimming
carbon monoxide	
	global climate change
particulates	
	breathing problems

02.5 Which gas causes acid rain? **[1 mark]**

Tick **one** box.

carbon dioxide	☐	sulfur dioxide	☐
carbon monoxide	☐	unburnt hydrocarbons	☐

03 An international organisation suggests three ways in which to reduce the rate of global climate change.
Evaluate each suggestion (**03.1**, **03.2**, and **03.3**) in terms of how effective it would be in reducing global climate change, and what socioeconomic effects it could have.

03.1 All governments invest in alternatives to fossil fuels. **[4 marks]**

03.2 Stop South American countries from cutting down the rainforest for farmland. **[3 marks]**

03.3 Tax cars to encourage use of other modes of transport. **[4 marks]**

04 **Figure 2** shows the gases that make up the atmosphere of the planet Mars.

Figure 2

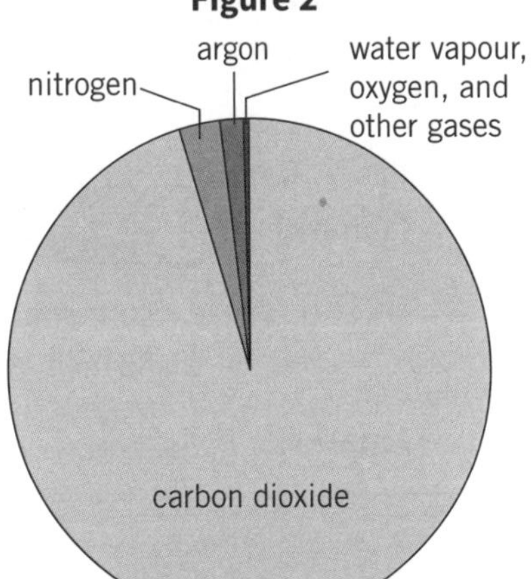

04.1 Compare the composition of the atmosphere of Mars to the composition of the atmosphere of the Earth. **[6 marks]**

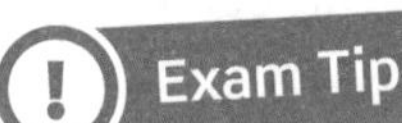

Compare means you need to give similarities *and* differences between the two planets.

04.2 Methane gas is also present in the atmosphere of Mars. The concentration of methane was measured at 0.7 parts per billion in August 2013. In June 2019 it was measured again at 21.0 parts per billion.
How many times greater was the concentration of methane in June 2019 compared to August 2013? **[1 mark]**

04.3 Suggest why scientists cannot be certain about the reasons for the changes in methane concentration in the atmosphere of Mars. **[1 mark]**

04.4 The average surface temperature of Mars is around −60 °C. The atmosphere of Mars is about 100 times less dense than the atmosphere of Earth.
Explain why the surface temperature of Mars is significantly lower than on Earth. **[4 marks]**

04.5 During the Martian winter, carbon dioxide in the atmosphere condenses to form polar ice caps made from carbon dioxide. During the summer, this carbon dioxide transforms back into a gas and returns to the atmosphere.
Name the process by which carbon dioxide changes state from a solid to a gas. **[1 mark]**

05 The Earth's atmosphere contains oxygen gas.

05.1 Draw a dot and cross diagram to show the bonding in an oxygen molecule. **[2 marks]**

05.2 Explain why the percentage of oxygen in the atmosphere changed from about 2.7 billion years ago to the present.
Include a balanced symbol equation in your answer. **[6 marks]**

Exam Tip

Don't forget oxygen gas is a diatomic molecule with a double bond between the oxygen atoms.

05.3 Suggest how planting trees could help reduce the effects of global climate change. **[3 marks]**

05.4 Explain how acid rain can contribute to global climate change. **[2 marks]**

06 Carbon dioxide is a greenhouse gas.

06.1 What is meant by the term greenhouse gas? **[1 mark]**

06.2 Name **one** other greenhouse gas. **[1 mark]**

Exam Tip

06.4 is worth three marks, so three short effects are all that's needed, *not* long explanations of each effect.

06.3 Give **two** human activities that increase the amount of carbon dioxide in the atmosphere. **[2 marks]**

06.4 Increasing amounts of greenhouse gases result in an increase in average global temperature. This is a major cause of climate change. Give **three** effects of global climate change. **[3 marks]**

07 This question is about the carbon footprint of a journey by road. **Table 2** shows carbon dioxide emissions data for a car and a bus.

Table 2

Vehicle	Mass of CO_2 emitted by the vehicle in grams per kilometre
car	100
bus	1050

07.1 A car travels 120 km. Use data from **Table 2** to calculate the mass of CO_2 emitted by the car on this journey.
Give your answer in kg. **[2 marks]**

Exam Tip

Don't forget to convert from grams to kg.

07.2 Two people are travelling in the car during the 120 km journey. Calculate the mass of CO_2 emitted by the car per person for this journey. Give your answer in kg. **[1 mark]**

07.3 A bus travels on the same 120 km journey as the car.
Calculate the minimum number of people that must be on the bus in order for the mass of CO_2 emitted per person to be **less than** the mass emitted for two people travelling the same journey in the car. **[3 marks]**

07.4 Suggest why some people do not travel by bus instead of by car, even though CO_2 emissions can be smaller by bus. **[1 mark]**

08 **Figure 3** shows values for the global annual mean surface temperature change between 2000 and 2018.

Figure 3

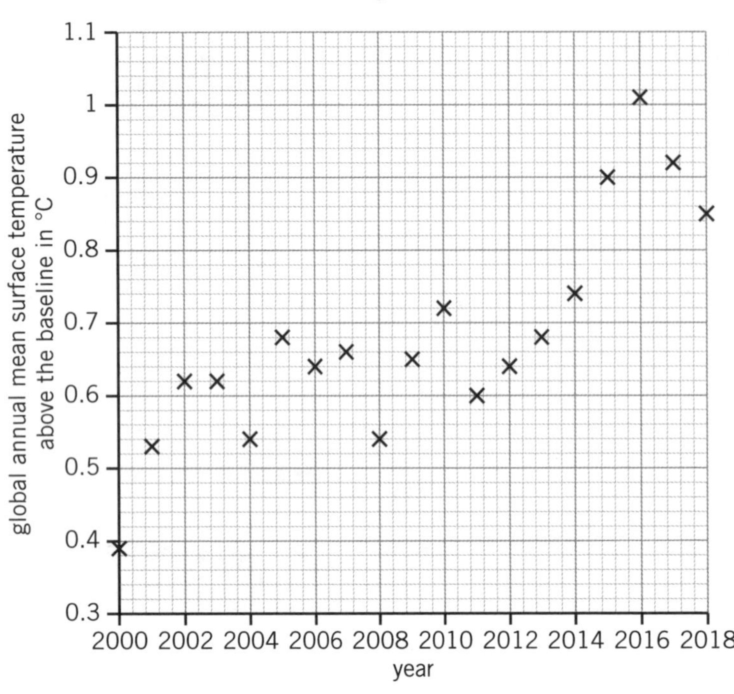

08.1 Give the temperature above the baseline in 2005. **[1 mark]**

08.2 Give the **four** years with the highest temperatures. **[1 mark]**

08.3 Give the year in which the global annual mean surface temperature above the baseline was 0.53 °C. **[1 mark]**

08.4 Describe the overall trend shown by **Figure 3**. **[1 mark]**

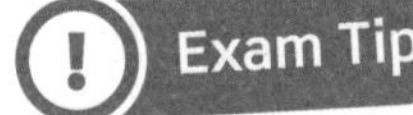

Draw a line of best fit to help you with the overall trend.

08.5 Explain how human activities have contributed to the trend shown in **Figure 3**. **[2 marks]**

08.6 A student says that **Figure 3** shows that global temperature is now decreasing. Evaluate this statement. **[3 marks]**

09 A healthy diet must include protein. **Table 3** gives the carbon footprint for the production of some foods that are high in protein.

Table 3

Food	Typical CO_2 emissions to produce 100 g of food in kg
beef	16
cheese	12
chicken	7
egg	5
nuts	1
beans and peas	1

09.1 Suggest why data for food carbon footprints is published. **[1 mark]**

09.2 People that follow a vegetarian diet do not eat meat.
Evaluate swapping from a meat-based diet to a vegetarian diet as a way of reducing an individual's carbon footprint. **[3 marks]**

09.3 Use data from **Table 3** to calculate the total mass of CO_2 emissions when 50 g of beef and 25 g of cheese are produced. **[2 marks]**

09.4 Beef and cheese are produced from cattle.
Suggest why **Table 3** is not an accurate representation of the carbon footprint of these foods. **[1 mark]**

10 The composition of the Earth's atmosphere has changed since the Earth formed about 4.6 billion years ago.

10.1 Why is there little evidence about the early atmosphere? **[1 mark]**

10.2 Explain how the percentages of carbon dioxide and oxygen in the atmosphere have changed over the past 4.6 billion years. **[6 marks]**

> **Exam Tip**
>
> Split your answer to **10.2** into two paragraphs: one about carbon dioxide and the other about oxygen.

10.3 Name **two** greenhouse gases that are added into the atmosphere as a result of human activity. **[2 marks]**

10.4 Give **one** effect of human activity increasing the greenhouse gases in the atmosphere. **[1 mark]**

11 Carbon dioxide, methane, and water vapour all act as greenhouse gases in the atmosphere.

11.1 Explain how greenhouse gases maintain the temperature of the Earth. **[4 marks]**

11.2 The combustion of fossil fuels produces carbon dioxide.
Describe **one** other way in which burning fossil fuels can contribute to an increase in the percentage of carbon dioxide in the atmosphere. **[3 marks]**

> **Exam Tip**
>
> Don't just repeat the example given in the question.

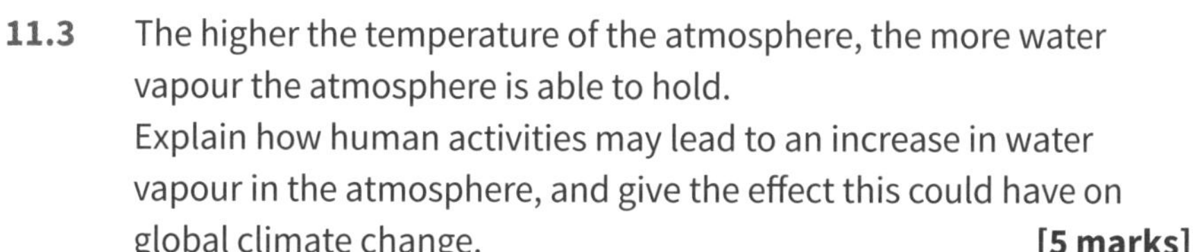

11.3 The higher the temperature of the atmosphere, the more water vapour the atmosphere is able to hold.
Explain how human activities may lead to an increase in water vapour in the atmosphere, and give the effect this could have on global climate change. **[5 marks]**

12 This question is about the elements in Groups 7 and 0 of the Periodic Table.

12.1 Give the electron configurations of fluorine and neon. Use the Periodic Table to help you to answer this question. **[2 marks]**

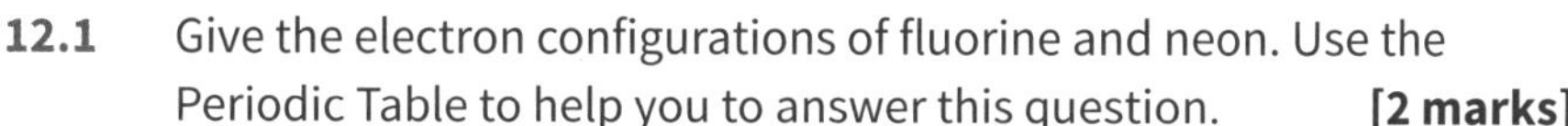

12.2 Explain why the Group 7 elements are very reactive but the Group 0 elements are unreactive. **[2 marks]**

12.3 Describe the pattern in the boiling points of the Group 7 and Group 0 elements. **[1 mark]**

Knowledge

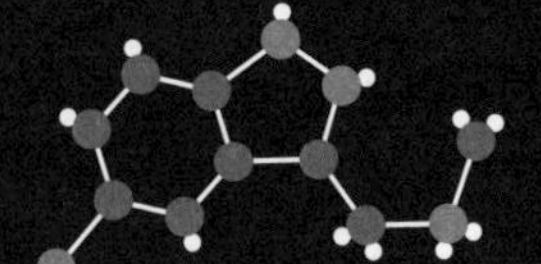

C15 Using the Earth's resources A

Natural and synthetic resources

We use the Earth's resources to provide us with warmth, fuel, shelter, food, and transport.

- Natural resources are used for food, timber, clothing, and fuels.
- Synthetic resources are made by scientists. They can replace or supplement natural resources.

When choosing and synthesising resources, it is important to consider **sustainable development**. This is development that meets the needs of current generations without compromising the ability of future generations to meet their own needs.

Finite and renewable resources

Some resources are **finite**. This means that they will eventually run out.

Fossil fuels are an example of a finite resource. They take so long to form that we use them faster than they are naturally formed.

Resources that will not run out are called **renewable** resources.

Wood is an example of a renewable resource. Trees can be grown to replace any that are cut down for wood.

Potable water

Water is a vital resource for life. **Potable** water is water that is safe to drink. However, most water on Earth is not potable.

Type of water	What it has in it
pure water	just water molecules and nothing else
potable water	water molecules, low levels of salts, safe levels of harmful microbes
salty water (sea water)	water molecules, dangerously high levels of salts, can have high levels of harmful microbes
fresh water (from rivers, lakes, or underground)	water molecules, low levels of salts, often has harmful microbes at high levels

Fresh water

In the UK, potable water is produced from rain water that collects in lakes and rivers.

To produce potable water:

1. Choose an appropriate source of fresh water.
2. Pass the water through filters to remove large objects.
3. **Sterilise** the water to kill any microbes using ozone, chlorine, or UV light.

Salty water

Some countries do not have lots of fresh water available. **Desalination** is the process to turn saltwater into potable water. This requires a lot of energy and can be done by:

- distillation
- **reverse osmosis**

Reverse osmosis involves using membranes to separate the salts dissolved in the water. The water needs to be pressurised and the salty water corrodes the pumps. As such, it is an expensive process.

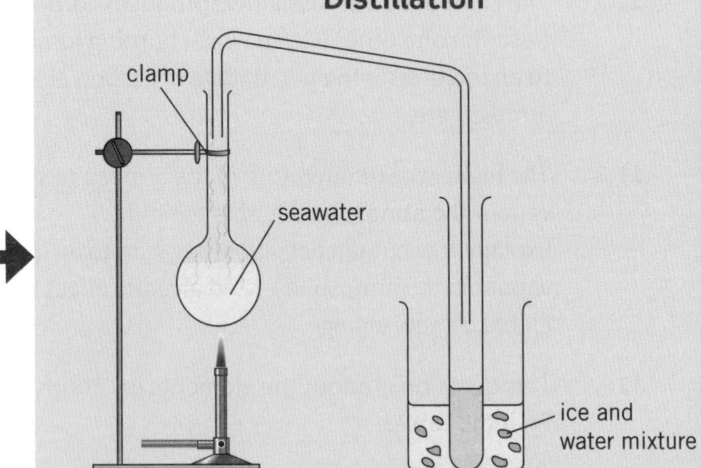

Key terms

Make sure you can write a definition for these key terms.

aerobic, anaerobic, distillation, effluent, finite resources, potable water, renewable resources, reverse osmosis, screening, sedimentation, sewage, sludge, sterilisation, sustainable development

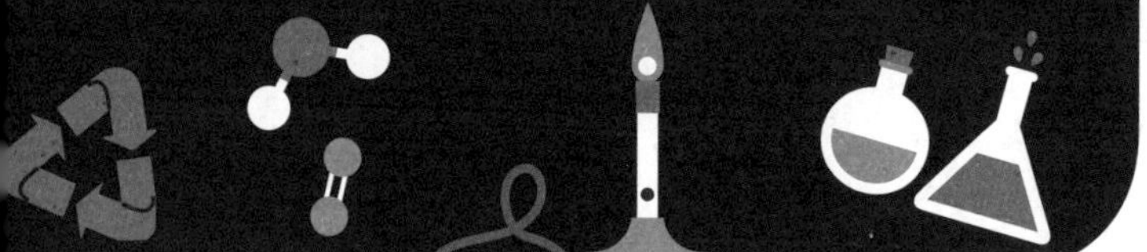

Waste water

Human activities produce lots of waste water as sewage, agricultural waste, and industrial waste.

- **Sewage** and agricultural waste contain organic matter and harmful microbes.
- Industrial waste contains organic matter and harmful chemicals.

These need to be removed before the water can be put back into the environment.

Treating sewage water

screening and grit removal

The sewage passes through a metal grid that filters out large objects.

sedimentation

The sewage is left so that solid sediments settle out of the water. The sediments sink to the bottom of the tank. The liquid sits above the sediment.

Treating sludge

sewage sludge

This sediment is called **sludge**. Sludge contains organic matter, water, dissolved compounds, and small solid particles.

anaerobic treatment

Bacteria are added to digest the organic matter. These bacteria break down the matter anaerobically – with a limited supply of oxygen.

biogas

The anaerobic digestion of sludge produces biogas. Biogas is a mixture of methane, carbon dioxide, and hydrogen sulfide. It can be used as fuel.

remaining sludge used as fuel

The remaining sludge can be dried out and can also be burnt as a fuel.

Treating effluent

effluent

The remaining liquid is called **effluent**. This effluent has no solid matter visible, but still contains some matter and harmful microorganisms.

aerobic treatment

Bacteria are added to the effluent. These bacteria feed on organic matter and the harmful microorganisms in the effluent. The bacteria break down the matter by aerobic respiration – oxygen needs to be present.

bacteria removed

The bacteria are allowed to settle out of the water.

discharged back to rivers

The water is now safe enough to be released back into the environment.

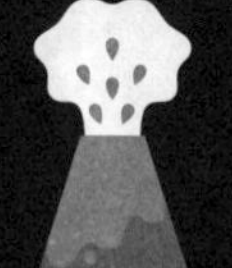
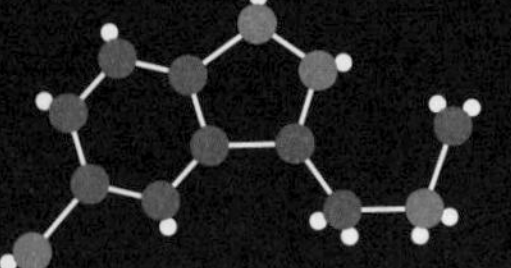

C15 Using the Earth's resources B

Metal extraction

Metals are used for many different things. Some metals can be extracted from their ores by reduction or electrolysis.

However, metal ores are a finite resource and these processes require lots of energy.

Scientists are looking for new ways to extract metals that are more sustainable.

Phytomining and **bioleaching** are two alternative processes used to extract copper from low grade ores (ores with only a little copper in them).

Phytomining

1. Grow plants near the metal ore.
2. Harvest and burn the plants.
3. The ash contains the metal compound.
4. Process the ash by electrolysis or displacement with scrap metal.

Bioleaching

1. Grow bacteria near the metal ore.
2. Bacteria produce leachate solutions that contain the metal compound.
3. Process the leachate by electrolysis or displacement with scrap metal.

Both of these methods avoid the digging, moving, and disposing of large amounts of rock associated with traditional mining techniques.

Life cycle assessment

A **life cycle assessment (LCA)** is a way of looking at the whole life of a product and assessing its impact on the environment and sustainability. It is broken down into four categories:

- extracting and processing raw materials
- manufacturing and packaging
- use and operation during its lifetime
- disposal at the end of its useful life, including transport and distribution at each stage.

Some parts of an LCA are objective, such as the amount of water used or waste produced in the production of a product. However, other parts of an LCA require judgements, such as the polluting effect, and so LCAs are not a completely objective process.

Revision tips

Practice Life cycle assessments can be long with a lot of data. If you are asked to compare two materials then most of the information you'll need will be in the question – carefully go over the text and pick out the information you need before you start.

Practice You might be asked to write a life cycle assessment for a common object. Remember to cover each part in the question and clearly show section by using mini headings for each separate paragraph.

Key terms

Make sure you can write a definition for these key terms.

biodegrade | bioleaching | life cycle assessment | phytomining | recycling

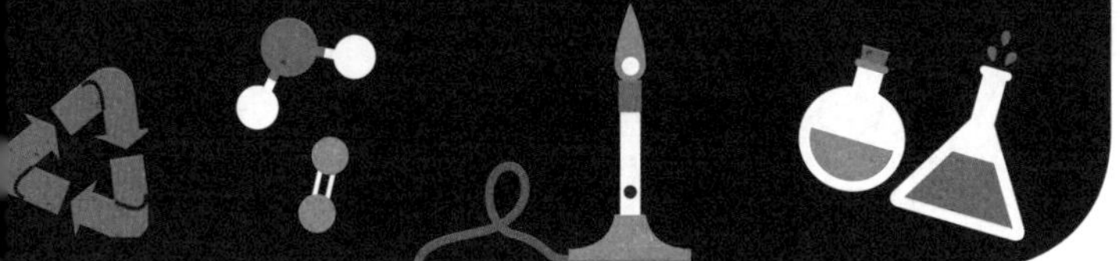

Disposal of products

When someone finishes with a product, it can be

- added to a landfill
  This can cause habitat loss and other problems in the local ecosystem. Some items persist in landfills as they do not **biodegrade** and could be there for hundreds of years.
- incinerated
  Some products can be incinerated to produce useful energy. However, the combustion can often be incomplete and result in harmful pollutants being released to the atmosphere.
- reused
  This is when an item is used again for a similar purpose.
- **recycled**
  Recycling requires energy, but conserves the limited resources and often requires less energy than needed to make brand new materials.

The table shows information about the extraction, processing, and disposal of some common materials. The are made from limited resources. This information is used when making a LCA.

Material	Extraction/processing	Disposal
metal	• quarrying and mining cause habitat loss • machinery involved in mining releases greenhouse gases • extraction from metal ores requires lots of energy	• metals can normally be recycled by melting them down and then casting them into new shapes • metals in landfill can persist for a long time
plastic	• normally come from fossil fuels that are non-renewable	• many plastic products can be reused and recycled • plastics often end up in landfills where they persist as they are not biodegradable • incinerating plastics releases lots of harmful pollutants like carbon monoxide and particulates
paper	• produced from trees that require land and lots of water to grow • lots of water also used in the production process	• many paper products can be recycled • paper products can also be incinerated or they can decay naturally in a landfill • incineration and decay release greenhouse gases
glass	• produced from sand, which is a finite resource • sand is heated, which requires a lot of energy	• many glass products can be reused, or crushed and recycled • if glass is added to landfills it persists as it is not biodegradable
ceramics	• made from clay and rocks, which are finite resources • generally obtained by quarrying, which requires energy, releases pollutants from heavy machinery, and causes habitat loss	• most ceramics are not commonly recycled in the UK, and once broken cannot be reused • ceramics tend to persist in landfills

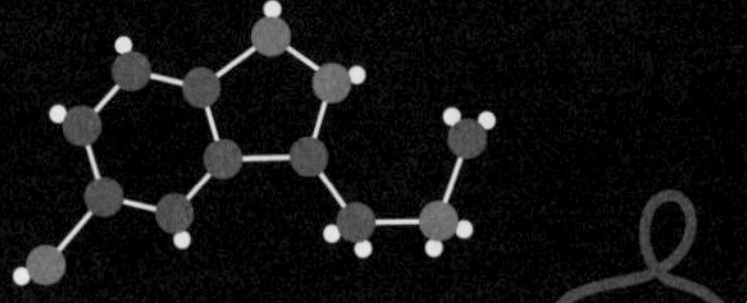

Retrieval

Learn the answers to the questions below, then cover the answers column with a piece of paper and write down as many as you can. Check and repeat.

	C15 questions	Answers
1	What do we use the Earth's resources for?	warmth, shelter, food, fuel, transport
2	What are some examples of natural resources?	cotton, wool, timber
3	What are some examples of synthetic resources?	plastic, polyester, acrylic
4	What is a finite resource?	a resource that will eventually run out
5	What is sustainable development?	development that meets the needs of current generations without compromising the ability of future generations to meet their own needs
6	What are the four main types of water?	pure water, salt water, fresh water, potable water
7	What is potable water?	water that is safe to drink
8	In the UK, how is potable water extracted from fresh water?	filtration and sterilisation
9	What is sterilisation?	killing microbes
10	What are three examples of sterilising agents?	chlorine gas, UV light, and ozone
11	How can potable water be produced from salt water?	desalination
12	How can desalination be carried out?	distillation or reverse osmosis
13	What are the three main types of waste water?	sewage, agricultural waste, industrial waste
14	What can waste water contain?	organic matter, harmful microbes, harmful chemicals
15	What is the first step in processing waste water?	screening and grit removal
16	What is sedimentation?	separating the waste water into sludge and effluent
17	How is sludge treated?	anaerobic respiration
18	How is effluent treated?	aerobic respiration
19	What is phytomining?	using plants to extract copper
20	What is bioleaching?	using bacteria to extract copper
21	What is a life cycle assessment?	a way of assessing the energy costs and environmental effect of a product across its lifetime
22	What are the four stages of a life cycle assessment?	• extracting and processing raw materials • manufacturing and packaging • use and operation during its lifetime • disposal at the end of its useful life
23	How can we reduce the amount of new materials manufactured?	by reducing, reusing, or recycling products
24	In what ways can materials that are not recycled be disposed?	landfill or incineration

Put paper here

Now go back and use the questions below to check your knowledge from previous chapters.

Previous questions / Answers

	Previous questions	Answers
1	What is the atmosphere?	a layer of gas surrounding the Earth
2	How did the amount of carbon dioxide in the atmosphere decrease to today's levels?	dissolved in the oceans, photosynthesis, converted to fossil fuels, precipitated as insoluble metal carbonates
3	How has the amount of nitrogen in the atmosphere changed over time?	increased slowly as it is a very stable molecule
4	What is a greenhouse gas?	a gas that traps radiation from the Sun
5	What is global warming?	an increase in the overall global average temperature
6	What is a carbon footprint?	the amount of carbon a product, process, or organism releases into the atmosphere over its lifetime
7	What are some examples of formulations?	fuels, cleaning agents, paints, medicines, alloys, fertilisers, and foods
8	What is chromatography?	a process for separating coloured mixtures
9	What is the test for carbon dioxide?	turns limewater milky if bubbled through it

Put paper here

Put paper here

Put paper here

Required Practical Skills

Practise answering questions on the required practicals using the example below. You need to be able to apply your skills and knowledge to other practicals too.

Water purification

You need to be able to describe how to analyse the purity of a water sample, and how to use distillation to purify the sample.

To do this, you need to know how to test pH, and describe the method of distillation for any solution. In an exam, you may also be asked about the purity and purification of different samples other than water.

You should also learn the different terms describing how water is made safe to drink.

Worked example

A student wanted to determine the identity of a salt dissolved in a sample of water. They evaporated away 100 cm^3 of the 1 M solution. The empty evaporating basin weighed 92.78 g and the basin containing the solids after evaporation weighed 98.63 g. Suggest how you could determine the identity of the salt.

mass of solid salt = 98.63 − 92.78 = 5.85 g

5.85 g of salt in 100 cm3 = 58.5 g in 1 dm^3

$$M_r = \frac{\text{mass}}{\text{moles}}$$

$$M_r = \frac{58.5}{1} = 58.5$$

The salt has an M_r of 58.5, so use the relative atomic masses on the Periodic Table to determine a potential identity: 23 (Na) + 35.5 (Cl) = 58.5, so the salt could be NaCl.

This could be confirmed using a flame test and a halide test.

Practice

1 Explain how you could use pH to determine if a sample of water is pure.

2 After carrying out a distillation experiment, a student re-distilled the distillate. Suggest what the student would have observed.

3 Describe the difference between pure and potable water.

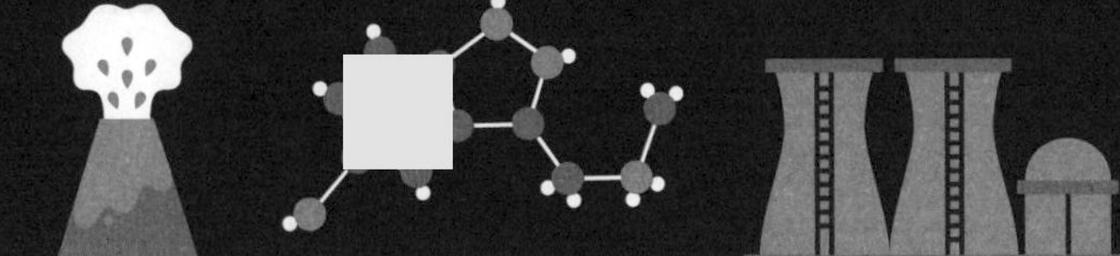

Practice

Exam-style questions

01 This question is about water treatment.

01.1 What is potable water? **[1 mark]**

Tick **one** box.

water that has nothing mixed with it	☐
water that is pure	☐
water that salt has been removed from	☐
water that is safe to drink	☐

> **Exam Tip**
>
> Each part of **01** tells you how many answers, ticks, or lines are required in bold. This is an important instruction. If you put too many ticks on then you won't get marks even if you've given the correct answers.

01.2 Draw **one** line from each water treatment process to the reason for the process. **[2 marks]**

Water treatment process	Reason for process
passing water through filter beds	kill microorganisms
sterilising	remove dissolved salts
desalination	remove pieces of solid

01.3 Name **two** sterilising agents that are used to make water safe to drink. **[2 marks]**

1 ______________________________

2 ______________________________

01.4 Give **one** advantage and **one** disadvantage of obtaining drinking water by desalination. **[2 marks]**

Advantage: ______________________________

____

Disadvantage: ______________________________

____

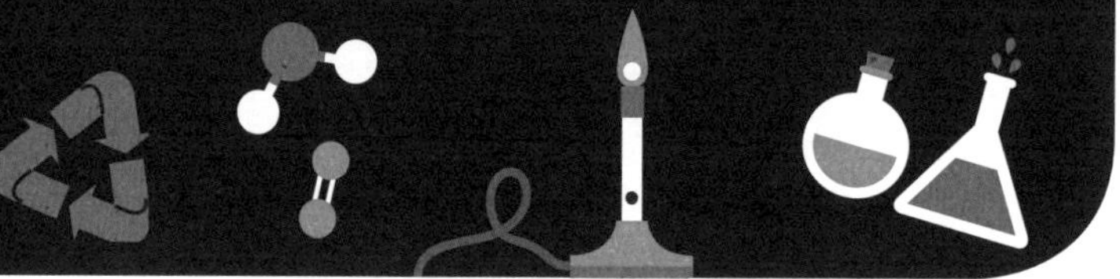

02 A student has an empty glass jar.

02.1 Which is an example of recycling? **[1 mark]**

Tick **one** box.

washing the jar and using it to store hairclips ☐

crushing and melting the jar to make a bottle ☐

putting the jar in landfill ☐

making an identical jar from raw materials ☐

02.2 **Table 1** lists the raw materials that are used to make glass.

Table 1

Raw material	Chemical formula
silicon dioxide	
calcium carbonate	
	Na_2CO_3

Complete **Table 1**. **[3 marks]**

Exam Tip

It is important that you have learnt the key ions from the specification. You can use the charge on the ions to work out the chemical formulae of ionic compounds. This is a skill that will come up throughout the chemistry course.

02.3 Outline **three** advantages of making glass objects from recycled glass, rather than from glass that has been newly made from its raw materials. **[3 marks]**

1 ______________________________

____

2 ______________________________

____

3 ______________________________

____

03 Some students are investigating water from different sources. They want to compare the mass of dissolved solids in three samples of water. They use the following method:

1. Find the mass of an empty evaporating basin.
2. Use a measuring cylinder to measure 10.0 cm^3 of one of the water samples into the evaporating basin.
3. Heat the evaporating basin and its contents until all the water has evaporated.
4. Find the mass of the evaporating basin again.

03.1 Suggest an improvement to step **2**.
Give a reason for this improvement. **[2 marks]**

03.2 Suggest an improvement to step **3**.
Give a reason for this improvement. **[2 marks]**

03.3 Give **two** safety precautions that the students should take. **[2 marks]**

> **! Exam Tip**
>
> Think about accuracy and safety.

03.4 **Table 2** shows the students' results. The mass of the empty evaporating basin was 95.24 g.

Table 2

Water sample	Mass of solid and evaporating basin after heating in grams
A	95.24
B	95.26
C	95.61

Identify the water sample that is pure water. **[1 mark]**

03.5 Identify the water sample that is most likely to be seawater. Give a reason for your decision. **[2 marks]**

04 A student is using distillation to purify a sample of seawater. **Figure 1** shows the apparatus the student used.

Figure 1

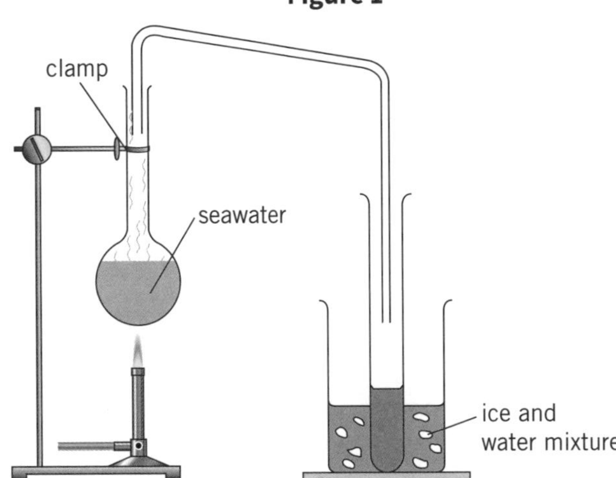

04.1 Give a reason for using a Bunsen burner, instead of a water bath, to heat the seawater. **[1 mark]**

04.2 Suggest a reason for using an ice–water mixture, not lumps of ice alone. **[1 mark]**

04.3 Identify the mistake the student has made in setting up the apparatus. **[1 mark]**

04.4 The student corrects the mistake, and starts the experiment again. Explain how the concentration of salt in the seawater changes as pure water is collected in the test tube. **[2 marks]**

05 Copper exists naturally on the Earth chemically bonded to non-metals. The pure metal can be extracted from these compounds.

05.1 Describe how copper is obtained from low-grade copper ore by phytomining. **[4 marks]**

05.2 Evaluate the advantages and disadvantages of obtaining copper by recycling scrap copper and bioleaching. **[6 marks]**

05.3 An ore of copper contains 22.1% copper. Calculate the mass of waste produced when 50.0 kg of copper is extracted from the ore. **[4 marks]**

Exam Tip

For this evaluate question you need to have six parts:

- the advantages of obtaining copper by recycling scrap copper
- the advantages of obtaining copper by bioleaching
- the disadvantages of obtaining copper by recycling scrap copper
- the disadvantages of obtaining copper by bioleaching
- your opinion on what is best
- a reason why you have that opinion.

06 Disposable water bottles are made from different materials. **Table 3** shows information on the life cycle assessments (LCAs) of two types of disposable water bottle. All quantities given are for the production of 12 bottles.

Table 3

Bottle material	PLA bottles	PET (plastic) bottles
Raw material	starch from plants	oil
Relative soil pollution	52.4	31.0
Land required in m^2	0.234	0.0565
Global warming in kg of CO_2 equivalent	3.58	3.87
Energy used in production in megajoules	62.1	69.4
Is the material biodegradable?	yes, but the process is slow and can only occur if the conditions are correct	no
Is the material recyclable?	no	yes

06.1 Evaluate the use of PLA compared with PET to make disposable water bottles. **[6 marks]**

06.2 Calculate the area of land required to make **one** PET bottle. Give your answer in standard form to three significant figures. **[3 marks]**

06.3 Disposable water bottles can also be made from recycled PET. Predict how the energy used in production compares for recycled PET bottles and ordinary PET bottles.
Suggest a reason for your prediction. **[2 marks]**

Exam Tip

An important part of life cycle assessments is being able to analyse them – use data from **Table 3** to compare PLA bottles and PET bottles.

07 The steps below describe the life cycle of a cotton T-shirt.

1. plant, grow, and harvest cotton plants
2. make cotton thread and fabric
3. sew T-shirt
4. put into plastic bags
5. transport to buyer
6. buyer wears T-shirt regularly
7. one year later, buyer puts T-shirt in dustbin, which is taken to landfill

Exam Tip

Be specific – this question is about a cotton T-shirt so refer to it in your answer and do not refer to other items of clothing.

07.1 Identify the **three** steps that are part of the manufacturing and packaging stage of the life cycle of the T-shirt. **[1 mark]**

07.2 Life cycle assessments assess the impact of products in four stages. Give the four stages of a life cycle assessment.
Identify **one** step in the lifetime of a cotton T-shirt for each stage in the life cycle assessment. **[4 marks]**

07.3 There are carbon dioxide emissions associated with the T-shirt when it is being used. Suggest why. **[1 mark]**

07.4 Suggest **one** action the buyer could take to reduce the environmental impact of the T-shirt at the disposal stage. **[1 mark]**

08 This question is about sewage treatment.

Exam Tip

This is a four-mark question asking for four steps so you don't need to go into too much detail about each part.

08.1 Name **two** types of substance that must be removed from household sewage and agricultural waste water, before the water is released back into the environment. **[2 marks]**

08.2 Give the **four** steps in the treatment of sewage. **[4 marks]**

08.3 Suggest why it is easier to obtain potable water from ground water than from sewage. **[1 mark]**

09 The metal tantalum is vital for making devices such as mobile phones. **Figure 2** shows the amounts of tantalum produced by different countries in one year.

Figure 2

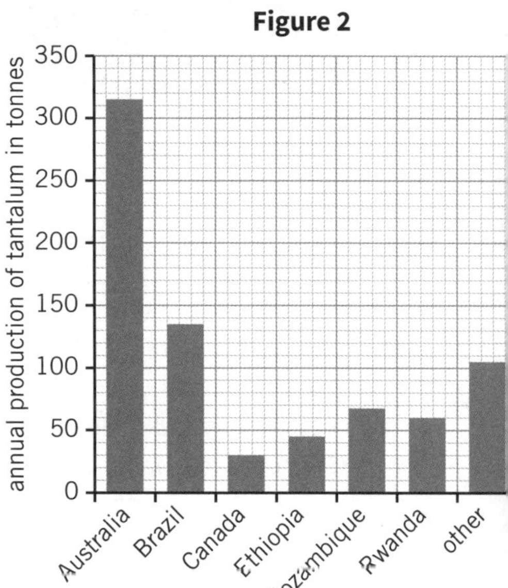

09.1 Calculate the total mass of tantalum produced. **[1 mark]**

09.2 Calculate the percentage of tantalum produced in Ethiopia. **[2 marks]**

09.3 A tantalum ore contains 72% Ta_2O_5.
Calculate the mass of tantalum in 80 kg of this ore.
Relative atomic masses A_r: Ta = 181, O = 16 **[3 marks]**

09.4 The reserves of tantalum are the ore deposits that have been discovered but not yet mined. Worldwide known reserves of tantalum are approximately 1.5×10^5 tonnes.
Estimate the year when known reserves of tantalum will run out, assuming annual production continues at the same rate as in **Figure 2**. **[2 marks]**

09.5 Suggest **two** reasons why tantalum might still be produced after the year given in **09.4**. **[2 marks]**

10 Garden chairs can be made from wood or plastic. Plastic is made from crude oil. Wood is obtained from trees. A student says that wooden chairs are better for sustainable development than plastic chairs.

Only write down arguments that *support* what the student says. Anything negative won't get you marks.

10.1 Define the term sustainable development. **[1 mark]**

10.2 Write down **two** arguments that support what the student says. **[2 marks]**

10.3 Suggest **one** way in which plastic chairs are better than wooden chairs for sustainable development. **[1 mark]**

11 **Table 4** shows the boiling points of a series of hydrocarbons.

You are told that all of the hydrocarbons are from *one* homologous series. Therefore, you only need to look at the first formula to identify the series.

Table 4

Formula of hydrocarbon	Boiling point in °C
CH_4	−162
C_2H_6	−89
C_3H_8	−42
C_4H_{10}	−1
C_5H_{12}	36
C_6H_{14}	69
C_7H_{16}	98
C_8H_{18}	126

11.1 Identify the homologous series that the hydrocarbons in **Table 4** belong to. **[1 mark]**

11.2 Give the formula of the hydrocarbon in this homologous series with 9 carbon atoms. **[1 mark]**

11.3 Name the hydrocarbon with the chemical formula C_4H_{10}. **[1 mark]**

11.4 A student mixed some C_4H_{10} with bromine water. Give the student's observation. **[1 mark]**

11.5 The student carries out complete combustion with C_4H_{10}. Write the balanced symbol equation with state symbols for the reaction. **[3 marks]**

11.6 Another student carries out catalytic cracking on C_8H_{18}. Give the **two** conditions needed for catalytic cracking. **[2 marks]**

11.7 Draw a dot and cross diagram for the hydrocarbon CH_4. **[2 marks]**

11.8 CH_4 is a greenhouse gas. Explain how CH_4 in the atmosphere maintains the temperature on the Earth. **[4 marks]**

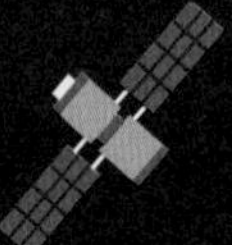

Knowledge

P1 Energy stores and transfers

Systems

A **system** is an object or group of objects.

Whenever anything changes in a system, energy is transferred between its stores or to the surroundings.

A **closed system** is one where no energy can escape to, or enter from, the surroundings. The total energy in a closed system never changes.

Energy stores

kinetic	energy an object has because it is moving
gravitational potential	energy an object has because of its height above the ground
elastic potential	energy an elastic object has when it is stretched or compressed
thermal (or internal)	energy an object has because of its temperature (the total kinetic and potential energy of the particles in the object)
chemical	energy that can be transferred by chemical reactions involving foods, fuels, and the chemicals in batteries
nuclear	energy stored in the nucleus of an atom
magnetic	energy a magnetic object has when it is near a magnet or in a magnetic field
electrostatic	energy a charged object has when it is near another charged object

Energy transfers

Energy can be transferred to and from different stores by:

Heating

Energy is transferred from one object to another object with a lower temperature.

Waves

Waves (e.g., light and sound waves) can transfer energy by radiation.

Electricity

When an electric current flows it can transfer energy.

Forces (mechanical work)

Energy is transferred when a force moves or changes the shape of an object.

Insulating buildings

Heating bills can be expensive so it is important to reduce the rate of heat loss from buildings.

Some factors that affect the rate of heat loss from a building include:

1. the thickness of its walls and roof
2. the thermal conductivity of its walls and roof.

lower thermal conductivity = lower rate of heat loss

The thermal conductivity of the walls and roof can be reduced by using thermal **insulators**.

A thermal insulator is a material which has a low thermal conductivity. The rate of energy transfer through an insulator is low.

The energy transfer per second through a material depends on:

1. the material's thermal conductivity
2. the temperature difference between the two sides of the material
3. the thickness of the material.

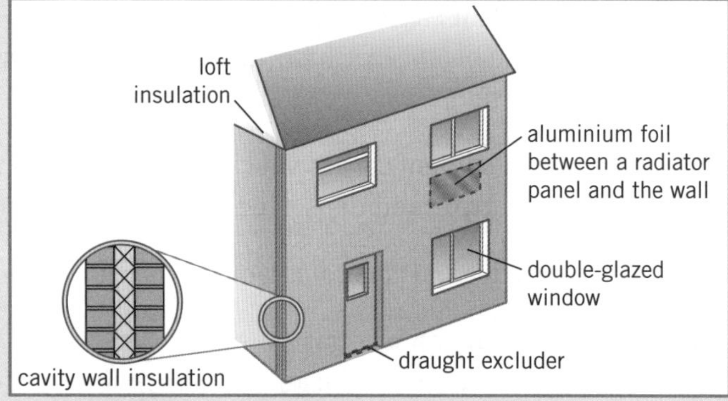

Energy equations

An object's gravitational potential energy store depends on its height above the ground, the gravitational field strength, and its mass.

gravitational potential energy (J) = mass (kg) × gravitational field strength (N/kg) × height (m)

$$E_p = mgh$$

An object's kinetic energy store depends on its mass and speed.

kinetic energy (J) = 0.5 × mass (kg) × (speed)^2 (m/s)

$$E_k = \frac{1}{2}mv^2$$

Power is how much work is done (or how much energy is transferred) per second. **Work done** means the same thing as energy transferred. The unit of power is the watt (W).

1 watt = 1 joule of energy transferred per second

$$\text{power (W)} = \frac{\text{energy transferred (J)}}{\text{time (s)}}$$

$$P = \frac{E}{t}$$

or

$$\text{power (W)} = \frac{\text{work done (J)}}{\text{time (s)}}$$

$$P = \frac{W}{t}$$

The elastic potential energy store of a stretched spring can be calculated using:

elastic potential energy (J) = 0.5 × spring constant (N/m) × (extension)^2 (m)

$E_e = \frac{1}{2}ke^2$ (assuming the limit of proportionality has not been exceeded)

This equation will be given to you on the equation sheet, but you need to be able to select and apply it to the correct questions.

Useful and dissipated energy

Energy cannot be created or destroyed – it can only be transferred usefully, stored, or **dissipated**.

Dissipated energy is often described as being wasted.

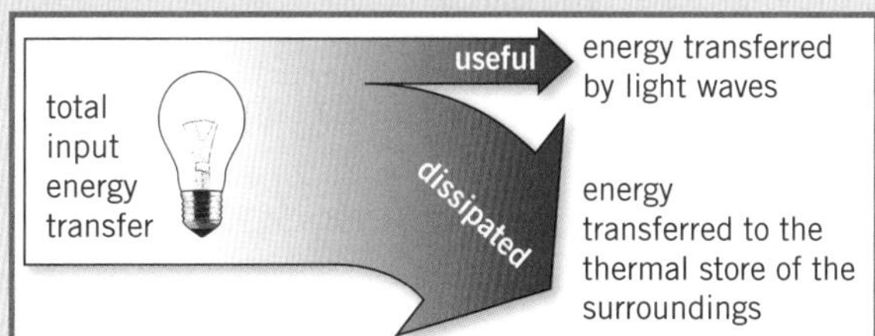

Energy is never entirely transferred usefully – some energy is always dissipated, meaning it is transferred to less useful stores.

All energy eventually ends up transferred to the thermal energy store of the surroundings.

In machines, work done against the force of friction usually causes energy to be wasted because energy is transferred to the thermal store of the machine and the surroundings.

Lubrication is a way of reducing unwanted energy transfer due to friction.

Streamlining is a way of reducing energy wasted due to air resistance or drag in water.

Use of thermal insulation is a way of reducing energy wasted due to heat dissipated to the surroundings.

Efficiency is a measure of how much energy is transferred usefully. You must know the equation to calculate efficiency as a *decimal*:

$$\text{efficiency} = \frac{\text{useful output energy transfer (J)}}{\text{total input energy transfer (J)}}$$

or

$$\text{efficiency} = \frac{\text{useful power output (W)}}{\text{total power input (W)}}$$

To give efficiency as a *percentage*, just multiply the result from the above calculation by 100 and add the % sign to the answer.

Key terms Make sure you can write a definition for these key terms.

chemical, closed system, dissipated, efficiency, elastic potential, electrostatic, gravitational potential, insulator, kinetic, lubrication, magnetic, nuclear, power, streamlining, system, thermal, work done

Retrieval

Learn the answers to the questions below, then cover the answers column with a piece of paper and write as many as you can. Check and repeat.

	P1 questions	Answers
1	Name the eight energy stores.	kinetic, gravitational potential, elastic potential, thermal, chemical, nuclear, magnetic, electrostatic
2	Name the four ways in which energy can be transferred.	heating, waves, electric current, mechanically (by forces)
3	What is a system?	an object or group of objects
4	What is a closed system?	a system where no energy can be transferred to or from the surroundings – the total energy in the system stays the same
5	What is work done?	energy transferred when a force moves an object
6	What is the unit for energy?	joule (J)
7	What is one joule of work?	the work done when a force of 1 N causes an object to move 1 m in the direction of the force
8	Describe the energy transfer when a moving car slows down.	energy is transferred mechanically from the kinetic store of the car to the thermal store of its brakes – some energy is dissipated to the thermal store of the surroundings
9	Describe the energy transfer when an electric kettle is used to heat water.	the electric current in a kettle transfers energy to the heating element's thermal store – energy is then transferred by heating from the heating element's thermal store to the thermal store of the water
10	Describe the energy transfer when a ball is fired using an elastic band.	energy is transferred mechanically from the elastic store of the elastic band to the kinetic store of the band – some energy is dissipated to the thermal store of the surroundings
11	Describe the energy transfer when a falling apple hits the ground.	energy is transferred from the kinetic store of the apple and dissipated to the thermal store of the surroundings by sound waves
12	Name the unit that represents one joule transferred per second.	watt (W)
13	What does a material's thermal conductivity tell you?	how well it conducts heat
14	Which materials have low thermal conductivity?	thermal insulators
15	Give three factors that determine the rate of thermal energy transfer through a material.	thermal conductivity of material, temperature difference, thickness of material
16	What factors affect the rate of heat loss from a building?	thickness of walls and roof, thermal conductivity of walls and roof, the temperature difference between the two sides of wall/roof

Put paper here

Required Practical Skills

Practise answering questions on the required practicals using the example below.
You need to be able to apply your skills and knowledge to other practicals too.

Specific heat capacity

To determine changes in specific heat capacity you need to measure mass, temperature rise, and energy transferred (work done).

To do this, you might use an energy meter, or measure time, current, and potential difference (to calculate power).

In the experiment, you need to:

- insulate the block or beaker, use a heatproof mat, and a lid (for a liquid)
- allow the material to heat up before taking measurements (due to thermal inertia)
- add water to make a good thermal contact between the thermometer and a solid material.

Calculated values for specific heat capacity will usually differ from given values because of energy transferred to the surroundings.

Worked example

A student uses a 12 V, 4 A heater to heat a 1 kg metal block. They measure the temperature of the block every minute for 10 minutes.

1 Calculate the work done.

power = potential difference × current
= 12 × 4
= 48 W

work done = power × time
10 min = 600 s
= 48 × 600
= 28 800 J

2 The temperature rise of the block is 75 °C.

Calculate the specific heat capacity of the material.

$$\text{specific heat capacity} = \frac{\text{energy transferred}}{\text{mass} \times \text{temperature rise}}$$

$$= \frac{28\,800}{1 \times 75}$$

= 384 J/kg°C

Practice

A student produces a graph of work done against temperature rise of 0.2 kg of a liquid.

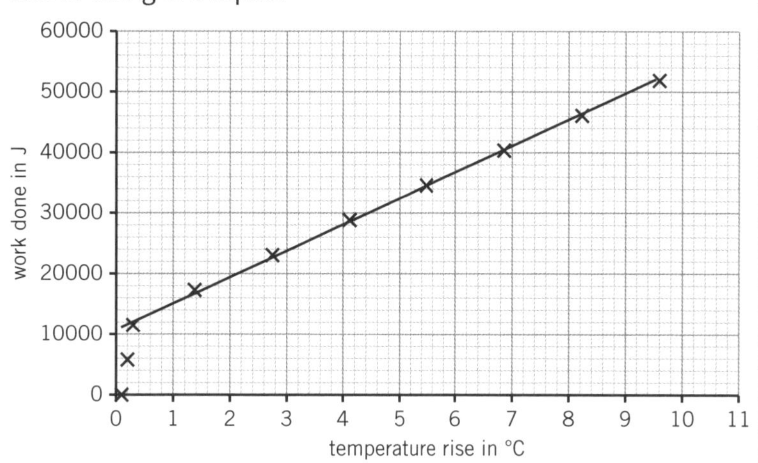

1 Explain why the graph does not go through (0,0).

2 Use the graph to calculate the specific heat capacity. Describe your method.

3 Suggest how you can tell from the graph that the material was well insulated.

Practice

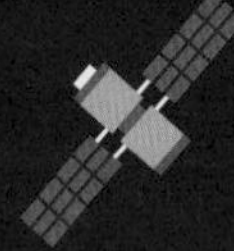

Exam-style questions

01 A student is playing with a slinky spring.

They hold one end and pull the other end of the spring.

01.1 There is energy in the elastic store of the spring.

Identify the energy store that had more energy in it before they pulled the spring, and where this energy has come from. **[2 marks]**

____

____

____

01.2 The spring has a spring constant of 20 N/m.

When the student pulls the spring it extends by 0.2 m.

Calculate the energy stored in the spring.

Use the correct equation from the *Physics Equations Sheet*. **[2 marks]**

> **Exam Tip**
> Always start your calculations by writing down the equation you're going to use.

Energy stored = ______________ J

02 This question is about conservation of energy.

02.1 Complete the statement of the law of conservation of energy. **[1 mark]**

Energy cannot ______________________________________

only transferred, stored, or dissipated.

02.2 When you consider energy changes, it is helpful to talk about the system that you are considering.

Define what a closed system is. **[1 mark]**

> **Exam Tip**
> Key definitions are really important to learn as they are easy marks in the exam.

____

____

02.3 A pendulum swings backwards and forwards. The pendulum gradually stops swinging.

Circle the correct bold word or words in this sentence.

A pendulum **is / is not** a closed system. **[1 mark]**

02.4 Explain why you have selected the word or words in this sentence. **[2 marks]**

____

____

____

03 A student investigates the energy transfers of a tennis ball when it is dropped onto the classroom floor.

She wants to calculate the energy transferred to the floor and surroundings when the ball first bounces.

03.1 Describe the measurements that she needs to make.

Suggest measuring instruments that she could use to do this. **[5 marks]**

> **Exam Tip**
>
> There are two parts to this question. For everything you want to measure you also have to say how you are going to measure it.

03.2 Suggest a problem that she may have with making the measurements and how it might be overcome. **[2 marks]**

03.3 Describe in detail how she can use the measurements to calculate the energy transferred to the floor/surroundings. **[5 marks]**

> **Exam Tip**
>
> The majority of the time problems in practicals can be overcome by using technology.

03.4 Suggest whether you can or cannot use the term efficiency when describing what happens when the ball bounces.

Justify your answer. **[2 marks]**

04 A gymnast runs and lands on a springboard.
Springs store energy when they are stretched or compressed. You can use the same equation to calculate energy in a stretched or compressed spring. You use compression instead of extension in your equation.

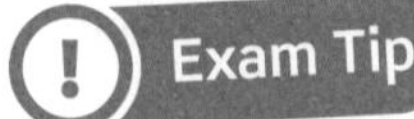

04.1 Write down the equation that links kinetic energy, mass, and speed. **[1 mark]**

Exam Tip

If you write down the symbol equation, ensure you write it down carefully and don't get the symbols mixed up with each other. It's ok to write the word equation down if you'll find it less confusing.

04.2 The gymnast is travelling at 10 m/s when they land on the springboard. The springboard contains a large spring that compresses when they land on it.
The mass of the gymnast is 40 kg.
Calculate the kinetic energy of the gymnast. **[2 marks]**

04.3 The spring constant of the spring is 20 000 N/m.
Assume that all of the energy in the kinetic energy store is transferred to the elastic potential energy store of the spring when the gymnast lands.
Calculate the compression of the spring. **[3 marks]**

Exam Tip

If you're confused, go back and read the hints given at the start of the question.

04.4 A manufacturer tests the spring in a springboard. They find that the spring does not compress by the distance predicted by the calculation.
Suggest whether the actual compression is bigger or smaller than the predicted compression. Explain your answer. **[3 marks]**

05 An Olympic archer can shoot an arrow at a target that is 80 m away. The archer draws back the string of a bow and releases it to shoot the arrow.

05.1 Describe the energy changes between the moment just before the archer releases the arrow and the moment when the arrow no longer has contact with the string.
Write down the method by which the energy is transferred. **[3 marks]**

05.2 The archer decides to calculate the energy stored in the string.
She makes the following estimates:

- the spring constant of the string is 10^5 N/kg
- the extension of the string is 5 cm.

Use the correct equation from the *Physics Equations Sheet* to calculate the energy stored in the string. **[2 marks]**

Exam Tip

Don't worry about the big numbers in this calculation. If you're not sure how to put 10^5 into your calculator then now is a great chance to practise.

05.3 The archer wants to find the speed of the arrow when it leaves the bow by direct measurement.
Suggest a technique for finding the speed of the arrow. **[1 mark]**

05.4 Suggest **one** reason why the speed of the arrow determined by this technique might be lower than the values from **05.2**. **[1 mark]**

05.5 The arrow hits the target and stops.
Give the name of the energy store that has gained energy as a result of this process. **[1 mark]**

06 The high-speed train in **Figure 1** travels at a top speed of 200 mph (90 m/s).

Figure 1

06.1 Suggest in terms of energy why the front of the train has the shape shown in **Figure 1**. **[1 mark]**

06.2 Write down the equation that links kinetic energy, mass, and speed. **[1 mark]**

06.3 Calculate the kinetic energy of the train when it is travelling at top speed. Write your answer in kJ. Give your answer to three significant figures. The mass of the train is 700 000 kg. **[4 marks]**

Exam Tip

Be careful with this equation, it's just the speed that is squared not the whole right-hand side.

06.4 Write down the work done by the brakes to bring the train to a complete stop. **[1 mark]**

07 An astronaut on the Moon is holding a hammer. He lets it go and it hits the ground.

Exam Tip

The energy at the start and the end will be different, be sure to use the correct terms to describe them.

07.1 Describe the energy changes from the moment when he drops the hammer to the moment before the hammer hits the ground. **[2 marks]**

07.2 Give the method of energy transfer that is producing the change. **[1 mark]**

07.3 Compare the speed of the hammer when it hits the ground on the Moon with the speed that it would hit the ground if it was on Earth.

- Assume the mass of the hammer is the same.
- The gravitational field strength of the Moon is less than that of Earth.
- The hammer is dropped from the same height.

Explain your answer. You do not need to do any calculations. **[5 marks]**

Exam Tip

The question has given you three bullet points to discuss – make sure you cover all of them in your answer.

08 A tall hotel building has a lift designed to carry guests and their luggage.

08.1 Write down the equation that links gravitational potential energy, mass, gravitational field strength, and height. **[1 mark]**

08.2 A family, the lift, and their luggage have a total mass of 1220 kg. Calculate the change in the gravitational potential energy store when the family moves up four floors. Each floor is 3.0 m high.
Gravitational field strength is 9.8 N/kg. **[2 marks]**

Exam Tip

Don't forget to calculate the total height first!

08.3 Write down the equation for efficiency. **[1 mark]**

08.4 The motor transfers a total energy of 280 kJ.
Calculate the efficiency of the lift motor as a percentage. **[3 marks]**

08.5 There is also a lift designed to carry trolleys of cleaning supplies and laundry. The power of this lift is 10 kW.
Suggest measurements that you could make to work out which lift motor is more efficient. Explain how you would use the measurements to calculate the efficiency. **[6 marks]**

Students often forget to convert the decimal to a percentage or forget the % sign after the answer – both of these are mistakes that will cost you marks.

08.6 Suggest why there would be uncertainty in your calculation of efficiency. **[1 mark]**

09 In a factory, a forklift truck does work lifting a box onto a shelf.

09.1 Write down the equation that links power, energy transferred, and time. **[1 mark]**

09.2 To lift the box onto the shelf, the motor of the forklift truck transfers 30 000 J of energy. The power of the truck motor is 15 000 W.
Show that it takes 2 seconds for the truck to lift the box onto the shelf. **[3 marks]**

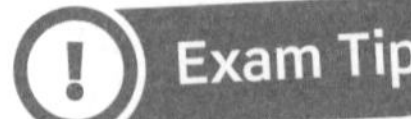

'Show' questions are amazing – you already know what the answer is, you just need to do the working. The great thing is if you don't get the right answer you can just try again!

09.3 A second truck lifts an identical box onto the same shelf.
The second truck takes longer to move the box onto the shelf.
Compare the power of the two trucks. **[1 mark]**

09.4 Write down the name of the store that has more energy in it after the truck has moved the box. **[1 mark]**

10 A teacher sets the students a challenge to check their understanding of energy. He puts a piece of track on the desk and raises one end. A marble rolls down the track and moves horizontally off the desk, as shown in **Figure 2**.

Figure 2

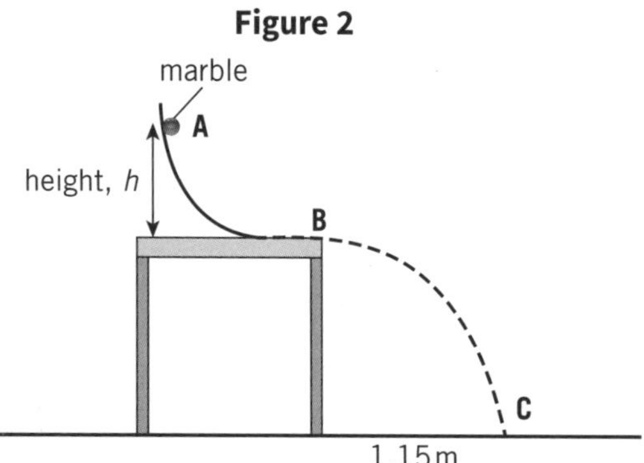

Try labelling the diagram at each point with the types of energy, it will help with later questions.

10.1 Describe the changes in energy between points **A** and **B**. **[2 marks]**

10.2 The ball is travelling at a horizontal speed of 1.3 m/s when it leaves the table.
Suggest the equipment that the students could use to measure the speed of the ball at the end of the track. **[1 mark]**

10.3 There is a target at point **C** on the floor that the students are aiming to hit. The horizontal distance of **C** from the edge of the table is 1.15 m. It takes 820 ms for the marble to move from **B** to **C**.
Calculate the distance travelled by the ball.
Write down **one** assumption that you made.
Write down whether or not it will hit the target. **[5 marks]**

There are three different parts to this question, make sure you include all of them in your answer.

10.4 Suggest how the students should adjust the equipment to make the ball hit the target.
Explain your answer in terms of energy. **[4 marks]**

11 A student researches the efficiency of different electric motors used in cars. In all system changes energy is wasted.

11.1 Describe what is meant by wasted energy. **[1 mark]**

11.2 The student knows that car **A** requires a total energy input of 20 J to move across the floor. It has a useful energy output of 12 J.
Write down the equation that links efficiency, total output energy, and total input energy. **[1 mark]**

11.3 Calculate the efficiency of car **A** as a decimal. **[2 marks]**

> **Exam Tip**
> This question has asked for the answer as a decimal, so don't multiply by 100 as that gives percentage efficiency.

11.4 The efficiency of car **B** is 50%.
Write down which car wastes more energy.
Explain your answer. **[2 marks]**

12 A student investigates how the height of a ramp affects the speed of a trolley. He puts the trolley at the top of a ramp. He releases the trolley and measures the speed of the trolley at the bottom of the ramp.

12.1 Explain why the student cannot use a ruler and stopclock to measure the speed at the bottom of the ramp.
Suggest the equipment that the student should use instead. **[2 marks]**

12.2 Write down the equation that links gravitational potential energy, mass, gravitational field strength, and height. **[1 mark]**

12.3 The student measures the height of the ramp. It is 0.12 m.
Gravitational field strength is 9.8 N/kg.
The mass of the trolley is 0.25 kg.
Calculate the gravitational potential energy of the trolley at the top of the ramp. **[2 marks]**

> **Exam Tip**
> You'll always be given the value for gravitational field strength, so you don't need to remember it.

12.4 The student measures the kinetic energy of the trolley at the bottom of the ramp. He discovers that the kinetic energy of the trolley is less than the gravitational potential energy.
He says: *'There is a mistake in the data. The answers should be the same.'*
Do you agree? Give reasons for your answer. **[2 marks]**

13 Houses have insulation to reduce unwanted energy transfers.

13.1 Describe how to reduce unwanted energy transfers through the roof of a house. **[1 mark]**

13.2 Older houses have one layer of bricks in their walls.
Newer houses usually have more than one layer of bricks.
Describe the link between the thickness of the layer of bricks and the rate of energy transfer through the bricks. **[1 mark]**

> **Exam Tip**
> There is generally a gap between the layers of brick and this has an effect on the way energy is transferred.

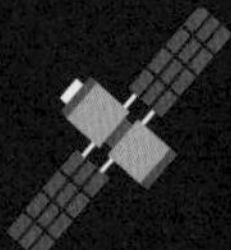

P2 National and global energy resources

Energy resources

The main ways in which we use the Earth's energy resources are:

- generating electricity
- heating
- transport.

Most of our energy currently comes from **fossil fuels** – coal, oil, and natural gas.

Reliability and environmental impact

Some energy resources are more reliable than others. **Reliable** energy resources are ones that are available all the time (or at predictable times) and in sufficient quantities.

Both **renewable** and **non-renewable** energy resources have some kind of **environmental impact** when we use them.

Non-renewable energy resources

- are not replaced as quickly as they are used
- will eventually run out.

For example, fossil fuels, and nuclear fission.

Renewable energy resources

- can be replaced at the same rate as they are used
- will not run out.

For example, solar, tidal, wave, wind, **geothermal**, **biofuel**, and **hydroelectric** energies.

Non-renewable energy resources

Resource	Main uses	Source	Advantages	Disadvantages
coal	generating electricity	extracted from underground	enough available to meet current energy demands reliable – supply can be controlled to meet demand relatively cheap to extract and use	will eventually run out release carbon dioxide when burned – one of the main causes of climate change release other polluting gases, such as sulfur dioxide (from coal and oil) which causes acid rain oil spills in the oceans kill marine life
oil	generating electricity transport heating			
natural gas	generating electricity heating			
nuclear fission	generating electricity	mining naturally occurring elements, such as uranium and plutonium	no polluting gases or greenhouse gases produced enough available to meet current energy demands large amount of energy transferred from a very small mass of fuel reliable – supply can be controlled to meet demand	produces nuclear waste, which is: • dangerous • difficult and expensive to dispose of • stored for centuries before it is safe to dispose of nuclear power plants are expensive to: • build and run • decommission (shut down)

Revision tip

Remember Nuclear fission is commonly confused as a renewable energy resource as it doesn't release polluting gases – but it's not!

Make sure you can write a definition for these key terms.

biofuel carbon neutral environmental impact fossil fuel geothermal hydroelectric non-renewable reliability renewable

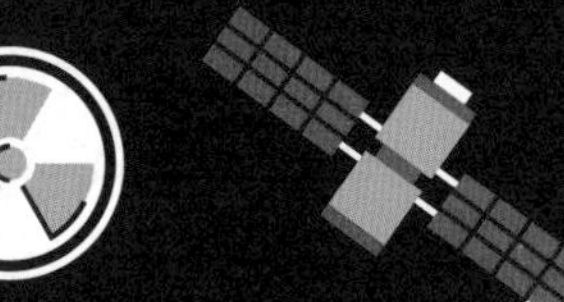

Renewable energy resources

Resource	Main uses	Source	Advantages	Disadvantages
solar energy	generating electricity heating	sunlight transfers energy to solar cells sunlight transfers energy to solar heating panels	can be used in remote places very cheap to run once installed no pollution/greenhouse gases produced	supply depends on weather expensive to buy and install cannot supply large scale demand
hydroelectric energy	generating electricity	water flowing downhill turns generators	low running cost no fuel costs reliable and supply can be controlled to meet demand	expensive to build hydroelectric dams need to flood a large area behind the dam, destroying habitats and resulting in greenhouse gas production from rotting vegetation
tidal energy	generating electricity	turbines on tidal barrages turned by water as the tide comes in and out	predictable supply as there are always tides can produce large amounts of electricity no fuel costs no pollution/greenhouse gases produced	tidal barrages: • change aquatic habitats and can harm animals • restrict access and can be dangerous for boats • are expensive to build and maintain cannot control supply supply varies depending on time of month
wave energy	generating electricity	floating generators powered by waves moving up and down	low running cost no fuel costs no pollution/greenhouse gases produced	floating generators: • change aquatic habitats and can harm animals • restrict access and can be dangerous for boats • are expensive to build, install, and maintain dependent on weather cannot supply large scale demand
wind energy	generating electricity	turbines turned by the wind	low running cost no fuel costs no pollution/greenhouse gases produced	supply depends on weather large amounts of land needed to generate enough electricity for large scale demand can produce noise pollution for nearby residents
geothermal energy	generating electricity heating	radioactive substances deep within the Earth transfer heat energy to the surface	low running cost no fuel costs no pollution/greenhouse gases produced	expensive to set up only possible in a few suitable locations around the world
biofuels	generating electricity transport	fuel produced from living or recently living organisms, for example, plants and animal waste	can be **carbon neutral** – the amount of carbon dioxide released when the fuel is burnt is equal to the amount of carbon dioxide absorbed when the fuel is grown reliable and supply can be controlled to meet demand	expensive to produce biofuels growing biofuels requires a lot of land and water that could be used for food production can lead to deforestation – forests are cleared for growing biofuel crops

Retrieval

Learn the answers to the questions below, then cover the answers column with a piece of paper and write as many as you can. Check and repeat.

	P2 questions	Answers
1	What is a non-renewable energy resource?	an energy source that will eventually run out, it is not replaced at the same rate as it is being used
2	What is a renewable energy resource?	an energy source that will not run out, it is being (or can be) replaced at the same rate as it is used
3	What are the main renewable and non-renewable resources available on Earth?	• renewable: solar, tidal, wave, wind, geothermal, biofuel, hydroelectric • non-renewable: coal, oil, gas, nuclear
4	What are the main advantages of using coal as an energy resource?	enough available to meet current demand, reliable, can control supply to match demand, cheap to extract and use
5	What are the main disadvantages of using coal as an energy resource?	will eventually run out, releases CO_2 which contributes to climate change, releases sulfur dioxide which causes acid rain
6	What are the main advantages of using nuclear fuel as an energy resource?	lots of energy released from a small mass, reliable, can control supply to match demand, enough fuel available to meet current demand, no polluting gases
7	What are the main disadvantages of using nuclear fuel as an energy resource?	waste is dangerous and difficult and expensive to deal with, expensive initial set up, expensive to shut down and to run
8	What are the main advantages of using solar energy?	can be used in remote places, no polluting gases, no waste products, very low running cost
9	What are the main disadvantages of using solar energy?	only available during hours of daylight, cannot control supply, initial set up expensive, cannot be used on a large scale
10	What are the main advantages of using tidal power?	no polluting gases, no waste products, reliable, can produce large amounts of electricity, low running cost, no fuel costs
11	What are the main disadvantages of using tidal power?	can harm aquatic habitats, initial set up expensive, cannot increase supply when needed, times the energy is available varies each day, hazard for boats
12	What are the main advantages of using wave turbines?	no polluting gases produced, no waste products, low running cost, no fuel costs
13	What are the main disadvantages of using wave turbines?	unreliable, dependent on weather, cannot control supply, initial set up expensive, can harm aquatic habitats, hazard for boats, cannot be used on a large scale
14	What are the main disadvantages of using wind turbines?	unreliable, dependent on weather, cannot control supply, take up a lot of space, can produce noise pollution
15	What are the advantages and the disadvantages of using geothermal energy?	• advantages: no polluting gases, low running cost • disadvantages: initial set up expensive, only available in a few locations
16	What are the main advantages and disadvantages of using biofuels?	• advantages: can be 'carbon neutral', reliable • disadvantages: expensive to produce, use land/water that might be needed to grow food
17	What are the main advantages and disadvantages of using hydroelectric power?	• advantages: no polluting gases, no waste products, low running cost, no fuel cost, reliable, can be controlled to meet demand • disadvantages: initial set up expensive, dams can harm/destroy aquatic habitats

Now go back and use the questions below to check your knowledge from previous chapters.

Previous questions

	Previous questions	Answers
1	Name the eight energy stores.	kinetic, gravitational potential, elastic potential, thermal, chemical, nuclear, magnetic, electrostatic
2	What is a system?	an object or group of objects
3	What is work done?	energy transferred when a force moves an object
4	Name the unit that represents one joule transferred per second.	watt (W)
5	What is the unit for energy?	joule (J)

Put paper here

Put paper here

Maths Skills

Practise your maths skills using the worked example and practice questions below.

Rearranging equations

You need to be able to rearrange and apply many equations in physics, for example, the equation for power.

Power is the rate at which energy is transferred or the rate at which work is done. It can be calculated using:

$$\text{power (W)} = \frac{\text{energy transferred (J)}}{\text{time taken (s)}}$$

Remember:

- a power of 1 W means a rate of energy transfer of 1 J per second
- the shorter the time taken for an energy transfer, the greater the power
- if the time taken to transfer energy is given in minutes or hours, you must convert it to seconds before calculating the power.

Worked example

A microwave is marked as having a power of 900 W. How long does it take to transfer 13 500 J of energy?

Step 1: write down the equation.

$$\text{power (W)} = \frac{\text{energy transferred (J)}}{\text{time taken (s)}}$$

Step 2: work out which information in the question relates to the variables in the equation.

power = 900 W, energy transferred = 13 500 J

Step 3: put the numbers into the equation.

$$900 = \frac{13\,500}{\text{time}}$$

Step 4: rearrange the equation.

Multiply both sides of the equation by t:

$$900 \times \text{time} = 13\,500$$

Then divide both sides of the equation by 900:

$$\text{time} = \frac{13\,500}{900} = 15\text{ s}$$

Alternatively:

Step 3: rearrange the equation first.

$$\text{time} = \frac{\text{energy}}{\text{power}}$$

Step 4: put the numbers into the equation.

$$= \frac{13\,500}{900} = 15\text{ s}$$

Practice

1. An LED lamp transfers 360 J of energy in 30 seconds. Calculate its power.
2. An electric cooker transfers 3 MJ of energy in 5 minutes. Calculate its power.
3. An electric kettle has a power of 3000 W. How much energy does it transfer in 45 seconds?
4. Rearrange the equation linking efficiency, useful power output, and total power input to calculate the total power output of a system.

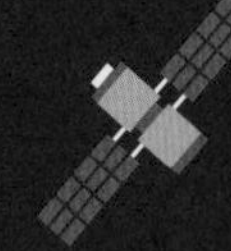

Practice

Exam-style questions

01 A student finds some data about electricity production and how it has changed over time.

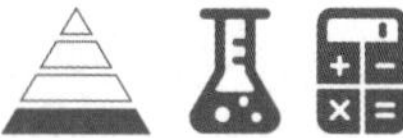

They plot the data on a bar chart, as shown in **Figure 1**.

Figure 1

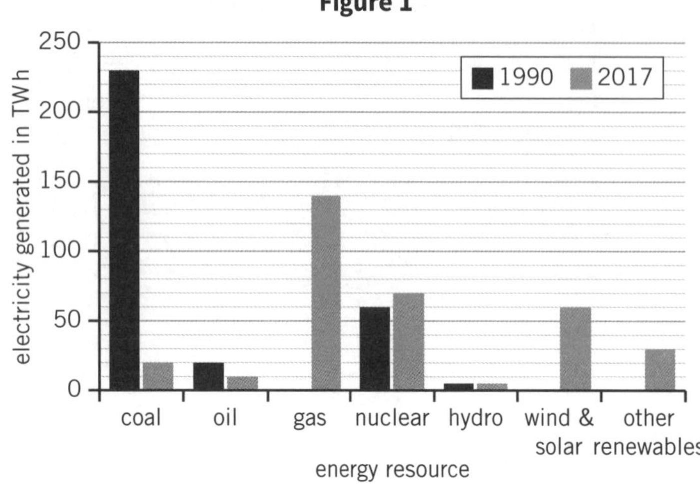

01.1 Explain why the student plotted the data as a bar chart and not a line graph. **[2 marks]**

____

____

01.2 Compare the number of renewable resources used in 1990 with the number used in 2017. **[2 marks]**

Use data from the graph.

____

____

____

01.3 Estimate the change in the use of fossil fuels between the two years in terawatt hours (TWh). **[3 marks]**

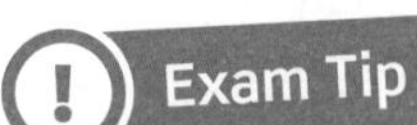

Don't worry if you've never heard of TWh before. Just use them as the unit for this question, treating them the same as you would any other unit.

Estimate = ______________ TWh

01.4 There was a large decrease in the use of one non-renewable resource for generating electricity between 1990 and 2017.

Identify this resource.

Suggest why use of this resource in power stations has decreased since 1990. **[2 marks]**

____

____

____

02 A student finds data relating to the cost of generating electricity and the grams of CO_2 produced (**Table 1**).

Table 1

Resource	Cost per unit in p	CO_2 produced per unit in g
solar (the Sun)	40.0	48
nuclear fuel	3.0	12
coal	1.5	820
natural gas	5.0	490
biomass	2.0	230

A unit is a measure of electricity generation. The CO_2 produced included emissions while the power station was being built and while it is in use.

02.1 Suggest why the cost per unit for solar power is so high. **[1 mark]**

Exam Tip

While the sun is free, it's not free to harvest that energy.

02.2 Suggest why the cheapest method in **Table 1** may cause environmental problems. Explain your answer. **[3 marks]**

02.3 **Table 1** shows that nuclear fuel is a relatively low-cost option, with the lowest emissions.

Suggest **two** disadvantages of using nuclear power stations to generate electricity. **[2 marks]**

Exam Tip

Think about safety and renewability.

1

2

02.4 The student thinks about how biomass is produced. She suggests that the impact of biomass in terms of CO_2 emissions is actually lower than that shown in **Table 1**. Suggest why. **[3 marks]**

03 A student is investigating how wind turbines work. The student measures the power output of a wind turbine for different wind speeds. The data for wind speed and power are shown in **Table 2**.

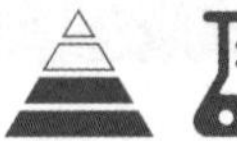

Table 2

Wind speed in m/s	Power output in W
0	0.0
2	0.0
4	0.1
6	1.2
8	2.4
10	3.6
12	3.6
14	3.6

03.1 Plot the data in **Table 2** on **Figure 2**. **[4 marks]**

Figure 2

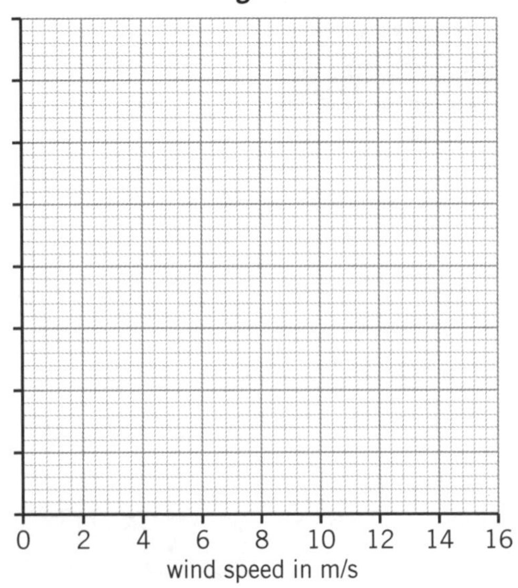

Exam Tip

One axis has been labelled for you, but don't forget to do the other one.

03.2 Describe the relationship between wind speed and power output. **[3 marks]**

03.3 Wind generators can be used to produce electricity used in homes. Suggest **one** advantage and **one** disadvantage of generating electricity using the wind. **[2 marks]**

04 A student collects data from a solar cell. They use a lamp to represent the Sun, and model the effect of clouds by putting sheets of transparent film on top of the solar cell. They make calculations to find the energy per second produced by the solar cell, as given in **Table 3**.

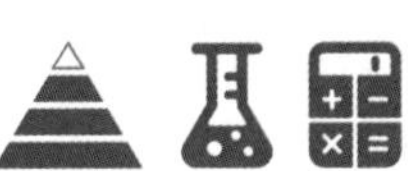

Table 3

Number of sheets of transparent film	Energy per second		
	Test 1	Test 2	Mean
0	5.24	5.15	5.20
1	4.12	4.32	4.22
2	3.65	2.11	2.88
3	3.21	3.32	3.27
4	2.50	2.40	2.45
5	1.70	1.60	1.65

Exam Tip

Independent variables are the ones that you change!

04.1 Write down the independent and dependent variables. **[2 marks]**

04.2 List **three** control variables. **[3 marks]**

04.3 Another student looked at the results in **Table 3**. They gave the following feedback.

Statement **1**: *'For two sheets, 2.11 is an outlier.'*

Statement **2**: *'The columns are not labelled correctly.'*

Statement **3**: *'The significant figures of the measurements are inconsistent.'*

Read each of the statements. Write down what action, if any, should be taken as a result. **[3 marks]**

Exam Tip

In your answer make it clear which statements you're referring to. Don't make it hard to mark your work by not laying it out in a neat manner.

04.4 Calculate the uncertainty in the measurement of energy when one sheet was used. **[2 marks]**

05 There are different methods of generating electricity. Some of the resources used to generate electricity are also used for transportation. Some are only used to generate electricity. Some are renewable and some are non-renewable.

05.1 Describe the difference between a renewable and a non-renewable resource. **[1 mark]**

05.2 Tick **all** the correct boxes in **Table 4**. There will be a minimum of two ticks in each column. **[3 marks]**

Table 4

Resource	Used to generate electricity	Used as a fuel in cars	Is a renewable resource
coal			
biomass			
oil			
wind			

05.3 Some non-renewable sources cause environmental problems, such as pollution. Describe **one** reason why, despite this fact, they are used to generate electricity. **[1 mark]**

06 The way in which electricity has been generated has changed over time. **Figure 3** shows the changes in the primary sources of energy in the United Kingdom (UK) between 1990 and 2015.

Figure 3

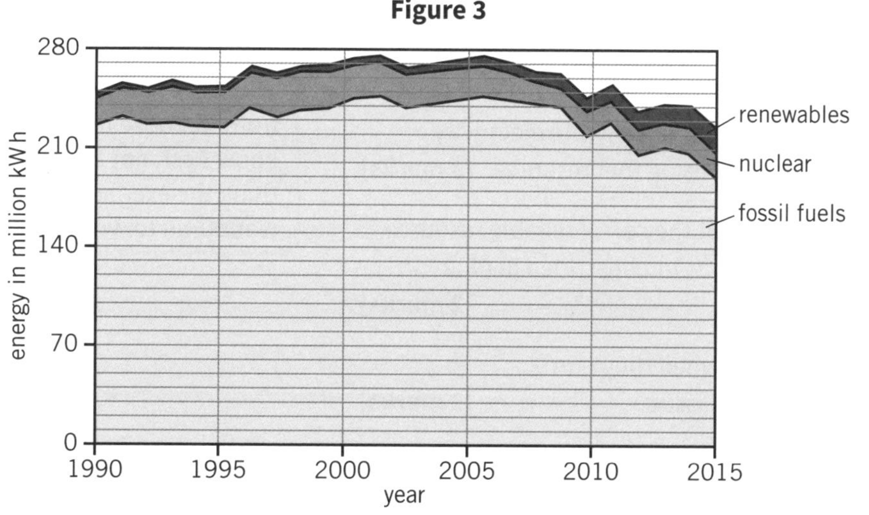

Exam Tip

This may not look like the graphs you're used to, but it's just a line graph shaded in.

06.1 Name **one** renewable source of energy. **[1 mark]**

06.2 Use data from **Figure 3** to compare the percentage energy use from fossil fuels in 1990 with the percentage use in 2015.
Show calculations to justify your answer. **[5 marks]**

> **Exam Tip**
> Use data from the graph and clearly link it to the statements you make.

06.3 Estimate the rate of decrease of energy use between 2010 and 2015. Use your estimate to determine the number of years it will take for the energy use in the UK to become half of the value in 2015. **[4 marks]**

06.4 Suggest **one** reason why the total energy use might halve in this time, and **one** reason why the total energy use might **not** halve in this time. **[2 marks]**

07 A village has a wind turbine. The output of the turbine varies between zero and 60 kW. The people in the village are considering increasing their use of renewables using either wind turbines or biomass generators. They collect the following data:

- annual energy requirement of village = 7000 MWh
- cost of wind turbine = £1 million
- cost per kW h generated with biofuel (installation and running) = £0.50

> **Exam Tip**
> There are lots of non-standard units in this question, so take it carefully step by step.

07.1 Calculate the annual energy requirement of the village in joules (J). **[2 marks]**

07.2 The mean power output of a wind turbine is 33 kW.
Calculate how many wind turbines are needed to produce the annual energy requirements of the village. **[4 marks]**

> **Exam Tip**
> Think about the cost of installation as well as ongoing costs.

07.3 Calculate which renewable resource would be cheaper to produce the annual energy requirements of the village. **[4 marks]**

07.4 Evaluate the use of each renewable resource in terms of their effect on the environment. **[6 marks]**

08 A student is comparing fossil fuels with energy resources that involve water.

08.1 Name **two** fossil fuels. **[2 marks]**

08.2 The student learns that electricity can be generated using the motion of waves at sea.
Name another resource that uses water to generate electricity.
Describe how electricity is generated using that resource. **[3 marks]**

> **Exam Tip**
> There are many you can pick from – choose the one you know best, not the one you think the examiner wants you to write about.

08.3 One benefit of using fossil fuels is that they are a reliable resource.
Compare the reliability of the resource you described in **08.2** with that of fossil fuels. **[2 marks]**

08.4 Fossil fuels produce carbon dioxide when they burn.
Explain why this is an environmental issue. **[2 marks]**

08.5 Describe **one** environmental issue associated with the resource you described in **08.2**. **[1 mark]**

09 A bungee jumper is standing on a platform attached to a 3.2 m bungee cord. They jump off the platform and touch some water 10 m below.

Figure 4 shows the jumper on the platform.

Figure 4

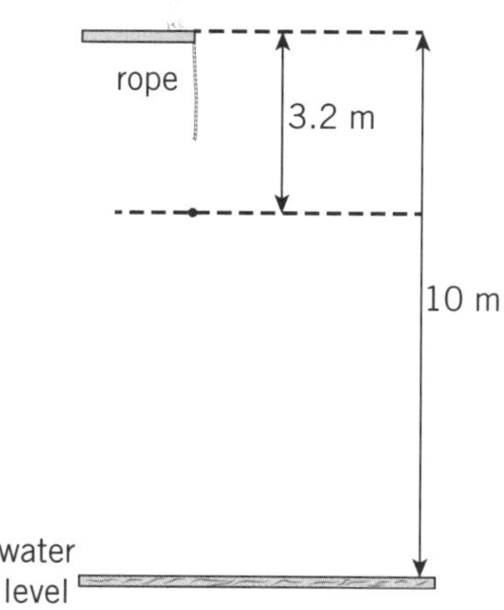

The mass of the bungee jumper is 60 kg.
Gravitational field strength is 9.8 N/kg.

Exam Tip

When you are asked to write an equation, you can use the words or the symbols.

09.1 Write down the equation that links gravitational potential energy, mass, gravitational field strength, and height. **[1 mark]**

09.2 Calculate the gravitational potential energy of the bungee jumper before they jump. **[2 marks]**

09.3 Calculate the spring constant of the bungee cord.
Use the correct equation from the *Physics Equations Sheet*. Assume that no energy is wasted during energy transfer. Give your answer to two significant figures. **[5 marks]**

10.1 What quantities do you need to find to work out kinetic energy?
Choose **one** answer. **[1 mark]**

mass and speed   mass and time   speed and time

10.2 Car **A** and car **B** are both moving.

- Car **A** accelerates under a constant force for 3 seconds at the start of a race.
- During the same 3 seconds car **B** is travelling at a steady speed on a motorway.

Compare:

- the ways in which energy is stored for each car at the start and end of the 3 seconds
- the way or ways in which the energy is transferred between those stores. **[6 marks]**

10.3 All cars require that you add oil to the engine.
Suggest **one** benefit of adding oil to the engine. Use the idea of energy to explain your answer. **[2 marks]**

Knowledge

P3 Supplying electricity

Mains electricity

A cell or a battery provides a **direct current (d.c.)**. The current only flows in one direction and is produced by a **direct potential difference**.

Mains electricity provides an **alternating current (a.c.)**. The current repeatedly reverses direction and is produced by an **alternating potential difference**.

The positive and negative terminals of an alternating power supply swap over with a regular frequency.

The frequency of the mains electricity supply in the UK is 50 Hz and its voltage is 230 V.

Plugs

The earth wire is a safety wire to stop the appliance becoming live. The potential difference of the earth wire is 0V. It only carries a current if there is a fault.

The neutral wire completes the circuit. It has a potential difference of 0V.

Plastic is used for the wire coatings and plug case because it is a good electrical insulator.

Fuse connected to the live wire. If the live wire inside an appliance touches the neutral wire a very large current flows. This is called a **short circuit**. When this happens the fuse melts and disconnects the live wire from the mains, keeping the appliance safe.

The live wire is dangerous because it has a high potential difference of 230V. This would cause a large current to flow through you if you touched it.

Most electrical appliances in the UK are connected to the mains using a three-core cable. Copper is used for the wires because it is a good electrical conductor and it bends easily.

The National Grid

The **National Grid** is a nationwide network of cables and transformers that links power stations to homes, offices, and other consumers of mains electricity.

Transformers are devices that can change the potential difference of an alternating current.

Power stations generate electricity at an alternating potential difference of about 25 000 V.

The cables in the National Grid transfer electrical power at a potential difference of up to 400 000 V.

Homes and offices use electrical power supplied at a potential difference of 230 V.

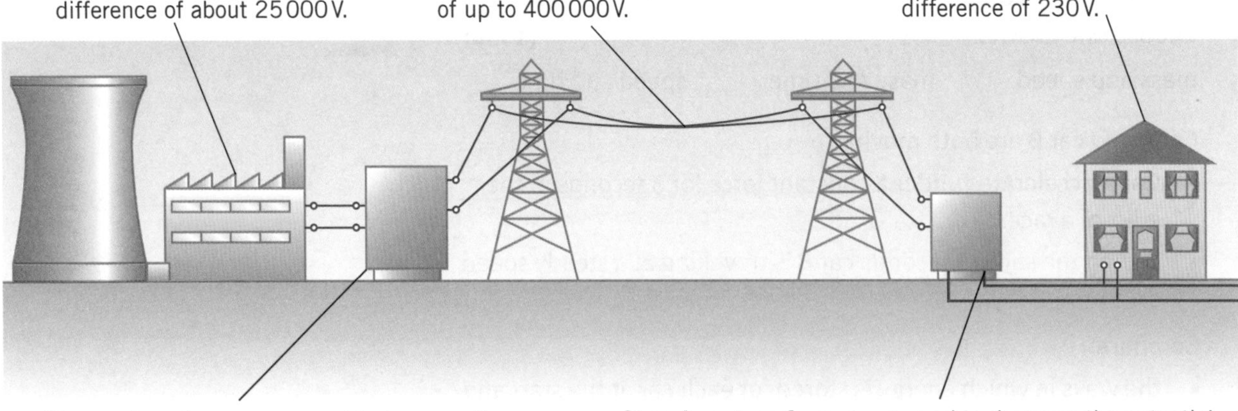

Step-up transformers are used to increase the potential difference from the power station to the transmission cables.

Step-down transformers are used to decrease the potential difference from the transmission cables to the mains supply in homes and offices so that it is safe to use.

Key terms

Make sure you can write a definition for these key terms.

alternating current · alternating potential difference · charge flow · short circuit · step-down transformer

Why do transformers improve efficiency?

A high potential difference across the transmission cables means that a lower current is needed to transfer the same amount of power, since:

power (W) = current (A) × potential difference (V)

$$P = IV$$

A lower current in the cables means less electrical power is wasted due to heating of the cables, since the power lost in heating a cable is:

power (W) = current² (A) × resistance (Ω)

$$P = I^2R$$

This makes the National Grid an efficient way to transfer energy.

If 100% efficiency is assumed:

primary potential difference × primary current = secondary potential difference × secondary current

$$V_pI_p = V_sI_s$$

Energy transfer in electrical appliances

Electrical appliances transfer energy.

For example, a hairdryer transfers energy electrically from a chemical store (e.g., the fuel in a power station) to the kinetic energy store of the fan inside the hairdryer and to the thermal energy store of the heating filaments inside the hairdryer.

When you turn an electrical appliance on, the potential difference of the mains supply causes charge (carried by electrons) to flow through it.

You can calculate the **charge flow** using the equation:

charge flow (C) = current (A) × time (s)

$$Q = It$$

You can find the energy transferred *to* an electrical appliance when charge flows through it using:

energy transferred (J) = charge flow (C) × potential difference (V)

$$E = QV$$

You can find the energy transferred *by* an electrical appliance using the equation:

$$\text{power (W)} = \frac{\text{energy transferred (J)}}{\text{time (s)}}$$

$$P = \frac{E}{t}$$

Revision tip

Practice This topic has the potential for some high level maths questions. If you see a question and you can't decide which equation you need to use to solve it, try looking at combinations of equations.

Revision tip

Remember There are lots of equations in this topic that you need to learn. Find the best way for you to remember them. It could be flashcards, a mnemonic, or changing the lyrics to your favourite song.

direct current | direct potential difference | fuse | National Grid | step-up transformer

Learn the answers to the questions below, then cover the answers column with a piece of paper and write as many as you can. Check and repeat.

	P3 questions	Answers
1	Why is the current provided by a cell called a direct current (d.c.)?	only flows in one direction
2	What is an alternating current (a.c.)?	current that repeatedly reverses direction
3	What kind of current is supplied by mains electricity?	alternating current
4	What is the frequency and voltage of mains electricity?	50 Hz, 230 V
5	What colours are the live, neutral, and earth wires in a three-core cable?	live = brown, neutral = blue, earth = green and yellow stripes
6	What is the function of the live wire in a three-core cable?	carries the alternating potential difference from the supply
7	What is the function of the neutral wire in a three-core cable?	completes the circuit
8	What is the function of the earth wire in a three-core cable?	safety wire to stop the appliance becoming live
9	When is there a current in the earth wire?	when there is a fault
10	Why is the live wire dangerous?	provides a large p.d. that would cause a large current to flow through a person if they touched it
11	What is the National Grid?	nationwide network of cables and transformers that link power stations to customers
12	What are step-up transformers used for in the National Grid?	increase the p.d. from the power station to the transmission cables
13	What are step-down transformers used for in the National Grid?	decrease the p.d. from the transmission cables to the mains supply in buildings so that it is safe to use
14	How does having a large potential difference in the transmission cables help to make the National Grid an efficient way to transfer energy?	large p.d. means a small current is needed to transfer the same amount of power, small current in the transmission cables means less electrical power is wasted due to heating
15	What two things does energy transfer to an appliance depend on?	power of appliance, time it is switched on for
16	What are the units for power, current, potential difference, and resistance?	watt (W), amp (A), volt (V), ohm (Ω)

Put paper here

Now go back and use the questions below to check your knowledge from previous chapters.

Previous questions / Answers

	Previous questions	Answers
1	What is a non-renewable energy resource?	an energy source that will eventually run out, it is not replaced at the same rate as it is being used
2	Describe the energy transfer when a ball is fired using an elastic band.	energy is transferred mechanically from the elastic store of the elastic band to the kinetic store of the band – some energy is dissipated to the thermal store of the surroundings
3	What are the main renewable and non-renewable resources available on Earth?	• renewable: solar, tidal, wave, wind, geothermal, biofuel, hydroelectric • non-renewable: coal, oil, gas, nuclear
4	What are the main advantages and disadvantages of using biofuels?	• advantages: can be 'carbon neutral', reliable • disadvantages: expensive to produce, use land/water that might be needed to grow food
5	What does a material's thermal conductivity tell you?	how well it conducts heat
6	Name the four ways in which energy can be transferred.	heating, waves, electric current, mechanically (by forces)

Required Practical Skills

Practise answering questions on the required practicals using the example below. You need to be able to apply your skills and knowledge to other practicals too.

Resistance in electrical circuits

You need to be able to measure resistance in an electrical circuit. You can use current and potential difference (p.d.), or an ohmmeter.

Length, cross-sectional area, and material all affect the resistance of a wire.

The arrangement of components affects the resistance of a circuit.

When measuring the resistance of a wire, remember to:

- turn off the power supply when not taking readings to stop the wire getting hot
- fix the wire to a ruler so that the wire is straight
- use crocodile clips that make a good contact with the wire.

When measuring the resistance of a circuit in an experiment, remember to make sure the ammeter measures the total current.

Worked example

A student uses an ammeter and a voltmeter to measure the resistance of a piece of wire.

Length in cm	10	20	30	40	50
p.d. in V	0.47	0.59	0.64	0.69	0.72
Current in A	0.24	0.16	0.14	0.11	0.10
Resistance in Ω	2.0	3.7	4.6	6.3	

1 Calculate the resistance when the length is 50 cm.

$$\text{resistance} = \frac{\text{p.d.}}{\text{current}} = \frac{0.72}{0.10} = 7.2\ \Omega$$

2 Describe how resistance changes with length of a piece of wire.

As the length of the wire increases, the resistance increases proportionally.

3 Another student finds that resistance does not increase proportionally with the length of wire. Suggest why, and explain your answer.

The wire was heating up, so the resistance was also changing because of the increase in temperature, not just the change in length.

Practice

Describe how to set up an experiment to compare the resistance of a circuit containing three unequal resistors in parallel with the resistance of a circuit containing three resistors in series.

Include circuit diagrams in your answer.

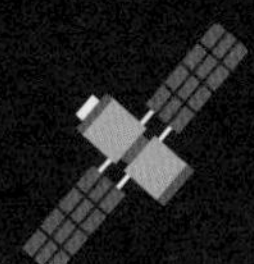

Exam-style questions

01.1 Draw **one** line from each statement beginning to the correct statement ending. You do not need to use all of the endings. **[3 marks]**

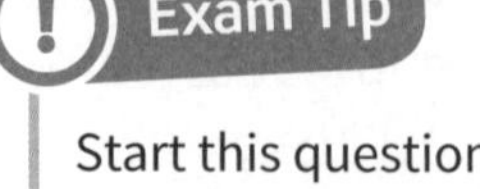

Start this question looking at the units – once you remember the unit for potential difference the answer should become clear.

Statement beginning	Statement ending
The potential difference of the mains electricity in the UK is…	…50 Hz.
	…direct.
The frequency of mains electricity in the UK is…	…about 230 V.
	…100 Hz.
The mains supply in the UK produces a current that is…	…alternating.

01.2 Complete the sentences below using the words in the box.
You will need to use some of the words more than once. **[5 marks]**

live	**earth**	**neutral**

The potential difference between the live and ______________ wires is 230 V.

The potential difference between the ______________ and ______________ wires is 0 V.

When an appliance is connected to the mains and turned on a current flows in the ______________ and ______________ wires.

01.3 Describe the reason for having an earth wire in a circuit. **[1 mark]**

____

____

____

02 A student has a small electric motor.

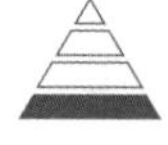

02.1 They connect the motor in a circuit with a 6 V battery.
A current of 1.5 A flows in the circuit.
Show that the power of the motor is 9 W. **[2 marks]**

'Show' questions are great! You already know the answer (9 W), so you just need to clearly show the examiner that you can use an equation to get this answer.

____

____

____

____

02.2 The student turns the motor on for 30 seconds.

Write down the equation that links power, energy, and time. **[1 mark]**

____

02.3 Calculate the energy transferred by the motor. **[3 marks]**

Exam Tip

For this question you need to use the answer from **02.1**. This is common in exams – you may have to look back at this question to get all the information you need.

Energy transferred = ______________ J

02.4 The student finds a lamp with the same power rating as the motor.

They connect the lamp to another 6 V battery.

They then turn both circuits on for 30 seconds.

Select the correct statement below. Tick **one** box. **[1 mark]**

The motor transfers more energy than the lamp.	☐
Both devices transfer the same amount of energy.	☐
The lamp transfers more energy than the motor.	☐

03 **Figure 1** shows how the motor that drives a desk fan is connected to the mains supply.

Figure 1

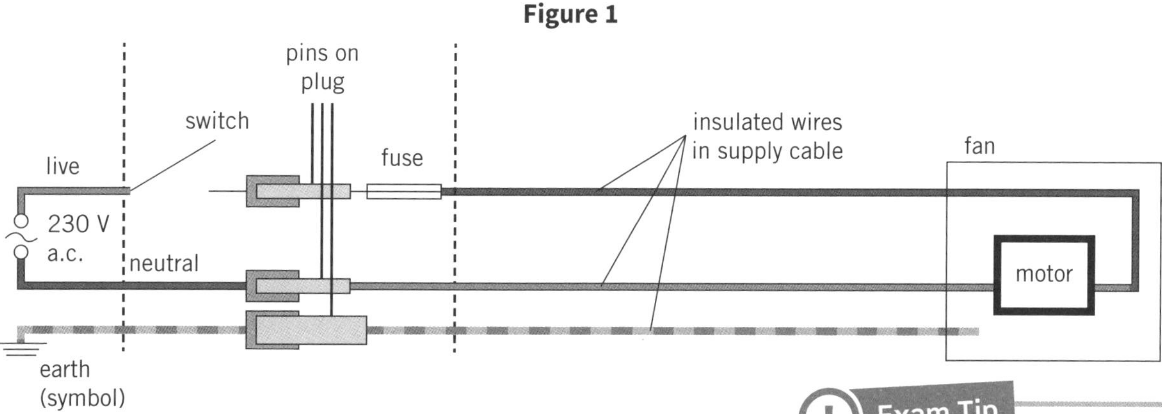

03.1 Use **Figure 1** to explain how the fuse and earth wire prevent a person being injured if there is a fault. **[5 marks]**

03.2 Suggest how to construct the fan so that an earth wire is not required.

Explain your suggestion. **[2 marks]**

Exam Tip

This question may seem easy, but look at the number of marks – 5.

To get full marks on this question you must refer back to the information in the figure.

03.3 When the motor is working the current in the wire is 4.5 A.

Calculate the power of the fan motor.

Give your answer to two significant figures. **[3 marks]**

Exam Tip

For this question you'll need to use two different equations to get the final answer. The first clue of this is the fact you're given three numbers in the question.

03.4 There is a fault and the current in the fuse reaches a value of 5.0 A.

The fuse melts in a time of 0.63 seconds.

The energy needed to melt the fuse is 5.4 J.

Calculate the resistance of the fuse wire to an appropriate number of significant figures. **[5 marks]**

04 The National Grid is made up of substations that contain transformers.

04.1 Describe the role of a transformer. **[1 mark]**

04.2 A power station supplies 80 MW to the National Grid. Some parts of the National Grid operate at very high potential differences.

Compare the power losses of transmitting power using a potential difference of 400 000 V with using a potential difference of 4000 V.

Assume that the wires have a resistance of about 4 Ω.

Use your calculations to explain why it is important to transmit power in the National Grid at a high potential difference rather than at a low potential difference. **[6 marks]**

You'll need to do two calculations for this question.

Make it clear which section of information each calculation is referring to in your answer.

05 A student looks at two appliances and produces **Table 1**.

Both appliances work when connected to the mains supply.

Exam Tip

Watch out for the change between W and kW in this question.

Table 1

Appliance	Power rating
toaster	1200 W
kettle	2.0 kW

05.1 Write down the equation that links power, potential difference, and current. **[1 mark]**

05.2 Use the potential difference of the mains supply and the data in **Table 1** to calculate the current flowing in the wires in the kettle when it is turned on.

Give your answer to two significant figures. **[6 marks]**

Exam Tip

There are two ways to approach this question: rearrange the equation and then put the numbers in, or put the numbers in and then rearrange the equation.

In an exam you can get marks for putting the numbers in the right places, so it's a good idea to do that bit first!

05.3 Give the equation that links current, potential difference, and resistance. **[1 mark]**

05.4 Show that the resistance of the kettle is approximately 26 Ω.

Give your answer to two significant figures. **[4 marks]**

05.5 Write the equation to calculate energy transfer from power and time. **[1 mark]**

05.6 It takes 2 minutes to boil water in the kettle.

Calculate the length of time that the toaster would take to transfer the same amount of energy as the kettle.

Give your answer in minutes. **[6 marks]**

Exam Tip

This answer needs to be given in minutes, so you don't have to convert time into seconds. Be careful if you get a decimal – remember there are 60 seconds in a minute not 100.

05.7 The student says:

'In terms of energy stores and transfers the toaster and kettle are identical.'

Do you agree? Explain your answer. **[2 marks]**

> **Exam Tip**
>
> 'Yes' or 'no' isn't going to be enough to get full marks on this question. You must explain your reasoning.

06 A student looks at the information on a hairdryer.

The power of the hairdryer is 2000 W.

The potential difference that the hairdryer needs to work is 230 V.

06.1 Write down what 2000 W means in terms of energy and time. **[1 mark]**

06.2 Write down what 230 V means in terms of energy and charge. **[1 mark]**

06.3 The student estimates that it takes 5 minutes to dry their hair.

Write down the equation that links time, power, and energy. **[1 mark]**

> **Exam Tip**
>
> Remember that the standard units for time are seconds!

06.4 Calculate the energy transferred from the mains during that time. **[2 marks]**

06.5 Write down the equation that links potential difference, charge, and energy. **[1 mark]**

06.6 Calculate the charge flowing in the hairdryer. Use your answer to **06.4** to help you. **[3 marks]**

07 A student is explaining how electricity gets to their house.

They draw a diagram to show this (**Figure 2**).

Figure 2

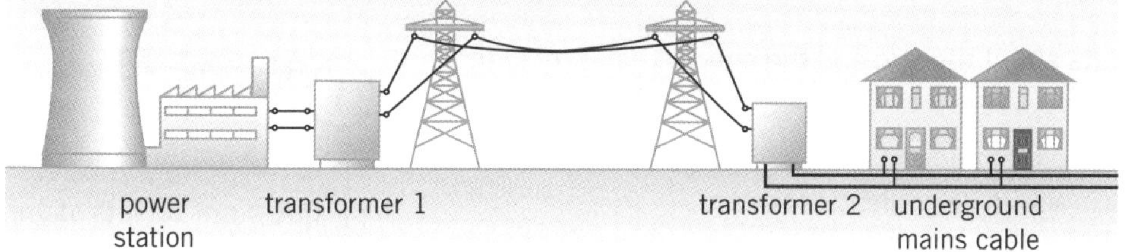

07.1 Write down the name of the system of transformers and power cables that provides electricity to businesses and houses. **[1 mark]**

07.2 A younger student asks:

'Why are there two transformers? Are they both the same?'

Answer these questions by comparing the transformers. **[3 marks]**

07.3 Give **one** reason why the system is an efficient way of transferring energy. **[2 marks]**

> **Exam Tip**
>
> It's important to look at the number of marks available for a question.
>
> This question asks for **one** reason but has **two** marks available. You can assume there is one mark available for your reason and one for why.

08 **Table 2** shows a survey of some electrical appliances in a student's house. All of the devices use mains p.d.

Table 2

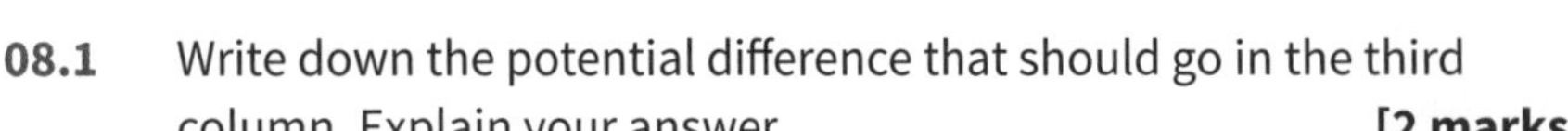

Appliance	Power rating in W	Potential difference in V
hairdryer	2200	
iron	2800	
toaster	2000	

> **Exam Tip**
>
> You may think you need a calculator and equations for this, but this is *not* a maths question. The key word in the question is *mains* p.d.

08.1 Write down the potential difference that should go in the third column. Explain your answer. **[2 marks]**

08.2 Name the type of energy store that fills when all the appliances are being used. **[1 mark]**

08.3 Put the appliances in order from largest to smallest current.

Explain your reasoning. **[2 marks]**

08.4 The current of the toaster is 8.7 A.

Calculate the resistance using the equation:

$$\text{power} = (\text{current})^2 \times \text{resistance}$$

Give your answer to two significant figures. **[4 marks]**

> **Exam Tip**
>
> Correct use of significant figures comes up frequently. Don't let the fact this is a topic you've covered in maths scare you.

09 A student is using a solar cell.

When they connect it to a voltmeter it produces a potential difference.

09.1 Explain why electricity generated with solar cells is 'renewable'. **[1 mark]**

09.2 The Sun radiates about 4×10^{26} joules per second.

Write down the power of the Sun. **[1 mark]**

09.3 Here are some data about the Sun and the energy that is incident on the Earth.

The energy that is incident upon 1 m^2 of the Earth's surface in northern Europe is about 500 joules per second.

There are 3.1×10^7 seconds in a year.

Calculate the energy absorbed by a solar cell in northern Europe with an area of 1 m^2 in one year. **[2 marks]**

> **Exam Tip**
>
> In the exam you'll get questions on lots of unfamiliar contexts – use a highlighter to pick out the key bits of information and you'll see this questions isn't as hard as it looks!

09.4 The world demand for electricity is about 7×10^{18} J per year.

Calculate the area of solar cells placed in northern Europe that would be needed to meet the world demand for energy. **[2 marks]**

10 A student learns that the oven in their kitchen works on a separate circuit to that of the toaster and other small electrical appliances.

They find the following information:

- the oven has a power of 9 kW
- the toaster has a power of 2 kW
- ovens are connected to the mains with much thicker wires than other appliances.

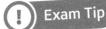

10.1 Calculate the current flowing in the oven. **[3 marks]**

10.2 Compare the current flowing in the oven with that of the toaster. **[4 marks]**

10.3 Suggest why the oven is connected with thicker wires. **[2 marks]**

10.4 Current larger than 0.1 A is dangerous to the human body.
Explain why the student can use both appliances safely. **[2 marks]**

> **Exam Tip**
> For **10.1** and **10.2**, you'll need to do two separate calculations and then compare them. Remember to make it very clear which calculation applies to which appliance, and then give the similarities and differences.

11 A student has found a box of metal rods.

The metal rods are numbered but the type of material that each rod is made of is not clear. The student wants to put the rods in order from best to worst conductor of thermal energy. They attach a small nail to the rod with wax.

Figure 3

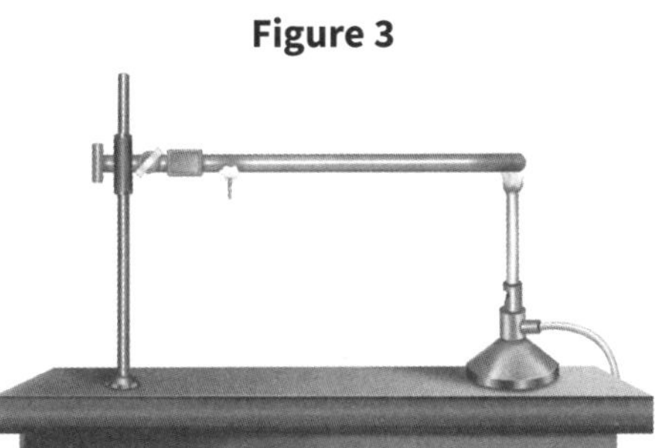

The equipment the student uses is shown in **Figure 3**.

11.1 Design a results table that could be used to collect the data in this experiment. **[3 marks]**

11.2 Write down **two** control variables in the experiment. **[2 marks]**

11.3 Explain why it would be difficult to collect valid data. **[2 marks]**

11.4 Suggest an improvement to this method that would improve the quality of the data. **[1 mark]**

> **Exam Tip**
> Control variables are the ones we keep the same.

12 A trampoline is made of a rubber sheet attached to a frame by springs.

Each spring stretches by 0.01 m when a person stands on the trampoline.

The spring constant of each spring is 500 N/m.

12.1 Calculate the energy stored in the spring. Use the correct equation from the *Physics Equations Sheet*. **[2 marks]**

12.2 A student bounces on the trampoline. On the first bounce they reach a height of 2 m above the trampoline. On the second bounce they reach a height of 1.5 m.

Describe the energy stores at the top of the first bounce and at the top of the second bounce.

Use your description to explain why the second bounce is lower than the first. **[3 marks]**

> **Exam Tip**
> Think about wasted energy when answering this question.

12.3 Describe **two** processes by which the energy is transferred between the energy stores in **12.2**. **[2 marks]**

Knowledge

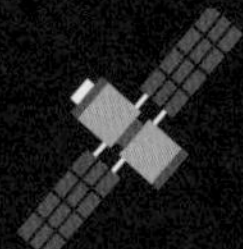

P4 Electric circuits

Charge

An atom has no charge because it has equal numbers of positive protons and negative electrons.

When electrons are removed from an atom it becomes *positively* charged. When electrons are added to an atom it becomes *negatively* charged.

Static charge

Insulating materials can become charged when they are rubbed with another insulating material. This is because electrons are transferred from one material to the other. Materials that gain electrons become negatively charged, and those that lose electrons become positively charged.

Positive charges do not usually transfer between materials.

Electric charge is measured in coulombs (C).

Sparks

If two objects have a very strong electric field between them, electrons in the air molecules will be strongly attracted towards the positively charged object. If the electric field is strong enough, electrons will be pulled away from the air molecules and cause a flow of electrons between the two objects – this is a spark.

Electric fields

A charged object creates an **electric field** around itself.

If a charged object is placed in the electric field of another charged object it experiences **electrostatic force**. This means that the two charged objects exert a non-contact force on each other:

- like charges repel each other
- opposite charges attract each other.

The electric field, and the force between two charged objects, gets stronger as the distance between the objects decreases.

Drawing electric fields

Electric fields can be represented using a diagram with field lines. These show the direction of the force that a small positive charge would experience when placed in the electric field.

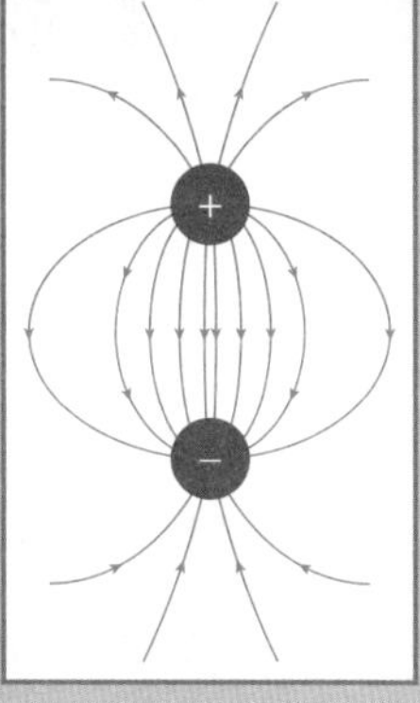

When drawing electric fields, make sure:

- field lines meet the surface of charged objects at 90°
- arrows always point away from positive charges and towards negative charges.

Electric current

Electric current is when **charge** flows. The charge in an electric circuit is carried by electrons.

The unit of current is the **ampere** (amp, A).

1 ampere = 1 ***coulomb*** *of charge flow per second*

In circuit diagrams, current flows from the positive terminal of a cell or battery to the negative terminal. This is known as conventional current.

In a single closed loop, the current has the same value at any point in the circuit.

Metals are good conductors of electricity because they contain delocalised electrons, which are free to flow through the structure.

Potential difference

Potential difference (p.d.) is a measure of how much energy is transferred between two points in a circuit. The unit of potential difference is the volt (V).

- The p.d. across a component is the work done on it by each coulomb of charge that passes through it.
- The p.d. across a power supply or battery is the energy transferred to each coulomb of charge that passes through it.

For electrical charge to flow through a circuit there must be a source of potential difference.

Key terms

Make sure you can write a definition for these key terms.

ampere
charge
coulomb
current
electric field
electrostatic force
parallel
potential difference
resistance
series
static

Resistance

When electrons move through a circuit, they collide with the ions and atoms of the wires and components in the circuit. This causes **resistance** to the flow of charge.

The unit of resistance is the ohm (Ω).

A long wire has more resistance than a short wire because electrons collide with more ions as they pass through a longer wire.

The resistance of an electrical component can be found by measuring the current and potential difference:

potential difference (V) = current (A) × resistance (Ω)

$$V = IR$$

Current-potential difference graphs

A graph of current through a component against the p.d. across it (I–V graph), is known as the component characteristic.

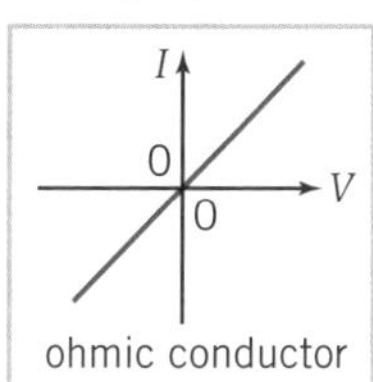

Current is directly proportional to the p.d. in an ohmic conductor at a constant temperature. The resistance is constant.

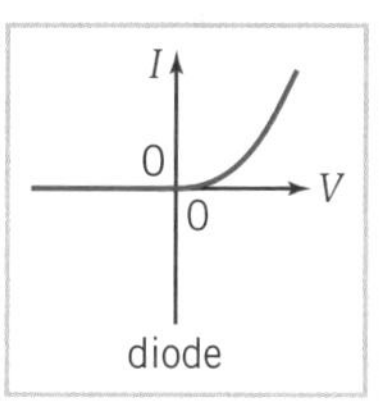

The current through a diode only flows in one direction – called the forward direction. There needs to be a minimum voltage before any current will flow.

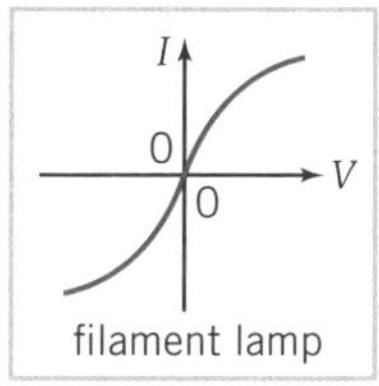

As more current flows through the filament, its temperature increases. The atoms in the wire vibrate more, and collide more often with electrons flowing through it, so resistance increases as temperature increases.

The resistance of an ohmic conductor can be found by calculating the gradient at that point and taking the inverse: $\text{resistance} = \frac{1}{\text{gradient}}$.

Circuit components

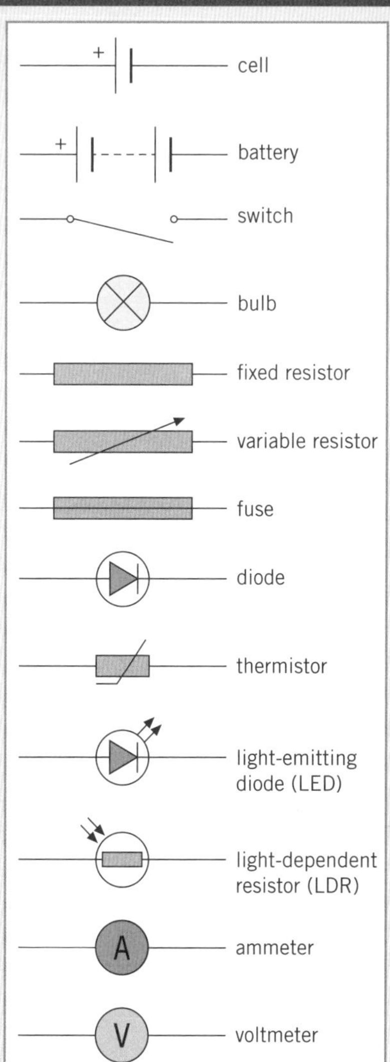

Series circuits

In a **series** circuit, the components are connected one after the other in a single loop. If one component in a series circuit stops working the whole circuit will stop working.

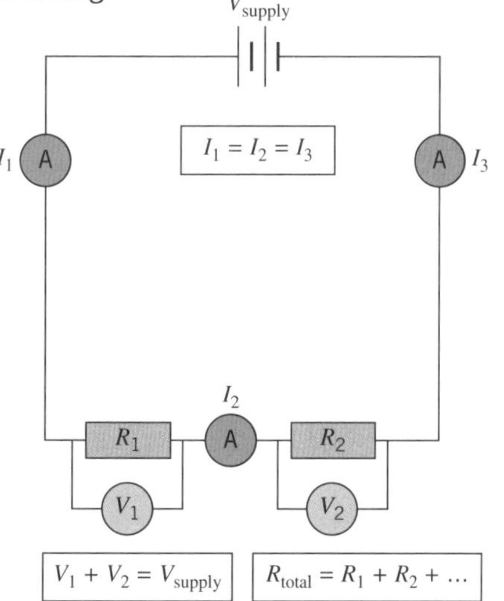

Components with a higher resistance will transfer a larger share of the total p.d. because $V = IR$ (and current is the same through all components).

Parallel circuits

A **parallel** circuit is made up of two or more loops through which current can flow. If one branch of a parallel circuit stops working, the other branches will not be affected.

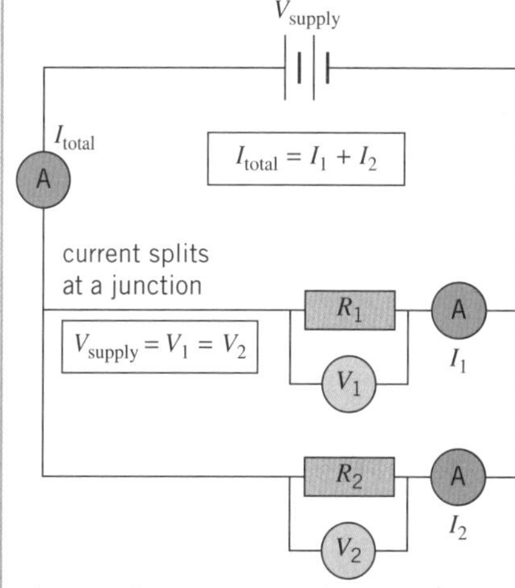

The total resistance of two or more components in parallel is always less than the smallest resistance of any branch. This is because adding a loop to the circuit provides another route for the current to flow, so more current can flow in total even though the p.d. has not changed. Adding more resistors in parallel decreases the total resistance of a circuit.

Learn the answers to the questions below, then cover the answers column with a piece of paper and write as many as you can. Check and repeat.

	P4 questions		Answers
1	How does a material become charged?	Put paper here	becomes negatively charged by gaining electrons, becomes positively charged by losing electrons
2	What will two objects carrying the same type of charge do if they are brought close to each other?		repel each other
3	What is an electric field?	Put paper here	region of space around a charged object in which another charged object will experience an electrostatic force
4	What happens to the strength of an electric field as you get further from the charged object?		it decreases
5	What is electric current?	Put paper here	rate of flow of charge
6	What units are charge, current, and time measured in?		coulomb (C), ampere (A), and second (s) respectively
7	What is the same at all points when charge flows in a closed loop?	Put paper here	current
8	What must there be in a closed circuit so that electrical charge can flow?		source of potential difference (p.d.)
9	Which two factors does current depend on and what are their units?	Put paper here	resistance unit: ohm (Ω) p.d. unit: volt (V)
10	What happens to the current if the resistance is increased but the p.d. stays the same?		current decreases
11	What is an ohmic conductor?	Put paper here	conductor where current is directly proportional to the voltage so resistance is constant (at constant temperature)
12	What happens to the resistance of a filament lamp as its temperature increases?		resistance increases
13	What happens to the resistance of a thermistor as its temperature increases?	Put paper here	resistance decreases
14	What happens to the resistance of a light-dependent resistor when light intensity increases?		resistance decreases
15	What are the main features of a series circuit?	Put paper here	same current through each component, total p.d. of power supply is shared between components – total resistance of all components is the sum of the resistance of each component
16	What are the main features of a parallel circuit?		p.d. across each branch is the same, total current through circuit is the sum of the currents in each branch – total resistance of all resistors is less than the resistance of the smallest individual resistor

Now go back and use the questions below to check your knowledge from previous chapters.

Previous questions | Answers

	Question		Answer
1	What are the units for power, current, potential difference, and resistance?	Put paper here	watt (W), amp (A), volt (V), ohm (Ω)
2	What is the National Grid?		nationwide network of cables and transformers that link power stations to customers
3	Why is the live wire dangerous?		provides a large p.d. that would cause a large current to flow through a person if they touched it

Required Practical Skills

Practise answering questions on the required practicals using the example below. You need to be able to apply your skills and knowledge to other practicals too.

I–V graphs

You need to be able to determine the relationship between current and potential difference (p.d.) for a lamp, resistor, and diode.

You should be able to draw and interpret *I–V* graphs – the shape of the graph is characteristic of the component.

The gradient of the graph is not related to the resistance, but resistance can be calculated from values for p.d. and current.

A variable power supply or resistor should be used to change the current in both directions.

The diode needs to be connected with a protective resistor so it does not get too hot.

Worked example

A student uses a circuit to measure values of current and p.d. for component **X**. They decide to use a variable resistor to change the current.

1 Below are some data for the component. Plot a graph of the data and draw a line of best fit.

p.d. in V	0.0	0.1	0.4	0.6	0.8	1.0
Current in A	0.2	0.38	0.59	0.64	0.69	0.72
p.d. in V	0.0	-0.1	-0.4	-0.6	-0.8	-1.0
Current in A	-0.2	-0.38	-0.59	-0.64	-0.69	-0.72

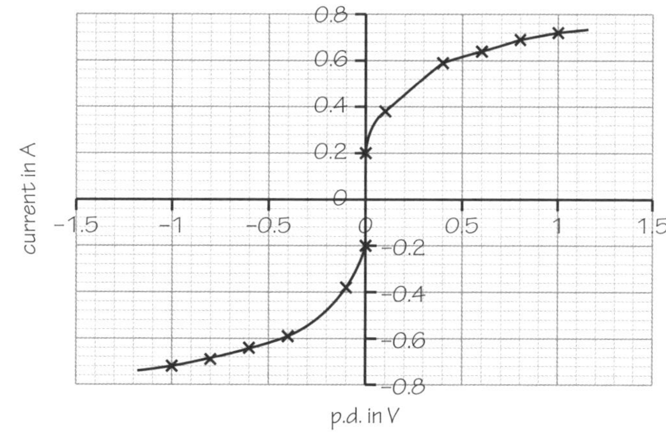

2 Suggest the name of component **X**. Use the graph and data to explain your answer.

X is a lamp as the graph is symmetrical:

$$\text{resistance} = \frac{\text{p.d.}}{\text{current}}$$

$$R = \frac{0.1}{0.38} = 0.26\,\Omega \qquad R = \frac{1}{0.72} = 1.39\,\Omega$$

So as p.d. increases, resistance increases.

Practice

A student has set up an experiment to collect data to plot an *I–V* graph for a piece of resistance wire.

1 Give two changes the student will need to make to repeat the experiment with a diode.

2 Sketch the *I–V* graph for a diode. Explain the shape of the graph in terms of resistance.

Practice

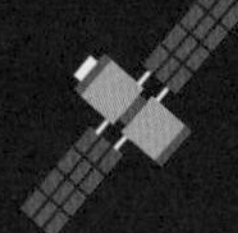

Exam-style questions

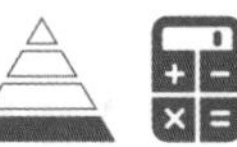

01 A student finds a box of different resistors. One of the resistors is not marked.

The student wants to find the resistance. They place the unknown resistor in the circuit shown in **Figure 1**.

Figure 1

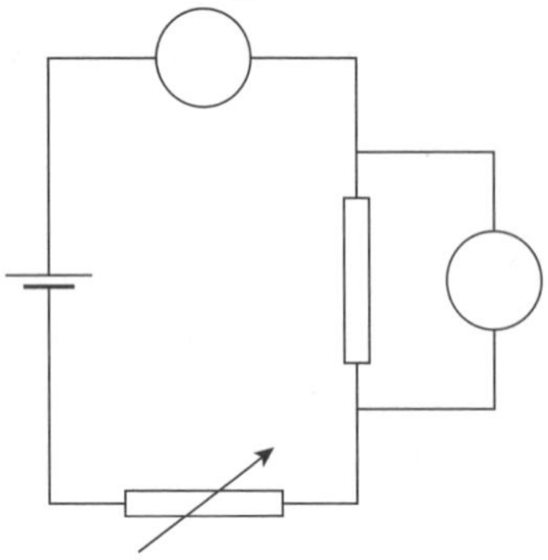

01.1 The student has not labelled the diagram.

The ammeter and voltmeter need to be in the correct places.

Write the letters **A** and **V** in the circles in **Figure 1** to show where to put the meters.

Label the resistor.

Label the variable resistor. **[4 marks]**

01.2 The student measures a current of 0.3 A.

Define current. **[1 mark]**

____

01.3 Write down the equation that links current, potential difference, and resistance. **[1 mark]**

____

01.4 The student measures a potential difference of 6 V.

Calculate the resistance of the resistor. Give the units. **[3 marks]**

Resistance = ____________

Unit = ____________

> **Exam Tip**
>
> Look back at the Knowledge page – this is practice, not the real exam, so you are allowed to look back!

> **Exam Tip**
>
> For all maths questions:
>
> Step 1 – write down the equation you are using (part **01.3**)
>
> Step 2 – put the numbers into the equation
>
> Step 3 – rearrange the equation
>
> Step 4 – do the maths
>
> Step 5 – write down the answer *with units*

02 **Figure 2** shows four circuits drawn by a student.

Figure 2

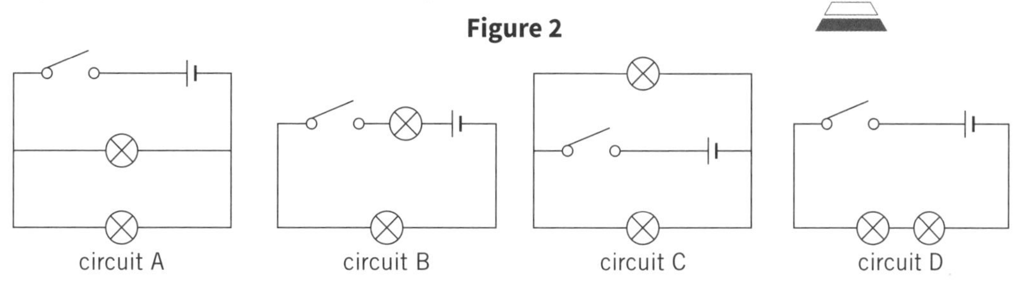

02.1 Here are some statements about the circuits in **Figure 2**. **[1 mark]**

Tick **one** box.

- Circuit **A** is a series circuit ☐
- Circuits **A** and **C** are parallel circuits ☐
- Only circuit **A** is a parallel circuit ☐
- Circuits **C** and **D** are series circuits ☐

02.2 Complete these sentences about the four circuits.

Use the letters **A**, **B**, **C**, or **D**. **[3 marks]**

The bulbs in circuits ____________ and ____________ are the brightest.

If one of the bulbs in circuit ____________ or ____________ breaks, the other bulb will go out.

An ammeter placed anywhere in circuit ____________ or ____________ will measure the same current.

02.3 The student looks at circuit **B** and says:

'I think that when you press the switch, the bulb nearer the battery will be brighter than the bulb that is further away.'

Do you agree? Explain your answer. **[3 marks]**

____

____

____

____

Exam Tip

Get into the habit of looking at the number of marks available, this will help you work out what the examiners are looking for.

This is a three-mark question, meaning a 'yes' or 'no' answer won't be enough – you need to explain why as well.

03 A student wants to demonstrate the difference between the equivalent resistances of two resistors in series and parallel circuits.

Describe how they could set up two circuits, one in series and one in parallel, to show the difference.

You need to:

- draw a circuit diagram for each circuit
- describe the measurements the student should make, and how the student should use those measurements to calculate the equivalent resistance of each circuit
- describe the differences in the equivalent resistance that the student should find. **[6 marks]**

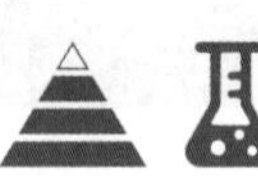

Exam Tip

Always use a ruler for circuit diagrams!

Exam Tip

Think about which equations you'll need to calculate resistance and which circuit components can give you the information you'll need.

04 A student is using a thermistor and a data logger to monitor the changes in temperature in the school greenhouse.

04.1 Describe how the resistance of a thermistor depends on temperature. **[1 mark]**

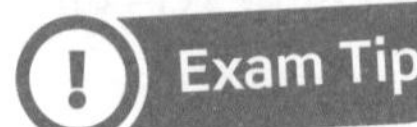

Exam Tip

04.1 is a 'describe' question, so you need to say *what* will happen but not *why*.

04.2 The student connects the thermistor in the circuit shown in **Figure 3**.
They think that if the temperature changes the reading on the voltmeter will change.
Explain why this would **not** happen. **[2 marks]**

Figure 3

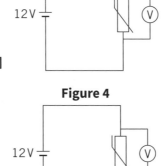

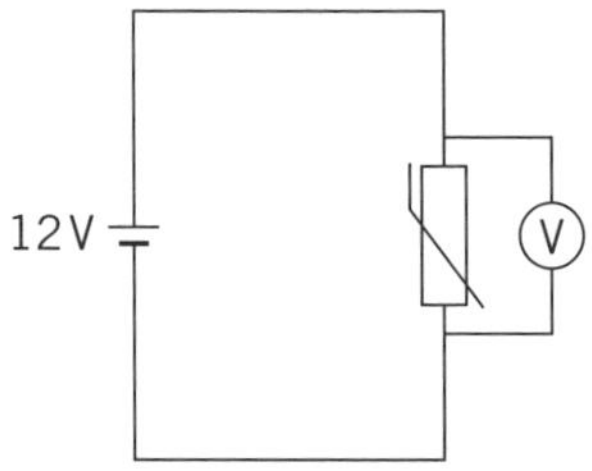

04.3 Another student sets up the circuit shown in **Figure 4**.
They measure the highest and lowest voltmeter readings.
The highest reading is 8 V.
The lowest reading is 3 V.
Use proportion to calculate the resistance of the thermistor when it is very hot, and when it is very cold.
Explain your method. **[7 marks]**

Figure 4

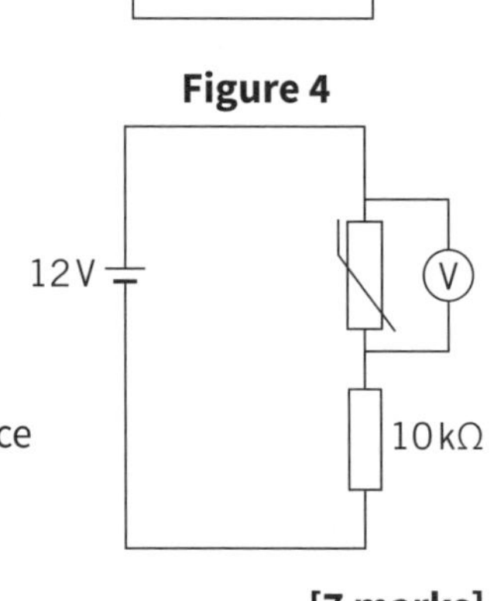

05 **Figure 5** shows a lamp and a resistor connected in series.

Figure 5

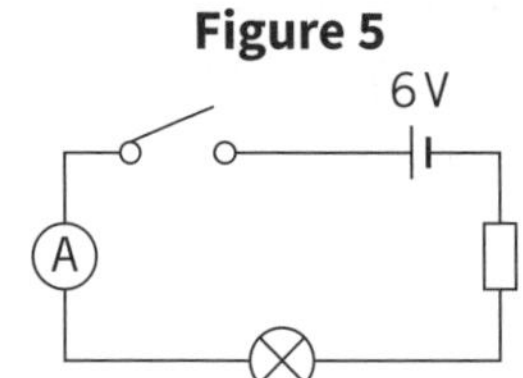

Exam Tip

To answer **05.3** you'll need to use your answer from **05.1** (p.d.) and the information in **05.2** (0.2 A). Show questions are great, because you know what the answer is, and if you write your working out clearly you know you've got the marks!

05.1 The potential difference across the lamp is 4 V.
Calculate the potential difference across the resistor. **[2 marks]**

05.2 The reading on the ammeter is 0.2 A.
Calculate the resistance of the lamp. **[3 marks]**

05.3 Show that the resistance of the resistor is 10 Ω. **[2 marks]**

05.4 The student now connects another identical resistor in series with the resistor and lamp in the circuit.

Select the correct bold word to complete this sentence:

The ammeter reading will **increase / stay the same / decrease**.

Explain your answer. **[2 marks]**

06 **Figure 6** shows the current against potential difference graph for two components: **A** and **B**.

Figure 6

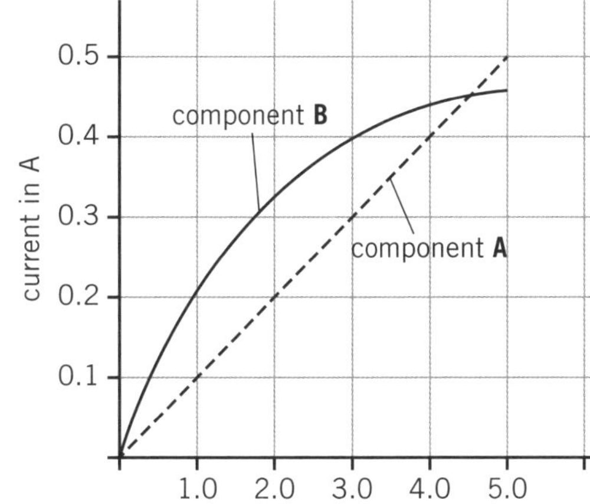

06.1 Write down which component is ohmic. **[1 mark]**

06.2 Calculate the resistance of component **A**. **[4 marks]**

Exam Tip

You need to find the gradient of the graph.

06.3 Describe what happens to the resistance of each component as the potential difference across it increases.
Explain how you used the graph to work out your answer. **[4 marks]**

06.4 A student connects the two components in parallel across a 3 V battery.
Calculate the total current in the circuit. **[2 marks]**

06.5 Calculate the resistance of the circuit.
Give your answer to two significant figures. **[2 marks]**

07 **Figure 7** shows a circuit with three resistors.

Figure 7

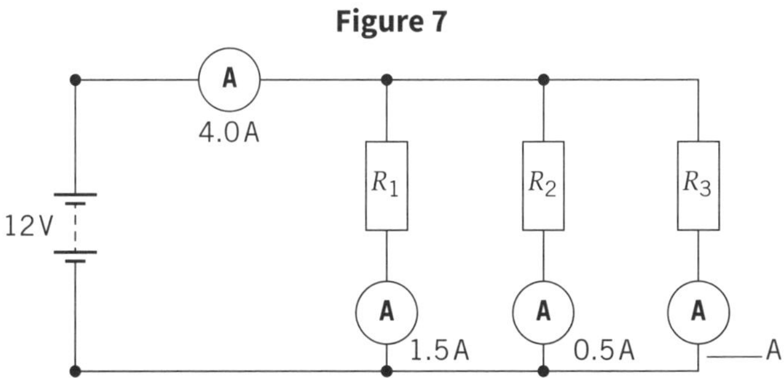

07.1 Use the readings from the ammeters to calculate the current passing through resistor R_3. **[2 marks]**

07.2 Identify which fact about this type of circuit you used to find the answer to **07.1**. **[1 mark]**

07.3 Write down the potential difference across R_2. **[1 mark]**

07.4 Identify which fact about this type of circuit you used to find the answer to **07.3**. **[1 mark]**

07.5 Look at the currents through resistors R_1 and R_2.
Without doing a calculation, determine which resistor has the bigger resistance. Explain how you worked out your answer. **[4 marks]**

07.5 specifically says 'without doing a calculation' which means if you're tempted to get that calculator out then you're not answering the question properly, and you won't get the marks.

08 A student connects an ammeter, a variable resistor, and a battery in a series circuit. The ammeter reads a current of 2 A.

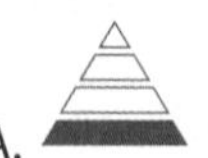

08.1 Write down the equation that links current, charge, and time. **[1 mark]**

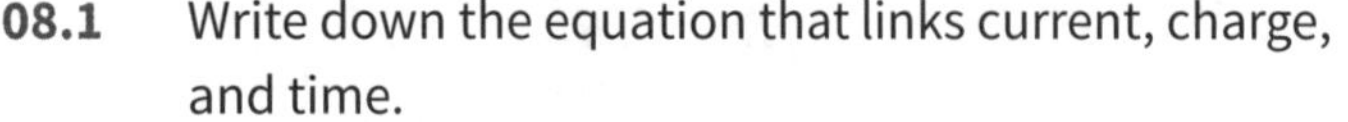

08.2 Calculate the charge flowing through the variable resistor in 25 seconds. Give the units with your answer. **[3 marks]**

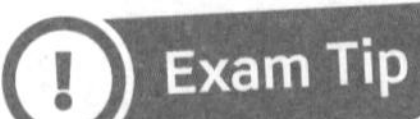

When you're trying to find the units needed for a calculation look at the units in the equation you've been using.

08.3 The student uses the variable resistor to change the resistance of the circuit. The current through the ammeter is now 1 A.
Write down what has happened to the resistance of the variable resistor. **[1 mark]**

08.4 Choose the correct bolded word to complete the sentence.
Justify your answer. **[2 marks]**
After the resistance has changed, the charge flowing through the variable resistor in 25 s will **increase** / **stay the same** / **decrease**.

09 A student has been given some samples of putty.
The putty conducts electricity because it has been made with salt.
The student connects one sample of putty in a series circuit with an ammeter and a battery marked 6 V, as shown in **Figure 8**.
The student then measures the current through the putty. The current is 15 mA.

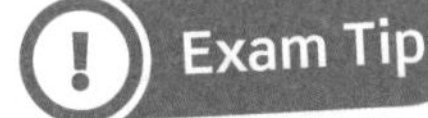

Look out for the non-standard units.

Figure 8

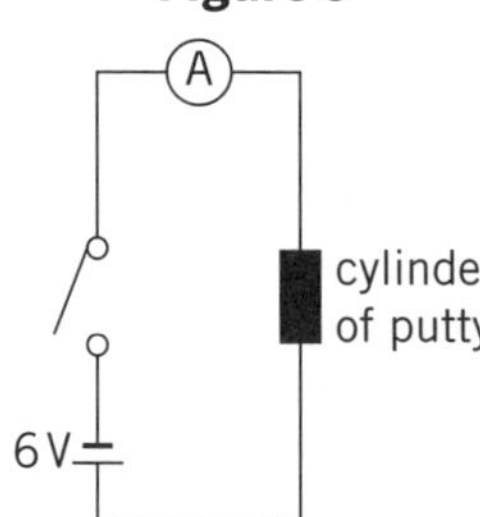

09.1 Calculate the time it takes 0.6 C of charge to flow through the putty. **[3 marks]**

09.2 The other samples of putty contain different masses of salt.
The student measures the current through these samples.
The data are shown in **Table 1**.

Table 1

Mass of salt per 100 g of putty in g	Current in mA
25	15
30	25
40	32
55	37
75	40
80	41

Sketch a graph of current against mass of salt from the data in **Table 1**. **[2 marks]**

Draw the graph in mA.

Trying to convert to amps will make the graph really small and hard to draw.

09.3 Use the data in **Table 1** to suggest how the resistance of the dough changes with the mass of salt.
Justify your answer with calculations. **[6 marks]**

> **Exam Tip**
> The only way to get full marks in the question is to use data from the table.

10 The resistance of a light dependent resistor (LDR) changes with light intensity. Light intensity is measured in lux.

> **Exam Tip**
> Don't worry if you've never come across lux before, it's just another unit!

10.1 Sketch a graph of the resistance of an LDR against light intensity. **[3 marks]**

10.2 Suggest a situation where you might need to use a light dependent resistor. **[1 mark]**

10.3 Using your answer to **10.2**, describe how the LDR can be used in that situation and explain why the changing resistance of the LDR would be useful.
You should include a circuit diagram to illustrate your answer. **[5 marks]**

> **Exam Tip**
> Your answer must refer to the situation you suggested in **10.2**!

11 Two students investigated the effect of length on the resistance of a wire.
They measured the resistance of different lengths of metal wire.

Table 2

Length in cm	Resistance in Ω
5	1.5
10	3.8
15	4.6
20	5.9
25	7.8

11.1 Plot the data from **Table 2** on graph paper. **[4 marks]**

11.2 Identify the independent variable, the dependent variable, and **one** control variable. **[3 marks]**

11.3 Estimate the resistance of a piece of wire that is 22 cm long. **[1 mark]**

> **Exam Tip**
> Draw lines on your graph to show your working!

11.4 Suggest **one** improvement that the student could make to improve the precision of the data. **[1 mark]**

11.5 Student **A** looked at the graph and said
'the resistance is directly proportional to length'.
Student **B** looked at the graph and said
'there is a linear relationship between resistance and length'.
Which student has made a correct statement?
student **A** student **B** both students
Explain your answer. **[3 marks]**

> **Exam Tip**
> Use evidence from the graph in your answer.

P5 Energy of matter

Changes of state and states of matter

Changes of state and conservation of mass

Changes of state are physical changes because no new substances are produced. The mass always stays the same because the number of particles does not change.

Particles and kinetic energy

When the temperature of a substance is increased, the kinetic energy store of its particles increases and the particles vibrate or move faster.

If the kinetic store of a substance's particles increases or decreases enough, the substance may change state.

Density

You can calculate the density of an object if you know its mass and volume:

$$\text{density (kg/m}^3\text{)} = \frac{\text{mass (kg)}}{\text{volume (m}^3\text{)}}$$

$$\rho = \frac{m}{V}$$

Solid	**Arrangement**	• particles held next to each other in fixed positions by strong forces of attraction
	Movement	• vibrate about fixed positions
	Properties	• high density • fixed volume • fixed shape (unless deformed by an external force)
Liquid	**Arrangement**	• particles are in contact with each other • forces of attraction between particles are weaker than in solids
	Movement	• free to move randomly around each other
	Properties	• usually lower density than solids • fixed volume • shape is not fixed so they can flow
Gas	**Arrangement**	• particles are spread out • almost no forces of attraction between particles • large distance between particles on average
	Movement	• move randomly at high speed
	Properties	• low density • no fixed volume or shape • can be compressed and can flow • spread out to fill all available space

Internal energy

Heating a substance increases its **internal energy**.

Internal energy is the sum of the total kinetic energy the particles have due to their motion and the total potential energy the particles have due to their positions relative to each other.

Latent heat

In a graph showing the change in temperature of a substance being heated or cooled, the flat horizontal sections show when the substance is changing state.

The energy transfers taking place during a change in state do not cause a change in temperature, but do change the internal energy of the substance.

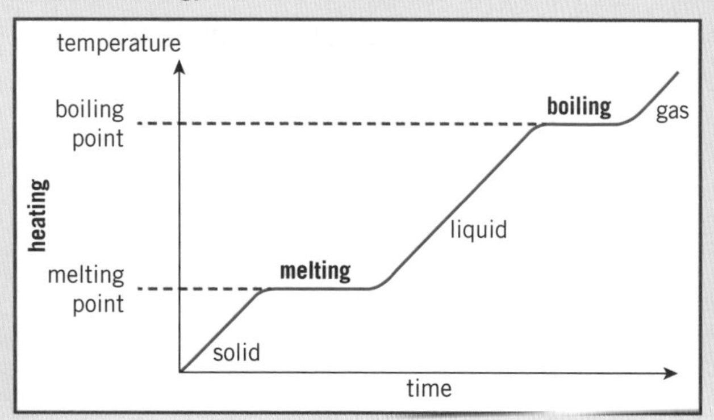

The energy transferred when a substance changes state is called the **latent heat**.

Specific latent heat – the energy required to change 1 kg of a substance with no change in temperature.

Specific latent heat of fusion – the energy required to melt 1 kg of a substance with no change in temperature.

Specific latent heat of vaporisation – the energy required to **evaporate** 1 kg of a substance with no change in temperature.

The energy needed to change the state of a substance can be calculated using the equation:

$$\text{thermal energy for a change in state (J)} = \text{mass (kg)} \times \text{specific latent heat (J/kg)}$$

$$E = ml$$

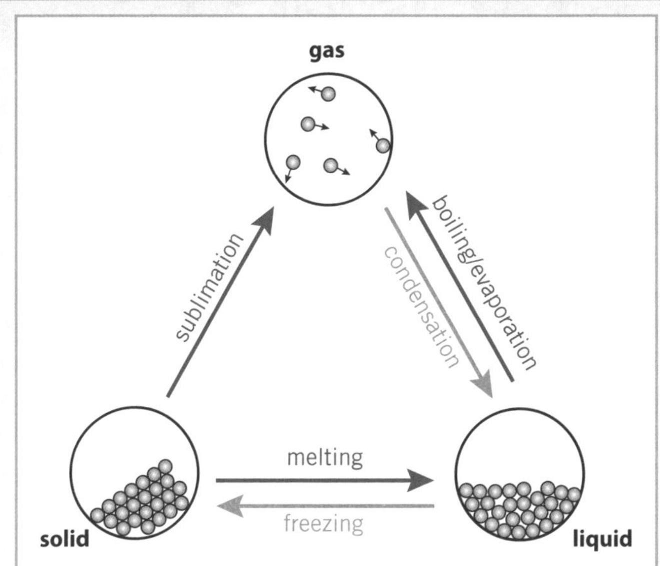

Specific heat capacity

When a substance is heated or cooled the temperature change depends on:

- the substance's mass
- the type of material
- how much energy is transferred to it.

Every type of material has a **specific heat capacity** – the amount of energy needed to raise the temperature of 1 kg of the substance by 1 °C.

The energy transferred to the thermal store of a substance can be calculated from the substance's mass, specific heat capacity, and temperature change:

change in thermal energy (J) = mass (kg) × specific heat capacity (J/kg°C) × temperature change (°C)

$$\Delta E = mc\Delta\theta$$

This equation will be given to you on the equation sheet, but you need to be able to select and apply it to the correct questions.

The relationship between temperature and pressure in gases

Gas temperature

The particles in a gas are constantly moving in random directions and with random speeds.

The temperature of a gas is related to the average kinetic energy of its particles.

When a gas is heated, the particles gain kinetic energy and move faster, so the temperature of the gas increases.

Gas pressure

The pressure a gas exerts on a surface, such as the walls of a container, is caused by the force of the gas particles hitting the surface.

The pressure of a gas produces a net force at right angles to the walls of a container or any surface.

If the temperature of a gas in a sealed container is increased, the pressure increases because

- the particles move faster so they hit the surfaces with more force
- the number of these impacts per second increases, exerting more force overall.

If a gas is compressed quickly, for example, in a bicycle pump, its temperature can rise. This is because

- compressing the gas requires a force to be applied to the gas – this results in work being done to the gas, since work done = force × distance
- the energy gained by the gas is not transferred quickly enough to its surroundings.

Key terms Write a definition for these key terms.

boiling condensation conservation of mass density evaporation freezing internal energy latent heat melting specific heat capacity specific latent heat sublimation

Revision tips

Practice Draw diagrams to show the arrangement of particles in solids, liquids, and gases, with labels to show the movement and forces of attraction. Cover up the page opposite and write down the properties of each type of substance.

Practice The units for specific heat capacity are tricky to remember, so practice writing them as units as well as words!

Retrieval

Learn the answers to the questions below, then cover the answers column with a piece of paper and write as many as you can. Check and repeat.

	P5 questions	Answers
1	Which two quantities do you need to measure to find the density of a solid or liquid?	mass and volume
2	What happens to the particles in a substance if its temperature is increased?	they move faster and the energy in their kinetic energy store increases
3	Why are changes of state physical changes?	no new substances are produced and the substance will have the same properties as before if the change is reversed
4	Why is the mass of a substance conserved when it changes state?	the number of particles does not change
5	What is the internal energy of a substance?	the total kinetic energy and potential energy of all the particles in the substance
6	What is the name given to the energy transferred when a substance changes state?	latent heat
7	What is the specific latent heat of a substance?	the energy required to change the state of one kilogram of that substance with no change in temperature
8	What is the specific latent heat of fusion of a substance?	the energy required to change one kilogram of the substance from solid to liquid at its melting point, without changing its temperature
9	What is the specific latent heat of vaporisation of a substance?	the energy required to change one kilogram of the substance from liquid to vapour at its boiling point, without changing its temperature
10	On a graph of temperature against time for a substance being heated up or cooled down, what do the flat (horizontal) sections show?	the time when the substance is changing state and the temperature is not changing
11	What property of a gas is related to the average kinetic energy of its particles?	temperature
12	What causes the pressure of a gas on a surface?	the force of the gas particles hitting the surface
13	Give two reasons why the pressure of a gas in a sealed container increases if its temperature is increased.	the molecules move faster so they hit the surfaces with more force and the number of impacts per second increases, so the total force of the impacts increases
14	Give two reasons why the temperature of a gas increases if it is compressed quickly.	the force applied to compress the gas results in work being done to the gas, and the energy gained by the gas is not transferred quickly enough to the surroundings
15	What is specific heat capacity?	the amount of energy needed to raise the temperature of 1 kg of a material by 1 °C

Now go back and use the questions below to check your knowledge from previous chapters.

Previous questions / Answers

	Previous questions	Answers
1	What is the same at all points when charge flows in a closed loop?	current
2	What are the units for power, current, potential difference, and resistance?	watt (W), amp (A), volt (V), ohm (Ω)
3	What colours are the live, neutral, and earth wires in a three-core cable?	live = brown, neutral = blue, earth = green and yellow stripes
4	What is an ohmic conductor?	conductor where current is directly proportional to the voltage so resistance is constant (at constant temperature)
5	What are the main disadvantages of using tidal power?	can harm aquatic habitats, initial set up expensive, cannot increase supply when needed, supply varies depending on time of month, hazard for boats
6	What factors affect the rate of heat loss from a building?	thickness of walls and roof, thermal conductivity of walls and roof, the temperature difference between the two sides of wall/roof

Put paper here

Required Practical Skills

Practise answering questions on the required practicals using the example below. You need to be able to apply your skills and knowledge to other practicals too.

Density

You need to be able to measure the masses and volumes of regularly and irregularly-shaped solid objects, and liquids.

To be accurate and precise in your investigation you need to:

- use dimensions to determine volume of regularly-shaped objects, and displacement for irregularly-shaped objects
- use a measuring cylinder to measure the volume of a liquid or displaced water
- choose a measuring cylinder that is just large enough for the object/liquid so that the divisions are as small as possible
- measure from the bottom of the meniscus of a liquid in a measuring cylinder.

Worked example

A student uses a measuring cylinder and digital balance to measure the density of an irregular lump of putty.

1 Describe how to use the equipment to make the measurements required.

Place the putty in the cylinder and cover it with water so that the putty is just covered. Record the volume, remove the putty, and record the new volume. Find the difference between the volumes in cm^3. Measure the putty mass with the digital balance in g.

2 For a putty mass of 65 g, the student recorded three volumes of 54, 56, and 57 cm^3. Calculate the mean volume and the density of the putty.

$$\text{mean volume} = \frac{(54 + 56 + 57)}{3} = 55.67\ \text{cm}^3$$

$$\text{density} = \frac{\text{mass}}{\text{volume}} = \frac{65}{55.67} = 1.17\ \text{g/cm}^3 \text{ to 3 significant figures}$$

Practice

A scientist has two samples of seawater. The volume of each is the same.

Sample **A** has a mass of 235 g and Sample **B** has a mass of 237 g.

Calculate the ratio of the densities of Sample **A** and **B**.

Show your working and explain your method.

Practice

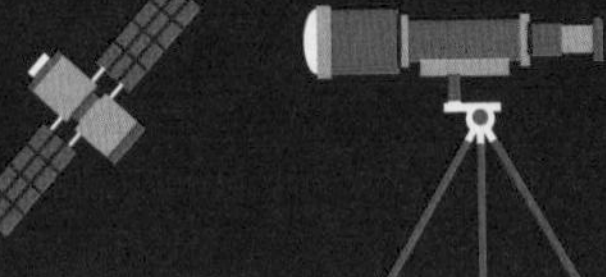

Exam-style questions

01 A student wants to calculate the density of modelling clay.

To do this, they take a mass of clay and put it into a measuring cylinder containing water.

Figure 1 shows the water in the measuring cylinder before (**A**) and after (**B**) the clay was added.

Figure 1

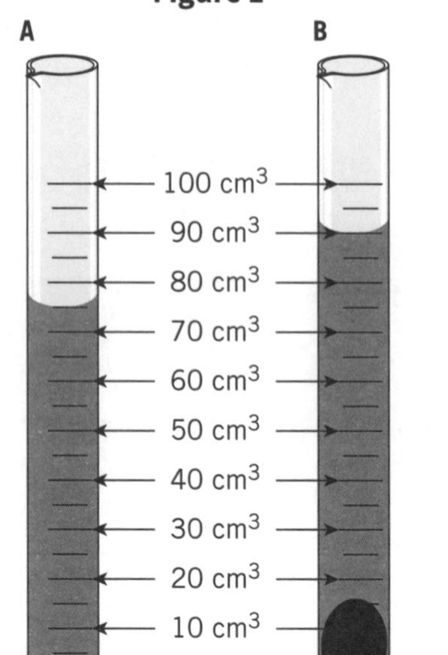

01.1 Use **Figure 1** to calculate the volume of the clay. **[2 marks]**

Volume = ________________ cm^3

01.2 Write down the resolution of the measuring cylinders.

Explain how you worked out your answer. **[2 marks]**

____

____

01.3 The student measures the mass of the clay.

The clay has a mass of 23.41 g.

Suggest the measuring instrument that the student used to find the mass. **[1 mark]**

____

01.4 Write down the equation that links density, mass, and volume. **[1 mark]**

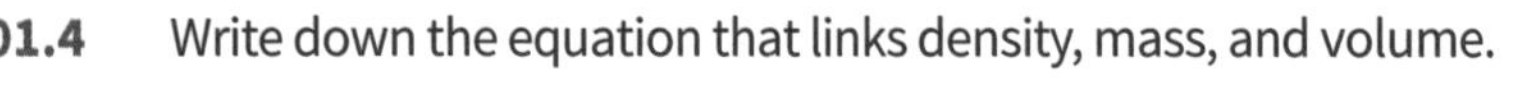

> **Exam Tip**
>
> An easy way to remember the equation in **01.4** is that the m and v can look like a heart:
>
> 

01.5 Calculate the density of the clay in g/cm^3. **[2 marks]**

Density = ________________ g/cm^3

01.6 Another student makes a cube out of the clay.

Suggest a method that this student could use to find the volume of the clay. **[2 marks]**

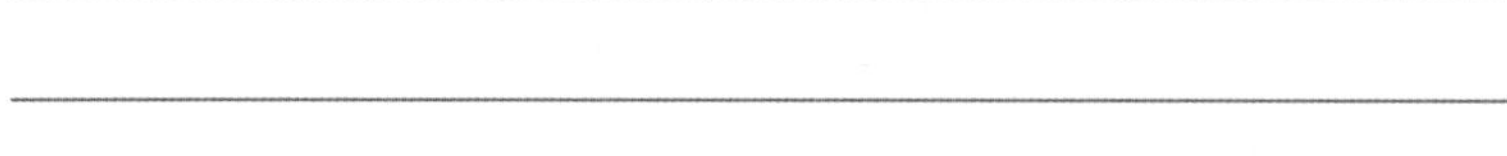

____

> **Exam Tip**
>
> A cube is a regular shape – you don't need to use a measuring cylinder for this.

02 A student is learning about internal energy.

They draw two diagrams, **A** and **B**, as shown in **Figure 2**.

Figure 2

A

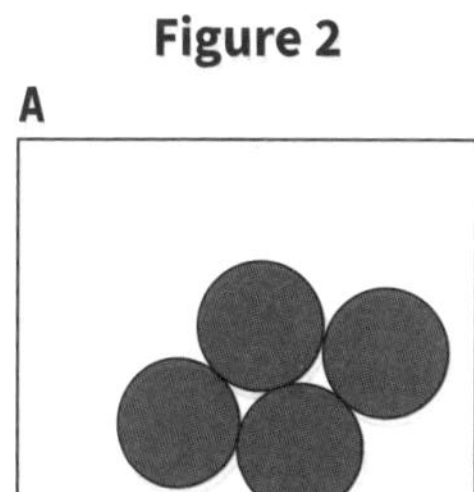

The particles in a solid.

B

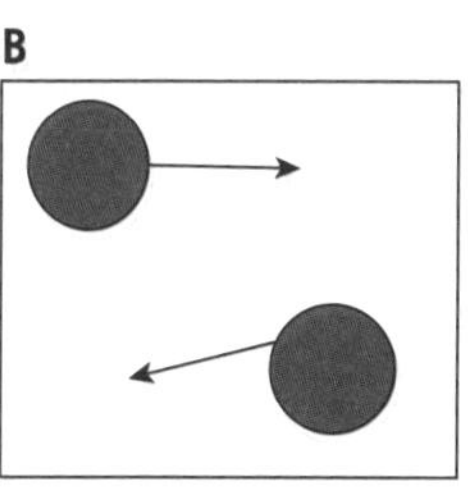

The particles in a gas.

02.1 Complete the sentences using the words in the box. **[4 marks]**

kinetic	vibrating	moving fast
potential	gravitational	moving slowly

In diagram **A** the particles are ____________. Most of the internal energy is due to the ____________ energy of the particles.

In diagram **B** the particles are ____________. Most of the internal energy is due to the ____________ energy of the particles.

02.2 The sample shown in **Figure 2 A** is heated for a long time.

Describe how the internal energy of the sample changes. **[2 marks]**

____

____

____

02.3 The sample shown in **Figure 2 B** is heated.

The student decides to use the particle model to describe and explain what happens.

Which statement is correct? **[1 mark]**

Tick **one** box.

As the gas is heated the average kinetic energy of the molecules decreases. ☐

The average kinetic energy of the molecules is independent of the temperature of the gas. ☐

If the temperature of a gas increases the pressure that the gas exerts decreases (if the volume stays the same). ☐

The particles in a gas are in random motion. ☐

03 A liquid is heated until it boils. The temperature is measured as it is being heated.

Figure 3 shows the graph of temperature against time for the liquid.

Figure 3

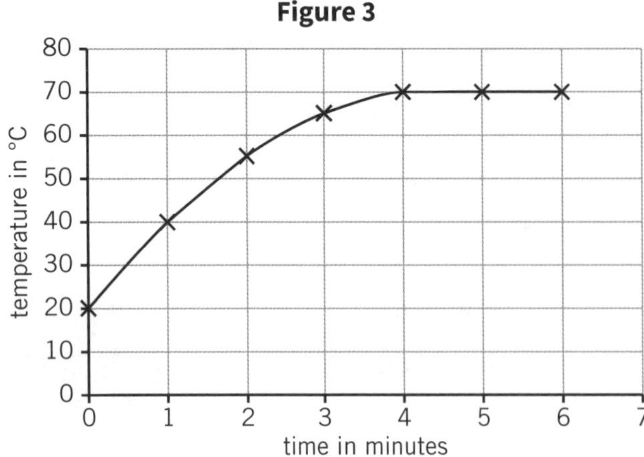

03.1 Write down the temperature of the room. **[1 mark]**

03.2 Write down the boiling point of the liquid. **[1 mark]**

03.3 Give the equation that links power, energy transferred, and time. **[1 mark]**

03.4 The power of the heater used to heat the liquid was 1 kW. The specific latent heat of vaporisation of the liquid is 365 kJ/kg. Calculate the mass of liquid that was vaporised between 4 and 6 minutes. Use an equation from the *Physics Equations Sheet*. **[5 marks]**

03.5 Suggest whether your answer to **03.4** is an overestimate or an underestimate of the actual mass of liquid that evaporated. Explain your answer. **[2 marks]**

03.6 Sketch a line on **Figure 3** to show what would happen if the power of the heater was doubled. **[3 marks]**

> **! Exam Tip**
>
> In **03.1** you can assume that the liquid was at room temperature before it started to be heated.

> **! Exam Tip**
>
> You need to use more than one equation to solve **03.4**.

04 A teacher is showing a class a method for finding the specific latent heat of vaporisation of water.
The teacher puts a kettle containing water on a set of digital scales and measures its mass. The kettle is turned on to allow the water to boil. At the same time, the teacher turns on a stopwatch. After two minutes the kettle is turned off and the teacher notes the new reading on the scales.

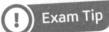

Table 1

Mass at the start of the two minutes	1.276 kg
Mass at the end of the two minutes	1.180 kg

The power of the kettle is 2 kW.

04.1 Write down the equation that links energy, power, and time. **[1 mark]**

04.2 Calculate the energy transferred from the kettle to the water. **[4 marks]**

04.3 Use your answer to **04.2** and the correct equation from the *Physics Equations Sheet* to calculate the specific latent heat of vaporisation of water. Give your answer in kJ/kg. **[5 marks]**

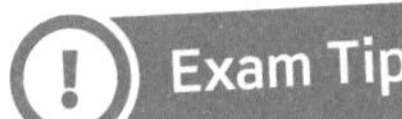

Look at the difference in values in **Table 1**.

04.4 The textbook value for the specific latent heat of vaporisation of water is 2265 kJ/kg.
Suggest a reason for the difference between the value that you have calculated and the textbook value. Explain your answer. **[3 marks]**

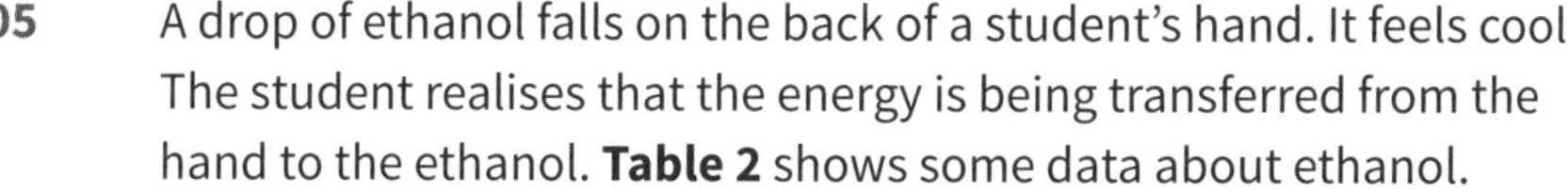

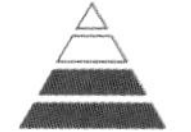

05 A drop of ethanol falls on the back of a student's hand. It feels cool. The student realises that the energy is being transferred from the hand to the ethanol. **Table 2** shows some data about ethanol.

Table 2

Specific heat capacity of ethanol	2460 J/kg °C
Specific latent heat of vaporisation of ethanol	838 000 J/kg

05.1 Explain what is meant by specific heat capacity and specific latent heat. **[2 marks]**

05.2 Compare the amount of energy needed to heat 0.01 kg of ethanol by 50 °C, with the energy needed to vaporise 0.01 kg of ethanol.
Use the correct equations from the *Physics Equations Sheet*. **[5 marks]**

05.3 Explain why, in general, the specific latent heat of vaporisation of a substance is bigger than its specific heat capacity when it is a liquid. **[2 marks]**

06 A student noticed that when they finished having a shower, the mirror is 'fogged up'.

06.1 Explain in terms of energy why the mirror is covered by a thin layer of water. **[3 marks]**

First use the equation for specific latent heat of vaporisation to find the mass of water.

06.2 The student estimates that the mirror is a square with sides measuring 60 cm. The density of water is 1×10^3 kg/m^3. The specific latent heat of vaporisation of water is 2265 kJ/kg. While the fog was forming, a total of 730 kJ of energy was transferred.
Calculate the thickness of the layer of water on the mirror. **[6 marks]**

07 A gas can be compressed or expanded by changes in pressure.

07.1 Describe how the arrangement of particles in a gas is different from that in a solid. **[4 marks]**

07.2 Explain, in terms of particles, why a gas exerts a pressure. **[4 marks]**

07.3 Sketch a graph to show how the pressure of a fixed mass of gas at constant volume varies with temperature. **[3 marks]**

08 One way to heat milk is to pass steam through it.

08.1 Suggest how a jet of steam heats a cup of milk. **[2 marks]**

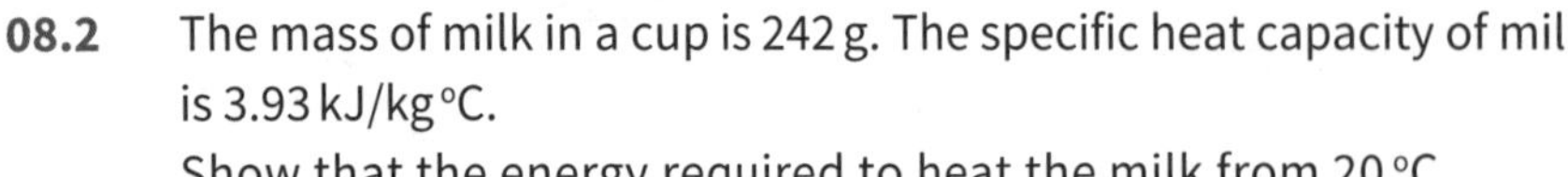

08.2 The mass of milk in a cup is 242 g. The specific heat capacity of milk is 3.93 kJ/kg °C.
Show that the energy required to heat the milk from 20 °C to 70 °C is about 48 kJ. Use an equation from the *Physics Equations Sheet*. **[4 marks]**

Exam Tip

Look out for non-standard units!

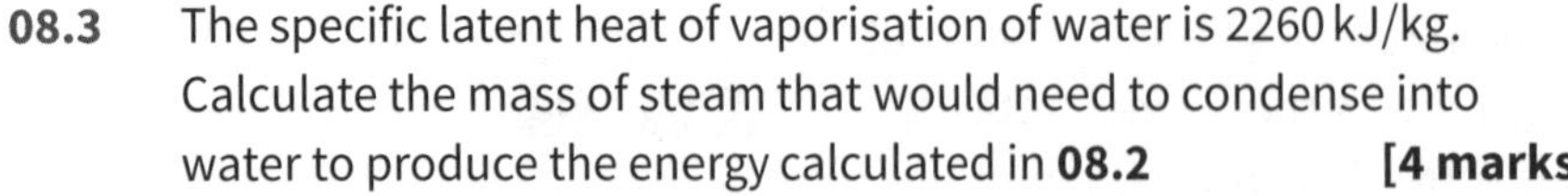

08.3 The specific latent heat of vaporisation of water is 2260 kJ/kg. Calculate the mass of steam that would need to condense into water to produce the energy calculated in **08.2** **[4 marks]**

08.4 Write down **one** assumption that you made when doing the calculation. **[1 mark]**

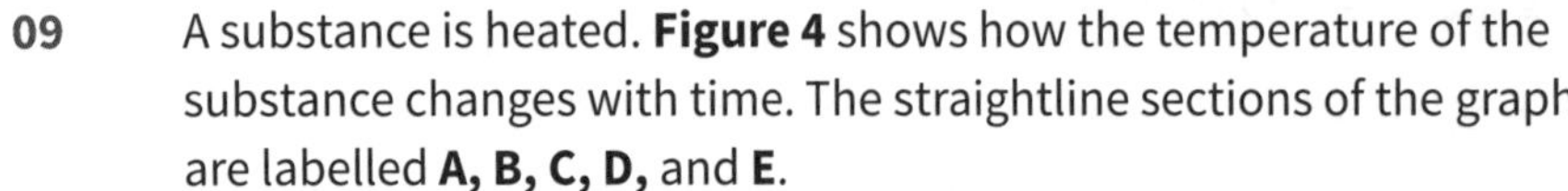

09 A substance is heated. **Figure 4** shows how the temperature of the substance changes with time. The straightline sections of the graph are labelled **A, B, C, D,** and **E**.

Figure 4

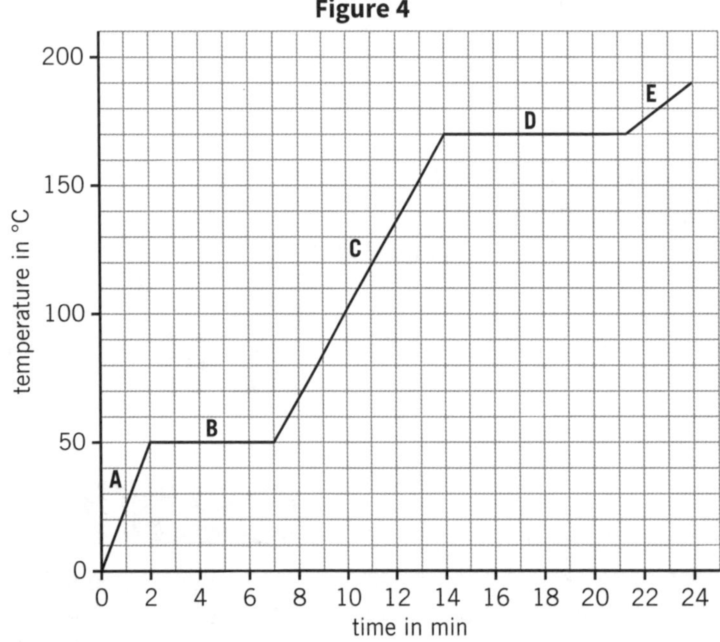

09.1 Write the letters of all the sections of the graph that show a change of state.
Explain why you have chosen these sections. **[4 marks]**

09.2 Did the substance start out as a solid or a liquid?
Explain your answer. **[2 marks]**

09.3 Write down the section of the graph where the vibration of the particles is increasing. **[1 mark]**

09.4 Write down the **two** sections of the graph where the kinetic energy of the particles is increasing. **[2 marks]**

Exam Tip

09.1 is worth four marks – it gives you a clue to what the examiner is looking for and helps structure your answer:

- 1st mark, give letter showing change of state
- 2nd mark, explain why you have chosen this letter
- 3rd mark, give letter showing second change of state
- 4th mark, explain why you have chosen this letter

10 A teacher has a cube of dry ice. Dry ice is solid carbon dioxide. The length of the sides of the cube is 5 cm.

10.1 Calculate the volume of the cube in cm^3. **[2 marks]**

10.2 The density of dry ice is 1.5 g/cm^3.
Calculate the mass of the cube of dry ice. **[4 marks]**

> **Exam Tip**
> The units in question **10.2** give you a big clue to the equation you need!

10.3 The dry ice changes from a solid to a gas without going through a liquid phase. Write down the name of this change of state. **[1 mark]**

10.4 Explain why the change is a physical change and not a chemical change. **[1 mark]**

10.5 Compare the internal energy of the carbon dioxide gas with the internal energy of the dry ice. Explain your answer.
Assume the gas and solid are at the same temperature. **[2 marks]**

11 A student wants to find out what happens when you put the human body into very cold water. To model this, the student uses a test tube filled with water and places it into a large beaker of iced water. The student sets up a circuit with a sensor to monitor the temperature of the water in the test tube over a period of time. The sensor is placed in the water in the test tube.

11.1 **Figure 5** shows the circuit the student used but the sensor is missing. Complete the diagram by drawing the correct circuit symbol for the sensor and label the component. **[2 marks]**

Figure 5

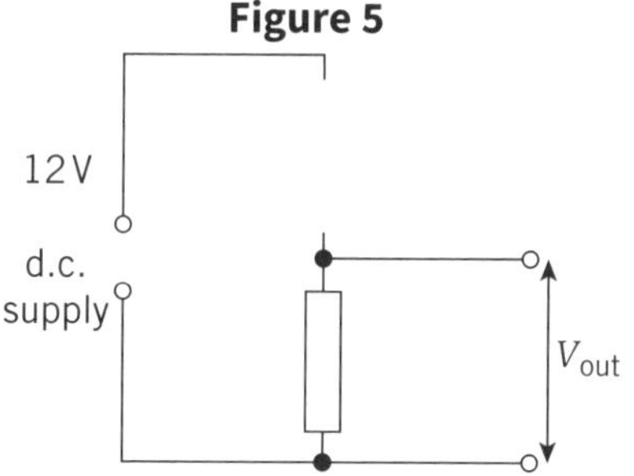

11.2 The student connects up the circuit. Initially V_{out} = 6 V.
Describe what will happen to V_{out} when they put the test tube into a large beaker of iced water. Explain your answer. **[5 marks]**

11.3 A data logger is used to monitor V_{out}. Eventually the data logger shows that V_{out} is no longer changing.
Describe how the student can use this measurement to calculate the temperature of the water. Include any additional data the student needs in order to do the calculation. **[4 marks]**

> **Exam Tip**
> You don't need to do the actual calculation, just describe how you would do it and what numbers you would need.

11.4 Suggest **one** limitation of this model for working out what happens to the temperature of a human body in cold water. **[1 mark]**

Knowledge

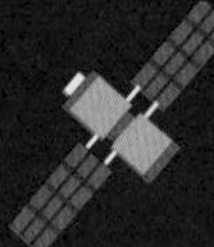

P6 Atoms

Modern model of an atom

The model of the atom we have today was developed over time with the help of evidence from experiments.

Future experiments may change our understanding and lead us to alter or replace this model of the atom.

Dalton's model

John Dalton thought of the atom as a solid sphere that could not be divided into smaller parts. His model did not include protons, neutrons, or electrons.

Plum pudding model

Scientists' experiments resulted in the discovery of charged sub-atomic particles. The first to be discovered were **electrons** – tiny, negatively-charged particles.

The discovery of electrons led to the **plum pudding model** of the atom – a cloud of positive charge, with negative electrons embedded in it.

Protons and neutrons had not yet been discovered.

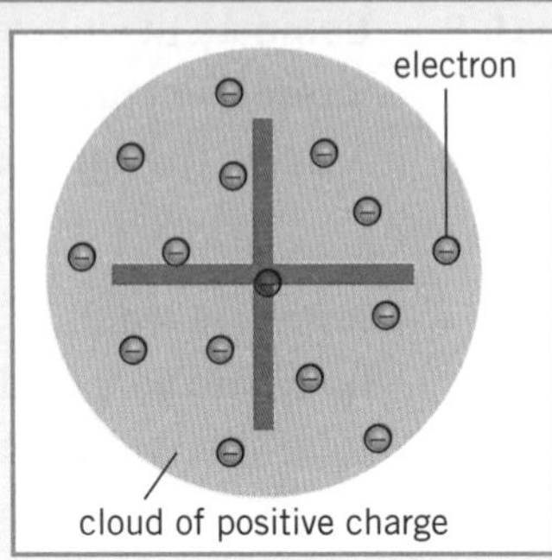

Alpha scattering experiment

1. Scientists fired small, positively-charged particles (called **alpha particles**) at a piece of gold foil only a few atoms thick.
2. They expected the alpha particles to travel straight through the gold.
3. They were surprised that a small number of the alpha particles bounced back and some were deflected (alpha scattering).
4. To explain why the alpha particles were repelled, the scientists suggested that the positive charge and mass of an atom must be concentrated in a very small space at its centre. They called this space the nucleus.

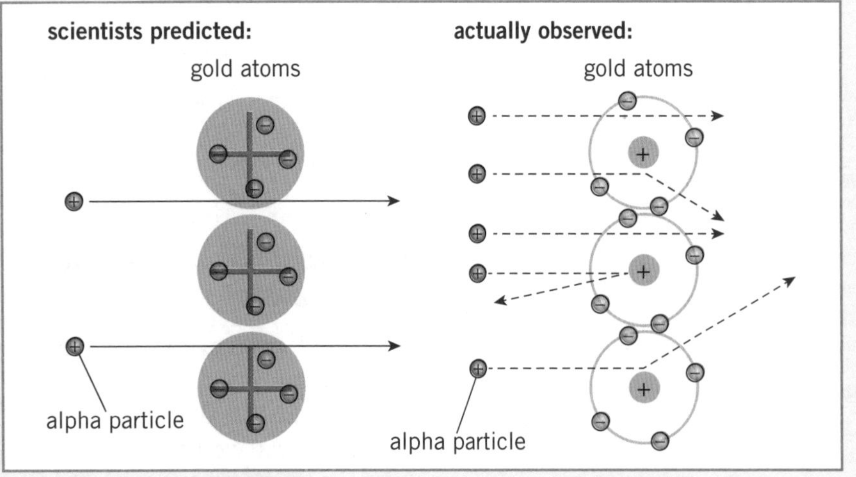

Nuclear model

Scientists replaced the plum pudding model with the **nuclear model**. They suggested that the electrons **orbit** (go around) the nucleus, but not at set distances, and that the mass of the atom was concentrated in the charged nucleus.

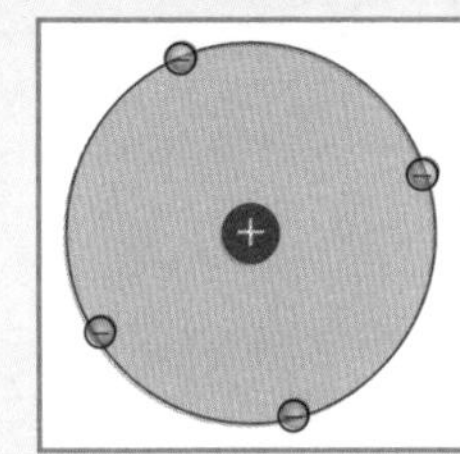

Bohr's model

Niels Bohr improved the nuclear model, and calculated that electrons must orbit the nucleus at fixed distances. These orbits are called shells or energy levels. These calculations agreed with experimental results.

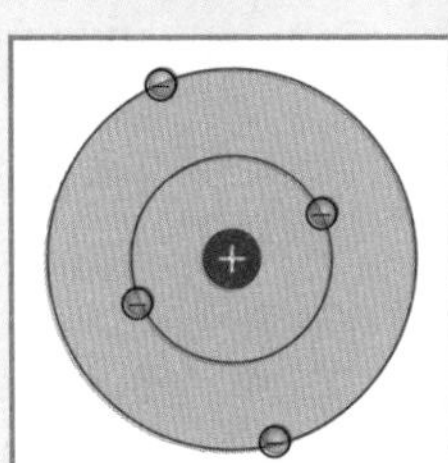

Revision tip

This content is also in chemistry. This can be a good thing and a bad thing – good because you have to learn less, and bad because it can be confusing in exams.

A few years ago there was a question about the structure of an atom in physics. If it had been in a chemistry exam everyone would have done brilliantly, but students panicked.

Protons

Later experiments provided evidence that the positive charge of a nucleus could be split into smaller particles, each with an opposite charge to the electron. These positively charged particles were called **protons**.

Neutrons

James Chadwick carried out experiments that provided evidence for a particle with no charge. Scientists called this the **neutron**. They concluded that the protons and neutrons are in the nucleus, and the electrons orbit the nucleus in shells.

Basic structure of an atom

An **atom** has a radius of about 1×10^{-10} metres.

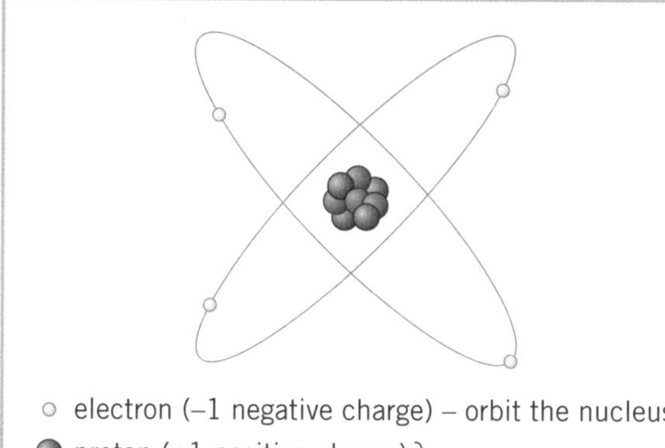

- electron (–1 negative charge) – orbit the nucleus
- proton (+1 positive charge) } in the nucleus
- neutron (no charge) } in the nucleus

An atom is uncharged overall, and has equal numbers of protons and electrons.

The nucleus

- has a radius about 10 000 times smaller than the radius of an atom
- contains protons and neutrons
- is where most of the mass of an atom is concentrated

Electrons

- Orbit the nucleus at different fixed distances called **energy levels**.
- Can gain energy by absorbing electromagnetic radiation. This causes them to move to a higher energy level.
- Can lose energy by emitting electromagnetic radiation. This causes them to move to a lower energy level.

Element symbols

mass number
= number of protons + neutrons
atoms of the same element can have different numbers of neutrons, so they can have different mass numbers

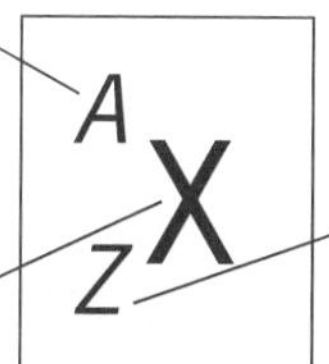

chemical symbol

atomic number
= number of protons
all atoms of the same element have the same number of protons in the nucleus, so they have the same atomic number

Isotopes are atoms of the same element, with the same number of protons but different numbers of neutrons.

Ionisation

Atoms can become charged when they lose or gain electrons. This process is called **ionisation**.

- A positive ion is formed if an uncharged atom *loses* one or more electrons.
- A negative ion is formed if an uncharged atom *gains* one or more electrons.

Key terms

Make sure you can write a definition for these key terms.

alpha particle atom atomic number electron energy level ionisation isotope mass number neutron nuclear model orbit plum pudding model proton

Learn the answers to the questions below, then cover the answers column with a piece of paper and write as many as you can. Check and repeat.

P6 questions		Answers
1	Describe the basic structure of an atom.	nucleus containing protons and neutrons, around which electrons orbit in fixed energy levels/shells
2	Describe the plum pudding model of the atom.	sphere of positive charge with negative electrons embedded in it
3	What charges do protons, neutrons, and electrons carry?	• protons = positive • neutrons = no charge • electrons = negative
4	Why do atoms have no overall charge?	equal numbers of positive protons and negative electrons
5	What is the radius of an atom?	around 1×10^{-10} m
6	How small is a nucleus compared to a whole atom?	around 10 000 times smaller
7	How can an electron move up an energy level?	absorb sufficient electromagnetic radiation
8	What is ionisation?	process which adds or removes electrons from an atom
9	What is formed if an atom loses an electron?	positive ion
10	How does an atom become a negative ion?	gains one or more electrons
11	What is the atomic number of an element?	number of protons in one atom of the element
12	What is the mass number of an element?	number of protons + number of neutrons
13	Which particle do atoms of the same element always have the same number of?	protons
14	What are isotopes?	atoms of the same element (same number of protons) with different numbers of neutrons
15	What were the two main conclusions from the alpha particle scattering experiment?	• most of the mass of an atom is concentrated in the nucleus • nucleus is positively charged

Put paper here

Now go back and use the questions below to check your knowledge from previous chapters.

Previous questions / Answers

	Previous questions	Answers
1	What is a renewable energy resource?	an energy source that will not run out, it is being (or can be) replaced at the same rate as it is used
2	Why are changes of state physical changes?	no new substances are produced and the substance will have the same properties as before if the change is reversed
3	What is the function of the earth wire in a three-core cable?	safety wire to stop the appliance becoming live
4	What are the main features of a parallel circuit?	p.d. across each branch is the same, total current through circuit is the sum of the currents in each branch – total resistance of all resistors is less than the resistance of the smallest individual resistor
5	How does a material become charged?	becomes negatively charged by gaining electrons and becomes positively charged by losing electrons
6	What is the specific latent heat of fusion of a substance?	the energy required to change one kilogram of the substance from solid to liquid at its melting point, without changing its temperature

Put paper here

Maths Skills

Practise your maths skills using the worked example and practice questions below.

Order of magnitude

Orders of magnitude are useful for comparing the size of numbers.

An order of magnitude is a factor of 10, so it is usually written as 10^n.

For example, if one number is roughly 10 times bigger than another number, it is one order of magnitude bigger.

If a number is 1000 times bigger than another number, it is three orders of magnitude bigger, because: $1000 = 10 \times 10 \times 10 = 10^3$.

Two numbers are of the same order of magnitude if dividing the bigger number by the smaller number gives an answer less than 10. For example, 12 and 45 are the same order of magnitude, but 13 and 670 are not.

If numbers are written in standard form, their orders of magnitude can be compared by dividing the larger power of ten by the smaller power of ten.

Worked Examples

1 A mouse has a mass of about 40 g, and an elephant has a mass of about 4×10^6 g. How many orders of magnitude heavier is an elephant compared to the mouse?

Divide the larger power of ten by the smaller power of ten:

$\frac{10^6}{10^1} = 10^5$, *or five orders of magnitude.*

2 The mass of the Sun is about 2.0×10^{30} kg. The mass of the Earth is 6.0×10^{24} kg. How many orders of magnitude bigger is the Sun's mass?

Divide the larger power of ten by the smaller power of ten:

$\frac{10^{30}}{10^{24}} = 10^6$, *or six orders of magnitude.*

Practice

1 How many orders of magnitude bigger is the mass of a lorry around 44 000 kg compared to a human body around 70 kg?

2 How many orders of magnitude smaller is the diameter of an atom around 0.1 nm compared to the diameter of a marble of 1 cm?

3 How many orders of magnitude smaller is 70 J compared to 450 MJ?

Practice

Exam-style questions

01 **Table 1** shows the number of protons and neutrons in the neutral atoms of three elements.

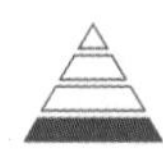

Table 1

Element	Number of protons	Number of neutrons
A	10	10
B	10	12
C	11	12

01.1 Write down the number of electrons in an atom of element **A**. **[1 mark]**

01.2 Explain your answer to **01.1**. **[2 marks]**

> **Exam Tip**
> Use data from **Table 1**.

01.3 Name the two elements that are isotopes. **[1 mark]**

1 ______________

2 ______________

> **Exam Tip**
> Isotopes have the same atomic number.

01.4 Explain your answer to **01.3**. **[2 marks]**

02 A student has drawn two diagrams that show the nuclei of isotopes of an element (**Figure 1**).

Figure 1

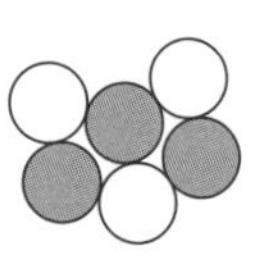

nucleus **1**

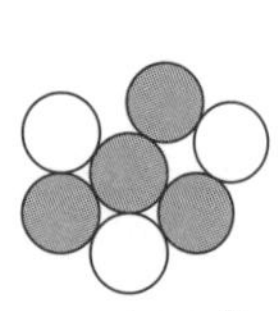

nucleus **2**

02.1 Write down which particle, **A** or **B**, is a proton.
Justify your answer. **[2 marks]**

02.2 Name the other type of particle. **[1 mark]**

____

02.3 Use **Table 2** to identify the element the student drew.

Table 2

Element	Atomic number
Lithium	3
Beryllium	4
Carbon	6
Nitrogen	7

Explain your answer. **[2 marks]**

____

____

____

02.4 Give the complete chemical symbol of both isotopes. **[2 marks]**

Isotope **1**: ______________

Isotope **2**: ______________

02.5 Compare the charge on nucleus **1** with the charge on nucleus **2**.
Justify your answer. **[2 marks]**

____

____

03 Atoms are very small.

03.1 Choose the approximate radius of an atom from the numbers in the box.

10^{15} m	10^{10} m	10^{1} m	10^{-10} m	10^{-15} m

[1 mark]

Exam Tip

Only select **one** answer – picking two will cause you to lose marks.

03.2 Atoms have electrons that are arranged in different energy levels. Define an energy level. **[1 mark]**

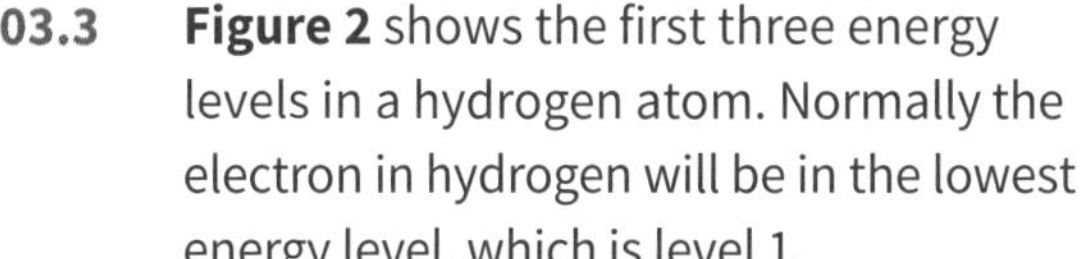

03.3 **Figure 2** shows the first three energy levels in a hydrogen atom. Normally the electron in hydrogen will be in the lowest energy level, which is level 1.

Compare what happens to the electron when an atom absorbs electromagnetic radiation with what happens when it emits electromagnetic radiation. Use **Figure 2** to provide examples. **[4 marks]**

Figure 2

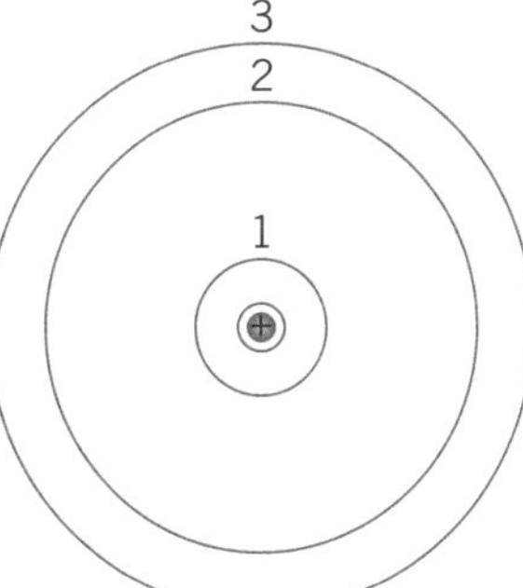

Exam Tip

Clearly label any lines you draw on the diagram to ensure the examiner can give you the marks for your answer.

04 A student is explaining what the symbols on the Periodic Table mean. She uses the example of the element nitrogen shown in **Figure 3**.

Figure 3

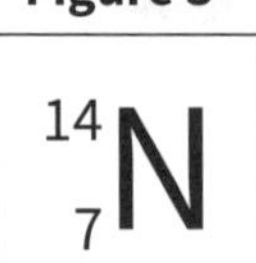

04.1 Complete the student's sentences.

You can work out the number of protons in an atom of this element by…

You can work out the number of neutrons in an atom of this element by…

You can work out the number of electrons in an atom of this element by… **[3 marks]**

Exam Tip

Remember the mass number is the larger number and the atomic number is the smaller number.

04.2 Another student says:

'The number of neutrons is always equal to the number of protons.'

Is this student correct? Explain your answer. **[2 marks]**

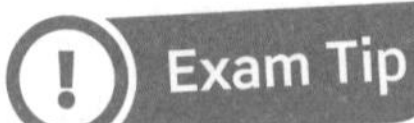

Exam Tip

You *must* use data to back up your answer.

05 In the development of the model of the atom, there have been many discoveries and different models have been proposed.

- The electron was discovered in 1899 by J. J. Thompson.
- The nuclear model of the atom was proposed by Ernest Rutherford in 1911.
- The proton was named in 1920 by Rutherford.
- The neutron was discovered in 1932 by James Chadwick.

Describe how it was possible for Rutherford to develop a nuclear model before the particles that make up the nucleus had been discovered or identified. **[6 marks]**

06 **Figure 4** shows the plum pudding model of an atom.

Figure 4

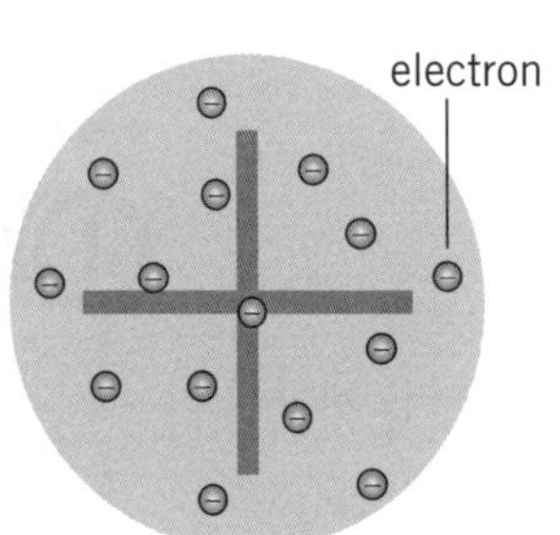

Exam Tip

To help you answer the next question try labelling any parts you can.

06.1 Use **Figure 4** to describe the plum pudding model. **[3 marks]**

Exam Tip

This is a great question – all the information you need to answer it is in the figure.

06.2 Describe the model of the atom that the plum pudding model replaced. **[1 mark]**

06.3 The plum pudding model could not explain some of the results of the alpha particle scattering experiment.
Describe **one** of the results that the plum pudding model could **not** explain. **[2 marks]**

07 **Figure 5** shows the experimental equipment that scientists working with Rutherford used to develop the nuclear model of the atom.

Figure 5

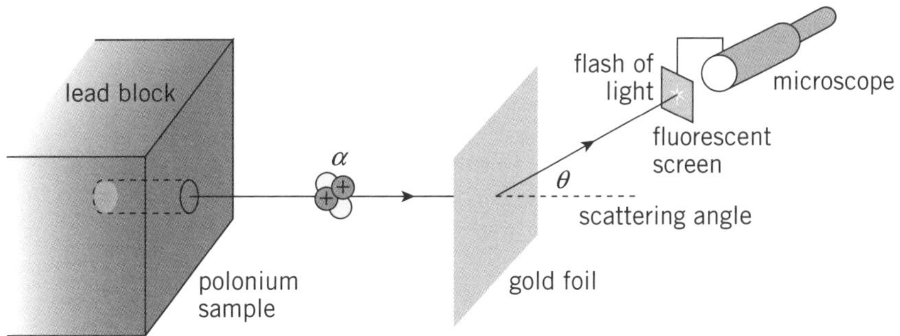

Table 3

Angle of deflection	Experimental count
150	33
135	43
120	52
105	70
75	211
60	477
45	1435
30	7800
15	132 000
	Total = 142 141

Table 3 shows the number of alpha particles deflected through different angles.

07.1 Use the data in **Table 3** to show that the percentage of alpha particles that were scattered back from the foil was approximately 0.14%. **[2 marks]**

07.2 Write down the percentage of alpha particles that went through the foil. **[1 marks]**

07.3 Suggest how the data in **Table 3** may have led Rutherford to propose the nuclear model. **[2 marks]**

07.4 The alpha particle is a helium nucleus.
Write down the charge on an alpha particle. **[1 mark]**

07.5 Suggest whether the data about the angle of deflection support the idea that the charge on the nucleus is positive or negative.
Justify your answer. **[4 marks]**

A helium nuclei has a mass of 4 and an atomic number of 2.

08 **Figure 6** shows transitions of electrons between different energy levels in an atom.

Figure 6

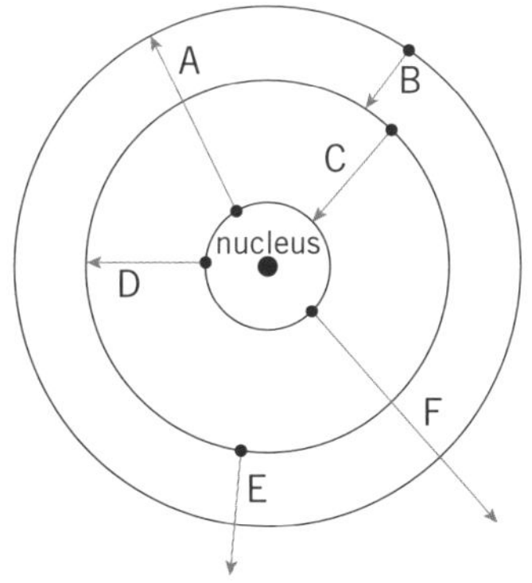

08.1 Write down the letters that show the transition of electrons when electromagnetic radiation is absorbed. **[2 marks]**

08.2 Write down the letters that show the transition of electrons when electromagnetic radiation is emitted. **[2 marks]**

08.3 Write down the letters that show ionisation of the atom. **[2 marks]**

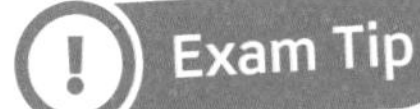

Make sure you check that the arrows are all going in the same direction – for example, either all pointing out, or all pointing in!

08.4 Write down the charge on the atom when the atom is ionised. **[1 mark]**

08.5 The nucleus in **Figure 6** is not drawn to scale. A student measures the diameter of the atom in a textbook and finds that it is 2 cm.

Estimate the diameter of the dot that would represent the nucleus if it was drawn to scale. Explain your calculation.
Suggest a reason why your answer may not be feasible. **[4 marks]**

09 A student investigates how a ball bounces. They use a metre rule and a ball (**Figure 7**). They drop a ball from different heights. They measure the height of the first bounce.

The results are in **Table 4**.

Figure 7

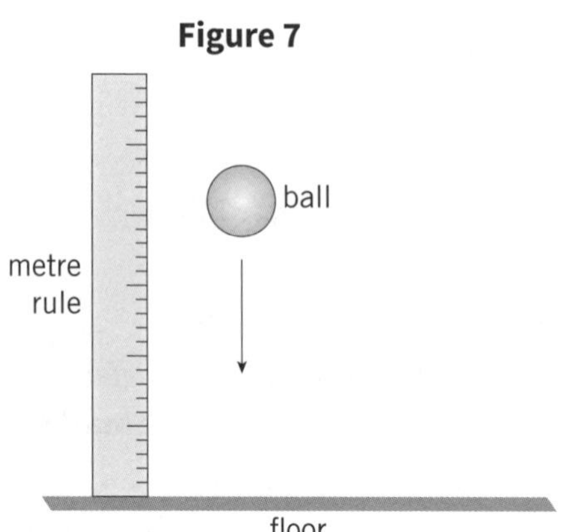

Table 4

Height of drop in cm	Height of bounce in cm
20	16
40	30
60	49
80	55
100	70

09.1 Explain in terms of energy why the ball does not bounce back to the height from which it was dropped. **[2 marks]**

09.2 Plot a graph of the results on **Figure 8**. **[3 marks]**

Figure 8

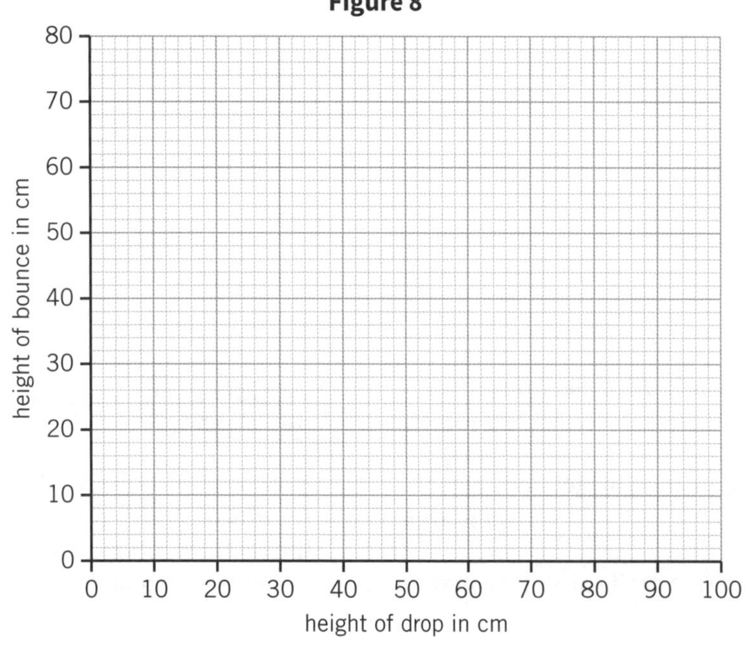

Exam Tip

Always mark points on the graph with crosses.

09.3 Identify the anomalous result. **[1 mark]**

09.4 Suggest whether the bounce height is proportional to the drop height. Explain your answer. **[2 marks]**

10 A student looks at a packet of fuse wires.
They notice that the wires have different thicknesses.

10.1 Describe the action of a fuse in a circuit where an appliance is connected to the mains. **[2 marks]**

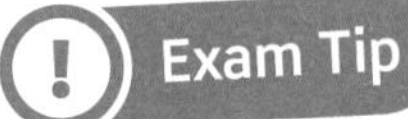

Think about the symbol for a fuse and the need for a complete circuit.

10.2 Suggest why the wires for different currents are different thicknesses. **[3 marks]**

10.3 **Table 5** shows some data relating to a particular fuse wire.

Table 5

Parameter	Fuse data
length	0.5 cm
cross-sectional area	1×10^{-6} m^2
density	7000 kg/m^3
specific heat capacity	230 J/kg °C
melting point of fuse metal	687 °C
specific latent heat	300 000 J/kg

Write down the equation that links density, mass, and volume. **[1 mark]**

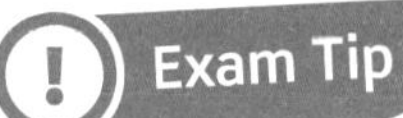

When you are asked to write the equation that links variables, you can write it in any correct arrangement. For example, for your answer to **10.3** you could write any of these:

- mass = density × volume
- mass = volume × density
- density = $\frac{\text{mass}}{\text{volume}}$
- volume = $\frac{\text{mass}}{\text{density}}$

10.4 Calculate the mass of the fuse wire using the data in **Table 5**. **[5 marks]**

10.5 Use the *Physics Equations Sheet* to calculate the energy needed to raise the temperature of the wire to its melting point, and melt the fuse. **[5 marks]**

10.6 Write down the equation that links energy transferred, power, and time. **[1 mark]**

10.7 Write down the equation that links power, current, and resistance. **[1 mark]**

10.8 The resistance of the fuse wire is 1.8 Ω and the fuse melts in about 0.5 s. Calculate the current in the wire when it melts. **[3 marks]**

Knowledge

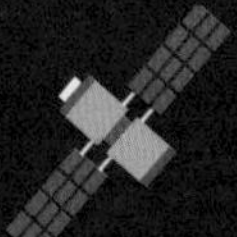

P7 Nuclear radiation

Radioactive decay

Radioactive decay is when nuclear radiation is emitted by unstable atomic nuclei so that they become more stable. It is a *random* process. This radiation can knock electrons out of atoms in a process called **ionisation**.

Type of radiation	Change in the nucleus	Ionising power	Range in air	Stopped by
α **alpha** particle (two protons and two neutrons)	nucleus loses two protons and two neutrons	highest ionising power	travels a few centimetres in air	stopped by a sheet of paper
β **beta** particle (fast-moving electron)	a neutron changes into a proton and an electron	high ionising power	travels ≈ 1 m in air	stopped by a few millimetres of aluminium
γ **gamma** radiation (short-wavelength, high-frequency electromagnetic radiation)	some energy is transferred away from the nucleus	low ionising power	virtually unlimited range in air	stopped by several centimetres of thick lead or metres of concrete

Activity and count rate

The **activity** of a radioactive source is the rate of decay of an unstable nucleus, measured in becquerel (Bq).

1 Bq = 1 decay per second

Detectors (e.g., **Geiger-Muller tubes**) record a **count rate** (number of decays detected per second).

$$\text{count rate after } n \text{ half-lives} = \frac{\text{initial count rate}}{2^n}$$

Revision tip

Practice Tips for working out half-lives from a graph:

1. Always draw your construction lines on. This helps examiners to follow your working even if you've made a mistake.
2. Calculate at least two half lives, the answers should be very similar both times and give you confidence in your answer.

Half-life

The **half-life** of a radioactive source is the time

- for half the number of unstable nuclei in a sample to decay
- for the count rate or activity of a source to halve.

The half-life of a source can be found from a graph of its count rate or activity against time.

To find the reduction in activity after a given number of half-lives:

1. calculate the activity after each half-life
2. subtract the final activity from the original activity.

Net decline can be given as a ratio:

$$\text{net decline} = \frac{\text{reduction in activity}}{\text{original activity}}$$

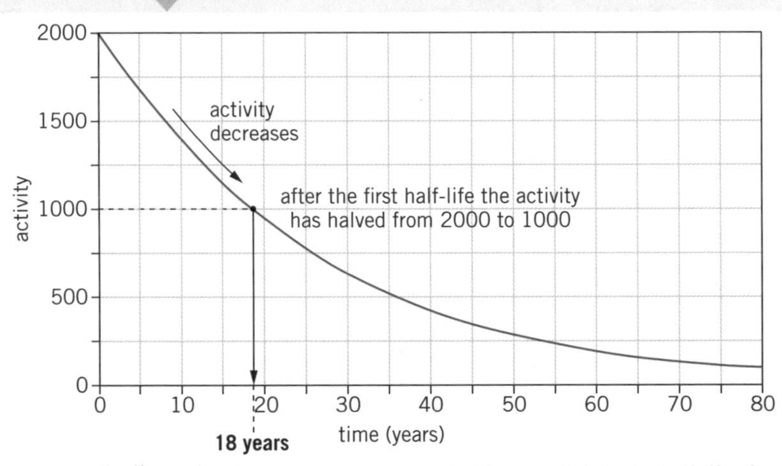

The time taken for the activity to halve is 18 years. This is the half-life of this substance.

P7

Nuclear equations

Nuclear equations are used to represent radioactive decay.

Alpha particles

Alpha particles can be represented as ${}^{4}_{2}\alpha$ or ${}^{4}_{2}\mathrm{He}$.

Equations are written in the form: ${}^{A}_{Z}\mathrm{X} \rightarrow {}^{(A-4)}_{(Z-2)}\mathrm{Y} + {}^{4}_{2}\alpha$

This shows us that alpha decay causes both the mass and the charge of the nucleus to change.

Beta particles

Beta particles can be represented as ${}^{0}_{-1}\beta$ or ${}^{0}_{-1}\mathrm{e}$.

Equations are written in the form: ${}^{A}_{Z}\mathrm{X} \rightarrow {}^{A}_{(Z+1)}\mathrm{Y} + {}^{0}_{-1}\beta$

This shows us that beta decay only causes the charge of the nucleus to change.

Ionising radiation

Living cells can be damaged or killed by ionising radiation.

The risk depends on the half-life of the source and the type of radiation.

Alpha radiation is very dangerous inside the body because it affects all the surrounding tissue. Outside the body it only affects the skin and eyes because it cannot penetrate further.

Beta and gamma radiation are dangerous outside and inside the body because they can penetrate into tissues.

Revision tip

Remember The mass number is at the top. Don't let the use of an A for mass number confuse you, it's not an A for atomic number!

Practice For decay equations, treat each line as a separate sum, and that should reduce any mistakes.

Irradiation versus contamination

irradiation	when an object is exposed to nuclear radiation	cause harm through ionisation	prevented by shielding, removing, or moving away from the source of radiation
contamination	when atoms of a radioactive material are on or in an object		object remains exposed to radiation as long as it is contaminated contamination can be very difficult to remove

Protection against irradiation and contamination

You can protect against irradiation and contamination by:

- maintaining a distance from the radiation source
- limiting time near the source
- shielding from the radiation.

Studies on the effects of radiation should be published, shared with other scientists, and checked by **peer review** as they are important for human health.

Key terms **Make sure you can write a definition for these key terms.**

alpha *activity* *beta* *contamination* *count rate* *gamma* *Geiger-Muller tube* *half-life* *ionisation* *irradiation* *net decline* *peer review* *radioactive decay*

Retrieval

Learn the answers to the questions below, then cover the answers column with a piece of paper and write as many as you can. Check and repeat.

	P7 questions		Answers
1	What is radioactive decay?	Put paper here	random emission of radiation from the nucleus of an atom
2	What are the three types of nuclear radiation?		alpha, beta, and gamma
3	What is gamma (γ) radiation?	Put paper here	electromagnetic radiation from the nucleus
4	Which type of nuclear radiation is the most ionising?		alpha
5	What is the range in air of alpha, beta, and gamma radiation?	Put paper here	a few cm, 1 m, and unlimited, respectively
6	Which materials can stop alpha, beta, and gamma radiation?		sheet of paper, thin aluminium sheet, and thick lead/concrete, respectively
7	Which type of radiation causes both the mass and charge of the nucleus to decrease?	Put paper here	alpha
8	Which type of radiation does not cause the mass to change but does cause the charge of the nucleus to increase?		beta
9	Which type of nuclear radiation does not cause a change in the structure of the nucleus when it is emitted?	Put paper here	gamma
10	What are the equation symbols for alpha and beta particles?		$^{4}_{2}\alpha$ and $^{0}_{-1}\beta$
11	What is radioactive activity?	Put paper here	the rate at which a source of unstable nuclei decays
12	What unit is used to measure the activity of a radioactive source?		becquerel (Bq)
13	What is meant by count rate?	Put paper here	number of decays recorded each second (by a detector, e.g., Geiger-Muller tube)
14	What is meant by the half-life of a radioactive source?		the time taken for half the unstable nuclei to decay, or the time taken for the count rate to halve
15	What is irradiation?	Put paper here	exposing an object to nuclear radiation
16	What is radioactive contamination?		unwanted presence of substances containing radioactive atoms on or in other materials

Now go back and use the questions below to check your knowledge from previous chapters.

Previous questions / Answers

	Previous questions	Answers
1	Describe the plum pudding model of the atom.	sphere of positive charge with negative electrons embedded in it
2	Give two reasons why the temperature of a gas increases if it is compressed quickly.	the force applied to compress the gas results in work being done to the gas, and the energy gained by the gas is not transferred quickly enough to the surroundings
3	What is the radius of an atom?	around 1×10^{-10} m
4	On a graph of temperature against time for a substance being heated up or cooled down, what do the flat (horizontal) sections show?	the time when the substance is changing state and the temperature is not changing
5	Why is the mass of a substance conserved when it changes state?	the number of particles does not change
6	What are step-up transformers used for in the National Grid?	increase the p.d. from the power station to the transmission cables
7	What are the main advantages of using solar energy?	can be used in remote places, no polluting gases, no waste products, very low running cost

Put paper here

Maths Skills

Practise your maths skills using the worked example and practice questions below.

Ratios, fractions, percentages

A **ratio** is a way of comparing the size of two quantities.

For example, a ratio of 2:4 of radioactive atoms to non radioactive atoms in a sample means for every 2 radioactive atoms, there are 4 non radioactive atoms.

A ratio can be simplified by dividing both numbers by their highest common factor.

A **fraction** can be a way of expressing part of a whole number, or a way of writing one number divided by another in an equation.

To find fractions from a ratio, each number in the ratio can be a numerator, and the denominator is the sum of both numbers. For example, if the ratio of apples to oranges is 2:3, the fraction of apples is $= \frac{2}{2+3} = \frac{2}{5}$

A **percentage** is a number expressed as a fraction of 100. For example, 45% $= \frac{45}{100}$

To find one number as a percentage of another divide the first number by the second and multiply by 100.

Worked example

1 A sample has a ratio of 8:20 radioactive atoms to non radioactive atoms. Simplify this ratio, and find the fraction that are radioactive atoms.

Find the greatest common factor for 8 and 12 = 4.

Divide both sides of the ratio by 4 = 2:5.

Fraction of radioactive atoms:

$$= \frac{2}{2+5} = \frac{2}{7}$$

2 The resistance of a thermistor changes from 250 Ω to 175 ohms when it is heated. Calculate the percentage change in its resistance.

Calculate the change in resistance: 250 − 175 = 75

Divide the change by the original value of the resistance: $\frac{75}{250}$ *= 0.3 × 100 = 30%*

Practice

1 A sample has 40 radioactive atoms for every 120 non radioactive atoms. Write this as a ratio in its simplest form.

2 In the above example, what fraction of atoms are not radioactive?

3 In the above example, what percentage of atoms are radioactive?

Practice

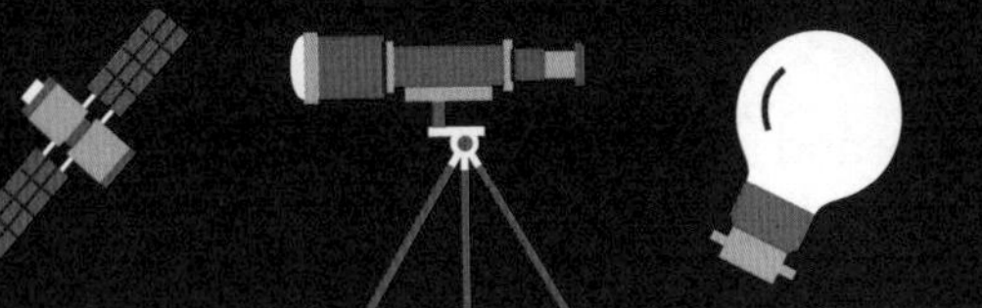

Exam-style questions

01 One of the uses of radioactive materials is in smoke detectors.

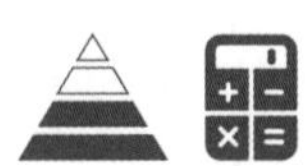

The isotope inside the smoke detector produces alpha radiation.

When there is smoke inside the detector, the smoke stops a current flowing in a circuit. This causes an alarm to go off.

01.1 Explain why the source needs to produce alpha radiation, and not beta or gamma radiation. **[2 marks]**

____

____

____

01.2 The decay of the isotope used in the smoke detector can be shown by the equation:

$$^{241}_{95}\text{Am} \rightarrow {}^{4}_{2}\alpha + {}^{\square}_{\square}\text{Np}$$

The equation shows how an americium nucleus decays into a neptunium nucleus.

Calculate the atomic number and atomic mass of the neptunium.

Show your working. **[4 marks]**

> **Exam Tip**
>
> The maths here may look hard but it's not. Take it one line at a time.

Atomic number = ____________

Atomic mass = ____________

01.3 Explain why americium decays into a different element. **[2 marks]**

____

____

____

> **Exam Tip**
>
> What is the one thing that all atoms and ions of an element have in common? What makes one element different from another?

02 One in every 10^{10} atoms of carbon is an atom of a carbon-14 isotope.

Figure 1 shows the count rate of carbon-14 against time.

Figure 1

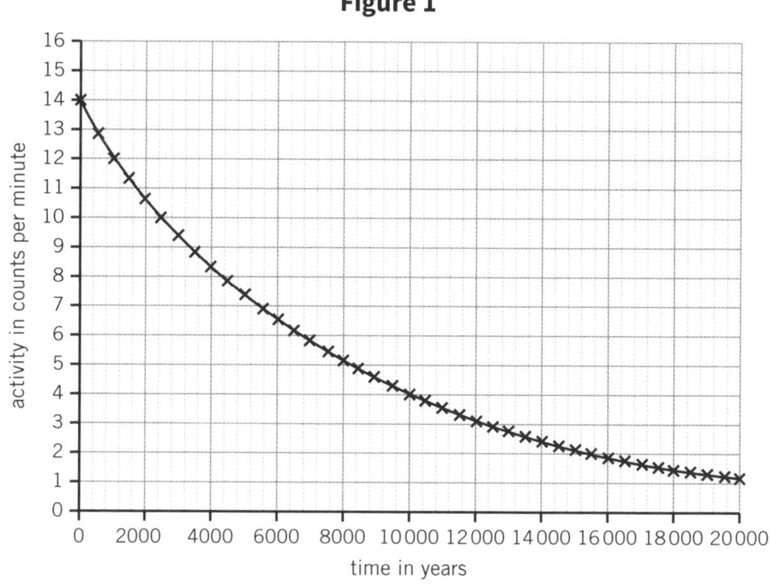

02.1 Deduce the half-life of carbon-14. **[1 mark]**

____

02.2 An archaeologist finds a fragment of a wooden spear. The spear contains carbon.

The fragment has an activity of 5 counts per minute.

Use **Figure 1** to deduce the age of the spear. **[1 mark]**

______________ years

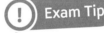

Exam Tip

You can simply read the answer off **Figure 1** for both **02.1** and **02.2**.

02.3 The last ice age ended around 11 000 years ago.

Is the spear old enough to have been used during the last ice age? Give a reason for your answer. **[2 marks]**

____

____

03 A teacher demonstrates how to measure the activity of a radioactive material.

03.1 Which **two** statements about activity are correct? **[2 marks]**
Choose **two** answers.

The activity of a sample is the number of particles it emits.

The activity of a sample is measured in becquerels (Bq).

The activity of a sample is the amount of radiation it emits.

The activity of a sample is the number of decays recorded per second.

Exam Tip

As you read through the options:

- cross out any you know are wrong
- put a question mark next to any you are unsure about
- put a tick next to the ones you are confident are correct.

That will only leave you a few to pick from.

03.2 Suggest a detector that the teacher could use to measure the activity. **[1 mark]**

03.3 The radiation emitted by a nucleus can

- be a particle or an electromagnetic wave
- be charged or have no charge.

Complete **Table 1** by ticking the correct boxes in the second and third columns. **[2 marks]**

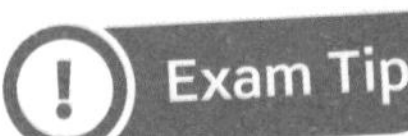

You can use the the marks available to determine what each mark will be awarded for. **03.3** has two marks available and has two columns to fill in, so there will be one mark available for each column, not for each tick.

Table 1

Type of radiation	Is a particle	Has no charge
alpha		
beta		
gamma		
neutron		

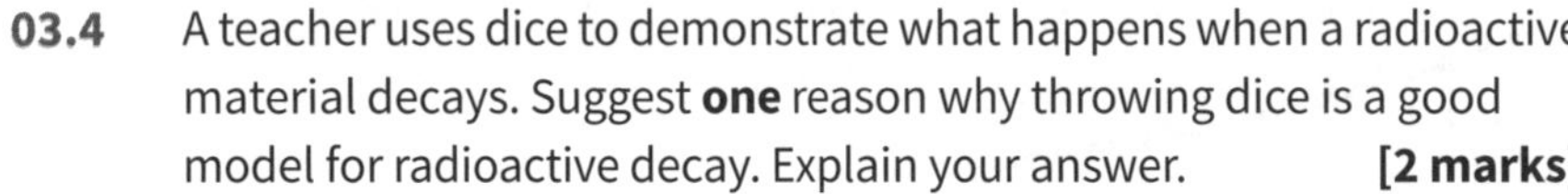

03.4 A teacher uses dice to demonstrate what happens when a radioactive material decays. Suggest **one** reason why throwing dice is a good model for radioactive decay. Explain your answer. **[2 marks]**

04 Different types of radiation can travel different distances through the air.

04.1 Complete **Table 2** with the words alpha, beta, and gamma. **[2 marks]**

Table 2

Type	Range in air
	>3 m
	1 m
	<10 cm

04.2 A student says:

'*There is a link between the ionising power of radiation and how far they go in air. If they do not go as far, that means that they are not as ionising.*'

Do you agree with the student? Explain your answer. **[3 marks]**

04.3 A teacher has a source that emits all three types of radiation. The activity of the source is 35 Bq. The teacher puts a sheet of aluminium between the source and the detector. The activity recorded is lower. Explain why the activity is lower, but radiation can still be detected. **[2 marks]**

05 Caesium-137, $^{137}_{55}\text{Cs}$, has a half-life 30 years.

05.1 Determine the mass of caesium-137 that remains in a 24 g sample after 90 years. **[3 marks]**

05.2 Complete the equation for the decay of caesium-137 when it emits a beta particle. **[2 marks]**

$$^{137}_{55}\text{Cs} \rightarrow {}^{137}_{\square}\text{Ba} + \square$$

05.3 Another isotope is caesium-134. Caesium-134 was emitted during an explosion at the Chernobyl nuclear reactor in Ukraine. Following the explosion, caesium-134 isotopes were found in fields in Wales. Sheep were farmed in these fields.
Explain why the presence of radioactive material on the grass is a hazard for sheep. **[2 marks]**

06 Strawberry fruits have microorganisms on them that cause the strawberries to decay. If the strawberries are irradiated, the radiation kills the microorganisms. Some people do not like to eat irradiated strawberries because they think that they themselves will become contaminated.

06.1 Describe the difference between contamination and irradiation in this context. **[2 marks]**

Exam Tip

The key part of this question is 'in this context'. You must refer to the context given, otherwise you won't gain full marks even if you correctly describe the difference between contamination and irradiation.

06.2 Explain why the hazard due to radiation is low when eating irradiated strawberries. **[1 mark]**

06.3 There are regulations that cover processes involving radioactive materials. The data that are used to produce the regulations come from reports published in peer-reviewed journals.
Describe the process of peer review. Explain why it is very important for regulations covering these processes to be based on peer-reviewed articles. **[3 marks]**

07 **Table 3** shows a list of radioisotopes and their half-lives.

Table 3

Radioisotope	Half-life
polonium-215	0.0018 seconds
bismuth-212	60.5 seconds
sodium-24	15 hours
iodine-131	8.07 days
cobalt-60	5.26 years
radium-226	1600 years
uranium-238	4.5 billion years

07.1 A scientist has a sample of sodium-24 with an activity of 100 Bq. Sketch a graph to show how the activity of the sample varies over a 48 hour period. Label the line 'sodium'. **[3 marks]**

Exam Tip

For a sketch graph you don't need to have the exact values – start at 100 Bq and estimate where the activity would be after each half-life.

07.2 On the same graph sketch a line to show the activity of a sample of radium over the same time period. Assume the sample of radium has the same initial activity as the sample of sodium. **[2 marks]**

07.3 Explain how you know that the polonium does **not** decay by alpha decay into the bismuth isotope shown in **Table 3**. **[2 marks]**

08 When a nucleus decays the mass of the nucleus might, or might not, change.

08.1 Write down a type of radiation that does **not** change the mass of the nucleus when it is emitted. **[1 mark]**

08.2 An equation that shows the decay of bismuth-214 is

$$^{214}_{83}\text{Bi} \rightarrow {}^{214}_{84}\text{Po} + \mathbf{X}$$

Name particle **X**. Give a description of this particle. **[2 marks]**

08.3 Explain why the mass of the nucleus does not change. **[2 marks]**

08.4 Describe how the decay equation shows what happens to the charge on the nucleus when particle **X** is emitted.
Explain your answer. **[2 marks]**

09 A machine can monitor the thickness of paper in a paper-making factory. The process is shown in **Figure 2**.

Figure 2

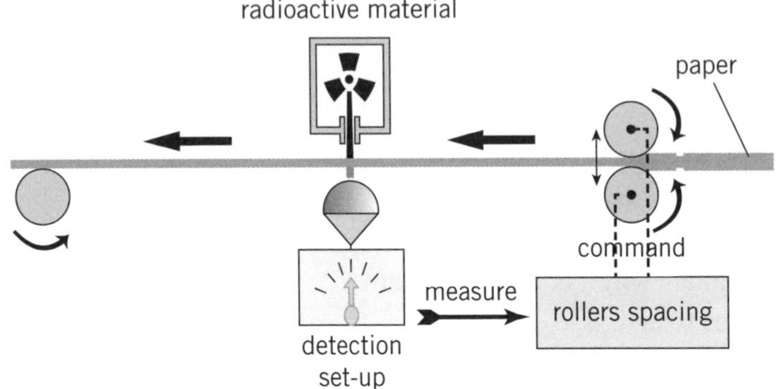

Describe the type of radiation that the radioactive material would need to emit in this process. Justify your answer.
Explain the consequences of choosing the wrong type of radioactive material. **[6 marks]**

! Exam Tip

You'll need to think about the type of radiation and the half-life – consider health and safety reasons, and cost effectiveness.

10 A student collects data on the activity of a sample of radioactive material. The data are shown in **Table 4** and **Figure 3** .

Table 4

Time in s	Count rate in Bq
0	42.6
20	35.2
40	24.9
60	20.9
80	17.7
100	15.2
120	10.7
140	8.7
160	4.5
180	6.1
200	4.3
220	3.7

Figure 3

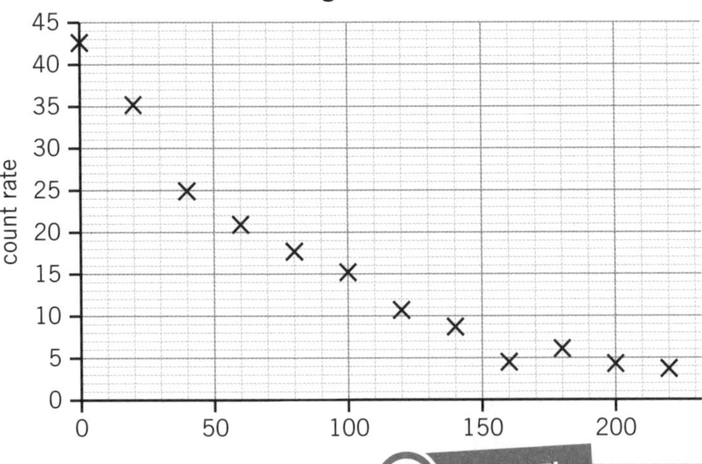

10.1 Draw a line of best fit on **Figure 3**. **[1 mark]**

10.2 Use **Figure 3** to find the half-life of the isotope. **[3 marks]**

10.3 A student says that the data is wrong because there are some points that are not on the line of best fit.
Do you agree? Justify your answer. **[2 marks]**

! Exam Tip

A line of best fit is *not* a dot-to-dot. You do not have to include every point in your line. It should show the trend of the data. Use a ruler to see if all the points will fit on a straight line. If they don't, draw a curved line.

10.4 Identify **one** thing that the student has done incorrectly when producing **Figure 3**. Assume that all the data points are correct. **[1 mark]**

11 The discovery of the electron led to the development of the plum pudding model of the atom by J.J. Thompson.

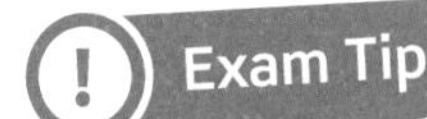

Plum pudding is like a fruit cake – think of how the fruit are distributed when you describe the model.

11.1 Describe the plum pudding model of the atom. **[2 marks]**

11.2 Explain why the discovery of the electron was important in the development of the model of the atom. **[2 marks]**

11.3 The plum pudding model was replaced by the nuclear model due to evidence from the alpha particle scattering experiment.
Suggest what a scientist would have expected to see in the alpha particle experiment if the plum pudding model was correct. **[1 mark]**

Practice at predicting results based on a model is great preparation for the exam!

11.4 Use your answer to **11.3** to explain why the alpha particle experiment resulted in a change to the model of the atom. **[1 mark]**

11.5 The results of the experiment were published in 1909, but the nuclear model was not proposed until 1911.
Suggest **one** reason why the model was proposed after the results were published. **[1 mark]**

12 A student sets up an experiment to compare the potential difference across components in series and parallel circuits.
The circuit diagrams are shown in **Figure 4**.

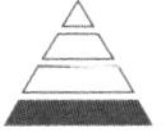

Figure 4

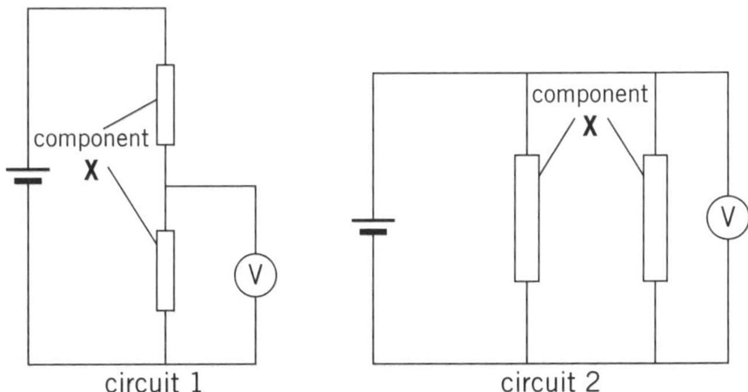

12.1 Identify component **X**. **[1 mark]**

12.2 The cell in each circuit has a potential difference of 6 V.
Compare the readings on the voltmeters in the two circuits.
Explain your answer. **[4 marks]**

12.3 The student replaces all of the components labelled **X** with bulbs.
The bulbs are identical.
Suggest what happens to the readings on the voltmeters. Explain your answer. **[2 marks]**

Knowledge

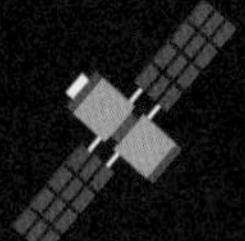

P8 Forces

Scalars and vectors

Scalar quantities only have a magnitude (e.g., distance and speed).

Vector quantities have a magnitude *and* a direction (e.g., velocity and force).

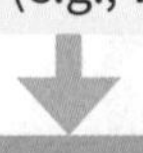

Forces

A **force** can be a push or pull on an object caused by an interaction with another object. Forces are vector quantities.

Gravity

The force of **gravity** close to the Earth is due to the planet's **gravitational field strength**.

Weight is the force acting on an object due to gravity.

The weight of an object

- can be considered to act at the object's **centre of mass**
- can be measured using a calibrated spring-balance (newtonmeter).

(L) weight (N) = mass (kg) × gravitational field strength (N/kg)

$$W = mg$$

Weight and mass are directly proportional to each other, which can be written as $W \propto m$, so as the mass of an object doubles, its weight doubles.

Contact forces	Non-contact forces
occur when two objects are touching each other	act at a distance (without the two objects touching)
examples: friction, air resistance, tension, normal contact force	examples: gravitational force, electrostatic force, magnetic force

When an object exerts a force on another object, it will experience an *equal and opposite* force.

Resultant forces

If two or more forces act on an object along the same line, their effect is the same as if they were replaced with a single **resultant force**. The resultant force is

- the sum of the magnitudes of the forces if they act in the same direction
- the difference between the magnitudes of the forces if they act in opposite directions.

If the resultant force on an object is zero, the forces are said to be balanced.

If the forces do not act along the same line, the resultant of two forces can be found by making a scale drawing using a ruler and a protractor.

Revision tip

Remember Too much time is wasted in exams drawing 'perfect' looking boxes or circles – this is physics not art so diagrams have to be scientifically accurate not works of art.

Drawing forces

Free body diagrams use arrows to show all of the forces acting on a single object. For example:

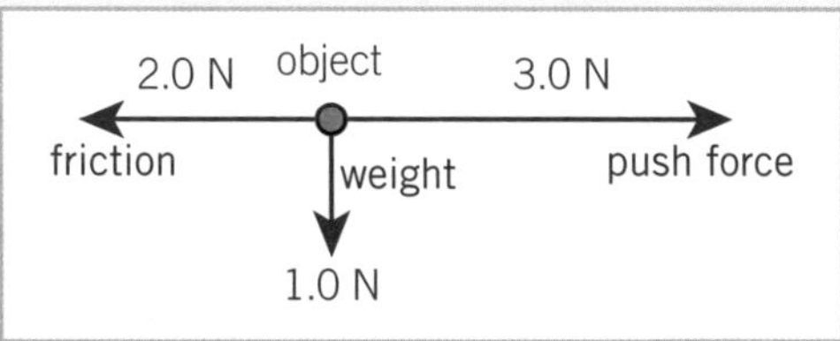

A dot or circle represents the object, with the forces drawn as arrows:

- the arrow length represents the magnitude of the force
- the arrow direction shows the direction of the force.

Scale drawings

Scale drawings can be used to find the resultant of two forces which are not acting along the same line.

The forces are drawn end to end. The resultant can then be drawn between the two ends, forming a triangle:

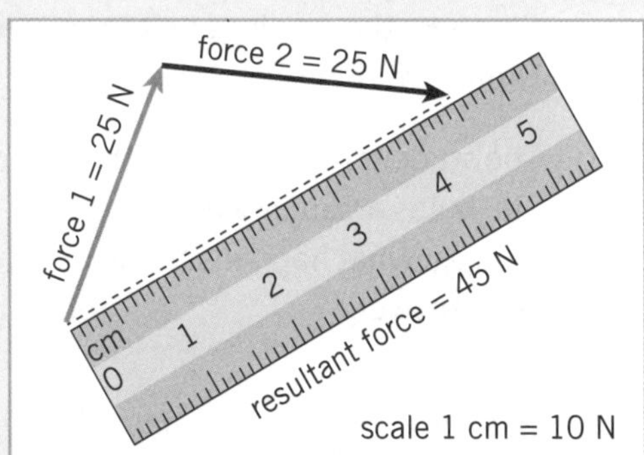

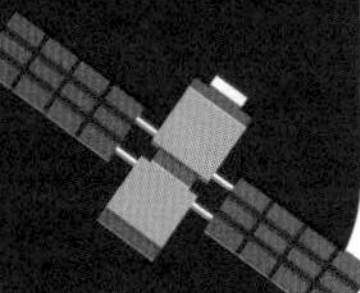

Deformation

Deformation is a change in the shape of an object caused by stretching, squashing (compressing), bending, or twisting.

More than one force has to act on a stationary object to deform it, otherwise the force would make it move.

Elastic deformation – the object can go back to its original shape and size when the forces are removed.

Inelastic deformation – the object does not go back to its original shape or size when the forces are removed.

Graphs of force against extension for elastic objects

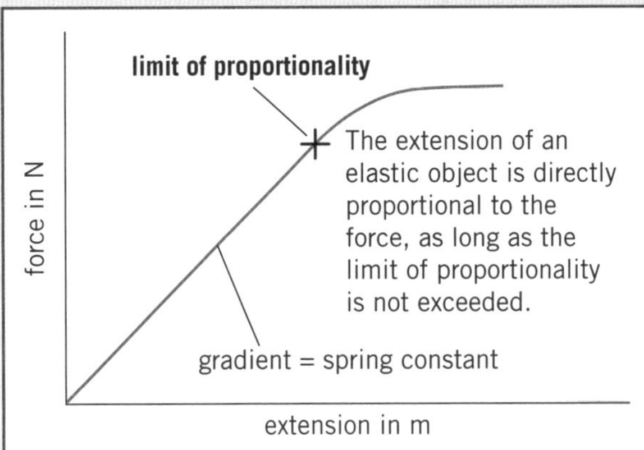

The spring constant can be calculated using the equation:

force applied (N) = spring constant (N/m) × extension (m)

$$F = ke$$

This relationship also applies to compressing an object, where *e* would be compression instead of extension.

Elastic potential energy

A force that stretches or compresses an object does work on it, causing energy to be transferred to the object's elastic potential store.

The elastic potential energy stored in an elastically stretched or compressed spring can be calculated using:

$$\text{elastic potential energy (J)} = \frac{1}{2} \times \text{spring constant (N/m)} \times (\text{extension})^2\ (\text{m}^2)$$

$$E_e = \frac{1}{2} k e^2$$

Revision tips

Remember your maths skills here. It is only the value for extension that is squared, not the whole answer.

BIDMAS is a good acronym to help you remember the order you should complete operations in mathematical equations.

Brackets

Indices

Division

Multiplication

Addition

Subtraction

Resolving forces

A single force can always be resolved (split) into two component forces at right angles to each other:

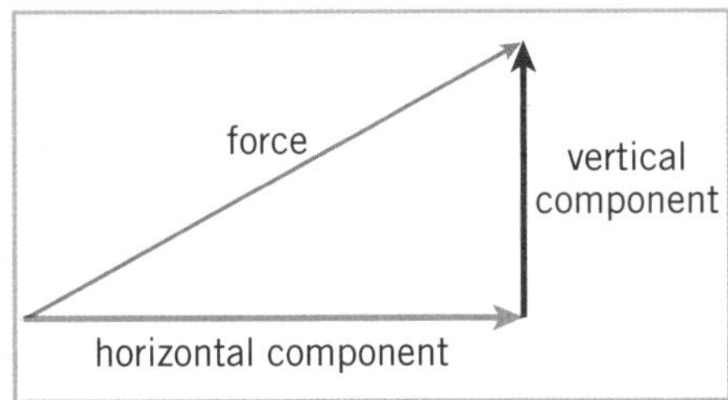

The two component forces added together give the same effect as the single force.

Key terms

Make sure you can write a definition for these key terms.

centre of mass, contact force, deformation, elastic, free body diagram, force, gravitational field strength, gravity, inelastic, limit of proportionality, non-contact force, resultant, scalar, vector, weight

Retrieval

Learn the answers to the questions below, then cover the answers column with a piece of paper and write as many as you can. Check and repeat.

	P8 questions	Answers
1	What is a scalar quantity?	only has a size (magnitude)
2	What is a vector quantity?	has both a size and direction
3	What is a force?	a push or pull that acts on an object due to the interaction with another object
4	Is force a vector or scalar quantity?	vector
5	What is a contact force?	when objects are physically touching
6	Name four contact forces.	friction, air resistance, tension, normal contact force
7	What is a non-contact force?	when objects are physically separated
8	Name three non-contact forces.	gravitational force, electrostatic force, magnetic force
9	What is the same about the interaction pair of forces when two objects interact with each other?	the forces are the same size
10	What is different about the interaction pair of forces when two objects interact with each other?	forces are in opposite directions
11	What is the size of the resultant force on an object if the forces on it are balanced?	zero
12	What is the name for the force acting on an object due to gravity?	weight
13	What instrument can be used to measure the weight of an object?	calibrated spring-balance (newtonmeter)
14	What is the centre of mass?	the point through which the weight of an object can be considered to act
15	What is elastic deformation?	when an object can go back to its original shape and size when deforming forces are removed
16	What is inelastic deformation?	when an object does not go back to its original shape and size when deforming forces are removed
17	How do you find the spring constant from a force–extension graph of a spring?	find the gradient of the straight line section

Put paper here

Now go back and use the questions below to check your knowledge from previous chapters.

Previous questions — Answers

	Previous questions	Answers
1	What are the equation symbols for alpha and beta particles?	${}^{4}_{2}\alpha$ and ${}^{0}_{-1}\beta$
2	Which particle do atoms of the same element always have the same number of?	protons
3	What is the specific latent heat of vaporisation of a substance?	the energy required to change one kilogram of the substance from liquid to vapour at its boiling point, without changing its temperature
4	Why do atoms have no overall charge?	equal numbers of positive protons and negative electrons
5	What is meant by count rate?	number of decays recorded each second (by a detector, e.g., Geiger-Muller tube)

Put paper here

Put paper here

Required Practical Skills

Practise answering questions on the required practicals using the example below. You need to be able to apply your skills and knowledge to other practicals too.

Extension of a spring

In this practical you measure the extension of a spring as different forces are applied to it.

To be accurate and precise you need to:

- measure extension using a pointer directed at the same position on the spring each time
- ensure that the ruler is positioned so that it is parallel to the spring
- make measurements by looking in a direction perpendicular to the ruler
- convert mass to weight (force) if necessary.
- use a measurement of zero force = zero extension
- use the gradient = $\frac{1}{\text{spring}}$ constant for a graph of force against extension

Worked example

A student records the following measurements for a spring.

Force in N						
Mass in kg	0	0.1	0.2	0.3	0.4	0.5
Length in cm	5.0	9.2	13.1	17.4	21	25
Extension in cm						

1 Calculate the spring extensions and forces.

weight (= force) = mass × gravitational field strength (10 N/kg)

extension = length − 5 (original length of spring)

Force in N	0	1	2	3	4	5
Extension in cm	0	4.2	8.1	12.4	16	20

2 Plot a graph of the results. Calculate the spring constant from your graph and give the unit.

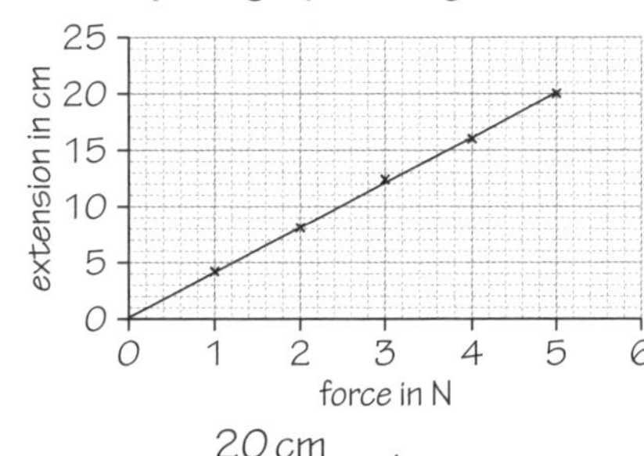

$$\text{gradient} = \frac{20\text{ cm}}{5\text{ N}} = 4$$

$$\text{gradient} = \frac{1}{\text{spring constant}}$$

$$\text{spring constant} = \frac{1}{\text{gradient}} = \frac{1}{4} = 0.25\text{ N/cm or } 25\text{ N/m}$$

Practice

1 A student measures an extension of 24 mm when she hangs a 40 g mass on a spring. Calculate the spring constant in N/m. Show your working.

2 Compare the meaning of the gradient of a graph of force against extension with the meaning of the gradient of a graph of extension against force.

Practice

Exam-style questions

01 A student investigates the extension of a spring.

01.1 Give the name of the pieces of equipment that they could use to measure force and extension. **[2 marks]**

> **Exam Tip**
> The units for force and extension might give you a clue.

01.2 Describe how they can use this equipment to make the measurements. **[4 marks]**

01.3 Explain why the student should take repeat measurements. **[1 mark]**

> **Exam Tip**
> If you only get one result how do you know that it is the correct result?

01.4 Suggest what the student should do if they see a result that does not fit with the pattern of their other results. **[1 mark]**

01.5 Describe the type of graph the student should plot.
Give reasons for your answer. **[2 marks]**

02 A student watches a video about forces.
The video shows a piece of wood floating in a tank of water.

02.1 Write down the name of the non-contact force acting on the wood and the name of the contact force acting on the wood. **[2 marks]**

02.2 The resultant force on the piece of wood is zero.
Describe what that means about the magnitude and direction of the two forces acting on the wood. **[2 marks]**

02.3 In the video the presenter shows that a piece of wood from an ironwood tree will sink rather than float.

The presenter shows this by placing the ironwood on the surface of the water.

It moves down through the water until it reaches the bottom of the tank.

Give the name of **one** other force that is acting on the wood as it moves through the water.

Write down whether it is a contact or a non-contact force. **[2 marks]**

Exam Tip

This question has two parts – make sure you answer both.

03 A child is sitting in a supermarket trolley. The brother is pushing the trolley.

The brother exerts a force of 20 N.

The total distance travelled by the trolley is 30 m.

03.1 Write down the equation which links work done, force, and distance. **[1 mark]**

03.2 Calculate the work done by the brother. **[2 marks]**

Work done = ________

03.3 Give the **two** units for work done. **[1 mark]**

1 ________ **2** ________

Exam Tip

The equation might give you a clue to one of the units in **03.3**.

03.4 When you lift an object, you do work against gravity.

The brother is doing work when he pushes the trolley at a steady speed.

Name the force against which he is doing work. **[1 mark]**

Exam Tip

What force would cause the trolley to slow down?

03.5 Describe the energy changes when the brother is moving the trolley at a steady speed. **[2 marks]**

04 A student investigates the deflection of a ruler. To do this, they put a ruler between two supports. They tie a piece of string in a loop and hang it in the centre of the ruler. They add weights to the loop, and the centre of the ruler is deflected.

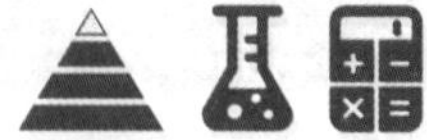

04.1 Suggest a problem the student might find when measuring the deflection of the ruler. **[1 mark]**

04.2 **Table 1** shows the measurements taken by the student.

Table 1

Weight in N	Deflection in mm			Mean deflection in mm
	Repeat 1	Repeat 2	Repeat 3	
0	0	0	0	0
2	3	2	2	2
4	4	5	6	5
6	10	12	17	
8	14	15	15	15
10	17	18	17	17
12	17	18	18	18

Calculate the mean deflection for the weight of 6 N. **[1 mark]**

> **Exam Tip**
> When ever you're asked to find a mean result be sure to look out for any anomalies.

04.3 Using the axes in **Figure 1**, plot a graph of the data in **Table 1**. Include a line of best fit. **[4 marks]**

> **Exam Tip**
> Plot your points using crosses.

Figure 1

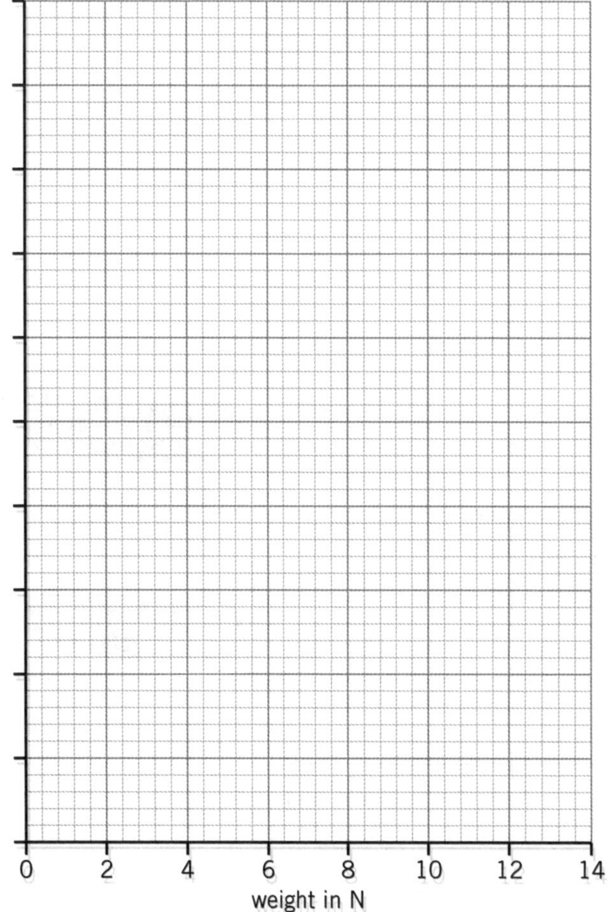

04.4 Determine whether the deflection is proportional to the force. Explain your answer. **[2 marks]**

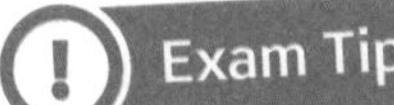

> **Exam Tip**
> It's important that you recognise the shape of direct proportion and indirect proportion on a graph as they frequently come up in exam questions.

05 A student is investigating material to make a newtonmeter. They collect data on the stretching of a sample of material.
The results are shown in **Table 2**.

Table 2

Weight in g	Length in cm			Average length in cm
	Repeat 1	Repeat 2	Repeat 3	
100	3.7	3.5	3.5	3.6
200	4.7	4.8	4.1	4.5
300	5.0	5.4	5.2	5.2
400	6.8	7.1	6.8	6.9
500	8.5	9.0	9.2	8.9

Exam Tip

The name of the equipment should give you a clue to the units needed.

05.1 Describe the error the student has made in the first column in **Table 2**. Suggest how to correct it. **[2 marks]**

Exam Tip

The question has given you the value for gravitational field strength. This should give you a clue that you need to do a calculation.

05.2 Plot a graph using **Figure 2** of weight against average length.
Gravitational field strength = 10 N/kg. **[4 marks]**

Figure 2

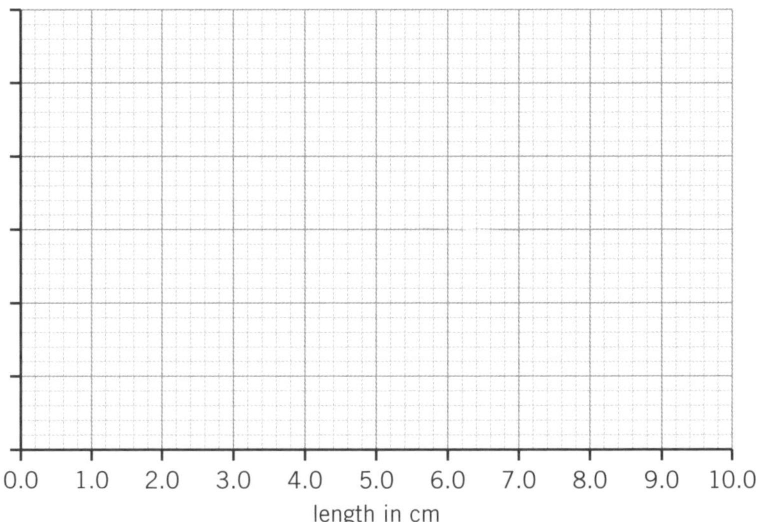

05.3 Estimate the original length of the sample.
Describe your method. **[2 marks]**

Exam Tip

You'll need to draw on the graph for this.

05.4 Use the shape of the graph to explain how the stiffness of the material changes as the force increases. **[1 mark]**

05.5 The student wants to use the material to make a newtonmeter.
Explain why the material would or would not be suitable. **[2 marks]**

06 A student is carrying heavy books in a plastic bag. This has caused the handles of the bag to stretch. Changing the shape of an object by stretching requires two forces. One of these forces is the force of the books on the bag.

06.1 Name the other force involved in stretching the bag. **[1 mark]**

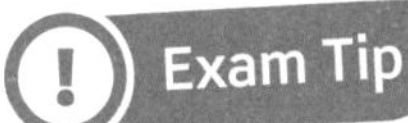

Exam Tip

Definitions of key words are easy marks in exams – learn them.

06.2 When the student takes the book out of the bag there is inelastic deformation of the handles.
Define inelastic deformation. **[1 mark]**

06.3 The student cuts the plastic bag into sections then applies different forces to the plastic sections and measures the extension. The student then repeats the experiment with a spring. They plot graphs of their data. One of the graphs is a curved line. The other graph is a straight line. Tick the **two** correct statements. **[2 marks]**

Statement	Correct
The graph for the plastic bag shows a non-linear relationship between force and extension.	
The graph for the plastic bag shows that force is proportional to extension.	
A graph that is a straight line is likely to be for a spring.	
The material that produced a linear graph has been inelastically deformed.	

07 A student attaches a spring to a retort stand and hangs a weight on the end of the spring. The unstretched length of the spring is 2 cm. The length of the spring when stretched is 3 cm.

Exam Tip

The question gives you numbers in centimetres, but the answer wants the number in metres. Be careful with your conversions here.

07.1 Calculate the extension of the spring in metres.
Show how you work out your answer. **[2 marks]**

07.2 Write down the equation which links force, extension, and spring constant. **[1 mark]**

07.3 The student used a weight of 2 N.
Show that the spring constant of the spring is 200 N/m. **[3 marks]**

07.4 Calculate the energy stored in the spring.
Use the correct equation from the *Physics Equations Sheet*. **[2 marks]**

07.5 The spring is not deformed inelastically.
Write down the work done on the spring.
Justify your answer. **[2 marks]**

08 A student wants to model how avalanches start. They put a tub with sand in it on an adjustable ramp.
Figure 3 shows the tub of sand when the ramp is flat on the workbench (left) and when it is raised (right).

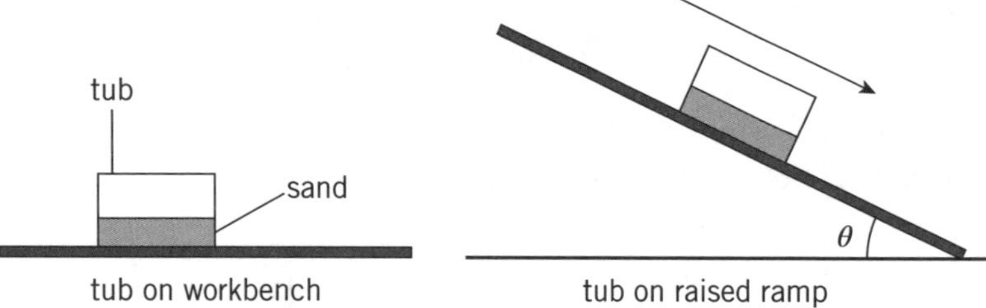

08.1 Draw a free body diagram for the tub of sand when it is flat on the workbench. Label your diagram. **[3 marks]**

08.2 The student raises the ramp as shown and writes down the angle (θ) when the tub just starts to move. When the ramp is raised further, the tub accelerates down the ramp.
Explain why there is a resultant force on the tub when the ramp is raised. Use ideas about components of forces and friction in your answer. **[3 marks]**

08.3 The student repeats the experiment with different masses of sand in the tub. The results show that the angle of the ramp needed to start the tub moving is independent of the mass of sand.
Sketch a graph of angle against mass of sand. **[2 marks]**

08.4 Suggest a reason for the shape of the graph. **[1 mark]**

09 A car is travelling on the road. The driving force is 18 000 N. The resistive forces add up to 12 000 N. The weight of the car is 15 kN. The car is travelling from right to left.

09.1 Draw a free body diagram for the car.
Label all of the arrows in your diagram. **[5 marks]**

> **Exam Tip**
> Look at the number of marks available for **09.1** – there are five marks, so if your diagram only has two things on it then you know you've missed something out.

09.2 Calculate the resultant forces in the vertical and horizontal directions. **[3 marks]**

09.3 Calculate the mass of the car.
The gravitational field strength is 9.8 N/kg. **[4 marks]**

09.4 The average value of the gravitational field strength on Earth is 9.8 N/kg. The gravitational field strength varies between the equator and the poles of the Earth.
Suggest how your free body diagram would change if the gravitational field strength was not 9.8 N/kg. **[3 marks]**

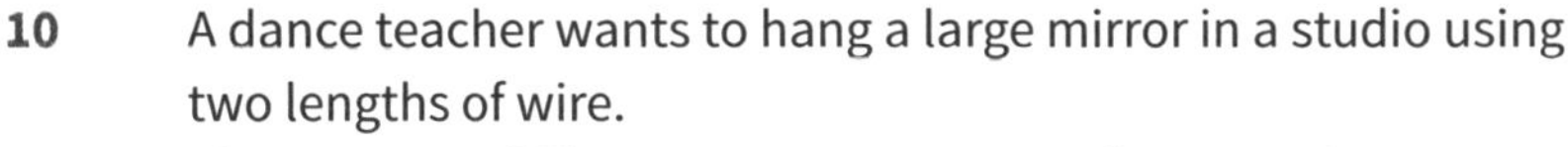

10 A dance teacher wants to hang a large mirror in a studio using two lengths of wire.
They use two different arrangements as shown in **Figure 4**.

Figure 4

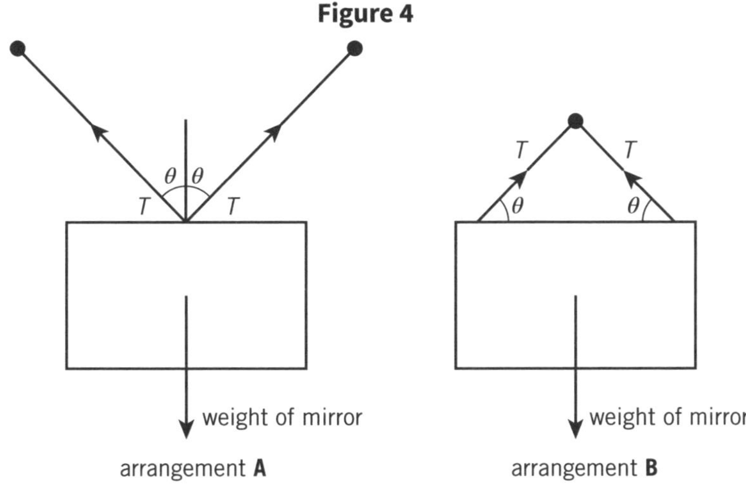

> **Exam Tip**
> You may be more used to using these skills in maths, but don't be surprised when they turn up in physics.

In arrangement **A** the tension in each string = 100 N.
The angle $\theta = 40°$. The mirror is hanging and is stationary.

10.1 Use a scale diagram to calculate the weight of the mirror in arrangement **A**. **[3 marks]**

10.2 Suggest what happens to the tension in the strings when the angle increases in arrangement **A**. Give reasons for your answer. **[2 marks]**

10.3 Another teacher suggests that the force in the string would be less if the mirror was fixed using arrangement **B**.
Compare the tensions in the strings in the two arrangements.
Assume that the angles are the same. **[2 marks]**

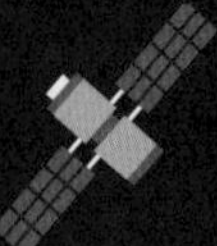

P9 Speed

Distance and displacement

Distance:

- is how far an object moves
- is a scalar quantity so does not have direction.

Displacement is a vector and includes the *distance* and *direction* of a straight line from an object's starting point to its finish point.

Velocity

The **velocity** of an object is its speed in a given direction.

Velocity is a vector quantity because it has a magnitude and direction.

An object's velocity changes if its direction changes, even if its speed is constant.

An object moving in a circle can have a constant speed but its velocity is always changing because its direction is always changing.

Speed

distance travelled (m) = speed (m/s) × time (s)

$$s = vt$$

The symbol for distance is s, and the symbol for speed is v.

In reality, objects rarely move at a constant speed. So it can be useful to calculate average speed:

$$\text{average speed (m/s)} = \frac{\text{total distance travelled (m)}}{\text{total time taken (s)}}$$

Some typical average speeds are:

- walking ≈ 1.5 m/s
- running ≈ 3 m/s
- cycling ≈ 6 m/s

The speed of sound and the speed of the wind also change depending on the conditions.

- speed of sound in air is ≈ 330 m/s

Acceleration

Acceleration is the change in velocity of an object per second. It is a vector quantity.

The unit of acceleration is metres per second squared, m/s^2.

An object is accelerating if its speed or its direction (or both) are changing. A negative acceleration means an object is slowing down, and is called **deceleration**.

Acceleration can be calculated using:

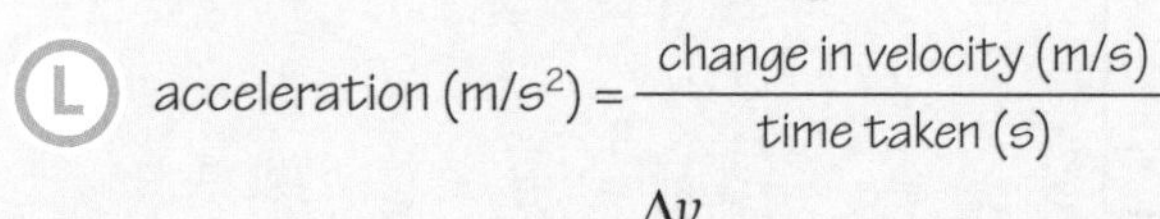

$$\text{acceleration (m/s}^2\text{)} = \frac{\text{change in velocity (m/s)}}{\text{time taken (s)}}$$

$$a = \frac{\Delta v}{t}$$

Near the Earth's surface any object falling freely under gravity has an acceleration of about 9.8 m/s^2.

Uniform acceleration is when the acceleration of an object is constant.

The following equation applies to objects with uniform acceleration:

$$\text{(final velocity)}^2 - \text{(initial velocity)}^2 = 2 \times \text{acceleration} \times \text{distance}$$

$$v^2 - u^2 = 2as$$

Revision tip

Practice Try going over all the formulae we use in physics and seeing which quantities are vector and which are scalar.

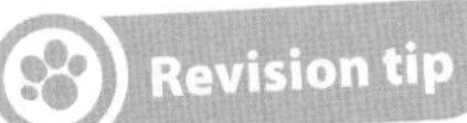

Revision tip

Remember $s = vt$ can be a confusing equation – students frequently get the s for distance travelled confused with speed. Make sure you don't fall into this trap!

Key terms

Make sure you can write a definition for these key terms.

acceleration   air resistance   deceleration   displacement   distance

Distance–time graphs

A distance–time graph shows how the distance travelled by an object travelling in a straight line changes with time.

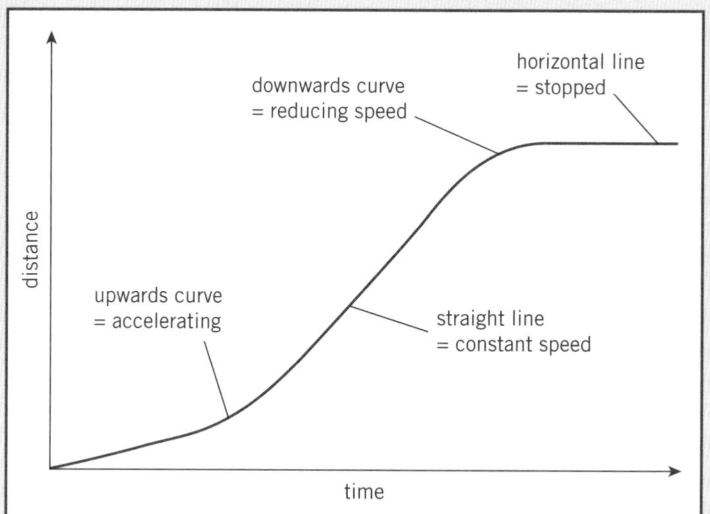

The gradient of the line in a distance–time graph is equal to the object's speed.

If the object is accelerating, the speed at any time can be found by calculating the gradient of a tangent to the curved line at that time.

Velocity–time graphs

A velocity–time graph shows how the velocity of an object changes with time.

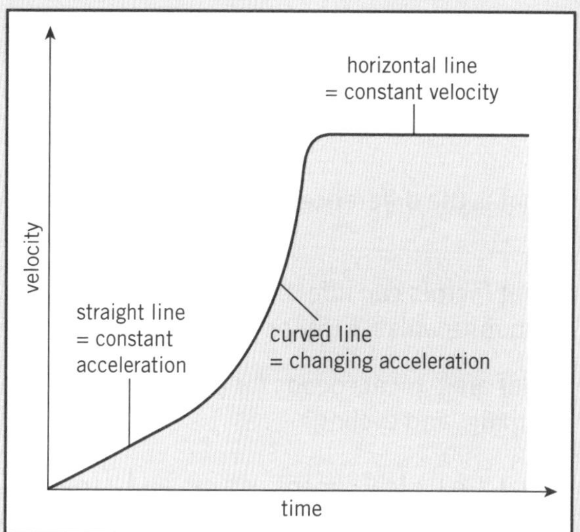

The gradient of the line in a velocity–time graph is equal to the object's acceleration.

The area under the line on a velocity–time graph represents the distance travelled (or displacement).

Drag forces

When an object moves through a fluid (liquid or gas) a frictional force drags on it.

These drag forces:

- always act in the opposite direction to an object's movement
- increase with the object's speed – the greater the speed, the greater the frictional force
- depend on the shape and size of the object.

The frictional drag force in air is called **air resistance**. **Streamlining** an object reduces the drag it experiences.

Terminal velocity

For an object falling through a fluid:

- there are two forces acting – its weight due to gravity and the drag force
- the weight remains constant
- the drag force is small at the beginning, but gets bigger as it speeds up
- the resultant force will get smaller as the drag force increases
- the acceleration will decrease as it falls
- if it falls for a long enough time, the object will reach a final steady speed.

Terminal velocity is the constant velocity a falling object reaches when the frictional force acting on it is equal to its weight.

streamlining *terminal velocity* *uniform acceleration* *velocity*

Retrieval

Learn the answers to the questions below, then cover the answers column with a piece of paper and write as many as you can. Check and repeat.

	P9 questions		Answers
1	What is the difference between distance and displacement?	Put paper here	distance is a scalar quantity and only has a magnitude (size), displacement is a vector quantity and has both magnitude and direction
2	What is the difference between speed and velocity?		speed is a scalar quantity and only has a magnitude (size), velocity is a vector quantity and has both magnitude and direction
3	What factors can affect the speed at which someone walks, runs, or cycles?	Put paper here	age, fitness, terrain, and distance travelled
4	What are typical speeds for a person walking, running, and cycling?		1.5 m/s, 3.0 m/s, and 6.0 m/s respectively
5	What are typical speeds of a car and a train?	Put paper here	13–30 m/s and 50 m/s respectively
6	What is a typical speed for sound travelling in air?		330 m/s
7	What is acceleration?		change in velocity of an object per second
8	What is the unit of acceleration?	Put paper here	m/s^2
9	How can an object be accelerating even if it is travelling at a steady speed?		if it is changing direction
10	What is happening to an object if it has a negative acceleration?	Put paper here	it is slowing down
11	What information does the gradient of the line in a distance–time graph provide?		speed
12	What information does the gradient of the line in a velocity–time graph provide?	Put paper here	acceleration
13	How can the distance travelled by an object be found from its velocity–time graph?		calculate the area under the graph
14	What is the name for the steady speed a falling object reaches when the resistive force is equal to its weight?	Put paper here	terminal velocity
15	What is the general name for the frictional forces an object experiences when moving through a fluid (liquid or gas)?		drag
16	In which direction does the drag on an object always act?	Put paper here	in the direction opposite to which it is moving
17	What happens to the drag on an object as its speed increases?		the drag increases
18	What can be done to reduce the drag on an object?		streamlining

Now go back and use the questions below to check your knowledge from previous chapters.

Previous questions / Answers

	Previous questions	Answers
1	What is a force?	a push or pull that acts on an object due to the interaction with another object
2	What is meant by the half-life of a radioactive source?	the time taken for half the unstable nuclei to decay or the time taken for the count rate to halve
3	How can an electron move up an energy level?	absorb sufficient electromagnetic radiation
4	What does a material's thermal conductivity tell you?	how well it conducts heat
5	Which two quantities do you need to measure to find the density of a solid or liquid?	mass and volume

Put paper here

Put paper here

Maths Skills

Area of graphs

The area between the line of a graph and the x-axis sometimes represents a useful quantity.

To find the area under a graph made up of straight lines, split the shape under the line into rectangles and triangles and add their individual values together.

If the graph has curved sections, estimate the area under the curve by following these steps:

1. calculate the area of a single small square on the graph
2. count the whole and half squares under the curved part of the line
3. multiply the number of squares by the area per square.

Worked example

The graph shows how the velocity of an object changes with time. How far does the object travel during 24 seconds?

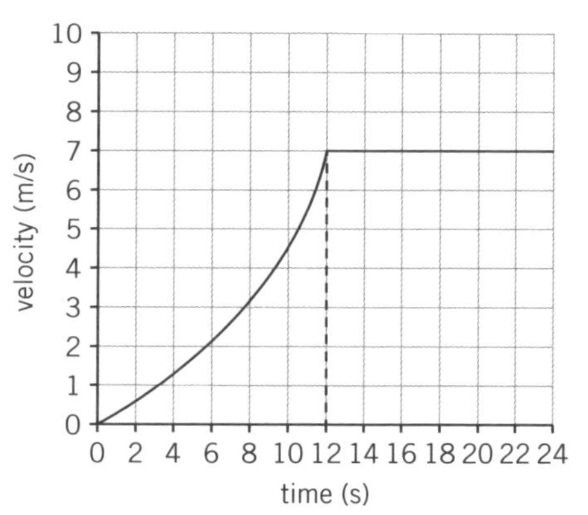

Calculate the area of the rectangular section:

$$7\,\text{m/s} \times (24 - 12)\,\text{s} = 7 \times 12 = 84\,\text{m}$$

Calculate the area a single square represents:

$$1\,\text{m/s} \times 2\,\text{s} = 2\,\text{m}$$

Count the number of whole squares under the curved part of the line (adding any half squares together) = 16

Multiply the number of squares under the curved line by the area one square represents:

$$16 \times 2 = 32\,\text{m}$$

Add the area under the curved section to the area of the rectangular section:

$$84 + 32 = 116\,\text{m}$$

Practice

The graph below shows a velocity-time graph for a cyclist:

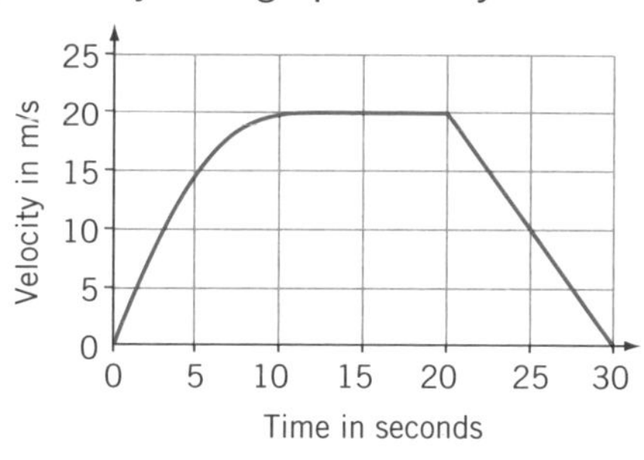

1. Describe the cyclist's motion in the time between 10 and 20 seconds.
2. Calculate the acceleration of the cyclist at 8 seconds.
3. Calculate the total distance travelled by the cyclist in the first 20 seconds.

Practice

Exam-style questions

01 A student sets up some equipment to measure the acceleration due to gravity as shown in **Figure 1**.

Figure 1

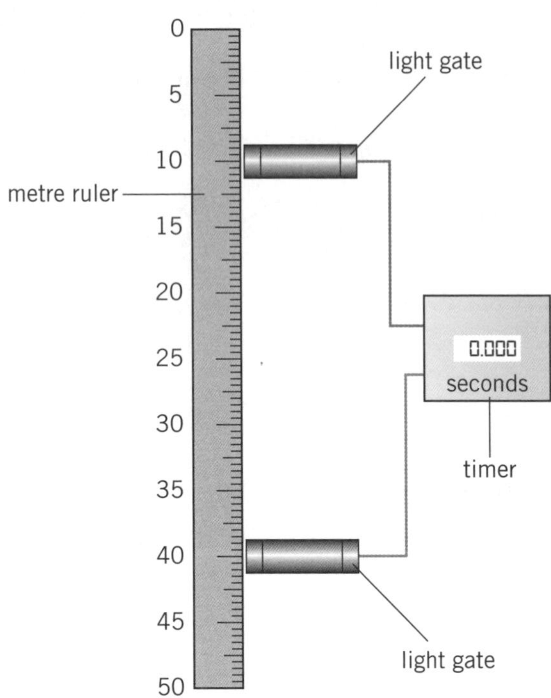

They use the ruler to measure the distance between the light gates. The distance is 30.0 cm. The student drops a piece of card from the top of the ruler. The light gates are connected to a data logger.

The student records the measurements in **Table 1**.

> **Exam Tip**
>
> Look out for non-standard units. Here, the distance is measured in cm, not m.

Table 1

Attempt	Velocity at light gate 1 in m/s	Velocity at light gate 2 in m/s
1	1.376	2.987
2	0.254	2.664
3	1.769	3.187

01.1 Describe how they should use the ruler to get an accurate measurement of the distance between the light gates. **[2 marks]**

____

____

____

01.2 Suggest why the velocities of the card at light gate 1 are different. **[1 mark]**

____

____

> **Exam Tip**
>
> Look at the equipment used to record each piece of data.

01.3 Explain why there are more significant figures in the velocities recorded in **Table 1** than in the distance measurements. **[3 marks]**

01.4 Calculate the acceleration due to gravity using the measurements for attempt **1**. Use the correct equation from the *Physics Equations Sheet*.

Give your answer to an appropriate number of significant figures. **[4 marks]**

Acceleration = ______________ m/s^2

01.5 Suggest **one** reason why the measured value of the acceleration due to gravity is different from the agreed value. **[1 mark]**

> **Exam Tip**
> Do not be tempted to write two reasons for question **01.5**. If you write two answers and one of them is wrong, you will get no marks.

02 Two students are travelling to school. Student **A** is walking. Student **B** is cycling.

02.1 Write down the typical speeds for students **A** and **B**. **[2 marks]**

Student **A** ______________

Student **B** ______________

> **Exam Tip**
> These estimated values come straight from the specification.

02.2 Write down the equation that links distance travelled, speed, and time. **[1 mark]**

02.3 Both students travel 1.5 km.

They leave their houses at the same time.

Calculate the difference in the times that they take to reach the school. Give your answer in minutes. **[6 marks]**

> **Exam Tip**
> You need to carry out two different calculations, so make sure you lay out your working clearly. If the examiner can't read your answer, they can't give you the marks.

Difference in time = ______________ minutes

02.4 Student **B** monitors their speed using an app on his phone. He sees that his fastest speed is much faster than his average speed.

Explain why. **[2 marks]**

____

____

____

03 **Table 2** shows the data for a student in a race on sports day.

Table 2

Time in s	Distance in m
0	0
2	2
4	5
6	8
8	14
10	20
12	22

03.1 Plot the data on **Figure 2**. **[2 marks]**

Figure 2

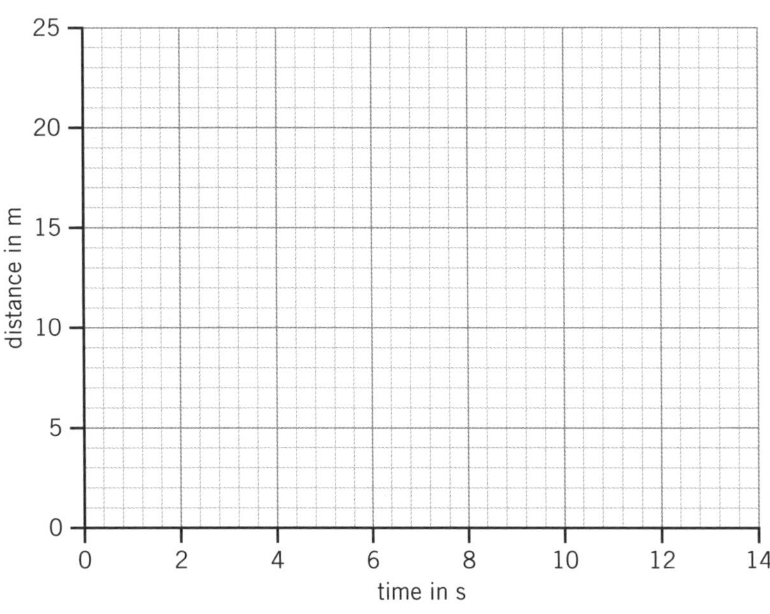

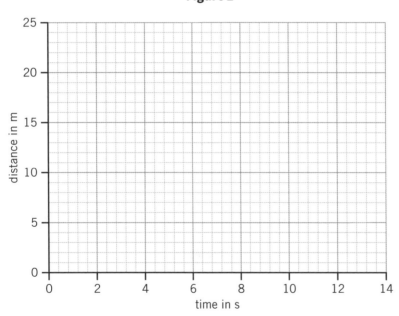

Exam Tip

Always plot points using crosses and use a pencil in case you make a mistake.

03.2 Calculate the speed of the student at a time of 4 seconds. **[3 marks]**

Exam Tip

You should show your working on the graph.

03.3 Describe the motion of the student between 6 seconds and 12 seconds. **[2 marks]**

04 A group of students collect data for a car journey. The journeys are shown as lines in **Figure 3**.

Figure 3

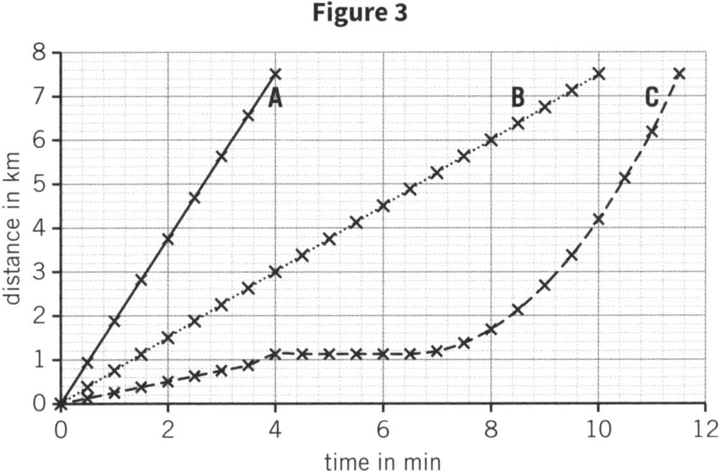

> **Exam Tip**
>
> You might find it helpful to annotate the graph with notes on when the cars are not moving, moving at a steady speed, or accelerating.

04.1 Which car travelled at the highest steady speed? Give reasons for your answer. **[2 marks]**

04.2 Which car or cars stopped at some point during the journey? Give reasons for your answer. **[2 marks]**

04.3 Which car or cars accelerated? Give reasons for your answer. **[2 marks]**

04.4 All three cars travelled the same overall distance. Which car has the highest average speed? Give reasons for your answer. **[2 marks]**

04.5 Use **Figure 3** to calculate the highest average speed. **[4 marks]**

05 A runner uses video analysis to analyse the first few seconds of a race.

Figure 4

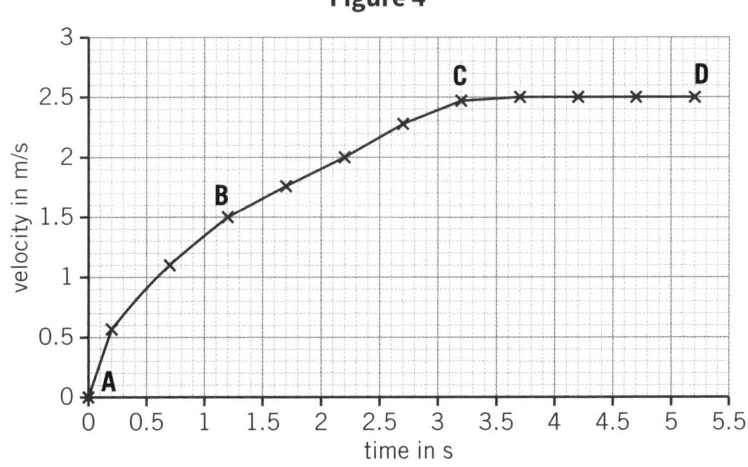

05.1 Suggest one advantage of using video analysis compared with light gates to analyse motion. **[1 mark]**

05.2 The runner divides the graph into three sections: **AB**, **BC**, and **CD**. Describe the motion of the runner in each of these sections. **[3 marks]**

05.3 Calculate the greatest acceleration of the runner. **[3 marks]**

05.4 Use **Figure 4** to calculate the distance travelled by the runner in the first 5 seconds of the race. Explain your method. **[4 marks]**

> When you are calculating the distance, treat the graph as three sections (**AB**, **BC**, and **CD**), turn each into a shape, and work from there.

06 A person needs to travel 20 miles to work. They have a choice of three different methods of transport to use – car, bicycle, and train.

Compare the time it would take, on average, to travel 20 miles by these methods. Choose suitable units in which to do your calculations. There are 1609 m in 1 mile. Write down any assumptions that you make. Suggest the effect on your answers if you do not make these assumptions. **[6 marks]**

07 Many drivers use satellite navigation (satnav) devices when driving to a destination. The satnav communicates with a global positioning system (GPS) satellite. A GPS satellite is at a distance of 20 200 km above the surface of the Earth. The signals from the satnav device to the satellite travel at a speed of 3×10^8 m/s.

In a 'show' question, you've already been given the answer. If you're not exactly sure what to do, work backwards from the numbers given using the correct equations.

07.1 Show that the time it takes the signal to travel from the car to the satellite and back is about 0.1 s. **[4 marks]**

07.2 A car is travelling at 55 mph.
Calculate the distance the car would have moved in the time it takes the signal to travel to the satellite and back.
There are 1609 m in 1 mile. There are 3600 s in 1 hour. **[3 marks]**

07.3 To pinpoint the position of the car, the satnav device communicates with at least three satellites. This reduces the error in the position to about 30 cm. Suggest whether the error is a systematic or a random error. Explain your answer. **[2 marks]**

07.4 Suggest how the satnav device calculates the speed of the car. **[3 marks]**

07.5 The GPS satellite is orbiting the Earth at a constant speed. Explain how it can be accelerating at the same time as it is moving with a constant speed. **[2 marks]**

08 A block of stone has a mass of about 10 tonnes. One tonne = 10^3 kg. The block has to be moved a vertical distance of 2 m.

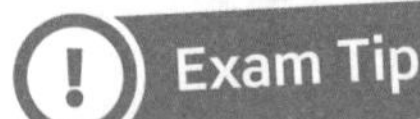

You will always be given the value that you need to use for gravitational field strength. Highlight all the different numbers you need to use for these calculations – it will save you time and stop you rereading the text several times.

08.1 Write down the name of the force that work is done against to move the block vertically 2 m. **[1 mark]**

08.2 Calculate the weight of the block.
Gravitational field strength = 9.8 N/kg. **[2 marks]**

08.3 Calculate the work done lifting the block a vertical distance of 2 m. **[2 marks]**

08.4 The block is pulled up a 4 m long ramp. The top of the ramp is 2 m above the ground.
Describe how a student can use a scale diagram to calculate the magnitude of the component of the weight parallel to the slope. **[3 marks]**

08.5 The student works out that the component of the weight parallel to the slope is 49 000 N. As the block is being pulled, the force acting on the block due to friction is 3000 N.
Calculate the work done pulling the stone up the ramp using the resultant of these two forces. **[3 marks]**

08.6 The work done using the ramp is larger than the work done lifting the stone directly. Suggest why a ramp is used. **[1 mark]**

09 A student collects data by stretching a spring and measuring the extension. They plot the graph shown in **Figure 5**.

09.1 Suggest which reading is an outlier. **[1 mark]**

09.2 Write the equation that links force, spring constant, and extension. **[1 mark]**

09.3 Use **Figure 5** to find the spring constant of the spring. **[4 marks]**

Figure 5

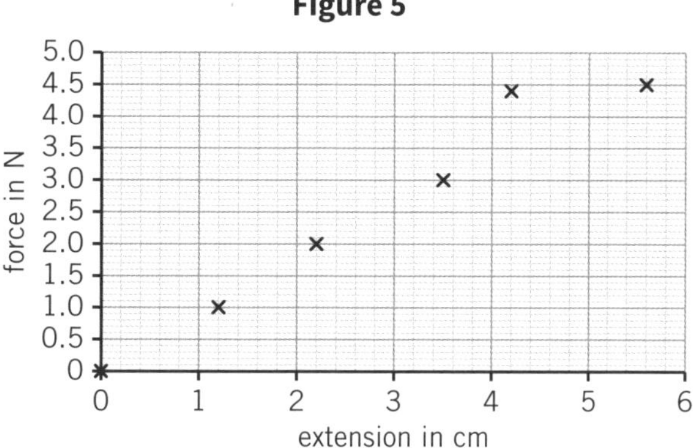

Exam Tip

You need to draw a line of best fit first. Make sure you do not include the outlier from **09.1** when drawing it.

09.4 Describe the shape of the graph if the limit of proportionality is exceeded. **[1 mark]**

10 A student puts a trolley at the top of a ramp. Two light gates are placed on the ramp so that the trolley can move through them. One light gate is placed close to the top of the ramp. The other is placed at the bottom of the ramp. Each light gate measures the velocity of the trolley as it passes:

- initial velocity = 1.12 m/s
- final velocity = 7.12 m/s
- time taken to travel between the light gates = 1.25 s

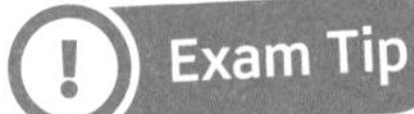

Exam Tip

This is a required practical, but there are lots of different ways this can be done. You can get the same data without light gates if your school doesn't have them.

10.1 Write down the equation that links acceleration, velocity, and time. **[1 mark]**

10.2 Calculate the acceleration of the trolley on the ramp. Give the correct unit with your answer. **[3 marks]**

10.3 Compare this acceleration with the acceleration due to gravity. Give your answer as a ratio. **[2 marks]**

10.4 The trolley leaves the ramp with the final velocity and moves on a rough section of the floor. The trolley takes 5 seconds to stop. The data logger plots a velocity–time graph for the trolley when it is both accelerating and decelerating. Sketch the graph the datalogger makes. Assume that the acceleration and deceleration are constant. Explain the shape of the graph. **[5 marks]**

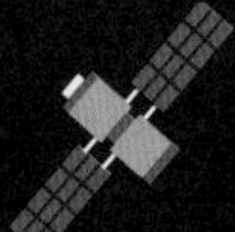

Knowledge

P10 Newton's laws of motion

Newton's First Law

The **inertia** of an object is its tendency to remain in a steady state, i.e., at rest or moving in a straight line at a constant speed.

Newton's First Law says that the velocity, speed, and/or direction of an object *will only change if a resultant force is acting on it*.

This means that:

- If the resultant force on a stationary object is zero, the object will remain stationary.
- If the resultant force on a moving object is zero, it will continue moving at the same velocity, in a straight line.
- If the resultant force on an object is not zero, its velocity *will* change.

When a car is travelling at a steady speed, the resistive forces (e.g., friction and air resistance) must be balanced with the driving forces.

A change in velocity can mean an object:

- starts to move
- stops moving
- speeds up
- slows down
- changes direction.

There *must* be a resultant force acting on an object if it is doing *any* of the things listed above.

Newton's Second Law

Newton's Second Law says that the acceleration a of an object:

- is proportional to the resultant force on the object

$$a \propto F$$

- is inversely proportional to the mass of the object

$$a \propto \frac{1}{m}$$

Resultant force, mass, and acceleration are linked by the equation:

resultant force (N) = mass (kg) × acceleration (m/s²)

$$F = ma$$

The inertial mass of an object is a measure of how difficult it is to change the velocity of an object. It can be found using:

$$\text{inertial mass (kg)} = \frac{\text{force (N)}}{\text{acceleration (m/s}^2\text{)}}$$

$$m = \frac{F}{a}$$

Newton's Third Law

Newton's Third Law states that whenever two objects interact with each other, they exert *equal and opposite* forces on each other.

This means that forces always occur in pairs.

Each pair of forces:

- act on separate objects
- are the same size as each other
- act in opposite directions along the same line
- are of the same type, for example, two gravitational forces or two electrostatic forces.

Momentum

Momentum is a property of all moving objects. It is a vector quantity.

Momentum depends on the mass and velocity of an object and is defined by the equation:

momentum (kg m/s) = mass (kg) × velocity (m/s)

$$p = mv$$

The Law of Conservation of Momentum says that:

In a closed system, the total momentum before an event (e.g., a collision or an explosion) is *equal* to the total momentum after the event.

If two moving objects collide the law of conservation can be written as:

$$m_1u_1 + m_2u_2 = m_1v_1 + m_2v_2$$

m_1 = mass of object 1 $\quad$ m_2 = mass of object 2

u_1 = initial velocity of object 1 $\quad$ u_2 = initial velocity of object 2

v_1 = final velocity of object 1 $\quad$ v_2 = final velocity of object 2

Revision tip

Remember The m means mass, while the symbol for momentum is p. Don't get them mixed up!

Remember the unit for stopping distance, m, is metres not miles.

Stopping distance

The distance it takes a body, such as a car, to stop is made up of **thinking distance** and **braking distance**.

Stopping distance = thinking distance + braking distance

Thinking distance is the distance the vehicle travels during the driver's **reaction time**. Thinking distance is proportional to the speed of the vehicle.

Stopping distance is the distance the vehicle travels once the brakes have been applied. Braking distance is not proportional to speed.

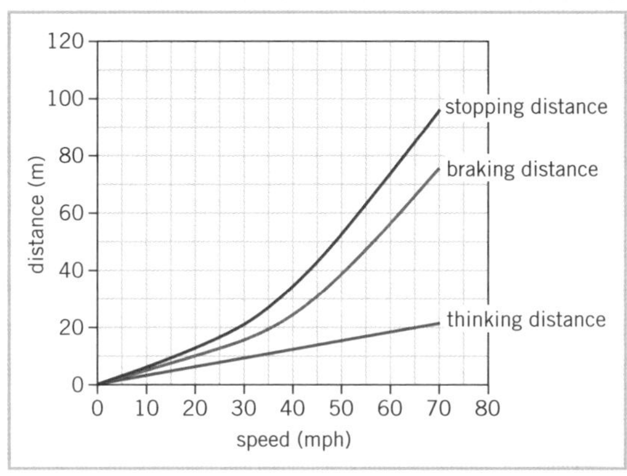

Speed has a bigger effect on braking distance than on thinking distance.

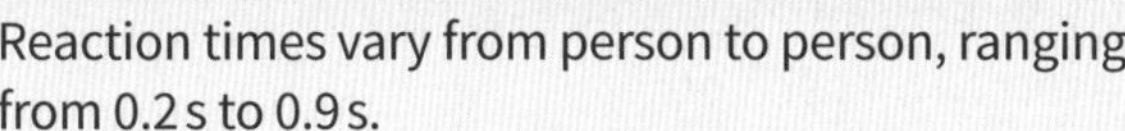

Reaction time

Reaction times vary from person to person, ranging from 0.2 s to 0.9 s.

Reaction time can be affected by:

- tiredness
- drugs
- alcohol
- distractions

Reaction times can be measured in a number of ways, including:

Computer

A computer is used to time how long someone takes to respond to a sound or image on the screen.

Ruler drop test

The ruler is dropped between someone's fingers and the distance it falls before they catch it is used to calculate their reaction time.

Factors affecting braking distance

The braking distance of a vehicle can be affected by:

- the speed of the vehicle
- road conditions
- the condition of brakes and tyres.

Any condition that causes less friction between the tyres and the road can lead to skidding, which increases the braking distance.

When the brakes of a vehicle are applied a frictional force is applied to its wheel.

Work done by the frictional force between the brakes and wheel transfers energy from the kinetic energy store of the car to the thermal energy stores of the brakes.

This increases the temperature of the brakes.

The braking force, braking distance, and energy transferred are related by the equation:

L *work done (J) = braking force (N) × distance (m)*

$$W = Fs$$

The faster a vehicle moves or the greater its mass:

- the greater the amount of energy in its kinetic energy store
- the more work that has to be done to transfer the energy to slow it down
- the greater the braking force needed to stop it in a certain distance
- the greater the distance needed to stop it with a certain braking force.

Make sure you can write a definition for these key terms.

braking distance *inertia* *momentum* *reaction time* *stopping distance* *thinking distance*

Learn the answers to the questions below, then cover the answers column with a piece of paper and write as many as you can. Check and repeat.

	P10 questions	Answers
1	What do we mean by inertia?	the tendency of an object to remain in a steady state (at rest or in uniform motion)
2	What does Newton's First Law say?	the velocity of an object will only change if a resultant force is acting on it
3	What is the resultant force on a stationary object?	zero
4	What is the resultant force on an object moving at a steady speed in a straight line?	zero
5	What will an object experience if the resultant force on it is not zero?	acceleration / change in velocity
6	What forces are balanced when an object travels at a steady speed?	resistive forces = driving force
7	According to Newton's Second Law, what is the acceleration of an object proportional to?	the force acting on it
8	According to Newton's Second Law, what is the acceleration of an object inversely proportional to?	mass
9	What is the inertial mass of an object?	how difficult it is to change an object's velocity
10	What does Newton's Third Law say?	when two objects interact they exert equal and opposite forces on each other
11	What is the name given to the distance a vehicle travels to safely come to a stop after the driver has spotted a hazard?	stopping distance
12	What is thinking distance?	distance vehicle travels during driver's reaction time
13	What is braking distance?	distance vehicle travels once brakes have been applied
14	What is the relationship between stopping distance, thinking distance, and braking distance?	stopping distance = thinking distance + braking distance
15	What are three factors that can affect the braking distance of a vehicle?	speed, road conditions, condition of tyres and brakes
16	What can happen if the braking force used to stop a vehicle is very large?	brakes may overheat / the car may skid
17	What is the law of conservation of momentum?	in a closed system, the total momentum before an event is equal to the total momentum after it
18	How is the force acting on an object related to its momentum?	force acting on an object = rate of change of momentum

Put paper here

Now go back and use the questions below to check your knowledge from previous chapters.

Previous questions / Answers

	Previous questions	Answers
1	What is an alternating current (a.c.)?	current that repeatedly reverses direction
2	What is a scalar quantity?	only has a size (magnitude)
3	Which materials have low thermal conductivity?	thermal insulators
4	Which type of nuclear radiation is the most ionising?	alpha
5	What is the centre of mass?	the point through which the weight of an object can be considered to act
6	How do you find the atomic number of an element?	number of protons in one atom of the element

Put paper here

Put paper here

Required Practical Skills

Practise answering questions on the required practicals using the example below. You need to be able to apply your skills and knowledge to other practicals too.

Force, mass, and acceleration

You need to be able to measure and explain how the acceleration of an object is linked to changes in force and mass.

For this practical, you can use two light gates to measure acceleration, or measure the time to travel a set distance. In the latter case the acceleration will be inversely proportional to the time.

To produce accurate and precise measurements you should:

- only change either the force or mass at one time
- use a video recording if not using light gates
- take repeat measurements and find the mean.

Worked example

A student sets up a trolley on a track. The trolley is attached to string, which goes over a pulley to a weight stack.

They set up light gates to record the acceleration as the force is changed.

Force in N	0	1	2	3	4	4
Acceleration in m/s^2	0	4	8.1	12	16.2	20.2

1 Calculate the mass of the system.

force = mass × acceleration

$$\text{mass} = \frac{\text{force}}{\text{acceleration}}$$

for example, $\frac{1\text{ N}}{4\text{ m/s}^2} = 0.25\text{ kg}$

2 Suggest how the student kept the mass of the system the same even though the number of weights on the stack increased.

They moved masses from the weight stack to the trolley.

3 What other force could be acting on the trolley, and how would this affect its acceleration?

Friction, which would cause the trolley's acceleration to be lower than expected.

Practice

A student connects a trolley to a piece of string attached to a weight stack. The weight stays the same, but the student increases the mass of the trolley.

She times how long it takes the trolley to travel 50 cm using a stop clock.

1 Sketch a graph of time against mass. Describe and explain the shape.

2 Describe how the student could ensure that the results are reproducible.

3 Suggest one benefit of using a larger distance.

Practice

Exam-style questions

01 A student wants to investigate the relationship between the mass of an object and its acceleration.

01.1 Describe an experiment that would enable the student to collect data to plot a graph of acceleration against mass. **[5 marks]**

01.2 Write down Newton's Second Law. **[1 mark]**

> **Exam Tip**
>
> It can be hard to remember which law was first, second, or third. Try looking at the first part of this question for clues.

01.3 Define the term inertia. **[1 mark]**

01.4 The student plotted their data on **Figure 1**. The student notices that a 0.2 kg mass does not have an acceleration of 20 m/s^2.

Figure 1

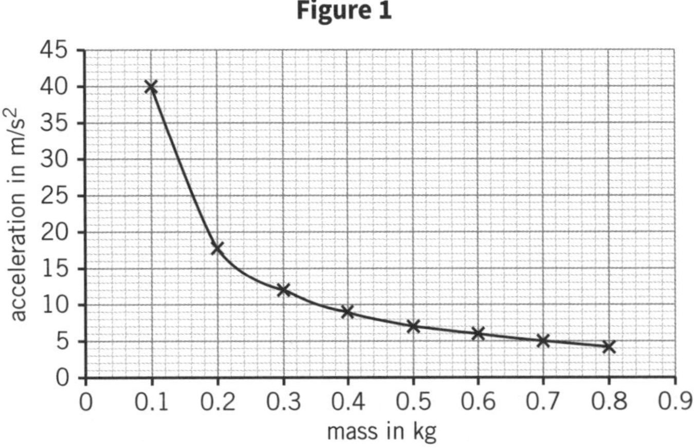

Suggest why the student expected that the acceleration would be 20 m/s^2.

Justify your answer. **[2 marks]**

01.5 Another student suggests that increasing the mass may have increased the friction, which would have affected the acceleration.

Do you agree with this student? Explain your answer. **[3 marks]**

02 An ice hockey puck is moving along the ice at a steady speed.

02.1 Student **A** says:
'If the speed is steady, there are no forces acting on the puck'.
Do you agree with student **A**? Justify your answer. **[2 marks]**

Exam Tip

Thinking about Newton's laws will help with these next few questions. Try writing them all down on the side here.

02.2 Student **B** says:
'The puck will only stop when the force it is carrying runs out'.

Do you agree with student **B**? Justify your answer. **[2 marks]**

02.3 One of the players hits the puck with a hockey stick and the puck moves in the opposite direction.

Student **C** says:
'While the stick is in contact with the puck, the stick exerts a bigger force on the puck than the puck exerts on the stick'.

Do you agree with student **C**? Justify your answer. **[2 marks]**

02.4 Determine whether the puck experienced an acceleration while in contact with the stick. Give reasons for your answer. **[2 marks]**

03 A company that transports food to supermarkets requires that lorry drivers are aware of how fast they are accelerating.
The acceleration of a lorry should not exceed 1.5 m/s^2.

03.1 The engine of a lorry produces a force of 10 kN. Typical resistive forces are about 2 kN. A lorry and its load have a total mass of 8400 kg. A driver uses the maximum force possible.

Determine whether the acceleration of their lorry exceeds the acceleration expected by the company.
Justify your answer with a calculation. **[5 marks]**

Be careful with the non-standard units here.

03.2 The lorry starts off fully loaded. The mass of the load is 3200 kg. The lorry stops at two supermarkets. It drops off half the load at each supermarket before going back to the depot.

Calculate the acceleration of the lorry on its way to the second supermarket, and on its way back to the depot. Each time the driver uses the maximum force.
Suggest whether this would be safe to do so. **[6 marks]**

Exam Tip

You were given the mass of the lorry *and* the load in the previous question. You have now been given the mass of just the load. The load will decrease at each supermarket. Read the question carefully to make sure you understand how it decreases.

04 A teacher demonstrates how changing the force applied to an object changes its acceleration.
Figure 2 shows a graph of the results.

Figure 2

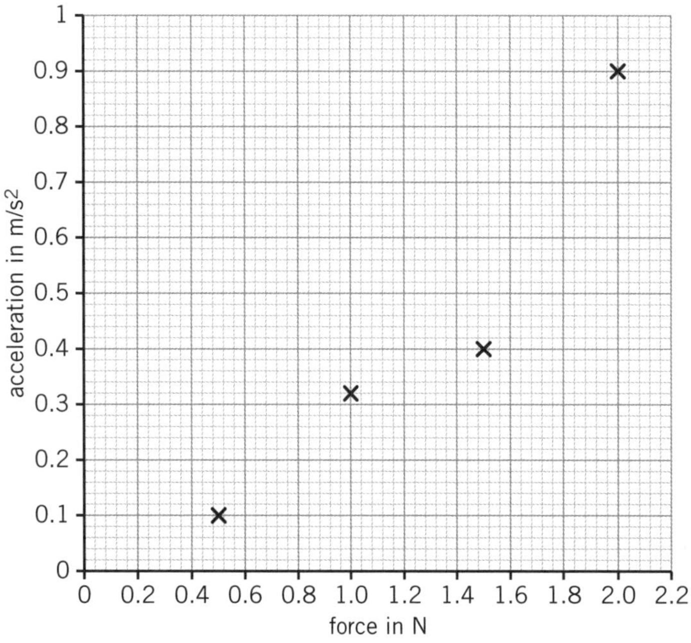

acceleration in m/s^2 (0 to 1); force in N (0 to 2.2)

04.1 On **Figure 2** circle the measurement that is an outlier. **[1 mark]**

Your line of best fit should best represent the data. This does not have to include all the points.

04.2 On **Figure 2** draw a line of best fit. **[1 mark]**

04.3 After the data has been plotted the teacher realises that the newtonmeter that they used does not read zero when there is no force applied.
Identify the type of error that this problem produces. **[1 mark]**

04.4 Give the reason why you can tell that there is this type of error by looking at the graph. Use the graph to write down the reading on the newtonmeter when no force is applied. **[2 marks]**

04.5 Write down the equation that links force, mass, and acceleration. **[1 mark]**

04.6 Use one of the points on your line of best fit to calculate the mass of the object. Explain how you have dealt with the error described in **04.3** and **04.4**. **[4 marks]**

> **Exam Tip**
> Draw on your graph to ensure you use the correct values.

05 The driver of a car reacts to a car braking suddenly in front of them. The car is initially travelling at 45 mph (20 m/s) and comes to a complete stop.

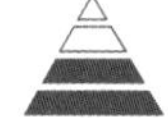

05.1 Describe the process by which energy is transferred from a kinetic energy store to a thermal energy store. **[1 mark]**

05.2 When energy is transferred to a thermal energy store, objects get hot.
Write down which objects get hotter when the driver brakes. **[1 mark]**

05.3 The speed of the car changes over a time of 4.3 seconds.
Calculate the deceleration of the car.
Give **one** assumption that you make when you do this calculation.
Suggest and explain whether this assumption is likely, or not likely, to be correct. **[5 marks]**

> **Exam Tip**
> You make assumptions for most calculations even if you don't realise it. Think about the motion of a car and what assumption you could have made.

05.4 The mass of the car is 1250 kg. Calculate the braking force.
Compare your answer with the typical driving force of a car. **[3 marks]**

06 It is very important to be able to stop a road vehicle quickly in an emergency. **Figure 3** shows a graph of braking distance against speed for a car in normal conditions and in an emergency.

Figure 3

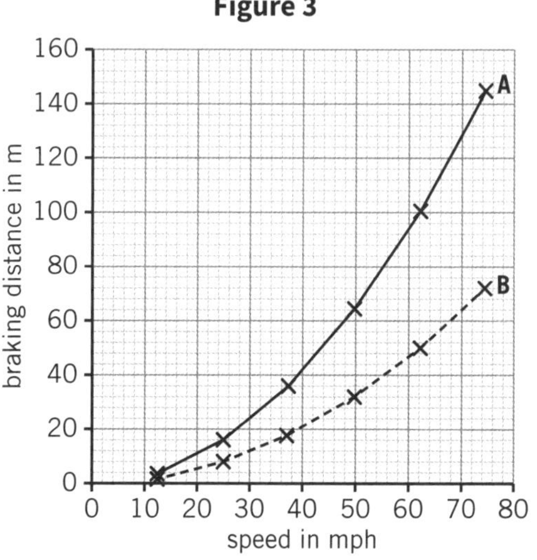

06.1 Write down which curve on **Figure 3**, **A** or **B**, relates to an emergency stop. Use the words force and acceleration to explain your answer. **[4 marks]**

> **Exam Tip**
> The question tells you some key words to use so make sure that you remember to use them.

06.2 Suggest **one** harmful effect of having to do an emergency stop. **[1 mark]**

06.3 **Figure 3** does not include the thinking distance.
Compare the thinking distance when stopping in normal conditions to when doing an emergency stop. **[2 marks]**

07 A student models the effect of road conditions on stopping distance using a trolley, a ramp, and different floor coverings (carpet, tiles, etc.).

There are four marks for **07.1**, so one mark for each variable. You can still pick up marks if you can't work out all the variables.

07.1 Identify the independent variable, the dependent variable, and **two** control variables in this investigation. **[4 marks]**

07.2 Write an experimental method to obtain sufficient data to plot a graph. **[5 marks]**

07.3 Identify a source of error in the experiment.
Suggest an improvement to reduce its effect. **[2 marks]**

07.4 Evaluate to what extent this is a good model of the effect of surface on the stopping distance of a car.
Use ideas about work and friction in your answer. **[3 marks]**

07.5 Suggest a limitation of this model.
Give a reason for your answer. **[2 marks]**

08 A helicopter is collecting an object from a remote location. A rope, hanging down from the helicopter, is attached to the object.
The object has a mass of 110 kg. The helicopter accelerates upwards with an acceleration of 2.0 m/s^2.
Gravitational field strength = 9.8 N/kg.

There is a lot of information in the main body of this question. Write down a list of the key values:

- mass =
- acceleration =
- weight =
- force =

08.1 Calculate the weight of the object. **[3 marks]**

08.2 Calculate the force needed to accelerate the object at 2.0 m/s^2. **[3 marks]**

08.3 Show that the total force that the helicopter must exert on the object is about 1300 N. **[2 marks]**

08.4 Describe what happens to the object if the helicopter exerts a force of 1078 N. Give reasons for your answer. **[3 marks]**

09 A medical journal published an article on injuries due to falling coconuts. Here is a summary of the study as reported in the journal.

'A four-year review of trauma admissions to the Provincial Hospital, Alotau, Papua New Guinea, reveals that 2.5 % of such admissions were due to being struck by falling coconuts. Since mature coconut palms may have a height of up to 35 meters and an unhusked coconut may have mass of up to 4 kg, blows to the head of a force exceeding 1 metric tonne, or 1000 kg, are possible.'

Exam Tip

Sort out which information is useful and what is just a distraction by crossing out information that will not help you answer the question. For example, the fact that this happened in a Provincial Hospital, Alotau, Papua New Guinea is not helpful for the physics. This can be crossed out. However, the height that the coconuts fall is useful for the physics.

09.1 When the scientists completed their investigation, they wrote a paper and submitted it to the journal. Describe what happens to an article before it is published. Give the name of this process. **[2 marks]**

09.2 Suggest why the statement *'a force exceeding 1 metric tonne'* is incorrect. **[1 mark]**

09.3 Write down the equation that links gravitational field strength, mass, and weight. **[1 mark]**

09.4 Calculate the force exerted by a mass of 1000 kg.
Gravitational field strength = 9.8 N/kg. **[2 marks]**

09.5 Suggest why the authors chose to describe the force in this way in the summary. **[1 mark]**

09.6 A coconut of mass 2.5 kg falls from a tree in 2.5 seconds. Calculate the momentum of the coconut just before it hits the ground. **[4 marks]**

10 Some animals can accelerate very quickly. **Table 1** shows the acceleration and top speed of a leafhopper (an insect) and a cheetah.

Table 1

Animal	Acceleration in m/s^2	Top speed in m/s	Mass of animal
leafhopper	1000	4	2 mg
cheetah	5	30	50 kg

10.1 Write down the equation that links acceleration, force, and mass. **[1 mark]**

10.2 Show that the force generated by the cheetah is 125 000 times greater than the force generated by the leafhopper. **[6 marks]**

10.3 Use **Table 1** to suggest whether the acceleration of the animal and the top speed of the animal are directly proportional.
Justify your answer with calculations. **[4 marks]**

10.4 A company makes an acceleration suit for a human. The suit allows the wearer to have the same level of acceleration as a leafhopper.
A human tries on the suit. They have a mass of 70 kg.
Calculate the force produced by the suit. Compare your answer with the forces produced by vehicles in everyday road transport. Forces produced by cars are about 40 kN. **[4 marks]**

> **! Exam Tip**
>
> In a show question, you know what the answer should be. So if you don't get that answer when you're doing your working out then you can try again until you get there. Just be careful of the amount of time you have in an exam.

11 A person buying a car is comparing the performance of some cars. **Table 2** shows data from a magazine.

Table 2

Car	Mass in kg	Time to go from 0 to 60 mph in s	Acceleration in m/s^2
Model A	1611	5.6	4.79
Model B	1565	7.1	3.78
Model C	1864	4.8	5.59

11.1 The buyer wonders whether the forces produced by the engines of the three cars are the same.
Use **Table 2** to compare the forces. **[5 marks]**

11.2 They test the Model B. It travels at a steady speed of 50 mph with a driving force of 3 kN.
Write down the resistive force acting on the car. **[1 mark]**

11.3 They take their foot off the accelerator pedal so that the only force acting on the car is the resistive force. Assume that the positive direction is in the direction of the driving force.
Calculate the acceleration of the car. **[4 marks]**

> **! Exam Tip**
>
> This question is testing your data interpretation skills. Use the data from **Table 2** and refer to it in your answer.

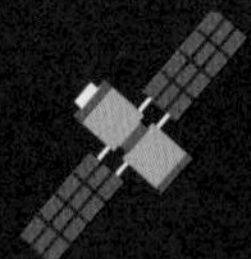

P11 Mechanical waves

Waves in air, liquids, and solids

Waves transfer energy from one place to another without transferring matter. Waves may be **transverse** or **longitudinal**.

For waves in water and air, it is the energy and not the substance that moves.

- When a light object is dropped into still water, it produces ripples (waves) on the water which spread out, but neither the object nor the water moves with the ripples.
- When you speak, your voice box vibrates, making sound waves travel through the air. The air itself does not travel away from your throat, otherwise a vacuum would be created.

Mechanical waves require a substance (a medium) to travel through.

Examples of mechanical waves include sound waves, water waves, waves on springs and ropes, and seismic waves produced by earthquakes.

When waves travel through a substance, the particles in the substance **oscillate** (vibrate) and pass energy on to neighbouring particles.

Transverse waves

The oscillations of a transverse wave are *perpendicular* (at right angles) to the direction in which the waves transfer energy.

Ripples on the surface of water are an example of transverse waves.

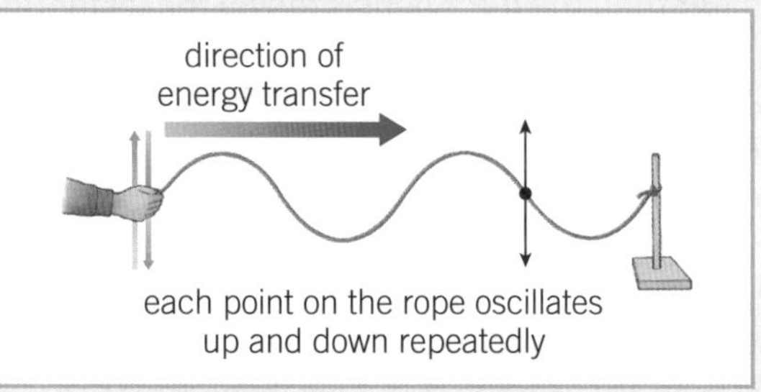

Longitudinal waves

The oscillations of a longitudinal wave are *parallel* to the direction in which the waves transfer energy.

Longitudinal waves cause particles in a substance to be squashed closer together and pulled further apart, producing areas of **compression** and **rarefaction** in the substance.

Sound waves in air are an example of longitudinal waves.

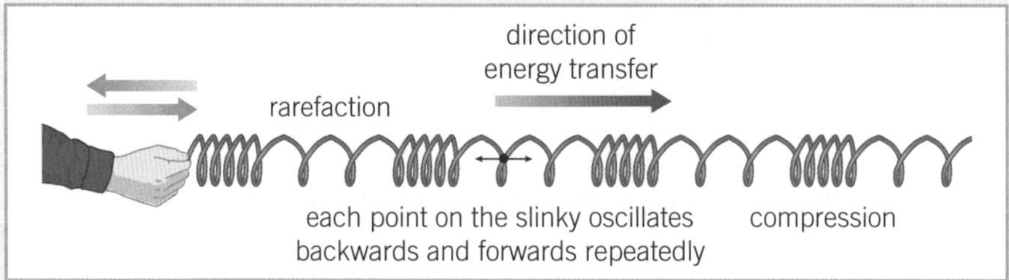

Revision tips

Remember Longitudinal waves can be drawn as particles, don't get confused if you see it in the exam as a lot of dots!

Practice drawing the diagrams for both waves and adding on the wavelength and amplitude.

Key terms

Make sure you can write a definition for these key terms.

amplitude compression frequency longitudinal mechanical wave oscillate

Properties of waves

Frequency and period are related by the equation:

$$\text{period (s)} = \frac{1}{\text{frequency (Hz)}}$$

$$T = \frac{1}{f}$$

All waves obey the wave equation:

L wave speed (m/s) = frequency (Hz) × wavelength (m)

$$v = f\lambda$$

When waves travel from one medium to another, their speed and wavelength may change but the frequency always stays the same.

The speed of ripples on water can be slow enough to measure using a stopwatch and ruler, and applying the equation:

L $$\text{speed (m/s)} = \frac{\text{distance (m)}}{\text{time (s)}}$$

The speed of sound in air can be measured by using a stopwatch to measure the time taken for a sound to travel a known distance, and applying the same equation.

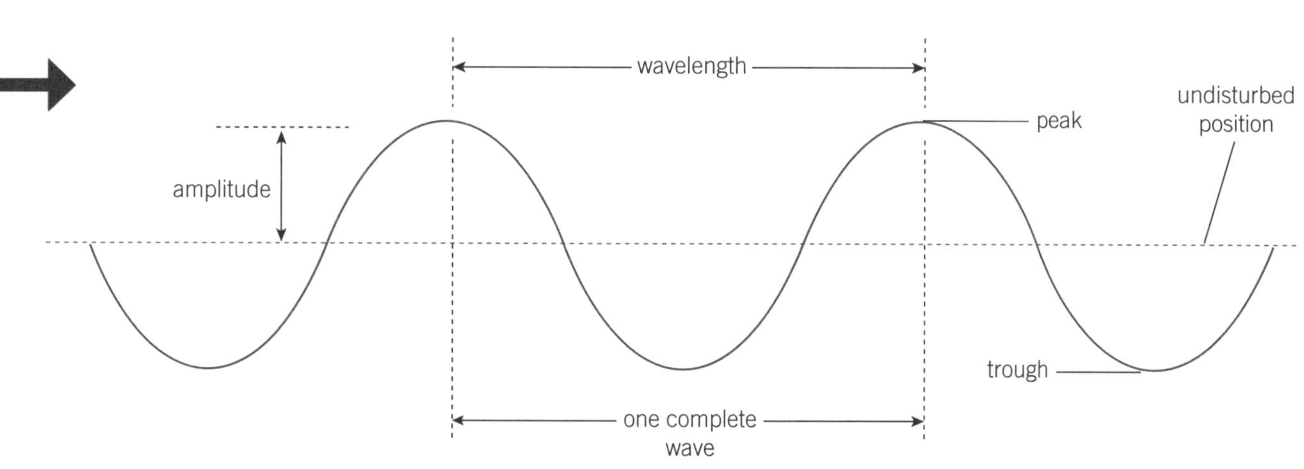

Wave motion is described by a number of properties.

Property	Description	Unit
amplitude A	maximum displacement of a point on a wave from its undisturbed position	metre (m)
frequency f	number of waves passing a fixed point per second	hertz (Hz)
period T	time taken for one complete wave to pass a fixed point	second (s)
wavelength λ	distance from one point on a wave to the equivalent point on the next wave	metre (m)
wave speed v	distance travelled by each wave per second, and the speed at which energy is transferred by the wave	metres per second (m/s)

period rarefaction transverse wavelength wave speed

Learn the answers to the questions below, then cover the answers column with a piece of paper and write as many as you can. Check and repeat.

	P11 questions	Answers
1	What is a transverse wave?	a wave with oscillations/vibrations perpendicular (at right angles) to the direction of energy transfer
2	What is a longitudinal wave?	a wave with oscillations/vibrations parallel to the direction of energy transfer
3	Give an example of a transverse wave.	electromagnetic waves
4	Give an example of a longitudinal wave.	sound waves
5	What is a compression?	area in longitudinal waves where the particles are squashed closer together
6	What is a rarefaction?	area in longitudinal waves where the particles are pulled further apart
7	What is the amplitude of a wave?	maximum displacement of a point on the wave from its undisturbed position
8	What unit is amplitude measured in?	metre (m)
9	What is the wavelength of a wave?	distance from a point on one wave to the equivalent point on the adjacent wave
10	What unit is wavelength measured in?	metre (m)
11	What is the frequency of a wave?	number of waves passing a fixed point per second
12	What unit is frequency measured in?	hertz (Hz)
13	What is wave speed?	speed at which the energy is transferred (or the wave moves) through a medium
14	What unit is wave speed measured in?	metres per second (m/s)

Put paper here

Now go back and use the questions below to check your knowledge from previous chapters.

Previous questions / Answers

	Previous questions	Answers
1	What do we mean by inertia?	the tendency of an object to remain in a steady state (at rest or in uniform motion)
2	What is acceleration?	change in velocity of an object per second
3	What is the unit of acceleration?	m/s^2
4	What is a non-contact force?	when objects are physically separated (e.g., gravitational, electrostatic, magnetic)
5	What is inelastic deformation?	an object does not go back to its original shape and size when deforming forces are removed

Put paper here

Put paper here

Required Practical Skills

Practise answering questions on the required practicals using the example below. You need to be able to apply your skills and knowledge to other practicals too.

Investigating waves

You need to be able to measure the frequency and wavelength of waves through a liquid and a solid. A ripple tank will be used to make water waves, and a vibration generator to make standing waves on a string.

To be accurate and precise in your investigation you need to:

- count and measure the length of multiple water waves
- measure the length of multiple waves on a string
- repeat your measurements and find the mean.

You should be able to evaluate the suitability of the equipment used to measure wave speeds in liquids and solids.

Worked example

A student sets up a ripple tank.

A lamp above the tank produces this image of the waves on a piece of paper below the tank.

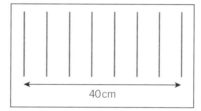

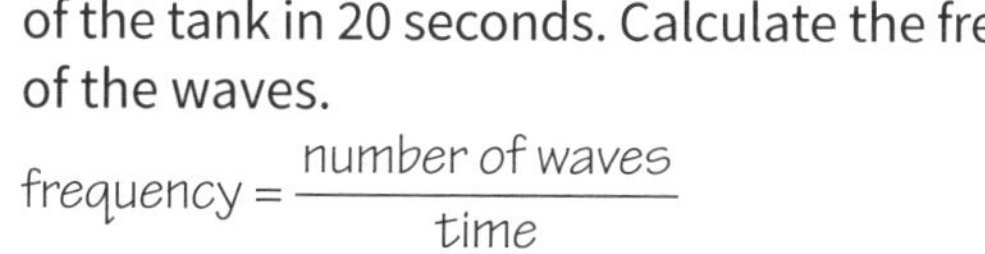

1 Calculate the wavelength of the waves.

Number of waves = 7

wavelength $= \frac{40}{7} = 5.7\text{ cm} = 0.057\text{ m}$

2 The student counts 25 waves reaching the end of the tank in 20 seconds. Calculate the frequency of the waves.

frequency $= \frac{\text{number of waves}}{\text{time}}$

$\frac{25}{20} = 1.25\text{ Hz} = 1.3\text{ Hz}$ *to 2 s.f.*

3 Calculate the speed of the waves.

speed = frequency × wavelength

$1.3 \times 0.057 = 0.0741\text{ m/s} = 0.074\text{ m/s}$ *to 2 s.f.*

4 Suggest one improvement the student could make to improve the accuracy of their speed measurement.

Repeat all measurements of wavelength and frequency and take the average.

Practice

A teacher connects a vibration generator to a piece of elastic.

She changes the frequency of the vibration generator and measures the wavelength of the elastic, producing the data below.

Frequency in Hz	Wavelength in m
4	4.86
8	2.51
12	1.25
16	1.29
20	1.02

1 Plot a graph of these data. Identify the outlier.

2 Use the data to calculate the average wave speed in m/s. Show your working.

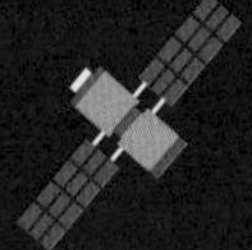

Practice

Exam-style questions

01 A student makes a wave on a long thin spring.

The spring is attached to the wall.

The wave is shown in **Figure 1**.

Figure 1

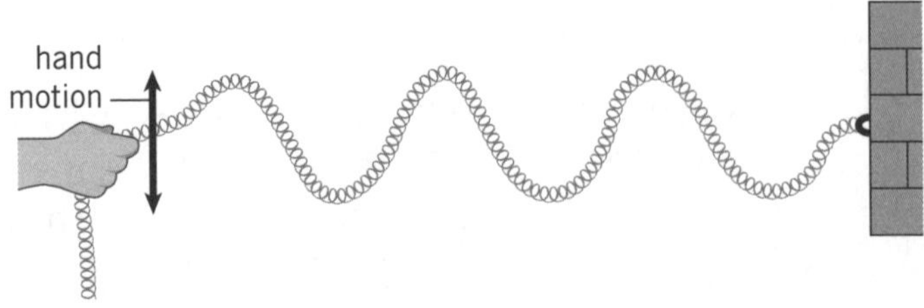

01.1 Write down the type of wave that the student produces. **[1 mark]**

____

01.2 On **Figure 1** draw an arrow to show the wavelength of the wave. **[1 mark]**

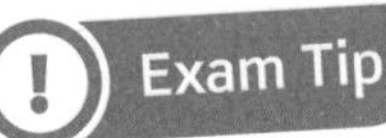

There is a big clue in the diagram!

01.3 Describe what the student should do to produce waves with a smaller amplitude.

Explain your answer. **[2 marks]**

____

____

____

02 One of the highest measured ocean waves was measured at a height of 34 metres from peak to trough.

The period of the wave was 14.8 s.

The wavelength was calculated to be 342 m.

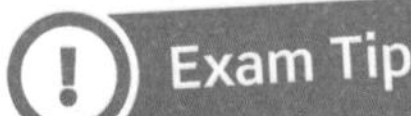

Don't be distracted by all the numbers in the question, not all of them are needed in every section of this question.

02.1 Calculate the amplitude of the wave. **[2 marks]**

Amplitude = ______________ m

02.2 Calculate the speed of the wave.

Use an equation from the *Physics Equations Sheet*.

Show your working. **[4 marks]**

Speed = ______________ m/s

02.3 A student compares this wave with the waves seen in a ripple tank. A ripple tank is a tray of water on four legs.

Estimate the amplitude of waves in a ripple tank. **[1 mark]**

02.4 The speed of waves in a ripple tank is found to be 50 cm/s.

Suggest whether the speed of a wave is proportional to its amplitude. **[3 marks]**

Exam Tip

Look out for non-standard units.

Exam Tip

The height was given in the question stem – 34 metres from peak to trough.

03 A child is throwing stones into a pond. The ripples move across the surface of the water.

03.1 Compare the motion of the surface of the water with the motion of the wave. **[1 mark]**

Exam Tip

There are two different types of waves in action here – work this out first and that will help you answer the question on particles.

03.2 The stone makes a sound when it hits the water. The sound wave and the ripple move towards the child.
Describe the difference between the motion of the particles on the surface of the water and the motion of the air particles in the sound wave. **[2 marks]**

03.3 Write down the equation that links wave speed, frequency, and wavelength. **[1 mark]**

03.4 The frequency of the sound that the stone makes is 400 Hz.
The speed of sound in air is 340 m/s.
Calculate the wavelength of the sound waves. **[3 marks]**

04 You can use a slinky coil to model waves. The wave on the slinky coil has compressions and rarefactions.

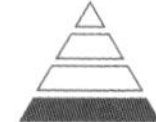

04.1 On **Figure 2** write the letter **C** above a compression, and the letter **R** above a rarefaction. **[2 marks]**

Figure 2

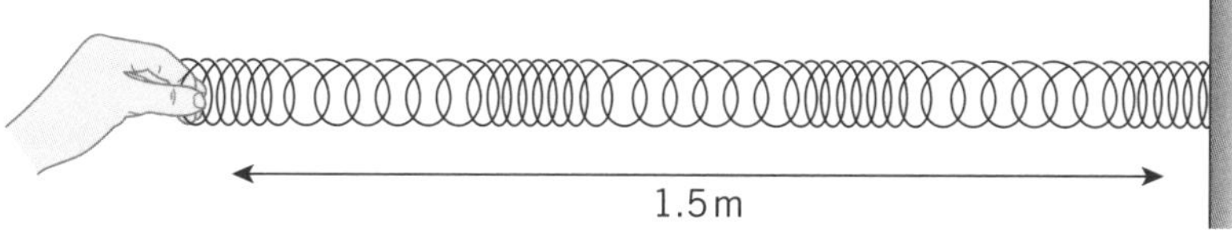

04.2 Show that the wavelength of the wave is 0.5 m. **[2 marks]**

04.3 Write down the equation that links wave speed, frequency, and wavelength. **[1 mark]**

04.4 The wave is travelling at 1.0 m/s.
Calculate the frequency of the wave. State the unit.
Explain what this means in terms of the motion of the person's hand. **[5 marks]**

05 A student watches a video about different types of wave.
The video describes ripples on a water surface and sound waves.

05.1 Write down which of these types of wave is longitudinal. **[1 mark]**

Exam Tip

This is related to one of the Required Practicals – try to use those to think about how you can measure the wave moving.

05.2 Describe an experiment to show that, as the wave travels, the air and water particles are not carried with it.
Describe the observations that you would make and what those observations show. **[6 marks]**

06 A scientist attempted to measure the speed of sound experimentally by measuring the time difference between spotting the flash of a gun and hearing the sound produced by the gun.
The experiment was carried out over a long distance on a day without any wind.
The value obtained was 478.4 m/s.

06.1 Describe **one** assumption made when doing this experiment. **[1 mark]**

06.2 Describe the measurements made and how they were used to calculate the speed of sound. **[2 marks]**

Exam Tip

Whenever you're doing calculations, always write down the equation first and then add in the numbers and rearrange it last, this is the best way to pick up marks.

06.3 The accepted speed of sound is 330 m/s.
Calculate the percentage difference between the accepted value and the value first calculated. Show your working. **[3 marks]**

06.4 Another scientist stood 29 km away from a cannon. The scientist measured the time interval between the cannon being fired and the scientist hearing the cannon.
They calculated the speed of sound as 332 m/s.
Calculate the time interval between hearing the sound from the cannon. Use the speed of sound calculated by the scientist. **[4 marks]**

06.5 Suggest why the difference between the accepted value of the speed of sound and the value calculated in this experiment is much smaller than for the first scientist's experiment. **[2 marks]**

07 A student sets up a ripple tank to measure the speed of water waves. The student takes a bar with a motor attached to it to make it vibrate. The bar is attached to a power supply and is partly submerged in a tray of water. A lamp above the tray of water projects an image of the ripples onto the desk below the ripple tank.

07.1 Describe a hazard associated with this experiment. Describe a strategy to reduce the risk of injury due to the hazard. **[2 marks]**

07.2 The student turns on the motor and sees the image of ripples moving across the desk.
The student records that the number of waves passing a point in 10 s is 5 and that the number of waves in 20 cm on the desk is 15.
Suggest what can be calculated from this data.
Include the units. **[2 marks]**

07.3 Describe how to perform the calculations you have suggested using the data collected by the student. Explain your reasoning. **[4 marks]**

07.4 Write down the equation that links wave speed, frequency, and wavelength. **[1 mark]**

07.5 Use the data recorded by the student to calculate the speed of the ripples in the tank. Give your answer in standard form.
Explain why the answer should be given to one significant figure. **[6 marks]**

> **! Exam Tip**
>
> You should always match the resolution of your answer to the data given in the question.

08 A student wants to investigate the deflection of a beam. They clamp a ruler to the edge of a table, and attach a mass to the end of the ruler as shown in **Figure 3**.

Figure 3

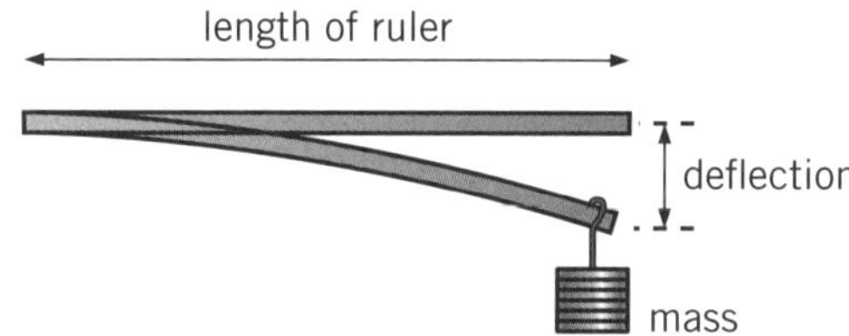

They decide to investigate how the length of the ruler affects the deflection.

08.1 Write down the independent variable, the dependent variable, and **two** control variables. **[4 marks]**

08.2 Describe a method that the student could use to collect data to find a relationship between the length of the ruler and the deflection. Assume that the equipment is set up as in **Figure 3**. **[3 marks]**

> **! Exam Tip**
>
> Remember:
> - independent variable – what you change
> - dependent variable – what you measure
> - control variables – what you keep the same.

08.3 The student collects the data in **Table 1**.

Table 1

Length of ruler in m	Deflection in cm
0.20	3.5
0.30	3.8
0.40	4.2
0.50	5.3

The deflection is not proportional to the length. Use the data in **Table 1** to show this. **[2 marks]**

08.4 Suggest a different investigation that the student could carry out using the same equipment. **[1 mark]**

09 A baker uses their car to travel to work, and back home at the end of the day.

09.1 Write down the total displacement from the baker's home. **[1 mark]**

09.2 The distance from the baker's home to their workplace is 4.5 miles. There are 1609 m in one mile. Calculate 4.5 miles in metres. **[1 mark]**

09.3 The total time the baker spends in the car each day is 20 min. Calculate the average speed they travel. **[4 marks]**

09.4 Describe why **09.3** is an average speed. **[1 mark]**

> **Exam Tip**
>
> The total displacement over the day is the difference between where they started and where they end up.

10 A wave can be modelled by a person running. The runner's stride length is 2.0 m. The runner takes 180 strides per minute.

10.1 Use the information to work out the speed of the runner in metres per second. **[3 marks]**

10.2 Write down which quantity is analogous to the wavelength. **[1 mark]**

10.3 Write down which quantity is analogous to frequency. Explain your answer. **[2 marks]**

10.4 Compare the method of working out the speed of a wave used in **10.1** with using the wave equation to work out the speed of a wave. **[3 marks]**

> **Exam Tip**
>
> Analogous means 'the same as' or 'very similar to' – so for **10.2** the question could read 'which quantity is very similar to frequency?'

11 An oscilloscope can be used to display sound waves. The oscilloscope is connected to a microphone. The microphone converts sound waves into an alternating potential difference which is displayed on the screen (**Figure 4**).

Figure 4

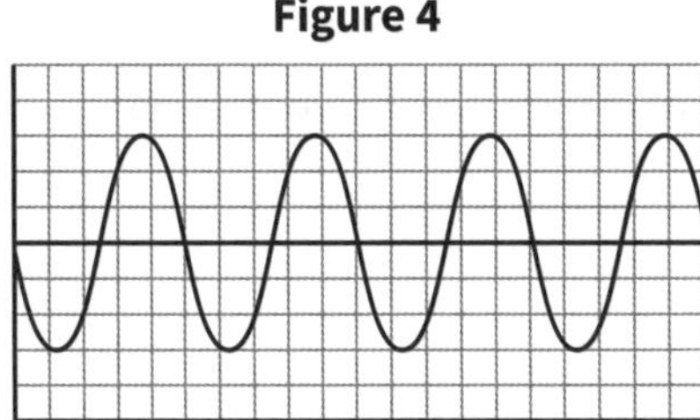

11.1 Each square on the horizontal axis represents a time of 0.1 ms. Calculate the period of the sound waves. Give your answer in standard form. **[3 marks]**

11.2 Write down the equation that links wave speed, frequency, and wavelength. **[1 mark]**

11.3 The speed of sound waves in air is 340 m/s. Calculate the wavelength of the wave. **[3 marks]**

11.4 Each square on the vertical axis of **Figure 4** represents a potential difference of 2 V. Calculate the amplitude of the waves in volts. **[2 marks]**

> **Exam Tip**
>
> ms is milliseconds, not to be confused with m/s, which is speed in metres per second.

> **Exam Tip**
>
> If it helps, you can draw axes on **Figure 4** and label them with the values given to help you work out **11.4**.

12 A sound wave travels from a transmitter to a receiver. The period of the wave is 1 millisecond. The wavelength of the wave is 34 cm.

12.1 Define period. **[1 mark]**

12.2 Calculate the frequency of the sound wave.
Use an equation from the *Physics Equations Sheet*. **[3 marks]**

12.3 Write down the equation that links wave speed, frequency, and wavelength. **[1 mark]**

12.4 Calculate the speed of the waves. Show your working. **[2 marks]**

> **Exam Tip**
> The units for frequency can be tricky – the only way you'll get marks for them is if the correct combination of capital and lowercase letters is used.

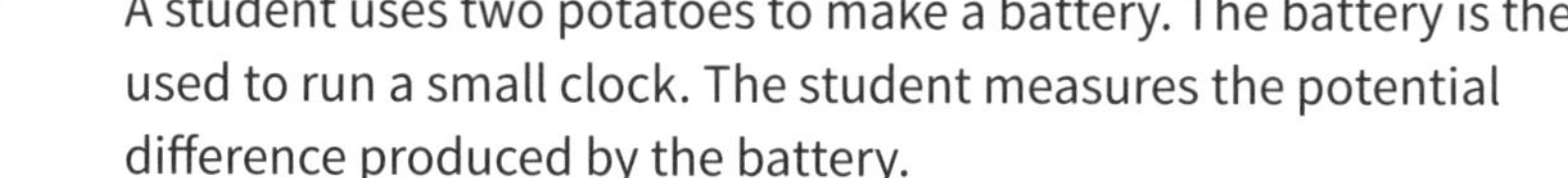

13 A student uses two potatoes to make a battery. The battery is then used to run a small clock. The student measures the potential difference produced by the battery.

13.1 Name the measuring instrument that is used to measure potential difference. **[1 mark]**

13.2 Write down the equation that links potential difference, current, and resistance. **[1 mark]**

13.3 Calculate the potential difference that you need to produce a current of 0.15 A in a clock with a resistance of 10 Ω. **[2 marks]**

13.4 Write down the equation that links charge flow, current, and time. **[1 mark]**

13.5 Calculate the charge that flows through the clock every minute. Write the correct unit with your answer. **[3 marks]**

13.6 A student decides to use four potatoes instead of one. Describe what would happen to the current flowing in the clock. Give a reason for your answer. **[2 marks]**

> **Exam Tip**
> In **13.1** think about the units for potential difference.

> **Exam Tip**
> The standard unit for time is seconds, so remember to convert minutes to seconds before you start **13.5**.

14 A light bulb is powered by a generator. The power of the light bulb is 0.24 W. The generator is powered by a falling 300 g mass attached to the generator by a string, as shown in **Figure 5**.

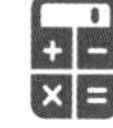

Figure 5

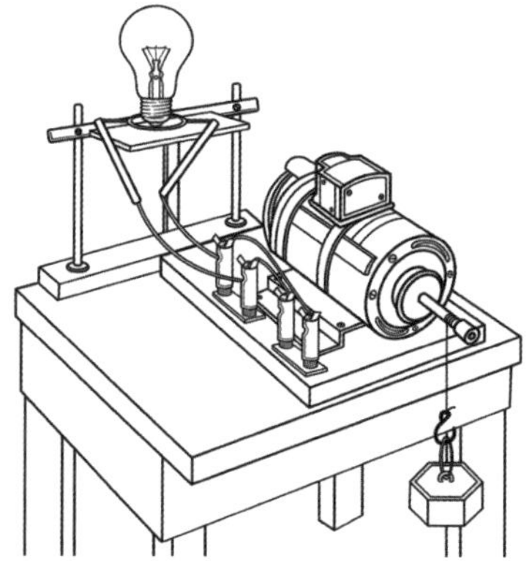

The generator is 90 % efficient. The bulb needs to be powered at full brightness for 1 minute.
Calculate how far the mass must fall. Explain the reasons for your calculations. Gravitational field strength = 9.8 N/kg **[6 marks]**

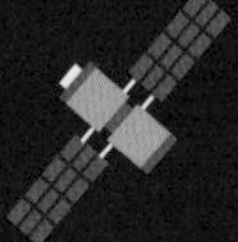

P12 Electromagnetic waves

The electromagnetic spectrum

Electromagnetic (EM) waves are **transverse** waves that transfer energy from their source to an absorber. For example, infrared waves emitted from a hot object transfer thermal energy.

EM waves form a continuous **spectrum**, and are grouped by their wavelengths and frequencies.

EM waves all travel at the same velocity through air or a vacuum. They all travel at a speed of 3×10^8 m/s through a vacuum.

Different substances may absorb, transmit, refract, or **reflect** EM waves in ways that vary with wavelength.

Refraction occurs when there is a difference in the velocity of an EM wave in different substances.

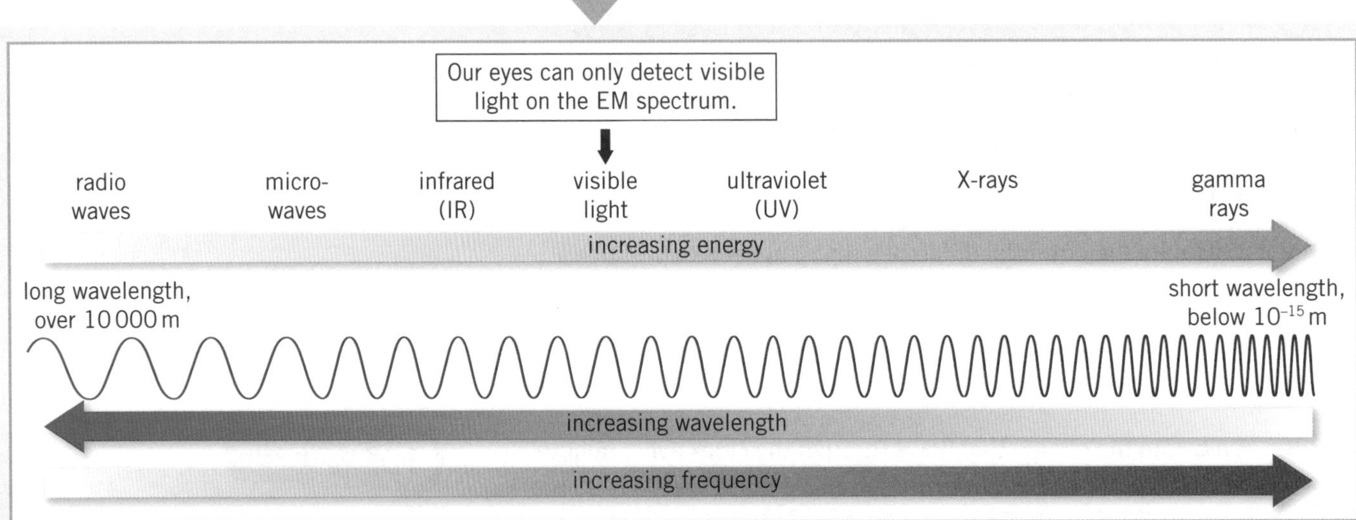

Refraction of electromagnetic waves

Ray diagrams show what happens when a wave is refracted (changes direction) at the boundary between two different substances.

- If a wave slows down when it crosses the boundary, the refracted ray will bend towards the normal.
- If a wave speeds up when it crosses the boundary, the refracted ray will bend away from the normal.
- If a wave travels at a right angle to the boundary (along the normal), it will change speed but not direction.

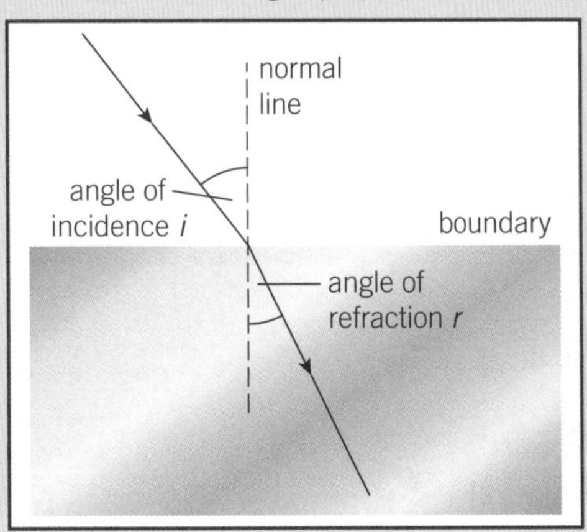

Wave front diagrams can be used to explain refraction in terms of the change of speed that occurs when a wave travels from one substance to another.

The wave front is an imaginary line at right angles to the direction the wave is moving.

- If a wave slows down as it crosses a boundary, the wave fronts become closer together.
- When a wave crosses a boundary at an angle, one end of the wave front changes speed before the other, so the wave changes direction.

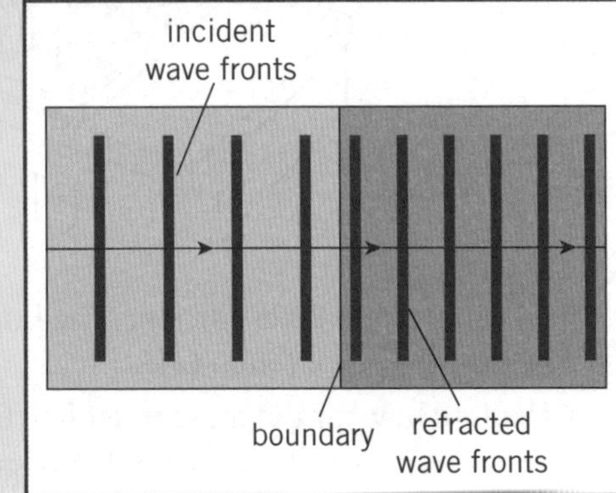

Properties of EM waves

EM waves of a wide range of frequencies can be absorbed or produced by changes inside an atom or nucleus. For example, gamma rays are produced by changes in the nucleus of an atom.

When electrons in an atom move down between energy levels, they emit EM waves.

Properties of radio waves

Radio waves can be produced by **oscillations** in an electrical circuit.

When radio waves are absorbed by a receiver aerial, they may create an alternating current with the same frequency as the radio waves.

Uses of EM waves

EM waves have many practical applications, but exposure to some EM waves (such as those that are forms of ionising radiation) can have hazardous effects.

Radiation dose (measured in sieverts) is the risk of harm from exposure of the body to a particular radiation.

Type of EM wave	Use	Why is it suitable for this use?	Hazards
radio waves	television and radio signals	• can travel long distances through air • longer wavelengths can bend around obstructions to allow detection of signals when not in line of sight	can penetrate the body and cause internal heating
microwaves	satellite communications and cooking food	• can pass through Earth's atmosphere to reach satellites • can penetrate into food and are absorbed by water molecules in food, heating it	
infrared (IR)	electrical heaters, cooking food, and infrared cameras	• all hot objects emit infrared waves – sensors can detect these to turn them into an image • can transfer energy quickly to heat rooms and food	can damage or kill skin cells due to heating
visible light	fibre optic communications	• short wavelength means visible light carries more information	can damage the retina
ultraviolet (UV)	energy efficient lights and artificial sun tanning	• carries more energy than visible light • some chemicals used inside light bulbs can absorb UV and emit visible light	can damage skin cells, causing skin to age prematurely and increasing the risk of skin cancer, and can cause blindness
X-rays	medical imaging and treatments	• pass easily through flesh, but not denser materials like bone • high doses kill living cells, so can be used to kill cancer cells – gamma rays can also be used to kill harmful bacteria	form of ionising radiation – can damage or kill cells, cause mutation of genes, and lead to cancers
gamma rays			

Key terms **Make sure you can write a definition for these key terms.**

electromagnetic wave *electromagnetic spectrum* *oscillation* *radiation dose* *ray diagram* *reflection* *refraction* *transverse* *wave front diagram*

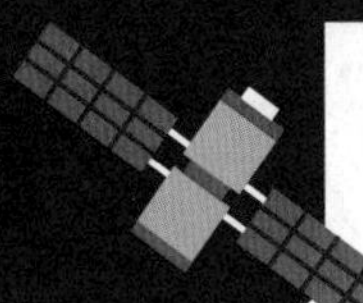

Learn the answers to the questions below, then cover the answers column with a piece of paper and write as many as you can. Check and repeat.

	P12 questions		Answers
1	Are electromagnetic (EM) waves longitudinal or transverse waves?	Put paper here	transverse
2	Explain why EM waves are not mechanical waves.		they can travel through a vacuum (don't need a substance to travel through)
3	What do EM waves transfer from their source to an absorber?	Put paper here	energy
4	List the different types of waves in the EM spectrum in order of decreasing wavelength (increasing frequency).		radio, microwave, infrared, visible, ultraviolet, X-rays, gamma
5	Which part of the EM spectrum can humans see?	Put paper here	visible light
6	How can EM waves be produced?		changes inside an atom/atomic nucleus
7	How are gamma rays produced?		changes in the nucleus of an atom, for example during radioactive decay
8	How can radio waves be produced?	Put paper here	oscillations in an electrical circuit
9	How can we detect radio waves?		waves are absorbed and create an alternating current with the same frequency as the radio wave
10	What are radio waves used for?	Put paper here	transmitting television, mobile phone, Bluetooth signals
11	What are microwaves used for?		satellite communications, cooking food
12	What is infrared radiation used for?		heating, remote controls, infrared cameras, cooking food
13	Which types of EM waves are harmful to the human body?	Put paper here	ultraviolet, X-rays, gamma rays
14	What are the hazards of being exposed to ultraviolet radiation?		damage skin cells, sunburn, increase risk of skin cancer, age skin prematurely, blindness
15	Why are X-rays used for medical imaging?	Put paper here	they pass through flesh but not bone
16	Why are gamma rays used for treating cancer and sterilising medical equipment?		high doses kill cells and bacteria
17	What is refraction?	Put paper here	waves change speed and direction as they cross the boundary from one substance to another due to the change in velocity
18	What happens to the direction of a refracted EM wave when it slows down as it crosses the boundary from one substance to another?		bends towards the normal

Now go back and use the questions below to check your knowledge from previous chapters.

Previous questions

	Previous questions	Answers
1	Give an example of a longitudinal wave.	sound waves
2	What can be done to reduce the drag on an object?	streamlining
3	What is a rarefaction?	area in longitudinal waves where the particles are pulled further apart
4	Give an example of a transverse wave.	electromagnetic waves
5	Is force a vector or scalar quantity?	vector
6	What is the name of the tendency of an object to remain in a steady state at rest or moving in a straight line at a constant speed?	inertia

Put paper here

Put paper here

Required Practical Skills

Practise answering questions on the required practicals using the example below. You need to be able to apply your skills and knowledge to other practicals too.

Infrared radiation

This practical investigates the rates of absorption and radiation of infrared radiation from different surfaces.

You should be able to plan a method to determine the rate of cooling due to emission of infrared radiation, and evaluate your method.

To be accurate and precise in your investigation you need to:

- use an infrared detector with a suitable meter, where possible
- ensure that you always put the detector the same distance from the surface
- repeat measurements and calculate an average.

Worked example

A student wants to investigate the infrared radiation emitted by a surface coated with different colours of paint.

1 Describe a method to investigate the effect of surface colour on infrared emission rate.

Paint identical containers with different colours of paint. Fill each container with the same volume of water at the same temperature, and place on a heatproof mat. Place an infrared detector at the same distance and position relative to each container. Record the reading on the detector. Repeat three times.

2 Describe the type of graph the student should plot. Explain your answer.

A bar chart, because the surface colours are categoric data.

Practice

A student paints four jars with shiny and matt black paint, and shiny and matt white paint. They fill the jars with water at room temperature (20°C), and set the jars outside in the sun. After one hour they record the temperature increase of each jar.

Jar	A	B	C	D
Temperature increase in °C	5.5	8.0	7.0	1.5

1 Suggest the resolution of the instrument used to measure temperature.

2 Write down which jar (A, B, C, or D) is covered with matt black paint. Explain your answer.

3 Suggest two improvements the student could make to the experiment. Give an explanation for each improvement.

Practice

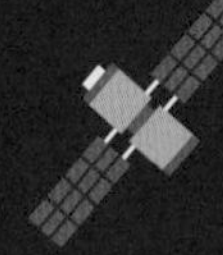

Exam-style questions

01 There are lamps that can be used to produce a suntan without needing to sunbathe.

The lamps emit ultraviolet radiation.

01.1 Name an electromagnetic wave with a longer wavelength than ultraviolet radiation. **[1 mark]**

____

01.2 Name an electromagnetic wave with a higher frequency than ultraviolet radiation. **[1 mark]**

____

01.3 Describe one hazard of using an ultraviolet lamp. **[1 mark]**

____

____

01.4 People who work outside are exposed to ultraviolet radiation from the Sun.

Suggest one method of reducing the risk of injury. **[1 mark]**

____

____

02 A teacher demonstrates how different materials absorb electromagnetic radiation.

They use a high power lamp and a solar cell to investigate how sheets of transparent film absorb visible light.

They fix the lamp 10 cm from the solar cell, and connect the solar cell to a voltmeter. The solar cell produces a potential difference that is proportional to the intensity of the light that falls on it.

Table 1 shows the data that they obtained.

Table 1

Number of sheets	Potential difference in V			
	Repeat 1	Repeat 2	Repeat 3	Mean
0	5.87	5.05	6.12	5.68
1	4.12	3.61	4.55	4.10
2	3.74	6.75	4.40	
3	3.12	2.81	3.13	3.02
4	2.89	2.02	3.86	2.92
5	2.67	2.64	3.21	2.84

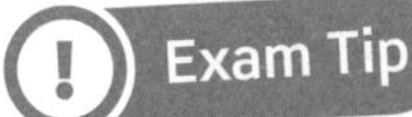

Go through the text and pick out the key points before attempting the questions. You may want to highlight the important information.

02.1 Explain why the potential difference decreases as the number of sheets of transparent film increases. **[2 marks]**

____

____

____

____

02.2 Calculate the missing mean in **Table 1**. **[1 mark]**

Mean = ______________ V

Exam Tip

Whenever you're asked to calculate a mean, always check for any outliers.

02.3 Suggest how a source of systematic error might arise in the experiment, and how it could be reduced. **[2 marks]**

____

____

____

Exam Tip

The marks for this question are for giving an error *and* how to reduce it. Do not list two errors, you will only gain one mark.

02.4 The teacher repeats the experiment with a gamma radiation source.

Suggest why the teacher ensures that all students are standing at least 1 m from the gamma source. **[2 marks]**

____

____

____

02.5 Compare the way that visible light is produced by the lamp with the way that gamma rays are produced by the source.

Use ideas about atoms, electrons, and nuclei in your answer. **[2 marks]**

____

____

____

____

03 Radiographers use X-ray machines in hospitals for medical imaging, for example computerised tomography (CT) scans.

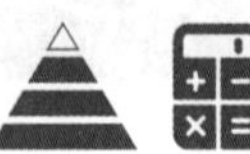

A narrow X-ray beam circles around one part of your body. It produces lots of 'slices' of the body which the computer puts together to make a detailed image of an organ, bone, or blood vessel.

Table 2 shows the radiation doses from different types of CT scan.

Table 2

Examination	Average effective dose in mSv
head	2
spine	6
chest	15

03.1 A radiographer must leave the room when a CT scan is being taken. Explain why they should leave the room. **[2 marks]**

03.2 Define the term radiation dose. **[1 mark]**

03.3 A traditional X-ray of a foot delivers an effective radiation dose of 0.001 mSv.
Suggest why the dose is much smaller than a CT scan of the head. **[1 mark]**

03.4 Calculate the number of foot X-rays that would give a patient the same dose as a CT scan of the head. **[2 marks]**

03.5 We also receive radiation from natural sources. This is called background radiation. In the UK, the average annual dose is 2.7 mSv.
Calculate the number of years of background radiation that is equivalent to a CT scan of the chest. **[2 marks]**

04 A student has made a list of appliances in his house that use different electromagnetic waves.

He identifies the television and the electrical heater as two appliances that use electromagnetic waves. However, he cannot find appliances for some of the other waves in the electromagnetic spectrum.

Explain how televisions and heaters use electromagnetic waves. Suggest uses for **two** of the waves for which the student cannot find appliances. **[6 marks]**

There are lots of parts to question **04**. First, identify the electromagnetic radiation that can be used in the home. Then work out which electromagnetic waves are left over and think of uses for them. The answer needs to have *two* different sources of electromagnetic waves included.

05 The atmosphere only allows certain wavelengths of the electromagnetic spectrum to reach the Earth's surface.

05.1 Write down the electromagnetic wave that our eyes detect. **[1 mark]**

05.2 Radio waves also reach the Earth's surface. People sometimes confuse radio waves and sound waves.
Complete the sentences with words from the box below. The words can only be used once. **[5 marks]**

transverse	330 m/s	matter	air	300 000 km/s
longitudinal	energy			

Waves of the electromagnetic spectrum are ______________ waves that travel at ______________.

Sound waves are ______________ waves and travel at ______________.

All waves transfer ______________ without transferring ______________.

> **! Exam Tip**
> Cross off each word as you use it – this way you won't get confused and use a word twice.

05.3 Some microwaves reach the surface of the Earth from the Sun. Write down which wave, radio or microwave, has the lower frequency. **[1 mark]**

05.4 We sometimes use the power of microwaves to cook food.
Write down a use of microwaves other than cooking. **[1 mark]**

> **! Exam Tip**
> Learning the order of the electromagnetic waves is really important. There are lots of fun mnemonics to help you remember, you just need to find one you like and can remember!

06 **Figure 1** shows the change in direction of waves as they move between two different media.

Figure 1

medium **1**

medium **2**

06.1 Add **three** lines to show the wavefronts of waves moving in medium **1**. **[2 marks]**

06.2 Add **three** lines to show the wavefronts of waves moving in medium **2**. **[3 marks]**

06.3 Describe what happens to the speed and frequency of the waves when they move from medium **1** to medium **2**. **[2 marks]**

06.4 Suggest a situation where waves would behave as shown in the diagram. **[1 mark]**

> **! Exam Tip**
> Whether the waves bend towards or away from the normal depends on whether the waves speed up or slow down as they pass into medium 2. This is the first thing you have to work out.

07 Electromagnetic waves have many different uses.
We use visible light to communicate.

07.1 Name **two** other electromagnetic waves that are used for communication. In each case describe the use. **[2 marks]**

> **! Exam Tip**
> The question gives you visible light as an example, so you won't get any marks for using that in your answer to **07.1**.

07.2 Some waves, such as gamma rays, can penetrate the human body. Describe a use of another electromagnetic wave that can penetrate the body. **[2 marks]**

07.3 Compare the changes in the atom that produce gamma rays with the changes in the atom that produce visible light. **[2 marks]**

08 A driver in a car sees an obstacle ahead on the road. The motion of the car is shown in **Figure 2**.

Figure 2

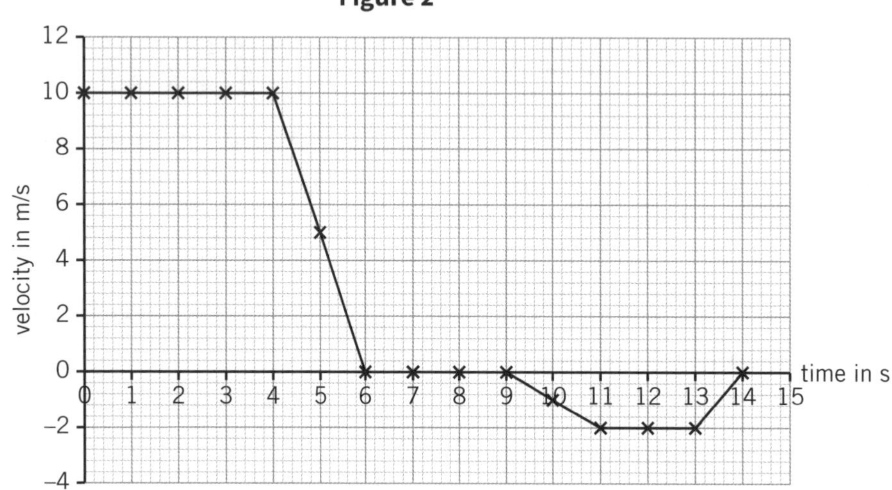

08.1 Identify the time at which the driver saw the obstacle. Give a reason for your answer. **[2 marks]**

08.2 Calculate the distance travelled by the car when it was travelling at its initial constant speed. **[2 marks]**

08.3 Calculate the acceleration of the car between 4 and 6 seconds. Comment on whether the answer is positive or negative. **[3 marks]**

Exam Tip

Draw lines on the graph to help with your working.

08.4 Compare the acceleration of the car between 9 and 11 seconds with the acceleration that you calculated in **08.3**. **[2 marks]**

09 In 1867 James Clark Maxwell developed a model that linked electricity and magnetism. Maxwell predicted that it was possible to produce electromagnetic waves even though no one had ever detected them.

09.1 Describe one difference between a model and a description. **[2 marks]**

Exam Tip

09.1 is a two mark question. You'll need to say how it refers to a model and then use words like 'whereas' or 'however' to contrast a model to a description.

09.2 Radio waves were first produced and detected by Heinrich Hertz in 1887.
Describe why it was important for Hertz to produce and detect the waves. **[1 mark]**

09.3 Today we can use an alternating current to produce radio waves. Radio waves can be detected using an aerial. An aerial is attached to a device, such as a radio, that needs an alternating current to work.
Describe what happens inside the aerial when the radio wave is absorbed. **[3 marks]**

10 A student makes the following observation:

'Black clothing gets hotter faster than white clothing because it attracts heat'.

10.1 Re-write the sentence so that it is correct. **[1 mark]**

Exam Tip

The number of marks give you important clues as to what you need to do in a question. **10.1** is worth 1 mark so you only need to make a small change.

10.2 The student makes a second observation:

'Silver surfaces only reflect radiation. They do not absorb or emit radiation.'

Suggest a situation where we use the fact that silver surfaces reflect radiation. **[1 mark]**

10.3 The student sets up a silver can and a black can. They fill the cans with hot water, put a lid on each can, and record the temperature of the water using a datalogger.

Describe **two** variables that they need to control in order to make a comparison between the cans. **[2 marks]**

10.4 Sketch the graph of temperature against time that the student would obtain from their experiment. **[4 marks]**

10.5 Suggest whether the experiment supports the student's second observation in **10.2**. **[2 marks]**

11 A group of students are on a camping trip. They sit around a fire to cook their food over the fire.

11.1 Write down the type of electromagnetic wave that is emitted by the fire and used to cook the food. **[1 mark]**

11.2 Describe another example of the transfer of energy by an electromagnetic wave.

Describe the object that absorbs the radiation. **[2 marks]**

11.3 The fire also emits visible light. The light from the fire enables people to see.

Describe another use of visible light apart from seeing. **[2 marks]**

12 A student is comparing the brightness of two bulbs connected in different types of circuit.

Bulb **A** has a resistance of 5 Ω.

Bulb **B** has a resistance of 10 Ω.

They connect the two bulbs in series with a 12 V battery.

Then they connect the same two bulbs in parallel with the same 12 V battery.

Compare the brightness of the bulbs in the series and parallel circuits.

Justify your answer with calculations. **[6 marks]**

Exam Tip

Brightness is dependent on power, which is current × voltage.

In a series circuit the current is the same everywhere, but not in a parallel circuit.

Knowledge

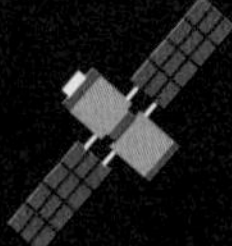

P13 Magnets and electromagnets

Magnets

Magnets have a north (N) and a south (S) pole.

When two magnets are brought close together, they exert a non-contact force on each other.

Repulsion – If the poles are the same (N and N, or S and S), they will repel each other.

Attraction – If the poles are different (N and S, or S and N), they will attract each other.

The force between a magnet and a magnetic material (iron, steel, cobalt, or nickel) is always attractive.

Magnetic fields

A **magnetic field** is the region around a magnet where another magnet or magnetic material will experience a force due to the magnet.

A magnetic field can be represented by magnetic field lines.

Field lines show the direction of the force that would act on a north pole at that point.

Field lines always point from the north pole of a magnet to its south pole.

A magnetic field's strength is greatest at the poles and decreases as distance from the magnet increases.

The closer together the field lines are, the stronger the field.

Electromagnetism

If an electric current flows through a wire (or other conductor), it will produce a magnetic field around the wire.

The field strength increases:

- with greater current
- closer to the wire.

The field around a straight wire takes the shape of concentric circles at right angles to the wire.

Reversing the direction of the current reverses the direction of the field.

Induced and permanent magnets

A **permanent** magnet produces its own magnetic field which is always there.

An **induced** magnet is an object that becomes magnetic when it is placed in a magnetic field.

The force between an induced magnet and a permanent magnet is always attractive (it doesn't matter which pole of the permanent magnet the induced magnet is near).

If the induced magnet is removed from the magnetic field it will quickly lose most or all of its magnetism.

Plotting magnetic fields

A magnetic compass contains a small bar magnet that will line up with magnetic field lines pointing from north to south.

A compass can be used to plot the magnetic field around a magnet or an **electromagnet**:

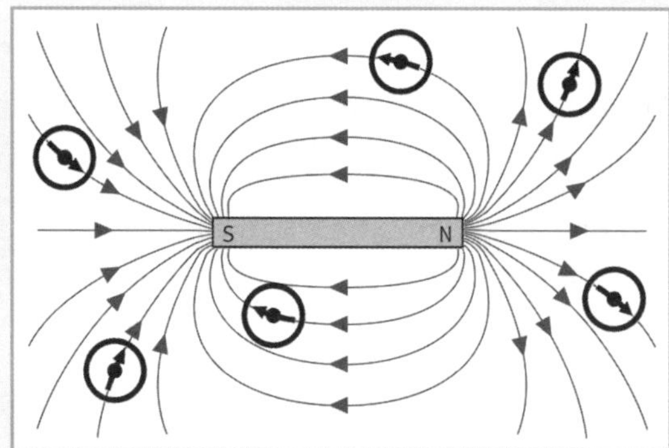

If it is not near a magnet, a compass will line up with the Earth's magnetic field, providing evidence that the Earth's core is magnetic.

As a compass points towards a south pole, the magnetic pole near the Earth's geographic North Pole is actually a south pole.

Magnetic flux density

The magnetic flux density of a field is a measure of the strength of the magnetic field.

For a current-carrying wire at right angles to a magnetic field, the size of the force on it is given by the equation:

force (N) = magnetic flux density (T) × current (A) × length (m)

$$F = BIl$$

Solenoids

A **solenoid** is a cylindrical coil of wire.

Bending a current-carrying wire into a solenoid increases the strength of the magnetic field produced.

The shape of the magnetic field around a solenoid is similar to a magnetic field around a bar magnet.

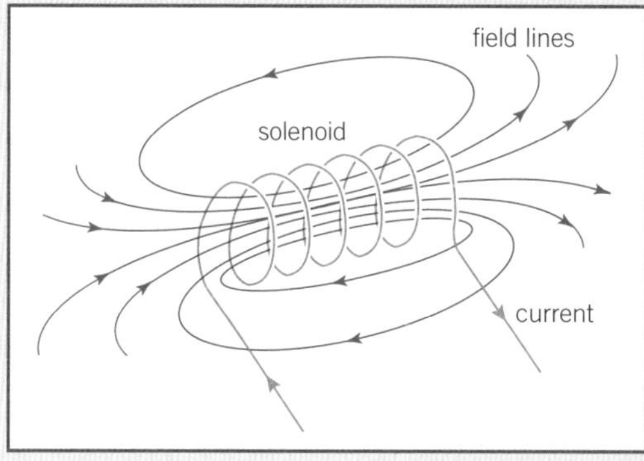

Inside a solenoid the magnetic field is strong and uniform, which means it has the same strength and direction at all points.

The strength of the magnetic field around a solenoid can be increased by putting an iron core inside it.

If the wire was gripped by someone's right hand so that the fingers curl in the direction of the current in the coil, the thumb will point towards the north pole of the field.

Electromagnets are often solenoids with an iron core.

Advantages of electromagnets

- An electromagnet can be turned on and off.
- The strength of an electromagnet can be increased or decreased by adjusting the current.

The motor effect

When a current-carrying wire (or other conductor) is placed in a magnetic field, it experiences a force.

The force is due to the interaction between the field created by the current in the wire and the magnetic field in which the wire is placed.

The magnet producing the field will experience an equal-sized force in the opposite direction.

The direction of the force is reversed if the current is reversed or if the direction of the magnetic field is reversed.

Key terms

Make sure you can write a definition for these key terms.

attraction electromagnet induced magnetic field permanent repulsion solenoid

Revision tip

Remember The lines on a diagram that show magnetic field lines will always point from north to south.

Electric motors

A current-carrying coil of wire in a magnetic field will tend to rotate.

This is the basis of an electric motor.

When there is a current in the wire, it spins because:

- each side of the coil experiences a force due to being a current-carrying conductor in a magnetic field
- the forces on each side of the coil are in opposite directions.

The motor can be made to spin

- faster – by increasing the current in the coil or increasing the strength of the magnetic field.
- in the opposite direction – by reversing the direction of the current or reversing the direction of the magnetic field.

Fleming's left-hand rule

The direction of the force/motion of the wire is always at right angles to both the current and the direction of the magnetic field it is within.

It can be worked out using Fleming's left-hand rule:

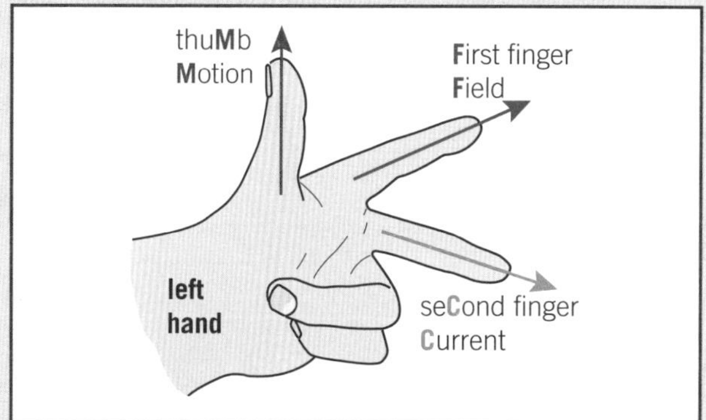

Learn the answers to the questions below, then cover the answers column with a piece of paper and write as many as you can. Check and repeat.

	P13 questions	Answers
1	What is a magnetic field?	the region of space around a magnet where a magnetic material will experience a force
2	What happens when like and unlike poles are brought together?	like = repel, unlike = attract
3	What happens to the strength of the magnetic field as you get further away from the magnet?	decreases
4	Where is the magnetic field of a magnet strongest?	at the poles
5	In which direction do magnetic field lines always point?	north to south
6	What does the distance between magnetic field lines indicate?	strength of the field, closer together = stronger field
7	What is a permanent magnet?	material that produces its own magnetic field
8	What is an induced magnet?	material that becomes magnetic when it is put in a magnetic field
9	What does a magnetic compass contain?	small bar magnet
10	What is produced around a wire when an electric current flows through it?	magnetic field
11	What factors does the strength of the magnetic field around a straight wire depend upon?	size of current, distance from wire
12	What effect does shaping the wire into a solenoid have on the magnetic field strength?	increases strength of magnetic field
13	How can the strength of the magnetic field inside a solenoid be increased?	put an iron core inside
14	What does Fleming's left-hand rule show?	relative orientation of the force, current in the conductor, and magnetic field for the motor effect
15	What is the symbol for magnetic flux density and what unit is it measured in?	B, tesla (T)
16	What is the motor effect?	when a conductor placed in a magnetic field experiences a force
17	What causes the motor effect?	interaction between the magnetic field created by current in a wire and the magnetic field in which the wire is placed

Put paper here

Now go back and use the questions below to check your knowledge from previous chapters.

Previous questions / Answers

	Previous questions	Answers
1	What does Newton's Third Law say?	when two objects interact they exert equal and opposite forces on each other
2	What are the typical speeds for a person walking, running, and cycling?	1.5 m/s, 3.0 m/s, and 6.0 m/s respectively
3	What instrument can be used to measure the weight of an object?	calibrated spring-balance (newtonmeter)
4	What is irradiation?	exposing an object to nuclear radiation
5	Explain why EM waves are not mechanical waves.	they can travel through a vacuum (don't need a substance to travel through)
6	List the different types of waves in the EM spectrum in order of decreasing wavelength (increasing frequency).	radio, microwave, infrared, visible, ultraviolet, X-rays, gamma
7	Which types of EM waves are harmful to the human body?	ultraviolet, X-rays, gamma rays

Put paper here Put paper here Put paper here Put paper here

Maths Skills

Practise your maths skills using the worked example and practice questions below.

Significant figures

We use significant figures (s.f.) to make sure we are not introducing error by giving a false level of accuracy.

When answering questions you use the same number of s.f. as the data with the fewest s.f. in the question. You may also be asked to give your answer to a given number of figures.

For example:

- 4.57 to two significant figures is 4.6 – the 5 after the decimal point is rounded up
- 12 345 to two significant figures is 12 000 – the number is rounded down
- 0.093 to two significant figures is 0.09 – the zero *before* the decimal point is *not* a significant figure, but the zero *after* the decimal point is.

Worked example

A metal ball has a mass of 13.4 kg and a volume of 5.3 m^3.

Calculate the density of the metal ball.

Give your answer to an appropriate number of significant figures.

First calculate the density using:

$$\text{density} = \frac{\text{mass}}{\text{volume}}$$

$$\frac{13.4}{5.3} = 2.52830$$

To work out the appropriate number of significant figures, work out which value in the question has the smallest number of significant figures.

- 13.4 = 3 significant figures
- 5.3 = 2 significant figures

So you should give your answer to 2 significant figures.

density = 2.5 kg/m^3

Practice

1 Give 67 812 to 3 s.f.

2 Give 0.567 to 2 s.f.

3 A person has a mass of 55.25 kg.

Calculate the weight of the person. Give your answer to 3 s.f.

Gravitational field strength = 10 N/kg

4 A plane flies from London to Perth in Australia, a distance of 8977 miles. It takes 17 hours and 45 minutes.

Calculate the average speed of the plane in metres per second. Give your answer to 4 s.f.

1 mile = 1609 metres

Practice

Exam-style questions

01 A student sets up a simple motor.

They connect the motor to a battery as shown in **Figure 1**.

Figure 1

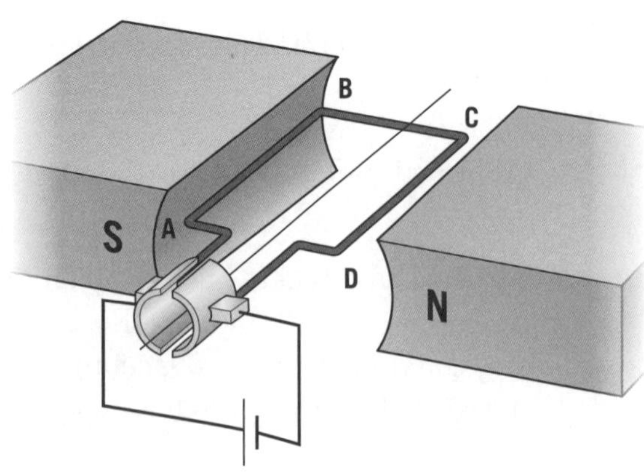

01.1 Describe the direction of the current in the coil of wire in terms of **A**, **B**, **C**, and **D**. **[1 mark]**

Exam Tip

You are asked to use the letters in your answer, so make sure you do!

01.2 Compare the force on side **AB** with the force on side **CD**.

Use your answer to describe which way the coil spins. **[3 marks]**

Exam Tip

You will need to use Fleming's Left Hand rule for **01.2**. The only way to find the answer is by getting that hand in shape.

01.3 Explain why there is no force on side **BC**. **[2 marks]**

01.4 When the coil is vertical, the contacts are no longer in contact with the battery and a current no longer flows in the coil.

Explain why the coil continues to move. **[2 marks]**

02 A student uses a magnetic field sensor.

Investigate how the magnetic field strength varies with distance from an electric wire.

02.1 When there is no current flowing in the wire the field sensor measures a magnetic field of 49 μT.

$1\,\mu T = 10^{-6}\,T$

Write down what the sensor is measuring when there is no current passing through the wire.

Write down the name of this type of error. **[2 marks]**

Exam Tip

μT are micro teslas. There are 1 000 000 μT in one tesla.

02.2 The student records their data in **Table 1**.

Table 1

Distance in cm	Magnetic field strength in mT			
	1	2	3	Mean
1	0.190	0.210	0.210	0.203
2	0.095	0.105	0.105	0.102
3	0.063	0.070	0.070	0.068
4	0.048	0.053	0.053	0.051

Suggest what the student should do about the sensor reading in **02.1** before recording the data. **[1 mark]**

Exam Tip

The error will have shown up in every result that the student recorded.

02.3 Suggest why the student does not start measuring at zero centimetres. **[1 mark]**

02.4 The student concludes that the magnetic field strength is inversely proportional to the distance from the wire.

Use the data in **Table 1** to explain why. **[3 marks]**

03 A tool set contains a screwdriver. The screwdriver attracts the screw so that the person using it is less likely to lose it.

03.1 The end of the screwdriver is magnetic. The screw is an induced magnet.
Explain the difference between a permanent magnet and an induced magnet. **[2 marks]**

03.2 There is a magnetic field around the end of the screwdriver.
Predict whether there is a magnetic field around the screw when it is attached to the screwdriver. Justify your answer. **[2 marks]**

03.3 On **Figure 2** write N (north) and S (south) in the blank boxes to show the induced poles on the screw. **[1 mark]**

Figure 2

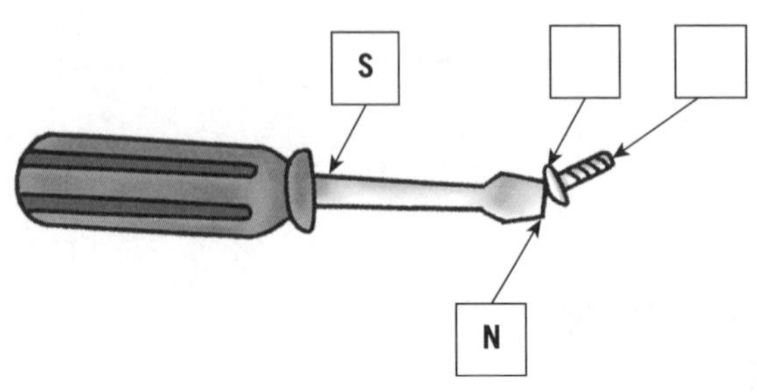

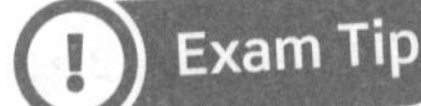

Remember, opposite poles attract.

03.4 The screw is put back into a box containing other screws.
Predict whether it will attract the other screws in the box.
Justify your answer. **[2 marks]**

04 A student investigates the strength of an electromagnet. They make a solenoid with different materials for the core and measure the mass of iron filings that the solenoid can pick up.

04.1 Write down the independent and dependent variables. **[2 marks]**

04.2 Write down **two** control variables. **[2 marks]**

The control variables are the things you need to keep the same to ensure it is a fair test.

04.3 The results are in **Table 2**.

Table 2

Material	Mass of iron filings in g			
	1	2	3	Mean
nickel alloy	0.10	1.0	0.10	0.10
steel	1.20	1.38	1.36	1.31
aluminium	0.03	0.02	0.02	0.02
iron	1.26	1.43	1.38	1.36

One of the values is an outlier. Identify the outlier.
Write down what the student did about this outlier when they calculated the mean. **[2 marks]**

04.4 Use **Table 2** to estimate the uncertainty in the mass of iron filings that the solenoid with a steel core picks up. **[2 marks]**

04.5 The student decides to draw a graph to show the results of the experiment.
Name the type of graph the student should draw. Explain the reason for your choice. **[2 marks]**

04.6 An alloy is a combination of two or more metals.
Suggest whether the amount of nickel in the nickel alloy is large or small. Give a reason for your answer. **[3 marks]**

05 A student winds some wire around a wooden rod to make a coil and connects the coil to a battery.

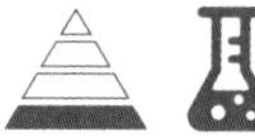

05.1 Identify a hazard when doing this experiment.
Suggest a method of reducing the risk of harm. **[2 marks]**

05.2 On solenoid **1** in **Figure 3**, draw lines to show the shape of the magnetic field around the coil. You do **not** need to draw arrows on the field lines. **[1 marks]**

Figure 3

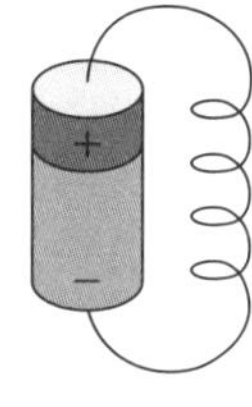

solenoid **1**

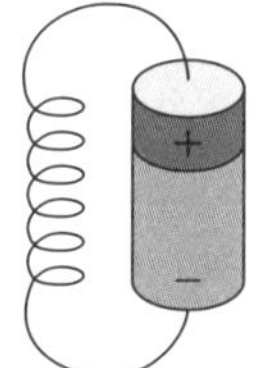

solenoid **2**

05.3 Write down which solenoid, **1** or **2**, has the strongest magnetic field around it. Give reasons for your answer. **[2 marks]**

05.4 The student takes a compass and places it in the centre of the solenoid. They move it up and down in the middle of the coil.
Will the compass needle move when it is in the solenoid?
Justify your answer. **[2 marks]**

06 There is a region around a magnet where there is a magnetic field.

06.1 Describe what is meant by magnetic field. **[1 mark]**

06.2 A student puts two magnets, **P** and **Q**, together so that their north poles are facing each other.
Draw a diagram to show the magnetic field between the two magnets.
Draw arrows to show the direction of the magnetic field. **[2 marks]**

06.3 The magnetic field is stronger near the poles.
Describe how this is shown on a diagram. **[1 mark]**

06.4 There is a 'neutral point' between the magnets where you can place a piece of magnetic material and it will not move.

Suggest where the point is in relation to the two magnets, **P** and **Q**, when

- the magnets are equally strong
- magnet **Q** is stronger than magnet **P**.

Explain your answers. **[5 marks]**

Exam Tip

A carefully annotated diagram can get marks in **06.4**. If you struggle to explain things with words then this is a perfect question to use a diagram.

07 There are craters produced from the impact of asteroids with the Earth's surface. Astronomers try to work out the position of asteroids that could collide with the Earth using telescopes. They send a pulse of radio waves to an asteroid. The radio waves are reflected by the asteroid. They use the time it takes to detect the reflected radio waves to work out the distance to the asteroid.

07.1 A telescope detects a reflected wave from an asteroid 0.2 s after a pulse of radio waves is emitted. Calculate the distance to the asteroid. The speed of electromagnetic radiation is 3.0×10^8 m/s. **[4 marks]**

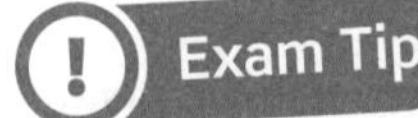

If you're not used to using standard form in science then take time to look it up in your maths books and practise it.

07.2 The uncertainty in the measurement of time is 1×10^{-4} s. Define uncertainty in this context. **[1 mark]**

07.3 The asteroid is moving. Suggest how the astronomers could use pulses of radio waves to calculate the speed of the asteroid. **[3 marks]**

08 A student connects a long thin strip of aluminium foil in a circuit with a battery. They lay the foil on the desk and bring a very strong magnet close to the foil. The foil moves.

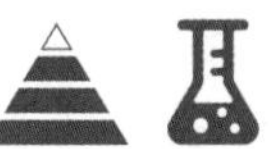

08.1 Suggest why the foil moves. **[1 mark]**

08.2 The student notices that as they move the magnet further away from the foil it no longer moves. Explain why. **[2 marks]**

08.3 The student also has a magnetic field sensor attached to a datalogger which measures magnetic field strength. The student wants to collect data to find the relationship between the magnetic field strength around the foil and the distance from the foil. Describe a method of collecting data to find this relationship. **[3 marks]**

08.4 is a two mark question. One mark will be for the correct shape of the line on the graph and the other for explaining why you drew it like that.

08.4 Sketch the graph the student would plot with the data they collected. Explain the shape of the graph. **[2 marks]**

09 A scientist notices that a compass needle is deflected when they turn on a circuit containing a battery and a wire.

09.1 Which direction was the compass pointing before the scientist turned on the circuit? Explain why the compass points in this direction. **[2 marks]**

09.2 Compare the strength of the Earth's magnetic field with the strength of the magnetic field around the wire. Give reasons with your answer. **[2 marks]**

09.3 Choose the correct description of a compass needle. Choose **one** answer. **[1 mark]**

a compass needle always points to the south pole

a compass needle is a magnet

a compass needle can be made from any metal

10 The Earth has a magnetic field.

10.1 Explain the difference between geographic North and magnetic north. **[2 marks]**

10.2 In the year 1600, William Gilbert published a paper in which he proposed that the Earth behaved like a giant magnet. Gilbert used a small physical model of the Earth with a magnet inside it.
Suggest the equipment he could have used to develop his ideas about the Earth. **[2 marks]**

10.3 Since Gilbert's idea was published, different scientists have proposed different models to explain the mechanism behind the bar magnet.
Suggest **one** reason why the models have changed. **[2 marks]**

10.4 Give **one** reason why scientists publish papers in journals. **[1 mark]**

Exam Tip

Think about the limitations of collecting and analysing data in 1600.

11 A student watches a video that shows that some insects can detect ultraviolet light.

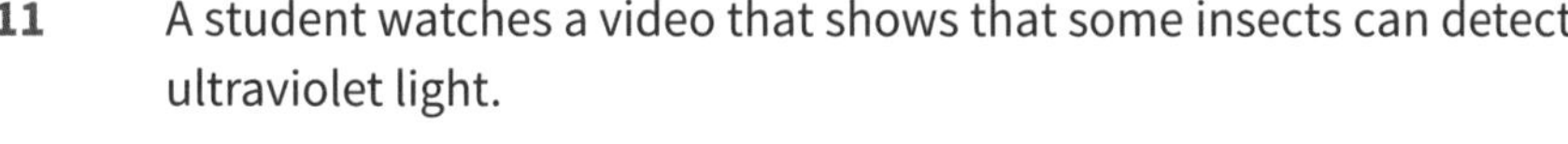

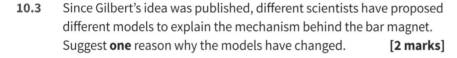

11.1 Explain why you cannot write down a single number for the wavelength of UV light. **[1 mark]**

11.2 The video explains that humans can see red light but some insects cannot.
Describe the difference between red light and ultraviolet light in terms of frequency and wavelength. **[2 marks]**

11.3 Ultraviolet light is hazardous to the human body.
Describe **one** reason why. **[1 mark]**

11.4 Describe **one** use of ultraviolet light. **[1 mark]**

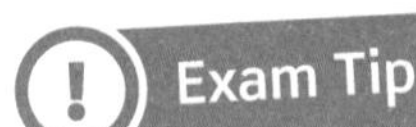

Exam Tip

You need to give two differences between red light and UV light in **11.2**. You can structure your answer like this:

The frequency of red light is ... whereas for ultraviolet it is ... .

The wavelength of red light is ... whereas for ultraviolet it is ... .

12 A student accelerates a toy car. They use a newtonmeter to apply a constant force. They use light gates to measure the speed at two different times.

12.1 Write down the equation that links change in velocity, time, and acceleration. **[1 mark]**

12.2 The initial velocity is 0.5 m/s. The final velocity is 2.7 m/s.
The time between the measurements of velocity is 0.4 s.
Calculate the acceleration of the trolley. **[2 marks]**

12.3 Write down the equation that links mass, force, and acceleration. **[1 mark]**

12.4 The student applies a force of 2.0 N.
The mass of the trolley is 400 g (0.4 kg).
Calculate the acceleration of the trolley. **[3 marks]**

12.5 Suggest **one** practical reason why the two values of acceleration are not the same. **[1 mark]**

Exam Tip

Even if it doesn't specifically ask you to, get into the habit of writing down the equation you are using whenever you do a calculation. You often get a mark for writing the correct equation.

Physics equations

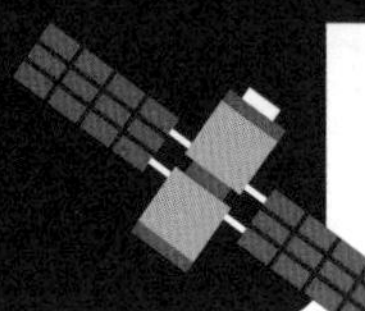

You need to be able to recall the following equations in your exams.

	Questions	Answers	
1	What is the equation for weight?	weight = mass × gravitational field strength	$W = m\,g$
2	What is the equation for work done?	work done = force × distance (along the line of action of the force)	$W = F\,s$
3	What is the equation for force on a spring?	force applied to a spring = spring constant × extension	$F = k\,e$
4	What is the equation for distance?	distance travelled = speed × time	$s = v\,t$
5	What is the equation of acceleration?	acceleration = $\frac{\text{change in velocity}}{\text{time taken}}$	$a = \frac{\Delta v}{t}$
6	What is the equation for resultant force?	resultant force = mass × acceleration	$F = m\,a$
7	What is the equation for momentum?	momentum = mass × velocity	$p = m\,v$
8	What is the equation for kinetic energy?	kinetic energy = 0.5 × mass × (speed)^2	$E_k = \frac{1}{2} m\,v^2$
9	What is the equation for gravitational potential energy?	gravitational potential energy = mass × gravitational field strength × height	$E_p = m\,g\,h$
10	What equation links power, energy transferred, and time?	power = $\frac{\text{energy transferred}}{\text{time}}$	$P = \frac{E}{t}$
11	What equation links power, work, and time?	power = $\frac{\text{work done}}{\text{time}}$	$P = \frac{W}{t}$
12	What are the equations for efficiency?	efficiency = $\frac{\text{useful output energy transfer}}{\text{total input energy transfer}} = \frac{\text{useful power output}}{\text{total power input}}$	
13	What is the equation for wave speed?	wave speed = frequency × wavelength	$v = f\,\lambda$
14	What is the equation for charge flow?	charge flow = current × time	$Q = I\,t$
15	What is the equation for potential difference?	potential difference = current × resistance	$V = I\,R$
16	What equation links power, potential difference, and current?	power = potential difference × current	$P = V\,I$
17	What equation links power, current, and resistance?	power = (current)^2 × resistance	$P = I^2\,R$
18	What equation links energy transferred, power, and time	energy transferred = power × time	$E = P\,t$
19	What equation links energy transferred, charge flow, and potential difference?	energy transferred = charge flow × potential difference	$E = Q\,V$
20	What is the equation for density?	density = $\frac{\text{mass}}{\text{volume}}$	$\rho = \frac{m}{V}$

Put paper here

You will be provided with a *Physics Equations Sheet* that contains the following equations. You should be able to select and apply the correct equation to answer the question.

1	(final velocity)^2 – (initial velocity)^2 = 2 × acceleration × distance	$v^2 - u^2 = 2\,a\,s$
2	elastic potential energy = 0.5 × spring constant × (extension)^2	$E_e = \frac{1}{2}\,k\,e^2$
3	change in thermal energy = mass × specific heat capacity × temperature change	$\Delta E = m\,c\,\Delta\theta$
4	period = $\frac{1}{\text{frequency}}$	
5	force on a conductor (at right angles to a magnetic field) carrying a current = magnetic flux density × current × length	$F = B\,I\,l$
6	thermal energy for a change of state = mass × specific latent heat	$E = m\,L$
7	potential difference across primary coil × current in primary coil = potential difference across secondary coil × current in secondary coil	$V_p\,I_p = V_s\,I_s$

Periodic Table

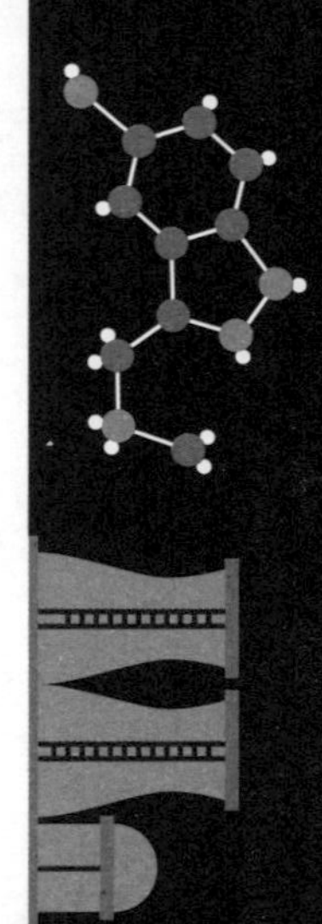

key

relative atomic mass **atomic symbol** name atomic (proton) number

1	2											3	4	5	6	7	0
							1 **H** hydrogen 1										4 **He** helium 2
7 **Li** lithium 3	9 **Be** beryllium 4											11 **B** boron 5	12 **C** carbon 6	14 **N** nitrogen 7	16 **O** oxygen 8	19 **F** fluorine 9	20 **Ne** neon 10
23 **Na** sodium 11	24 **Mg** magnesium 12											27 **Al** aluminium 13	28 **Si** silicon 14	31 **P** phosphorus 15	32 **S** sulfur 16	35.5 **Cl** chlorine 17	40 **Ar** argon 18
39 **K** potassium 19	40 **Ca** calcium 20	45 **Sc** scandium 21	48 **Ti** titanium 22	51 **V** vanadium 23	52 **Cr** chromium 24	55 **Mn** manganese 25	56 **Fe** iron 26	59 **Co** cobalt 27	59 **Ni** nickel 28	63.5 **Cu** copper 29	65 **Zn** zinc 30	70 **Ga** gallium 31	73 **Ge** germanium 32	75 **As** arsenic 33	79 **Se** selenium 34	80 **Br** bromine 35	84 **Kr** krypton 36
85 **Rb** rubidium 37	88 **Sr** strontium 38	89 **Y** yttrium 39	91 **Zr** zirconium 40	93 **Nb** niobium 41	96 **Mo** molybdenum 42	[98] **Tc** technetium 43	101 **Ru** ruthenium 44	103 **Rh** rhodium 45	106 **Pd** palladium 46	108 **Ag** silver 47	112 **Cd** cadmium 48	115 **In** indium 49	119 **Sn** tin 50	122 **Sb** antimony 51	128 **Te** tellurium 52	127 **I** iodine 53	131 **Xe** xenon 54
133 **Cs** caesium 55	137 **Ba** barium 56	139 **La*** lanthanum 57	178 **Hf** hafnium 72	181 **Ta** tantalum 73	184 **W** tungsten 74	186 **Re** rhenium 75	190 **Os** osmium 76	192 **Ir** iridium 77	195 **Pt** platinum 78	197 **Au** gold 79	201 **Hg** mercury 80	204 **Tl** thallium 81	207 **Pb** lead 82	209 **Bi** bismuth 83	[209] **Po** polonium 84	[210] **At** astatine 85	[222] **Rn** radon 86
[223] **Fr** francium 87	[226] **Ra** radium 88	[227] **Ac*** actinium 89	[261] **Rf** rutherfordium 104	[262] **Db** dubnium 105	[266] **Sg** seaborgium 106	[264] **Bh** bohrium 107	[277] **Hs** hassium 108	[268] **Mt** meitnerium 109	[271] **Ds** darmstadtium 110	[272] **Rg** roentgenium 111	[285] **Cn** copernicium 112	[286] **Nh** nihonium 113	[289] **Fl** flerovium 114	[289] **Mc** moscovium 115	[293] **Lv** livermorium 116	[294] **Ts** tennessine 117	[294] **Og** oganesson 118

*The lanthanides (atomic numbers 58–71) and the actinides (atomic numbers 90–103) have been omitted.

Relative atomic masses for **Cu** and **Cl** have not been rounded to the nearest whole number.